Object-Oriented Programming with Java

Second Edition

Barry J. Holmes
Oxford Brookes University

Daniel T. Joyce
Villanova University

JONES AND BARTLETT PUBLISHERS

Sudbury, Massachusetts

BOSTON   TORONTO   LONDON   SINGAPORE

World Headquarters
Jones and Bartlett Publishers
40 Tall Pine Drive
Sudbury, MA 01776
978-443-5000
info@jbpub.com
www.jbpub.com

Jones and Bartlett Publishers
Canada
2406 Nikanna Road
Mississauga, ON L5C 2W6
CANADA

Jones and Bartlett Publishers
International
Barb House, Barb Mews
London W6 7PA
UK

Library of Congress Cataloging-in-Publication Data

Holmes, Barry (Barry J.)
    Object-oriented programming with Java / Barry Holmes, Daniel Joyce.
      p. cm.
    Includes bibliographical references and index.
    ISBN 0-7637-1435-6
    1. Java (Computer program language)   2. Object-oriented programming (Computer
Science) I. Joyce, Daniel T. II. Title.

QA76.73.J38 H62 2000
005.13'3—dc21   00-062545

Cover image © Peter R. Harris

The computer programs presented in this book have been included for their instructional value. They have been computer-tested with considerable care and are not guaranteed for any particular purpose. The authors do not offer any warranties or representations, nor do they accept any liabilities with respect to the computer programs.

Chief Executive Officer: Clayton Jones
Chief Operating Officer: Don W. Jones, Jr.
Executive Vice President and Publisher: Tom Manning
V.P., Sales and Marketing: Paul Shepardson
V.P., College Editorial Director: Brian L. McKean
V.P., Managing Editor: Judith H. Hauck
V.P., Design and Production: Anne Spencer
V.P., Manufacturing and Inventory Control: Therese Bräuer
Director of Media Services: W. Scott Smith
Senior Acquisitions Editor: Michael Stranz
Development and Product Manager: Amy Rose
Cover Design: Night & Day Design
Composition: Northeast Compositors, Inc.
Text Design: Delgado Design, Inc.
Printing and Binding: Courier Westford
Cover printing: John Pow Company, Inc.

This book was typeset in Quark 4.1 on a Macintosh G4. The font families used were Adobe Caslon, Franklin Gothic, and Prestige Elite. The first printing was printed on 45 lb. Utopia Book Matte.

Printed in the United States of America
04 03 02 01 00   10 9 8 7 6 5 4 3 2 1

This book is dedicated to all
of our students, past, present, and future

Preface

Our Intended Audience

Object-Oriented Programming with Java is written for first-year college/university programming courses worldwide. It introduces you to object-oriented design and programming and can be used in computing programs for a first course. The book is aimed at a broad audience of students in science, engineering, and business, where a knowledge of programming is thought to be essential.

We have assumed that you have no prior knowledge of computer programming; however, you are expected to be familiar with the fundamentals of operating a home computer.

Our Philosophy

We believe students should be exposed to sound, modern software development practices from the very start of their studies. Several features of this textbook support this philosophy:

- Our audio-visual interface (avi) package, described in more detail later, allows you to create interesting screen-oriented user interfaces from the very start. For example, you will use check boxes, radio buttons, sliders, and dialogue boxes for input and will be able to output images and sounds.

- In addition to allowing modern I/O approaches, the avi package provides good practice in the use of abstraction and third-party packages.

- Since Java is an object-oriented programming language, we introduce objects from the word *go!* In Chapter 2 we show you how to use classes from the Java Application Programming Interface (API) and how to create objects. By Chapter 3 we introduce you to object-oriented programming and the creation of your own classes and objects.

- We introduce a systematic approach to program design, implementation, and testing in Chapter 3, and this approach is used in examples and case studies throughout the rest of the text.

- We present the Unified Modeling Language (UML) and use it throughout the text on an as-needed basis, allowing you to gradually learn this universally accepted modeling language as you also learn the fundamentals of object-oriented programming with Java.

- We provide an early introduction to object-oriented design approaches, such as using noun and verb analysis to help identify objects and methods.

- As the problems addressed become more complex, we turn to CRC cards to drive the analysis stage.

- We provide many nontrivial programs throughout the text to clarify topic coverage and to provide examples of substantial programs.

The AVI Package

One of the difficulties we have found in the past in teaching Java to beginners is the complexity of the Java input/output scheme, whether it is in the context of a simple windowing system or a full-blown graphical user interface.

To overcome this problem, Barry Holmes has written an audio-visual interface package in Java called `avi`, to enable beginner programmers to create and use windowing components for input and output. In addition to the input and output of text, the `avi` package will permit you to input from predefined check boxes, radio buttons, and scrolling lists; display pictures; and play prerecorded sound. This approach allows us to use more interesting examples than do most introductory textbooks and will increase your interaction with the text. By the end of the book you will have enough knowledge to understand fully how this package was written and the functionality of its Java code.

Use of the `avi` package is introduced gradually throughout the early chapters of the text:

- In Chapter 2 we give an overview of the package, and you learn how to create a window to hold your input and output objects, how to obtain an input String from the user, and how to output text to the window.

- Chapter 3 covers the output of images and sounds, and includes the use of a "timer" so that you can control when these items are shown in the window. Example programs include one that features a slide show of vacation spots and another that simulates rolling a die, complete with the image of the die face that turns up and an announcement of what was rolled.

- Chapter 4 provides more input and output options: `Sliders`, `Radio-Buttons`, and `Memo` boxes.

- Chapter 5 completes the presentation of the `avi` by introducing the `Checkbox` input object. Examples in this chapter include an "alarm clock" program.

The `avi` package is included on the CD-ROM bundled with this book.

Overview of the Book

This textbook includes material typically covered in a first course in computer programming, which is sometimes referred to as "CS1." The CS1 material can be found in Chapters 1 through 7, and should be enough material to build a first course around. Additionally, Chapters 8 through 11 introduce graphical user interface programming in Java, a topic that is increasingly finding its way into the early part of the CS curriculum. Finally, Chapter 12 provides an introduction to more advanced data structure and algorithm topics.

Comparing the book's topics to the current draft of the IEEE/ACM Computing Curricula 2001, we can safely claim that it provides complete coverage of Programming Fundamentals areas 1 (Algorithms and problem-solving), 2 (Fundamental programming constructs), and 3 (Basic data structures), and most of areas 5 (Abstract data types), 6 (Object-oriented programming), 7 (Event-driven and concurrent programming), and 8 (Using modern APIs). Note that we do not cover area 4 (Recursion), since we believe that topic is more suited to a later course. A more detailed description of the contents follows.

Chapters 1 to 5 provide a gradual introduction to the fundamentals of programming. Here, much emphasis is placed upon good practice involving object-oriented program design, testing, and implementation. These chapters broadly cover: primitive data types, arithmetic, classes, objects, and input and output via an audio-visual interface; class methods, constructors, and instance methods; program design, UML notation, implementation, compilation and error correction; `if` and `switch` selection statements; `while`, `do`, and `for` loop statements; and one-dimensional arrays.

Once you understand the fundamentals of programming and can create and use classes competently, you can then explore the Java language and object-oriented programming to a much greater depth. Chapters 6 and 7 cover the topics of encapsulation, abstract data types, object properties, inheritance, polymorphism, genericity, exception handling, and data streams.

Graphical user interfaces are so important in the development of modern software that Chapters 8 and 9 are devoted to the production of graphical interfaces using the classes supplied by the Java Abstract Windowing Toolkit.

These chapters also explain how some of the `avi` package components that have been used throughout the book for input and output are written in Java.

Since program and class design feature strongly in this book, Chapter 10 covers the topic of objects working together as well as further UML notation.

Chapter 11 provides a complete coverage of writing and running Java Applets on a web browser.

Finally, Chapter 12 introduces the topics of sorting, searching, and dynamic data structures.

Language and Computer Requirements

The most effective way to learn Java programming with this book is to use your computer to run the example programs and case studies, and to check your answers to the programming problems.

All the programs written in this book have been compiled and tested using Sun Microsystems, Inc. Java Development Kit (SDK) version 1.2 (release 1.2.2) on both a PC-compatible microcomputer under Windows 98 and a Sun Workstation under Solaris.

The Introduction explains how to download and install the latest version of the Java Development Kit from the World Wide Web to your computer.

Pedagogical Features

Objectives

Each chapter begins with a set of learning objectives.

Case Studies

Many chapters contain fully designed case studies with comprehensive documentation, program listings, and output.

Example Programs

All chapters contain complete example programs used to demonstrate the key features of the chapter. All computer programs are followed by a listing of the output from the program.

End-of-Chapter Summary

Every chapter contains a summary of its key points. This provides you with a check-list of topics you should understand before you progress to the next chapter.

Review Questions

All chapters contain review questions to enable you to test and reinforce your knowledge.

Exercises

All chapters contain pencil-and-paper exercises that are designed to test your understanding of the programming topics introduced in the chapter. The exercises should normally be tackled before the programming problems. Solutions to the exercises appear in Appendix C.

Programming Problems

All chapters contain a robust set of programming problems that require the use of a computer to solve.

Icons

The chapters include icons or special design elements for quick reference:

SYNTAX

These statements express the grammar of the language, and illustrate how language statements are constructed.

 This icon signals information the authors feel should be brought to your attention.

 Pay special attention to this cautionary advice.

NOW DO THIS Throughout the chapters you are asked to experiment with the language features that have been introduced. Experimentation can take the form of modifying an existing program to gain insight into its functionality, or writing a new program to reinforce knowledge gained. This feature can form the focus for many laboratory exercises.

Supplements to the Text

Compact Disk

A CD-ROM accompanies this book and contains the following software:

- The audio-visual interface.

- All of the example and case-study computer programs used throughout the book.

- All of the image and sound files required to support the example programs.

Instructor's Guide

A comprehensive web-based instructor's guide is available, free of charge, to adopters of *Object-Oriented Programming with Java*. The instructor's guide is accessible via a password protected page on the Jones and Bartlett web site. This guide contains hints and tips on teaching the material, together with all of the answers to the review questions, and many of the programming problems. To utilize this guide, qualified instructors should contact their Jones and Bartlett Publisher's Representative at (800) 832-0034 or info@jbpub.com to receive a URL and password.

Acknowledgments

The authors would like to express their thanks to the following technical reviewers, whose comments they found to be most constructive and helpful, and who have contributed toward shaping this book into its present form: Robert Burton, Brigham Young University; Michael Fry, Lebanon Valley College; David Hughes, Brock University; Pamela Lawhead, University of Mississippi; Dale Skrien, Colby College.

In addition, the authors would like to express their thanks to Amy Rose and Michael Stranz at Jones and Bartlett and to Mike and Sigrid Wile at Northeast Compositors for their professional insight and team approach to the development and the production of the book.

Barry Holmes—Oxford, England
Daniel Joyce—Philadelphia, USA

Contents

Chapter 0 **Introduction   1**

0.1   What is Java?   2
0.2   Using the Internet   3
0.3   Downloading the Java 2 SDK for Windows, Unix (Solaris), and Linux Users   4
0.4   Downloading Java 2 SDK Documentation   4
0.5   Creating a Java Software Development Environment   5
0.6   Copying and Installing the Audio-Visual Interface (AVI)   7
0.7   How to Input and Save a Java Program in the Computer   9
0.8   How to Compile a Java Program   10
0.9   How to Execute (run) a Java Program   12
0.10 SDK Tools   14
0.11 Copying and Editing Programs from the CD   15
      Summary   17

Chapter 1 **Primitive Data Types and Arithmetic   19**

1.1   Data   20
1.2   Data Storage   21
      Number Systems   23
1.3   Identifiers   27
1.4   Syntax   29
1.5   Variables and Constants   31

1.6   The Format of a Simple Program   33
1.7   Arithmetic   35
          Unary Operators   35
          Binary Multiplicative Operators   35
          Binary Additive Operators   35
1.8   Operator Precedence   40
1.9   Casting   42
          Summary   45
          Review Questions   46
          Exercises   47
          Programming Problems   49

Chapter 2   **Objects   51**
2.1   Introduction to Objects   52
2.2   The String Class   53
          Declaring Objects   54
          Methods and Parameters   54
          Constructors   56
          String Assignment   58
          Instance Methods   58
2.3   The Anatomy of a Simple Program Revisited   61
          Heading Giving Details of the Name and Purpose of the
                Program   62
          Import List   62
          Class Name   63
          Main Method   63
2.4   The AVI Package   63
2.5   The Window Class   65
2.6   Input to a Dialog Box   69
2.7   Converting Strings to Numbers   72
2.8   Command Line Arguments   75
2.9   Errors   78
          Syntax Errors   78
          Run-Time Errors   82
          Logical Errors   82
          Summary   82
          Review Questions   83
          Exercises   84
          Programming Problems   85

Chapter 3   **Object-Oriented Programming   87**
3.1   Abstract Data Type   88
3.2   Constructors   90
3.3   Instance Methods   93
3.4   Class Methods   101

3.5   Scope and Lifetime of Identifiers   104
3.6   Software Development   106
3.7   Object-Oriented Program Design   108
        Identify the Classes and Methods   109
        Algorithm Development   111
        Testing   112
        Compilation and Execution   112
        Documentation   113
        Case Study: Cutting Logs   116
3.8   The AVI Package Revisited   124
        The Audio Class   125
        The Timer Class   128
        The Filmstrip Class   130
        Case Study: A Simulation of Rolling a Die   135
        Summary   144
        Review Questions   146
        Exercises   147
        Programming Problems   150

Chapter 4   **Selection   153**
4.1   More AVI Classes   154
        The Slider Class   154
        The RadioButtons Class   156
4.2   If..else Statement   161
4.3   Nested If Statement   166
4.4   Conditional Expressions   172
4.5   Else if Statements   176
4.6   Boolean Data Type   177
4.7   Switch   179
4.8   Wrapper Classes   184
        Case Study: Body Mass Index   185
4.9   Yet another AVI Class!   194
        The Memo Class   194
4.10   The This Object   195
        Case Study: Validation of Dates including Leap
            Years   196
        Summary   209
        Review Questions   210
        Exercises   210
        Programming Problems   212

Chapter 5   **Repetition and One-Dimensional Arrays   217**
5.1   Loop Structure   218
5.2   While Loop   220

While Loop Controlled by a Counter   220

While Loop Controlled by Data   220

5.3   Do..while Loop   227

5.4   Increment/Decrement Operators   232

5.5   For Loop   235

5.6   Which Loop?   239

while   240

do..while   240

for   240

5.7   Arrays Revisited   241

5.8   Declaring and Initializing One-Dimensional Arrays   242

Three Methods   242

5.9   Using Arrays   245

Case Study: Palindrome   253

5.10 Our Last AVI Class: CheckBoxes   261

The CheckBox Class   261

5.11 Formatting Numbers for Output   264

Case Study: Ben's Breakfast Bar   267

Summary   282

Review Questions   283

Exercises   283

Programming Problems   285

Chapter 6   Advanced Concepts with Classes   289

6.1   Inheritance   290

6.2   An Example of Inheritance   292

6.3   Overriding Superclass Methods   299

6.4   Polymorphism   303

6.5   Instanceof Operator   307

6.6   Shadowed Variables   309

6.7   Inner Classes   312

6.8   Abstract Methods and Classes   312

Case Study: Boats   317

6.9   Interfaces   339

6.10 Constructors Revisited   345

6.11 Instance Methods Revisited   347

6.12 Object Properties   348

Comparing Objects   348

Copying Objects   350

Passing Objects as Parameters   352

Case Study: Arithmetic of Rational Numbers   353

6.13 Garbage Collection and Object Finalization   361

Summary   363

Review Questions   365
Exercises   366
Programming Problems   371

Chapter 7   **Exceptions and Streams   375**

7.1   Introduction   376
7.2   Exception Classes   377
7.3   Catching an Exception   379
7.4   Catching Multiple Exceptions   383
7.5   Creating Your Own Exception Class   387
7.6   Throwing an Exception   390
7.7   Finally Blocks   394
7.8   Using Exception Handling   396
7.9   Stream Input and Output   398
7.10   The StreamTokenizer Class   404
7.11   Text File Processing   407
        Book Example Problem   412
        Another Example: Using a File Viewer   417
7.12   The FileDialog Class   419
        Case Study: Reporting on the Statistics of a
        Text File   422
        Summary   433
        Review Questions   434
        Exercises   435
        Programming Problems   438

Chapter 8   **An Introduction to the java.awt Package   443**

8.1   Creating a Container   444
8.2   Handling an Event   448
8.3   Adding a Button to the Container   451
8.4   Adding Labels, Fonts, and Text Fields to a
        Container   457
        Labels   457
        Fonts   458
        Text Fields   461
8.5   Adding Check Boxes, Radio Buttons, and Lists to a
        Container   465
        Check Boxes   465
        Radio Buttons   468
        List   472
8.6   Creating a Reusable Container   476
8.7   Creating a Reusable WritingPad Component   480

8.8   Creating a Reusable DialogBox Component   486
8.9   Creating a Reusable CheckBoxes Component   491
8.10   Java Swing   497
        Summary   497
        Review Questions   499
        Exercises   500
        Programming Problems   500

Chapter 9   **Vectors, Serialization, and the java.awt Graphics Class   501**

9.1   Vectors   502
        Case Study: Chemical Elements   508
9.2   Saving and Loading Serializable Objects   520
9.3   The Graphics Class   524
9.4   Mouse Events   527
9.5   Pop-Up Menus   534
9.6   Painting the Screen   544
9.7   Printing Objects   548
        Summary   558
        Review Questions   558
        Exercises   559
        Programming Problems   560

Chapter 10   **Objects Working Together   563**

10.1   Packages   564
10.2   Associations   570
10.3   CRC Cards   582
10.4   Aggregation   586
10.5   Composition   598
10.6   Building a Student Management System   599
10.7   Menus Revisited   604
10.8   Testing the Student Management System   608
        Summary   613
        Review Questions   614
        Exercises   615
        Programming Problems   616

Chapter 11   **Applets and Threads   619**

11.1   Introduction   620
11.2   Applets   622
11.3   Input to Applets   628
11.4   Playing Sounds   634
11.5   Displaying Images   637

11.6   Loading Images   639
11.7   Arrays Revisited   641
11.8   Image Maps   645
11.9   Threads   649
       Case Study: An Example of Multithreading   657
11.10 Animation   668
11.11 Restrictions   673
11.12 Sound and Images with Applications   674
       Sound   675
       Images   675
11.13 Conclusion   676
       Summary   677
       Review Questions   679
       Exercises   680
       Programming Problems   682

Chapter 12   Sorting, Searching, and Dynamic Data Structures   685

12.1   Sorting   686
12.2   Class java.util.Arrays—Sort
12.3   Sequential Search   700
12.4   Class java.util.Arrays—Binary Search
12.5   Linked Lists   708
       LinkedList Class   718
12.6   Stacks   726
       Case Study: Using a Stack for Converting Algebraic
       Expressions   728
       Summary   738
       Review Questions   739
       Exercises   739
       Programming Problems   739

Appendix A   Tables   743

A.1   ASCII Characters   743
A.2   Java Primitive Data Types   744
A.3   Operator Priorities   745
A.4   Escape-Sequence Characters   746

Appendix B   Syntax of Java   747

B.1   Productions of Lexical Structures   747
B.2   Productions from Types, Values, and Variables   747
B.3   Productions from Names   748
B.4   Productions from Packages   748

B.5   Productions Used Only in the LALR(1)
        Grammar   749
B.6   Productions from Classes   749
            Productions from Class Declarations   749
            Productions from Field Declarations   750
            Productions from Method Declarations   751
            Productions from Static Initializers   751
            Productions from Constructor Declarations   751
B.7   Productions from Interfaces   752
            Productions from Interface Declarations   752
B.8   Productions from Arrays   752
B.9   Productions from Blocks and Statements   753
B.10   Productions from Expressions   756

Appendix C   Answers to Exercises   761

Index   805

Introduction

Welcome to the world of Object-Oriented Programming with Java.

Please take your time to read this introduction. It will help you set up your computer system so that you can execute the Java program examples used throughout this book and so that you will be able to create and execute your own Java programs.

The chapter begins by instructing you how to download and install the Java 2 Software Development Kit (SDK) from Sun Microsystems, Inc. onto your computer. The SDK is free of charge, and subject to the licensing agreement set out by Sun Microsystems, Inc. Sun's SDK will be used exclusively throughout this book; therefore, it is important that you get off to the right start by installing all the Java software and documentation that will you need to build and run Java programs on your computer.

The CD that accompanies this text includes a package of Java routines, the Audio-Visual Interface package (AVI). It will enable you to easily use screen-oriented user interfaces in your programs. You will learn how to set up your computer so that your programs can automatically use this package. You will also learn how to access the book's example programs, which are also contained on the CD. (Note that everything contained on the CD is also available at the text-book's Web site.)

Additionally, you will be instructed on how to edit, save, create, compile, and execute Java programs. By the end of this introduction you should have an understanding of the following topics.

- A brief history of Java.

- How to download the Java 2 SDK from Sun Microsystems, Inc.

- How to configure your computer to use the Java 2 SDK.

- How to install the Audio-Visual Interface (AVI).

- How to create and save a Java program using an editor.

- How to compile and run your first Java program.

- Java 2 SDK Tool support.

- How to copy, modify, and save programs from the CD.

0.1   What is Java?

Java is a computer language, designed and implemented by Sun Microsystems, Inc. The term Java is not an acronym; it was adopted to reflect a favorite drink (coffee) of many programmers—hence Sun's logo for Java is a cup of steaming coffee.

Java is a very young language in comparison with such languages as Pascal and C (both developed in the early 1970s). Although Java was first brought to the attention of the public in 1995, it started life back in 1990. A team at Sun, headed by James Gosling, designed a new programming language known as Oak (allegedly named after a tree outside the window of its main designer) for the development of consumer electronics software.

In 1993, the World Wide Web appeared on the Internet. The Sun development team soon realized that the Java language would be suitable for writing programs to run on different computers connected to the Internet. This was a milestone, since Java was the first language to provide features to allow programs to be downloaded as part of a web page and run on a user's computer. To demonstrate this new feature, Sun developed the first web browser to support Java applets (a Java program designed to run using a Java-enabled web browser); they named it HotJava.

In addition to applets, the Java language can be used to develop standalone application programs that do not involve the use of web pages.

Java is an object-oriented language, unlike Pascal and C, which are procedural languages. As a programmer, object-oriented programming means that you focus on building classes to represent the data in your application, rather than on the solution to a problem as a set of procedures that must be followed in a set order.

The Java language is small in size and simple to learn and to use. The power of the language comes from the extensive library of utilitarian software components that a programmer may use.

You are not restricted to developing and running your programs on just one type of computer. Java programs are portable. For example, a program written and compiled for a PC may be transferred without modification to run on, say, a Sun Workstation.

Java offers improvements over other computer languages in that it is robust, secure, and may be used for networking applications.

As a young language, Java is still evolving. Although the core of the language is small, the evolution appears to be coming from the addition of more and more useful libraries to the development environment. The language in 1995 used version 1.0, followed by major additions to the libraries and minor modification to the core language, leading to version 1.1 in 1997.

In 1998, Java version 1.2 was launched and was popularly dubbed Java 2. All the programs in the book and on the enclosed CD have been developed using Java 2 version 1.2.2. Since version 1.3.0 also became available at the time of writing this book, all the programs have also been tested using this new edition of the language.

0.2 Using the Internet

If you already have access to the Internet on your computer, please go to the next section on downloading the Java 2 SDK for Windows, Unix, and Linux users. However, if you are new to computers and would like to know how to link your computer to the World Wide Web, then please read on.

There are three essential requirements you need to fulfill before you can connect to the Web.

- Your computer must have a *modem* installed in order to connect it with your domestic phone line or mobile phone. If you don't have such equipment, then contact your computer dealer for more information.

- You need an account with an *Internet provider*; this is an organization that your computer will dial into and enable you to gain access to the Internet. There are many Internet providers all competing for your account. Many providers will allow you hours and hours of free connect time before they start billing you for their service. Many Internet providers advertise in popular computer magazines, so read around and make your own informed choice as to which provider to choose. Once you have an account, you will be given a *user id* and a *password*, which must be used each time you need to gain access to the Internet via the provider.

- You need an *Internet browser*. A browser is a computer program that will enable you to move around the World Wide Web looking for information. There are several popular browsers available, for example Microsoft Internet Explorer, Sun HotJava, and Netscape Navigator.

To connect with the World Wide Web on the Internet, use your browser to connect with your Internet provider. You may need to type your password when prompted. Once you are connected with your Internet provider you have access to all those many millions of people and companies who subscribe to the Internet worldwide.

0.3 Downloading the Java 2 SDK for Windows, Unix (Solaris), and Linux Users

If you want to use Java 2, version 1.2.2 or later, on a Windows, UNIX, or Linux platform, then once you have logged onto the Internet, input the following address (URL) to your Web browser:

```
http://java.sun.com
```

Browse through the web pages, mouse-clicking on the following hot links:

```
Products & APIs
Java 2 Platform, Standard Edition
```

You now have a choice of which version of the Java 2 SDK (Software Development Kit) to download. Since all the programs on the enclosed CD were developed using version 1.2.2, we will use this version in the explanation. You are, of course, free to choose a later version.

```
Java 2 SDK, Standard Edition, v 1.2.2
```

You then have to choose a platform:

```
Java 2 SDK v 1.2.2 005 Windows 95/98/NT Production Release
Java 2 SDK Solaris Production Release
Java 2 SDK v 1.2.2 for Linux Production Release
```

By following the instructions on the screen, the software and documentation will be downloaded to the hard drive on your computer, unless you request otherwise. The time needed to download the complete development kit will vary considerably, since this depends upon the speed of your connection to your provider, and the time of day you access the Internet.

0.4 Downloading Java 2 SDK Documentation

In addition to downloading the SDK, you may also want to download the associated documentation. It is also free of charge, and we strongly suggest you download it so that you have easy access to it while pursuing your study of object-oriented programming with Java. Assuming you are still connected to the Internet, use your web browser to return to the page that contained the options for downloading the Java 2 SDK. Further down this page you will see hot links to the documentation. Choose:

```
English Java 2 SDK documentation
```

This will take you to the Java 2 SDK documentation. Follow the instructions for downloading the documentation.

Note: If you are a Windows user, you will need access to a zip utility such as `WinZip`.

> *i* By using the Sun Microsystems Web site you can always keep in touch with the latest developments to the Java language.

0.5   Creating a Java Software Development Environment

All the instructions that follow assume that you are using a PC running either Microsoft's 95/98 (or later) or NT Windows operating systems. For Unix and Linux platforms, use the equivalent platform-dependent instructions.

If you are using the Windows platform, the file `jdk1_2_2-win` should already be downloaded if you have followed the previous directions. This file is known as a self-extracting program. Running it will cause it to extract from itself the many files that make up the Java 2 system. Mouse-click on the filename to run the program. Follow the on-screen instructions to install the Java 2 SDK on your computer. Use Windows Explorer to inspect the files that have been added to your C drive under the directory `jdk1.2.2` (or a later version of your choice). A listing of this directory is given in Figure 0.1. The `docs` folder should not appear since it has not yet been included in the environment.

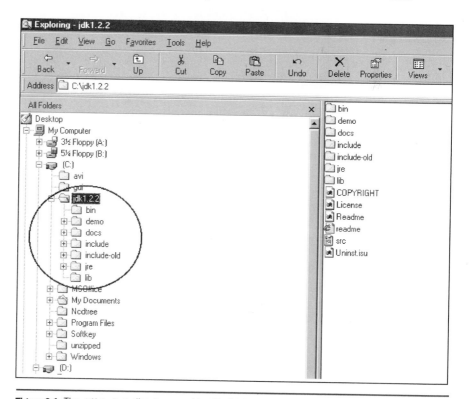

Figure 0.1 The `jdk1.2.2` directory on drive C with its subdirectories and files

If you chose to download the Java SDK documentation, then you should follow this next step that describes how to install the documentation. A file called `jdk1_2_2-doc` should have been downloaded. If you are using a Windows platform, then mouse-click on this file and it should invoke the `WinZip` utility. Request to extract the files and store them on drive C. Do not specify a subdirectory. When the extraction is complete, the `jdk1.2.2` directory will contain the `docs` subdirectory. If you open the `docs` subdirectory and mouse-click on the `index`, your default Web browser will be invoked, providing you access to the Java SDK, Standard Edition Documentation. Figure 0.2 illustrates the opening page of this documentation.

If you scroll through the page illustrated in Figure 0.2 to the heading <u>API & Language Documentation</u> and mouse-click on the <u>Java 2 Platform API Specification</u>, you will see the page illustrated in Figure 0.3. API stands for application programming interface.

Be curious, look around, explore. For example, examine what is contained under the packages named `java.lang`, `java.string`, and `java.util`. You may not understand the technical content of the documentation at this stage; however, you will start to get a feel for how to access the documentation and how it is organized.

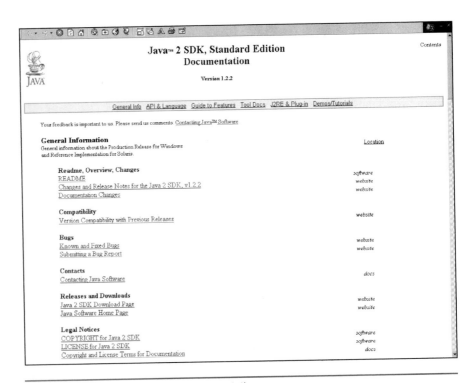

Figure 0.2 Opening page of the Java Documentation

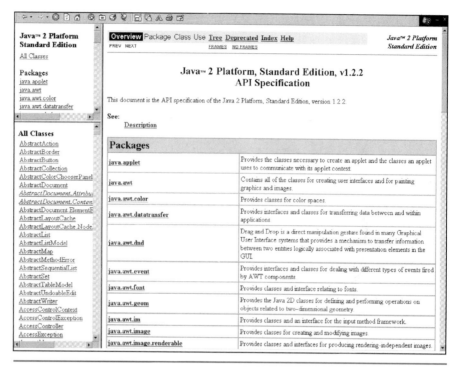

Figure 0.3 Java 2 Documentation, introductory page

i You are strongly advised to keep the documentation iconized on your computer, ready for reference when you start to develop your own programs.

0.6   Copying and Installing the Audio-Visual Interface (AVI)

The CD that accompanies this text includes a package of Java routines (the AVI package) that will enable you to easily use screen-oriented user interfaces in your programs. Most of the book's examples also use this package. It is important that the package be installed properly on your computer.

The following instructions are intended for Windows users. Unix and Linux users are advised to use the equivalent platform-dependent instructions.

Copy the `avi` directory and its contents from the CD included with this book and store it as a directory on the C drive. Figure 0.4 shows a listing of the entries in the `avi` directory.

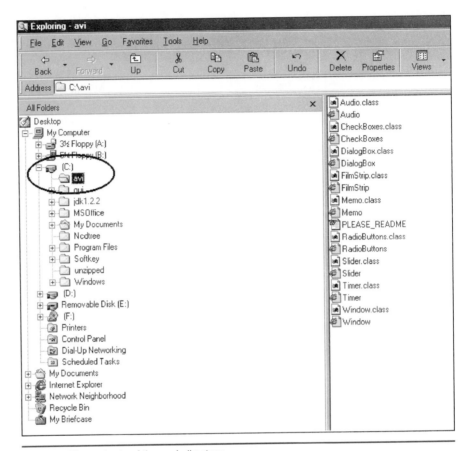

Figure 0.4 The contents of the `avi` directory

Now that the SDK and the AVI package have been installed on your computer, you must set up your computer so that these programs can be located when needed. Use the `NotePad` utility to open the `autoexec.bat` file that is stored on your C drive. Amend the file to include the `jdk1.1.2` directory in the `path` entry. Also include a `CLASSPATH` entry. The following listing of an `autoexec.bat` file illustrates how the `path` and `CLASSPATH` entries have been modified to include `jdk1.2.2` and the `avi` package.

```
@C:\PROGRA~1\NORTON~1\NAVDX.EXE /Startup
set CLASSPATH=.;c:\
path=c:\jdk1.2.2\bin
```

The interpretation of the CLASSPATH entry follows. The pathways are separated by the semicolon, hence there are two pathways the computer should use when searching for the named packages. The first pathway is signified by the use of a period (.), which implies the current directory. The computer will search all subdirectories of the current subdirectory to find the subdirectory of the avi package.

The second pathway is signified by c:\, which is the root directory of the C drive. The computer will search all the subdirectories of the root directory to find the subdirectory of the avi package. If you use software that also requires a CLASSPATH entry, append the entry to the one shown here. Separate the entries with a semicolon, and set the CLASSPATH only once.

The path entry signifies where on the C drive the computer can find the Java development environment. Once again, if you use software that requires a path entry, append the entry to the one shown here, separating different path-names by a semicolon.

Save the modified autoexec.bat file, and finally restart your computer.

0.7 How to Input and Save a Java Program in the Computer

In order to type a Java program at the keyboard and save the program on a disk, it is necessary to run a program called an *editor* or *word processor*. In addition to enabling program entry, an editor allows a program to be retrieved from disk and amended as necessary. A Java program is stored in text mode so that the programmer can read the program as it was written.

Once again, the following illustration assumes a Windows platform. Unix and Linux users should use the equivalent platform-dependent commands and software.

Try the following. From your Microsoft Windows environment, mouse-click on Start, and then select Programs from the menu, followed by Accessories from the next menu, then mouse-click on WordPad from the final menu.

WordPad is a simple word processor to use; you are advised to use this software to create all your Java programs. WordPad is not the only word processing package—you may also have NotePad, Word, or other word processing programs on your computer.

Use WordPad to type the following program so that it appears on your screen. Don't worry that you cannot yet understand the meaning of the statements in the program. A full explanation of this program will be given in Chapter 2.

```
// program to write the text literal "HELLO WORLD" centrally on the screen

import avi.*;

class Example_1
{
     public static void main(String[] args)
     {
          // create a window object screen
          Window screen = new Window("Example_1.java","bold","red",72);

          screen.showWindow();
          screen.write("\n\n\n               HELLO WORLD");
     }
}
```

The next step is most important. You must save the program as a *text document*, having a filename appended with `.java`. For example, the program that you have just typed must be saved under the filename `Example_1.java`, as a text file.

 In reality it doesn't matter which word processing software you use as an editor to input your program as long as you save the program as a text file with a `.java` suffix.

Figure 0.5 shows you how to save the file `Example_1.java` as a text document in the subdirectory `Introduction`.

0.8   How to Compile a Java Program

Before a program can be run on your computer, it first must be compiled. Compilation is a process that will transform your program into a form the computer can execute.

The computer cannot execute the Java statements as they currently appear in the program; the statements must be translated to an intermediate form for execution. The compiler is resident in the memory of the computer and uses the Java source program code as input data. The output from the compiler is the same program, now represented by a set of Java byte codes. *Java byte codes* are a set of instructions written for a hypothetical computer, known as the *Java virtual machine*. Regardless of the computer you are using, whether it is a PC, Apple™, or Sun™ computer, the compiler will generate the same Java bytecode program. For this reason programs written in Java are portable. A program written in Java to run on, say, a PC that also runs without modification on a different computer, for example, a Sun, and produces exactly the same results, is said to be *portable* between the two computers.

In addition to translation, a compiler reports on any grammatical errors made by the programmer in the language statements of the program. If errors

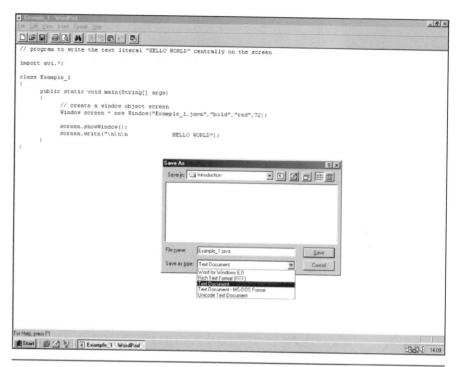

Figure 0.5 Using WordPad to save a Java program as a text document

are reported, it is necessary to return to the editor to correct the errors, resave the program, and then recompile the program.

If you are working on a PC using Microsoft's Windows environment, then open an MSDOS window and change your subdirectory to wherever you saved your Java program Example_1.java. In this scenario, the program is stored in the subdirectory Java\disk\Introduction on the D drive.

The command to compile a Java program using the Java 2 SDK is javac. To compile the first program listed, you would issue the following command:

```
javac Example_1.java
```

Figure 0.6 illustrates how to use the compilation command in an MSDOS window. Unix and Linux users will use the same command but from a terminal window.

The byte code produced by the compiler will be stored in a file called Example_1.class. You should *not* try to edit or print a class file.

If you get errors listed in the MSDOS window, they could be caused by the following problems.

- You have not modified the path entry of your autoexec.bat file correctly and the computer cannot execute the command javac to compile your program.

Figure 0.6 Using the compile command `javac` to compile a program in an MSDOS window

- You have not modified the `CLASSPATH` entry in your `autoexec.bat` file correctly and the computer cannot find any reference to the `avi` sub-directory.

- You have made a mistake when typing the program, and the syntax of at least one statement might be incorrect.

You should carefully examine all three cases and make any necessary amendments before you recompile the program.

0.9   How to Execute (run) a Java Program

The program stored as Java byte codes is loaded into the memory of the computer, and is read and translated by an interpreter. An interpreter will read the byte code one "line" at a time, and translate each line, in turn, into a sequence of commands that can be directly executed by the computer. There exist different interpreters for different computers; for example, the interpreter for a PC will be different from the interpreter for an Apple. Each of these interpreters can read the same byte code, i.e., the same `.class` file, but will produce a different set of executable instructions since each computer supports a different machine-instruction set. The interpreter reads the respective byte codes and instructs the computer to execute the meanings of the instructions.

If the compilation is successful, you can execute (run) the program. The command to execute or run a Java program using the Java 2 SDK is `java`. To execute the HELLO WORLD program you would issue the following command in the same window where you compiled the program:

```
java Example_1
```

Figure 0.7 illustrates how to execute the program by typing the command `java Example_1` at the prompt in the MSDOS window. Unix and Linux users will use the same command but from a terminal window. By default, the `java` command will use the appropriate `.class` file.

If the program has executed correctly, the output should appear as illustrated in Figure 0.8. You can stop the program by clicking on the X in the upper-right

Figure 0.7 Using the execute command `java` to run a program from an `MSDOS` window

corner of the window, by choosing Close from the pull-down menu that appears when you click on the coffee-cup icon in the upper-left corner of the window, or by pressing the Alt-F4 key combination.

To summarize, the sections on inputting and saving a program (phase 1), compiling a program (phase 2), and executing a program (phase 3) are illustrated in Figure 0.9.

It is possible for a program to fail during the execution phase, in which case it must be stopped from any further execution. If modifications to the program are required, it is necessary to perform the amendments at phase 1, and repeat phases 2 and 3.

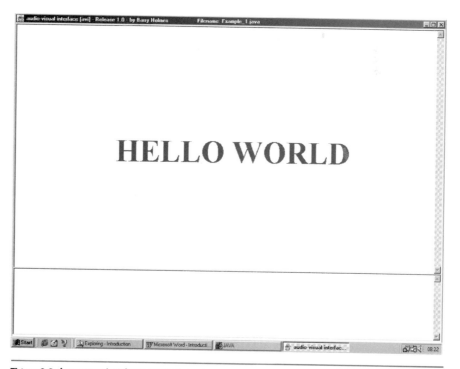

Figure 0.8 A screen shot from running program `Example_1`

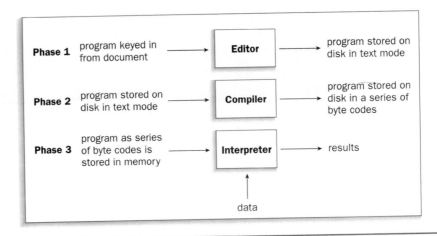

Figure 0.9 Three phases of program implementation

NOW DO THIS   Using the editor, modify program `Example_1` as follows.

(1) Locate the line of the program that contains the text HELLO WORLD and modify this line to display a message of your own choice on the screen.

(2) Save and re-compile the amended program. If the program is error free after compilation, then run the program.

0.10 SDK Tools

In order to build Java programs on your computer, the SDK contains a set of tools for compiling and executing your programs, plus a variety of other utilitarian features. Return to the index page of your documentation (now you know why we said iconize the index page for future use), and search down the index page for the heading <u>SDK Tool Documentation</u>. Under the heading, mouse-click on the hot link <u>Tool Documentation</u>. The two tools that you used in this chapter and that you will use extensively throughout this book are:

- `javac`—the **Java Language Compiler** that you use to compile programs written in the Java programming language into bytecodes.

- `java`—the **Java Interpreter** that you use to run programs written in the Java programming language.

Take your time to browse through the SDK tool documentation using your mouse pointer to click on the hot links for each tool command. This way you will be given a full explanation of the function of each tool.

Look up the `javadoc` entry and read how to document Java code.

0.11   Copying and Editing Programs from the CD

In addition to containing the AVI, the CD that accompanies this book contains all of the book's example programs and numerous sound and image files that are used by those programs. As you work through the book, it is crucial for you to copy the sample programs and support files from the CD onto your computer. You will then be able to execute and interact with the programs. Additionally, we have included throughout the book many hands-on exercises related to the example programs. Performing these exercises (many are contained in "Now Do This" sections while others are included in end-of-chapter exercises) will help you learn object-oriented programming with Java.

Load the CD into your computer's CD drive now and use your operating system tools to examine the directory structure of the CD. (Remember, if you do not have a CD drive, all of the files are also available on the textbook's Web site.) You will see that the sample program files are organized by chapter number.

Depending on how you prefer to work, you may want to copy the entire sample program directory structure right now onto a suitable location on your computer. Alternatively, you could copy the files on an as-needed basis, as you progress through the book. In any case, you should probably use the same file subdirectory structure on your hard drive as is used on the CD.

For purposes of this introduction, you should now use your operating system's copy command to copy the file `Example_2.java` from the `Introduction` subdirectory of the CD into an appropriate directory on your computer's hard drive. It's up to you whether you take this opportunity to copy all of the files or not. Altogether, the program and support files require about 30 MB of memory.

> ⚠ You may need to change the properties of the programs you copied from the CD, from Read-only to Archive. Failure to do this will result in your not being able to save any modifications you make to the programs on your hard disk.

Following the same steps described previously for the first example, compile and run `Example_2.java`.

You should see a window called `Example_2.java` open on your screen with a dialog box asking you to enter your name. Type your name into the dialog box, and press the Return key. If the name Mickey Mouse is input into the box, the dialog box would appear the same as shown in Figure 0.10.

The output on the screen should appear to be similar to the screen-shot of Figure 0.11 if the name Mickey Mouse was entered into the dialog box.

Figure 0.10 A dialog box used to input a name

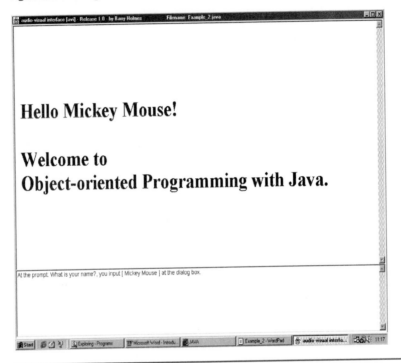

Figure 0.11 Screen shot from running program `Example_2`

NOW DO THIS

1. Using your editor, open program `Example_2.java`.

2. Locate those lines in the program that print the message, and change the message to one of your own choice.

3. Save the program (remember the original file must be saved in Archive mode).

4. Compile and run the modified program.

Congratulations. You are now set to begin your study of Object-Oriented Programming with Java.

SUMMARY

You should now be able to perform the following tasks:

- Gain access to the Internet to download software from the `java.sun.com` Web site.

- Install the Java 2 Software Development Kit on your computer.

- Install the Audio-Visual Interface package that is used throughout the book to simplify input and output.

- Implement a program on a computer:

   —by using an editor to key a program into the computer.

   —by compiling the program into byte codes.

   —by using an interpreter to execute or run the byte-code program.

- Copy the files from the CD enclosed with this book to your computer. Load and run one of the copied programs.

- Modify an existing program.

CHAPTER 1

Primitive Data Types and Arithmetic

We start our exploration of the Java language by examining the different characteristics of data such as type and size, and introduce you to the data types for numbers and characters. We also examine how to perform arithmetic on numbers in Java.

To reinforce these concepts, the chapter contains several example programs to show you how to declare data types and perform calculations.

By the end of the chapter you will have an understanding of the following topics.

- Recognizing data and classifying it by type

- The identification of variables and constants and their representation in a program

- The construction of arithmetic expressions for the purpose of making calculations

- Writing simple programs

1.1 Data

Before we attempt to write any computer programs, we must be able to classify information into various types. We are surrounded by information; just look at the assortment of signs in Figure 1.1 that we may encounter. This information can be classified as either characters or numbers. From the signs you can identify single characters such as P (for Parking) or T (weight limit in Tons); you can also see groups of characters such as WEAK BRIDGE, CAFÉ, breakfast, or soups; and numbers such as 10 (in the 10 T weight limit for the weak bridge) or 2 (in the waiting limited to 2 hours).

Figure 1.2 contains information from a newspaper and from a bank statement. In the newspaper extract you can find a listing of world share markets that contains groups of characters representing a name of a market, followed by a numerical value. For example, FTSE All-Share yield (%) −0.03 and Dow Jones Industrial +91.36 both show the change in the value of portfolios of shares over a week. From the bank statement a similar format exists; for example, BALANCE BROUGHT FORWARD 1225.11 shows the balance from the previous bank statement, and BRITISH GAS 21.00 tells the charge for a direct debit on the cost of gas.

Data is the name given to characters and quantities operated upon by a computer. For example, in the bank statement in Figure 1.2, the name of the company is a group of characters and the charge for gas is a quantity. A computer *program* consists of a series of instructions for the computer to execute and provides a method for processing data. The data from bank transactions can be processed by a computer into information for bank statements.

From the information shown in the two figures, we can identify four data types: *integer* (a positive or negative whole number), *real* (a positive or negative number with a decimal fraction), *character* (a single character), and a *string* (a

Figure 1.1 An assortment of signs

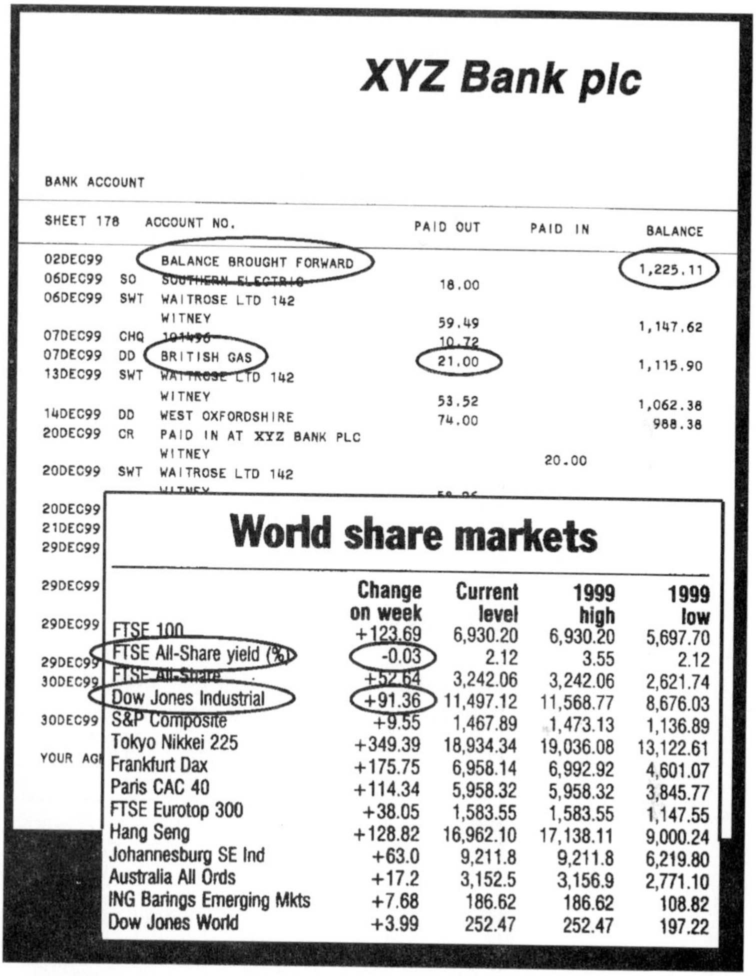

XYZ Bank plc

BANK ACCOUNT

SHEET 178		ACCOUNT NO.	PAID OUT	PAID IN	BALANCE
02DEC99		BALANCE BROUGHT FORWARD			1,225.11
06DEC99	SO	SOUTHERN ELECTRIC	18.00		
06DEC99	SWT	WAITROSE LTD 142 WITNEY	59.49		1,147.62
07DEC99	CHQ	101496	10.72		
07DEC99	DD	BRITISH GAS	21.00		1,115.90
13DEC99	SWT	WAITROSE LTD 142 WITNEY	53.52		1,062.38
14DEC99	DD	WEST OXFORDSHIRE	74.00		988.38
20DEC99	CR	PAID IN AT XYZ BANK PLC WITNEY		20.00	
20DEC99	SWT	WAITROSE LTD 142			

World share markets

	Change on week	Current level	1999 high	1999 low
FTSE 100	+123.69	6,930.20	6,930.20	5,697.70
FTSE All-Share yield (%)	-0.03	2.12	3.55	2.12
FTSE All-Share	+52.64	3,242.06	3,242.06	2,621.74
Dow Jones Industrial	+91.36	11,497.12	11,568.77	8,676.03
S&P Composite	+9.55	1,467.89	1,473.13	1,136.89
Tokyo Nikkei 225	+349.39	18,934.34	19,036.08	13,122.61
Frankfurt Dax	+175.75	6,958.14	6,992.92	4,601.07
Paris CAC 40	+114.34	5,958.32	5,958.32	3,845.77
FTSE Eurotop 300	+38.05	1,583.55	1,583.55	1,147.55
Hang Seng	+128.82	16,962.10	17,138.11	9,000.24
Johannesburg SE Ind	+63.0	9,211.8	9,211.8	6,219.80
Australia All Ords	+17.2	3,152.5	3,156.9	2,771.10
ING Barings Emerging Mkts	+7.68	186.62	186.62	108.82
Dow Jones World	+3.99	252.47	252.47	197.22

Figure 1.2 Information from a newspaper and bank statement

group of characters). For example, in Figure 1.1 the numbers 2 and 10 are both whole numbers and can be classified as integers. In the same figure, the single characters P and T can be classified as characters, and the groups of characters WEAK BRIDGE, CAFÉ, sandwiches, and soups can be classified as strings. In Figure 1.2, the numbers 1225.11, 21.00, −0.03, and +91.36 are positive or negative numbers containing a decimal fraction and can be classified as reals.

1.2 Data Storage

Figure 1.3 shows two memory chips from a digital computer. The term *digital* implies that all information is represented by numbers within the computer. Computer memory is composed of many millions of storage cells. The unique

The smallest memory component can physically represent a binary digit (**bit**). These components are grouped together in units of eight to form a **byte** of memory. Each memory chip shown here has a storage capacity of over four million bytes.

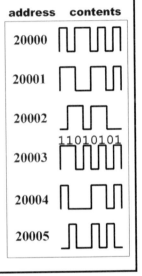

Each byte of memory has a unique numeric address to enable data to be written to or read from specific locations in memory.

A binary digit is stored as a representation of some physical property of the circuitry being used, for example as levels of electrical charge.

The diagram shows that at any memory address the eight bits are represented in one of two states as either a peak or a trough, where a peak represents the binary digit 1 and a trough the binary digit 0. For example the contents of address 20003 can be interpreted as the binary value 11010101.

Figure 1.3 Computer memory

numeric address of a group of cells identifies the location of the cells within the memory. Figure 1.3 also illustrates several storage cell groups with addresses from 20000 to 20005, which contain information represented by levels of electrical charge. The levels are shown as a series of peaks and troughs.

> *i* A *chip* is a small section of a single crystal of semiconductor, usually silicon, that forms the substrate upon which is fabricated a single semiconductor device or all the individual devices comprising an integrated circuit. Chip is also an informal name for an integrated circuit.

A *binary digit* or *bit* has one of two possible values and is the smallest unit of memory available on a computer. In a computer, a bit is represented by some physical property that can be in one of two states: on or off, open or closed, high charge or low charge (as shown in Figure 1.3). It is standard practice to represent the contents of a bit with the numbers 0 or 1.

A single bit can therefore distinguish between two values. For example, it could represent a door being open as a 0 and the door being closed as a 1. It could represent the temperature being cold with a 0 and being hot with a 1. To represent more than two values we need to use more bits. For example, we could classify the temperature into four categories by using two bits as follows: 00 = cold, 01 = pleasant, 10 = warm, and 11 = hot.

Every time we add a bit, we double the number of values we can represent. With three bits we can represent 2^3 = 8 values (000, 001, 010, 011, 100, 101, 110, 111), with four bits we can represent 2^4 = 16 values, and so on. A collection of eight bits is called a *byte* and can represent 2^8 = 256 values. Bytes are often used as the unit of addressing in computers, and therefore we describe the size of computer memories in terms of bytes. Figure 1.3 illustrates the storage of several bytes. The figure illustrates that within memory address 20003, the levels of electrical charge represent the series of bits 11010101. Each memory address in the illustration is capable of holding a byte of information. Each memory chip pictured in the figure has a storage capacity of four megabytes! A megabyte is 1,048,576 bytes (2^{20} bytes) and not 1,000,000 as the name implies.

In many programming languages, including Java, programmers use variables to hold data whose values can change during the execution of a program. A *variable* is a named memory location that can hold a particular type of data. For example, the following statement in a Java program will reserve a memory location called count that can hold data of type integer.

```
int count;
```

This statement is called a *type declaration* since it declares that the variable count must hold data of type integer. We say that the *data type* of count is int. We will return to this discussion of variables and type declarations in Java soon. First we continue our general discussion of data storage.

Number Systems

We use the decimal number system (base 10) in our everyday lives for our numerical calculations. There is nothing sacred about the number 10, and number systems using a different number of digits have been used throughout human history. In particular, with computers it is more efficient to use the *binary number system* (base 2) for calculations inside the machine.

Despite all information being stored in the computer in a binary format, there is no equivalent representation for binary numbers in Java. The hexadecimal number system is used in Java as a shorthand representation of binary numbers. Figure 1.4 shows that a hexadecimal digit can be conveniently represented by four bits; for example, the four bits 0000 represent hexadecimal digit 0, the four bits 0001 represent hexadecimal digit 1, the four bits 0010 represent hexadecimal digit 2, and, finally, the four bits 1111 represent hexadecimal digit F.

Binary	Decimal	Hexadecimal
0000	0	0
0001	1	1
0010	2	2
0011	3	3
0100	4	4
0101	5	5
0110	6	6
0111	7	7
1000	8	8
1001	9	9
1010	10	A
1011	11	B
1100	12	C
1101	13	D
1110	14	E
1111	15	F

Figure 1.4 Representation of 0 to 15 in binary, decimal, and hexadecimal

From Figure 1.4 you will notice that the hexadecimal digits 0 to 9 are the same as those for a decimal number, however, to represent the six extra hexadecimal digits, it is necessary to use the letters A to F, which are equivalent to the decimal numbers 10 to 15.

The decimal system is a positional number system that uses the ten digits from 0 to 9 to represent numbers. The binary and hexadecimal number systems work exactly the same way as the decimal number system. Just as the decimal number 573 really means $5 \times 10^2 + 7 \times 10^1 + 3 \times 10^0$, the binary number 101 means $1 \times 2^2 + 0 \times 2^1 + 1 \times 2^0$, and the hexadecimal number 31E means $3 \times 16^2 + 1 \times 16^1 + 14 \times 16^0$. In Java, hexadecimal integer numbers are prefixed by 0x, for example, 0x31E.

The remainder of this section explains how data of types called character, integer, and real are organized in the computer's memory. The explanation of the data type for a string is covered in Chapter 2.

Characters Many computer languages use the ASCII character code to represent characters. ASCII stands for the American Standard Code for Information Interchange. Its extended version uses a byte to represent a character and can therefore represent $2^8 = 256$ different characters. This is enough to represent all the characters on a typical keyboard but is not enough to represent all the special symbols we might want to use with computers, especially when you consider the different symbols used around the world in all the different languages.

Therefore, the creators of Java decided to base their language on the Unicode character set, a set that uses 16 bits per character. Each character requires two bytes of storage space in memory. The Unicode character set can represent $2^{16} = 65,536$ different symbols and contains the ASCII character set as a subset! The complete mapping of codes onto symbols is not yet complete.

The type declaration for a character is declared in Java as `char`. For example, the following Java statement declares a variable called `myChar`, of type `char`. This variable can hold a character as a value, and in fact is initialized to the character `'A'` in this statement.

```
char myChar = 'A';
```

Again, we will return to variables and type declarations in more detail soon.

A character literal is always delimited by single quotes; for example, the character literal A is written as `'A'`. The term *literal* refers to the stated value. In Java, a character literal may also be expressed by its Unicode character. A Unicode character is prefixed by \u to distinguish it from a numeric literal. The character literal `'A'` may also be written as `'\u0041'` (see Figure 1.5 for the appropriate unicode and corresponding character); however, this representation is not as clear as using the literal value of the character. Refer to Appendix A, Table A.1 for the character subset from `'\u0000'` to `'\u007E'`.

i

The *Unicode Worldwide Character Standard* is a character coding system designed to represent the characters of the languages of the modern world. Currently, the Unicode standard contains 34,168 distinct coded characters. The characters used in the computer programs in this book are confined to those illustrated in Figure 1.5. This character set is known as the ASCII character set. Notice that each Unicode character has been defined as a four-digit hexadecimal number.

Integer numbers   An integer is stored as a binary number. In Java there are several integer data types. The one we will be using most frequently is declared as `int` and uses four bytes of computer memory. Therefore, an `int` can represent any of $2^{32} = 4,294,967,296$ different integers. The range of `int` values is $-2,147,483,648$ to $+2,147,483,647$.

If you want to store an integer number that lies outside of the range for `int` types, then use the Java type `long`. These numbers are represented with eight bytes (64 bits) and have a range of $-9,223,372,036,854,775,808$ to $+9,223,372,036,854,775,807$.

The use of a plus sign (+) is optional for positive integer literals. All decimal integer literals must begin with a digit in the range from 1 to 9 after the sign (if a sign is present). Integer literals must not begin with 0 (zero). A `long` integer literal, either decimal or hexadecimal, has the character `1` or `L` appended immediately after the number.

Unicode	Character	Unicode	Character	Unicode	Character
0020	space	0040	@	0060	`
0021	!	0041	A	0061	a
0022	"	0042	B	0062	b
0023	#	0043	C	0063	c
0024	$	0044	D	0064	d
0025	%	0045	E	0065	e
0026	&	0046	F	0066	f
0027	'	0047	G	0067	g
0028	(	0048	H	0068	h
0029	)	0049	I	0069	i
002A	*	004A	J	006A	j
002B	+	004B	K	006B	k
002C	'	004C	L	006C	l
002D	–	004D	M	006D	m
002E	.	004E	N	006E	n
002F	/	004F	O	006F	o
0030	0	0050	P	0070	p
0031	1	0051	Q	0071	q
0032	2	0052	R	0072	r
0033	3	0053	S	0073	s
0034	4	0054	T	0074	t
0035	5	0055	U	0075	u
0036	6	0056	V	0076	v
0037	7	0057	W	0077	w
0038	8	0058	X	0078	x
0039	9	0059	Y	0079	y
003A	:	005A	Z	007A	z
003B	;	005B	[	007B	{
003C	<	005C	\	007C	|
003D	=	005D	]	007D	}
003E	>	005E	^	007E	~
003F	?	005F	_		

Figure 1.5 Printable character set

Real numbers   A real number is stored in the computer memory in two parts, a mantissa (the fractional part) and an exponent (the power to which the base of the number must be raised in order to give the correct value of the number when multiplied by the mantissa). For example, 437.875 can be rewritten as 0.437875 $\times 10^3$, where 0.437875 is the mantissa and 3 is the exponent. A four-byte representation of a real number will give a maximum value of $\pm 3.40282347 \times 10^{38}$ and the smallest value as $\pm 1.40239846 \times 10^{-45}$. The majority of decimal fractions do not convert exactly into binary fractions; therefore, the representation of a real number is not always accurate.

In Java, the type real is declared as `float`.

If the float range is too restrictive for the real numbers being stored, Java can store much larger real numbers using the type `double`. The number of bytes used to store a double-precision number is increased to eight. This increase in storage space will give a maximum value of $\pm 1.79769313486231570 \times 10^{+308}$ and the smallest value as $\pm 4.94065645841246544 \times 10^{-324}$.

A real-number literal can be written in one of two ways. For example, the literal -123.456 can be written as depicted or using a scientific notation $-1.23456E+2$. The character E represents the base 10, so the number can be interpreted as -1.23456×10^2, which, of course, evaluates to -123.456 when you adjust the decimal point.

> *i* All real literals in Java are stored in double-precision (`double`) by default. To distinguish a single-precision literal, that is, a real number stored as `float`, from its default value, append the letter f or F after the number. For example, $-123.456f$ or $-1.23456E+2f$. Although it is not strictly necessary, a double-precision real literal may have the letter d or D appended after the number.

The data types `char`, `int`, `long`, `float`, and `double` are known as *primitive* data types. Only a selection of the primitive data types that you are likely to use in this book have been presented. For the complete set of primitive data types, turn to Appendix A, Table A.2.

1.3 Identifiers

Data may be thought of as occupying areas of the computer's memory in the same way as people occupy houses in a street. To distinguish different families in different houses, we could use either the surname of the family or the number of the house. To distinguish data in different areas of memory, we could give the data a name or use the numeric memory address of the first byte of the address in which the data is stored.

In Java it is much easier to refer to data by name and let the computer do the work of finding out where in memory the data is stored. Figure 1.6 illustrates the use of names to represent data stored at memory addresses. The generic term for the name you give to a datum is an identifier. Java uses the following rules for the composition of identifiers.

An identifier may contain combinations of the letters of the alphabet (both uppercase A-Z and lowercase a-z), an underscore character _, a dollar sign $, and decimal digits 0-9. The identifier may start with any of these characters with the exception of a decimal digit.

Java is a *case-sensitive* language, meaning that uppercase letters and lowercase letters of the alphabet are treated as different letters. Identifiers can normally be of any practicable length. An identifier must not be the same as those Java keywords listed in Figure 1.7. A programmer uses keywords to construct statements

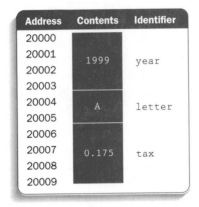

Address	Contents	Identifier
20000		
20001		
20002	1999	year
20003		
20004	A	letter
20005		
20006		
20007	0.175	tax
20008		
20009		

Figure 1.6 Use of identifiers to represent data

abstract	default	goto	operator	synchronized
boolean	do	if	outer	this
break	double	implements	package	throw
byte	else	import	private	throws
byvalue	extends	inner	protected	transient
case	false	instanceof	public	true
cast	final	int	rest	try
catch	finally	interface	return	var
char	float	long	short	void
class	for	native	static	volatile
const	future	new	super	while
continue	generic	null	switch	

Figure 1.7 Keywords

in a program for the computer to obey. Therefore, we will use keywords in program statements, but not as identifiers.

The words in Figure 1.7 that appear in black are reserved by Java, but are currently unused.

A programmer should always compose identifiers so they convey meaning. The identifiers name, street, town, and zipcode imply the meaning of the data that they represent, unlike the non-descriptive identifiers N, S, T, and Z. When an identifier is constructed from more than one word, each successive word should begin with an uppercase letter; an identifier should be easy to read, and its meaning should be clear.

Examples of legal identifiers are subTotal, salesTax, unitCost, and rateOfPay.

Resist the temptation of beginning an identifier with an underscore _ or using a dollar sign $ in your identifiers. Often such characters are used in other variables by the computer.

1.4 Syntax

· ·

In the Introduction, it was stated that one cause of your program not compiling correctly was making a mistake when typing the program and causing the syntax of at least one statement to be incorrect. The syntax is the grammar of the statement construction. Java, like the majority of computer languages, has specific rules on how you construct programs using the language.

Throughout each chapter you will come across syntax icons identical to the one shown here.

SYNTAX

· ·

The syntax described under this icon is for quick reference only—the full syntax of the language can be found in Appendix B.

Many beginners to computer programming find difficulty in getting the syntax of a program correct, even after several attempts. To the student, not being able to understand the syntax of the language is one of the most frustrating areas in programming, since it becomes difficult to interpret the syntax errors that are listed by the compiler.

As an example of how we will describe syntax, we will look at the Java assignment statement. An assignment statement assigns a value to a variable. For example, if `count` has been declared as a variable of type `int` as shown in Section 1.2, then the following statement assigns the value 7 to `count`.

```
count = 7;
```

The syntax of the assignment statement is given as follows.

SYNTAX

· ·

Assignment Statement: *identifier* = *literal*;
                                             identifier = *identifier*;
                                             identifier = *expression*;

These statements express the grammar of assignment and illustrate how language statements are constructed. Within the syntax description we use both terminal symbols and non-terminal symbols. The terminal symbols are shown in a color monospace font, and non-terminal symbols in an *italic typeface*. Terminal symbols cannot be defined further, unlike non-terminal symbols that can be defined in other syntax definitions.

If an identifier is specified by the word `tax`, then according to the rules of the syntax of an assignment statement the following statements are legal.

```
tax = 135.86;
tax = incomeTax;
tax = 0.175*cost;
```

where `135.86` is a numeric literal
where `incomeTax` is another identifier
where `0.175*cost` is an expression

By using the rules of assignment, it is easy to understand that the following statements are illegal.

```
135.86 = tax;
tax = incomeTax
0.175*cost = tax;
```

this implies the syntax *literal = identifier* (wrong)
statement delimiter ; missing (wrong)
this implies *expression = identifier* (wrong)

The terminal symbols in these examples are the assignment symbol =, the multiplication operator *, and the statement delimiter ; The identifiers are `tax`, `incomeTax` and `cost`.

As described in the previous section, an identifier is an unlimited-length sequence of Java letters and Java digits, the first of which must be a Java letter. An identifier cannot have the same spelling as a keyword, Boolean literal, or a null literal. These facts are represented formally by the following notation found in Appendix B.

Identifier:
    IdentifierChars but not a *Keyword* or *BooleanLiteral* or *NullLiteral*

IdentifierChars:
    JavaLetter
            IdentifierChars JavaletterOrDigit

JavaLetter:
            any Unicode character that is a Java letter

JavaLetterOrDigit:
    any Unicode character that is a Java letter-or-digit

From these definitions it should be clear that examples of acceptable identifiers are:

`tax`, `incomeTax` and `cost`.

Examples of illegal identifiers would be:

```
0Finance    begins with a digit; this violates the rule that an
            identifier must begin with a Java letter.
Mr.Jones    the period is not a legal identifier character.
final       this is a Java keyword and cannot be used as an
            identifier.
```

1.5   Variables and Constants

A Java program contains data declarations and instructions. The data declarations must appear before the instructions, since the declarations describe the type of data used by the instructions. Although a declaration may appear anywhere in a program, subject to the restrictions mentioned, you should attempt to group your declarations before the instructions that use them.

If the values of the data in the storage cells can be changed by the instructions in a computer program, the values of the data will vary, and the data identifiers are known as *variables*. The syntax for making a variable declaration follows.

SYNTAX

Variable Declaration: `data-type identifier;`
`data-type identifier-list;`

For example, the data declarations for a sample of the information displayed in Figures 1.1 and 1.2 might be:

```
int   weightLimit;
int   parkingTime;
float balance;
float costOfGas;
float valueOfShares;
```

When variables are of the same type, you may declare the type followed by a list of identifiers separated by commas, for example:

```
int   weightLimit, parkingTime;
float balance, costOfGas, valueOfShares;
```

Variables can be initialized (set to an initial value) by the programmer at their point of declaration, using the following syntax. Note that these statements both declare and initialize the variables.

SYNTAX

Variable Initialization: `data-type identifier = literal;`

For example, the data of Figures 1.1 and 1.2 can be initialized as follows:

```
char     parkingSymbol = 'P';
int      weightLimit  = 10;
float    balance      = 1225.11f;
```

Reminder! Notice the use of f after the value `1225.11`. The f signifies that the numeric literal is stored as a single-precision value. This is an important point to remember since real numeric literals are stored in double-precision form by default.

Many programs have data values that remain constant during the running of the program. Examples of constants are sales tax at 5% (`0.05f`), mathematical PI at 3.14159, and Earth's gravitational constant (`G`) at the surface, 9.80665 ms^{-2}. Rather than using the literal value of a constant in an expression, it is far better to name the constant, thus giving greater clarity to the expression in which the constant is found. If you use this technique, your program does not become littered with numbers that have meanings that can be difficult to understand.

The syntax for a constant declaration follows.

SYNTAX

Constant Declaration: `final data-type identifier = literal;`

Such constants can be declared in Java as follows.

```
final float   SALES_TAX = 0.05f;
final double PI         = 3.14159;
final float   G         = 9.80665f;
```

The keyword `final` implies that the constant identifier is initialized to a value that will not change during the execution of the program. Convention dictates that constant identifiers should be coded in uppercase letters to distinguish them from variables in a program—hence the identifiers SALES_TAX, PI, and G.

1.6   The Format of a Simple Program

Before we look at the first of three short programs in this chapter, it is necessary to give you a feel for how a simple Java application program is constructed. The following template may be used for constructing a simple Java application program, and will be used in this and the next chapter to provide you with a framework for inserting statements into the program.

---

heading giving details of the name and purpose of the program

import *list*

class *name*
{
      main *method*
      {
            declarations of constants
            declarations of variables
            program statements
      }
}

For the moment, we ask you to accept the contents of the template. By the end of Chapter 2, each component in this template will have been explained.

In the first of the three programs, three variables are initialized at their point of declaration, and their values are output to the screen.

From the template you can see that the declaration of variables is performed within an area of the program characterized by a statement that contains the keyword main.

In the following program, the text in color illustrates where declarations of the variables can be written in the context of a complete program. In general, declarations of variables must always be made before the variables are used. At this stage you are not expected to understand the remainder of the statements in the program.

```
// program to illustrate the declaration and initialization of
// variables

import avi.*;

class Example_1
{
    public static void main(String[] args)
    {
        char parkingSymbol = 'P';
        int weightLimit = 10;
        float balance = 1225.11f;

        Window screen = new
            Window("Example_1.java","bold","blue",36);
        screen.showWindow();
        screen.write("\n\tParking symbol is "
                    +parkingSymbol+"\n\n");
        screen.write("\n\tWeight limit is "+weightLimit+
                    "tons\n\n");
        screen.write("\n\tBalance is $"+balance+"\n");
    }
}
```

The following screen shot shows the program's results.

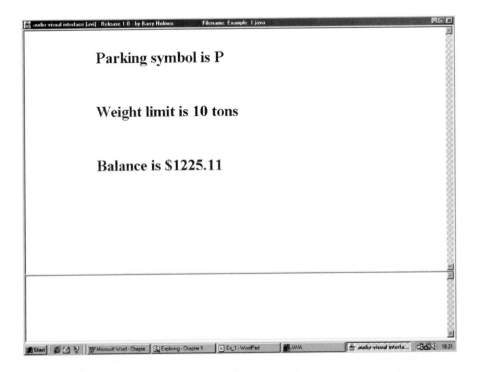

NOW DO THIS▶   Modify the statements in program `Example_1.java`.

(1) Replace the variables with the constants `SALES_TAX`, `PI`, and `G` that are described in the previous section.

(2) Modify the `screen.write` statements to display the values of the three constants on the screen.

(3) Compile and run the modified program.

1.7 Arithmetic

Arithmetic operations are among the most fundamental instructions that can be included in a program. The following symbols are used to perform arithmetic on data stored in memory.

Unary Operators

+ unary plus
− unary minus

Unary operators have one operand and are used to represent positive or negative numbers.

Binary Multiplicative Operators

* multiplication
/ division
% remainder

Note that the % operator will compute the remainder after the division of two numeric values; for example, `33%16` computes the remainder 1 after 33 is divided by 16; `16%33` computes the remainder 16 after 16 is divided by 33. (The result of the division is 0, remainder 16.)

Binary Additive Operators

+ addition
− subtraction

Both multiplicative and additive operators have two operands.

To understand arithmetic operations, it is helpful to conceptualize how a computer uses memory. In the previous section we saw how data can be referred to by name in the memory of a computer. Figure 1.8 illustrates numbers being referred to by the names `total`, `subTotal`, and `tax` in three separate locations in memory before arithmetic operations are applied to the data.

Arithmetic may be performed on this data and the result assigned to a memory location, using the assignment operator = . The syntax of an assignment statement has already been given in Section 1.4.

Figure 1.8 Numbers stored by identifier

For example, the assignment statement `total = subTotal + tax` adds the contents of `subTotal` to the contents of `tax` and stores the result in `total`, destroying or overwriting the previous contents of `total`. Therefore, after the computer executes the statement `total = subTotal + tax`, the contents of `total` is changed. The result of the computation is shown in Figure 1.9.

Similar before-and-after situations can be applied to the following computations.

```
total = score - penalty;
tax = price * taxRate;
time = distance / speed;
result = sum % divisor;
counter = counter + 1;
```

The results of the arithmetic from these statements are illustrated in Figure 1.10.

The destination of an assignment will always be on the left-hand side of an assignment statement. For example, `score = 9` implies that `score` is assigned the value 9. The statement `9 = score` has no meaning since 9 is not a legal identifier. However, `score = result` implies that `score` is assigned the value of `result`, whereas `result = score` implies that `result` is assigned the value of `score`.

In the last example in Figure 1.10, the expression `counter = counter + 1` may seem a little unusual since the variable `counter` appears on both sides of the expression. The statement should be read as follows: On the right-hand side of the expression, the current value of `counter` (3) is increased by 1, giving a result of (4). This result is then assigned to the variable on the left-hand side of the expression, which also happens to be the variable `counter`. The old value of `counter` (3) is overwritten or destroyed by the new value (4). The effect of this statement has been to increase the value of the variable `counter` by 1.

Figure 1.9 Result of the computation `total = subTotal + tax`

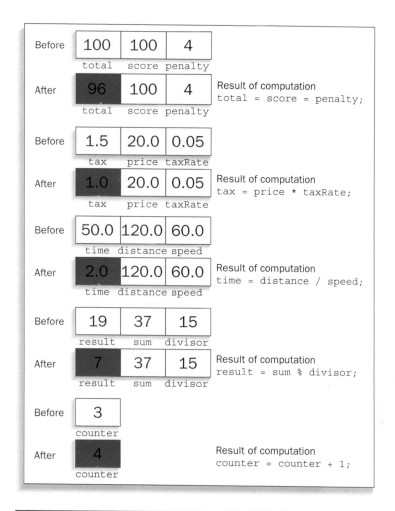

Figure 1.10 Results of various computations

The second program illustrates how to use a constant in a program. In Europe, there is a taxation known as the value added tax (VAT). This tax is applied to the cost of many goods and services, and, in the UK, currently stands at 17.5%. The second program illustrates a simple shopping bill where the costs of three consumer products are summed, VAT is applied to the sum, and the total for the purchases is displayed.

Those statements that you are expected to understand at this stage are shown in color in the program.

```
// program to illustrate the use of arithmetic statements

import avi.*;

public class Example_2
{
      public static void main(String[] args)
      {
            // declaration of a constant
            final float VAT = 0.175f;

            // declaration of variables
            float cdPlayer;
            float amplifier;
            float speakers;
            float subTotal;
            float tax;
            float total;

            // assign values to the goods purchased
            cdPlayer = 75.00f;
            amplifier = 99.00f;
            speakers = 56.00f;

            // calculate sub total of goods
            subTotal = cdPlayer+amplifier+speakers;

            // calculate value added tax
            tax = VAT * subTotal;

            // calculate total cost
            total = subTotal + tax;

            // display shopping bill
            Window screen = new Window("Example_2.java","plain","blue",36);
            screen.showWindow();

            screen.write("HI FI Bulk Discount Stores\n\n");
            screen.write("CD Player\t\t"+cdPlayer+"\n");
            screen.write("amplifier\t\t"+amplifier+"\n");
            screen.write("speakers\t\t"+speakers+"\n\n");
            screen.write("sub-total\t\t"+subTotal+"\n");
            screen.write("VAT\t\t"+tax+"\n");
            screen.write("TOTAL    \t\t"+total+"\n");
      }
}
```

The results appear as follows.

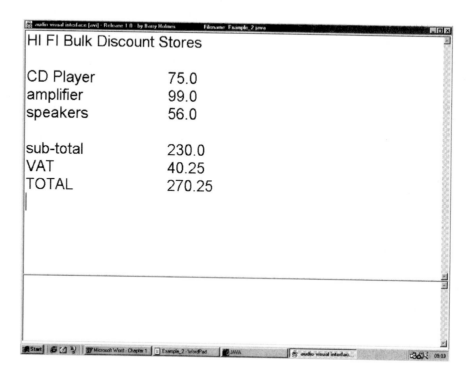

NOW DO THIS Using the editor, modify the program `Example_2` as follows.

(1) Change the name and value of the tax to the name used in your country. Remember to change all references to the name in the program.

(2) Alter the purchases to five items of your own choice. Initialize the prices of these five articles at the point of declaration.

(3) Modify the lines to calculate the sub-total, tax, and total.

(4) Change the name of the store to one applicable for your purchases.

(5) Change the names of the variables in the `screen.write` statements to match the names of your chosen variables.

(6) Re-compile the program. If there are no errors, then run the program.

1.8   Operator Precedence

Suppose an expression is written as A+B*C-D/E. How would it be evaluated? There is a need to introduce a set of rules for the evaluation of such expressions. All operators have an associated hierarchy that determines the order of precedence for evaluating expressions. Unary operators have a higher order of precedence than multiplicative operators, and multiplicative operators have a higher order of precedence than additive operators (see Figure 1.11). A complete list of operator priorities is given in Appendix A, Table A.2.

Expressions are evaluated by using operators with a higher priority before those of a lower priority. Generally, where operators are of the same priority, the expression is evaluated from left to right. Expressions in parenthesis will be evaluated before nonparenthesized expressions. Parentheses, although not an operator, can be considered as having an order of precedence after unary operators.

The expression A+B*C-D/E can be evaluated by inspecting the operators and grouping operations according to the above rules. Since there are no parentheses, this expression is parsed from left to right, evaluating those operands whose operators have the highest priority first. B*C is evaluated first, followed by D/E. In parsing the expression for a second time, A is added to the result of B*C, and finally the result of D/E is subtracted from this value. This process is illustrated in Figure 1.12; the numbers indicate the order of evaluation. The equivalent algebraic expression is given at each stage of the evaluation.

The expression (X*X+Y*Y)/(A+B) can be evaluated in the same way, as illustrated in Figure 1.13. Since this expression is parenthesized, the contents of both pairs of parentheses must be evaluated first. As multiplication has a higher priority than addition, the X*X and Y*Y are evaluated before the two results are added together. Similarly, A is added to B before the result is divided into the result of the first parenthesized expression.

You should adopt the habit of using parentheses in order to make the meaning of an expression as clear as possible. For example, the algebraic expression

$\frac{uv}{wx}$ can be written in Java as U*V/W/X; however, it is easier to understand (U*V)/(W*X).

Priority level	Operator	Operand type(s)	Associativity	Operation performed
1	+ −	arithmetic	R	unary plus, unary minus
	(type)	any	R	cast
2	* / %	arithmetic	L	multiplication, division, remainder
3	+ -	arithmetic	L	addition, subtraction
13	=	variable any	R	assignment

Figure 1.11 Priority levels of operators

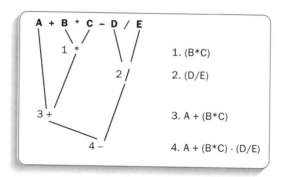

Figure 1.12 Evaluation of A + B * C - D / E

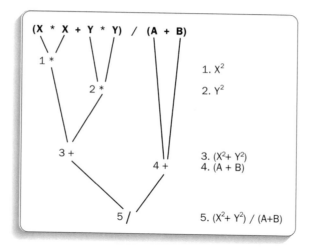

Figure 1.13 Evaluation of (X * X + Y * Y) / (A + B)

Similarly, $x^2 + y^2 + \dfrac{4}{z^2}(x + y)$ can be written in Java as

(X*X)+(Y*Y)+4*(X+Y)/(Z*Z).

With the exception of the % remainder operator, which must have integer operands, all other operators can have integer or real operands or a mixture of both types. In a division, if both the operands are integer, then the result will also be an integer, i.e., the fractional remainder in the result will be truncated.

1.9 Casting

As described previously, the storage of integer and real numbers is organized differently, and may use different amounts of memory. For example, the internal representation of the types `int` and `float` are organized differently, and `int` and `long` as well as `float` and `double` use different amounts of memory. Therefore, when operands are of different types, one or more of the operands must be converted to a type that can safely accommodate all values before any arithmetic can be performed.

Type conversion is performed automatically when the type of the expression on the right-hand side of an assignment can be *safely* promoted to the type of the variable on the left-hand side. For example,

```
long  largeInteger = 123456789012345;
int   smallInteger = 987654;


largeInteger = smallInteger;
```

This assignment involves the value of the variable `smallInteger` of type `int` being promoted to type `long` for the purpose of performing the assignment. However, the original type declaration `int` for the variable `smallInteger` does not change.

Note that the assignment `smallInteger = largeInteger;` is not allowed, since the value of the variable `largeInteger` cannot be promoted from type `long` to type `int` without possible loss of digits.

Type conversion may also be explicit through the use of a cast operation. A **cast** is an explicit conversion of a value from its current type to another type. The syntax of this operation follows:

SYNTAX

Cast operation: `(data-type) expression;`

---

where data-type in parentheses indicates the type to which the expression should be converted. For example,

```
float money = 158.05;
int   looseChange = 275;
money = (float) looseChange;
```

The cast expression `(float)looseChange` is used to convert the value of the variable `looseChange` to a number of type `float`. This does not imply that `looseChange` has altered its type from `int` to `float`; only the value has been converted to type `float` for the purpose of the assignment.

> ⚠️ Java will allow the statement `smallInteger = (int)largeInteger;` even though digits may be lost in the assignment. However, it is the responsibility of the programmer to ensure that casting will not result in any inaccuracy.

In the third example program of this chapter, two variables are declared and assigned the values of 15 and 7, respectively. Calculations on the sum, difference, product, quotient, and remainder of these numbers are performed and the results of these calculations are displayed on the screen.

```
// program to calculate the sum, difference, product, quotient,
// and remainder of two numbers

import avi.*;

public class Example_3
{
    public static void main(String[] args)
    {
        // declare variables
        int first;
        int second;
        int sum;
        int difference;
        int product;
        int quotient;
        int remainder;

        // assign values to variables
        first = 15;
        second = 7;
```

```
// perform computations
sum = first+second;
difference = first - second;
product = first*second;
quotient = first/second;
remainder = first%second;

// output results of calculations
Window screen = new Window("Example_1.java","plain","blue",36);
screen.showWindow();

screen.write("Simple Mathematics\n\n");
screen.write(first+"+"+second+"="+sum+"\n");
screen.write(first+"-"+second+"="+difference+"\n");
screen.write(first+"*"+second+"="+product+"\n");
screen.write(first+"/"+second+"="+quotient+"\n");
screen.write(first+"%"+second+"="+remainder+"\n");
  }
}
```

The following screen shot shows the results from running this program.

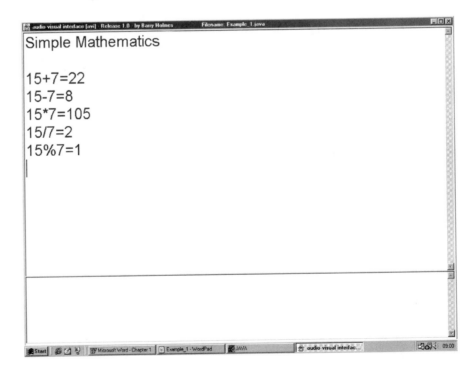

NOW DO THIS   Recompile and rerun the program after each suggested change.

(1) Compile and run the program as it is and note the output.

(2) Change the program so that the variable first is set to 25 instead of 15.

(3) Add two more integer variables called `value1` and `value2` to the program.

Assign `value1` the expression `10 + 5 * 6`.

Assign `value2` the expression `(10 + 5) * 6`.

Add the appropriate output statements, so that you can see what values end up being assigned to the two variables.

(4) Change the declarations of the variables `quotient` and `remainder` to type `float`. What effect does that have on the program?

(5) Use casting within the computations of `quotient` and `remainder`. For example, the calculation of the quotient could be written as:

```
quotient = (float) first / second;
```

What effect does that have on your program?

SUMMARY

- *Data* is the name given to characters and quantities operated upon by a computer.

- The integer data types are `int` and `long`; the real data types are `float` and `double`; the character data type is `char`. All five data types are known as primitive types in Java.

- Integers may be represented as either decimal or hexadecimal numbers.

- The range of data that can be stored in a computer's memory is limited by the data's type.

- Data stored in the memory of a computer can be accessed through an identifier invented by the programmer. Identifier names should be self-documenting.

- Data names must conform to the rules for identifiers.

- Numeric data that reside in memory locations can be manipulated by use of the following operators: + (addition); - (subtraction); * (multiplication); / (division); % (remainder).

- Arithmetic operations in Java are evaluated in order of highest to lowest operator precedence. Expressions in parentheses have higher precedence than nonparenthesized expressions. Where operators have equal precedence, the expressions are generally evaluated from left to right.

■ The result of a computation is assigned to a variable using the = operator.

■ When operands are of different types, one or more of the operands must be converted to the type that can safely accommodate the values before the operation can be performed. The conversion can occur in one of two ways: (1) implicitly, by which Java automatically converts the value on the right-hand side of the assignment to the type of the variable on the left-hand side, or (2) by the use of a *cast* operation, which the programmer must write into the program code.

■ Variable declaration specifies the type of data followed by the name of the data.

■ Variables may be initialized at the point of declaration.

■ Data values that do not change during the running of a program may be declared as constants.

■ Constants must be initialized at the point of declaration.

Review Questions

True or False

1. Real numbers may be described as type `float`.

2. A character is stored as an integer value.

3. An identifier may begin with an underscore.

4. An identifier described as being constant may have its initial value changed by statements in a program.

5. `0x3GF` is a legal hexadecimal literal.

6. `032767` is a legal decimal literal.

7. Single-precision real constants contain the letter `f` after the number.

8. The multiplication operator has a higher priority than the subtraction operator.

9. The word `return` is a keyword.

Short Answer

10. Describe the meaning of the data types integer, real, and character.

11. How are the three types listed in Question (10) represented as data types in Java?

12. How would you declare an integer variable that had an initial value of 67AF?

13. Distinguish between the mantissa and exponent of a real number.

14. What range of integers can be stored within four bytes?

15. What is the smallest real number that can be stored as type `float`?

16. What is a variable?

17. What is a constant?

18. Is the declaration of a constant `final PI = 3.14159;` correct?

19. Which operator calculates the remainder after the division of two integer numbers?

20. What is the result of the integer division 3/2?

21. If the variable counter has an initial value of 8, what is the value of
    `counter = counter + 1`?

22. Describe the term operator precedence.

23. What is the result of evaluating the expression `2 * 6 + 20 / 4`?

24. What does the expression `(int)alpha` do, if `alpha` is declared as a real number?

25. What is the difference when the expressions `(float)(x/y)` and `(float)x/(float)y` are evaluated? Assume that both `x` and `y` are integers.

26. What is the Unicode representation for the letter H?

Exercises

27. From the illustration in Figure 1.14, discuss what you consider to be data and classify the data by type as variables declared in Java.

28. Identify the illegal variable names in the following list of identifiers. Explain why the names are illegal.

    (a) `priceOfBricks` (b) `net-pay`   (c) `x1`   (d) `cost of paper`

    (e) `INTEGER`   (f) `?X?Y`   (g) `1856AD`   (h) `float`

29. Describe the Java types for the following items of data:

    (a) -64 (b) `';'`   (c) `+156`   (d) `+2147483648`

    (e) `247.9`   (f) `0.732E+01f`   (g) `0xAB0`   (h) `23.96f`

30. Use Figure 1.5 to determine the Unicodes of the following characters:

    (a) `A`   (b) `M`   (c) `*`   (d) `a`   (e) `m`   (f) `9`

31. Write the following numbers using E notation for real numbers; only one nonzero digit should precede the decimal point.

    (a) -874.458 (b) $+0.00123456$ (c) 123456789.0

COMMUTER RAIL FARES				
Zone	One-way	Half-fare	Monthly Pass	Family Fare
1	2.00	1.00	64.00	8.00
2	2.25	1.10	72.00	9.00
3	2.50	1.25	82.00	10.00
4	3.00	1.50	94.00	12.00
5	3.25	1.60	104.00	13.00
6	3.50	1.75	112.00	14.00
7	3.75	1.85	120.00	15.00
8	4.00	2.00	128.00	16.00

Figure 1.14 Commuter rail fares

32. Evaluate the following expressions.

    (a) $10/4$ (b) $10.0f/4.0f$ (c) $5+7*3$ (d) $5*7+3$

33. Write suitable type declarations for the following constants:

    (a) -45678 (b) 0xFABC   (c) 3.14159   (d) '\u0041'

34. Convert the following hexadecimal numbers into decimal numbers, and convert the following binary numbers into hexadecimal numbers. Hint: To convert a binary number into a hexadecimal number, split the binary number into groups of 4 bits starting from the right-hand side of the binary number. Evaluate each group from the information given in Figure 1.4.

    (a) 0xFF   (b) 0x1A2C   (c) 01110011   (d) 0111001100001111

35. Given the original values as shown, what are the values of the following variables after the execution of the respective assignments?

    (a) B = A;

A	B	C	D
36	98	45	29

    C = A;

    D = A;

    (b) D = A + B + C + D;

A	B	C	D
10	14	29	36

    (c) A = B - 2;

A	B
17	50

    (d) Y = X - Y;

X	Y
19	32

(e) `Z = X * Y;`   X   Y   Z

                           18   3   27

(f) `B = B / A;`   A   B

                           12.5   25.0

(g) `X = A / B;`   A   B   X

                           16   3   25

(h) `Y = C % D;`   C   D   Y

                           19   5   2

(i) `D = D + 1`   D

                           34

36. Write the following expressions in Java.

(a) $\dfrac{A+B}{C}$ (b) $\dfrac{W-X}{Y+Z}$ (c) $\dfrac{D-B}{2A}$ (d) $\dfrac{\left(A^2+B^2\right)}{2}$

(e) $(A-B)(C-D)$ (f) B^2-4AC (g) AX^2+BX+C

37. Rewrite the following Java expressions as algebraic expressions.

(a) `X + 2 / Y + 4`   (b) `A * B / (C + 2)`   (c) `U / V * W / X`

(d) `B * B - 4 * A * C`   (e) `A / B + C / D + E / F`

Programming Problems

Refer to the three example programs in the text to help you to write programs as answers to the next three questions. Compile and run the programs.

38. Write a program to calculate and output the distance traveled by a car on a tank of gas. Assume figures for the capacity of the tank and the average rate of gas consumption per mile by the car.

39. Write a program to convert any amount of US dollars into any chosen world currency and output your results. Write the conversion factor for the currency of your choice as a constant.

40. Write a program to convert a temperature in degrees Fahrenheit to degrees Celsius. The formula for conversion is Celsius = (Fahrenheit − 32) * (5/9).

CHAPTER 2

Objects

This chapter introduces you to classes, which are the primary building blocks for Java programs. A class is an extension of a data type. Classes are used to create objects.

The first example of a class that you will see is the `String` class. Unlike the primitive data types discussed in the previous chapter, strings are declared by using a class. This chapter explains the format of a class, and shows how a class may be used to create an application program.

We also look at the input of data to a program and the output of information from a program, and the structure of simple Java programs. We introduce our audio-visual interface package `avi` that allows beginning Java programmers to create interesting multimedia interfaces to programs.

By the end of the chapter you should have an understanding of the following topics.

- Some fundamentals of packages, classes, objects, and methods

- Input and output using a graphical user interface

- Writing simple programs

- Using the command line to input data

- Syntax, run-time, and logical errors

2.1 Introduction to Objects

In an object-oriented language such as Java, the emphasis is on combining (known in computing jargon as encapsulating) data with segments of program code that access and manipulate the data. Objects permit this encapsulation and form the backbone of the Java language. In this section we will introduce several object-related terms and ideas, using strings as an example. You should not worry if at first you feel somewhat overwhelmed with the terminology and concepts. As we progress through the book you will become more comfortable with the ideas.

As mentioned above, an *object* encapsulates data and a set of operations that access and manipulate the data. For example, a program to help manage a bank might maintain thousands of `BankAccount` objects, each holding data (`owner name`, `balance`, `interest rate`) about a particular bank account and each allowing a set of operations (`deposit`, `withdraw`, `balance`, `printStatement`) that affect the data or return information about the data. A `String` object will hold a string such as `"HELLO WORLD"` and allow the programmer to perform operations that return information about the string such as its length, or to return new strings related to the original string, such as a copy of the string in all lowercase letters.

Objects are created from templates, called *classes*. A class may define both the type of data and the operations that can be performed on the data. These operations are segments of program code, known as *methods*. Once a class is defined, it can be used to create, or *instantiate*, many objects. Sometimes we refer to these objects as *instances* of the class. As a Java programmer, you will define your own classes and use them to instantiate objects to help you solve problems—but more of this in the next chapter! There are also numerous predefined classes for your use as a programmer.

If you inspect the Java documentation you were asked to install during the Introduction, you will find listings of all the predefined classes found in the Java language. You will see that the Java API is arranged in a hierarchical structure. Figure 2.1 attempts to capture the nature of this hierarchy.

In the Java API, classes that are related to each other are grouped together into packages. In fact the number of packages increases with every new release

---

NOW DO THIS   Using your Java documentation and a Web browser, follow these instructions.
(1) Open the installed directory `jdk1.2.2`, then open the `docs` folder. Mouse-click on the `index` within this folder, and this should take you into the Java 2 SDK, Standard Edition Documentation.

(2) Scroll down to the section marked API & Language Documentation and mouse-click on Java 2 Platform API Specification (API is an acronym for Application Programming Interface). Mouse-click on the `java.lang` package, and mouse-click again on the `String` class.

(3) Investigate the documentation of this class.

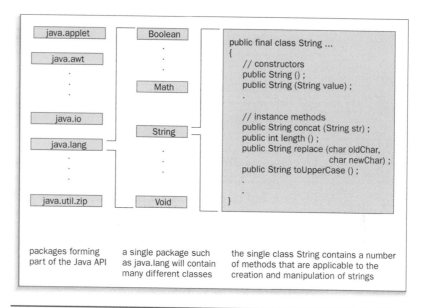

Figure 2.1 Packages and classes

of the Java language. A *package* is a convenient way of grouping together many different classes that have a common purpose. For example, the `java.lang` package contains the classes that are most central to the Java language. In learning Java we will concentrate on a minimum number of these packages in order to focus your understanding on the essentials of package and class design and use. Once you have mastered the use of packages and classes, you can apply these principles to all the packages within the language.

To review:

- The Java API is composed of many packages.

- A package consists of a set of related classes.

- Classes act as templates for objects. They define both data and operations (methods).

- Specific objects are instantiated from a class.

- Objects and primitive data values are the two kinds of information manipulated by Java programs.

Now, we will further explore the concepts of classes and objects using strings as an example.

2.2   The String Class

A *string* is a group of characters that are stored as consecutive items in the memory of a computer, with each character being represented by a 16-bit Unicode.

A string literal in Java is delimited by double quotes. For example the string literal ABC is written as "ABC", or by using the Unicodes as "\u0041\u0042\u0043".

In Chapter 1 you were introduced to the basic data types used for storing primitive data such as numbers and single characters; however, no type was explicitly mentioned for a string. The reason for postponing the introduction of strings is because in Java they are not represented as primitive data, but as objects.

Declaring Objects

How can we declare a string object? By using the name of the class `String` in the same way as you would use the names of any of the primitive types. A class may be thought of as a data type.

For example, you can declare a `String` object called `alphabet` as follows:

```
String alphabet;
```

The declaration on its own is not much use, since the memory location `alphabet` does not refer to any data. It simply reserves a location in memory for a reference to the object. Java recognizes this fact, and has designated the contents of this location as `null` (other null designations are shown in Figure 2.3).

So, the next question is how to assign a value to the string object and how to perform operations on the object. The answer lies in understanding the methods of the object's class.

Methods and Parameters

Recall that a class may define both data and segments of program code, known as methods, to operate upon the data contained in the class. A method's *signature* is the first line of a method, terminated by a semicolon. The purpose of a signature is to uniquely identify a method in terms of its name and formal parameter list. The syntax of a signature is:

SYNTAX
• •

Method Signature: `modifier(s) return-type`
`method-name(formal-parameter-list);`

---

which is interpreted as follows:

`modifier(s)`—usually indicates the visibility of the method, i.e., where it can be activated from. If you inspect the partial listing of the `String` class in Figure 2.1, you will notice that the modifier defined for those methods is `public`; this implies that the methods are visible (accessible) anywhere the class is visible.

return-type—the `return` type specifies the data type of the value that is returned by the method. This can be a primitive data type or a class. If no data is returned by the method, then the keyword `void` is used for the `return` type. For example, the `length()` method of the String class returns the length of the string as an `int`. You will see an example of the use of this method in the sample program at the end of this section.

method-name—an identifier that defines the name of the method.

formal-parameter-list—declares the data variables that are passed to and used by the method. If no data is passed to the method, then the parentheses remain empty. A method will typically perform some action on its object, or return some information about its object. Parameters can be used to modify the action or affect the information that is returned. For example, the string method `replace(char oldChar, char newChar)` includes two parameters, `oldChar` and `newChar`. As you can probably guess, these parameters affect the action of the method—they determine what kind of replacement will take place.

Method signatures are used in the documentation of a class. Consider the following partial listing taken from the `String` class.

```
public final class String ...
{
    // constructors
    public String();
    public String(String value);
    .

    .


    // instance methods
    public String concat(String str);
    public int length();
    public String replace(char oldChar, char newChar);
    public String toUpperCase();
    .

    .

}
```

From the partial listing of the class `String`, it is evident that a class contains at least two different categories of methods. (There is a third category, but this will be dealt with in the next chapter.) For now we need to consider the differences between two concepts:

- a constructor

- an instance method

Constructors

You may wonder about the methods that have the same name as the class. These are special methods known as *constructors*, and their purpose is to initialize data of the type `String` to specified values. A constructor does not return a value.

Recall that we declared a `String` object called `alphabet` as follows:

```
String alphabet;
```

Once it is declared, we can initialize `alphabet` by using either of the constructors. This initialization is known as creating an *instance* of the class or creating an *object*.

The syntax of the instantiation of a class or the creation of an object follows.

SYNTAX
··

Instantiation:

object-name = new *class-constructor*();
object-name = new *class-constructor*(*argument-list*);

where `argument-list` consists of one or more values used by the constructor to initialize the data of the object.

Examples of creating the object `alphabet` follow.

```
alphabet = new String();
```

The above uses the first `String` constructor with no arguments.

```
alphabet = new String("abcdefghijklmnopqrstuvwxyz");
```

The above uses the second `String` constructor that accepts a string as an argument.

The first of these two statements will initialize `alphabet` to the empty string `""` and the second statement will initialize `alphabet` to the string `"abcdefghijklmnopqrstuvwxyz"`.

Since the declaration and initialization of objects are so frequently performed one right after the other, the Java language provides a way to do both together in a single statement. The following will both declare and instantiate the `String` object `alphabet`:

```
String alphabet = new String("abcdefghijklmnopqrstuvwxyz");
```

In any of these situations we might ask, What is the purpose of the reserved word `new`? Let us recall for a moment how primitive data types are stored.

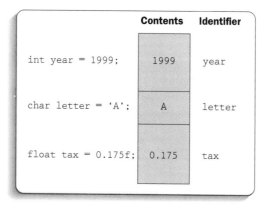

Figure 2.2 Primitive types stored by value

Figure 2.2 illustrates how three primitive types `int`, `char`, and `float` can be conceptually represented in the memory of the computer.

In Figure 2.2, the *values* of the identifiers `year`, `letter`, and `tax` are stored at the memory locations depicted by the names of the identifiers. Hence, the primitive data is *stored by value*.

Figure 2.3 illustrates that when an identifier of the type `String` is initialized, the value of the string is not stored at the memory location depicted by the identifier, but it is stored in a different location pointed at or *referenced* by the identifier. The object `alphabet` is *stored by reference*.

The purpose of the reserved word `new` is to allocate a new memory storage area for holding the value of the string. Notice in Figure 2.3 that the memory

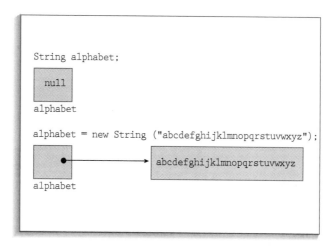

Figure 2.3 An object is stored by reference

location `alphabet` contains a reference to the memory area that stores the string.

> ℹ️ Since the `String` data type is so commonly used, Java provides a shortcut method for initializing a string. The reserved word `new` may be omitted and an object `alphabet` of type `String` can be declared as follows.
>
> `String alphabet = "abcdefghijklmnopqrstuvwxyz";`

String Assignment

If you wish to assign one string to another, then the assignment does not provide a copy of the value but merely a copy of the *reference* to the value. For example, Figure 2.4 illustrates that although the string `alphabet` is assigned to the string `lowerCase` by the assignment statement `lowercase = alphabet`, `lowerCase` only references the same object as `alphabet` and does not obtain a new copy of the string `"abcdefghijklmnopqrstuvwxyz"`.

Instance Methods

From the partial listing of the class `String` you can see a group of methods that appear to describe the characteristics and operations you might associate with an object such as a string of characters. For example, the identifier `length` suggests that it returns the characteristic of the number of characters in a string; the identifier `concat` suggests the operation of concatenation or appending of one

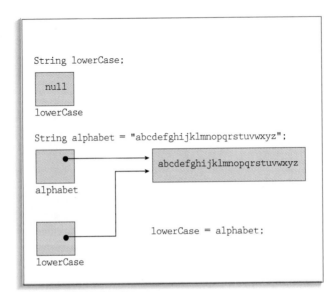

Figure 2.4 Assignment of strings

string after another; the identifier `replace` suggests the operation of replacing every occurrence of one character with another; and the identifier `toUpperCase` suggests the operation of converting the characters in the string to the uppercase letters if appropriate.

Conceptually, an object is a thing you interact with. You send it various messages and it will react. There are two kinds of messages:

- a command message

- a query message

From the partial listing of the `String` class, examples of command messages are `concat`, `replace`, and `toUpperCase`; an example of a query message is `length`. These messages are implemented as *instance methods*.

Messages in Java are passed by using the name of the object to receive the message, followed by the message itself. A period is used to separate the object name and the message as depicted by the following syntax.

SYNTAX
• •

Passing a Message to an Object by an Instance Method:

```
object.method-name();
object.method-name(argument-list);
```

The statement `alphabet.length()` will return the length of the `alphabet` string as 26.

The statement `alphabet.toUpperCase()` will change every character of the alphabet string to uppercase letters:

```
"ABCDEFGHIJKLMNOPQRSTUVWXYZ".
```

In Java, a string is immutable or constant; that is to say, once a string has been defined, its contents cannot be changed. To conform with this requirement, for `String` methods such as `toUpperCase`, Java makes a copy of the original string and changes the contents of the copy to reflect the operation. Consider the following statements:

```
String oldString = "Have a nice day!";
String newString = oldString.replace('a','-');
```

The second statement replaces every occurrence of the character `'a'` in the old string with the character `'-'`. As a result, the variable `newString` will contain the following characters:

```
"H-ve - nice d-y!"
```

Given the following declarations:

```
String first = "Java is ";
String second = "a useful programming language.";
String sentence;
```

then the statement `sentence = first.concat(second)` will assign the following string to the variable `sentence`:

```
"Java is a useful programming language".
```

> ⚠ Once an object of a particular class has been declared, you are allowed to perform message passing upon objects of that class, only using the instance methods defined by the class.

The following program is intended to reinforce the technique of creating a string object, using some of the instance methods to manipulate and gain information about the string. You are expected to understand those statements that are in color in the program.

```
// program to demonstrate the String class and some of its instance methods

import avi.*;

class Example_1
{
      public static void main(String[] args)
      {
            String oldString = "Have a nice day!";
            String newString = oldString.replace('a','-');
            String capitalString = oldString.toUpperCase();
            int lengthOfString = oldString.length();

            Window screen = new Window("Example_1.java","bold","blue",36);
            screen.showWindow();

            screen.write("\n\tOld string: " + oldString + "\n");
            screen.write("\n\tNew string: " + newString + "\n");
            screen.write("\n\tOld string in upper case: " + capitalString +
                        "\n");
            screen.write("\n\tLength of old string: " + lengthOfString +
                        " characters\n");
      }
}
```

The following is the resulting screenshot.

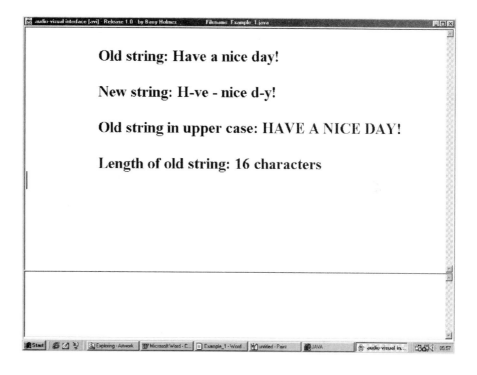

Modify the program Example_1 as follows.

(1) Declare and initialize two strings containing your first name and your family name (surname).

(2) Write a statement to concatenate both strings, leaving a space between the names. Hint—concatenate the first name with a space, and then concatenate the result with the family name.

(3) Write the concatenated names to the screen.

(4) Capitalize the names and write them to the screen.

(5) Write the number of characters in the concatenated names to the screen.

(6) Save, compile, and run your new program.

2.3   The Anatomy of a Simple Program Revisited

A template for constructing a Java program was already given to you in Chapter 1 so that you had a framework for inserting statements into the program. We are now ready to discuss the general structure of a Java program. This should help you to understand many of the program constructs that you have seen in the previous example programs, but that have not yet been addressed.

The same template for constructing a Java application program is illustrated below. I say application program because Java code can be written as either an application or an applet. However, don't concern yourself at the moment with applets; these are dealt with in detail much later in the book. For the moment, you need to concentrate on application programming.

In the explanation that follows, the key parts of the template illustrated in the following figure are used as suitable section subheadings.

heading giving details of the name and purpose of the program

import *list*

class *name*
{
      main *method*
      {
           declarations of constants
           declarations of variables
           program statements

      }

}

Heading Giving Details of the Name and Purpose of the Program

This is simply a set of comments written on as many lines as necessary. Comments are used to provide information to someone who is reading the program code. They are ignored by the computer and do not affect the execution of the program. In Java, a comment begins with a double slash // at the start of every line. The heading comments normally document the name and purpose of the program. They may also include the name of the author of the program and the date it was written, plus other facts you care to document.

You are not limited to using comments at the beginning of a class. Comments should be used throughout your program to clearly describe the purpose of either a single statement or groups of executable program statements.

Import List

The import statement makes Java classes available to the program. You can specify each class in the import statement, for example avi.DialogBox and avi.Window, but it is a lot simpler to use an asterisk as a wildcard to make all the classes of the package avi available; hence the statement avi.* that is used in many of the programs in this book.

A *wildcard* is a character that can represent a number of different characters. The wildcard * may represent any of the class names.

> ℹ️ The `java.lang` package is automatically imported; therefore, there is never any need to include it in the import list.

Class Name

The name of the class containing the `main` method must be the same as the name given to the program file (omitting the `.java` suffix). The naming of the class must follow the same rules as for the naming of any other identifier. The use of braces { } indicate the beginning and ending of the class.

> ⚠️ When creating a name for a class, be careful about the rules for naming identifiers in Java and the naming of program files for the operating system being used. The Java convention also dictates that the name of a class should always begin with an uppercase letter.

Main Method

In the construction of a Java application program there must be one `main` method present in one of the classes. The computer will start the execution of the program at the first statement in the `main` method and terminate execution after the last statement. The `main` method is a class method with the following signature:

```
public static void main(String[] args);
```

The `static` modifier implies that the `main` method is not an instance method requiring an object for its invocation—but more of this in the next chapter. The keyword `void` implies that the `main` method does not return a value. The formal parameter list will allow arguments to be passed to the `main` method at the time of giving the command to execute the program—but more of this later in this chapter.

Notice that the beginning and ending of the `main` method are denoted by the use of an open { and a closed } brace respectively. Notice also from the template how the declaration of the variables is kept separate from the program statements.

2.4 The AVI Package

The Java language was not designed for beginners to programming, and, as a consequence, the level of programming associated with the input and output of data to the computer is not trivial. To understand the program statements that permit input and output requires an understanding of object-oriented concepts that are not covered until at least halfway through this book.

To enable you to use and understand a modern approach to input and output, we have written a package called `avi` (an acronym for audio-visual interface). This package was written in Java 2, and you should have already installed it according to the instructions given in the Introduction.

By the time you have read through this book, you will be able to understand how the `avi` package was written, and you will have enough knowledge of the Java language to write your own package for input and output.

Figure 2.5 indicates the names of the classes within the `avi` package that are available for public use. This figure uses the Universal Modeling Language (UML) notation for describing a package. The package name is contained within a tab drawn on the top left-hand side of a larger rectangle, thus representing a folder icon. Each class is labeled within an inner rectangle. The + sign in front of the name of a class indicates that the class has been written for public use.

> The Unified Modeling Language (UML) is a general-purpose visual modeling language that is used to specify, visualize, construct, and document the artifacts of a software system. The notation will be gradually introduced in context, from a programming perspective, as you progress through the book.

In the following two sections you will become familiar with the use of the `Window` and `DialogBox` classes. The remainder of the `avi` classes will be explained in their correct context as you progress through the book.

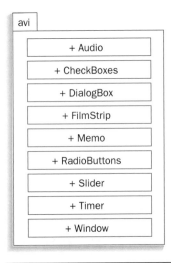

Figure 2.5 UML representation of the `avi` package

2.5   The Window Class

The `Window` class is used for *output* and is analogous to a pane of glass in a window frame. You can write on the glass or fix objects, such as posters, to the glass. By creating a `Window` object, you are creating a container for both a writing area and for displaying other graphical objects. The class `Window` contains the following methods:

```
public class Window
{
      // first constructor
      public Window(String filename);

      // second constructor
      public Window(String filename,
                    String style,
                    String color,
                    int    fontSize);

      public void showWindow();
      public void clearTextArea();
      public void closeWindowAndExit();
      public int getWidth();
      public int getHeight();
      public void write(String datum);
      public void write(char datum);
      public void write(int datum);
      public void write(long datum);
      public void write(float datum);
      public void write(double datum);
}
```

To create a `Window` container object, you must first use one of the class constructors. The first constructor requires just one argument that can be a literal constant or a variable:

`filename`—is normally the name of the main application file associated with the program. This parameter is for documentation purposes only.

The constructor automatically uses by default a monospaced, Courier font, with a plain style, and font size 16 for text output. The color of the text on the screen is dark gray. Use this constructor if you need a font similar to that produced by a typewriter. To create a window object that represents the screen of the monitor, you would code the constructor as follows:

```
Window screen = new Window("Example.java");
```

However, if you need to change either the style or size of the font, or change the color of the text, then use the second constructor. The second constructor requires four parameters. The arguments you supply can be either literal constants or variables.

filename—is normally the name of the main application file associated with the program. This parameter is for documentation purposes only.

style—is either "PLAIN", "BOLD", "ITALIC" or "BOLD+ITALIC". You may use either uppercase or lowercase characters. An empty string "" will default to a BOLD+ITALIC style.

color—is either "red", "blue", or "black". You may use either uppercase or lowercase characters. An empty string "" will default to the color black.

fontSize—is a positive integer that represents the point size of the output text. Values less than 10 default to a point size of 10. A font size of 72 points will produce uppercase characters approximately 1 inch in height.

The second constructor uses the Java Dialog font by default. To create a Window object that represents the screen of the monitor and permits textual output on the screen to appear in a bold typeface with a point size of 72 and with the text in red, you would code the constructor as follows:

```
Window screen = new Window("Example.java","bold","red",72);
```

Having created a Window object screen, you must issue a message to show the object:

```
screen.showWindow();
```

An illustration of a Window object is shown in Figure 2.6. Notice that the screen is split into two text areas. The upper text area is the larger of the two and is used for textual output. The second-lower text area is used by the avi system to echo and display all input data.

You may output to the screen any of the primitive data types or the String type described in this chapter by using the write method. For example,

```
screen.write("Hello World");
```

will display the text Hello World on the screen and leave the cursor on the same line.

The strings that you output can have special characters embedded into them. These are known as escape sequence characters, the most common being \t for tabulation and \n for a new line. Turn to Appendix A, Table A.4 for the full list of escape sequence characters.

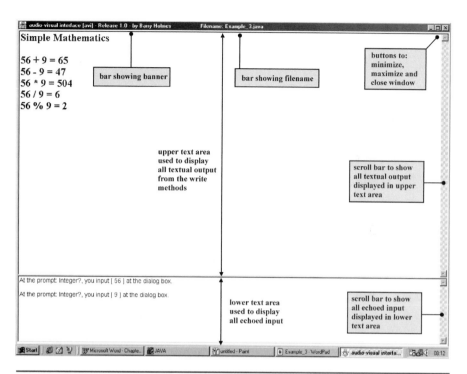

Figure 2.6 Format of a `Window` object

To display the `"Hello World"` string and place the cursor on the next line, you would embed the escape sequence for the new-line character into the output string as follows:

```
screen.write("Hello World\n");
```

If you examine the class `Window` you will see that there is a `write` method for every data type discussed in this chapter. The methods, where necessary, convert the various Java primitive types to string representations, then output the resulting string. This means that the `write` method can not only be used to display primitive data types, but it also can be used for combinations of primitive data types and strings. For example, the following segment of Java code can be used to output text and the value of an initialized variable.

```
float grossWage = 250.0f;
```

```
screen.write("Gross weekly wage = $" + grossWage);
```

Java allows a plus sign + to be used as a *string concatenation operator*. The Java primitive type `float` will automatically be converted to a string representation before being concatenated to the string defined between the quote marks. Therefore, `"Gross weekly wage = $"` is appended with the string value of `grossWage` before the entire string is displayed on the screen.

 There is no limit to the number of strings that can be concatenated to form the argument of the instance method `write`.

The text areas of the window contain scroll bars on the right-hand side of the window. As the upper text area fills up with text, it automatically scrolls vertically upwards and a scroll bar appears. Whenever you input data into the program via an object such as a dialog box, the input is automatically echoed and displayed to the lower text area. As this lower text area fills up with text, it also automatically scrolls vertically upwards and a scroll bar appears. When your program finishes, you can use the scroll bars to inspect all the text output to the upper text area and match it to all the echoed input displayed in the lower text area.

The instance method `clearTextArea()` will allow you to clear the entire text area of all the text in the upper window. The scroll bar disappears and you can start writing more text from the top left-hand corner of the text area.

The instance methods `getWidth()` and `getHeight()` allow you to inspect the width and height of the window.

Finally, the instance method `closeWindowAndExit()` does as the name suggests; it will close the window object and cause the computer to exit back to your operating system prompt. Do not use the `closeWindowAndExit()` method if you want to spend time inspecting the echoed input and output from your program in the respective text areas. In such circumstances, it is better to use the close window icon X in the top right-hand corner of the window only when you want to return to the operating system.

The use of the `window` class is illustrated by the next program. You have already seen this program in the Introduction. It displays the message HELLO WORLD across the screen in red.

```
// program to write the text literal "HELLO WORLD" centrally
// on the screen

import avi.*;

class Example_2
{
    public static void main(String[] args)
    {
```

```
// create a window object screen
Window screen = new Window(
              "Example_2.java","bold","red",72);

screen.showWindow();
screen.write("\n\n\n              HELLO WORLD");
    }
}
```

NOW DO THIS   Compile and re-run program `Example_2` after each of the following modifications.

(1) Delete the line `screen.showWindow();` and note the outcome.

(2) Experiment by changing the style of text, color of text, and font size.

2.6   Input to a Dialog Box

The `DialogBox` class is used for the input of any string value via the keyboard. The constructor creates a `DialogBox` object that appears on the `Window` object. The dialog box is modal, implying that no other interaction either with the window pane or with other objects on the pane is possible until data has been input at the dialog box and the box has been closed. Figure 2.7 illustrates a dialog box.

The class `DialogBox` contains the following methods:

```
public class DialogBox
{
      public DialogBox(Window parent,
                       String prompt);

      public void showDialogBox();
      public String getString();
      public char getChar();
      public int getInteger();
      public long getLongInteger();
      public float getFloat();
      public double getDouble();
}
```

To create a `DialogBox` object you must use the class constructor. Notice that the constructor requires two data items in the formal parameter list:

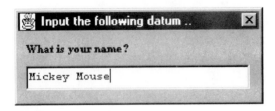

Figure 2.7 An example of a dialog box

parent—a `Window` type that specifies the container onto which to place the dialog box.

prompt—a string, used as a cue to prompt for input. For example, in Figure 2.7 the prompt is `"What is your name?"`.

Assuming that you have already created a screen `Window` object, create a dialog box named `input` like the one depicted in Figure 2.7 by coding the constructor as follows:

```
DialogBox input = new DialogBox(screen, "What is your name?");
```

However, having created the dialog box object, remember to display it on the screen using the `showDialogBox()` instance method, as in `input.showDialogBox();`.

To retrieve the name `Mickey Mouse`, input by the user at the dialog box, it is necessary to use the appropriate instance method, in this example, `getString()`. Notice that the method returns a string; therefore, retrieval of the input data is possible by using either of the following statements:

```
String name;
name = input.getString();
```

or by shortening this to:

```
String name = input.getString();
```

Note that both coding techniques have used the shorthand form of `String` instantiation.

If you forget to show a dialog box and use any of the methods to get the appropriate datum, the `avi` system will issue an error message and abandon the execution of your program.

After inputting the data, the user must close the dialog box by either pressing the Return key (the most natural operation after typing the string) or by using the mouse to press the close box button X in the top right-hand corner of the dialog box. Despite the dialog box being closed, it is only hidden from view and not destroyed. To make the dialog box visible again, the programmer can use the instance method `showDialogBox()` and it will return to the screen with the text field for inputting the blank, ready for new input.

You have already seen the following program in the Introduction. The same program is presented to you now so that you may understand the input statements that are in color.

```
// program to input your name and display a welcome message on
// the screen

import avi.*;

class Example_3
{
      public static void main(String[] args)
      {
            // declare name as a string
            String name;

            // create a window object screen
            Window screen = new
            Window("Example_3.java","bold","blue",48);
            screen.showWindow();

            // create a dialog box object for user input
            DialogBox inputName = new
            DialogBox(screen,"What is your name?");
            inputName.showDialogBox();

            // get the name from the dialog box
            name = inputName.getString();

            // display a welcome message on the screen
            screen.write("\n\n\n Hello "+name+"!");
            screen.write("\n\n Welcome to");
            screen.write("\n Object-oriented Programming with Java.");
      }
}
```

NOW DO THIS   Modify the previous program to:

(1) Input your name and address into two different dialog boxes.

(2) Change all the alphabetic characters of the name to uppercase letters.

(3) Change all the alphabetic characters of the address to lowercase letters.

(4) Display the modified name and address to the screen.

2.7 Converting Strings to Numbers

Figure 2.8 indicates that numerical data has been input into the dialog box.

If the dialog box was coded using:

```
DialogBox input = new DialogBox(screen,"Integer?");
input.showDialogBox();
```

then the number is retrieved from the dialog box using the appropriate instance method. In this example, an integer value has been input; therefore, the method `getInteger()` will be used as follows.

```
int number = input.getInteger();
```

If the number had been any of the other primitive types described in this chapter, then the appropriate instance method would be used from the `DialogBox` class. For example, if a single-precision real was input, then use `getFloat()`; if the number was a long integer, then use the instance method `get-LongInteger()`, and so on.

You may wonder what would happen if you input a noninteger string and attempted to convert it to an integer type through one of the instance methods. For example, if you attempted to convert the real `1.234` to an integer, then you would get the error message shown in Figure 2.9 displayed on the screen.

Figure 2.8 Input of a number into a dialog box

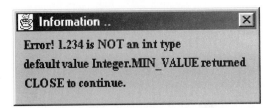

Figure 2.9 An error message issued when data is not in the correct format

Similarly, if you input any number in an incorrect format for the type of data required, the `DialogBox` class will automatically issue a warning message and set your data to the specified default value of the minimum value for its data type.

The programs you were asked to write as answers to questions 38, 39, and 40 at the end of Chapter 1 all suffered from one severe drawback—the data you used was written into the program. This is known as *hard-coding* data, and does not allow the program to respond to a range of data values that you might want to use when running the program.

The next program demonstrates how a dialog box may be used to input two integers and display their sum, difference, product, quotient, and remainder after division. Read through the program and see if you can understand all of the code with the aid of the descriptions and examples you have read so far. The code in color indicates how the strings input to the dialog box have been converted into integers.

```
// program to input two integer operands and perform the
// arithmetic operations of +, - *, /, and % upon them

import avi.*;

class Example_4
{
    public static void main(String[] args)
    {
        // declare two variables of type integer
        int first, second;

        // create a window object screen
        Window screen = new Window("Example_4.java","bold","blue",24);
        screen.showWindow();

        // display a heading on the screen
        screen.write("Simple Mathematics\n\n");

        // create a dialog box object to input numbers
        DialogBox inputNumber = new DialogBox(screen,"Integer?");

        // show dialog box twice to input two integers
        inputNumber.showDialogBox();
        first = inputNumber.getInteger();
        inputNumber.showDialogBox();
        second = inputNumber.getInteger();
```

```
// display the results of calculations
screen.write(first+" + "+second+" = "+(first+second)+"\n");
screen.write(first+" - "+second+" = "+(first-second)+"\n");
screen.write(first+" * "+second+" = "+(first*second)+"\n");
screen.write(first+" / "+second+" = "+(first/second)+"\n");
screen.write(first+" % "+second+" = "+(first%second)+"\n");
    }
}
```

Note: Arithmetic statements may be specified within the parameter of the instance method, however, you must parenthesize each numeric expression.

After compilation, the execution of the program results in the following screen shot, assuming the user has responded to the two Dialog Box queries with 56 and 9.

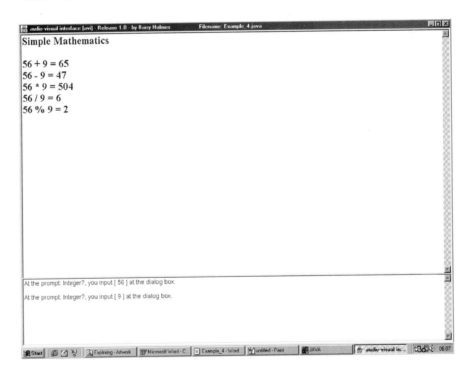

Whenever you use the audio-visual interface, a text file is automatically created to record all the echoed input and output as your program executes. This log file is very useful if you need a paper copy of your results. The name of the file is `LOG_FILE.TXT`, and may be opened by any text processing program to enable you to print the textual output from your program. Figure 2.10 illustrates the contents from the log file that was generated when program `Example_4` was executed.

```
=====================================================================================
                     L  O  G      F  I  L  E
        audio-visual interface [avi] - Release 1.0 - by Barry Holmes
          filename: Example_4.java    date: 6/25/2000  time: 5:7:44
=====================================================================================


Simple Mathematics


At the prompt: Integer?, you input [ 56 ] at the dialog box.


At the prompt: Integer?, you input [ 9 ] at the dialog box.


56 + 9 = 65
56 - 9 = 47
56 * 9 = 504
56 / 9 = 6
56 % 9 = 2
```

Figure 2.10 An example of a log file

NOW DO THIS⯈   Modify program `Example_4` as follows.

(1) Declare four variables first, second, third, and mean as `float`. Declare a fifth variable, count, as `int`, and initialize count to zero.

(2) Use dialog box objects to input real numbers for the variables first, second, and third, respectively. After each input, increase the variable count by 1.

(3) Calculate the arithmetic mean of the three values first, second, and third.

(4) Modify `screen.write` statements to output the values of the variables first, second, third, and mean.

(5) Compile the program.

(6) Run the program several times; on each occasion use different values for the variables.

2.8   Command Line Arguments

The command line provides another means of inputting *string* data to a program at the point at which you issue the command to run the program. For example, in the Introduction you were instructed to use the following command to run the HELLO WORLD program:

```
java Example_1
```

This program can be rewritten to allow command-line input. For example, it could be written to allow the user to change the style and the color of the text being used to output the message HELLO WORLD. In that case, two parameters could be appended to the command line as follows:

```
java Example_1 italic blue
```

The two string arguments "italic" and "blue" are passed as parameters to the main method. You may recall that this parameter is defined as String[] args. Clearly, this is a modification to the syntax for defining a variable of type string; the String type now has brackets [] appended to it. What does all this mean?

The square bracket notation is reserved to indicate that the data is stored, not at a single memory location—for this would be impossible for two items of data—but at continuous memory locations in a configuration that conceptually may be thought of as a set of pigeon holes numbered from 0 to 1. Figure 2.11 illustrates this concept.

The set of pigeon holes is known as a *one-dimensional array*. An array is a special kind of object. It has no class and it is not defined as part of the Java API documentation. The object is an inherent data structure in the Java language.

Since the array args is an object, it uses a reference to point to the pigeon holes. (Remember all objects are stored by reference and not by value.)

However, the data to be stored are a set of strings, which themselves are objects. Since the strings are objects, they cannot be directly stored in the pigeon holes; instead, references from each of the pigeon holes point to the respective string objects.

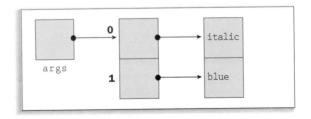

Figure 2.11 An illustration of the main method formal parameter args

An *array* is a named collection of one or more items of data of the same type. Each element of data can be accessed by the name of the array and the numbered index indicating its position within the array. Within the `main` method the arguments that are passed are stored as strings in the array `args`. The first parameter is stored at `args[0]`, the second at `args[1]`, and so on. In other words, `args[0]` has the value `"italic"`, and `args[1]` has the value `"blue"`.

The size of the array `args` is clearly dependent upon the number of parameters being passed to the `main` method. The size of any array is always returned by the instance variable `length`. Therefore, the size of the `args` array is `args.length`.

Program `Example_1`, from the Introduction, can be rewritten and renamed as `Example_5` to take into account the command-line parameters as follows.

```
// program to use command line parameters to specify the style and color
// of the text on the window at run time, and write the text literal
// "HELLO WORLD" centrally on the screen

import avi.*;

class Example_5
{
      public static void main(String[] args)
      {
            // create a Window object screen
            Window screen = new
            Window("Example_5.java",args[0],args[1],72);

            screen.showWindow();
            screen.write("\n\n\n              HELLO WORLD");
      }
}
```

The program is executed using the command line:

```
java Example_5 italic blue
```

You may wonder how to pass a numerical value to the `main` method in order to control the size of the font. This must be passed as a string and then converted into a number. The conversion of a string to a numerical value will be considered in Chapter 4, in the section on wrapper classes. However, for now you will not need to use this feature.

2.9   Errors

Syntax Errors

There are many traps for the unwary programmer to avoid when writing a computer program. The first of these concerns the misuse of the syntax (grammar) of the language. It is very easy, even for the experienced programmer, to type a lowercase letter when an uppercase letter was required, omit a semicolon at the end of a statement, incorrectly type the wrong number of arguments in a constructor or method, and so on. The list of grammatical errors that you can make is endless. The compiler will detect the misuse of the syntax and list the source of the errors for you, as the next program demonstrates.

The following program is written to find the total cost and average price of three newspapers. The names of the newspapers are input at the command line, and each name is used as part of the prompt in a dialog box to input the price of that paper. Notice that it is necessary to instantiate three dialog boxes, since each dialog box has a different prompt.

Can you find the errors from the listing of the program? Line numbers have been deliberately inserted into the listing of the program to make reference to the syntax errors easier.

```
1:    // program to input the names of three newspapers at the
2:    // command line, and input the prices of the newspapers
3:    // via dialog boxes, calculate and output the total cost
4:    // and average price of the newspapers
5:
6:    import avi.*;
7:
8:    class Example_6
9:    {
10:        public static void main(String[] args)
11:        {
12:            // declare prices of newspapers
13:            int pricePaper1, pricePaper2, pricePaper3;
14:
15:            // declare total cost and average price of papers
16:            int totalCost, averagePrice;
17:
18:            // declare a dialog box for each paper
19:            DialogBox inputPricePaper1, inputPricePaper2,
20:                        inputPricePaper3;
21:
22:            // create a window object screen
23:            Window screen = new
24:            Window("Example_6.java","blue");
25:            screen.showWindow();
26:
27:            // input prices of papers
28:            inputPricePaper1 = new DialogBox(screen,"Price of "+
29:                                    args[0]+"?");
30:            inputPricePaper1.showDialogBox();
31:            pricePaper1 = inputPricePaper1.getInteger()
32:
33:            inputPricePaper2 = new DialogBox(screen,"Price of "+
34:                                    args[1]+"?");
35:            inputPricePaper2.showDialogBox();
36:            pricePaper2 = inputPricePaper2.getInteger();
37:
38:            inputPricePaper3 = new DialogBox(screen,"Price of "+
39:                                    args[2]+"?");
40:            inputPricePaper3.showDialogBox();
41:            pricePaper3 = inputPricePaper3.getInteger();
42:
```

```
43:                   // calculate total cost and average price
44:                   totalcost = pricePaper1 + pricePaper2 + pricePaper3;
45:                   averagePrice = totalCost / args.length;
46:
47:                   // display statistics about newspapers
48:                   screen.write("Statistics about newspapers\n\n");
49:                   screen.write("Total cost of "+args.length+" papers is "+
50:                                   totalCost+" cents\n");
51:                   screen.write("Average price of papers is "+averagePrice+
52:                                   " cents\n");
53:           }
54:   }
```

When the program was compiled, the compiler listed the following errors.

On lines 23 and 24, the constructor for the `Window` requires four arguments. The missing arguments are the style and font size. The statement should be written as:

```
Window screen = new
Window("Example_6.java","plain","blue",36);
```

Line 31 is a confusing error message since it does not specify the cause of the error. Because the semicolon has been omitted at the end of the line, the compiler assumes that the expression continues onto lines 32 and 33. Hence, line 33 is flagged as containing an error when the error is only on line 31. The statement in line 31 should be written as:

```
pricePaper1 = inputPricePaper1.getInteger();
```

The error message relating to line 44 is informative. However, you can be forgiven for thinking that the variable `totalcost` has already been defined in line 16. But look again, and remember that Java is a case-sensitive language. The declaration in line 16 defines the variable as `totalCost` (with an uppercase letter C), yet the identifier in line 44 contains a lowercase c.

This error also had a knock-on effect, i.e., the compiler found errors that did not exist in the remainder of the line, and because the identifier was not correctly coded, the identifier `totalCost` in line 45 has also been flagged as not being initialized. To eliminate these errors, the statement in line 44 should be written as:

```
totalCost = pricePaper1 + pricePaper2 + pricePaper3;
```

In the final analysis, three real syntax errors were reported as six errors by the compiler!

NOW DO THIS

(1) Correct and recompile program `Example_6`.

(2) If you have no more syntax errors, then run the program on a computer using the command line:

```
java Example_6 Courier Mercury Globe
```

The following screen shot illustrates the result from running the corrected program.

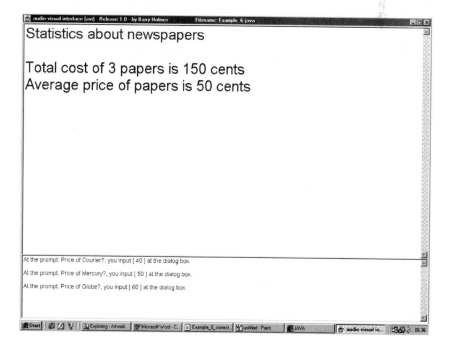

Run-Time Errors

The second category of error you may encounter occurs when the program compiles correctly, yet fails during program execution. There are numerous reasons why this can happen; however, we will consider just one case here. Consider what would happen if you did not input the three command-line parameters when attempting to run the previous example on a computer, and input:

```
java Example_6
```

The interpreter would generate the following error message.

```
Exception in thread "main" java.lang.ArrayIndexOutOfBoundsException: 0
at Example_6.main(Example_6.java:27)
```

If you run this program in the manner described, you will notice that despite the window being opened, no dialog box appeared for you to input any data. There were no values supplied as command-line parameters. Consequently the length of the `args` array was 0 since it contained no values. Therefore, the reference to `args[0]` in the program generated the run-time error.

Logical Errors

The third category of error you are likely to encounter is when the program compiles correctly, yet does not perform in the manner expected. This could happen, for example, if you coded a minus sign somewhere you meant to code a plus sign. Your program would compile and run to completion but would probably give incorrect output. These are logical errors that may be avoided by carefully checking the logical solution behind your programmed solution. Such errors can normally be weeded out during the testing stage of programming; however, despite many of our best efforts, some errors may still creep through into the final code.

SUMMARY

- A package is a convenient structure for grouping together classes that represent some common purpose.

- A class containing a constructor and instance methods may be used as a data type.

- An instance method is invoked by an object of the same class.

- The instance methods of a class are used to perform a variety of operations that pertain to the object.

- A variable declared as a class type does not become an object until a constructor within the class has been executed.

- The assignment of one object to another of the same type does not create a copy of the object.

- A data type `String` is a class and not a primitive data type.

- The only operator a `String` type may use is + for concatenation.

- To reuse any method it is necessary to import the appropriate class. A class can be imported by specifically stating the name of the package and class in an `import` statement. Alternatively, to make all the classes of a package available in a program, use only the package name followed by the wildcard symbol `*`.

- A program may contain just one class that contains the `main` method.

- Data may be input to the `main` method at run-time through the use of command-line arguments.

- The formal parameter list of the `main` method is a `String` array. Each string argument is stored in consecutive locations of this array.

- A program should contain many comments explaining the purpose of not only the program but groups of statements contained therein.

- A program may contain syntax errors when the grammar of the Java language is not used correctly, logical errors when the functionality of the program has not been correctly tested, and run-time errors when the program fails owing to unpredictable circumstances.

Review Questions

True or False

1. An object is created by executing a class constructor.

2. Assigning one string object to another string will result in a copy of the string object being made.

3. You may invoke an instance method in the same way as you call a class method.

4. The arguments passed to a `main` method from a command line are stored as strings in a one-dimensional array.

5. You interpret a program before you compile it.

6. A byte-code file may be used on a different computer from the one that produced the file.

Short Answer

7. Write the signature of any `String` constructor listed in this chapter.

8. What is the meaning of `args.length`, where `args` is the formal parameter of the `main` method?

9. Why is the `main` method declared as void?

10. What does a Java compiler do?

11. Why are Java programs portable?

12. Distinguish between syntax and logical errors.

13. What is the purpose of a package?

Exercises

14. From the illustration in Figure 2.12 discuss what you consider to be data and classify the data by type as variables declared in Java.

World Forecasts	
City	**Today**
Acapulco	90/97 s
Athens	79/59 pc
Bangkok	90/78 pc
Beijing	62/38 pc
Berlin	63/51 r
Bermuda	81/74 pc
Budapest	72/52 pc
Buenos Aires	83/62 pc
Cairo	89/68 pc
Dublin	53/39 c
Frankfurt	63/56 sh
Hong Kong	84/74 s

Figure 2.12 World forecasts

In Figure 2.12 the numbers refer to high and low temperatures in degrees Fahrenheit, and the abbreviations describe the following weather conditions: s- sunny, pc - partial cloud, r- rain, sh- showers and c - cloud.

15. What are the errors in the following statements?

    a. `Window = new Window("Question 15a");`

    b. `Window screen = new Window("Question 15b","plain");`

c. `Window screen = new Window("red","BOLD",18);`

d. `DialogBox input = new DialogBox("screen","temperature?");`

e. `DialogBox input = new DialogBox("");`

f. `DialogBox input = new DialogBox(screen);`

16. How would you expect the following output statements to display information?

a. `screen.write("Hello World");`

b. `screen.write("\tname: ");`

c. `screen.write("\tname:    " +   name);` where `name` is declared as `String name = "Mickey Mouse";`

d. `screen.write("a=" + a + " b=" + b + " c=" + c+"\n");` where a=3, b=4, and c=5.

e. `screen.write("area covered " + area);` where area = 635.8658.

f. `screen.write("\u0041\u0042\u0043");`

17. If a `DialogBox` object was created as `inputData`, state the errors in the following statements.

a. `String datum = inputData.getString;`

b. `int datum = inputData.getFloat();`

c. `String datum = inputData.getChar();`

d. `Double datum = inputData.getDouble();`

e. `float datum = inputData.getDouble();`

Programming Problems

18. Run program `Example_5` using command-line arguments to investigate every combination of font style and color of text.

19. Write a `main` method to input a phrase, convert it to uppercase letters of the alphabet, and write the phrase to the screen.

20. Write a `main` method to input a phrase, replace the occurrence of the letter `'e'` with `'?'`, and write the phrase to the screen.

21. Write a `main` method to input three phrases, concatenate the phrases into one phrase, and write the result to the screen.

22. Input a phrase at the command line, and write a `main` method to write the number of words in this phrase to the screen.

23. Write a `main` method to input the radius of a circle, calculate the circumference and area of the circle, and write these values to the screen. Assume π to be 3.14159.

24. Write a `main` method to input the maximum cross-sectional radius of a sphere, calculate the surface area and volume of the sphere, and write these values to the screen. Assume π to be 3.14159.

25. Write a `main` method to input a weight in kilograms, convert this to pounds, and write both weights on the screen. 1 kg = 2.2 pounds.

26. Write a `main` method to input a length in meters, convert this to feet and inches, and write both lengths on the screen. 1 meter = 39.4 inches.

27. Write a `main` method to input a velocity in miles per hour (mph), a distance in miles, calculate the time (in hours) it would take to cover the distance, and write all three quantities on the screen.

28. Write a `main` method to input two times in a 24-hour format, calculate the time (in hours and minutes) between the two times, and write the result on the screen. In this question assume that the second time to be input is greater than the first time.

29. Write a program to calculate and output the distance traveled by a car on a tank of gas. Input the capacity of the tank, and input the average rate of gas consumption per mile by the car.

30. Write a program to input any amount of US dollars and convert the amount into any chosen world currency and output your results. Input the conversion factor for the currency of your choice.

31. The wind chill temperature is based upon the air temperature and the speed of the wind. The National Weather Service uses the following expression to calculate the wind chill.

    $T(wc) = 0.0817(3.71V^{**}0.5 + 5.81 - 0.25V)(T-91.4) + 91.4$; where

    T(wc) is the wind chill;
    V is the wind speed in statute miles per hour;
    T is the temperature in degrees Fahrenheit.

    Write a computer program to input the wind speed and temperature and calculate and display the wind chill temperature.

---

i   The term wind chill goes back to the Antarctic explorer Paul A. Siple, who coined the term in a 1939 dissertation "Adaptation of the Explorer to the Climate of Antarctica." The wind chill factor describes how cold the wind makes us feel. As the wind blows, it draws heat from our bodies. The stronger the wind blows, the faster the heat is taken away. Thus, wind chill increases as the wind speed increases in cold temperatures. The calculation of the wind chill temperature is based upon a scientific formula that uses the air temperature and wind speed. This and more information is available on the Environmental Protection Agency Web site
http://www.usatoday.com/weather/wchilfor.htm

CHAPTER 3

Object-Oriented Programming

In this chapter you will be shown how to create your own classes and their constructors and methods, and you will be introduced to some of the techniques for writing programs using the object-oriented programming paradigm.

By the end of this chapter you should have an understanding of the following topics.

- The creation of an abstract data type

- Creating constructors, instance methods, and class methods

- Returning a value from a method

- Passing data as arguments in a method call

- The scope and life of identifiers

- The `Audio`, `FilmStrip`, and `Timer` classes from the `avi` package

- Designing and writing basic object-oriented programs

3.1   Abstract Data Type

Computer programs can be very complex, perhaps the most complicated arti-facts ever created by humans. One way to manage and control this complexity is with *abstraction*. An abstraction of something is a simplified view of it—the abstraction "hides" the unnecessary details and allows us to focus only on the parts of interest to us. For example, a chart in a newspaper might be an abstrac-tion of how world money markets are behaving.

We use many abstractions in our day-to-day lives. Consider a car. Most of us have an abstract view of how a car works. We know how to interact with it to get it to do what we want it to do: we put in gas, turn a key, press some pedals, and so on. But we don't necessarily understand what is going on inside the car to make it move—and we don't need to. Millions of us use cars everyday without under-standing the details of how they work. Abstraction helps us get to school or work!

A program can be designed as a set of interacting abstractions. In Java, these abstractions are captured in classes. The creator of a class obviously has to know all the details of the class. But once the class is created, other programmers can use the class without knowing its internal details. They only have to know its interface, just as the driver of a car can use the vehicle without knowing how the engine works. For example, you can use the classes of the book's `avi` package to do neat audio-visual output without knowing the details of how the classes work.

Abstract data types (ADTs) are an important form of program abstraction. An ADT consists of some hidden or protected data and a set of methods to perform actions on the data. When we hide data in a class, we say that the data have been *encapsulated*. Encapsulation is illustrated in Figure 3.1. The figure shows a class that defines `private` data, `public` methods, and `public` constructors. It shows that objects can be instantiated from the class with the `new` operator. Finally, it shows that the private data is "hidden" inside the objects, as indicated by the heavy circle surrounding the data, and that it can be accessed only through the `public` instance methods. The implementation of the data, constructors, and methods is normally hidden from a programmer who uses the class. The class acts as a boundary surrounding the constructor, methods, and data.

Why should we want to hide the implementation details of a class? By deny-ing other programmers, or even other parts of your program, access to the implementation details, you can safely modify the implementation without wor-rying that you may inadvertently introduce errors into other code that uses the class. As long as the interface and functionality do not change, the rest of the system should not be affected by changes you make within the class.

Another reason for encapsulation is to preserve the integrity of the data in your class. Direct access to the class data can result in variables not being cor-rectly updated. Access to the data must be through trusted methods of the class.

In documenting the interface of an encapsulated class, there is no need to reveal the constants, variables, and methods that programmers cannot access.

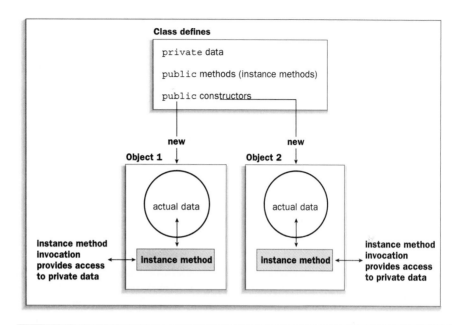

Figure 3.1 ADTs encapsulation data and methods

The appearance of the interface becomes uncluttered and helps to improve the documentation of the class.

The concept of an abstract data type is not new. Consider for a moment the class `String`. A variable of type `String` can be instantiated, using the `String` constructors, to reference a `String` object; this object can invoke many predefined instance methods such as `length`, `concat`, `replace`, `toUpperCase`, and so on. The method of implementing the data type `String` is hidden from the programmer. Without consulting with the author of the class `String`, there is no way of knowing the internal format of a `String`. We can of course guess that it might be stored as an array of characters! However, even if it is represented in this manner, we are precluded from accessing the array directly and must rely upon access through those instance methods that are supplied for the class.

Similarly, the implementations of the constructors and instance methods are hidden from the programmer. As a programmer, there is no way of inspecting how these operations are carried out since the class will be stored as Java byte codes. Only the implementers of the classes should have access to the Java source code, to prevent other programmers from changing well-engineered software.

A programmer may declare variables of type `String` and apply any of the set of instance methods to objects of this type.

The `String` example demonstrates the following features that embody the requirements of the abstract data type.

- The abstraction has created a data type, for example, `String`.

- It is possible to declare variables of the type, for example, `String alpha-bet`.

- The type contains a set of instance methods for the access and manipulation of data of the said type, for example, `length`.

- The implementation of the type, behind the scenes, uses whatever data and methods are necessary.

- Access to the type is through a restricted interface with the implementation details being hidden from the programmer who uses the type.

> *i* A `private` variable or method is visible only within its own class. Classes may not be `private`. A `public` class is visible anywhere; it can be seen, depending on the file accessibility. A `public` variable or method is visible anywhere its class is visible.

In creating classes, we will be creating abstract data types that conform to the above requirements. In the construction of an abstract data type, the data should be kept `private` to prevent access and hence changes to the values from outside of the class. The constructors and instance methods that are to be accessed from outside the class should be defined as `public`.

3.2 Constructors

The instantiation of an object is understood to be the allocation of memory for storing the object's data and the initialization of this memory space with appropriate values.

> *i* A class may contain a number of *instance variables* that represent the data for a particular object. Each object will have its own set of instance variables, which represent the state of an object.

Instantiation is made possible by the use of a constructor, which serves several purposes.

- A constructor is given the same name as the class to allow for the data type of objects to be declared.

- A constructor is normally used in conjunction with the keyword `new`, which allocates memory space from the heap. The *heap* is an area of memory set aside for the dynamic allocation of computer memory to objects during run time.

- A constructor provides the storage in memory and the initialization of the instance variables allocated to the object.

- For each separate invocation of the constructor, a new object will become instantiated.

The syntax of a constructor follows.

SYNTAX
··
Constructor:

```
public class-name ( formal-parameter-list )
{
        declarations
        statements
}
```

A constructor must be defined as being `public`, otherwise there is no means of using the constructor from outside of its class. The name of the constructor is always the same as its class name. Data values that specify a particular object are passed to the constructor via the formal parameter list. It is these values that are used to initialize the instance variables of the class.

In Chapter 2, when you used command-line arguments to pass data to the `main` method, you were transferring data to the formal parameter list (`String[] args`) of the `main` method. At the end of the Chapter 2 programming exercises, you were asked to experiment with different arguments for the `Window` class. By inputting different values for the color and type of font, you had the ability to change the color and style of text on the screen.

Passing different arguments to the formal parameters of a method gives you the power to reuse the method again and again with different data sets.

We will use the solution to the following problem to demonstrate the use of constructors and other Java constructs that are discussed later in this chapter.

Statement of the Problem

Write a program to input the length, width, depth at the shallow end, and depth at the deep end of a rectangular swimming pool. Then calculate the time it takes in hours to fill the swimming pool. Assume the rate of flow of water into the pool is 50 U.S. gallons per minute and that a cubic foot of water has a capacity of 7.48 U.S. gallons. Assume a uniform increase in depth when moving from the shallow end to the deep end.

The solution involves calculating the volume of the swimming pool (remember that a pool is not always a cuboid), and multiplying the volume by 7.48 to obtain the capacity of water in U.S. gallons of the pool. The time it takes to fill the pool with water is calculated by dividing the capacity of the pool by rate of flow of water into the pool, and then dividing this result by 60 to return a time in hours.

We can create a class `SwimmingPool` that represents the boundary of an abstract data type and contains the data about any pool.

```
public class SwimmingPool
{
      // instance variables
      private float lengthOfPool;
      private float widthOfPool;
      private float shallowDepthOfPool;
      private float deepDepthOfPool;
}
```

To this class we need to add a constructor to enable the instance variables of the class to be initialized when the constructor is used to create an object of type `SwimmingPool`.

```
public SwimmingPool(float length,
                    float width,
                    float shallowEndDepth,
                    float deepEndDepth)
{
      lengthOfPool        = length;
      widthOfPool         = width;
      shallowDepthOfPool  = shallowEndDepth;
      deepDepthOfPool     = deepEndDepth;
}
```

The constructor can be used to create swimming pools of various sizes. For example, the execution of:

```
SwimmingPool largePool = new SwimmingPool(100.0f,30.0f,3.0f,8.0f);
```

will first assign the four actual parameters (`100.0f,30.0f,3.0f,8.0f`) to the four formal parameters (`length`, `width`, `shallowEndDepth`, `deepEndDepth`) and then initialize the instance variables `lengthOfPool`, `widthOfPool`, `shallowDepthOfPool`, and `deepDepthOfPool` to the real values `100.0f`, `30.0f`, `3.0f`, and `8.0f` respectively. Similarly, the statement:

```
SwimmingPool smallPool = new SwimmingPool(50.0f,20.0f,5.0f,5.0f);
```

initializes the instance variables `lengthOfPool`, `widthOfPool`, `shallow-DepthOfPool`, and `deepDepthOfPool` to the real values `50.0f`, `20.0f`, `5.0f`, and `5.0f`, respectively. Note in this last example that the swimming pool is of uniform depth.

Let's look more closely at how the parameters behave. The call to the constructor using `SwimmingPool(100.0f,30.0f,3.0f,8.0f);` passes four arguments to the formal parameter list of the constructor.

- The number of arguments in the actual parameter list of a method call *must be the same* as the number of parameters specified by the formal parameter list of the method, in this example, the constructor.

- The data types of the arguments *must be the same* as those data types in the formal parameter list. However, you will see later in the book that there are exceptions to this rule.

- The order of the arguments in the actual parameter list *must be the same* as the order of the parameters in the formal parameter list.

In the swimming pool example, the actual parameter list for a large pool was

```
(100.0f, 30.0f, 3.0f, 8.0f);
```

which corresponds with the formal parameter list of

```
(float length, float width, float shallowEndDepth, float deepEndDepth)
```

Notice that between the two lists the number of arguments and parameters is the same; the data types between the corresponding arguments and parameters are the same, and the order in which the arguments and parameters appear is the same.

3.3   Instance Methods

As you are well aware, instance methods relate to some aspect of the instantiated object. For example, the `length` of a string, the conversion of a string `toUpperCase` characters, and so on. In the class `SwimmingPool`, suitable instance methods are of the "query" type rather than the "command" type and might be:

```
public float volumeOfWater();
public float capacityOfPool();
public float timeToFillPool(float rateOfFlow);
```

These return the volume of the pool, the capacity of water in the pool, and the time taken to fill the pool with water, respectively. Notice that these methods return single values, and only the instance method `timeToFillPool` requires a formal parameter, called `rateOfFlow`. Note that we did not have to use a parameter for the rate of flow but that we have chosen to do so to show how parameters work.

Instance methods pass a message to the object, and the object responds accordingly. Therefore, we can find the volume, capacity, and time to fill the pool by invoking the instance methods as follows.

```
largePool.volumeOfWater();
largePool.capacityOfPool();
largePool.timeToFillPool(RATE_OF_FLOW);
```

The syntax of a method definition follows.

SYNTAX

....

Method:

```
modifier(s) return-type method-name ( formal-parameter-list )
{
        declarations
        statements
}
```

The modifier used in the swimming pool example is `public`; however, as you will soon discover, it is possible to apply other modifiers to a method. Remember a method described as `public` means that it can be accessed from outside of the class. The return-type identifies the type of value that the method will return. This can be a primitive type or a class. If no data is returned by the method, the keyword `void` is used for the return-type.

The formal-parameter-list indicates the data types for any arguments the function expects to receive from the caller. Each individual argument passed to the method must have its own corresponding parameter. If no arguments are being passed to the method, then the parentheses remain empty.

Declarations refer to local constant and variable declarations for use within the method, and statements refer to the executable instructions within the method.

The return-type identifies the type of the value that the method will return with its return statement.

The syntax of the return statement is:

SYNTAX

••

Return Statement:

```
return expression;
```

---

where the expression may be omitted depending upon the use of the statement.

The three instance methods of the `SwimmingPool` class are constructed as follows

```
public float volumeOfWater()
{
     volume =
     0.5f*(lengthOfPool*widthOfPool)*(shallowDepthOfPool+deepDepthOfPool);
     return volume;
}


public float capacityOfPool()
{
     capacity = volume * CAPACITY_CUBIC_FOOT;
     return capacity;
}

public float timeToFillPool(float rateOfFlow)
{
     return (capacity / rateOfFlow)/60.0f;
}
```

where the constant `CAPACITY_CUBIC_FOOT` is declared within the class `SwimmingPool`. Both `volume` and `capacity` must be declared as instance variables within the class.

The following computer listing defines the completed `SwimmingPool` class. This code may be stored in a text file with the name `SwimmingPool.java`. The class is compiled using the `javac` command that you used in the Introduction.

```java
// The creation of the SwimmingPool class

public class SwimmingPool
{
      // constant
      private final float CAPACITY_CUBIC_FOOT = 7.48f;

      // instance variables
      private float lengthOfPool;
      private float widthOfPool;
      private float shallowDepthOfPool;
      private float deepDepthOfPool;
      private float volume;
      private float capacity;


      // constructor
      public SwimmingPool(float length,
                          float width,
                          float shallowEndDepth,
                          float deepEndDepth)
      {
            lengthOfPool       = length;
            widthOfPool        = width;
            shallowDepthOfPool = shallowEndDepth;
            deepDepthOfPool    = deepEndDepth;
      }

      // instance methods
      public float volumeOfWater()
      {
            volume = 0.5f*(lengthOfPool*widthOfPool)*
                        (shallowDepthOfPool+deepDepthOfPool);
            return volume;
      }

      public float capacityOfPool()
      {
            capacity = volume * CAPACITY_CUBIC_FOOT;
            return capacity;
      }

      public float timeToFillPool(float rateOfFlow)
      {
            return (capacity / rateOfFlow)/60.0f;
      }
}
```

It would be illogical to attempt to execute this class on the computer. Do you know why? What we have achieved is to create an abstract data type of a SwimmingPool. In other words, we can create objects of this type and send various messages to these objects. However, we have not created a complete program. To do that we need a separate class that contains a main method.

To test the SwimmingPool class we create a class similar to those introduced in Chapter 2. Such a class is often called a *driver class* since it lets us "drive" the class we wish to test. The driver class will contain a main method. Within the main method it is possible to instantiate a SwimmingPool object and write to the screen the results of the state of a pool with respect to the volume of water (cubic feet), capacity (U.S. gallons), and time to fill the pool (hours).

The following listing is contained in a text file with the name Example_1.java and is compiled using the javac command. Since this file contains a main method, it is possible to execute the program using the java command.

For the present time, adopt the practice of ensuring that every class you have written, as part of a program, must be stored in the same directory or subdirectory. Later in the book you will be shown how to group all related classes into a package.

```java
// program to demonstrate using the SwimmingPool class

import avi.*;

class Example_1
{
    public static void main(String[] args)
    {
        final float RATE_OF_FLOW = 50.0f;
        float volume, capacity, time;

        Window screen = new Window("Example_1.java","bold","blue",24);
        screen.showWindow();

        SwimmingPool largePool = new
        SwimmingPool(100.0f,30.0f,3.0f,8.0f);

        volume = largePool.volumeOfWater();
        capacity = largePool.capacityOfPool();
        time = largePool.timeToFillPool(RATE_OF_FLOW);

        screen.write("Large Pool\n\tVolume: "+volume+" cubic feet\n");
        screen.write("\tCapacity: "+capacity+" US gallons\n");
        screen.write("\tTime to fill: "+time+" hours\n\n");
    }
}
```

A screen shot of the results from `Example_1` follows.

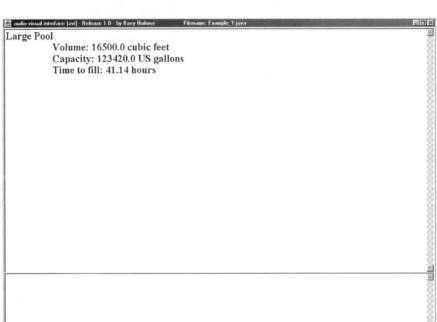

NOW DO THIS   Using the `SwimmingPool` class for reference, create a class `DecorateARoom` that contains the following.

(1) A constructor to initialize instance variables for the length, width, height, window area, and door area of a room.

(2) Instance methods to return all of the instance variables initialized by the parameters of the constructor.

(3) An instance method to return the total surface area of the walls of the room.

(4) An instance method to return the number of rolls of wallpaper needed to paper the walls, given that a roll of paper is 25 feet in length and 3 feet wide.

(5) An instance method to return the number of cans of paint required to cover the walls (as an alternative to wallpaper), given that a 1 gallon can contains enough paint to cover an area of 100 square feet.

(6) Compile the `DecorateARoom` class; if there are no syntax errors then progress to Step (7).

(7) Write and execute a driver program to test all the methods of the `DecorateARoom` class.

Note that due to the way the `SwimmingPool` class has been defined, it is necessary to invoke its exported methods in a specific order, namely `volumeOfWater`, `capacityOfPool`, and `timeToFillPool`. Otherwise the instance variables `volume` and `capacity` will not be properly initialized. Order restrictions such as this should usually be avoided and are allowed in some early examples just to keep the code relatively uncomplicated.

Although the declaration of the variables `volume`, `capacity`, and `time` in the `main` method were included here for clarity, they are superfluous. The use of the variables `volume`, `capacity`, and `time` in the `write` statements may be replaced by a direct invocation of the corresponding instance method, as shown in the code of `Example_2`.

```java
// program to demonstrate using the SwimmingPool class

import avi.*;

class Example_2
{
     public static void main(String[] args)
     {
          final float RATE_OF_FLOW = 50.0f;

          Window screen = new Window("Example_2.java","bold","blue",24);
          screen.showWindow();

          SwimmingPool largePool = new
          SwimmingPool(100.0f,30.0f,3.0f,8.0f);

          screen.write("Large Pool\n\tVolume: "+
                    largePool.volumeOfWater()+" cubic feet\n");
          screen.write("\tCapacity: "+largePool.capacityOfPool()+
                    " US gallons\n");
          screen.write("\tTime to fill: "+
                    largePool.timeToFillPool(RATE_OF_FLOW)+
                    " hours\n\n");
     }
}
```

The next iteration of the same problem shows you how two swimming pool objects are created and how the state of each swimming pool is written to the screen in `Example_3`.

```java
// program to demonstrate using the SwimmingPool class

import avi.*;

class Example_3
{
      public static void main(String[] args)
      {
            final float RATE_OF_FLOW = 50.0f;

            Window screen = new Window("Example_3.java","bold","blue",24);
            screen.showWindow();

            SwimmingPool largePool = new
            SwimmingPool(100.0f,30.0f,3.0f,8.0f);

            screen.write("Large Pool\n\tVolume: "+
                        largePool.volumeOfWater()+" cubic feet\n");
            screen.write("\tCapacity: "+largePool.capacityOfPool()+
                        " US gallons\n");
            screen.write("\tTime to fill: "+
                        largePool.timeToFillPool(RATE_OF_FLOW)+
                        " hours\n\n");

            SwimmingPool smallPool = new
            SwimmingPool(50.0f,20.0f,5.0f,5.0f);

            screen.write("Small Pool\n\tVolume: "+
                        smallPool.volumeOfWater()+" cubic feet\n");
            screen.write("\tCapacity: "+smallPool.capacityOfPool()+
                        " US gallons\n");
            screen.write("\tTime to fill: "+
                        smallPool.timeToFillPool(RATE_OF_FLOW)+
                        " hours\n\n");
      }
}
```

A screen shot follows showing the results of `Example_3` being executed.

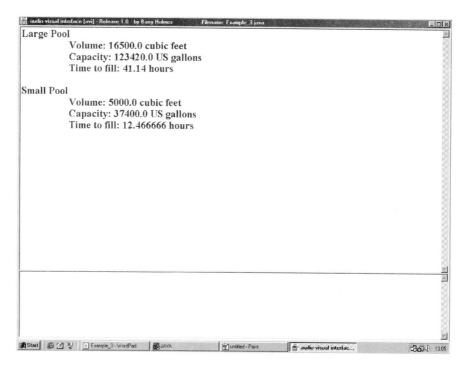

Clearly the disadvantage in this coding is the amount of similar code that has to be repeated for each pool. To reduce this duplication it is possible to code a new method, local to the driver class, known as a *helper* method, which will be called from the `main` method every time the `volume`, `capacity`, and `time` are to be written to the screen. This approach is described in the next section.

3.4   Class Methods

An instance method such as the `volumeOfWater` method of the `SwimmingPool` class is invoked through an object of the class, for example, `"volume = largePool.volumeOfWater();"`. A *class* method, also known as a *static* method, is one that *cannot* be invoked through an object. To differentiate an instance method from a class method, one of the modifiers used in the signature of the class method is declared as `static`.

A Java application consists of at least one class method, the `main` method. In `Example_4`, a second class method has been introduced to write the `volume`, capacity, and time on the screen. The program illustrates how to define a second class method within a class, how to call (invoke) this method, and how the computer returns to the main method after the method has been executed.

```
// program to demonstrate using the SwimmingPool class
// and to demonstrate the creation of a helper method

import avi.*;

class Example_4
{
        // a 'helper' method to display the statistics of the pool
        private static void displayStatistics(Window screen,
                                              String nameOfPool,
                                              float   volume,
                                              float   capacity,
                                              float   time)
        {
            screen.write(nameOfPool+"\n\tVolume: "+volume+" cubic feet\n");
            screen.write("\tCapacity: "+capacity+" US gallons\n");
            screen.write("\tTime to fill: "+time+" hours\n\n");
        }

        public static void main(String[] args)
        {
            final float RATE_OF_FLOW = 50.0f;

            Window screen = new Window("Example_4.java","bold","blue",24);

            screen.showWindow();

            // create a large SwimmingPool object
            SwimmingPool largePool = new
            SwimmingPool(100.0f,30.0f,3.0f,8.0f);


            displayStatistics(screen,
                        "Large Pool",
                        largePool.volumeOfWater(),
                        largePool.capacityOfPool(),
                        largePool.timeToFillPool(RATE_OF_FLOW));

            // create a small SwimmingPool object
            SwimmingPool smallPool = new
            SwimmingPool(50.0f,20.0f,5.0f,5.0f);
```

```
displayStatistics(screen,
                  "Small Pool",
                  smallPool.volumeOfWater(),
                  smallPool.capacityOfPool(),
                  smallPool.timeToFillPool(RATE_OF_FLOW));
   }
}
```

Those methods that are part of the class, yet are not accessed from outside of the class, but used to help a `public` method achieve its goal, should be `private`. We will often refer to such methods as *helper* methods.

The `main` method is executed before any other method. Having created a window object and shown this object on the screen, a large swimming pool object is created. The computer then calls (branches to) the `displayStatistics` method, passing across the data for the large swimming pool, found in the actual-parameter list of the class method call.

After the `displayStatistics` class method has been executed, the computer automatically returns to the next statement after the call to the class method. This is one case in which you do not explicitly need to code a return statement because this class method does not return a value. The computer returns to the statement in the `main` method to create a small swimming pool object. Notice that comments are ignored by the computer when executing the program.

The computer then calls (branches to) the `displayStatistics` method for a second time, passing across the data for the small swimming pool, found in the actual-parameter list of the class method call. Once again the statements of the `displayStatistics` class method are executed, and the computer returns to the next statement after the call to the class method. But this is now then end of the `main` method; therefore, the computer returns to the operating system prompt.

Class methods should be defined as `static` and `public` if they are to be accessed from outside of the class; otherwise, they should be labeled as `static` and `private`.

In effect, at this point we have identified two ways of classifying methods:

■ A method defined as `static` is called a class method; a method not defined as `static` is called an instance method.

■ A `private` method other than the `main` method is often called a helper method; for now, if a method is not `private`, it is `public`; later we will learn more categories of protection for methods.

So, a method can be either a class method or an instance method, and it can be either a `private` method or a `public` method. We can redraw Figure 3.1, so that its modified form appears as Figure 3.2, to reflect the most interesting possibilities. The figure emphasizes that `public` class methods are invoked through the class itself, whereas instance methods are invoked through an instance of the class, i.e., through an object. Furthermore, you can see that helper methods can

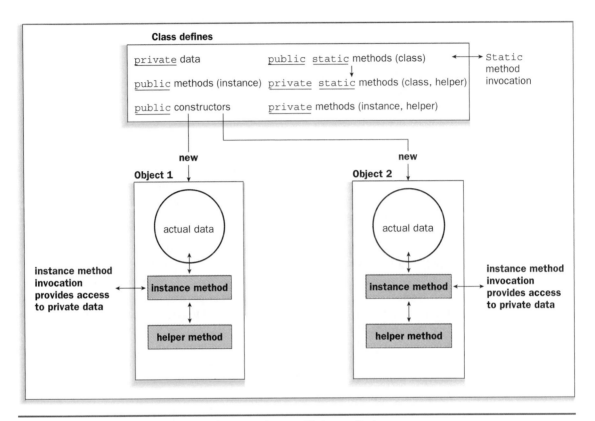

Figure 3.2 A class may define constructors, instance, class, and helper methods

be invoked only from other methods defined within the class; they cannot be invoked from outside the class like `public` methods. Note also that it is possible for a class to contain more than one constructor. This fact was obvious from the `String` class; however, it is a feature that we have not used in defining our own classes. We will use this feature in later chapters.

3.5   Scope and Lifetime of Identifiers

The class `Example_4` can be rewritten as `Example_5`, so that there is no need to explicitly pass the object screen as a `Window` parameter. This requires that the declaration of the screen object is moved so that it is "visible" from both the `main` method and the `displayStatistics` class method. In doing this, it is necessary to qualify the screen object as being `static`. You will notice from the computer listing that there is no need to include the screen as a parameter in the signature of the `displayStatistics` class method.

```
// program to demonstrate class scope for a window object

import avi.*;

class Example_5
{
      static Window screen = new Window("Example_4.java","bold","blue",24);

      // a 'helper' method to display the statistics of the pool
      private static void displayStatistics(String  nameOfPool,
                                            float    volume,
                                            float    capacity,
                                            float    time)
      {
           screen.write(nameOfPool+"\n\tVolume: "+volume+" cubic feet\n");
           screen.write("\tCapacity: "+capacity+" US gallons\n");
           screen.write("\tTime to fill: "+time+" hours\n\n");
      }

      public static void main(String[] args)
      {
           final float RATE_OF_FLOW = 50.0f;


           screen.showWindow();

           // create a large SwimmingPool object
           SwimmingPool largePool = new
           SwimmingPool(100.0f,30.0f,3.0f,8.0f);


           displayStatistics("Large Pool",
                        largePool.volumeOfWater(),
                        largePool.capacityOfPool(),
                        largePool.timeToFillPool(RATE_OF_FLOW));

           // create a small SwimmingPool object
           SwimmingPool smallPool = new
           SwimmingPool(50.0f,20.0f,5.0f,5.0f);

           displayStatistics("Small Pool",
                        smallPool.volumeOfWater(),
                        smallPool.capacityOfPool(),
                        smallPool.timeToFillPool(RATE_OF_FLOW));
      }
}
```

class scope

The *scope* of an identifier refers to the region of a program in which an identifier can be used. An identifier can have either class scope or block scope. An identifier with *class scope* is accessible from its point of declaration throughout the entire class. `Example_5` illustrates that the object `screen` may be used by any method declared within the class. The arrowed line drawn along the left-hand side of the code indicates the scope of the identifier `screen` within the class.

By contrast, an identifier with *block scope* is accessible only from the point of declaration to the end of the block. A *block* begins with an open brace { and ends with a close brace } and contains declarations and executable statements. `Example_5` illustrates the block scope of the constant `RATE_OF_FLOW`. This identifier is not accessible outside of the `main` method.

Block scope is not always defined by the use of braces { }. This will become evident in later chapters on selection and repetition.

The *lifetime* of an identifier is the period during which the value of the identifier exists in computer memory. The lifetime of an identifier will vary according to the nature of the identifier. Identifiers declared as being `static` exist for the life of the program, such as the object `screen` in `Example_5`, whereas parameters and identifiers having block scope exist only during the execution of the method. For example, in `Example_5`, the value of the parameters `nameOfPool`, `volume`, `capacity`, and `time` will be destroyed when the `displayStatistics` method is not being executed.

When an object goes out of scope, the amount of memory allocated to storing that object is returned back to the heap for future use by other objects.

The Java system automatically returns memory to the heap when it is no longer required. This process is known as *garbage collection*.

3.6 Software Development

The stages in the development of a software project are illustrated in Figure 3.3. Notice that although the software development cycle consists of a set of four phases, each phase is not deemed to be entirely completed before moving on to the next phase. Because the development of software evolves through the experience gained at each stage, it is possible to go back to any of the stages and modify the solution to the problem.

During *analysis*, the customer who commissioned the system to be built and the software developers who construct the system meet to agree upon a description of the problem. The outcome of the analysis phase is a description of the functionality of the system, which conveys the behavior of the software system

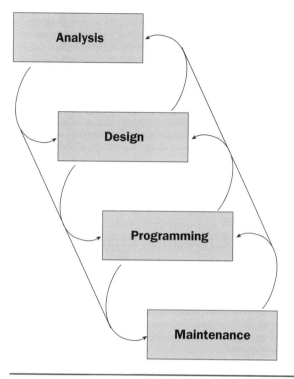

Figure 3.3 Software development life cycle

to be constructed. It is often desirable at this stage to identify a set of test cases, i.e., input for the program and the corresponding expected output. This process helps clarify the description of the system and can be used later during the design and programming stages.

In the *design* phase, plans are generated for building the system. This stage may, for example, include the identification of classes and their interfaces. After a design is completed, it is possible to look for any shortcomings in the proposed system, iterate back to the analysis phase, and, if necessary, make appropriate modifications to the requirements.

The *programming* of a software project combines coding, testing, and the integration of the various software components to construct the software system. Together, the design and programming phases are the phases you will concentrate on most as you work through this book.

A software system is not static. With use, and with changes in requirements, the system may need to be modified to meet changing demands. The *maintenance* phase may take the form of simply changing and retesting small amounts of code. Alternatively, a modification to the software system may require further analysis, design, coding, and testing.

Identify the classes and methods - decide on how to solve the problem, and identify the classes, their relationships and dependencies; and the methods required to manipulate the data. Draw the class diagrams.

Algorithm development - for each method devise an appropriate algorithm and code this into the Java language.

```java
public float timeToFillPool(float rateOfFlow)
{
        return (capacity / rateOfFlow)/60.0f;
}
```

Testing - Invent suitable test data, and desk check each method for logical errors.

Test data: capacities 37400, 123420

Desk check

rateOfFlow	capacity	timeToFillPool
50.0	37400	12.46
50.0	123420	41.14

Compilation and program execution - compile each class and detect and correct any syntax errors.

Run the computer program using the same suite of test data that you used during the desk checking stage.

Documentation

Figure 3.4 The programming phase in software development

Figure 3.4 illustrates five major activities that form the *design and programming* parts of the software development life cycle.

3.7   Object-Oriented Program Design

Before attempting to design and code Java classes we need to state a few guidelines. These guidelines will be used in the case studies and should help you to develop a systematic approach to problem solving and good programming habits.

Identify the Classes and Methods

Document in English how you plan to tackle the problem from the information provided. Problem analysis should include sifting through the information and determining what classes and methods are required. Show any calculations that will be used on the data since this will be helpful when coding methods that use these calculations.

In object-oriented programming we tend to focus upon the production of classes at an early stage in the design. We identify the data used in the problem and analyze which methods should operate upon data of this type.

You may find the following technique useful in determining the classes in your program.

The identification of classes and objects is the hardest part of object-oriented design. One simple technique for identifying classes is to write a description of the problem, list all the *nouns* that appear in the description, and then choose your possible classes from the list.

For example, "Write a *program* to input the *dimensions* of a *swimming pool* and calculate and display the *volume, capacity,* and *time* to fill the pool." From the list of possible nouns only *swimming pool* can be considered as a viable class. We can visualize a swimming pool as an object and instantiate many swimming pool objects of different dimensions.

The nouns *dimensions, volume, capacity,* and *time* (to fill) all represent attributes of a swimming pool and can hardly be visualized as objects.

Figure 3.5 illustrates that a class may be represented in UML by a rectangle containing only the name of the class.

Once you have identified a class, the next step is to determine the operations that an object of that class can perform or can have performed upon itself, and also the information an object of the class must maintain.

If we identify all the *verbs* in the description of the problem, we can choose a list of possible actions that an object may perform or have performed upon itself. For example, "*Write* a program to *input* the dimensions of a swimming pool and *calculate* and *display* the volume, capacity and time to *fill* the pool." From the list of verbs, *input, calculate,* and *display* are possible candidate methods for an object of type `SwimmingPool`.

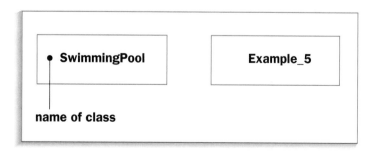

Figure 3.5 The simplest UML representation of classes

Data representing the dimensions of the swimming pool will be input to the object using the class constructor. In the `SwimmingPool` class the dimensions of the pool represent the instance data of the class. The attributes of `lengthOfPool`, `widthOfPool`, and `depthOfPool` describe the data of the `SwimmingPool` class.

The verb *calculate* applies to calculating the volume, capacity, and time to fill the pool; therefore, `volumeOfPool`, `capacityOfPool`, and `timeToFillPool` are all methods that return further attributes of a swimming pool. The verbs *display* and *fill* may be dismissed since the three methods already identified incorporate all the functionality required to acquire information about the pool.

> The technique of identifying the nouns and verbs from the description to the problem is by no means the only approach, and it definitely does not apply well to anything beyond simple problems. However, the method is sufficient for the majority of the problems appearing in this book. Another approach to discovering classes, methods, and associations between classes will be explained in Chapter 10.

An alternative UML representation of classes is depicted in Figure 3.6. Notice that the rectangle is split into three parts. The top part is used, as before, to identify the class by name; the middle part describes the attributes or data for the class; the bottom part lists the operations contained within the class. Notice from the `Example_5` class that it is possible to leave the attributes part of the diagram blank.

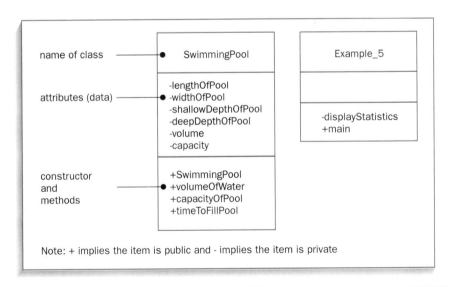

Figure 3.6 An expanded UML representation of classes, their attributes, and methods

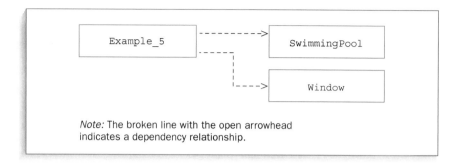

Figure 3.7 The UML representation of dependencies between classes

The next stage looks for any dependencies that may exist between classes. Classes can build upon and cooperate with other classes. Often one class depends upon another class because it cannot be used unless the other class exists.

Figure 3.7 illustrates how the `Example_5` class is dependent upon the existence of a `SwimmingPool` class and a `Window` class (found in the `avi` package). Note the use of broken lines with open arrow heads to denote the dependency relationship.

Algorithm Development

An algorithm is a solution to a problem and is expressed as a series of operations for the computer to obey. Each constructor and method will have its own algorithm. Normally, both the constructors and methods are reasonably short in length and may be coded directly into the Java language. However, when an algorithm is particularly complex, it is advisable to represent the algorithm as a narrative of the solution written in English, known as *pseudocode*, rather than in Java code. You can then sort out the logical order of operations before coding the algorithm into Java code. The pseudocode can, if necessary, be refined into further pseudocode, showing more detail about the solution to the problem, until eventually the pseudocode can be mapped directly into Java code. At this stage it is also possible to identify what helper methods, if any, are required.

As an example of the use of pseudocode, consider the following generalization of the statements to create two swimming pools. Do realize, however, that designing algorithms using pseudocode is beneficial only before the Java code is written and not afterwards!

1. create a window object—screen

2. create a swimming pool object—large pool

3. write the statistics of the large pool to the screen

4. create a swimming pool object—small pool

5. write the statistics of the small pool to the screen

This initial design of the statements to be used by the `main` method shows an obvious repetition of writing the statistics of the pool to the screen twice in the same method. If we assume the creation of a helper method to write the statistics of a swimming pool to the screen, the pseudocode design can be rewritten to take this fact into account.

1. create a window object—screen

2. create a swimming pool object—large pool

3. **call static method** to write the statistics of the large pool to the screen

4. create a swimming pool object—small pool

5. **call static method** to write the statistics of the small pool to the screen

The use of pseudocode will also be demonstrated in later case studies in the book.

Testing

Having designed a solution and coded it into the Java language, the next step is to trace through the algorithm with test data to verify that the solution contains no logical errors. *Logical errors* are mistakes in the design of the program, such as a branch to a wrong statement, or the use of a wrong mathematical formula.

Programs can be tested, either by the programmer tracing through the design and program code, known as desk checking, or by peer-group inspection.

To *desk check* a program, invent suitable test data such that the type and nature of the data is representative of the problem. Numerical data should be chosen for ease of calculation. Use the variables defined in the method being tested to construct headings for the desk-check table. Use the test data to trace through the algorithm line-by-line, obeying the instructions, and modifying the values of the variables in the table as required. The desk check makes it possible to predict the results before the program is run on the computer.

In *peer-group* inspection, members of the programming team review the accuracy of a design or program and determine whether it meets the original specification.

Compilation and Execution

During compilation, errors may be detected in the way the grammar of the computer language has been used. These errors, known as *syntax errors*, are associated with the wrong construction of computer language statements.

When the compilation is successful, and regardless of the testing technique adopted, further testing, often using the same test data as in the desk check, is always carried out by running the program with test input and checking if the output is correct. This testing phase should be much more extensive than the desk-checking stage and therefore additional test cases should be identified. When completed, the programmer should be confident that the code will perform to meet the original requirements specification.

Documentation

Despite documentation being discussed as the fifth activity in programming, it is used and produced during the other four activities, and for this reason documentation can be regarded as an activity that occurs throughout the entire programming cycle.

Over a period of time a program may be changed, and indeed evolve, as the computer project to which it contributes evolves. Documentation involves stating the purpose of the program, the method of solution (both pseudocode, if applicable, and program code), the stages of testing that it has undergone, and other necessary facts.

The documentation of a program will usually conform to the in-house standards of an organization.

The standard Java tools include a documentation aid called `javadoc`, the Java API documentation generator. The full details of the `javadoc` tool are given in the documentation you were instructed to download from the Sun Web site in the Introduction. However, we include the following brief description of its use, to encourage you to use it to document all your classes and methods.

Before the coding of a method, even before the constructor, include a comment as follows.

```
/**
```

Textual annotation of the purpose of the method.

```
@param
```

Name of parameter followed by a description of its purpose. (This line must be repeated for each parameter the method contains.)

```
@return
```

Description of the data being returned. (This line is omitted if the method returns `void`.)

```
*/
```

For example, these new-style comments were incorporated into the coding of the `SwimmingPool` class as follows.

```
// program to demonstrate the creation of a class

public class SwimmingPool
{
    // constant
    private final float CAPACITY_CUBIC_FOOT = 7.48f;

    // instance variables
    private float lengthOfPool;
```

```java
private float widthOfPool;
private float shallowDepthOfPool;
private float deepDepthOfPool;
private float volume;
private float capacity;

// constructor
/**
The SwimmingPool class enables an object that represents any
rectangular-shaped swimming pool to be created.
@param length is the length of the pool.
@param width is the width of the pool.
@param shallowEndDepth is the depth of the pool at the shallowest end
@param deepEndDepth is the depth of the pool at the deepest end
*/
public SwimmingPool(float length,
                    float width,
                    float shallowEndDepth,
                    float deepEndDepth)
{
    lengthOfPool       = length;
    widthOfPool        = width;
    shallowDepthOfPool = shallowEndDepth;
    deepDepthOfPool    = deepEndDepth;
}


// instance methods
/**
Calculates the volume of water in the pool.
@return The volume of water in cubic feet.
*/
public float volumeOfWater()
{
    volume = 0.5f*(lengthOfPool*widthOfPool)*
                (shallowDepthOfPool+deepDepthOfPool);
    return volume;
}

/**
Calculates the capacity of the pool.
@return The capacity of the pool in US gallons.
*/
public float capacityOfPool()
{
```

```
        capacity = volume * CAPACITY_CUBIC_FOOT;
        return capacity;
    }


    /**
    Calculates the time to fill the pool.
    @param rateOfFlow rate of flow of water into the pool in US gallons
    per minute.
    @return Time to fill the pool in hours.
    */
    public float timeToFillPool(float rateOfFlow)
    {
        return (capacity / rateOfFlow)/60.0f;
    }
}
```

The documentation is normally generated after the compilation phase is satisfactorily completed with no errors present in the source code. Use the same window (MS-DOS or terminal) that you used for compilation to input the `javadoc` command. A simplified form of the syntax to produce Java documentation is:

```
javadoc classname.java
```

Notice the amount of information that is output by this command during the automated documentation process.

```
C:\chap_3>javadoc SwimmingPool.java
Loading source file SwimmingPool.java...
Constructing Javadoc information...
Building tree for all the packages and classes...
Building index for all the packages and classes...
Generating overview-tree.html...
Generating index-all.html...
Generating deprecated-list.html...
Building index for all classes...
Generating allclasses-frame.html...
Generating index.html...
Generating packages.html...
Generating SwimmingPool.html...
Generating serialized-form.html...
Generating package-list...
Generating help-doc.html...
Generating stylesheet.css...
```

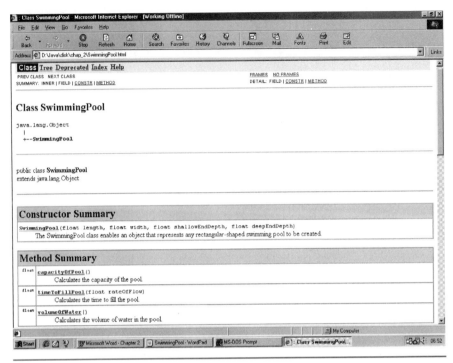

Figure 3.8 An illustration of the online documentation being viewed by a browser

A small sample of the online documentation generated by `javadoc` for the `SwimmingPool` class is shown in Figure 3.8.

To conclude, the design and programming stages contain the activities of identifying classes and methods, designing and coding constructors and methods, testing the code, compiling and testing the program on the computer, and last but not least, continually documenting all of these activities.

CASE STUDY

Cutting Logs

Statement of the Problem. An automated sawmill uses computer-controlled equipment to cut logs to set sizes and report on the amount of wasted timber. In the absence of the equipment, write a program to input the length of a log and the size of the pieces to be cut from the log. Calculate the number of whole pieces cut from the log and the length of wasted timber. Repeat the process for any number of different-sized logs to be cut to individual set sizes for each log.

Calculate the total number of whole pieces of log that are cut to size and the accumulated waste (off-cuts) from all the logs. Display the information about the logs at the end of the program.

Given the length of a log and the size that each log must be cut, the number of pieces that may be cut from a log is computed using the expression:

```
numberOfPieces = (int)(lengthOfWood / cutSize);
```

The length of wasted wood from this log would be

```
lengthOfWood - (numberOfPieces * cutSize);
```

The total length of wasted wood is therefore calculated using the expression:

```
totalWasted = totalWasted + lengthOfWood - (numberOfPieces * cutSize);
```

Identification of Classes and Methods

By analyzing the nouns in the specification of the problem it is possible to identify a number of candidate classes.

Write a *program* to input the *length* of a *log* and the *size* of the *pieces* to be cut from the *log*. Calculate the *number* of *whole pieces* cut from the *log* and the *length* of *wasted timber*. Repeat the *process* for any *number* of *different-sized logs* to be cut to *individual* set *sizes* for each *log*. Calculate the *total number* of *whole pieces* of *log* that are cut to *size* and the *accumulated waste* (off-cuts) from all the *logs*. Display the *information* about the *logs* at the *end* of the *program*.

The noun *log* specifies a real-world object, a piece of timber, that you can touch (and smell). This is a natural candidate for a class. The nouns such as *length* and *size* are attributes of the whole log before it is cut, and the nouns *whole pieces* and *wasted timber* are attributes of a log after it has been cut.

A second candidate class is the program, in this case, `Example_6`. It is in this class that we can input data on a log and, after the log has been cut, display information on the number of whole pieces and wasted timber. We conclude that suitable classes are `Log` and `Example_6`.

By performing an analysis on the verbs in the problem specification, it is possible to determine candidate methods for the class log.

Write a program to *input* the length of a log and the size of the pieces to be *cut* from the log. *Calculate* the number of whole pieces *cut* from the log and the length of wasted timber. *Repeat* the process for any number of different-sized logs to be *cut* to individual set sizes for each log. *Calculate* the total number of whole pieces of log that are *cut* to size and the accumulated waste (off-cuts) from all the logs. *Display* the information about the logs at the end of the program.

The verb *input*, to input the length and size of a log, can be implemented as the constructor to input this data and initialize attributes of the `Log` class. The verb *cut*, to cut a log into a number of pieces, can be implemented as an instance method, since it is a command to change the state of a log. This method is responsible for performing the calculations on the number of whole pieces cut from a log and the amount of waste wood from a log.

However, it is also necessary to calculate the total number of whole pieces cut and the accumulated waste from many logs. These methods do not relate to a single object and, therefore, cannot be invoked using a single object. The methods are class methods that return the total number of whole pieces and the accumulated waste timber.

We conclude that suitable methods for the Log class are: the constructor Log, the instance method cut, and the class methods totalCut and waste.

The only method in the class Example_6 is the main method. This is essentially a driver to test the validity of the code in the Log class.

The representation of classes is shown in Figure 3.9.

Algorithm Development

Every object has its own set of instance variables. In this example, if three Log objects were instantiated, each would have its own value for the length of the log and the size of the pieces that each log was to be cut. The problem demands that we keep a tally on the total number of whole pieces cut from all the logs and the amount of accumulated waste from all the logs. These variables cannot be instance variables since they relate to more than one object. The variables are *class variables*, they are defined as being static, and they only have *one set of data values* regardless of the number of Log objects that are instantiated. The Log class, therefore, contains the following class and instance variables.

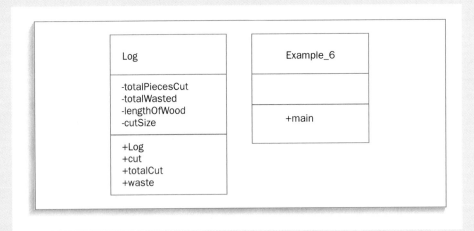

Figure 3.9 UML representation of classes

```
class Log
{
        // class variables
        private static int totalPiecesCut = 0;
        private static float totalWasted = 0.0f;
```

```
        // instance variables
        private float lengthOfWood;
        private float cutSize;
            .

            .
}
```

The constructor simply initializes the instance variables `lengthOfWood` and `cutSize` from values passed via the formal parameter list as follows.

```
// constructor
public Log(float length, float size)
{
        lengthOfWood = length;
        cutSize = size;
}
```

The instance method `cut` must not only calculate the number of whole pieces that can be cut from a single object, but it must also update the class variables, showing the total number of whole pieces cut from many logs and the accumulated waste from many logs.

```
// instance method
public int cut()
{
        int numberOfPieces;

        numberOfPieces = (int)(lengthOfWood / cutSize);
        totalPiecesCut = totalPiecesCut + numberOfPieces;
        totalWasted = totalWasted+lengthOfWood - (numberOfPieces * cutSize);

        return numberOfPieces;
}
```

The class methods return the total number of whole pieces cut for all logs and the accumulated waste for all logs, respectively.

```
// static class methods
public static int totalCut()
{
        return totalPiecesCut;
}


public static float waste()
{
        return totalWasted;
```

}

Testing

Before continuing with the coding of the program it is a good idea to check over its most important parts. To do this we first devise a set of test data that represents the standard conditions of the problem.

Test data used to create Log **objects**

Log **Object**	**Length**	**Size of Pieces**
first log	36.0	17.0
second log	58.5	19.0
third log	42.75	12.0

Next we will use this data to desk check the critical method cut. We build a table of the variables accessed by cut, including its local variable numberOfPieces, the two class variables, and the two instance variables. We list these variables across the top of our table. We will now fill out the rows of the table with the values of the variables over time. We will add two rows to the table for each time the method cut is invoked—one row for the values of the variables before the execution of any of the statements and one row for the values of the variables after the execution of the statements.

Desk check of the instance method cut()

totalPiecesCut	totalWasted	lengthOfWood	cutSize	numberOfPieces
0	0.0	36.0	17.0	0
2	2.0			2
2	2.0	58.5	19.0	0
5	3.5			3
5	3.5	42.75	12.0	0
8	10.25			3

The act of carefully filling out this table by tracing through our design will hopefully either expose errors in our logic or give us confidence that the program is designed correctly.

A listing of the completed class Log follows.

```
public class Log
{
        // static variables
        private static int totalPiecesCut = 0;
        private static float totalWasted = 0.0f;

        // instance variables
        private float lengthOfWood;
        private float cutSize;
```

```
// constructor
/**
The Log class will create a timber log object of a fixed length
and set the size the log is to be cut to.
@param length is the length of a log.
@param size is the length a log is to be cut.
*/
public Log(float length, float size)
{
     lengthOfWood = length;
     cutSize = size;
}


// instance method
/**
The method cut() is used to cut the log into set lengths.
@return The number of logs cut to size from a single piece of
timber.
*/
public int cut()
{
     int numberOfPieces;

     numberOfPieces = (int)(lengthOfWood / cutSize);
     totalPiecesCut = totalPiecesCut + numberOfPieces;
     totalWasted = totalWasted + lengthOfWood -
                   (numberOfPieces * cutSize);
     return numberOfPieces;
}


// static class methods
/**
The method totalCut() returns the total number of logs cut to
various sizes.
@return The total number of logs.
*/
public static int totalCut()
{
     return totalPiecesCut;
}


/**
The method waste() returns the total length of wasted timber
```

```
        (offcuts).
        @return Returns the total length of wasted timber.
        */
        public static float waste()
        {
                return totalWasted;
        }
}
```

The second class `Example_6` is used to test the constructor and methods of the `Log` class. The algorithm for this class may be stated as follows.

1. create a window object—screen
2. create a log object—first log
3. display the number of pieces cut from the first log
4. create a log object—second log
5. display the number of pieces cut from the second log
6. create a log object—third log
7. display the number of pieces cut from the third log
8. display the total number of logs cut
9. display the total waste wood

From the algorithm it is possible to state the dependencies that the class `Example_6` will have on other classes. The class depends upon the existence of the `Window` class and `Log` class as illustrated in Figure 3.10.

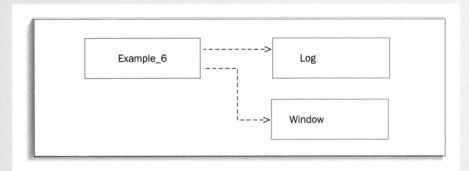

Figure 3.10 UML representation of dependencies

```
// program to demonstrate using the Log class

import avi.*;

class Example_6
{
        public static void main(String[] args)
        {
```

```
Window screen = new
Window("Example_6.java","bold","blue",24);
screen.showWindow();

Log firstLog = new Log(36.0f, 17.0f);
screen.write("Number of pieces cut from the first log is "+
            firstLog.cut()+"\n");
Log secondLog = new Log(58.5f, 19.0f);
screen.write("Number of pieces cut from the second log is "+
            secondLog.cut()+"\n");
Log thirdLog = new Log(42.75f, 12.0f);
screen.write("Number of pieces cut from the third log is "+
            thirdLog.cut()+"\n");

screen.write("Total number of logs cut "+Log.totalCut()+"\n");
screen.write("Total waste wood "+Log.waste()+"\n");
    }
}
```

A screen shot of the results of program `Example_6` as it is running follows.

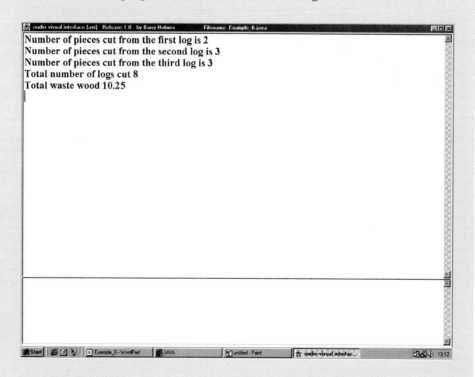

NOW DO THIS   Return to the `DecorateARoom` class you created earlier in the chapter.

(1) Modify the class to contain static variables to store the total number of rolls of wallpaper, and the total number of cans of paint required to decorate a number of rooms in a house.

(2) Create class methods to return the total number of rolls of wallpaper and the total number of cans of paint.

(3) Invent suitable test data and desk check all the methods of the `DecorateARoom` class.

(4) Write a new driver program that instantiates several room objects and test every method in the modified `DecorateARoom` class.

3.8   The AVI Package Revisited

Before we proceed with another example, it is worth taking time out to explain about three more classes from the `avi` package. These classes are the `Audio`, `FilmStrip`, and `Timer` classes.

One feature of the `Audio` and `FilmStrip` classes is they both use arrays in their constructors. You already know how to initialize the array `args` using command-line string data; however, it is also possible to initialize arrays other than `args` with string data at the point of declaration of the array.

For example, if we wanted to declare an array named `filename` and store just the one name of a sound file in the first cell (indexed as 0), then we would code:

```
String[] filename = {"funky.wav"};
```

The representation of the data in memory is depicted in Figure 3.11. Remember an array is an object. Therefore, it is stored by reference and not by value—hence the arrow from the memory location filename to the first (and only) cell of the array. However, a string is also an object, and again is stored by reference—hence the arrow from the only cell (indexed 0) to the memory containing the string representation of the name of the file.

If we wanted to declare another array named `sounds` and store the names of seven sound files in the cells of the array indexed from 0 through to 6, respectively, then we would code:

```
String[] sounds = {"chord0.wav","chord1.wav","chord2.wav","chord3.wav",
        "chord4.wav","chord5.wav","chord6.wav"};
```

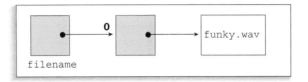

Figure 3.11 Array `filename`

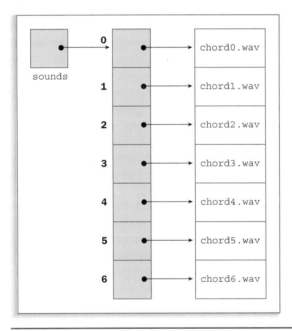

Figure 3.12 Array `sounds`

Once again, the array `sounds` is an object and is stored by reference—hence the arrow from the memory location sounds to cell 0 of the array (see Figure 3.12). Notice that the consecutive cells, indexed 0 through 6, of the array all contain references to the string representation of the name of each sound file.

The `Audio` Class

The `Audio` class contains the following constructor and instance methods:

```
public class Audio
{
      public Audio(Window parent, String[] filenames);

      public void playSound(int index);
      public static void beep(WindowPane parent);
}
```

To create an `Audio` object, you must use the class constructor that requires two items of data in the formal parameter list:

`parent`—a `Window` type that specifies the container onto which to display any information or error messages about the sound files.

`filenames`—a string array containing the names of the sound files that are to be played.

Assuming that you have already created a `screen` window object and a string array `filename`, to create an object named `output` of the `Audio` class, the `Audio` constructor would be coded as

```
Audio output = new Audio(screen, filename);
```

The sound files whose names are in the string array can then be played using the instance method `playSound`. For example, if you wanted to play the sound file stored in cell 0 of the array, code

```
output.playSound(0);
```

The following program will play a short piece of music.

```
// program to play a wav sound file

import avi.*;

class Example_7
{
    static public void main(String[] args)
    {
        String[] filename = {"funky.wav"};

        // create window
        Window screen = new Window("Example_7.java","bold","blue",16);
        screen.showWindow();
        // create sound object and play sound
        Audio output = new Audio(screen, filename);
        output.playSound(0);
        // display information
        screen.write("You should hear sweet music!\n\n");
        screen.write("This music is copyright-free and was "+
                    "published by:\n");
        screen.write("Future Publishing on their CD - "+
                    "16th February 2000\n\n\n\n");
        screen.write("WHEN THE MUSIC STOPS CLOSE THE WINDOW.");
    }
}
```

Since program `Example_7` plays music, there is little point in displaying a screen shot. However, the contents of the log file will show you what was displayed during the running of the program.

```
===================================================  ============  ===============
                    L O G      F I L E
       audio-visual interface [avi] - Release 1.0 - by Barry Holmes
         filename: Example_7.java   date: 3/11/2000   time: 1:14:55
===============================================================================


< memo contained  Sound file(s) are loading, there will be a short pause. >
< audio file funky.wav played >
You should hear sweet music!

This music is copyright-free and was published by:
Future Publishing on their CD - 16th February 2000


WHEN THE MUSIC STOPS CLOSE THE WINDOW.
```

> *i*   Only `wav` and `au` format audio files can be successfully played using the `Audio` class.
> All `wav`-formatted files follow the RIFF (Resource Information File Format) specification. The standard Windows PCM-waveform contains PCM-coded data, which is pure uncompressed pulse code modulation-formatted data. The `wav`-formatted files tend to eat up your hard drive if you are a real sound bug. This format allows 16-bit stereo samples up to 44.1 KHz.
> The most common use for the `au` file format is for compressing 16-bit data to 8-bit data; therefore, `au` files tend to consume less hard drive space. The quality cannot approach that of `wav` files.

NOW DO THIS

(1) Either download from the Internet a copyright-free sound clip, or create your own sound clip on your computer. If you want to create your own sound clip and you are using a Microsoft Windows environment, provided your computer has a sound card, connect a microphone to the card and start recording.

(2) Make appropriate modifications to `Example_7` to play your sound clip and change the text on the screen to inform of the sound being played.

The Timer Class

The `Timer` class contains the following class or `static` methods:

```
public class Timer
{
      public static void delay(int seconds);
      public static int getHour();
      public static int getMinute();
      public static int getSecond();
      public static String getTime();
      public static String getDate();
}
```

This class is important to the `avi` package since it offers a `delay` class method that allows a pause between playing sounds or showing pictures. Since the method is `static`, you do not use an object to invoke the method. Instead it is called directly, for example by `Timer.delay(5)`, if you require a delay of five seconds.

Other `static` methods in this class will allow you to get the current hour, minute, and second from the computer's clock—these are `getHour()`, `getMinute()`, and `getSecond()`, respectively. Should you want to get the current time of day, then use `getTime()`. This method returns a string giving the time in hours, minutes, and seconds.

The final `static` method, `getDate()`, returns the current date as a string of characters.

The following program shows how to play a succession of sounds, each with a delay between the time of the sound starting to play. Notice that a `static` class method is used as a helper method for playing the music. The `filenames` array containing the names of the audio files is illustrated in Figure 3.12.

```
// program to demonstrate the Timer class and playing sounds
// one after another

import avi.*;

class Example_8
{
      static private void music(Audio output, int index)
      {
            final int DURATION = 3;
            output.playSound(index);
            Timer.delay(DURATION);
```

```
        }

        static public void main(String[] args)
        {
                String[] filenames = {"chord0.wav","chord1.wav","chord2.wav",
                                      "chord3.wav","chord4.wav","chord5.wav"};

                // create window
                Window screen = new Window("Example_8.java","bold","blue",16);
                screen.showWindow();

                // create sound object and play sound
                Audio output = new Audio(screen, filenames);

                // display information
                screen.write("These sounds are copyright-free and "+
                             "were published by:\n");
                screen.write("Future Publishing on their CD - "+
                             "16th February 2000\n\n\n\n");

                // play music
                music(output,0);
                music(output,1);
                music(output,2);
                music(output,3);
                music(output,4);
                music(output,5);

                screen.write("WHEN THE SOUNDS STOP CLOSE THE WINDOW.");
        }
}
```

The following LOG_FILE was created during the execution of the program.

```
===============================================================================
                      L  O  G      F  I  L  E
       audio-visual interface [avi] - Release 1.0 - by Barry Holmes
          filename: Example_8.java   date: 3/11/2000   time: 1:19:5
===============================================================================


< memo contained  Sound file(s) are loading, there will be a short pause. >
These sounds are copyright-free and were published by:
Future Publishing on their CD - 16th February 2000
```

```
< audio file chord0.wav played >
< audio file chord1.wav played >
< audio file chord2.wav played >
< audio file chord3.wav played >
< audio file chord4.wav played >
< audio file chord5.wav played >
WHEN THE SOUNDS STOP CLOSE THE WINDOW.
```

NOW DO THIS

(1) Either download from the Internet copyright-free sound clips, or create your own sound clips on your computer.

(2) Modify `Example_8` to play a number of sounds of your choice in succession allowing a suitable delay between clips.

The FilmStrip Class

This class is used to output JPEG, GIF, or animated GIF images onto the screen. The class contains the following constructor and methods:

```
public class FilmStrip
{
      public FilmStrip(Window parent,
                       String[] filenames,
                       int widthOfFrame,
                       int heightOfFrame);

      public void showFilmStrip();
      public void hideFilmStrip();
      public void showFrame(int frame);
      public void showFrames(int[] frames);
      public void clearImages();
}
```

To create a `FilmStrip` object you must first use the class constructor. Notice that the constructor requires four data items in the formal parameter list. The arguments that you supply can be literal constants or variables.

parent—a `Window` type that specifies the container onto which to place the picture or pictures.

`filenames`—a string array containing the names of the image files that are to be output.

`widthOfFrame` and `heightOfFrame`—the width and height, respectively, of the image, in pixels.

> **ⓘ** The image files that can be successfully shown with the `FilmStrip` class are `jpg` and `gif` (including animated `gif`) files only.
>
> JPEG is an acronym for Joint Photographic Experts Group. This committee works on the storage and transmission of still images. Notice that JPEG files have the suffix `jpg`. GIF is an acronym for the graphics image format developed by CompuServe Inc. It is designed for efficient online transmission of color images.

Figure 3.13 illustrates how the strings defined by the following declaration are stored in the array `cities`.

```
String[] cities = {"NewYork.jpg","Paris.jpg","Venice.jpg"};
```

Assuming that a `screen` object has already been created, it is possible to create a `FilmStrip` object by coding:

```
FilmStrip capitals = new FilmStrip(screen, cities, IMAGE_WIDTH, IMAGE_HEIGHT);
```

All the images represented by the three filenames in the array `cities` can be displayed as a film strip by coding: `capitals.showFilmStrip()`.

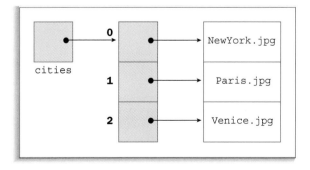

Figure 3.13 Array `cities`

You may show an individual frame from the film strip by specifying the index to the array cities, where the name of the file is to be shown is stored. For example, the code `capitals.showFrame(1)` will output the image of Paris.

Up to now you have only created an array of strings, for example, the array `cities` depicted in Figure 3.13. However, an array can store primitive data types such as integers. Therefore, it is possible to declare and initialize an array of integers as follows:

```
int[] chosenCities = {0,2};
```

Figure 3.14 illustrates the creation and storage of this integer array containing the values 0 and 2 at cells 0 and 1, respectively.

To show a selection of frames from the film strip you must first initialize an integer array with the indexed positions of the selected images from the cities array. For example, if you wanted to show the images for New York and Venice only, then you must first create an array of indices that correspond to the positions of the filenames of these images in the `cities` array.

```
int[] chosenCities = {0,2};
```

You may show the images for New York and Venice by coding:

```
capitals.showFrames(chosenCities);
```

All of the images may be cleared from the screen by using the instance method `clearImages()`.

The film strip may be temporarily hidden from view by using the method `hideFilmStrip()`. The film strip may be brought back into view by the method `showFilmStrip()`.

The following program illustrates the methods described for the `FilmStrip` class.

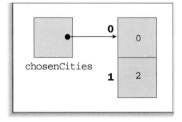

Figure 3.14 An array of integers

```java
// program to display images

import avi.*;

class Example_9
{
    public static void main(String[] args)
    {
        // store the names of the three image files
        String[] cities = {"NewYork.jpg","Paris.jpg","Venice.jpg"};

        // create a Window object screen
        Window screen = new Window("Example_9.java");
        screen.showWindow();

        // declare size of image
        final int IMAGE_WIDTH = screen.getWidth()/5;
        final int IMAGE_HEIGHT = (int)((float)IMAGE_WIDTH * 0.667);

        // create a film strip object containing the three images
        // found in the files
        FilmStrip capitals = new
        FilmStrip(screen,cities,IMAGE_WIDTH,IMAGE_HEIGHT);
        screen.write("image files are\ncopyright "+
                    "(c) 2000 Barry Holmes");

        // show the film strip on the screen for 5 seconds
        capitals.showFilmStrip();
        Timer.delay(5);
        capitals.clearImages();

        // show only Paris for 5 seconds from the filmstrip
        capitals.showFrame(1);
        Timer.delay(5);
        capitals.clearImages();

        // show both NewYork and Venice from the film strip
        int[] chosenCities = {0,2};
        capitals.showFrames(chosenCities);
        Timer.delay(5);

        // destroy window and exit
        screen.closeWindowAndExit();

    }
}
```

The following screen shot illustrates the appearance of the three images on the screen. Only by running the program will you see how the remaining images appear at set times on the screen.

The log file for the program `Example_9` follows.

```
=================================================================================
                    L  O  G      F  I  L  E
         audio-visual interface [avi] - Release 1.0 - by Barry Holmes
           filename: Example_9.java    date: 3/11/2000    time: 1:25:24


=================================================================================


< memo contained  Image file(s) are loading, there will be a short pause. >
image files are
copyright (c) 2000 Barry Holmes< image file NewYork.jpg shown >
< image file Paris.jpg shown >
< image file Venice.jpg shown >
< image file Paris.jpg shown >
< image file NewYork.jpg shown >
< image file Paris.jpg shown >
```

NOW DO THIS

(1) Either download from the Internet a number of copyright-free images, or digitize your own images to create image files in either a JPEG or GIF format.

(2) Modify `Example_9` to show a series of single images on the screen in succession with a 5 second delay between each image changing.

CASE STUDY

A Simulation of Rolling a Die

Statement of the Problem. Write a program to simulate rolling a die (singular of dice). Play the sound of the die being rolled, use the value of the die to display an image of the die, and announce this value.

Unless a die is biased (loaded) how do we simulate any value on the face of a die appearing at random? The answer is to use a random-number generator from the class `Random`, found in the Java package `util` (utilities) to simulate the occurrence of a digit in the range 1 through 6. An object of type `random` is instantiated using:

```
Random value = new Random();
```

The instance method `nextInt()` returns an integer random number that lies in the range of all integer numbers. Therefore, `value.nextInt()` will return a pseudo-random integer anywhere in the permissible range of integers, including negative values as well as positive values. To change the random number into a number between 1 and 6 (the values on the faces of the die), use the following expression:

```
Math.abs(value.nextInt() % NUMBER_OF_SIDES) + 1;
```

By dividing the random number by the constant `NUMBER_OF_SIDES` (the six sides of the die) and finding the remainder, you will always get a number in the range 0 through 5. However, this number, apart from zero, could be either positive or negative. To ensure that the number returned is positive, use the `abs` class method found in the Java `Math` class. Since we are attempting to simulate a number in the range 1 through 6, it is then necessary to add 1 to this result.

Identification of Classes and Methods

If we analyze the English in the problem, then the following nouns all represent candidate classes.

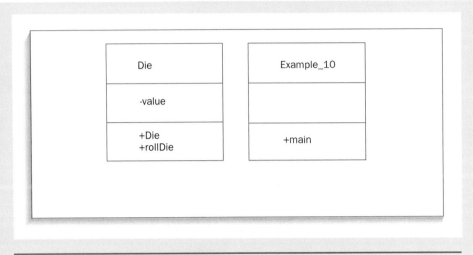

Figure 3.15 UML class diagrams

Write a *program* to simulate rolling a *die* (singular of dice). Play the *sound* of the *die* being rolled, use the *value* of the *die* to display an *image* of the *die*, and announce this *value*.

The likely candidate classes are *program*, *die*, *sound*, and *image*. The noun *value* represents an attribute of the die (a value in the range 1 to 6). From this analysis, Die and program (Example_10) are the most viable classes. The Audio class will provide for the class sound, and the FilmStrip class will provide for the class image.

If we analyze the English in the problem, then the following verbs all represent candidate methods.

Write a program to *simulate rolling* a die. *Play* the sound of the die being *rolled*, use the value of the die to *display* an image of the die, and *announce* this value.

Remember the verbs are an indication of the methods of a class. The only viable method of the class Die is *rolled*, or in this example rollDie. The verbs *play* and *announce* are taken care of by the instance method playSound in the class Audio; the verb to *display* an image is taken care of by the instance method showFrame in the class FilmStrip.

Figure 3.15 illustrates the Die and Example_10 classes.

Algorithm Development

There is just one instance variable in the class Die, and that is the object value representing a stream of random numbers. The purpose of the constructor is to instantiate the random-number object.

```
class Die
{
      // instance variable
      private Random value;
```

```
    public Die()
    {
        value = new Random();
    }

           .
           .

}
```

The only method of this class is `rollDie`, which returns a random number in the range 1 through 6.

```
public int rollDie()
{
    return Math.abs(value.nextInt() % NUMBER_OF_SIDES) + 1;
}
```

The class `Die` is dependent upon the class `Random`, as illustrated in Figure 3.16.

Testing

Test data. The `nextInt()` method in the `Random` class will return an integer within the range of all integers represented in Java. If this integer had the value −234789, say, then the value for the face of the die is calculated as follows.

```
-234789 % 6 = -3  (remainder after division by 6)
abs(-3) =3
3 + 1 = 4
```

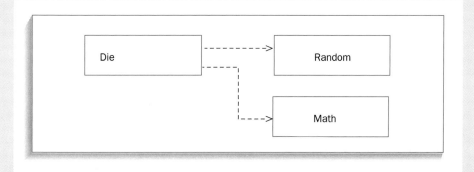

Figure 3.16 UML dependency diagram

Hence, the value returned by the instance method `rollDie()` is 4.

A complete listing of the class `Die` follows.

```java
import java.util.Random;

public class Die
{
     // class constant
     static final int NUMBER_OF_SIDES = 6;

     // instance variable
     private Random value;

     // constructor
     /**
     The Die class generates a stream of pseudo random numbers on
     demand to represent an order of each face of the die appearing
     uppermost.
     */
     public Die()
     {
          value = new Random();
     }


     // instance method
     /**
     The method rollDie simulates the rolling of a die.
     @return An integer value in the range 1..6 that represents a
     single face of the die.
     */
     public int rollDie()
     {
          return Math.abs(value.nextInt() % NUMBER_OF_SIDES) + 1;
     }
}
```

The name of the sound file of the die being rolled is stored in the first cell (index 0) of the array `sounds`, illustrated in Figure 3.17. Hence the instance method `playSound(0)` will play the sound file `"rollDie.wav"`.

From the test data, the simulated value of the face of the die was 4. This is used as an index to the array `sounds` to select a filename to announce the value scored. Hence the

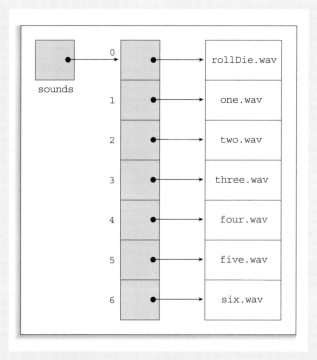

Figure 3.17 Array sounds used in the case study

instance method `playSound(4)` will play the sound file `"four.wav"`. In this example, 4 would index the fifth cell (remember an array is indexed from 0), which contains the file-name `"four.wav"`. See Figure 3.17 for clarification.

The filename of the image of each face of the die is stored in the array `dieSides`. Cell 1 (indexed by 0) deliberately contains an empty string, so that cell 2 (indexed by 1) will contain the image file for face 1 of the die, cell 3 (indexed by 2) will contain the image file for face 2 of the die, and so on. Inclusion of an empty string in the first cell simplifies access to the correct image file since the value returned by the instance method `throwDie()` is used to access the `dieSides` array. The instance method `showFrame(value)` will display the image whose filename is `"die4.jpg"` when `value` is 4. See Figure 3.18 for further clarification.

The algorithm for class `Example_10` follows.

1. create window object—screen
2. create filmstrip object—faces
3. create audio object—output
4. create die object—gamble
5. play sound of die being rolled

6. delay for 1 second

7. show face of die

8. announce the score on the face of the die

9. delay for 5 seconds

10. close window object and exit

From the algorithm it is possible to define the classes on which Example_10 is dependent (see Figure 3.19).

A completed listing of the class Example_10 follows. The purpose of this class is to simulate the rolling of a die using the Die, WindowPane, Audio, FilmStrip, and Timer classes.

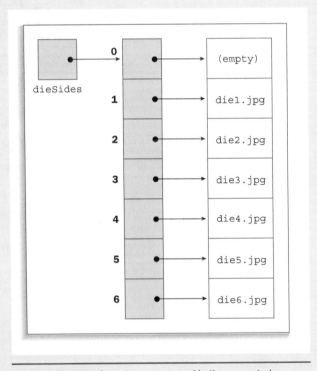

Figure 3.18 Array dieSides used in the case study

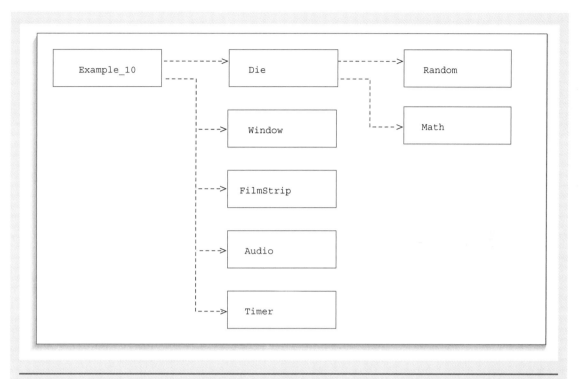

Figure 3.19 UML dependency diagrams

```
// program to simulate rolling a die

import avi.*;
import Die.*;

class Example_10
{
    public static void main(String[] args)
    {
        // store the filenames of the images that represent the
        // six faces of a die
        String[] dieSides = {"die1.jpg","die2.jpg","die3.jpg",
                            "die4.jpg","die5.jpg","die6.jpg"};
        // store the filenames of the sounds for rolling a die
        // and announcing the score
```

```
String[] sounds   = {"rollDie.wav","one.wav","two.wav",
                     "three.wav","four.wav","five.wav",
                     "six.wav"};

// create a window pane object and show the window
Window screen = new Window("Example_10.java");
screen.showWindow();

// create a filmstrip object of the six faces of a die
final int WIDTH_OF_IMAGE = screen.getWidth()/12;
FilmStrip faces = new
FilmStrip(screen,dieSides,WIDTH_OF_IMAGE, WIDTH_OF_IMAGE);

// create an audio object to play the various sounds
Audio output = new Audio(screen, sounds);

// create a die object
Die gamble = new Die();
int value = gamble.rollDie();

// play sound of die being rolled
output.playSound(0);
Timer.delay(1);

// show face of die
faces.showFrame(value-1);

// announce score on die
output.playSound(value);

// delay and then exit
Timer.delay(5);
screen.closeWindowAndExit();
    }
}
```

A screen shot of program Example_10 being run follows, together with a listing of the log file.

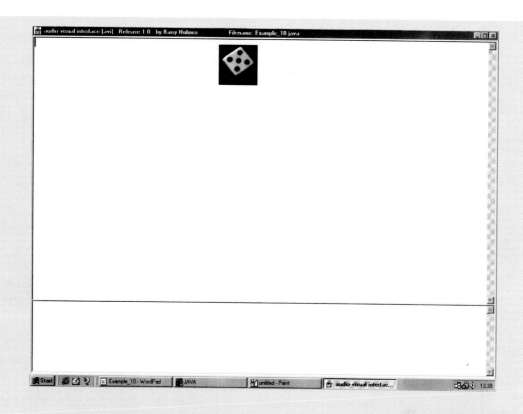

```
===============================================================================
                        L O G    F I L E
            audio-visual interface [avi] - Release 1.0 - by Barry Holmes
              filename: Example_10.java   date: 3/11/2000  time: 1:29:58
===============================================================================

< memo contained  Image file(s) are loading, there will be a short pause. >
< memo contained  Sound file(s) are loading, there will be a short pause. >
< audio file rollDie.wav played >
< image file die5.jpg shown >
< audio file five.wav played >
```

We should mention that naming a class `Example_10` as we did here is a good idea only in the context of a textbook. It is usually recommended to use as descriptive a name as possible. For example, we could have named the above class `VirtualDie`, to nicely differentiate from the other class we defined in this section, `Die`.

SUMMARY

- Encapsulation is the grouping together of data and a set of methods to perform actions on data of that class type. An encapsulated group is called an abstract data type.

- A constructor is used to initialize an object with data. Every instance of a class is an object of the class. Every object has its own data set.

- A constructor is used to initialize the instance variables of a class.

- For each invocation of a constructor, a new object with its own set of instance variables is instantiated.

- Instance methods and class methods are constructed using the same techniques for returning a value and passing parameters.

- Modifiers are used to alter the behavior of a class, method, or variable. A `public` class is visible anywhere. A `public` method or variable is visible anywhere its class is visible. A `private` method or variable is visible only within its own class. Classes may not be `private`.

- The `static` modifier is reserved for methods that cannot be invoked by an object; these are known as class methods. The `static` modifier may also be used with variables that do not belong to a single object.

- A method should be written as a self-contained unit that represents a single programmed activity.

- When calling a method, the list of literals or variables, enclosed in parentheses after the method name, is known as the actual parameter list.

- When declaring a method, the list of declarations, enclosed in parentheses after the method name, is known as the formal parameter list.

- The number of actual parameters must be the same as the number of corresponding formal parameters.

- The order of the actual parameters and the formal parameters must be the same.

- The data types of the corresponding actual parameters and formal parameters must be the same.

- The names of the identifiers in the actual parameter list and the formal parameter list can be the same or different.

- After executing a method, the computer will return to the next executable statement after the method call.

- The computer will return to the calling method by either executing a return statement or by reaching the physical end of the method.

- The `return` statement may assign a value to the method and exit from the method.

- A method may contain parameters and local variables.

- Constants and variables may have either block scope or class scope.

- When an object has gone out of scope, the automatic garbage collector will release the memory occupied by an object's data to the heap.

- In designing object-oriented programs, it is important to analyze classes at an early stage in the development of the software. The analysis of classes can be divided into the activities of: identifying classes, identifying class data and methods, and finding relationships and dependencies between classes.

- A Java program is constructed from a number of classes. A class may contain any combination of data declarations, constructors, and class and instance methods. The implementation of methods within a class may reuse the methods defined in the Java API.

- To reuse any method defined by the Java API, it is necessary to import the appropriate class. A class can be imported by specifically stating the name of the package and class in an `import` statement. Alternatively, to make all the classes of a package available in a program, use only the package name followed by the wildcard symbol *.

- Software development consists of the stages of analysis, design, programming, and maintenance. Because software development evolves through the experience gained at each stage, it is possible to go back to any of the stages and modify the solution to the problem.

- Programming consists of analyzing the problem, designing an algorithm, coding the algorithm into a computer program, testing the computer program, and supplying sufficient documentation so that the program can easily be understood and modified by others.

- As a means of checking program accuracy, a program should be run for the first time with the same test data used during the desk check.

Review Questions

True or False

1. Data abstraction permits programmers to access data using their own methods.

2. Every method has a formal parameter list.

3. A class may be defined as being `private`.

4. A `private` method or variable is only visible within its own class.

5. A method may have many `return` statements.

6. A method may have no `return` statements.

7. A `static` identifier has life for the duration of the program in which it is declared.

8. An instance variable is `static`.

9. A Java program may be constructed from several classes.

10. A class may contain declarations and methods.

11. Pseudocode is written in Java.

12. A desk check is used after the program has been written.

Short Answer

13. What is an abstract data type?

14. Why should instance methods be defined as `public`?

15. Comment upon how instance methods and class methods are invoked.

16. State the names of at least two predefined classes that contain class methods.

17. What is the syntax of a programmer-defined method?

18. Does every method return a value?

19. What is a formal parameter list?

20. What is an actual parameter list?

21. Where does the computer return to upon exiting a method?

22. What is the scope of an identifier?

23. What is a block?

24. Distinguish between block scope and class scope.

25. What is the lifetime of an identifier?

26. What is meant by garbage collection?

27. What is a constructor?

28. What is the purpose of the `import` list?

29. Name the four main activities associated with the software development life cycle.

30. List the activities involved in programming.

31. What is a desk check?

32. What is peer-group evaluation?

33. What is pseudocode?

34. At what stages in programming would test data be used?

Exercises

35. Desk check the following code. What is output from the `main` method?

```
public static void main(String[] args)
{
        screen.write(sum());
}

static int sum()
{
        int A = 12;
        int B = 13;

        return A+B;
}
```

36. Desk check the following code. What is output from the method `display`?

```
public static void main(String[] args)
{
        display("Hello World");
}

static void display(String message)
{
        screen.write(message+"\n");
}
```

37. Desk check the following code. What is output from method `display`?

```
public static void main(String[] args)
{
        display(25,13);
        display(12,17);
```

```
}

static void display(int A, int B)
{
        int C = A+B;

        screen.write(C+"\n");
}
```

38. Desk check the following code. What is output from the methods `valueOnly` and `main`?

```
public static void main(String[] args)
{
        int A=41;
        int B=29;

        valueOnly(A,B);
        screen.write("A=" + A + " B=" + B+"\n");
}

static void valueOnly(int A, int B)
{
        A--;
        B++;
        screen.write("A=" + A + " B=" + B+"\n");
}
```

39. State the errors in the following method calls and method signatures.

Class method call	Class method signature
(a) `alpha;`	`static void alpha();`
(b) `beta(A,B,C);`	`static void beta();`
(c) `delta(18,'*');`	`static void delta(char X, int Y);`
(d) `gamma(X,Y);`	`static void gamma(int[] data);`

40. What is the error in the following method?

```
static void alpha(int number)
{
        return 2*number;
}
```

41. In the following code, what is the value of `global` inside the method `overRide`?

```
class example
{
        static final int global = 29;      // constant with class scope

        static void overRide()
        {
                int global = 56;           // variable with block scope

                .

                .

}
```

42. Desk check the following program and determine what values are output for x.

```
class StaticTest
{
        private static int x = 0;
        public StaticTest(){}
        public void increaseX() {x++;}

        public void printX()
            {screen.write("value of x is " + x+"\n");}
}


class Question_42
{
        public static void main(String[] args)
        {
                StaticTest objectA = new StaticTest();
                StaticTest objectB = new StaticTest();

                objectA.printX();
                objectA.increaseX();
                objectA.printX();
                objectB.increaseX();
                objectB.printX();


        }
}
```

43. If the code in Question (42) is changed by deleting the modifier `static` in the declaration of the variable x, desk check the code again and determine what values of x are output.

Programming Problems

44. Modify class `Example_5` to input the parameters for a swimming pool using

    (a) command-line parameters

    (b) dialog boxes

45. Modify class `Example_7` to input the name of a sound file of your choice as a command-line parameter and then play the audio file.

46. Modify class `Example_10` to roll two dice, display each respective jpeg image and announce the score on each die.

47. Create a class `MinimumNotes` to input an amount of money as a whole number, for example $157, and display an analysis of the minimum number of $20, $10, $5, and $1 bills that make up this amount. Test the class.

48. We all keep loose change in our pockets. Write a class `MoneyBags` to calculate the total value of your loose change. You will need to input the number of half dollars, quarters, dimes, nickels, and pennies and then display the total value of the coinage in dollars and cents. Test the class.

49. The interest payable on a loan is calculated according to the following equation:

$$\text{interest} = \text{principal} \cdot \frac{\text{rate}}{100} \cdot \frac{\text{time}}{365}$$

    Write a class `SimpleInterest` to input the principal amount borrowed, the rate of interest as a percentage, and the time of the loan in days. Calculate and output the value of the interest. Test the class.

50. Write a class `PersonalDetails` to input your name, height (in inches), and weight (in pounds); convert the height to centimeters and weight to kilograms and display the following results. *Note:* 1 inch = 2.54 centimeters and 1 pound = 0.4546 kilograms. Test the class.

Personal Details

Name	Henry Smith
Height	180 cm
Weight	75 kg

51. A person is paid a gross weekly wage based upon the number of hours worked per week and the hourly rate of pay. Calculate the net pay for an employee after the following deductions:

Federal income tax	15% of gross pay
Social security tax	6.2% of gross pay
Payroll savings	3% of gross pay
Retirement pension	8.5% of gross pay
Health insurance	$5.75 per employee

    Write a class `Deductions` to input the hourly rate of pay and the number of hours worked in a week; calculate the deductions and supply enough information to display the pay check. Test the class.

52. An estimate for framing a photograph is based upon the following information.

    The outside edge of the wooden frame is 6 inches longer and 6 inches wider than the photograph. The cost of the wood to make the frame is $2.50 per foot.

    Two backing cards are required to be mounted with the photograph. Each card is 5.5 inches longer and 5.5 inches wider than the photograph. The cost of the backing card is $1.50 per square foot.

    The photograph is to be protected under glass. The size of the glass is the same as a backing card. The cost of the glass is $5.50 per square foot.

    Write a class `CostOfFraming` and computerize the process of supplying a fully item-ized quotation for framing a photograph.

53. Write a class `MyHolidays` that will store images and sounds from a memorable holiday. Write a program to create a holiday object that shows images from your holiday, plays the appropriate sound to accompany the image, and writes information on the screen about the occasion.

CHAPTER 4

Selection

All the programs in the previous chapters were constructed from a sequence of statements. Each time a program was run, the computer would execute the same statements in the same order. A natural question is: How do you write a program that will allow different statements to be executed under different conditions?

This chapter introduces the techniques of coding conditions and branching on the result of a condition to alternative statements in a program. By the end of the chapter you should have an understanding of the following topics.

- The `awt` package components that allow for graphical selection

- The syntax and use of the two-way branch statement `if..else`

- The construction and evaluation of a conditional expression

- The use of nested, or embedded, selection statements

- The use of logical operators in the construction of conditional expressions

- The `boolean` data type

- The syntax and use of the multiway branch statement `switch`

- Wrapper classes

- The `this` object

- Error detection

4.1 More AVI classes

Before getting into the main topics of this chapter, we will introduce a few more classes of the `avi`.

The Slider Class

A `slider` object is illustrated in Figure 4.1. The figure shows that the slider bar has been moved to a position that corresponds to an input value of 25 degrees Celsius. Sliders are used for the input of integer values. The advantage of a slider over a dialog box is that you can guarantee that a user will input data only within predefined limits. Erroneous data cannot be input since the user is constrained to move the slider between preset limits.

The `Slider` class contains the following constructor and `public` instance methods:

```
public class Slider
{
        public Slider(Window parent,
                      String prompt,
                      int minValue,
                      int maxValue,
                      int increment);

        public void showSlider();
        public int getValue();
}
```

To create a `Slider` object you must use the class constructor that requires five items of data in the formal parameter list:

`parent`—a `Window` type that specifies the container on which to display a slider object.

`prompt`—a description of the quantities being represented; it will be written in the slider box as a prompt.

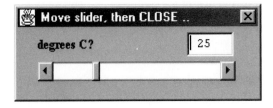

Figure 4.1 A `Slider` object from the `avi` package

minValue, maxValue, and increment are the smallest integer value, largest integer value, and smallest graduation that the slider can recognize, respectively.

Assuming that you have already created a screen window object, then the slider object shown in Figure 4.1 can be created using the constructor as:

```
Slider input = new Slider(screen,"degrees C?",0,100,1);
```

The slider is displayed on the screen using the instance method showSlider, for example:

```
input.showSlider();
```

After using the mouse-pointer to move the slider to any position, the user closes the slider's own window to indicate that input is complete. The input value is read by using another instance method, getValue(), for example:

```
celsius = input.getValue();
```

The following program will input, using a slider, a temperature in degrees Celsius, convert the temperature to degrees Fahrenheit, and write the result to the screen.

```
// program to demonstrate the use of a slider to input a temperature
// in degrees Celsius and convert the value to degrees Fahrenheit

import avi.*;

public class Example_1
{
      public static void main(String[] args)
      {
          int celsius;

          // create and show window
          Window screen = new Window("Example_1.java");
          screen.showWindow();

          // create and show slider
          Slider inputTemperature = new
          Slider(screen,"degrees C?",0,100,1);
          inputTemperature.showSlider();

          // input temperature in degrees celsius
          celsius = inputTemperature.getValue();
```

```
// convert temperature to degrees Fahrenheit and display
// the value on the screen
screen.write("Temperature input was "+celsius+" C; ");
screen.write("equivalent temperature is "+
            ((celsius)*(9.0f/5.0f)+32)+" F\n");
    }
}
```

Since the screen output of this program changes dynamically as the program is executing, it is hard to capture the feel of it in a figure. We suggest while you are working through the book that you compile and execute all examples as they are encountered, to see how they run. The source code is included on the CD that was bundled with the book, and is also available on the book's Web site. To show the results of a program in the book, we will often show the contents of an example's log file, which captures everything that occurred during the run of the program. The contents of the log file after running the `Example_1` program follows.

```
===================================================================
              L  O  G      F  I  L  E
     audio-visual interface [avi] - Release 1.0 - by Barry Holmes
       filename: Example_1.java   date: 3/12/2000    time: 6:42:56
===================================================================


At the prompt: degrees C?, you selected [ 25 ] from the slider.


Temperature input was 25 C; equivalent temperature is 77.0 F
```

NOW DO THIS⯈   Using `Example_1` for reference, write a program to perform the following.

(1) Create a slider object to input a number of dollars in the range $10 .. $1000 in increments of $10.

(2) Taking the input from the slider, calculate and display the amount of money in a foreign currency of your choice.

The RadioButtons Class

A group of radio buttons may be used for the input of just *one* item of data selected from many items. The mouse-pointer is used to depress a button. The key feature of radio buttons is that only one button may indicate a choice. If you

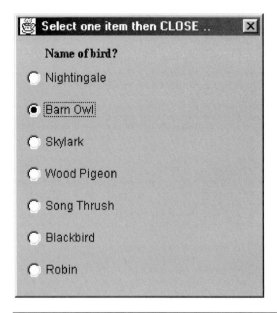

Figure 4.2 A `RadioButtons` object from the `avi` package

change your mind about a selection, then simply select a different item and the button on the original selection is cancelled.

Figure 4.2 illustrates a radio buttons object used to indicate a choice of names of birds. From Figure 4.2 it is clear that the choice is for a Barn Owl. When the final selection has been made, the radio button's window is closed.

The `RadioButtons` class contains the following constructor and `public` instance methods.

```
public class RadioButtons
{
    public RadioButtons(Window parent,
                        String prompt,
                        String[] itemsInList);

    public void showRadioButtons();
    public void getNameOfButton();
    public int getPositionOfButton();
}
```

To create a radio-buttons object you must use the class constructor that requires three items of data in the formal parameter list:

parent—a `Window` type that specifies the container on which to display a radio-buttons object.

prompt—a string that is used as a cue to inform the user of the nature of the selection. For example, in Figure 4.2 the cue is `"Name of bird?"`.

itemsInList—a string array containing a list of all the names of the radio buttons.

Assuming that you have already created a screen window object, then the `RadioButtons` object shown in Figure 4.2 can be created with the constructor as:

```
RadioButtons input = new RadioButtons(screen,"Name of bird?",names);
```

where `names` is a `String` array.

```
String[] names = {"Nightingale","Barn Owl","Skylark","Wood Pigeon",
                  "Song Thrush","Blackbird","Robin"};
```

The radio buttons are displayed on the screen using the instance method `showRadioButtons`, as, for example:

```
input.showRadioButtons();
```

After using the mouse-pointer to select a button, the radio button's own window is closed to indicate that data has been input. The name of the selected radio button may be chosen using the instance method `getNameOfButton`, for example:

```
String nameOfBird = input.getNameOfButton();
```

The position of the selected radio button may be chosen using the instance method `getPositionOfButton`, for example:

```
int position = input.getPositionOfButton();
```

The position represents the index to the array `names` of button labels.

In the following program, radio buttons are used to offer a choice of bird songs. The names of the birds in the array `names` corresponds to the names of the bird `songs` in the array `songs`. Therefore, if a Barn Owl is chosen, the position of the button is returned as 1 (note that an array index always starts at 0) and this is used to index the songs array to select the correct sound file.

```java
// program to demonstrate the use of radio buttons for the selection
// of just one item of text from a list of items, then use the position
// of the selected button to select an audio file

import avi.*;

class Example_2
{
    public static void main(String[] args)
    {
        // store names of files of birdsong in an array
        String[] songs = {"Nightingale.wav","Barn Owl.wav",
                "Skylark.wav","Wood Pigeon.wav",
                "Song Thrush.wav","Blackbird.wav",
                "Robin.wav"};

        // store names of birds in an array
        String[] names = {"Nightingale","Barn Owl","Skylark",
                "Wood Pigeon","Song Thrush","Blackbird",
                "Robin"};

        // create and show window pane
        Window screen = new Window("Example_2.java");
        screen.showWindow();

        // create sound object
        Audio birdSong = new Audio(screen, songs);

        // create and show radio buttons
        RadioButtons input = new
        RadioButtons(screen, "Name of bird?", names);
        input.showRadioButtons();

        // select from radio buttons list
        int position = input.getPositionOfButton();

        // play sound of selected bird
        birdSong.playSound(position);
```

```
            // write information to the screen
            screen.write("You should be listening to the song of a "+
                         names[position]+".\n\n\n");
            screen.write("Sound files edited and digitized by Barry "+
                         "Holmes.\n\n\n");
            screen.write("Close the window when the bird song finishes.");
      }
}
```

The contents of the log file after running this program follows.

```
================================================================================
                          L  O  G     F  I  L  E
            audio-visual interface [avi] - Release 1.0 - by Barry Holmes
              filename: Example_2.java   date: 3/11/2000  time: 6:53:32
================================================================================


< memo contained  Sound file(s) are loading, there will be a short pause. >
At the prompt: Name of bird?, you selected [ Barn Owl ] from the radio but-
tons.

< audio file Barn Owl.wav played >

You should be listening to the song of a Barn Owl.


Sound files edited and digitized by Barry Holmes.


Close the window when the bird song finishes.
```

NOW DO THIS   Modify `Example_2` as follows.

(1) Search the Internet for copyright-free images of the birds listed. Download the images and store them in the same directory as your copy of the program `Example_2`. Store the names of the image files in the same order as the bird-song files.

(2) Create a `Filmstrip` object that contains the images of the birds.

(3) After the choice of bird has been made, show the image of the bird as well as playing the song of the bird.

4.2   If..else Statement

Consider the following problem in which you are to display radio buttons to offer a choice of weather conditions—dry or raining. If the user selects raining, then the program advises them what outer garments to wear before going outdoors.

The solution to the problem can be stated by the following statements written in pseudocode.

1. create and show window object

2. create and show radio buttons

3. get name of button

4. if name of button is raining

5.   advise to wear raincoat and take an umbrella

6. close window to exit

If the name of the radio button selected was raining, then the condition name of button is raining would be true, and statement number (5) to advise on what to wear in wet weather would be displayed on the screen. Program execution would then continue on line (6). However, if the name of the radio button selected was dry, then the condition name of button is raining would be false, and statement number (5) would be bypassed by the computer, with program execution being resumed at line (6). This split in the sequential line of flow when the condition is true is depicted by Figure 4.3.

The following program has been coded from the pseudocode and illustrates the if Java statement that will allow for single-branch selection.

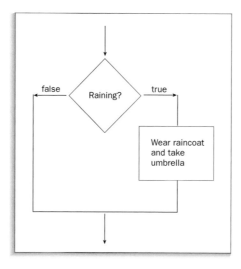

Figure 4.3 Single-branch selection

```
// program to demonstrate the if statement

import avi.*;

public class Example_3
{
      public static void main(String[] args)
      {
            String[] buttons = {"DRY","RAINING"};
            String   weather;

            // create and show window
            Window screen = new Window("Example_3.java","bold","blue",18);
            screen.showWindow();

            // create and show radio buttons
            RadioButtons inputWeather = new
            RadioButtons(screen,"Weather conditions?",buttons);
            inputWeather.showRadioButtons();

            // get selection from button
            weather = inputWeather.getNameOfButton();

            // display what to wear
            if (weather.equals("RAINING"))
            screen.write("It's raining outside wear your raincoat "+
                        "and take an umbrella.");

            screen.write("\n\n\nClose the window to exit.");
      }
}
```

The contents of the log file after running this program follows.

```
===============================================================================
                       L O G     F I L E
         audio-visual interface [avi] - Release 1.0 - by Barry Holmes
         filename: Example_3.java   date: 3/12/2000   time: 5:35:50
===============================================================================

At the prompt: Weather conditions?, you selected [ RAINING ] from the radio
buttons.

It's raining outside wear your raincoat and take an umbrella.


Close the window to exit.
```

You must use the instance methods `compareTo`, `equals`, and `equalsIgnoreCase` defined in the `String` class, if you need to compare the values of strings.

The syntax of the `if` statement follows:

SYNTAX

If statement: `if (conditional-expression)`
                         `statement(s);`

where the conditional-expression will equate to either true or false. If the conditional-expression is true, then the statement(s) will be executed; if the conditional expression is false, then the statement(s) will not be executed. Afterward, the computer will continue with the execution of the next statement after statement(s).

Clearly the program gives no advice on what to wear when the weather is dry. The pseudocode can be modified to take this fact into account. When the weather is dry, we shall advise to wear a jacket.

1. create and show window object

2. create and show radio buttons

3. get name of button

4. **if name of button is raining**

5.   advise to wear raincoat and take an umbrella

6. **else**

7.   advise to wear a jacket

8. close window to exit

This time if the name of the radio button selected was dry, then the condition name of button is raining would be false, and statement number (7) after the keyword `else` would be executed by the computer. In either situation the sequential flow of control of the program is resumed at statement number (8). This split in the sequential line of flow when the condition is true or false is depicted by Figure 4.4.

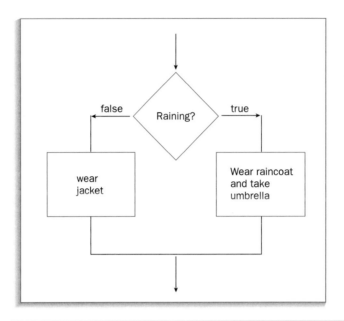

Figure 4.4 Double-branch selection

The following program has been coded from the pseudocode and illustrates the Java statement that will allow for two-way selection.

```
// program to demonstrate the if..else statement

import avi.*;

public class Example_4
{
      public static void main(String[] args)
      {
            String[] buttons = {"DRY","RAINING"};
            String    weather;

            // create and show window pane
            Window screen = new Window("Example_4.java","bold","blue",18);
            screen.showWindow();

            // create and show radio buttons
            RadioButtons inputWeather = new
            RadioButtons(screen,"Weather conditions?",buttons);
```

```
inputWeather.showRadioButtons();

// get selection from radio button
weather = inputWeather.getNameOfButton();

// write what to wear
if (weather.equals("RAINING"))
     screen.write("It's raining outside wear your raincoat and "+
                  "take an umbrella.");
else
     screen.write("The weather is dry wear your jacket.");

screen.write("\n\n\nClose the window to exit.");
    }
}
```

The contents of the log file after running this program follows.

```
================================================================
               L  O  G      F  I  L  E
     audio-visual interface [avi] - Release 1.0 - by Barry Holmes
      filename: Example_4.java    date: 3/12/2000    time: 5:34:15
================================================================


At the prompt: Weather conditions?, you selected [ DRY ] from the radio
buttons.


The weather is dry wear your jacket.


Close the window to exit.
```

The syntax of the if..else statement follows:

SYNTAX
··

If .. else Statement: if (*conditional-expression*)
                                     statement(s)-1;
                               else
                                     statement(s)-2;

where the conditional-expression will equate to either true or false. If the conditional-expression is true, then statement(s)-1 will be executed; if the conditional expression is false, then statement(s)-2 will be executed. After either statement has been executed, the computer will continue with the execution of the next statement after statement(s)-2.

4.3 Nested If Statements

The problem of what to wear can be extended to cater for temperature variations, as well as it being either raining or dry. Figure 4.5 illustrates the logic behind the various selections.

The following observations can be made by reading Figure 4.5.

- If it *is* raining and the temperature is less than 50 degrees, then you should wear a hat and coat; else if the temperature is greater than or equal to 50 degrees, then you should wear a raincoat and take an umbrella.

- If it is *not* raining and the temperature is less than 50 degrees, then you should wear a hat, coat, and scarf; else if the temperature is greater than or equal to 50 degrees, then you should wear a jacket and take your sunglasses.

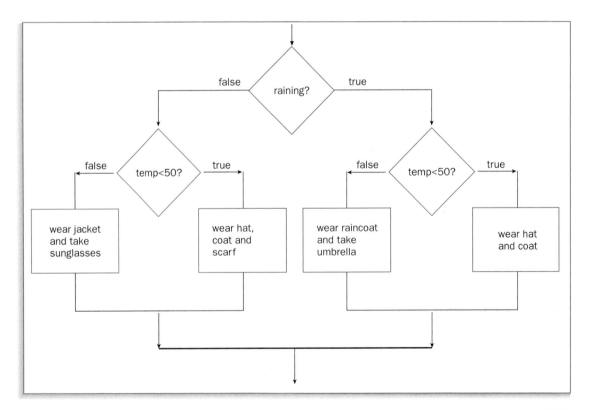

Figure 4.5 Selections within selections, known as nested selections

The statement that follows the conditional expression after the keyword `if`, or the statement that follows the keyword `else`, can also be an `if` statement.

The previous program can be modified to take these changes into account. Notice that a slider object has been included for the input of the temperature.

```java
// program to demonstrate the use of nested if .. else statements

import avi.*;

class Example_5
{
      public static void main(String[] args)
      {
            String[] buttons = {"DRY", "RAINING"};
            String   weather;

            // create and show window
            Window screen = new Window("Example_5.java","bold","blue",18);
            screen.showWindow();

            // create and show radio buttons
            RadioButtons inputWeather = new
            RadioButtons(screen,"Weather conditions?",buttons);
            inputWeather.showRadioButtons();

            // get selected weather button
            weather = inputWeather.getNameOfButton();

            // create and show slider
            Slider inputTemperature = new
            Slider(screen,"Temp. degrees F?",40,70,1);
            inputTemperature.showSlider();

            // get temperature
            int temperature = inputTemperature.getValue();

            // write what to wear
            if (weather.equals("RAINING"))
            {
                  if (temperature < 50)
                        screen.write("It's cold and wet outside, "+
                                  "wear an overcoat and hat.");
                  else
                        screen.write("The weather is warm and wet, wear "+
                                  "a raincoat and take an umbrella.");
            }
```

```
        else
        {
                if (temperature < 50)
                        screen.write("It's cold but dry, wear a hat, "+
                                        "coat and scarf.");
                else
                        screen.write("The weather is just great, wear a "+
                                        "jacket and take sunglasses");
        }

        screen.write("\n\n\nClose the window to exit.");
    }
}
```

> *i* You should adopt the habit of indenting code within an `if` statement. Indentation shows
> which statements are associated with the conditional expression being true (after the `if`)
> and which statements are associated with it being false (after the `else`). Indentation of the
> statements after the `else` also indicates to the reader where the `if` statement finishes, since
> the next statement after the `if` statement will be indented the same distance from the left-hand
> margin as the keywords `if` and `else`. Indentation is ignored by the compiler.

The contents of the log file after running this program follows.

```
================================================================================
                            L O G     F I L E
            audio-visual interface [avi] - Release 1.0 - by Barry Holmes
               filename: Example_5.java    date: 3/12/2000  time: 5:40:50
================================================================================


At the prompt: Weather conditions?, you selected [ RAINING ] from the radio
buttons.

At the prompt: Temp. degrees F?, you selected [ 50 ] from the slider.

The weather is warm and wet, wear a raincoat and take an umbrella.


Close the window to exit.
```

In the previous two program examples, only one statement was executed
regardless of whether the conditional expression evaluated to true or false. What
if more than one statement is to be executed? The answer is to treat the group of
statements as a *block* by introducing braces { }.

For example, if a string array called `instructions` contains the filenames of four different audio files:

```
String[] instructions = {"coldWet.wav","warmWet.wav","coldDry.wav","warmDry.wav"};
```

then an `Audio` object can be created for playing the contents of any of the four files.

```
Audio whatToWear = new Audio(screen, instructions);
```

If you wanted to announce that it is cold and wet, then you can code `whatToWear.playSound(0)`; however, if you wanted to announce that it is cold but dry, then you can code `whatToWear.playSound(2)`, and so on.

If the instructions of what to wear are spoken in addition to appearing on the screen, the code would be modified as follows.

```
// write what to wear
if (weather.equals("RAINING"))
{
      if (temperature < 50)
      {
            whatToWear.playSound(0);
            screen.write("It's cold and wet outside, wear an overcoat "+
                  "and hat.");
      }
      else
      {
            whatToWear.playSound(1);
            screen.write("The weather is warm and wet, wear a raincoat "+
                  "and take an umbrella.");
      }
}
else
{
      if (temperature < 50)
      {
            whatToWear.playSound(2);
            screen.write("It's cold but dry, wear a hat, coat and scarf.");
      }
      else
      {
            whatToWear.playSound(3);
            screen.write("The weather is just great, wear a jacket "+
                  "and take sunglasses");
      }
}
```

Even if only one statement is executed in a selection statement, the use of braces can improve the clarity of the code, even though the braces are themselves redundant. In program `Example_5` and the related example above, braces have been included in the outer selection statement purely to improve the readability of the code.

NOW DO THIS

(1) Record your own sound files to correspond with the on-screen instructions given in program `Example_5`.

(2) Modify program `Example_5` to include a sound object to announce the instructions as well as displaying them on the screen.

The relational operator < is not the only operator that can be used in a conditional-expression. Figure 4.6 lists the seven relational operators that can be used with primitive data types in a conditional-expression. See also Appendix A, Table A.3.

Remember, if you need to compare strings, then you must use the appropriate method in the `String` class (see previous cautionary advice box).

Notice that the test for equality is a double equals sign ==. Be careful not to use the single equals sign when testing for equality. Remember = is reserved for assignment.

Operator	Meaning
>	greater than
<	less than
==	equal
!=	not equal
>=	greater than or equal
<=	less than or equal
!	not

Figure 4.6 Relational operators

i   The storage of real numbers in the memory of a computer may not always be done pre-
cisely. For example, the storage of 0.33 in binary can only be an approximation to the true
value of the number. For this reason you should exercise extreme caution when comparing two
real numbers for equality. For example if f and g are both numbers of type `float` then instead of
coding

```
if (f == g)
```

it might be better to code

```
if ((Math.abs(f - g)) < epsilon)
```

where `epsilon` is an appropriately small constant, for example 0.0001.

In Java, `if` statements can be nested to any depth; however, you should pay
particular attention to the use of indentation and the grouping of the `else` keywords. In the following example, to which `if` statement does the single `else`
statement belong?

```
if (alpha == 3)
    if (beta == 4)
        screen.write("alpha 3, beta 4");
else
    screen.write("alpha not 3");
```

The indentation suggests that the `else` belongs to `if (alpha == 3)`; however, as you might guess, this is wrong. The rule in Java regarding which `else`
belongs to which `if` is simple. An `else` clause belongs to the nearest `if` statement that has not already been paired with an `else`. The preceding example can
be rewritten taking into account the correct indentation:

```
if (alpha == 3)
    if (beta == 4)
        screen.write("alpha 3, beta 4");
    else
        screen.write("alpha not 3");
```

If the `else` clause did belong to `if (alpha == 3)`, then braces would be introduced into the coding as follows:

```
if (alpha == 3)
{
    if (beta == 4)
        screen.write("alpha 3, beta 4");
}
else
    screen.write("alpha not 3");
```

4.4 Conditional Expressions

From the discussions so far, it should be clear to you that the conditional expressions can equate to one of two values, either true or false. Examples of conditional expressions given so far are `(reply.equals("RAINING"))` and `(temperature < 50)`.

In a new example, a program is written to select an applicant for medical trials provided the applicant is female, has blood group O, is between 18 and 40 years of age, and is between 90 and 180 pounds in weight.

The logic behind the solution to this problem can be expressed by the following pseudocode.

1. create and show window

2. create and show dialog box to input name of applicant

3. create and show radio buttons to input gender of applicant

4. create and show radio buttons to input blood group of applicant

5. create and show slider to input age of applicant

6. create and show slider to input weight of applicant

7. if gender is female

8.   if blood group is O

9.   if age is between 18 and 40

10.   if weight is between 90 and 180

11.   write on screen that applicant is successful

The conditions used in this logic are gender is female, blood group is O, age is between 18 and 40, and weight is between 90 and 180. The first two conditions may be coded as follows:

```
(gender.equals("FEMALE"))
(bloodGroup.equals("O"))
```

However, if we want to test a piece of data for its validity between a range of values, then we should use the logical operator && (AND) in the coding of the conditions as follows:

```
(age >= 18 && age <= 40)
(weight >= 90 && weight <= 180)
```

Note that the && operator has a lower priority than the comparison operators like >=, so that the comparisons are performed first, before the logical AND. See Appendix A, Table A-2, for a list of operator priorities.

This logic can be coded into the following program.

```
// program to demonstrate the use of conditional statements

import avi.*;

class Example_6
{
      public static void main(String[] args)
      {
            String[] genderButtons = {"MALE","FEMALE"};
            String[] bloodButtons = {"A","B","AB","O","not listed"};

            String name, gender, bloodGroup;
            int     age, weight;

            // create and show window pane
            Window screen = new
            Window("Example_6.java","bold","blue",18);
            screen.showWindow();

            // create and show dialog box and input name of applicant
            DialogBox inputName = new DialogBox(screen,"Name?");
            inputName.showDialogBox();
            name = inputName.getString();

            // create and show radio buttons and input gender
            RadioButtons inputGender = new
            RadioButtons(screen,"Gender?",genderButtons);
            inputGender.showRadioButtons();
            gender = inputGender.getNameOfButton();

            // create and show radio buttons and input blood group
            RadioButtons inputBloodGroup = new
            RadioButtons(screen,"Blood Group?",bloodButtons);
            inputBloodGroup.showRadioButtons();
```

```
bloodGroup = inputBloodGroup.getNameOfButton();

// create and show slider and input age
Slider inputAge = new Slider(screen,"Age in years?",10,80,1);
inputAge.showSlider();
age = inputAge.getValue();

// create and show slider and input weight
Slider inputWeight = new
Slider(screen,"Weight in pounds?",50,250,1);
inputWeight.showSlider();
weight = inputWeight.getValue();

// analyze applicant for suitability in trial
if (gender.equals("FEMALE"))
    if (bloodGroup.equals("O"))
        if (age >= 18 && age <= 40)
            if (weight >= 90 && weight <= 180)
                screen.write(name+" your application "+
                             "for the medical trial "+
                             "was successful.");


    }
}
```

The contents of the log file after running this program follows.

```
===============================================================================
                         L O G     F I L E
        audio-visual interface [avi] - Release 1.0 - by Barry Holmes
         filename: Example_6.java   date: 3/12/2000   time: 5:42:59
===============================================================================


At the prompt: Name?, you input [ Lucy Lockett ] at the dialog box.

At the prompt: Gender?, you selected [ FEMALE ] from the radio buttons.

At the prompt: Blood Group?, you selected [ O ] from the radio buttons.

At the prompt: Age in years?, you selected [ 32 ] from the slider.

At the prompt: Weight in pounds?, you selected [ 125 ] from the slider.

Lucy Lockett your application for the medical trial was successful.
```

Condition X	**Condition** Y	X && Y
false	false	false
false	true	false
true	false	false
true	true	true

Figure 4.7 Truth table for logical AND

A truth table for logical AND is given in Figure 4.7. This table tells us that the combination of two conditions with an AND is true only if both the original conditions are true.

We can now analyze the conditions listed in the program. If the gender is female, then the computer executes the next statement to test the condition `bloodGroup.equals("O")`.

If `(age >= 18)` is condition X and `(age <= 40)` is condition Y, then X && Y can only be true if both condition X is true and condition Y is true. In other words, both conditions `(age >= 18)` and `(age <= 40)` must be true for the expression to be true. Therefore, if either condition X or condition Y or both happen to be false, the complete expression given by X && Y is false.

Similarly, both conditions in the expression `(weight >= 90 && weight <= 180)` must be true for the conditional expression to be true. If either one condition or both conditions is false, then the conditional expression is false.

In the program, if the age is between 18 and 40 years, then the computer executes the next `if` statement, and if the weight is between 90 and 180 pounds, then the computer writes to the screen that the applicant was successful.

The program can be reconstructed by omitting the last three `if` statements and combining all the conditions as follows:

```
if ((gender.equals("FEMALE")) &&
    (bloodGroup.equals("O")) &&
    (age >= 18 && age <= 40) &&
    (weight >= 90 && weight <= 180))

        screen.write(name+" your profile for the medical trial "+
                "is acceptable.");
else

        screen.write(name+" your application for the medical "+
                "trial was not successful.");
```

Notice that the redesign of the code to use a single `if` statement allows us to easily use a corresponding `else` statement to provide output even in the situation in which the applicant is not accepted.

4.5   Else if Statements

The complexity of nested `if` statements can be reduced by combining conditions and using logical AND. For example, the following is part of the nested selection in `Example_5`.

```
if (buttons[position].equals("RAINING"))
{
      if (temperature < 50)
            screen.write("It's cold and wet outside, wear an overcoat "+
                    "and hat.");
      else
                        screen.write("The weather is warm and wet, wear a "+
                                "raincoat and take an umbrella.");
}
else
{
      if (temperature < 50)
            screen.write("It's cold but dry, wear a hat, coat and scarf.");
      else
            screen.write("The weather is just great, wear a jacket "+
                    "and take sunglasses");
}
```

can be recoded as

```
if      (buttons[position].equals("RAINING")) && (temperature < 50)
            screen.write("It's cold and wet outside, "+
                    "wear an overcoat and hat.");
else if (buttons[position].equals("RAINING")) && (temperature >= 50)
            screen.write("The weather is warm and wet, "+
                    "wear a raincoat and take an umbrella.");
else if (buttons[position].equals("DRY")) && (temperature < 50)
            screen.write("It's cold but dry, wear a hat, coat and scarf.");
else
            screen.write("The weather is just great, wear a jacket "+
                    "and take sunglasses");
```

An `else` keyword followed by an `if` keyword is very common in programming. In fact, in many computer languages, except for Java, there is an *elseif* statement. In Java we can write the `else` keyword, separated by a space and on the same line as the `if` keyword, as if it is one keyword, *elseif*. It is not a single keyword, but indentation produces a very clear multibranch structure that is actually made of multiple two-branch `if else` statements.

4.6 Boolean Data Type

A variable of primitive type `boolean` is permitted to have only one of two values, either `true` or `false`. A `boolean` variable is initialized by Java to be `false` (see Appendix A, Table A.2).

The conditional expression in an `if` statement must evaluate to a `boolean` value that is either `true` or `false`.

A variable may be declared as `boolean` and initialized at its point of declaration to either `true` or `false`. This variable may be reassigned either of the `boolean` values at a later stage in the program.

The medical trial applicant program can be reconstructed yet again using different conditions and the logical operator `||` (OR). By considering the negation (in some cases using the NOT operator "`!`") of the criteria for selection, it is possible to construct the following conditional expressions:

```
// initialize boolean flag to trap any unsuitable criteria
boolean reject = false;

// analyze applicant for suitability in trial
if       (!gender.equals("FEMALE"))
{
     reject = true;
}
else  if (!bloodGroup.equals("O"))
{
     reject = true;
}
else   if (age < 18 || age > 40)
{
     reject = true;
}
else   if (weight < 90 || weight > 180)
{
     reject = true;
}
else
     screen.write(name+" your profile for the medical trial is "+
               "acceptable.");

if (reject) screen.write(name+" your application for the medical trial was "+
               "NOT successful.");
```

The truth table for logical OR is given in Figure 4.8. It shows that an OR expression is false only if both its components are false. Looking at the code we see that if (`age < 18`) is condition X and (`age > 40`) is condition Y, then X`||`Y is

Condition X	**Condition** Y	X || Y
false	false	false
false	true	true
true	false	true
true	true	true

Figure 4.8 Truth table for logical OR

true if X is true or Y is true or both are true (clearly both conditions cannot be true in this example).

Similarly, if (weight < 90) is condition X and (weight > 180) is condition Y, then X||Y is true if X is true or Y is true or both are true. Once again both conditions cannot be true in this example.

The conditions for gender, blood group, age, and weight can also be combined into

```
(! gender.equals("FEMALE") || ! bloodGroup.equals("O") ||
(age <18 || age > 40) || (weight < 90 || weight > 180))
```

Thus, if any one of the conditions is true, the entire conditional expression is true, and the applicant is not accepted for the medical trial. However, if all the conditions are false, then the entire conditional expression must be false, the applicant is FEMALE, has blood group O, is between 18 and 40 years of age, is between 90 and 180 inches tall, and has fulfilled the criteria for selection.

i   By examining the truth tables for logical AND and logical OR, Figures 4.7 and 4.8 respectively, it is clear there are occasions when only the condition X need be evaluated. For example, when using logical AND, if condition X is false, there is no need for the computer to evaluate condition Y. Similarly, when using logical OR, if condition X is true, there is no need for the computer to evaluate condition Y. The evaluation of only the first condition in a logical expression is known as *short-circuit evaluation*. In Java, both logical operators && and || use short-circuit evaluation. If you need to avoid short-circuit evaluation, then you may use the corresponding logical operators & and |.

!   When using the logical operators && and ||, be careful which condition to write as the first condition in a logical expression. Using short-circuit evaluation, the conditions in the remainder of a logical expression may not be evaluated, and as a result your program may not run as predicted!

4.7 Switch

An ordinal variable has a value that belongs to an ordered set of items. For example, integers are ordinal types since they belong to the set of values from −2,147,483,648 to +2,147,483,647. A character is an ordinal type since it belongs to the Unicode character set. Real numbers and strings are not ordinal types.

If selection is to be based upon an ordinal type, then a `switch` statement can be used in preference to multiple `if` statements.

The syntax of the `switch` statement follows.

SYNTAX

Switch Statement:
```
switch (expression)
{
          case c1:  statement(s);
          case c2:  statement(s);
                  .

                  .

          default:  statement(s);
}
```

The expression must evaluate to an ordinal value. Each possible ordinal value is represented as a case label that indicates the statement to be executed corresponding to the value of the expression. Those values that are not represented by case labels will result in the statement after the optional default being executed. For example,

```
int number = inputData.getInteger(); // input from a dialog box
switch (number)
{
   case 1:   screen.write("one"); break;
   case 2:   screen.write("two"); break;
   case 3:   screen.write("three"); break;
   default:  screen.write("number not in the range 1..3");
}
```

In this example, a number is input at the keyboard. If this number is 1, then the string one will be output; if it is 2, then the string two will be output; if it is 3, then the string three will be output. If the number is not 1, 2, or 3, then the string number not in range 1..3 will be output.

It is necessary to include a way of exiting from the `switch` statement at the end of every `case`.

 Failure to exit from the `switch` will result in the execution of all the `case` statements following the chosen `case`.

One method of exiting from a `switch` statement is through the use of a *break* statement at the end of every `case` list. The keyword `break` causes the `switch` to terminate, and execution resumes with the next statement (if any) following the end of the `switch` statement.

If the optional `default` statement was not present and the value of number had not been in the range 1 to 3, then the computer would branch to the end of the `switch` statement.

In program `Example_7`, a user is invited to input a value for an exit number on Highway 6 at Cape Cod. Depending upon the value, from 1 to 12, of the exit number, the names, numbers, or both of the adjoining roads at that exit are displayed. If the value input is not in the range 1 to 12, the statement after the default will warn the user of the data error. The multiple selection in this problem can be highlighted by the illustration in Figure 4.9.

```java
// program to demonstrate the switch statement

import avi.*;

class Example_7
{
    public static void main(String[] args)
    {
        // create and show window
        Window screen = new Window("Example_7.java","bold","blue",18);
        screen.showWindow();

        // create and show dialog box and input exit number
        DialogBox inputExitNumber = new
        DialogBox(screen,"Exit number on Highway 6?");
        inputExitNumber.showDialogBox();
        int exitNumber = inputExitNumber.getInteger();

        screen.write("Exit "+exitNumber+" on Highway 6 connects with ");

        // select on the value of the exit number
        switch (exitNumber)
        {
```

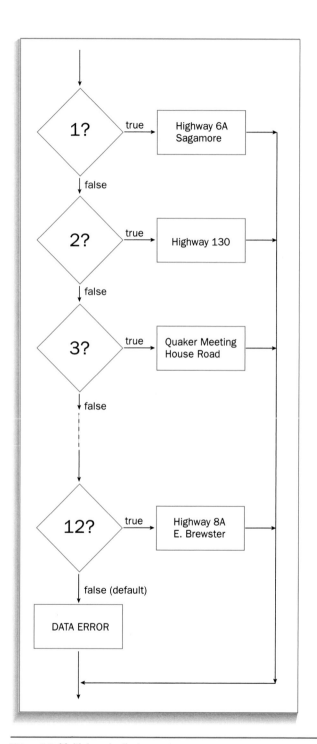

Figure 4.9 Multiple selection

```
        case 1:   screen.write("Highway 6a/ Sagamore Bridge"); break;
        case 2:   screen.write("Highway 130"); break;
        case 3:   screen.write("Quaker Meeting House Road"); break;
        case 4:   screen.write("Chase Road/ Scorten Road"); break;
        case 5:   screen.write("Highway 149/ Martons Mills"); break;
        case 6:   screen.write("Highway 132/ Hyannis"); break;
        case 7:   screen.write("Willow Street/ Higgins Crowell Road"); break;
        case 8:   screen.write("Union Street/ Station Avenue"); break;
        case 9:   screen.write("Highway 134/ S.Dennis"); break;
        case 10:  screen.write("Highway 124/ Harwich Port"); break;
        case 11:  screen.write("Highway 137/ S.Chatham"); break;
        case 12:  screen.write("Highway 6A/ E.Brewster"); break;
        default:  screen.write("DATA ERROR - incorrect exit number");
                  Audio.beep(screen);
        }
    }
}
```

The contents of the log file after running this program twice follows.

```
================================================================================
                      L O G     F I L E
         audio-visual interface [avi] - Release 1.0 - by Barry Holmes
            filename: Example_7.java    date: 3/12/2000  time: 5:48:19
================================================================================


At the prompt: Exit number on Highway 6?, you input [ 7 ] at the dialog box.

Exit 7 on Highway 6 connects with Willow Street/ Higgins Crowell Road
```

```
================================================================================
                      L O G     F I L E
         audio-visual interface [avi] - Release 1.0 - by Barry Holmes
            filename: Example_7.java    date: 3/12/2000  time: 5:49:45
================================================================================


At the prompt: Exit number on Highway 6?, you input [ 13 ] at the dialog box.

Exit 13 on Highway 6 connects with DATA ERROR - incorrect exit number
```

By comparing the `switch` statement in the program with the syntax notation, you should note the following points.

- An expression is any expression that will evaluate to an ordinal type. In this example the expression consists of a single variable `exitNumber` of type `integer`, which is expected to evaluate to an integer in the range 1..12.

- A case label is any value that corresponds to the ordinal type in the expression. Case labels in this example represent the junctions numbers 1, 2, 3, 4, 5, 6, 7, 8, 9, 10, 11, and 12. Case labels must be unique.

- The optional default traps any values of the expression that are not represented as case labels. Without this option, no action would occur when a value was out of range.

In program `Example_7`, only one case value was associated with a set of statements. What if more than one case value is used for the same set of statements?

For example, if the requirement was to compute the number of days in a particular month in the year, a `switch` statement could be used. The variable month is an integer in the range 1..12, indicating the months January..December. Different case labels, separated by a colon, are used for each month of the year, for the month containing 31 days, 30 days, and 28 days (assuming a nonleap year).

```
switch (month)
{
    // test for months Jan, Mar, May, Jul, Aug, Oct, Dec
    case 1:
    case 3:
    case 5:
    case 7:
    case 8:
    case 10:
    case 12: daysInMonth = 31; break;

    // test for months Apr, Jun, Sep, Nov
    case 4:
    case 6:
    case 9:
    case 11: daysInMonth = 30; break;

    // test for Feb (or use default)
    case 2:  daysInMonth = 28;
}
```

4.8 Wrapper Classes

All the primitive types have corresponding classes that provide some general methods that are useful when dealing with data of the specified type. The classes are known as *wrapper* classes since they literally wrap the primitive data type in a class. Inspect your Java documentation for a full listing of wrapper classes. A partial listing of the Integer class follows.

```
public final class Integer
{
    public static final int MIN_VALUE = 0x80000000;
    public static final int MAX_VALUE = 0x7fffffff;
    .

    .

    // constructors
    public Integer(int value);
    public Integer(String s);

    // instance method
    public int intValue();
    .

    .


}
```

From this listing you can see the class Integer contains useful maximum and minimum constants that define the size (in hexadecimal notation) of the largest negative int MIN_VALUE and the largest positive int MAX_VALUE; constructors to convert an int or a String to an Integer object; and a method intValue to convert an Integer object to a primitive int value.

Given a declaration such as:

```
String dateString = "2001";
```

the string value can be converted into an integer using a constructor and method of the Integer wrapper class.

An Integer object is instantiated using a constructor that takes a string type as its argument, for example:

```
Integer number = new Integer(dateString);
```

Once the object number has been created, it can be used to convert the Integer object into an int by using the instance method intValue():

```
int date = number.intValue();
```

These facts are illustrated in Figure 4.10.

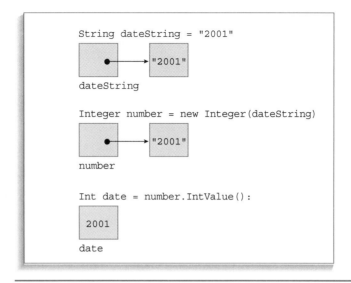

Figure 4.10 Use of the `Integer` wrapper class

You may recall from Chapter 2 that data was input as strings on the command line. At that time we could only process string data in the program. By using the wrapper classes it is now possible to pass data as command-line argument strings and convert the strings, using wrapper classes, to any primitive data type.

There is a wrapper class in Java for every primitive data type. These classes are `Boolean`, `Byte`, `Character`, `Double`, `Float`, `Integer`, `Long`, and `Short`. Read the appropriate Java documentation for further details about these wrapper classes and see Appendix A, Table A.2 for the corresponding primitive types.

CASE STUDY

Body Mass Index

Statement of the Problem.   Your body-mass index (BMI) is a measure of the ratio of your weight to height. It is your weight in kilograms divided by the square of your height in meters.

For instance, if your height is 1.82 meters, the divisor of the calculation will be (1.82*1.82) = 3.3124. If your weight is 70.5 kilograms, then your BMI is 21.28 (70.5/ 3.3124).

Body-mass index has been the medical standard for obesity measurement since the early 1980s. Government researchers developed it to take height into account in weight measurement. Figure 4.11 indicates the medical interpretation of weight with regard to the BMI.

BMI	Interpretation
<20	underweight
20 to <25	appropriate weight
25 to <30	overweight
30 to <39	obese

Figure 4.11 BMI value analysis

Write a program to input the name, weight, and height of a person; calculate their body-mass index, and use this statistic to interpret their weight category according to Figure 4.11.

Identification of Classes and Methods

A noun analysis of the sentence "Write a program to … " indicates that *program, name, weight, height, person, body-mass index, index, category* are possible candidate classes. These can be narrowed down to just two classes: *program* and *person*. The class program is `Example_8` and contains the statements to test the constructor and methods of the `Person` class.

A verb analysis on the same sentence indicates that *write, input, calculate,* and *interpret* are possible candidate methods.

In the final analysis, the calculation of the body-mass index should be performed by the constructor to ensure that every object (person) has a BMI. This value will need to be retrieved by the instance method `getBMI`. The value of the BMI for a person should also be interpreted according to the values in Figure 4.11; therefore, a second instance method `interpretBMI` is also required. If you need to write the name, height, and weight for a person, there will be three additional instance methods: `getName`, `getHeight`, and `getWeight`, respectively, to return these three values.

The instance variables of the `Person` class are `name`, `weight`, `height`, and `bmi`.

Figure 4.12 illustrates the classes `Person` and `Example_8`.

Algorithm Development

The class `Person` contains the following variables.

```
public class Person
{
    // instance variables
    private String name;        // name of person
    private float height;       // metric units only (m)
```

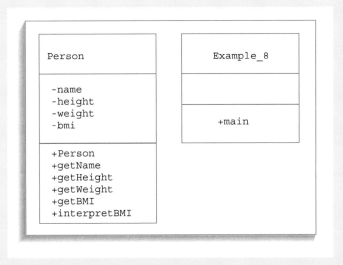

Figure 4.12 UML representation of classes

```
private float weight;          // metric units only (kg)
private float bmi;             // body mass index
```

```
        .
        .
}
```

The constructor initializes the instance variables name, height, and weight from the values passed via the formal parameter list and calculates the body-mass index. By calculating the BMI in the constructor, you will ensure that every object (person) has a BMI.

```
public Person(String nameOfPerson, float bodyHeight, float bodyWeight)
{
    name   = nameOfPerson;
    height = bodyHeight;
    weight = bodyWeight;
    bmi    = weight / (height*height);
}
```

There are a number of instance methods to just return information: getName(), getHeight(), getWeight(), and getBMI(). These are trivial to code and are not included here; however, they are included in the final listing of the class Person.

The final instance method interprets the body-mass index that was originally calculated by the constructor.

```
public String interpretBMI()
{
    if      (bmi < 20.0f)
        return "underweight";
    else if (bmi >= 20.0f & bmi < 25.0f)
        return "an appropriate weight";
    else if (bmi >= 25.0f & bmi < 30.0f)
        return "overweight";
    else if (bmi >= 30.0f & bmi <= 39.0f)
        return "obese";
    else
        return "you should consult a physician";
}
```

Testing

Test data used to create different Person objects (people)

Person object	Name	Height (m)	Weight (kg)	BMI
anybody	Fred Smith	1.73	84.5	28.23
anybody	Charlie Gomez	1.65	92.7	34.05
anybody	Betty Ramirez	1.69	65.5	22.93
anybody	Sonia Wall	1.75	59.7	19.49

Desk check on the instance methods getBMI and interpretBMI for different objects (people)

Name	BMI	Interpretation
Fred Smith	28.23	overweight
Charlie Gomez	34.05	obese
Betty Ramirez	22.93	appropriate weight
Sonia Wall	19.49	underweight

A listing of the completed Person class follows.

```
public class Person
{
    // instance variables
    private String name;      // name of person
    private float height;     // metric units only (m)
```

```
private float weight;       // metric units only (kg)
private float bmi;          // body-mass index

// constructor
/**
The Person class will create a person object.
@param nameOfPerson is the person's name.
@param bodyHeight is the height of the person in meters.
@param bodyWeight is the weight of the person in Kilograms.
*/
public Person(String nameOfPerson,
              float bodyHeight,
              float bodyWeight)
{
     name = nameOfPerson;
     height = bodyHeight;
     weight = bodyWeight;
     bmi    = weight / (height*height);
}


// instance methods
/**
getName is used to return the name of the person.
@return The name of the person.
*/
public String getName()
{
     return name;
}


/**
getHeight is used to return the height of the person in meters.
@return The height of the person in meters.
*/
public float getHeight()
{
     return height;
}


/**
getWeight is used to return the weight of the person in kilograms.
@return The weight of the person in kilograms.
*/
public float getWeight()
```

```
      {
            return weight;
      }


      /**
      getBMI is used to return the body-mass index of the person.
      @return The body-mass index of the person.
      */
      public float getBMI()
      {
            return bmi;
      }


      /**
      interpretBMI is used to return an interpretation of the body-
      mass index for the person.
      @return An interpretation of the body-mass index for the person.
      */
      public String interpretBMI()
      {
            if       (bmi < 20.0f)
                  return "underweight";
            else if (bmi >= 20.0f & bmi < 25.0f)
                  return "an appropriate weight";
            else if (bmi >= 25.0f & bmi < 30.0f)
                  return "overweight";
            else if (bmi >= 30.0f & bmi <= 39.0f)
                  return "obese";
            else
                  return "you should consult a physician";
      }
}
```

The class `Example_8` is used to test the constructor and the methods of the class `Person`. The design of this class may be represented by the following pseudocode.

1. create a window object screen

2. create a dialog box and input the name

3. create a slider object to input the height in centimeters

4. convert the height to meters

5. create a slider object to input the weight in kilograms X 10

6. convert the weight to kilograms

7. create a person object

8. display the name, height, and weight of the person

9. calculate and display the body-mass index, and interpretation of bmi

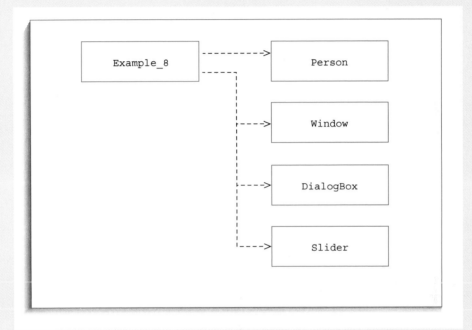

Figure 4.13 UML representation of dependencies

From the pseudocode it is possible to draw the UML dependency diagram shown in Figure 4.13.

The first slider will input a height in centimeters, and the second slider will input a weight in kilograms multiplied by a factor of 10. In both cases the fine graduation of scales is to allow for a height to be input to an accuracy of 1 cm, and a weight to an accuracy of $\frac{1}{10}$th of a kilogram.

Notice that the data input from both sliders needs to be in the correct units (m) and (kg), respectively, before they can be used as arguments in the constructor.

```
// case study on body-mass index

import avi.*;

class Example_8
{
    public static void main(String[] args)
```

```
{
        String name;
        float height, weight;

        // create and show window
        Window screen = new Window("Example_8.java","bold","black",24);
        screen.showWindow();

        // create dialog box and input name
        DialogBox inputName = new DialogBox(screen,"Name?");
        inputName.showDialogBox();
        name = inputName.getString();

        // create and show slider and input height
        Slider inputHeight = new
        Slider(screen,"Height (cm)?",135,230,1);
        inputHeight.showSlider();

        // convert height to (m)
        height = (float)inputHeight.getValue()/100.0f;

        // create and show slider and input weight
        Slider inputWeight = new
        Slider(screen,"Weight (Kg)x10 ?",300,1900,1);
        inputWeight.showSlider();

        // convert weight to (kg)
        weight = (float)inputWeight.getValue()/10.0f;

        // create person, calculate bmi and interpret the result
        Person anybody = new Person(name, height, weight);

        // display statistics about person
        screen.write("Name: "+anybody.getName()+"\n");
        screen.write("Height  m: "+anybody.getHeight()+"\n");
        screen.write("Weight kg: "+anybody.getWeight()+"\n");
        screen.write("Body-mass index is "+anybody.getBMI()+"\n");
        screen.write("Interpretation of BMI means that you are "+
                        anybody.interpretBMI());
    }
}
```

A screen shot of the program being run follows.

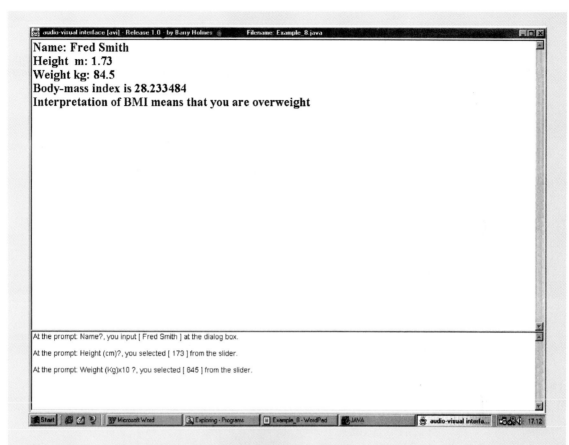

The contents of the corresponding log file follows.

```
==========================================================================
                      L  O  G      F  I  L  E
        audio-visual interface [avi] - Release 1.0 - by Barry Holmes
            filename: Example_8.java  date: 3/12/2000  time: 9:0:2
==========================================================================


At the prompt: Name?, you input [ Fred Smith ] at the dialog box.

At the prompt: Height (cm)?, you selected [ 173 ] from the slider.

At the prompt: Weight (Kg)x10 ?, you selected [ 845 ] from the slider.

Name: Fred Smith
Height  m: 1.73
Weight kg: 84.5
Body-mass index is 28.233484
Interpretation of BMI means that you are overweight
```

Modify program `Example_8` as follows.

(1) Use radio buttons to give a person a choice as to whether they want to input a height in inches and a weight in pounds or a height in meters and a weight in kilograms. Remember the BMI is calculated using height in meters and weight in kilograms.

(2) According to the choice made, use the appropriate scales on the sliders.

4.9   Yet another AVI Class!

The Memo Class

A `Memo` object is illustrated in Figure 4.14. The object is an output window. Its purpose is to inform the user of any events that are happening when a program is running. You have seen this object many times before since the `avi` uses it when loading sound files, loading image files, informing users about inputting the wrong format for numbers in a dialog box, and so on.

The `Memo` class contains the following constructor and `public` instance methods:

```
public class Memo
{
     public Memo(Window parent,
               String firstLine,
               String secondLine,
               String thirdLine,
               boolean mode);

     public void showMemo();
     public void hideMemo();
}
```

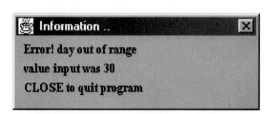

Figure 4.14 An example of a `Memo` object

To create a `Memo` object, you must use the class constructor that requires five items of data in the formal parameter list:

`parent`—a `Window` type that specifies the container on which to display a `Memo` object.

`firstLine`, `secondLine`, and `thirdLine`—string types that allow for textual information to be displayed by the `Memo` object. You do not have to fill every line; it is permissible to use an empty string (`""`) where required.

`mode`—a `boolean` type that specifies whether the memo is to remain on the screen until the memo's window is closed. If the mode is set to `true`, the only way to advance to the next executable statement in the program is by closing the memo's window.

If the mode is set to `false`, then the computer will advance to the next executable program instruction without waiting for you to even read what is contained in the memo object. For this reason it is necessary to introduce a timed-delay after the statement to show the memo on the screen.

Assuming that you have already created a screen window-pane object, then to represent the memo depicted in Figure 4.14, the `Memo` constructor may be coded as:

```
Memo message = new Memo(screen,
                "Error! day out of range",
                "value input was "+day,
                "CLOSE to quit program",
                true);
```

The memo is displayed on the screen using the instance method `showMemo()`, for example:

```
message.showMemo();
```

The memo may be hidden from view using the instance method `hideMemo()`.

4.10   The This Object

Suppose you have created an instance method within a class. For the sake of reuse of code, you want to call that method from another method within the same class. However, instance methods are only invoked by passing a message to an object. How, within a class, do you invoke an instance method of that class when the object is declared outside of the class?

The keyword `this` refers to the current object, which is the object being instantiated in the case of the constructor.

The `this` keyword may be used within a class to refer to any object of that class type.

For example, suppose the instance method `isALeapYear` had been defined within a class to return `true` if a year was a leap year and otherwise return `false`:

```
public boolean isALeapYear();
```

This instance method may be reused in another instance method, `daysInMonth`, to calculate and return the number of days in a month. Part of the coding for the `daysInMonth` method is listed here.

```
public int daysInMonth()
{
        .
        .


    // test for Feb being a Leap Year
    case 2:if (this.isALeapYear())
                return 29;
            else
                return 28;
        .
        .

}
```

We will use the above code in the case study of the next section.

CASE STUDY

Validation of Dates including Leap Years

Statement of the Problem.   Write a program to input a date, as a string, in the format MMD-DYYYY where MM represents a two-digit month, DD represents a two-digit day, and YYYY represents a four-digit year. Check the validity of the date, and report on any errors. For valid dates only, divide the date up into its three numerical components of month, day, and year, and write these values to the screen. Determine whether the year is a leap year, and report on your findings. Calculate the number of days in the month and write your result on the screen.

Identification of Classes and Methods

Finding a relevant class using noun analysis is not particularly helpful in this problem. Basically, the solution to the problem depends on validating a date string and finding attributes about the date. The only two classes that appear relevant are a program class which we will name Example_9, and a class containing tests and calculations on the date string, which we will name DateString.

A verb analysis proves a little more fruitful, since the problem contains many actions such as checking the validity of a date, dividing the date into month, day, and year, and outputting these values. Other activities include reporting on leap years and the number of days in a month.

If we assume that the month, day, and year are instance variables, then the constructor will take the date string as a formal parameter and check on the numerical validity of the contents of the string before assigning the values to the instance variables.

Since we need to output the month, day, and year, it makes sense to have three instance methods to perform this activity—getMonth, getDay, and getYear.

Other instance methods that may be derived from the verb analysis are isALeapYear and daysInMonth. The functionality of these methods should be obvious from their names (see Figure 4.15).

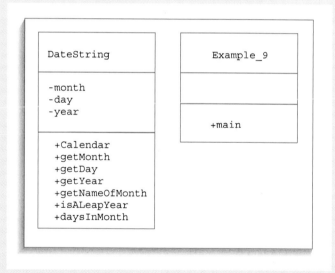

Figure 4.15 UML class diagrams

Algorithm Development

The DateString class contains the following constants and instance variables.

```
public class DateString
{
     private static final String[] NAMES_OF_MONTHS =
```

```
                        {"January","February","March","April",
                        "May","June","July","August",
                        "September","October","November","December"};

        private int month;
        private int day;
        private int year;
          .

          .

}
```

Notice that an array containing the names of the months has been declared as a `static` constant. The instance method `nameOfMonth` will use the numerical value of the month as an index to the string array, to locate the correct name. Remember that array indexes start at cell 0, so the numerical value of the month will need to be reduced by 1 before you attempt to use it as an index to the array.

The constructor of the class `DateString` has to perform the following operations.

1. validate the length of the formal parameter
2. if length of date != 8
3.   report error and quit program
4. convert the date string to an integer using a wrapper class
5. split up the date into month, day, and year
6. if month <1 or month > 12
7.   report error and quit program
8. if day < 1 or day > number of days in month
9.   report error and quit program

This pseudocode can be written in Java as follows.

```
public DateString(WindowPane screen, String dateString)
{
        // validate date
        Memo message;

        if (dateString.length() != 8)
        {
                Audio.beep(screen);
                message = new Memo(screen,
                                "Error! date format not 8 digits",
                                "value input was "+dateString,
                                "CLOSE to quit program",
                                true);
                message.showMemo();
```

```
        screen.closeWindowAndExit();
}
// use a wrapper class to convert the string to an integer
Integer number = new Integer(dateString);
int date = number.intValue();

// split up date into MM DD and YYYY
month = date / 1000000;
day   = (date % 1000000) / 10000;
year  = (date % 10000);

if (month < 1 || month > 12)
{
        Audio.beep(screen);
        message = new Memo(screen,"Error! month out of range",
                                  "value input was "+month,
                                  "CLOSE to quit program",true);
        message.showMemo();
        screen.closeWindowAndExit();
}

if (day < 1 || day > this.daysInMonth())
{
        Audio.beep(screen);
        message = new Memo(screen,"Error! day out of range",
                                  "value input was "+day,
                                  "CLOSE to quit program",true);
        message.showMemo();
        screen.closeWindowAndExit();
}
}
```

The instance methods to getMonth, getDay, and getYear are trivial to code since they simply return the numerical value of the instance variables month, day, and year respectively. These methods will appear in the final listing of the DateString class. The instance method isALeapYear relies upon the following algorithm to test whether a year is a leap year or not.

1. if the year is evenly divisible by 4 and the year is not a century
        or the year is a century that is divisible by 400 then
2.   the year is a leap year
3. else
4.   the year is NOT a leap year

This algorithm can be expressed as follows:

```
public boolean isALeapYear()
{
        if (((year%4 == 0) && (year%100 != 0)) || (year%400 == 0))
            return true;
        else
            return false;
}
```

The instance method `daysInMonth` relies upon the following algorithm to return the correct number of days in a given month.

```
public int daysInMonth()
{
        // calculate number of days in month
        switch(month)
        {
            // test for Jan, Mar, May, Jul, Aug, Oct, Dec
            case 1:
            case 3:
            case 5:
            case 7:
            case 8:
            case 10:
            case 12:    return 31;

            // test for Apr, Jun, Sep, Nov
            case 4:
            case 6:
            case 9:
            case 11:    return 30;

            // test for Feb being a Leap Year
            case 2:if (this.isALeapYear())
                        return 29;
                    else
                        return 28;
            default:    return 0;
        }
}
```

Testing

Test data used to create `DateString` **objects**

DateString **object**	dateString	**Month**	**Day**	**Year**	**Error message**
anyDate	262000				date format not 8 digits
anyDate	03181997	3	18	1997	
anyDate	02121992	2	12	1992	
anyDate	02301987	2	30	1987	day out of range
anyDate	20091999	20	9	1999	month out of range
anyDate	02062001	2	6	2000	
anyDate	06141999	6	14	1999	

Desk check of instance method `daysInMonth`

DateString **object**	**Month**	**Day**	**Year**	isALeapYear	daysInMonth
anyDate	3	18	1997	false	31
anyDate	2	12	1992	true	29
anyDate	2	6	2001	false	28
anyDate	6	14	1999	false	30

The dependencies of the `DateString` class are shown in Figure 4.16.

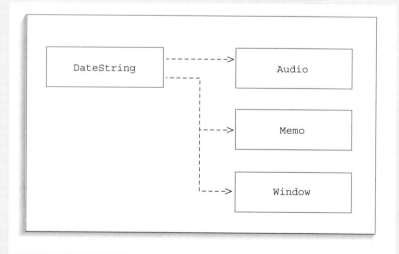

Figure 4.16 The UML representation of the dependencies

A listing of the completed class `DateString` follows.

```
import avi.*;

public class DateString
{
      // class constants
      private static final String[] NAMES_OF_MONTHS =
                    {"January","February","March","April",
                     "May","June","July","August",
                     "September","October","November","December"};


      // instance variables
      private int month;
      private int day;
      private int year;


      // constructor
      /**
      The DateString class enables an object to be created that represents
      a date in the format MMDDYYYY.
      @param screen is the container for any memo objects that might be
       shown.
      @param dateString is the date in the format MMDDYYYY.
      */
      public DateString(Window screen, String dateString)
      {
            // validate date
            Memo message;

            if (dateString.length() != 8)
            {
                  Audio.beep(screen);
                  message = new Memo(screen,"Error! date format not 8 "+
                                            "digits",
                                            "value input was "+dateString,
                                            "CLOSE to quit program",true);
                  message.showMemo();
                  screen.closeWindowAndExit();
            }
```

```
// use a wrapper class to convert the string to an integer

Integer number = new Integer(dateString);
int date = number.intValue();

// split up date into MM DD and YYYY
month = date / 1000000;
day   = (date % 1000000) / 10000;
year  = (date % 10000);

if (month < 1 || month > 12)
{
      Audio.beep(screen);
      message = new Memo(screen,"Error! month out of range",
                                "value input was "+month,
                                "CLOSE to quit program",true);
      message.showMemo();
      screen.closeWindowAndExit();
}

if (day < 1 || day > this.daysInMonth())
{
      Audio.beep(screen);
      message = new Memo(screen,"Error! day out of range",
                                "value input was "+day,
                                "CLOSE to quit program",true);
      message.showMemo();
      screen.closeWindowAndExit();
}
}


// instance methods
/**
getMonth returns the month as an integer.
@return The value of the month as an integer.
*/
public int getMonth()
{
      return month;
}
```

```
/**
getDay returns the month as an integer.
@return The value of the day as an integer.
*/
public int getDay()
{
      return day;
}


/**
getYear returns the year as an integer.
@return The value of the year as an integer.
*/
public int getYear()
{
      return year;
}


/**
getNameOfMonth returns the name of the month.
@return The name of the month as string.
*/
public String getNameOfMonth()
{
      return NAMES_OF_MONTHS[month-1];
}


/**
isALeapYear determines whether the year is a Leap year
@return true if the year is a Leap year.
*/
public boolean isALeapYear()
{
      if (((year%4 == 0) && (year%100 != 0)) || (year%400 == 0))
            return true;
      else
            return false;
}


/**
daysInMonth returns the number of days in a month
@return The number of days in the month as an integer.
```

```
        */
        public int daysInMonth()
        {
                // calculate number of days in month
                switch(month)
                {
                        // test for Jan, Mar, May, Jul, Aug, Oct, Dec
                        case 1:
                        case 3:
                        case 5:
                        case 7:
                        case 8:
                        case 10:
                        case 12:    return 31;

                        // test for Apr, Jun, Sep, Nov
                        case 4:
                        case 6:
                        case 9:
                        case 11:    return 30;

                        // test for Feb being a Leap Year
                        case 2:if (this.isALeapYear())
                                        return 29;
                                   else
                                        return 28;
                        default:    return 0;
                }
        }
}
```

The design of class Example_9 is given by the following pseudocode.

1. create a window object screen
2. create a dialog box and input the date
3. create a DateString object
4. display details about the date
5. if date is a leap
6.   display leap year
7. else
8.   display NOT leap year
9. display number of days in the month

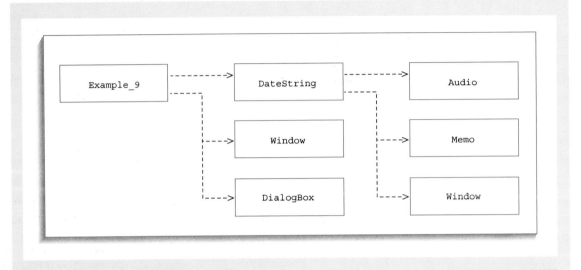

Figure 4.17 UML dependency diagrams

The UML dependency diagram for the classes `Example_9` and `DateString` is shown in Figure 4.17.

The complete listing of class `Example_9` follows.

```java
// case study - validate date

import avi.*;

class Example_9
{
    public static void main(String[] args)
    {
        String date;

        // create and show window
        Window screen = new Window("Example_9.java","bold","blue",24);
        screen.showWindow();

        // create and show dialog box and input date in format MMDDYYYY
        DialogBox inputDate = new DialogBox(screen,"date as MMDDYYYY");
        inputDate.showDialogBox();
        date = inputDate.getString();
```

```
        // create DateString object
        DateString anyDate = new DateString(screen,date);

        // write details to the screen about the date
        screen.write("Date input was "+anyDate.getMonth()+
                  "/"+anyDate.getDay()+"/"+anyDate.getYear()+";\n");

        if (anyDate.isALeapYear())
            screen.write(anyDate.getYear()+" is a Leap year;\n");
        else
            screen.write(anyDate.getYear()+" is NOT a Leap year;\n");

        screen.write("The month "+anyDate.getNameOfMonth()+" has "+
                  anyDate.daysInMonth()+" days.");
    }
}
```

A screen shot from the program running follows, together with the contents of the log file.

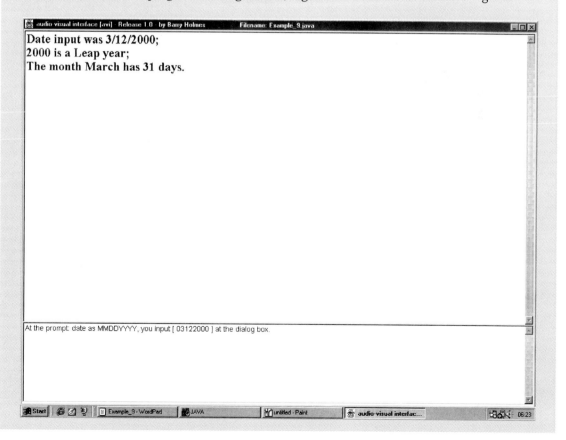

```
================================================================
                    L  O  G      F  I  L  E
      audio-visual interface [avi] - Release 1.0 - by Barry Holmes
        filename: Example_9.java    date: 3/12/2000  time: 9:40:11
================================================================


At the prompt: date as MMDDYYYY, you input [ 03122000 ] at the dialog box.

Date input was 3/12/2000;
2000 is a Leap year;
The month March has 31 days.
```

A second screen shot from the program running with error data follows, together with the contents of the log file.

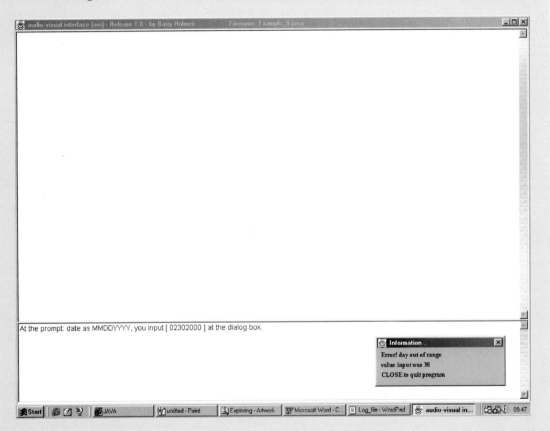

```
===================================================================
                    L O G     F I L E
       audio-visual interface [avi] - Release 1.0 - by Barry Holmes
            filename: Example_9.java    date: 3/12/2000  time: 9:47:37
===================================================================

At the prompt: date as MMDDYYYY, you input [ 02302000 ] at the dialog box.

< memo contained Error! day out of range value input was 30 CLOSE to quit
program >
```

SUMMARY

- A conditional expression evaluates to either `true` or `false`.

- Depending upon the result of the conditional expression, it is possible for the computer to select different statements in an `if` statement.

- Comparison of real numbers for equality should be avoided, since real numbers are not always accurately stored by the computer.

- Conditional expressions can be combined into one expression by using the logical operators `&&` (AND) and `||` (OR).

- Short-circuit evaluation will result in conditions not being evaluated in a conditional expression.

- Both `&&` and `||` use short-circuit evaluation. If long evaluation is required, use `&` and `|`, respectively.

- `if` statements may be nested within each other.

- In nested `if` statements, an `else` keyword belongs to the nearest `if` keyword that has not already been paired with an `else`.

- When selection is based upon an ordinal type, a `switch` statement may be used.

- All `case` labels must be unique and of the ordinal type compatible with the selector type.

- Wrapper classes are used to provide constants and general methods for the primitive data types.

- The `this` keyword refers to the current object for which the instance method or constructor is called.

Review Questions

1. What is the syntax of an `if` statement?

2. Distinguish between the operators = and ==.

3. How many statements are allowed after the `if` keyword?

4. How many statements are allowed after the `else` keyword?

5. What is a conditional expression?

6. What symbols are used for the logical operators AND and OR?

7. What is short-circuit evaluation?

8. Why do we indent statements in an `if` statement?

9. What are nested `if` statements?

10. Explain the purpose of the `switch` statement.

11. Why should a `break` statement be used within a `switch` statement?

12. What are `case` labels?

13. When is the `default` label used in a `switch` statement?

14. If a statement corresponds to many `case` labels in a `switch` statement, how are the `case` labels organized?

Exercises

15. If A = 1, B = -2, C = 3, D = 4, E = 'S', and F = 'J', state whether the following conditions are true or false.

    (a) A==B

    (b) A>B

    (c) (A<C && B<D)

    (d) !(A<C && B>D)

    (e) (A>B || C<D)

    (f) E>F

    (g) ((A+C)>(B-D)) && ((B+C)<(D-A))

16. Code the following conditions in Java. Assume all variables are of type `int`.

    (a) X is equal to Y.

    (b) X is not equal to Y.

(c) A is less than or equal to B.

(d) Q is not greater than T.

(e) X is greater than or equal to Y.

(f) X is less than or equal to Y and A is not equal to B.

(g) A is greater than 18 and H is greater than 68 and W is greater than 75.

(h) G is less than 100 and greater than 50.

(i) H is less than 50 or greater than 100.

17. Trace through the following segment of code for each of (a), (b), and (c) and state the output in each case.

(a) A = 16, B = 16,   C = 32

(b) A = 16, B = -18, C = 32

(c) A = -2, B = -4,   C = 16

```
if (A>0)
{
    if (B<0)
        screen.write("x");
    else
        if (C>20)
            screen.write("y");
}
else
    screen.write("z");
```

18. Trace through the following segment of code for each new value of the variable character and state the output.

(a) character = 'B';   (c) character = 'a';

(b) character = '4';

```
switch (character)
{
    case 'a': case 'b': case 'c': screen.write("small letter");
                                  break;
    case 'A': case 'B': case 'C': screen.write("capital letters");
                                  break;
    case '1': case '2': case '3': screen.write("digits"); break;
    default                     : screen.write("error in data");
}
```

19. Correct the syntax in this program segment.

```
if y > 25
    x == 16;
    screen.write("x = " + x);
else
    y = 20
```

20. The lengths of the four sides of a quadrilateral and the measure of one internal angle are input into a computer. Design an algorithm using pseudocode to categorize the shape of the quadrilateral as a square, rhombus, rectangle, parallelogram, or irregular quadrilateral. Remember to give your algorithm a desk check using suitably chosen data.

The rules for determining the shape of the quadrilateral follow.

Name	All sides equal?	Opposite sides equal?	Internal angle is a right angle.
square	true	true	true
rectangle	false	true	true
rhombus	true	true	false
parallelogram	false	true	false
irregular	false	false	-

Programming Problems

21. Return to Question 18 in Chapter 2. Rewrite the program to allow for a change in the size of the font in addition to the change in the style of the font and color of the text. You should use command-line input to change the values of the parameters to the `Window` constructor. Use a wrapper class to convert the size of the font from a string to an integer.

22. A worker is paid at the hourly rate of $8 per hour for the first 35 hours worked. Overtime is paid at 1½ times the hourly rate for the next 25 hours worked and paid at 2 times the hourly rate for additional hours worked. Write a program to input the number of hours worked; then calculate and output the total amount paid, broken into regular pay and overtime pay.

23. A student traveling to Florida for Spring Break will consider a particular airline if the round trip ticket costs less than $200 and has a layover of no longer than four hours, or if the ticket costs between $200 and $300 and has no layover. Write a program to input the name of an airline, cost of ticket, and layover time; output the name of the airline only if it meets the student's criteria.

Value of sales	Commission
$1–999	1%
$1000–$9999	5%
$10000–$99999	10%

Figure 4.18 Scale of commission

24. A student choosing among payment plans for a college loan wants to keep the monthly payments to less than $200. If the initial amount of the loan is $5,000, then write a program to calculate which plans are acceptable given different loan lengths and simple interest rates.

25. Write a program to implement the algorithm that you designed and tested in Question 20.

26. A salesperson earns a commission on the value of sales. Figure 4.18 shows the scale of the commission. Write a program to input a figure for the value of the sales, and then calculate and output the commission.

27. Write a program to mimic a calculator. Input two real numbers and state whether the numbers are to be added, subtracted, multiplied, or divided. Consider the possibility of a denominator being zero in the division of two numbers.

28. A bicycle shop in Hyannis rents bicycles by the day at different rates throughout the year, according to the season (see Figure 4.19). The proprietor also gives a 25% discount if the rental period is greater than 7 days. Renters must also pay a $50 returnable deposit for each bicycle rented. Write a program to input the season and the number of days of rental, and then calculate and display a total charge that includes the deposit.

29. Create a set of digitized images relating to your favorite hobby or sport. For example, with a sport such as golf, get a friend to take pictures of your progress (or frustration) over, say, 9 holes. Record a set of sound clips to describe how you played each hole. Write a program to display radio buttons for each hole. On pressing a button, show the image of you playing the hole, and play the accompanying sound commentary.

30. Create a program that will use two radio-button boxes to query the user about their preferences for a vacation. (For example, do they prefer sports, scenery, or sightseeing and do they prefer to be adventurous or not?) Based on the user's responses, have the

Season	Charge
Spring	$5.00
Summer	$7.50
Autumn	$3.75
Winter	$2.50

Figure 4.19 Rental rates

program suggest a vacation spot by writing out a short description of a location and providing a picture or two of the location. For example, if the person prefers scenery on a budget, you might "advertise" a local nature trail.

31. Use the Internet to search for a table of the Beaufort Wind Speed Scale. Try the following URL that was current at the time of writing:

    http://www.iesd.dmu.ac.uk/ ~slb/wc111t1.html

    Create the following class.

    ```
    public class Beaufort
        {
        // constructor
        public Beaufort(float windSpeedLow, float windSpeedHigh);

        // instance methods
        public int windForce();
        public String description();
    }
    ```

    For example, according to the Beaufort Wind Speed Scale, a wind speed between 55.2 mph (windSpeedLow) and 74.8 mph (windSpeedHigh) would be classified as wind force 10 and described as a strong gale.

    Write a driver program to create Beaufort objects relating to different wind speeds and display the corresponding wind force values and descriptions.

32. During hot weather it is commonplace for weather reports to include information on the strength of the ultra-violet (UV) radiation from the sun, and the burning effect of this radiation upon your skin.

i   In the U.S., the UV Index is computed using forecasted ozone levels, a computer model that relates ozone levels to UV incidence on the ground, forecasted cloud amounts, and the elevation of the forecast cities.

The calculation starts with measurement of current total ozone amounts for the entire globe, obtained via two satellites operated by the National Oceanic and Atmospheric Administration (NOAA). These data are then used to produce a forecast of ozone levels for the next day at various points around the country. A radiative transfer model is then used to determine the amount of UV radiation reaching the ground from 290 to 400 nm in wavelength, using the time of day (solar noon), day of the year, and latitude. This and more information is available on the Environmental Protection Agency Web site:

http://www.epa.gov/sunwise/uvindex/uvcalc.html

Create the following class.

```
public class Sunburn
{
        // constructor
        public Sunburn(int uvRadiationlevel,
                        String cloudCover,
                        int heightAboveSea);

        // instance methods
        public int getUVIndex();
        public String interpretUVIndex();
}
```

The getUVIndex method assumes the total amount of UV radiation for one day on a person's skin has already been calculated. For the purpose of this question the measure of this radiation will be limited to within the range 250 .. 350 units. The question also assumes that the hottest weather occurs during the summer months when the sun is closest to the location being used to measure the weather.

The final figure for UV radiation is adjusted for the height of the location above sea level. UV at the surface increases about 6% per kilometer above sea level.

The amount of UV radiation changes with the cloud coverage. Clear skies permit 100% of the incoming UV radiation to reach the surface; scattered clouds transmit 89%; broken clouds transmit 73%; overcast conditions transmit 31%.

The final figure for the UV index is then scaled by a factor of 25 to result in a UV index from 0 .. 22.

The UV Index provides a daily forecast of the expected risk of overexposure to the sun. The UV index can be interpreted into the following risk categories. However, the table shown in Figure 4.20 does not take into account the color of a persons skin. Fair-skinned people are at a greater risk from UV radiation than dark-skinned people.

Write a driver program to create Sunburn objects and test the various methods within the class.

UV Index	Risk
0 – 2	Minimal
3 – 4	Low
5 – 6	Moderate
7 – 9	High
10+	Very High

Figure 4.20 Risk from UV radiation levels

CHAPTER 5

Repetition and One-Dimensional Arrays

$\blacksquare$n the previous chapters, it was necessary to run some programs several times to demonstrate the effect that different items of input data would have on the results. At the time, you might have thought this approach was a little cumbersome. How much better it would be if we had a structure in the program that would allow statements to be repeated.

The purpose of this chapter is to introduce you to three methods for repeating statements that are based on the control structures known as `while`, `do..while`, and `for`. The chapter also revisits arrays and introduces the `avi` `CheckBox` class, the last of the `avi` classes. By the end of the chapter you should have an understanding of the following topics.

- The concept of a loop

- The syntax and appropriate use of `while`, `do..while`, and `for` loop statements

- The use of postfix increment and decrement operators

- One-dimensional arrays

- The `avi` `CheckBox` class

- The Java library `NumberFormat` class

217

5.1 Loop Structure

In writing a computer program it is often necessary to repeat part of a program a number of times. One way to achieve repetition is to write out that part of the program as many times as it is needed. This method is very impractical since it produces a very lengthy computer program and the number of repetitions is not always known in advance.

A better way to repeat part of a program a number of times is to introduce a loop into the code. The illustration in Figure 5.1 shows one mechanism for setting up a loop.

In this example, a counter is used as a loop control variable to record the number of times part of the program is repeated. The following operations take place on the loop control variable.

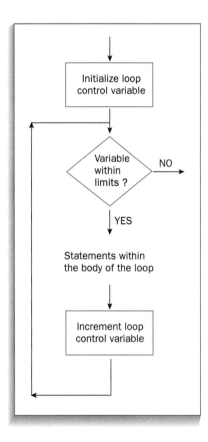

Figure 5.1 Loop variable controlled by a counter

1. The loop control variable must be initialized before the computer enters the loop.

2. The value of the loop control variable is tested to see whether it is within specified limits for looping to continue. If the loop control variable is not within these limits, then the computer must exit from the loop.

3. The statements within the body of the loop are executed.

4. The value of the loop control variable is incremented by 1 to indicate that the statements have been performed once.

5. Go back to step 2, thereby completing the loop.

Notice from Figure 5.1 that if the loop control variable is initialized to a value that is outside of the limits, then the loop will never be entered and the statements within the body of the loop will never be executed.

The loop control variable does not have to be assigned values from within the program. The initialization and incremental increase of this variable can be replaced by reading data from an input object such as a dialog box. The illustration in Figure 5.2 shows that values of the loop control variable are input rather

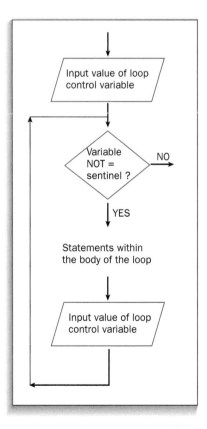

Figure 5.2 Loop variable controlled by data

than assigning values from within a program. Notice that a certain value input will trigger the exit from the loop. This value is known as a *sentinel* value.

5.2   While Loop

A `while` loop will allow a statement to be repeated zero or more times and behaves in the same manner as depicted by the illustrations in Figures 5.1 and 5.2. The syntax of the `while` loop follows.

SYNTAX

While Loop: `while (conditional-expression) statement(s);`

Notice that many statements may follow the conditional expression. If more than one statement is to be repeated, it is necessary to enclose the statements within braces { } so the computer treats the statements as a block.

While Loop Controlled by a Counter

The following segment of code uses a `while` loop and a loop variable controlled by a counter, as illustrated in Figure 5.1.

```
counter = 1;                          // initialize loop control variable
while (counter <= 5)                  // test if variable is within limits
{
    screen.write(counter + "\n");
    counter = counter + 1;            // increment loop control variable
}
```

The value of counter is initialized to 1; the condition (counter<=5) is true; therefore, the value of the counter is output. The counter is incremented by 1 to the value 2; the condition (counter<=5) is true, so the value of counter is output again. The process continues while the condition (counter<=5) remains true. When counter is incremented to the value 6, the condition (counter<=5) becomes false and the computer exits from the `while` loop. The loop body will execute five times.

While Loop Controlled by Data

Consider the use of a `while` loop to read in a set of numbers when the numbers are not zero, display each number on the screen, and output the sum of the numbers. The numbers are input from a slider, and the value 0 (zero) is the sentinel value. The following segment of code uses a `while` loop and a loop variable controlled by data, as illustrated in Figure 5.2.

```
// input value of loop control variable from slider
input.showSlider();
number = input.getValue();

while (number != 0)                      // test if variable is a sentinel value
{
    screen.write(number + "\n");
    sum = sum + number;

    // input value of loop control variable from slider
    input.showSlider();
    number = input.getValue();
}
```

If the first number to be input is zero, then the conditional expression (num-ber!=0) will be false. The computer will not enter the loop but branch to the next executable statement after the end of the compound statement delimited by the braces {}. Since the loop was not entered, the loop is said to be repeated zero times.

However, if the first number to be input is nonzero, the conditional expression would be true and the computer would execute the statements contained within the loop. To this end, the number would be displayed on the screen, the sum would be incremented, and the next number input at the slider. The computer then returns to the line containing the conditional expression, which is reevaluated to test whether the new number is not zero. If the condition is true, the computer continues to execute the statements in the body of the loop. If the condition is false, the computer will branch to the next executable statement after the end of the compound statement.

To restate the behavior of the while loop: If the first number read is zero, then the loop is not entered, and the statements within the loop are repeated zero times. If the second number to be read is zero, the statements in the loop will be repeated once. If the third number to be read is zero, the statements in the loop will be repeated twice, and so on. Therefore, if the hundredth number to be read is zero, the statements inside the loop will have been repeated 99 times.

> *i* Note that for clarity, the body of the while loop is indented. Therefore, when other kinds of loops are introduced in this chapter, we will follow the same pattern of indentation. In addition, we will utilize indentation in writing the pseudocode. Getting into the habit of identifying the structure of a loop at the algorithm stage of program design will facilitate the eventual coding of the loop.

The following Java program uses the data controlled loop described above.

```java
// program to demonstrate a while loop controlled by input data

import avi.*;

class Example_1
{
    static public void main(String[] args)
    {
        // sum will hold the sum of the numbers input so far
        int sum = 0;

        Window screen = new Window("Example_1.java");
        screen.showWindow();

        Slider input = new
        Slider(screen,"zero terminates loop",-100,+100,1);
        input.showSlider();

        // input value of loop control variable from slider
        int number = input.getValue();

        while (number != 0)
        {
            screen.write("non-zero number input is "+number+"\n");
            sum = sum + number;

            // input value of loop control variable from slider
            input.showSlider();
            number = input.getValue();
        }

        screen.write("\n.. computer has exited from the while loop");
        screen.write("\n The sum of the numbers is " + sum);
    }
}
```

Run the program twice. The first time, input 0 (zero) as the first number and notice that the contents of the loop body are never executed. The second time, input up to 10 different, nonzero numbers in the range −100 to +100 before inputting 0 (zero). The statements within the `while` loop should be repeated up to 10 times.

The log files for each run follow.

```
================================================================
                  L O G     F I L E
     audio-visual interface [avi] - Release 1.0 - by Barry Holmes
        filename: Example_1.java date: 6/29/2000   time: 7:40:52
================================================================


At the prompt: zero terminates loop, you selected [ 0 ] from the slider.

.. computer has exited from the while loop
 The sum of the numbers is 0
```

```
================================================================
                  L O G     F I L E
     audio-visual interface [avi] - Release 1.0 - by Barry Holmes
        filename: Example_1.java   date: 6/29/2000   time: 7:49:25
================================================================
At the prompt: zero terminates loop, you selected [ 89 ] from the slider.

non-zero number input is 89
At the prompt: zero terminates loop, you selected [ 20 ] from the slider.

non-zero number input is 20
At the prompt: zero terminates loop, you selected [ -72 ] from the slider.

non-zero number input is -72
At the prompt: zero terminates loop, you selected [ -20 ] from the slider.

non-zero number input is -20
At the prompt: zero terminates loop, you selected [ 33 ] from the slider.

non-zero number input is 33
At the prompt: zero terminates loop, you selected [ 59 ] from the slider.

non-zero number input is 59
At the prompt: zero terminates loop, you selected [ -68 ] from the slider.

non-zero number input is -68
At the prompt: zero terminates loop, you selected [ 94 ] from the slider.

non-zero number input is 94
At the prompt: zero terminates loop, you selected [ 40 ] from the slider.

non-zero number input is 40
At the prompt: zero terminates loop, you selected [ 0 ] from the slider.

.. computer has exited from the while loop
The sum of the numbers is 175
```

A screen shot of the running program follows.

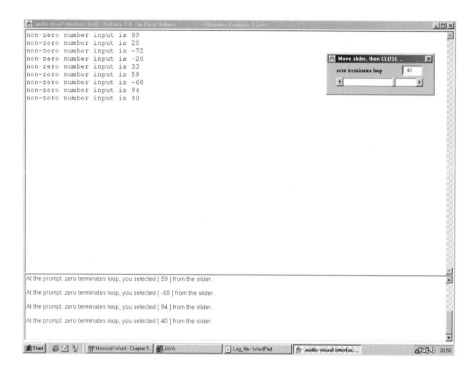

NOW DO THIS   Modify program `Example_1`.

(1) Include a counter in the program to count the number of nonzero numbers input.

(2) Include a statement to calculate the arithmetic mean of the list of numbers and output this value.

(3) Recompile and run the program.

A `while` loop can be used with elements of the `avi` package to implement some interesting programs. For example, we can simulate a simple alarm clock. The `Timer` class in the `avi` package contains class methods that return the current hour, minute, and second as integer values, respectively. In the next example, the user inputs the time in hours and minutes at the command line, for the time the alarm clock is expected to wake you. A `Memo` object stays on the screen, informing you of the time the alarm is set to wake you.

The computer gets the current hours and minutes and compares these values with the values of the command line hours and minutes in a conditional statement of a `while` loop. For example:

```
while (hour != currentHour ||
      (hour == currentHour) && (minute != currentMinute))
```

While this condition is true, the computer writes the current time on the screen, in hours, minutes, and seconds; it delays for one second, clears the screen, then gets the current hours and minutes again. This process is continuously repeated until the `while` condition becomes false. The `while` loop is then exited, the computer writes a message on the screen, and then plays an appropriate alarm sound.

```
// program to demonstrate a while loop for an alarm clock

import avi.*;

class Example_2
{
      static public void main(String[] args)
      {
            // time of alarm clock is input as two command line
            // parameters; these are converted from their string
            // values into hour and minute
            int hour = new Integer(args[0]).intValue();
            int minute = new Integer(args[1]).intValue();

            Window screen = new Window("Example_2.java","bold","red",36);
            screen.showWindow();

            // create audio object as alarm sound
            String[] soundFile = {"wakeup.wav"};
            Audio wakeUp = new Audio(screen,soundFile);

            // display wake up time on memo object
            Memo wakeUpTime = new
            Memo(screen,"","Alarm set for "+hour+":"+minute,"",false);
            wakeUpTime.showMemo();

            // get current time from Timer class
            int currentHour = Timer.getHour();
            int currentMinute = Timer.getMinute();

            while (hour != currentHour || (hour == currentHour) &&
                  (minute != currentMinute))
```

```
        {
                // display current time
                screen.write(currentHour+":"+currentMinute+":"+
                            Timer.getSecond()+"\n");
                Timer.delay(1);
                screen.clearTextArea();
                // get current time from Timer class
                currentHour = Timer.getHour();
                currentMinute = Timer.getMinute();
        }
        // display message and sound alarm
        screen.write("Wakey .. Wakey !!\n");
        wakeUp.playSound(0);
        Timer.delay(5);
        screen.closeWindowAndExit();
    }
}
```

The log file for the program, executed with the command `java Example_2 14 46`, at time 14:45:33 follows.

```
===================================================================================
                        L O G    F I L E
          audio-visual interface [avi] - Release 1.0 - by Barry Holmes
          filename: Example_2.java    date: 3/12/2000    time: 2:45:30
===================================================================================

< memo contained  Sound file(s) are loading, there will be a short pause. >
< memo contained  Alarm set for 14:46  >
14:45:33
14:45:34
14:45:35
14:45:36
14:45:37
14:45:38
14:45:39
14:45:40
14:45:41
14:45:42
14:45:43
14:45:44
14:45:45
14:45:46
```

```
14:45:47
14:45:48
14:45:49
14:45:50
14:45:51
14:45:52
14:45:53
14:45:54
14:45:55
14:45:56
14:45:57
14:45:58
14:45:59
Wakey .. Wakey !!
< audio file wakeup.wav played >
```

NOW DO THIS▶

(1) Run the program for yourself.

(2) Change the sound file and wake-up message.

(3) Recompile and run the program.

5.3 Do..while Loop

The illustration in Figure 5.3 shows another method for repeating statements within a program. Notice the absence of a decision symbol at the beginning of the loop, which implies that it is required to execute the statements within the loop at least once. The decision symbol appears at the end of the loop. Thus the computer will exit from the loop only when the condition associated with this symbol is false.

Unlike a `while` loop, a `do..while` loop always requires the statements within the loop to be executed at least once by the computer. The syntax of the `do..while` loop follows.

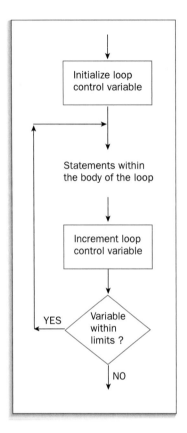

Figure 5.3 A loop that is executed at least once

SYNTAX

··

Do .. while Statement:

```
do statements(s) while (conditional-expression);
```

For example,

```
counter = 1;                          // initialize loop control variable
do
{
   screen.write(counter + "\n");
   counter = counter + 1;             // increment loop control variable
} while (counter <= 5);               // test if variable is within limits
```

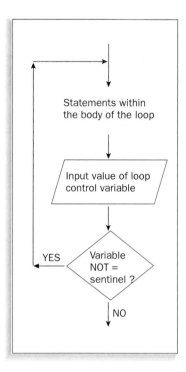

Figure 5.4 Loop controlled by data

The value of counter is initialized to 1; the `do..while` loop is entered and the value of counter is output. The counter is incremented by 1 to the value 2; the condition (`counter<=5`) is true, so the value of counter is output again. The process continues while the condition (`counter<=5`) remains true. When the counter is incremented to the value 6, the condition (`counter<=5`) becomes false and the computer exits from the `do..while` loop.

Notice that the computer enters the loop without any test for entry being made. Hence the contents of a `do..while` loop will always be executed at least once. There can be either a single statement or a compound statement between the key words `do` and `while`. Like the `while` loop, the `do..while` loop may also use a loop variable controlled by data, as illustrated in Figure 5.4.

NOW DO THIS   Modify program `Example_1` to:

(1) Input the number of numbers to add together. Insist that it be > 0.

(2) Replace the `while` loop with a `do..while` loop, and detect from the information given in (1) when all the numbers have been input.

(3) Calculate and display the arithmetic mean of the numbers.

As an example of the use of the `do..while` loop, the die rolling program from Chapter 3 is extended here. Radio buttons have been included to allow the user to either continue playing the simulation or quit the program. A `do..while` loop has been included to allow the die to be rolled again and again while the following condition is true:

```
while (choice.getNameOfButton().equals("Continue?"));
```

indicating that the user wishes to continue the simulation. The sentinel is the button labeled `"Quit"`; therefore, the statement reflects the variable `choice.getNameOfButton()` not equal to the sentinel.

```java
// program to simulate rolling a die

import avi.*;

class Example_3
{
    public static void main(String[] args)
    {
        // store the filenames of the images that represent the six
        // faces of a die
        String[] dieSides = {"die1.jpg","die2.jpg","die3.jpg",
                             "die4.jpg","die5.jpg","die6.jpg"};

        // store the filenames of the sounds for rolling a die and
        // announcing the score
        String[] sounds   = {"rollDie.wav","one.wav","two.wav",
                             "three.wav","four.wav","five.wav",
                             "six.wav"};

        // store the names of the radio buttons
        String[] buttons   = {"Continue?","Quit?"};

        // create a window pane object and show the window
        Window screen = new Window("Example_3.java");
        screen.showWindow();
```

```
// create a filmstrip object of the six faces of a die
final int WIDTH_OF_IMAGE = screen.getWidth()/12;
FilmStrip faces = new
FilmStrip(screen,dieSides,WIDTH_OF_IMAGE,WIDTH_OF_IMAGE);

// create an audio object to play the various sounds
Audio output = new Audio(screen, sounds);

// create radio buttons object to continue play
RadioButtons choice = new
RadioButtons(screen,"What next?",buttons);

// create a die object
Die luckyCube = new Die();
int value;

do
{
      value = luckyCube.rollDie();

      // play sound of die being rolled
      output.playSound(0);
      Timer.delay(1);

      // show face of die
      faces.showFrame(value-1);

      // announce score on die
      output.playSound(value);

      // show radio buttons
      choice.showRadioButtons();
} while (choice.getNameOfButton().equals("Continue?"));

screen.closeWindowAndExit();
   }
}
```

A screen shot of the running program follows.

5.4   Increment/Decrement Operators

At this point in the chapter it is worth digressing to the topic of incrementing and decrementing values, in particular in the context of control variables found in loops.

If you want to increase the value of an integer variable counter by 1, then you write

```
counter = counter + 1
```

The same result can be achieved by writing

```
counter++
```

Similarly, if you wanted to decrease the value of counter by 1, then you would write

```
counter = counter - 1
```

The same result can be achieved by writing

```
counter--
```

These new operators are known as the *increment* and *decrement postfix operators*; they are written after the variables as ++ and - -, respectively, and can be used to increase or decrease an integer numeric variable or a character variable by 1. The increment and decrement postfix operators are useful within loops, as the next program illustrates. The Java language also has increment and decrement prefix operators, but they are not used in this book.

The following program writes a character and its corresponding decimal Unicode value to the screen.

Two integer values between the numbers 32 and 127 are input via sliders. If the first value is less than the second, the computer will write to the screen all the Unicode characters with values that fall between these two numerical values, taken in ascending order. However, if the first value is greater than or equal to the second, then the Unicode characters and their corresponding numerical values are displayed in descending order. Notice how casting a Unicode to a char will result in a character being written to the screen.

To allow the whole process to be repeated, the program code is contained within a do..while loop.

```
// program to demonstrate the use of the while, do..while loops, and
// increment and decrement operators

import avi.*;

class Example_4
{
    static public void main(String[] args)
    {
        String[] buttons    = {"CONTINUE?","EXIT LOOP?"};

        // create window, sliders and radio buttons objects
        Window screen = new Window("Example_4.java","bold","blue",18);
        Slider inputFirstCode = new
        Slider(screen,"First decimal Unicode",32,127,1);
        Slider inputLastCode = new
        Slider(screen,"Last decimal Unicode",32,127,1);
        RadioButtons choice = new
        RadioButtons(screen,"What next?",buttons);

        int firstCode, lastCode, counter;

        screen.showWindow();

        do
        {
            // input range of Unicodes from two sliders
```

```
inputFirstCode.showSlider();
firstCode = inputFirstCode.getValue();
inputLastCode.showSlider();
lastCode = inputLastCode.getValue();

screen.clearTextArea();
screen.write("Decimal Unicode\tCharacter\n\n");
if (firstCode < lastCode)
{
        // display table of Unicodes and
        // respective characters
        // in ascending order of Unicode
        counter = firstCode;
        while (counter <= lastCode)
        {
                screen.write(counter+"\t\t"+
                                (char)counter+"\n");
                counter++;
        }
}
else
{
        // display table of Unicodes and
        // respective characters
        // in descending order of Unicode
        counter = firstCode;
        while (counter >= lastCode)
        {
                screen.write(counter+"\t\t"+
                                (char)counter+"\n");
                counter--;
        }
}

        choice.showRadioButtons();
}while (choice.getNameOfButton().equals("CONTINUE?"));
    }
}
```

A screen shot of the running program follows.

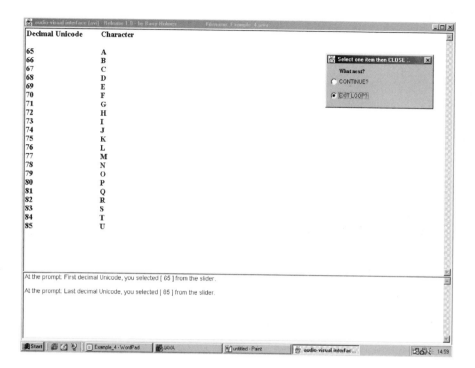

5.5   For Loop

The syntax of a `for` statement in Java follows:

SYNTAX

For Loop:

```
for ( expression1 ; expression2 ; expression3 ) statements(s)
```

---

where expression1 represents the declaration (if necessary) and initialization of the loop control variable; expression2 is a condition under which repetition will continue, and expression3 is a statement to increment or decrement the loop control variable. For example

```
for (int counter = 1; counter <= 5; counter++)
{
    screen.write(counter + "\t");
}
```

The output to the screen from this code is

```
1    2    3    4    5
```

Note that since the integer variable `counter` is declared "inside" the `for` loop, its scope of existence is only within the `for` loop, and it cannot be accessed outside of that scope. This rule helps protect the counter variable from being misused.

The `for` statement can be regarded as a shorthand version of the following `while` loop.

```
expression1;
while (expression2)
{
    statements(s);
    expression3;
}
```

The `while` loop and the `for` loop are interchangeable in that both types of loops can be used for counting. The following code produces exactly the same output as the `for` loop example.

```
int counter = 1;
while (counter <= 5)
{
    screen.write(counter + "\t");
    counter++;
}
```

The expressions in a `for` loop are optional.

1. If expression1 is omitted, the initialization (and declaration) of the loop control variable must take place before entry into the loop.

2. If expression2 is omitted, then the loop does not terminate unless it contains a `break` statement.

3. If expression3 is omitted, then increasing or decreasing the loop variable must take place within the body of the loop.

4. If all three expressions are omitted, then you will create an infinite loop!

> *i* By omitting all three expressions in a `for` loop, it is possible to set up an infinite loop—one that repeats without ending! Unless you deliberately want your program to run forever, such programming practice should be avoided.

For example, the following segment of code continues to print the message until the user interrupts the running program by either closing the window, or opening the MSDOS window/terminal window and pressing the Ctrl (control) and C keys simultaneously.

```
for ( ; ; )
{
    screen.write("forever and ever ... ");
}
```

Notice that even when the expressions are omitted in `for` loops, the semicolon separators must be present.

The following program demonstrates how the expressions of the `for` loop may be used (or abused, in the case of an infinite loop). The program demonstrates counting from 1 to 5 (twice), from 5 to 1 twice, then continuously displaying the current time of day.

```
// program to demonstrate counting

import avi.*;

class Example_5
{
    static public void main(String[] args)
    {
        Window screen = new
        Window("Example_5.java","bold+italic","red",72);
        screen.showWindow();

        // count from 1 to 5, display each value with a
        // timed delay of 1 second between each value
        for (int counter = 1; counter <= 5; counter++)
        {
            screen.write(counter);
            Timer.delay(1);
            screen.clearTextArea();
        }

        screen.write(".. and again ..");
        Timer.delay(1);
        screen.clearTextArea();

        int counter = 1;                    // (1) initialization
        for (; counter <= 5; counter++)
        {
```

```
        screen.write(counter);
        Timer.delay(1);
        screen.clearTextArea();
}

// count from 5 to 1, display each value with a
// timed delay of 1 second between each value
screen.write(".. counting backwards ..");
Timer.delay(1);
screen.clearTextArea();

for (counter = 5;; counter--)
{
        if (counter == 0) break;      // (2) condition to exit
        screen.write(counter);
        Timer.delay(1);
        screen.clearTextArea();
}

screen.write(".. and again ..");
Timer.delay(1);
screen.clearTextArea();

for (counter = 5; counter > 0;)
{
        screen.write(counter--);      // (3) decrement loop control
        Timer.delay(1);
        screen.clearTextArea();
}

// set up an infinite loop and display the value
// of the time once every second
screen.write(".. about time too ..");
Timer.delay(2);
screen.clearTextArea();

for (;;)                              // (4) infinite loop
{
        screen.write("\n"+Timer.getTime());
        Timer.delay(1);
        screen.clearTextArea();
}
    }
}
```

The log file of the executed program follows.

```
=========================================================================
                    L  O  G      F  I  L  E
        audio-visual interface [avi] - Release 1.0 - by Barry Holmes
        filename: Example_5.java   date: 3/12/2000   time: 4:26:48
=========================================================================

12345.. and again ..12345.. counting backwards ..54321.. and again ..54321..
about time too ..
4:27:14
4:27:15
4:27:16
4:27:17
4:27:18
4:27:19
4:27:20
4:27:21
4:27:22
4:27:23
4:27:24
```

NOW DO THIS▶   Modify program `Example_1`.

(1) Input the number of numbers to add together.

(2) Replace the `while` loop with a `for` loop, and detect from the information given in (1) when all the numbers have been input.

(3) Calculate and display the arithmetic mean of the numbers.

5.6   Which Loop?

By now you should understand the syntax and semantics of the three loop structures `while`, `do..while`, and `for`. Any task that can be accomplished with one of these loop constructs can also be accomplished with either of the others—we say that they have equivalent power. However, each of the approaches expresses the loop control in a different fashion, and in any given programming situation that requires a loop there is usually a "best" choice for loop structure.

While

The first statement in a `while` loop contains a condition to exit from the loop. This condition guards entry into the loop. If the guarding condition evaluates to false, then entry into the loop will be denied, and the loop body will not be executed at all. Whenever there is the possibility that you do not want the program to execute the statements within the body of the loop, you should use the `while` loop structure.

In this example an input data string from a dialog box is used to control entry into the loop.

```
input.showDialogBox();
String inputData = input.getString();
while (! inputData.equals(sentinel))
{
    .
    .
    .

    input.showDialogBox();
    inputData = input.getString();
}
```

Notice that when data is used to control entry into a loop, it is necessary to read ahead for data in order to test the guarding conditional statement. It is also necessary to include a second read statement within the body of the loop to supply data for testing the conditional statement.

Do..while

The feature of this loop is that it is not guarded by any condition, and the computer will always execute the statements within the loop at least once. This feature can be useful when validating data. In the following example, the body of the loop will continue to be executed until a number that lies within the range 0..100 is input from a dialog box.

```
do
{
    screen.write("input a number in the range 0..100 ");
    input.showDialogBox();
    number = input.getInteger();
} while (number < 0 || number > 100);
```

For

When a loop is to be controlled by some type of counter and both the initial and final values of the counter are known before the execution of the loop begins, the best choice is the `for` loop. In the following example, we want to write out the squares of the first 10 integers.

```
start = 1;  finish = 10;
for (int counter = start; counter <= finish; counter++)
{
    screen.write(counter + "\t" + (counter*counter));
}
```

5.7 Arrays Revisited

Consider for a moment how you would store five integer values in the memory of the computer. One solution is to create five variable names and assign a value to each variable. For example,

```
int number1 = 54;
int number2 = 26;
int number3 = 99;
int number4 = -25;
int number5 = 13;
```

If you adopted the same approach to storing 50 integer values, then the coding would become quite tedious. A better approach is to store the numbers in a one-dimensional array. This will lead to a reduction in the amount of code you need to write.

What do we already know about an array? A one-dimensional array was first introduced in Chapter 2 in the context of passing command-line arguments to the `main` method of a class. You may recall the following points from the work covered in the previous three chapters.

- An array is an implicit class of Java. In other words, Java arrays are objects.

- You may visualize an array as a set of numbered pigeon holes, each containing data of the same type.

- The first pigeon hole is always numbered as 0 (zero). Subsequent holes are numbered 1, 2, etc. A programmer must be careful of "off by one" errors when using arrays.

- An array may store both primitive data and objects such as an array of integers or an array of strings.

- The declaration of an array has the format `type[] arrayName` and may be initialized with data at the point of declaration; for example:

```
String[] reply        = {"continue","quit"};
int[]    chosenCities = {0,2,5};
```

- The length of an array may be found by using the implicit instance variable `length`. In the examples above, `reply.length` is 2 and `chosenCities.length` is 3.

■ Each element of data stored in an array can be accessed by the name of the array and the numbered index indicating the position of the data within the array. For example, `args[0]` and `args[1]` represent the first and second elements of the array declared as `String[] args` as the formal parameter of the `main` method.

5.8   Declaring and Initializing One-Dimensional Arrays

Three Methods

There are three approaches to declaring and initializing arrays. We briefly introduce them here, and revisit each of them later in examples. To simplify our approach, let's concentrate on declaring and initializing an integer array to hold the five values 54, 26, 99, −25, and 13.

Method 1   Declaring the array and instantiating the array as separate steps. As with other Java objects, we can declare an array with one statement and instantiate it later using the `new` operation.

Method 2   As with other Java objects, we can combine the declaration and instantiation of an array into a single statement. Methods 1 and 2 are shown in the following code fragments:

```
Method 1:

int[] numbers;
numbers = new int[5];
```

```
Method 2:

int[] numbers = new int[5];
```

Figure 5.5 illustrates the results of these statements. The first part of the figure shows what memory looks like after statement 1 of Method 1 is executed. The second part of the figure shows what memory looks like in either case, after the `new` command is used. Notice that the `int[] numbers` statement has created only one memory location to represent the identifier `numbers`. This location is automatically initialized to the value `null` indicated by a slash in the memory location for `numbers`. In order to allocate space for storing integers, it is necessary to use the `new` keyword and specify an amount of memory to allocate for the storage of, in this example, five integers. In the second part of Figure 5.5, each allocated memory cell is indexed with a value from 0 to 4, and the contents of the five cells have automatically been initialized to zero. Notice that the five cells are pointed at or referenced by the identifier `numbers`.

The syntax for the declaration of a one-dimensional array follows.

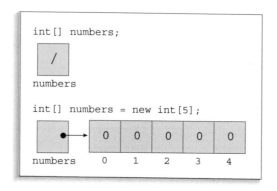

Figure 5.5 Declaration of an array of integers

SYNTAX

••

One-Dimensional Array Declaration:

```
type-specifier [] array-name =
  new type-specifier[ number-of-cells ];
```

Once the array has been instantiated, values can be inserted into the array using the assignment statement. As you might have guessed from our previous use of the `args` array, we can reference a specific element of an array by using the name of the array object, followed by the index of the array we wish to reference enclosed in brackets. So, the following code will "finish" the task we set ourselves for both Method 1 and Method 2 of array declaration:

```
numbers[1] = 54;
numbers[2] = 26;
numbers[3] = 99;
numbers[4] = -25;
numbers[5] = 13;
```

Figure 5.6 shows how the array looks after the assignment statements have been executed.

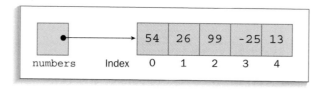

Figure 5.6 Conceptual representation of numbers in an array

Method 3   This is probably the easiest approach to declaring, instantiating, and initializing an array object. It combines all three into a single Java statement. As we have done for other Java types and objects, we can provide the initial set of values on the same line as the declaration, as follows:

```
int[] numbers = {54,26,99,-25,13}
```

Since the compiler can count the number of items of data in the list, there is no need to explicitly state how much memory to allocate in order to store the numbers. Again, Figure 5.5 illustrates how to conceptualize the storage of the five numbers in the array.

The syntax for the declaration of a one-dimensional array is modified as follows.

SYNTAX

....

One-Dimensional Array Declaration and Initialization:

        type-specifier [] *array-name* = { *list of numbers* };

In program `Example_6` that follows, the array `numbers` is declared and initialized as in Method 3. The numbers in the array are then displayed on the screen.

```
import avi.*;

class Example_6
{
      public static void main(String[] args)
      {
          Window screen = new
          Window("Example_6.java");
          screen.showWindow();

          // store integers in a one-dimensional array
          int[] numbers = {54,26,99,-25,13};

          // display numbers
          screen.write("cell 0 contains "+numbers[0]+"\n");
          screen.write("cell 1 contains "+numbers[1]+"\n");
          screen.write("cell 2 contains "+numbers[2]+"\n");
          screen.write("cell 3 contains "+numbers[3]+"\n");
          screen.write("cell 4 contains "+numbers[4]+"\n");
      }
}
```

The contents of the log file from the program being executed follows.

```
==========================================================================
                    L  O  G        F  I  L  E
          audio-visual interface [avi] - Release 1.0 - by Barry Holmes
            filename: Example_6.java   date: 3/12/2000   time: 4:29:32
==========================================================================


cell 0 contains 54
cell 1 contains 26
cell 2 contains 99
cell 3 contains -25
cell 4 contains 13
```

5.9   Using Arrays

The original idea of introducing an array to store integers was to reduce the amount of coding required to assign numbers to memory and output the numbers from memory. The previous program hardly inspires confidence that the original idea can be implemented! All it proves is that the same name `numbers`, using a different index value from 0 through to 4, can be used in place of the five different names. The program was introduced only to show you that it is possible to explicitly access any cell in the array.

Suppose we wanted to write a program where the values to be placed in the array were provided by the user through a slider box. We could continue to use the brute-force approach as in the previous program, that is, writing explicit code with a literal index for each element of the array. But that is not a very elegant approach, especially if the array is large. To reduce the amount of coding, it is necessary to replace the explicit use of the index by a control variable identifier. Instead of explicitly coding `numbers[0]`, `numbers[1]`, `numbers[2]`, `numbers[3]`, and `numbers[4]`, it is far easier to use `numbers[index]` and embed this statement in a `for` loop that changes the value of `index` from 0 to 4. For example, integers can be input from a slider and stored in an array using

```
for (int index=0; index != 5; index++)
{
    screen.write("Input number into cell "+index+"\n");
    input.showSlider();
    screen.clearTextArea();
    numbers[index] = input.getValue();
}
```

and the contents of each cell of the array can be displayed on the screen using

```
for (int index=0; index != 5; index++)
{
     screen.write("Cell "+index+" contains "+ numbers[index]+"\n");
}
```

where the array `numbers` was declared in Figure 5.6. In this declaration, the number of cells in the array was explicitly coded as 5.

> *i*   A good programming practice is to replace the numeric literal that defines the number of cells in the array with a constant. Consequently, if the size of the array changes, the only statement in the program that needs to be modified is the declaration of the constant. However, whenever possible you should use the implicit instance variable `length` to specify the size of an array.

The declaration should be modified to include

```
// size of array
static final int SIZE = 5;

// declaration of the array
int[] numbers = new int[SIZE];
```

The next program demonstrates using a constant `SIZE` to define the size of the array, and a loop control variable `index` to refer to the position of the individual cells within the array. Notice in this program that the constant `SIZE` is also used in the `for` loops to detect when the loop control variable `index` is about to go out of range.

```
import avi.*;

class Example_7
{
     public static void main(String[] args)
     {
          Window screen = new
          Window("Example_7.java","bold","blue",36);
          screen.showWindow();

          Slider input = new Slider(screen,"Number?",-100,+100,1);

          // declare constant size of array
          final int SIZE = 5;
```

```
// declare one-dimensional array
int[] numbers = new int[SIZE];

// input numbers
for (int index=0; index != SIZE; index++)
{
      screen.write("\n\n\tinput number into cell "+index+"\n");
      input.showSlider();
      screen.clearTextArea();
      numbers[index] = input.getValue();
}

// display contents of the array
for (int index=0; index != SIZE; index++)
{
      screen.write("\tcell "+index+" contains "+
                  numbers[index]+"\n");
}
    }
}
```

A screen shot of the running program follows.

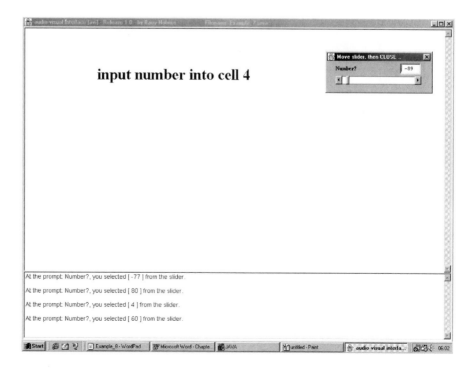

The contents of the log file from the program being executed follows.

```
=====================================================================
                    L  O  G      F  I  L  E
        audio-visual interface [avi] - Release 1.0 - by Barry Holmes
            filename: Example_7.java  date: 3/13/2000   time: 6:2:13
=====================================================================


     input number into cell 0
At the prompt: Number?, you selected [ -77 ] from the slider.

     input number into cell 1
At the prompt: Number?, you selected [ 80 ] from the slider.

     input number into cell 2
At the prompt: Number?, you selected [ 4 ] from the slider.

     input number into cell 3
At the prompt: Number?, you selected [ 60 ] from the slider.

     input number into cell 4
At the prompt: Number?, you selected [ -89 ] from the slider.


     cell 0 contains -77
     cell 1 contains 80
     cell 2 contains 4
     cell 3 contains 60
     cell 4 contains -89
```

The use of a `for` statement to control the index to an array is not confined to input and output but can also be used to compare data between cells. In this next program, five numbers are stored in an array, and the contents of the array are inspected to find the largest number.

The `for` loop controls the index so that it is possible to gain access to consecutive items of data and compare each item with the largest number found so far.

```
largest = numbers[0];
for (int index=1; index != SIZE; index++)
    if (numbers[index] > largest) largest = numbers[index];
```

The variable `largest` is assigned the first value in the array. The control variable identifier is then set to access the remaining cells in the array. If a number in one of these cells is greater than the current value of the variable `largest`, then `largest` is assigned this value.

```java
import avi.*;

class Example_8
{
      public static void main(String[] args)
      {
            Window screen = new
            Window("Example_8.java","bold","blue",36);
            screen.showWindow();

            Slider input = new Slider(screen,"Number?",-100,+100,1);

            // declare constant size of array
            final int SIZE = 5;
            // declare one-dimensional array
            int[] numbers = new int[SIZE];

            // input numbers
            for (int index=0; index != SIZE; index++)
            {
                  screen.write("\n\n\tinput number into cell "+index+"\n");
                  input.showSlider();
                  screen.clearTextArea();
                  numbers[index] = input.getValue();
            }

            // display contents of the array
            for (int index=0; index != SIZE; index++)
            {
                  screen.write("\tcell "+index+" contains "+
                              numbers[index]+"\n");
            }

            // find largest number in array
            int largest = numbers[0];
            for (int index=1; index != SIZE; index++)
                  if (numbers[index] > largest) largest = numbers[index];

            screen.write("\n\tlargest number in the array is "+largest);
      }
}
```

A screen shot of the running program follows.

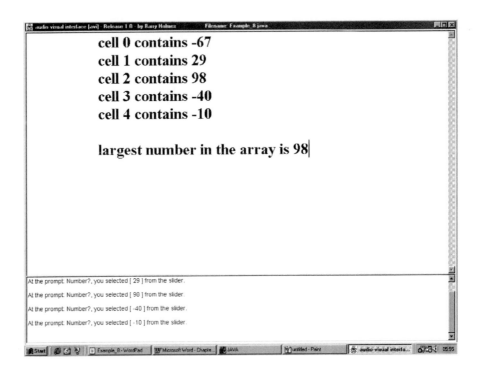

In the previous examples, the size of the array was stated at the time of writing the program. This need not always be the case. In Java it is possible to postpone assigning a value for the size of an array until program execution. By doing this you create a *dynamic array* and hence tailor the storage requirements to the amount of data available, as shown in `Example_9`. In this program the user enters the size of the array and each of the numbers to be inserted into the array, and the program outputs the arithmetic mean of the set of numbers.

```
import avi.*;

class Example_9
{
      public static void main(String[] args)
      {
            Window screen = new Window("Example_9.java","bold","blue",36);
            DialogBox inputSize = new DialogBox(screen,"Size of array?");
            Slider input = new Slider(screen,"Number?",-100,+100,1);
```

```
int sizeOfArray;
int sum = 0;

screen.showWindow();

// input size of array
do
{
    inputSize.showDialogBox();
    sizeOfArray = inputSize.getInteger();
} while (sizeOfArray < 1);

// declare one-dimensional array
int[] numbers = new int[sizeOfArray];

// input numbers
for (int index=0; index != sizeOfArray; index++)
{
    screen.write("\n\n\tinput number into cell "+index);
    input.showSlider();
    screen.clearTextArea();
    numbers[index] = input.getValue();
}

// display contents of the array
for (int index=0; index != sizeOfArray; index++)
{
    screen.write("\tcell "+index+" contains "+
                 numbers[index]+"\n");
}

// find arithmetic mean of numbers in array
for (int index=0; index != sizeOfArray; index++)
{
    sum = sum + numbers[index];
}

screen.write("\n\tarithmetic mean of numbers in array is "+
             (float)sum/sizeOfArray);
    }
}
```

A screen shot of the running program follows.

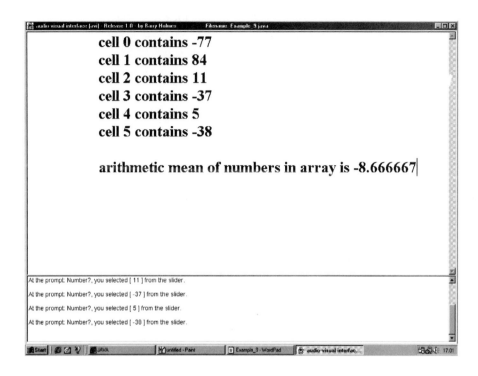

NOW DO THIS   Using `Example_8` and `Example_9` for reference, write a program to:

(1) Declare an array of maximum size 20 to store real numbers.

(2) Input any number of real numbers up to a maximum of 20, and store these numbers in the array. Terminate the numbers being input with a sentinel of zero.

(3) Find and display the maximum and minimum numbers in the array.

(4) Calculate and display the arithmetic mean of the numbers in the array.

Let's review the following points regarding one-dimensional arrays.

■ The contents of the array must be of the same data type. In other words, an array can contain all integers or all reals or all characters or all strings, but not a mixture of types.

■ Each item in the array is stored in a separate cell. If an array contained five integers, then each integer would occupy a single cell.

- Each cell has a unique location value that shows the cell's position within the array. This location is known as an index and starts at value 0.

- The array is given one name, no matter the number of items it contains.

- Before an array can be used, it must be declared like any other variable.

- Like other objects, an array must also be instantiated, either with the `new` operator or from a set of initial values provided by the programmer on the declaration line.

- An item of data within a cell is accessed by using the name of the array followed by the position, index, or subscript, within square brackets.

CASE STUDY

Palindrome

Statement of the Problem Write a program to test for a word being a palindrome, that is, a word spelled the same way forward and backward.

Identification of Classes and Methods

A noun analysis of the problem identifies three candidate classes—*program*, *word*, and *palindrome*. Of these, *program* and *word* appear to be the most plausible. The *palindrome* is what we are testing for, and might be a better candidate as a method. The class program is `Example_10` and contains statements to test the constructor and methods of the class `Word`.

A verb analysis on the problem identifies two candidate methods—*write* and *test*. Of these, *test* is the most obvious, and since you are testing a word for being a palindrome, we will elect to call this method `palindrome`. Figure 5.7 illustrates the class representation.

Algorithm Development

The first question to ask is, How should we analyze individual characters in a string? Java classes are very comprehensive, and it should come as no surprise that there is a method in the `String` class that will convert a string to individual characters stored in separate cells of a one-dimensional array. The method is `toCharArray()`. To convert a string contained by the object `datum` to individual characters stored in the one-dimensional array `characterArray`, the following code is required.

```
char[] characterArray = datum.toCharArray();
```

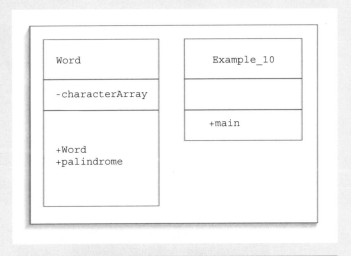

Figure 5.7 UML representation of classes

In testing a word for being a palindrome, is the word `Radar` equivalent to the word `RADAR`? If it is meant to be the same, then all the characters in the word must be converted to uppercase. The statement to store a word as single characters in each cell of an array can be modified to capitalize all alphabetic characters:

```
char[] characterArray = datum.toUpperCase().toCharArray();
```

This statement first creates a temporary string consisting of the characters of `datum` in all uppercase, then creates an array of characters out of the separate characters of this uppercase string, and finally assigns the reference in the variable `characterArray` to "point to" this array of characters.

We can now start to piece together the class `Word` as follows.

```
public class Word
{
    // instance variable
    private char[] characterArray;

    // constructor
    public Word(String datum)
    {
        characterArray = datum.toUpperCase().toCharArray();
```

```
                }

                .
                .
}
```

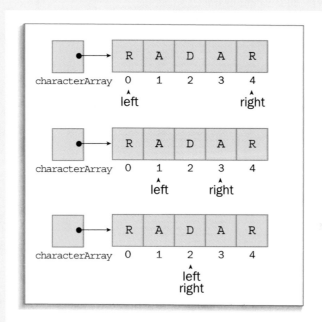

Figure 5.8 Comparison of characters in the array

The method used to test the `datum` for being a palindrome is to inspect the characters at either end of the word. If these characters are the same, then the next two characters at either end of the word are compared. The comparisons continue until there is no match between the characters or there are no further comparisons possible. The movement of the indexes is shown in Figure 5.8. Notice that when both indexes indicate the same array element, there is really no need to do a character comparison since you would just be comparing a character to itself.

In assigning `left` and `right` to the first and last indexes in the array, it is necessary to know the length of the array. In this example the expression `characterArray.length` will return the value 5, since there are five cells in the array. Assigning values to `left` and `right` becomes

```
left = 0;
right = characterArray.length-1;
```

Since the array is indexed from 0 (zero) it is necessary to deduct 1 from the length of the array in calculating a value for the `right` index.

The pseudocode for the algorithm to test a word for being a palindrome can be expressed as follows.

1. initialize left and right indexes
2. while left index is less than right index
3.   if left character equals right character
4.   move left index one cell to the right
5.   move right index one cell to the left
6.   else
7.   characters do not match
8. characters match

The pseudocode can be converted into the following instance method.

```java
public boolean palindrome()
{
      int left=0;
      int right = characterArray.length-1;

      // compare characters in the word
      while (left < right)
      {
            if (characterArray[left] == characterArray[right])
            {
                  left++;
                  right--;
            }
            else
            {
                  return false;
            }
      }

      return true;
}
```

Notice that as soon as a mismatch of characters is encountered, the `return false` statement will be executed, ending the method and returning the value false. But if no mismatch of characters is ever encountered, then the `return true` statement will be executed instead.

Testing

This is a good chance to discuss test data selection. Identifying a reasonable set of test data for desk checking and program run-time checking is crucial for successful software development. Normally, it is impossible to test a program on all potential inputs, so we must think carefully about the test cases we have time to use.

If possible, consider different dimensions of the input to your program and try to identify subclasses along each of those dimensions. The subclasses are meant to group together similar test cases so that if your program works correctly for a few of the test cases in a subclass, it will probably work correctly for all the rest of the possible input from that subclass.

In the current example we can list three dimensions of the input, with subclasses, as follows:

1. Length of word—1, 2, 3, 4, …, 20 characters long; alternatively, we could identify the subclasses as long, short, even number of letters, odd number of letters.
2. Expected result—palindromes and nonpalindromes.
3. Case used—all lowercase, all uppercase, mixed case.

This suggests the following robust set of test cases, with the palindromes on the left:

a	aaA	az
b	poop	bat
z	radar	suds
aa	RotaTOR	sUds
bb	AmanAPlanACanalPanama	Java

The test data we will use to desk check the instance method `palindrome` are *radar* and *suds*. The desk check would be as follows:

palindrome()			true			false	
datum	radar			suds			
characterArray	RADAR			SUDS			
left	0	1	2	0	1		
right	4	3	2	3	2		
(left<right)?	true	true	false	true	true		
characterArray[left]	R	A		S	U		
characterArray[right]	R	A		S	D		
(characterArray[left] == characterArray[right])?	true	true		true	false		

In the first test, the word *radar* is a palindrome, and the characters match; in the second test, the word *suds* is not a palindrome, since the characters u and d do not match.

A listing of the complete `Word` class follows.

```
public class Word
{
    // instance variable
    char[] characterArray;

    // constructor
    /**
    The Word class enables an object that represents a string
    of characters to be created.
    @param datum is a string of characters
    */
    public Word(String datum)
    {
        characterArray = datum.toUpperCase().toCharArray();
    }

    // instance method
    /**
    Inspects the characters of a word and determines whether the
    word is a palindrome.
    @return true if the word is a palindrome, otherwise returns false.
    */
    public boolean palindrome()
    {
        int left=0;
        int right = characterArray.length-1;

        // compare characters in the word
        while (left < right)
        {
            if (characterArray[left] == characterArray[right])
            {
                left++;
                right--;
            }
            else
            {
                return false;
            }
        }

        return true;
    }
}
```

The class `Example_10` is used to test the constructor and instance method of the class `Word`. The pseudocode design for this class follows.

```
 1. create and show window object screen
 2. create dialog box object to input word
 3. create radio buttons object to continue or quit
 4. do
 5.      show dialog box
 6.      get input string from dialog box
 7.      instantiate word object from input string
 8.      if word is a palindrome
 9.           display message to confirm
10.      else
11.           display message to reject
12.      show radio buttons
13. while reply to continue
14. close window and exit
```

From the pseudocode it is possible to determine which classes `Example_10` is dependent upon for its implementation. These are depicted in Figure 5.9.

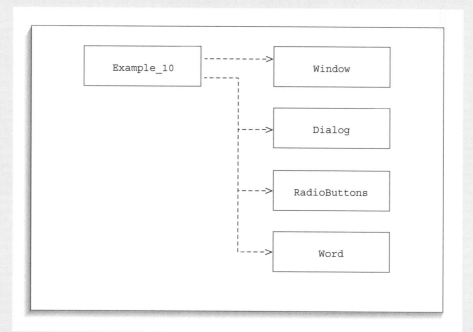

Figure 5.9 UML representation of dependencies

```
// case study - palindrome

import avi.*;

class Example_10
{
    public static void main(String[] args)
    {
        Window screen = new
        Window("Example_10.java","bold+italic","black",24);
        screen.showWindow();

        DialogBox inputWord = new DialogBox(screen,"Word?");

        String[] reply = {"continue","quit"};
        RadioButtons buttons = new
        RadioButtons(screen,"What next?",reply);

        String datum;
        Word word;

        do
        {
            // input word
            inputWord.showDialogBox();
            datum = inputWord.getString();
            word = new Word(datum);

            // check for palindrome
            if (word.palindrome())
                screen.write(datum+" is a palindrome\n");
            else
                screen.write(datum+" is NOT a palindrome\n");

            // request to continue or quit
            buttons.showRadioButtons();

        }while (buttons.getNameOfButton().equals("continue"));

        screen.closeWindowAndExit();
    }
}
```

A screen shot of the running program follows.

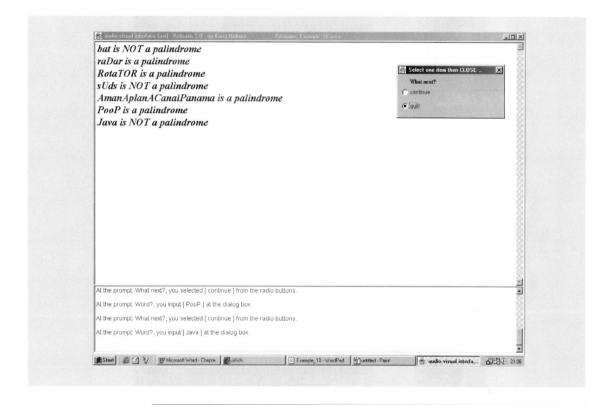

NOW DO THIS▶   The dictionary definition of a palindrome is "a word or *phrase* that reads the same backwards as forwards (e.g. rotator, *nurses run*). Modify the Case Study: Palindrome to cater for phrases as well as individual words being read from a text file.

5.10   Our Last AVI Class: CheckBoxes

The final `avi` class is the `CheckBox` class. Whereas the `RadioButtons` class allowed for only one selection from a list of items, the `CheckBox` class will allow for the selection of *more than one item* from a set list of items.

The CheckBox Class

A `CheckBox` object is illustrated in Figure 5.10. In the sections that follow you will be shown how to include a currency sign for the country in which you are using an application program. Figure 5.10 was the output from a program being run in the UK. As you will see later, if you run the same program in the USA then the £ currency sign will automatically be replaced by a $ currency sign.

The `CheckBox` class contains the following constructor and public instance methods.

Figure 5.10 A `CheckBox` object from the `avi` package

```
public class CheckBoxes
{
      public CheckBoxes(Window parent,
                        String prompt,
                        String[] itemsInList);

      public void showCheckBoxes();
      public boolean[] getCheckedBoxes();
}
```

To create a check-box object you must use the class constructor that requires three items of data in the formal parameter list:

parent—a `Window` type that specifies the container on which to display a check box object.

prompt—a string that is used as a cue to inform the user of the nature of the selection. For example, in Figure 5.10 the cue is "Ben's Breakfast Bar Menu."

itemsInList—a string array containing a list of all the names of the check boxes. For example, in Figure 5.10, if you only wanted the names of the food and beverages displayed and not the prices, the itemsInList argument would have been declared as the array:

```
String[] food = {"Eggs", "Blueberry Pancakes", "Bagels with Cream Cheese",
                 "English Muffin", "Yogurt", "Corned Beef Hash", "Toast",
                 "Fries", "Tea", "Coffee", "Hot Chocolate"};
```

Assuming that you have already created a screen window and the food array, then the CheckBoxes constructor may be coded as:

```
CheckBoxes menu = new CheckBoxes(screen,"Ben's Breakfast Bar Menu",food);
```

The check boxes are displayed on the screen using the instance method showCheckBoxes(); for example:

```
menu.showCheckBoxes();
```

After using the mouse-pointer to check (or uncheck) any number of items, the check-boxes window is closed to indicate that data selection is complete. The selected items are returned as being true within a boolean array by the instance method getCheckedBoxes(). The boolean array contains the same number of cells as there are items in the check-boxes list, with the first cell representing the first item in the list, the second cell the second item in the list, and so on. For each item selected in the check-boxes list, the corresponding cell in the boolean array is set to true (those not selected remain at false).

If a boolean array is declared as follows:

```
boolean[] choice;
```

then this array may be used to represent the selected items from the check boxes by the statement:

```
choice = menu.getCheckedBoxes();
```

In Figure 5.10, items that have been checked for selection are in the first, seventh, and ninth positions in the check boxes list. The cells in the corresponding array choice will be set to true, representing this selection. Remember that array indexing begins with 0. See Figure 5.11.

We can use the following code to inspect each cell of the array choice and display on the screen which of the boxes have been checked.

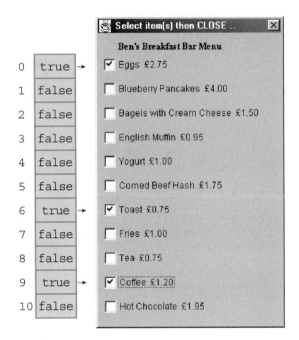

Contents of `boolean` array
set `true` for each box that is
checked (ticked)

Figure 5.11 An illustration of how the selected check boxes are represented by a `boolean`
array

```
for (int index=0; index != food.length; index++)
{
      if (choice[index]) screen.write(food[index]+"\n");
}
```

The above examples are used in our next case study.

5.11 Formatting Numbers for Output

To be useful, the output from a program should be easy to read. For example, if
a program outputs a large number, it might important for the number to be separated by commas at the appropriate places.

There are several standard Java library classes to help us format output. In
this section we will take a brief look at one of these: the `NumberFormat` class.
You can study this class in detail by examining the documentation available with
the Java 2 SDK environment.

The `NumberFormat` class helps us format numbers in a local, specific way. It is an abstract class, which means we will not instantiate an instance of the class using the `new` command. Instead, we will obtain a number-formatting object through one of the `static` class methods provided by the class. We will learn more about abstract classes in the next chapter. For now it will suffice to learn how to use the `NumberFormat` class to let us format the output of money and percentage data.

Three steps are needed for using the `NumberFormat` class:

1. Import the class from the standard text library.

2. Obtain a number formatting object using one of the "get" methods.

3. Apply the number formatting object to a specific number.

Each of these will be explained in turn, and they are all shown in `Example_11`. To import the class, simply include the statement

```
import java.text.NumberFormat;
```

at the top of your program.

There are several methods exported from the `NumberFormat` class that can be used to obtain a number-formatting object. The two we are most interested in are the `getPercentInstance` and the `getCurrencyInstance` methods. These will return an object that allows us to format numbers according to the local conventions for printing percentages or currency. For example, if the latter method is used on a computer in the United States, the final printed results will be in dollars ($), but if it is used in the United Kingdom, the results will be in pounds (£). An example of a statement to establish currency formatting is

```
NumberFormat outFormat = NumberFormat.getCurrencyInstance();
```

Once the number formatting object is obtained, it can be used to format numbers by passing the number to be formatted to its `format` method as follows:

```
outFormat.format(456.783f);
```

which will take the number 456.783 of type `float` and change it into a string formatted according to local currency standards.

Study `Example_11` and its output to see how all these things work together.

```
// program to test output format options

import avi.*;
import java.text.NumberFormat;
```

```java
class Example_11
{
      public static void main(String[] args)
      {
            // create a window object screen
            Window screen = new Window("Example_11.java","bold","black",24);

            screen.showWindow();

            float a = 52435.26f, b = 12f, c = -132.5f, d = 0.1f;

            screen.write("No formatting");
            screen.write("\n" + a);
            screen.write("\n" + b);
            screen.write("\n" + c);
            screen.write("\n" + d);
            screen.write("\n\n");

            NumberFormat myMoney = NumberFormat.getCurrencyInstance();

            screen.write("Formatted as currency");
            screen.write("\n" + myMoney.format(a));
            screen.write("\n" + myMoney.format(b));
            screen.write("\n" + myMoney.format(c));
            screen.write("\n" + myMoney.format(d));
            screen.write("\n\n");

            NumberFormat myPercent = NumberFormat.getPercentInstance();

            screen.write("Formatted as percent");
            screen.write("\n" + myPercent.format(a));
            screen.write("\n" + myPercent.format(b));
            screen.write("\n" + myPercent.format(c));
            screen.write("\n" + myPercent.format(d));
      }
}
```

The appearance of the output from Example_11 will depend on the configuration of your local computer. Compile and run the program to see how it appears. The NumberFormat class will be used in the case study in the following section.

CASE STUDY

Ben's Breakfast Bar

Statement of the Problem   The menu at Ben's Breakfast Bar is illustrated in Figure 5.12. Write a program to allow a customer to select items from the menu and to place an order for breakfast and be given the tab (bill) for the meal.

Identification of Classes and Methods

The noun and verb analysis works well on this problem, as you are about to discover. The list of nouns from the statement of the problem are *menu*, *program*, *customer*, *order*, *breakfast*, *tab*, and *meal*. Objects in Ben's Breakfast Bar that you can see with your eyes are a *customer* (person); a *menu* (either displayed on a board or as individual menus at tables); an *order* (piece of paper containing an itemized request for food); *breakfast* and *meal* both refer to the food being served; and the *tab* at the end of the meal.

In this problem we are not recording any data about a customer. Had we wanted to record customer details, then customer would have been a viable class, however, in this example the customer's details are not required and, therefore, *customer* is not a valid class.

The menu is used by the customer to select a meal, and may be regarded as a suitable class. Ben may want to change the contents of his menu from time to time; therefore, it is necessary that the class can accommodate a change in the contents of the displayed menu items. This approach also allows the `Menu` class to be more easily used for other restaurants.

Each customer will produce an order that is special to that customer. An order must be regarded as a class, since it will contain a meal based upon the selection from the menu by each

Ben's Breakfast Bar Menu	
Eggs	2.75
Blueberry Pancakes	4.00
Bagels with Cream Cheese	1.50
English Muffin	0.95
Yogurt	1.00
Corned Beef Hash	1.75
Toast	0.75
Fries	1.00
Tea	0.75
Coffee	1.20
Hot Chocolate	1.95

Figure 5.12 Menu at Ben's Breakfast Bar

customer. Within the `Order` class, it must be possible for a customer to state the quantities of food and beverages required.

Since Ben is in business to earn a living, he will present a customer with a tab (bill) at the end of the meal. This is an itemization of the food ordered and the total cost of the meal. For each customer (or group of customers) Ben will write and present a tab; therefore, the tab appears to be a valid candidate class.

We may conclude that suitable candidate classes are *menu*, *order*, *tab*, and the *driver* program, with the four candidate classes being expressed in the problem as the classes `Menu`, `Order`, `Tab`, and `Example_12`.

The list of verbs from the statement of the problem are *write*, *allow*, *select*, *place*, and *given*. From this list, suitable candidate methods are: *select* (from the menu), *place* (an order) and be *given* (the tab). In the context of the classes the verb *select* belongs to the class `Menu`, the verb *place* belongs to the class `Order`, and the verb *given* belongs to the class `Tab`. These verbs can translate into the instance methods `selection` in the class `Menu`, `quantityOrdered` in the class `Order`, and `pickUpTheTab` in the class `Tab`. See Figure 5.13.

Both the `Menu` class and the `Tab` class use the `NumberFormat` class from the `text` package to display the monetary values correctly, and with the appropriate currency sign. Since the output from the program displayed at the end of this section was created on a computer in the U.K., it features the British pound Sterling.

Algorithm Development

The class `Menu` contains two instance variables; the first, `menu`, is a `CheckBoxes` object for displaying the items in the menu and the second, `menuItems`, is a one-dimensional array containing a concatenation of the prices and names of the food and beverage items to be displayed in the check boxes. The class menu also contains two static one-dimensional array variables for storing the names of the foods and the prices of the foods; these are `foodNames` and `foodPrices` respectively.

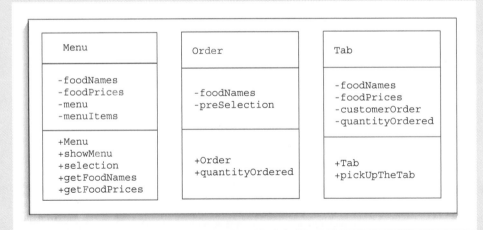

Figure 5.13 UML representation of classes

The constructor for the class `Menu` creates a `CheckBoxes` object containing the prices and names of the food and beverages. The instance method `selection` returns a one-dimensional boolean array indicating those items that have been selected by the user from the menu.

The class menu also contains static class methods to return the names of the foods and the prices of the foods.

```java
import avi.*;
import java.text.NumberFormat;

public class Menu
{

    // instance variables
    private CheckBoxes menu;
    private String[] menuItems;

    // class (static) variables
    private static String[] foodNames;
    private static float[] foodPrices;

    // constructor
    /**
    The Menu class enables an object to be created that represents a
    menu of food and beverages. The menu is represented as check boxes.
    @param screen is the container for the check boxes object.
    @param titleOfMenu is the title that appears across the menu.
    @param food is a one-dimensional array containing the names of the
    foods/ beverages that appear on the menu.
    @param prices is a one-dimensional array of the prices of the food
    and beverages.
    */
    public Menu(Window screen, String titleOfMenu,
                String[] food, float[] prices)
    {

        NumberFormat money = NumberFormat.getCurrencyInstance();

        foodNames = new String[food.length];
        foodNames = food;
        foodPrices = new float[prices.length];
        foodPrices = prices;

        menuItems = new String[food.length];
        // concatenate price and food description
        for (int index=0; index != food.length; index++)
        {
```

```
                    menuItems[index] = food[index]+
                "   "+money.format(prices[index]);
            }


        menu = new CheckBoxes(screen, titleOfMenu, menuItems);
    }


// class (static) methods
/**
Get the names of foods on the menu.
@return Returns an array of the names of the foods.
*/
public static String[] getFoodNames()
{
        return foodNames;
}


/**
Get the prices of foods on the menu.
@return Returns an array of the prices of the foods.
*/
public static float[] getFoodPrices()
{
        return foodPrices;
}


// instance methods
/**
Displays the menu on the screen.
*/
public void showMenu()
{
        menu.showCheckBoxes();
}


/**
Stores the checked items as true in a corresponding boolean array.
@return A boolean array with each cell set at true for each
respective check box ticked.
*/
public boolean[] selection()
{
        return menu.getCheckedBoxes();
}
}
```

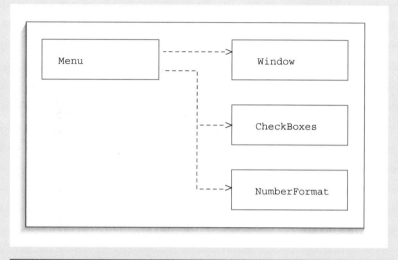

Figure 5.14 UML dependencies

Notice that the class `Menu` is dependent upon the classes `Window` and `CheckBoxes` from the `avi` package, and the class `NumberFormat` from the `text` package, as shown in Figure 5.14.

The class `Order` contains a static variable, `foodNames`, a one-dimensional array containing the names of the foods and beverages, and one instance variable, `preSelection`, a one-dimensional boolean array indicating those items that had been preselected by the customer from the menu.

The constructor for this class initializes the array `preSelection`. The instance method `quantityOrdered`, requests a user to input, via a slider, the quantities of food and beverages chosen from the menu. The method `quantityOrdered` returns a one-dimensional array of the quantities ordered for every item displayed in the menu.

```
import avi.*;

public class Order
{
    // instance variable
    private boolean[] preSelection;
    private static String[] foodNames;

    // constructor
    /**
    The Order class enables an object to be created that represents the
    quantities of food/beverages ordered from the menu.
    @param selectedItems is the one-dimensional array containing the
    selected items from the menu.
```

```
        */
        public Order(boolean[] selectedItems)
        {
                preSelection = selectedItems;
                foodNames = Menu.getFoodNames();
        }


        // instance method
        /**
        Stores the quantity of food/ beverages required from the selected
        items.
        @param screen is the container for the slider object
        @return An integer array with each cell corresponding to each of the
        items on the menu, and representing the quantity of food/ beverages
        ordered.
        */
        public int[] quantityOrdered(Window screen)
        {
                int[] quantity = new int[preSelection.length];

                Slider inputQuantity = new Slider(screen,"Quantity?",1,10,1);

                for (int index=0; index != preSelection.length; index++)
                {
                        if (preSelection[index])
                        {
                                screen.write("What quantity of "+foodNames[index]+
                                                " do you want to order?\n");
                                inputQuantity.showSlider();
                                quantity[index] = inputQuantity.getValue();
                        }
                        else
                        {
                                quantity[index] = 0;
                        }
                }

                screen.clearTextArea();

                return quantity;
        }
}
```

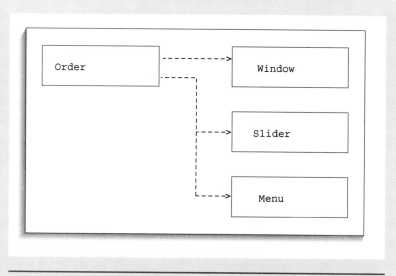

Figure 5.15 UML dependencies

Notice that the class `Order` is dependent upon the classes `Window` and `Slider` from the `avi` package, and the class `Menu`, as shown in Figure 5.15.

The purpose of the class `Tab` is to display an itemized tab on the screen. A typical layout for a tab is illustrated in Figure 5.16.

```
At Ben's Breakfast Bar you ordered:

Eggs 2 @ £2.75 = £5.50
Toast 4 @ £0.75 = £3.00
Coffee 2 @ £1.20 = £2.40


- - - - - - - - - - - - - - - - - - - - -
AMOUNT TO PAY     £10.90
- - - - - - - - - - - - - - - - - - - - -


Thank you - have a nice day.
```

Figure 5.16 An example of a tab

The class `Tab` contains instance variables that represent two one-dimensional arrays, and static variables that also represent two one-dimensional arrays. These arrays are initialized by the constructor to correspond with the quantities of food and beverages ordered and the customer order, and with the names and prices of the food and beverages from the menu, respectively.

   The instance method `pickUpTheTab` displays the tab on the screen in the format depicted in Figure 5.16.

```
import avi.*;
import java.text.NumberFormat;

public class Tab
{
      // instance variable
      boolean[] customerOrder;
      int[] quantityOrdered;

      // static variables
      private static String[] foodNames;
      private static float[] foodPrices;

      // constructor
      /**
      The Tab constructor creates an object from the customer's order for
      displaying as an itemized tab or bill.
      @param quantity is a one-dimensional array of the quantities of
      food/beverages chosen.
      @param choice is a one-dimensional array of the choice of
      food/beverages made by the customer.
      */
      public Tab(int[] quantity, boolean[] choice)
      {
            quantityOrdered = quantity;
            customerOrder = choice;
            foodNames = Menu.getFoodNames();
            foodPrices = Menu.getFoodPrices();
      }

      // instance method
      /**
      The method will display in the text area of the screen a fully
      itemized tab or bill.
      @param screen is the container for the text area on which to display
      the tab.
```

```
        @param name is the name of the bar or restaurant.
        */
        public void pickUpTheTab(Window screen, String name)
        {
                NumberFormat money = NumberFormat.getCurrencyInstance();
                float costOfItems;
                float total=0.0f;

                screen.write("At "+name+" you ordered:\n\n");

                for (int index=0; index != customerOrder.length; index++)
                {
                        if (customerOrder[index])
                        {
                                costOfItems = foodPrices[index]*
                                        quantityOrdered[index];
                                screen.write(foodNames[index]+" "+
                                        quantityOrdered[index]+
                                        " @ "+
                                        money.format(foodPrices[index])+
                                        " = "+
                                        money.format(costOfItems)+"\n");
                                total=total+costOfItems;
                        }
                }

                screen.write("\n-----------------------\n");
                screen.write("AMOUNT TO PAY\t"+money.format(total));
                screen.write("\n-----------------------\n\n");
                screen.write("Thank you - have a nice day.");
        }
}
```

Notice that the class `Tab` is dependent upon the class `Window` from the `avi` package and the class `NumberFormat` from the `text` package, and the `Menu` class, as illustrated in Figure 5.17.

Testing

The test data reflects the choice of meal shown in Figure 5.11. The choice of food from the menu was Eggs, Toast, and Coffee, which is encoded in the `customerOrder` instance variable as follows.

cell index	0	1	2	3	4	5	6	7	8	9	10
customerOrder	true	false	false	false	false	false	true	false	false	true	false

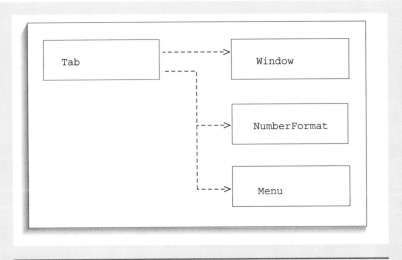

Figure 5.17 UML dependencies for the class Tab

The prices of the foods are stored in a one-dimensional array foodPrices as follows.

cell index	0	1	2	3	4	5	6	7	8	9	10
prices	2.75	4.0	1.5	0.95	1.0	1.75	0.75	1.0	0.75	1.20	1.95

The quantities of food and beverages ordered are stored in the one-dimensional array quantityOrdered as follows.

cell index	0	1	2	3	4	5	6	7	8	9	10
quantity	2	0	0	0	0	0	4	0	0	2	0

Desk check of the method pickUpTab

Index	customerOrder	quantityOrdered	foodPrices	costOfItems	**Total**
0	true	2	2.75	5.50	5.50
1	false				
2	false				
3	false				
4	false				
5	false				
6	true	4	0.75	3.00	8.50
7	false				
8	false				
9	true	2	1.20	2.40	10.90
10	false				

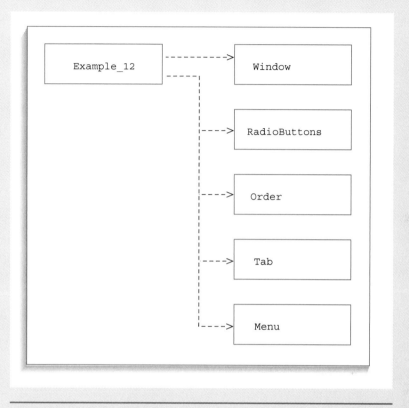

Figure 5.18 UML class dependencies for `Example_12`

The class `Example_12` is used to test the classes `Menu`, `Order`, and `Tab`. This class is constructed from the following algorithm.

1. create and show window object screen
2. create radio buttons object to continue or quit
3. do
4.   clear text area of screen
5.   create menu and select food and beverages
6.   create customer order and select quantities of food and beverages
7.   create customer tab
8.   display tab on the screen
9.   show radio buttons to prompt to continue
10. while request to continue

From the algorithm for class `Example_12` it is possible to list the class dependencies in Figure 5.18. Notice that the class `Example_12` is dependent upon the classes `Window` and

RadioButtons from the avi package and upon Menu, Order, and Tab from the current directory containing the class Example_12.

```java
import avi.*;

class Example_12
{
    static public void main(String[] args)
    {
        final String[] food = {"Eggs","Blueberry Pancakes",
                               "Bagels with Cream Cheese",
                               "English Muffin","Yogurt",
                               "Corned Beef Hash","Toast", "Fries",
                               "Tea","Coffee","Hot Chocolate"};
        final float[] prices = {2.75f,4.0f,1.5f,0.95f,1.0f,1.75f,
                                0.75f,1.0f,0.75f,1.20f,1.95f};

        boolean[] choice = new boolean[food.length];
        int[] quantity = new int[food.length];

        Window screen = new Window("Example_12.java");
        screen.showWindow();

        String[] reply = {"continue","quit"};
        RadioButtons buttons = new
        RadioButtons(screen,"What next?",reply);

        // declare menu, Order and Tab objects
        Menu menu;
        Order order;
        Tab   amount;

        do
        {
            // clear screen
            screen.clearTextArea();

            // instantiate menu
            menu = new Menu(screen, "Ben's Breakfast Bar Menu",
                            food, prices);

            // choose from menu
            menu.showMenu();
            choice = menu.selection();
```

```
                    // instantiate customer order
                    order = new Order(choice);
                    quantity = order.quantityOrdered(screen);

                    // instantiate customer tab
                    amount = new Tab(quantity, choice);

                    // display tab on screen
                    amount.pickUpTheTab(screen,"Ben's Breakfast Bar");

                    // request to continue or quit
                    buttons.showRadioButtons();
              } while (buttons.getNameOfButton().equals("continue"));
      }
}
```

A screen shot from the running program follows.

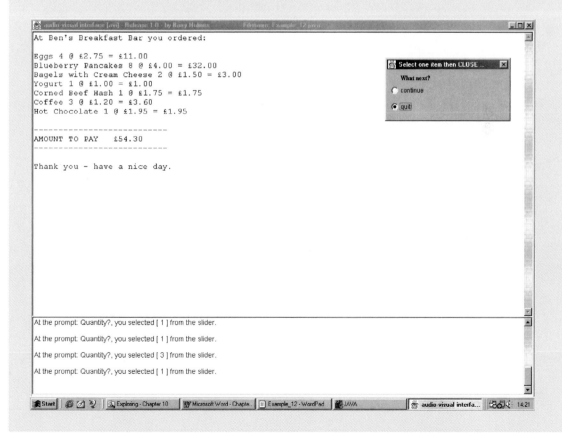

A listing of the log file appears below.

```
==============================================================================
                            L O G      F I L E
            audio-visual interface [avi] - Release 1.0 - by Barry Holmes
               filename: Example_12.java    date: 4/28/2000    time: 1:19:25
==============================================================================


At the prompt: Ben's Breakfast Bar Menu, you selected [ Eggs  £2.75   Toast
£0.75   Coffee   £1.20   ] from the check boxes.

What quantity of Eggs do you want to order?
At the prompt: Quantity?, you selected [ 2 ] from the slider.

What quantity of Toast do you want to order?
At the prompt: Quantity?, you selected [ 4 ] from the slider.

What quantity of Coffee do you want to order?
At the prompt: Quantity?, you selected [ 2 ] from the slider.

At Ben's Breakfast Bar you ordered:

Eggs 2 @ £2.75 = £5.50
Toast 4 @ £0.75 = £3.00
Coffee 2 @ £1.20 = £2.40


- - - - - - - - - - - - - - - - - - - - -
AMOUNT TO PAY      £10.90
- - - - - - - - - - - - - - - - - - - - -


Thank you - have a nice day.At the prompt: What next?, you selected [ con-
tinue ] from the radio buttons.

At the prompt: Ben's Breakfast Bar Menu, you selected [ Eggs  £2.75
Blueberry Pancakes   £4.00  Bagels with Cream Cheese   £1.50  Yogurt   £1.00
Corned Beef Hash   £1.75  Coffee   £1.20   Hot Chocolate   £1.95  ] from the
check boxes.

What quantity of Eggs do you want to order?
At the prompt: Quantity?, you selected [ 4 ] from the slider.

What quantity of Blueberry Pancakes do you want to order?
At the prompt: Quantity?, you selected [ 8 ] from the slider.
```

What quantity of Bagels with Cream Cheese do you want to order?
At the prompt: Quantity?, you selected [2] from the slider.

What quantity of Yogurt do you want to order?
At the prompt: Quantity?, you selected [1] from the slider.

What quantity of Corned Beef Hash do you want to order?
At the prompt: Quantity?, you selected [1] from the slider.

What quantity of Coffee do you want to order?
At the prompt: Quantity?, you selected [3] from the slider.

What quantity of Hot Chocolate do you want to order?
At the prompt: Quantity?, you selected [1] from the slider.

At Ben's Breakfast Bar you ordered:

Eggs 4 @ £2.75 = £11.00
Blueberry Pancakes 8 @ £4.00 = £32.00
Bagels with Cream Cheese 2 @ £1.50 = £3.00
Yogurt 1 @ £1.00 = £1.00
Corned Beef Hash 1 @ £1.75 = £1.75
Coffee 3 @ £1.20 = £3.60
Hot Chocolate 1 @ £1.95 = £1.95

- -
AMOUNT TO PAY   £54.30
- -

Thank you - have a nice day.At the prompt: What next?, you selected [quit] from the radio buttons.

NOW DO THIS   Modify `Example_12` to:

(1) Input the name of a cocktail bar to replace the name Ben's Breakfast Bar at run-time.

(2) Input the names and prices of cocktail drinks at run-time.

(3) Recompile and run the program.

SUMMARY

- The statements within a `while` loop can be executed zero or more times.

- The statements within a `do..while` loop are executed at least once.

- Both the `while` and `do..while` loops use conditional expressions to control the number of repetitions.

- All statements within a `while` loop and a `do..while` loop will be executed while the conditional expression is true.

- Counter variables may be increased or decreased by one by using the postfix increment ++ and the postfix decrement -- operators.

- If the first expression in a `for` loop is omitted, then the initialization (and declaration) of the loop control variable must take place outside of the loop.

- If the second expression in a `for` loop is omitted, then the loop does not terminate unless it contains a `break` statement.

- If the third expression in a `for` loop is omitted, then the loop control variable must be incremented or decremented within the body of the loop.

- By omitting all three expressions from within a `for` loop, it is possible to set up an infinite loop.

- An array is an implicit Java class; hence, an array is an object.

- Storage space is allocated to an array using the keyword `new`.

- The length of an array can be determined through the class variable `length`.

- A one-dimensional array is a data structure that can be used to store data of one type.

- An array is subdivided into cells. Each cell has a unique index value, and the first cell has an index of 0 (zero).

- If the array is static, it is a good practice to declare the number of cells of an array as a constant.

- Access to any item of data in the array is through the name of the array, followed by the position of the data in the array, that is, the index of the cell that contains the data.

- A loop control variable in a `for` statement is a useful way of representing the index of an array. By varying the value of the loop control variable, it is possible to access any cell within the array.

- We can use the `NumberFormat` class to help us format numbers according to local conventions.

Review Questions

1. What is the purpose of a loop?

2. Is the conditional expression true or false upon exiting from a `while` loop?

3. What is the minimum number of times a `do..while` loop can be repeated?

4. How is a sentinel value used to control a `while` loop?

5. State the fundamental operations associated with using a `while` loop as a counter.

6. At what point in the loop does each expression in a `for` statement execute?

7. True or false? The statement `counter=counter-1` is the same as the expression `counter--`.

8. What does the statement `x++` do?

9. What is an infinite loop?

10. True or false? An array stores data of different types.

11. What is an index to an array?

12. Is the index of the first cell in an array always 0?

13. Declare an array `realNumbers` to contain five floating-point numbers.

14. Modify the declaration in Question 13 to initialize the contents of respective cells to the real values 1.0, 2.0, 3.0, 4.0, and 5.0.

15. State an alternative method to that described in Question 14 for the initialization of the array.

16. Write a statement to show how you would display a number in the third cell of the array declared in Question 13.

17. What method in the `String` class is used to store a string as an array of characters?

Exercises

18. Desk check the following `while` loop. What is output from the program segment?

```
int counter = 1;
while (counter < 10)
{
    screen.write("\t" + counter);
    counter = counter + 2;
}
```

19. Desk check the following `do..while` loop using the test data 10, −1, and 9. What is the purpose of the loop?

```
do
{
    input.showDialogBox();
    digit = input.getInteger();
} while (digit < 0 || digit > 9);
```

20. Desk check the following `for` loop. What is output?

```
for (int counter = 0x61; counter <= 0x7A; counter++)
{
    screen.write((char)counter);
}
```

21. Discover the errors in the following segments of code.

    (a)
    ```
    int i = 10;
    while (i > 0);
    {
        screen.write("T minus " + i + " and counting\n");
        i--;
    }
    ```

    (b)
    ```
    for (int i=10; i > 0; i--);
        screen.write("T minus " + i + " and counting\n");
    ```

22. Use a `for` loop to rewrite the following segment of code.

```
int x = 30;
while (x >= 3)
{
    screen.write(x+"\n");
    x--;
}
```

23. Figure 5.19 illustrates the steps required to convert the decimal number 3947 to the hexadecimal number F6B.

    Design an algorithm, using pseudocode, to convert a decimal number to a hexadecimal number. Desk check your answer with the data shown in Figure 5.19.

24. Desk check the following segment of code. What is the final value of the identifier `value`?

```
int[] alpha = {-10,16,19,-15,20};
int value = 0;

for (int index=0; index != 5; index++)
    value = value + alpha[index];
```

25. What is the result of `alpha[3]-alpha[1]` in the array declared in Question 24?

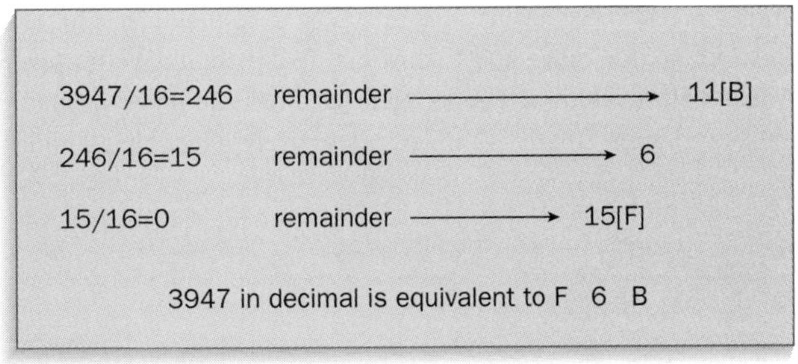

Figure 5.19 Conversion of a decimal to a hexadecimal

26. What is the error in the following segment of code?

```
char[] string = "abracadabra";
```

27. Given the declaration

```
String data = "Ten green bottles standing on the wall.";
```

describe the functionality of the following statement:

```
char [] string = data.toCharArray();
```

28. What is the value of `string.length` for the string declared in Question 27.

29. Desk check the following code and determine the final contents of the array.

```
int[] numbers = {5,2,8,7,0,3};
int left = 0;
int right = numbers.length()-1;

while (left <= right)
{
    numbers[right] = numbers[left];
    left++;
    right--;
}
```

Programming Problems

30. Write a program that uses a loop to display the message Hello, World 10 times on the screen.

31. Write a program to input a message of your choice and the number of times you want to repeat it; then display the message repeatedly.

32. Write a program to output a table of conversion from miles to kilometers. The table should contain column headings for miles and kilometers. Miles should be output as integer values between 1 and 50, in steps of 1 mile. New headings should be printed at the beginning of the table and after 20 and 40 miles, respectively. Note that 1 mile = 1.609344 kilometers.

33. Write a program using `while` loops to output the following:

    (a) The odd integers in the range 1 to 29

    (b) The squares of even integers in the range 2 to 20

    (c) The sum of the squares of the odd integers between 1 and 13

    (d) The alphabet in lowercase—without using the `toLowerCase` method

34. Repeat Question 33 using `for` loops.

35. Repeat Question 33 using `do..while` loops.

36. Write a class containing a `main` method to use a `do..while` loop for the validation of data from a dialog box. Use a `Memo` object to inform that the data is not legal.

37. Modify `Example_3`, the die rolling program, to check for pairs of dice that have the same value when rolled. You should announce only when the values are the same.

38. Write a new die rolling program to record the frequency of occurrence of each die as it is rolled. Create an array of these frequencies and display the contents of the array after:

    (a) 600 throws

    (b) 6,000 throws

    (c) 6,000,000 throws.

    Note you are not expected to use any audio-visual classes in this problem apart from the `Window` class.

39. Return to the Body-Mass Index Case Study from Chapter 4. Modify `Example_8` to input the data for many people, and store the frequency of people who fall into each of the four categories specified in Figure 4.11. At the end of the program, display the frequency analysis for each weight category.

40. Invent a `MultiplicationTable` class. You supply a positive nonzero integer N to the constructor, and a method within the class displays the multiplication table from N times 1 up to N times 12.

41. Return your answer to Question 23. Write a program to input a positive integer number and convert the value to a hexadecimal number. *Hint:* Since the solution will require you to display a number starting with the least significant digit through to the most significant digit, you will need to use the escape sequence \r (carriage return) to move the cursor to the beginning of a line without advancing to a new line.

Class	Carats
A	>100
B	>65
C	>35
D	>15
E	>5
F	<=5

Figure 5.20 Diamond classification

42. A diamond merchant has recently received a consignment of stones. The diamonds are to be categorized by weight according to Figure 5.20. At the end of the weighing, the merchant requires a print-out of the total number of stones in each category and the percentage weight of each category. Assume that the electronic scale the merchant uses is calibrated in milligrams. Write a program to input the weights of the diamonds and output the required statistics. *Note:* 200 mg is equivalent to 1 carat (SI).

43. You plan to take a walking holiday in the Canadian Rockies. The trip is expected to last five days (unless the bears get you!). From your map of the area, you measure the distances you want to walk each day. The Canadian map is metric, with 1 centimeter equivalent to 0.78 kilometers. You estimate that because of the mountainous terrain your average speed of walking will be 1.5 miles per hour (you think in miles per hour, not kilometers per hour!).

    Your task is to estimate how many miles you will walk each day and how long it will take you. Calculate the total distance you will have traveled by the end of the holiday and the total time you will spend walking between daily destinations. *Note:* 1 kilometer is equivalent to 0.625 miles.

    Computerize the process of estimating the distances and times.

    Write a program to input the map distances traveled on each leg of the journey and calculate the actual distances in miles and the time to walk between destinations.

44. Write a program to store the alphabet as characters in an array. The program should display

    (a) The entire alphabet

    (b) The first six characters of the alphabet

    (c) The last 10 characters of the alphabet

    (d) The tenth character of the alphabet

45. Write a program to input 10 integers in numerical ascending order into a one-dimensional array X; copy the numbers from array X to another one-dimensional array Y, such that array Y contains the numbers in descending order. Output the contents of array Y.

46. The monthly sunshine record for a holiday resort follows.

Month	Jan	Feb	Mar	Apr	May	Jun	Jul	Aug	Sep	Oct	Nov	Dec
Hours of Sunshine	100	90	120	150	210	250	300	310	280	230	160	120

Write a program to do the following.

(a) Store the names of the months and the hours of sunshine in two one-dimensional arrays.

(b) Calculate and display the average number of hours of sunshine over the year.

(c) Calculate and display the names of the months with the highest and lowest number of hours of sunshine.

47. Write a program to input a phrase and display the Unicode, in hexadecimal, for each character of the phrase.

48. Write a program to input a phrase that is guaranteed to contain an opening parenthesis and a closing parenthesis, in that order, and is possibly repeated. For example, such a phrase might be

```
for (int index=0; index != 5; index++) screen.write(index);
```

(a) Scan each character in the phrase and output only those characters that are contained between the opening and closing parentheses.

(b) Rescan the phrase and output only those characters that are outside of the opening and closing parentheses.

49. Write a `Survey` class that will support taking surveys on various topics. The class should make use of the `CheckBox` class for a survey in which a particular question that will posed, along with a list of potential answers. The class should allow the programmer to easily define, administer, and report the results of the survey.

Next write a program that uses the `Survey` class to survey a group of students about why they are studying computer programming and Java.

50. Create a new class `Table`, in the Case Study: Ben's Breakfast Bar, to record the order taken at a particular table in the bar. The new class will allow a customer to place as many orders as required before being presented with the tab.

CHAPTER 6

Advanced Concepts with Classes

In the previous chapters you were taught how to create your own classes. This chapter extends your knowledge of object-oriented programming including showing you how one class can inherit the characteristics of another class to build a hierarchical relationship between classes.

By the end of the chapter you should have an understanding of the following topics.

- The concept of inheritance

- Defining hierarchies of superclasses and subclasses

- Using methods appropriate to a class through polymorphism

- Using an abstract class to create a clearly defined and documented hierarchy

- The creation and use of interfaces

- Method overloading

- Object properties

- Passing objects as parameters

6.1 Inheritance

Inheritance is the process by which one class receives the characteristics of another class.

One of the identifying characteristics of object-oriented languages and systems is support for inheritance. With inheritance we can define a new class by allowing it to take on some of the characteristics of a previously defined class, usually reducing the amount of work required to define the new class.

Figure 6.1 illustrates how different car models are derived from a fundamental concept of a vehicle. The concept of the vehicle is a blueprint of the generic car and specifies such features as four wheels, an engine, a transmission unit, and a saloon body shell. Different car models can be derived from this concept of a vehicle, and each derivation incorporates a plan for a specific car such as a Corvette, VW Beetle, or Porsche. All three vehicles have inherited the characteristics of the generic car; that is to say, they all have four wheels, they all contain engines and transmission units, and they are all built with a saloon body shell. However, each particular model has a different set of four wheels, a different engine and transmission unit, and a different shape of body shell.

The concept or blueprint of the vehicle is the base class. The Corvette, VW Beetle, and Porsche all inherit characteristics from the base class and represent derived classes. The cars themselves are the objects since they are instances, created in the factory, of a particular model or class of car.

Figure 6.1 illustrates the class hierarchy between the base class vehicle and the derived classes Corvette, VW Beetle, and Porsche. By convention, the arrows in the figure always point from the derived class to the base class. The solid line with the hollow arrowhead represents a UML *generalization*. This is a taxonomic relationship between a more general element (the base class) and a more specific element (any one of the derived classes). This example illustrates some of the following fundamental features of inheritance.

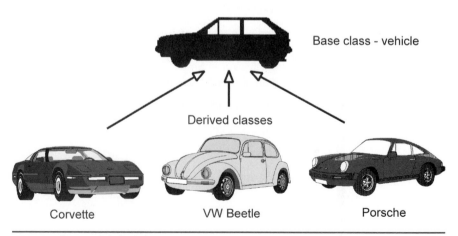

Figure 6.1 Base and derived classes

The initial class is called the base or parent class; in Java this is known as the *superclass*. The receiving class is called the derived or child class; in Java this is known as the *subclass*.

What are the benefits of using inheritance?

- Inheritance increases your ability to reuse classes. Software can be extended by reusing previously defined classes and adding new methods to the subclasses.

- Inheritance increases the level of abstraction in a program.

- Inheritance improves the clarity in the design of classes by allowing the implementation of methods to be postponed in superclasses and to appear in subclasses.

When you examined the partial listing for the `String` class you may have wondered about the inclusion of the keyword `extends` in the clause:

```
public final class String extends Object
```

The Java syntax for achieving inheritance follows.

SYNTAX

Inheritance:
```
class subclass-name extends superclass-name
```

The keyword `extends` implies that all the methods defined in the class `Object` are inherited by the class `String`. The class `Object` is known as a superclass of the subclass `String`. The superclass/subclass relationship may be represented in a *hierarchy diagram* as depicted in Figure 6.2. As explained previously, UML convention dictates that the arrowed-line in the figure always points up the hierarchy to the superclass and that the line is drawn solid, with a hollow arrowhead.

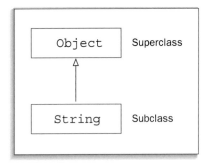

Figure 6.2 UML hierarchy diagram showing superclass and subclass relationship

All Java classes are ultimately derived from the `Object` class. A partial listing of the class `Object` follows.

```
public class Object
{
   // constructor
   public Object();

   // public instance methods
   public boolean equals(Object obj);
   public String toString();

   .
   .

   // protected instance methods
   protected Object clone() . . .
   protected void finalize() . . .
}
```

6.2   An Example of Inheritance

Consider a class that describes an employee for a company. The class should, at the very least, contain some form of reference to an individual employee, such as the name of a person being employed and the name of the department in which the person works. This class also contains the length of service, in years, the employee has worked for the company.

```
public class Employee
{
    // constant
    protected final static float holidayEntitlement = 20.0f;

    // instance variables
    protected String employeeName;
    protected String employeeDept;
    protected int lengthOfService;

    // constructor
    public Employee(String name, String department, int yearsService)
    {
        employeeName = name;
        employeeDept = department;
        lengthOfService = yearsService;
    }
```

```
// instance methods
public String getName()
{
      return employeeName;
}

public String getDepartment()
{
      return employeeDept;
}

public int getLengthOfService()
{
      return lengthOfService;
}

public float getHolidays()
{
      return holidayEntitlement;
}
}
```

Notice that the instance variables `employeeName`, `employeeDept`, and `lengthOfService` are not declared as `private` but declared as `protected`. Normally, variables are declared as `private` to prevent access from outside of the class. However, although `private` variables are inherited by subclass objects (in that each object has its own copy of that variable with its own value), such variables cannot be accessed directly by the subclass objects themselves. They can only be accessed through any `protected` or `public` access method of the superclass. A `protected` variable can be accessed from any method of any class in the same package. Recall that a *package* is a group of related classes. Thus, protected variables are safe from access from outside a controlled set of classes, yet can still be easily accessed from within the set, that is, from classes in the same package.

The `Employee` class is given a constructor for initializing the name of the employee, the name of the department in which the employee works, and the length of time spent working for the company. Instance methods are included that return the name of the employee, the name of the department in which the employee works, the length of service, and the holiday entitlement. Suppose there is a special type of employee, which we will call a technician, who has many of the characteristics of a standard employee but also has some additional characteristics, or a few characteristics that differ from the standard employee. Another class, `Technician`, may be defined that inherits all the characteristics of the class `Employee`.

For example, the statement `class Technician extends Employee` permits all the variables and methods of the class `Employee` to be inherited by the

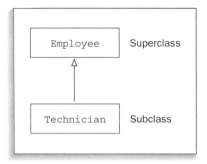

Figure 6.3 A hierarchy diagram between the `Employee` and `Technician` classes

class `Technician`. Failure to use inheritance would mean that all the variables and methods that are common to both an `Employee` and a `Technician` would need to be recoded as part of the definition of the class `Technician`. Figure 6.3 illustrates the hierarchical relationship between the two classes `Employee` and `Technician`.

```
public class Technician extends Employee
{
      // instance variable
      protected float holidays;

      // constructor
      public Technician(String name, String department, int yearsService)
      {
            super(name, department, yearsService);
      }
}
```

What has the class `Technician` inherited from the class `Employee`?

The answer is that it has inherited the constant `holidayEntitlement`, the instance variables `employeeName`, `employeeDept`, and `lengthOfService`, and the instance methods `getName()`, `getDepartment()`, `getLengthOfService`, and `getHolidays`. Inheritance allows both the variables and the instance methods to be used for objects of type `Technician` despite both the variables and methods not being explicitly defined in this class.

Figure 6.4 illustrates a more detailed hierarchy class diagram between the `Employee` and `Technician` classes. All the protected constants and instance variables, and public instance methods are inherited by the `Technician` class.

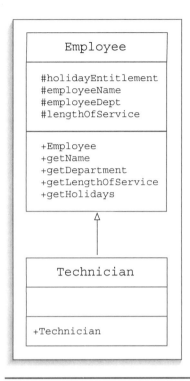

Figure 6.4 Inheritance by the `Technician` class

We must define a new constructor for the class `Technician` that includes the initialization of the name of a technician, their department of employment, and their length of service with the company. The coding of the `Technician` constructor has made use of the `Employee` constructor by making specific reference to the constructor of the superclass through the reserved word `super`.

> *i* The `super` keyword, if present in a constructor, must always be the first statement in a constructor body.

In the following program, notice that due to inheritance the instance methods `getName()`, `getDepartment`, `getlengthOfService`, and `getHolidays` have been invoked by an object of type `Technician`, even though the instance methods were defined in the class `Employee`.

Program Example_1—Demonstration of inheritance between Employee and Technician classes

```
import avi.*;

class Example_1
{
      public static void main(String[] args)
      {
            Window screen = new Window("Example_1.java");
            screen.showWindow();

            // instantiate an employee and a technician
            Employee caterer = new
            Employee("Millie Johnson","Catering", 7);
            Technician lineWorker = new
            Technician("Susan Schroeder","Electronics", 4);

            // use methods of superclass to display details of employee
            screen.write("Using the superclass methods \n");
            screen.write("Name: "+caterer.getName()+"\n");
            screen.write("Department: "+caterer.getDepartment()+"\n");
            screen.write("Service: "+caterer.getLengthOfService()+
                        " years\n");
            screen.write("Holidays: "+caterer.getHolidays()+" days\n\n");

            // use inherited methods of superclass to display details of a
            // technician
            screen.write("Using the inherited superclass methods \n");
            screen.write("Name: "+lineWorker.getName()+"\n");
            screen.write("Department: "+
                        lineWorker.getDepartment()+"\n");
            screen.write("Service: "+lineWorker.getLengthOfService()+
                        " years\n");
            screen.write("Holidays: "+lineWorker.getHolidays()+
                        " days\n\n");
      }
}
```

Here are the results from the log file after the program was executed.

```
================================================================
                    L O G      F I L E
      audio-visual interface [avi] - Release 1.0 - by Barry Holmes
      filename: Example_1.java     date: 7/8/2000   time: 11:26:45
================================================================


Using the superclass methods
Name: Millie Johnson
Department: Catering
Service: 7 years
Holidays: 20.0 days

Using the inherited superclass methods
Name: Susan Schroeder
Department: Electronics
Service: 4 years
Holidays: 20.0 days
```

i   When you construct an object of a subclass, the constructor for the superclass also gets invoked. Should you omit a call to the superclass constructor from your subclass constructor, Java will automatically insert this call for you. If the superclass does not contain a default (no argument) constructor, this will result in a compilation error.

Constructor calls are automatically chained. A sequence of constructor methods are invoked from subclass to superclass and eventually to the `Object` class. Because a superclass constructor is always invoked before the subclass constructor, the body of the `Object` constructor is executed first, followed by the execution of the bodies of the constructors down through the class hierarchy, and finally to the execution of the subclass constructor body.

Java is a *strictly typed language*. This implies that the compiler would never allow you to assign an object or primitive of one type to an object or primitive of a different type unless casting was used. What about the assignment of objects within a hierarchy? What will the compiler allow?

When one class inherits from another class anywhere in the hierarchy, an object of any subclass in the hierarchy is also a legal superclass object. Therefore, an object of a subclass may be assigned to an object of its superclass without a type violation.

An object referred to by a variable of type `Employee`, say, can be assigned to a variable of type `Technician`, where `Technician` is a subclass of `Employee`, if the object is really of type `Technician`. These two facts are illustrated in program `Example_2`.

Program Example_2—Demonstration of object assignment over a hierarchy

```
import avi.*;

class Example_2
{
     public static void main(String[] args)
     {
          Window screen = new Window("Example_2.java");
          screen.showWindow();

          Employee worker;
          Technician lineWorker;
          Technician laboratoryWorker = new
          Technician("Peter Potter","Micro Laboratory",7);

          // any object of a subclass (Technician) can be assigned to an
          // object of a superclass (Employee)
          worker = laboratoryWorker;
          screen.write("The employee's name is "+worker.getName()+"\n");
          screen.write("working in the "+worker.getDepartment()+
                    " department\n\n");

          // any object of a superclass (Employee) can be assigned to a
          // subclass (Technician) using an appropriate cast
          lineWorker = (Technician)worker;
          screen.write("The technician's name is also "+
                    lineWorker.getName()+"\n");
          screen.write("also working in the "+lineWorker.getDepartment()+
                    " department\n\n");
     }
}
```

Results from the log file follow:

```
================================================================
                   L O G      F I L E
      audio-visual interface [avi] - Release 1.0 - by Barry Holmes
         filename: Example_2.java    date: 7/2/2000   time: 5:12:49
================================================================


The employee's name is Peter Potter
working in the Micro Laboratory department

The technician's name is also Peter Potter
also working in the Micro Laboratory department
```

6.3   Overriding Superclass Methods

A subclass may replace an inherited method from a superclass. When a subclass defines a method with the same name, return type, and argument list as a method in a superclass, the superclass method is said to be *overridden*. When the overridden method is invoked for an object of the class, the new definition of the method is called and not the old definition from the superclass.

If the calculation of the holiday entitlement is different for a technician than an employee, then the inherited method `getHolidays` should be overridden in the `Technician` class. Assume that for every year of service in excess of 5 years, a technician receives an extra half-day holiday, then the method to calculate the new holiday entitlement must change. The following listing of the `Technician` class illustrates how the `getHolidays` method has been overridden.

```java
public class Technician extends Employee
{
      // instance variable
      protected float holidays;

      // constructor
      public Technician(String name, String department, int yearsService)
      {
            super(name, department, yearsService);
      }

      // overridden instance method
      public float getHolidays()
      {
            int service = this.getLengthOfService();
```

```
if (service > 5)
      holidays = (float)(holidayEntitlement+0.5f*(service-5));
else
      holidays = (float)holidayEntitlement;

return holidays;
    }
}
```

Figure 6.5 illustrates the addition of an instance variable and an overridden method in the `Technician` class.

The test program listed in class `Example_3` calculates and displays the holidays for a person in the `Employee` class and a person in the `Technician` class.

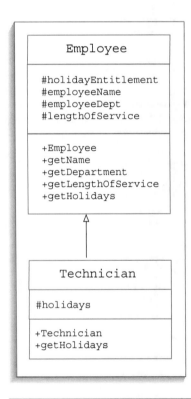

Figure 6.5 Modifications to the `Technician` class.

Program Example_3—To demonstrate overriding superclass methods

```
import avi.*;

class Example_3
{
      public static void main(String[] args)
      {
            Window screen = new Window("Example_3.java");
            screen.showWindow();

            Employee caterer = new
            Employee("Millie Johnson", "Catering", 7);
            Technician lineWorker = new
            Technician("Hans Neilsen", "Micro Laboratory", 7);

            screen.write(caterer.getName()+" in the "+
                    caterer.getDepartment()+" department has "+
                    caterer.getHolidays()+
                    " days holiday entitlement\n\n");

            // use overridden method getHolidays in the Technician class
            screen.write(lineWorker.getName()+" in the "+
                    lineWorker.getDepartment()+" department has "+
                    lineWorker.getHolidays()+
                    " days holiday entitlement\n\n");
      }
}
```

Results from the log file follow:

```
================================================================================
                        L  O  G      F  I  L  E
        audio-visual interface [avi] - Release 1.0 - by Barry Holmes
          filename: Example_3.java    date: 7/8/2000  time: 11:49:9
================================================================================


Millie Johnson in the Catering department has 20.0 days holiday entitlement

Hans Neilsen in the Micro Laboratory department has 21.0 days holiday enti-
tlement
```

In program `Example_3` it is clear which version of `getHolidays` is to be invoked by the type of the object being used in the call to the instance method. Thus `caterer.getHolidays()` and `lineWorker.getHolidays()` will invoke the methods for returning the holiday entitlement for an employee and a technician respectively.

 Inheritance lets us reuse the parts of a superclass that are applicable to the subclass, and redefine the parts that differ.

If you look back at the partial listing of the `Object` class, presented at the end of Section 6.1, you will notice that it contains a public instance method `toString`.

Java allows programmers to use objects as operands for string operations such as concatenation (+). When this occurs, Java will look for a programmer-defined `toString` method in the object's class, and will use it to convert the object into a string before proceeding with the concatenation. If such a method is not found, then Java will use a default `toString` operation that is defined for all objects.

The `Employee` class can be modified to include a `toString` method as follows.

```
public class Employee
{
        .
        .

    public String toString()
    {
        String temporary = new String("Name: "+employeeName+
                            "\nDept: "+employeeDept+
                            "\nService: "+lengthOfService);
        return temporary;
    }
}
```

Since all classes are subclasses of the `Object` class, we have overridden the `toString` method in the subclass `Employee`. Recall the purpose of the `toString` method is to represent the object as a string so that it may be written as part of a string. For example, to write the details of an employee we would code:

```
Employee caterer = new Employee("Millie Johnson", "Catering", 7);
screen.write(caterer+"\n");
```

In generating Java byte codes, the compiler searches for a `toString` method associated with the `Employee` class to enable a string to be written to the screen.

A `toString` method may also be included in the subclass `Technician`, as follows:

```
public class Technician extends Employee
{

        .
        .


    public String toString()
    {
        String temporary = new String("TECHNICIAN\t"+super.toString());
        return temporary;
    }
}
```

Notice that it is possible to make reference to an inherited method from a superclass, even when the method has been overridden in the subclass. The inherited method from the superclass can be invoked by using the keyword `super`. For example, within the class `Technician`, instead of writing the name, department, and length of service of the technician, it is possible to re-use the `toString` method in the `Employee` class by coding `super.toString()`.

6.4 Polymorphism

The Java engine is able to dynamically, at run time, choose one of several method definitions to execute for a single method call. This capability is called *polymorphism*.

Polymorphism is a way of giving a method one name that is shared up and down an object hierarchy, with each object in the hierarchy implementing the method in a way appropriate to itself. Polymorphism applies only to a specific set of methods. To write polymorphic classes we require two things:

- The classes must be part of the same inheritance hierarchy.

- The classes must support the same set of required methods.

Consider the creation of a `Manager` class that is also a subclass of the `Employee` class, as depicted by Figure 6.6. The holiday entitlement for a manager is dependent upon the length of service. For every year in excess of 10 years service, a manager receives an extra day of holiday time added to the normal holiday entitlement.

The coding of the `Manager` class follows.

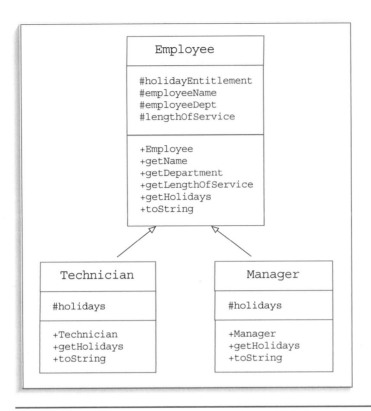

Figure 6.6 The addition of a `Manager` class as a subclass of the `Employee` class

```
public class Manager extends Employee
{
      // instance variable
      protected float holidays;

      // constructor
      public Manager(String name, String department, int yearsService)
      {
            super(name, department, yearsService);
      }

      // instance methods
      public float getHolidays()
      {
            int service = this.getLengthOfService();

            if (service > 10)
```

```
                holidays = (float)(holidayEntitlement + (service - 10));
        else
                holidays = (float)holidayEntitlement;

        return holidays;
    }

    public String toString()
    {
        String temporary = new String("MANAGER\t"+super.toString());
        return temporary;
    }
}
}
```

Consider what would happen if we wrote a general purpose class method to display the details of any employee, including technicians and managers.

```
static void displayDetails(Employee person)
{
    screen.write(person+"\n");
    screen.write("Holidays: "+person.getHolidays()+"\n");
}
```

How would the compiler know which `toString` method and which `getHolidays` method to use for either a technician or a manager? The answer is that the compiler doesn't know, and the decision on which `toString` method and `getHolidays` method to use is postponed until run-time! *Dynamic method lookup* is a technique where each object has a table of its methods, and Java searches for the correct versions of any overridden methods at run-time.

i   Dynamic method lookup is not as fast as invoking a method directly. Dynamic method lookup is not required for `static` or `private` methods and those methods and classes declared as `final`. A `final` method cannot be overridden and a `final` class cannot be extended.

Program `Example_4` uses the concepts discussed in this section to demonstrate polymorphism. Notice that it is perfectly legal for an object of a subclass to be passed as an argument to a method that requires a parameter of its superclass type.

Program Example_4—An example of polymorphism

```
import avi.*;

class Example_4
{
    static Window screen = new Window("Example_4");

    static void displayDetails(Employee person)
    {
        screen.write(person+"\n");
        screen.write("Holidays: "+person.getHolidays()+"\n\n");
    }

    public static void main(String[] args)
    {
        screen.showWindow();

        Technician lineWorker = new
        Technician("Franco Ramirez","Electronics",18);
        Manager computerManager = new
        Manager("Brian Biggins","Computing",21);

        displayDetails(lineWorker);
        displayDetails(computerManager);
    }
}
```

Following are the contents of the log file after program execution.

```
===========================================================================
                       L O G     F I L E
        audio-visual interface [avi] - Release 1.0 - by Barry Holmes
            filename: Example_4      date: 7/8/2000    time: 1:4:44
===========================================================================


TECHNICIAN    Name: Franco Ramirez
Dept: Electronics
Service: 18
Holidays: 26.5

MANAGER       Name: Brian Biggins
Dept: Computing
Service: 21
Holidays: 31.0
```

6.5   Instanceof Operator

If we had wanted to explicitly discriminate between a technician and a manager in the `displayDetails` method, we would have used the `instanceof` operator. The syntax of the operator follows.

SYNTAX

Instanceof Operator:
object `instanceof` *class*

The `instanceof` operator returns `true` if the object on its left-hand side is an instance of the class specified on its right-hand side; otherwise, `instanceof` returns `false`. The `instanceof` operator will also return `false` if the object is `null`.

The `displayDetails` method could be modified to provide explicit discrimination between the subclasses as follows. The conditional statement

```
(person instanceof Technician)
```

is `true` if the object being passed happens to be of the type `Technician`. Similarly, the condition

```
(person instanceof Manager)
```

is `true` if the object being passed happens to be of type `Manager`.

The only other type of object being passed is that for an `Employee`, in which case the conditional statements would be `false`.

If the statement

```
(person instanceof Employee)
```

is used, then the superclass `Employee` *cannot* act as a discriminator of subclass objects since all subclasses are, by their nature, instances of superclasses.

> ⚠ Ensure when you choose a discriminator class, the class contains methods, either directly or through inheritance, that can be used by objects of the class. Failure to comply with this requirement will cause a syntax error.

Program Example_5—Using the instanceof operator

```
import avi.*;

class Example_5
{
    static Window screen = new Window("Example_5");

    static void displayDetails(Employee person)
    {
        screen.write(person+"\n");
        screen.write("Holidays: "+person.getHolidays()+"\n");

        if (person instanceof Technician)
            screen.write("All technicians will receive a productivity "+
                        "bonus of $500.\n\n");
        else if (person instanceof Manager)
            screen.write("All managers will receive a productivity "+
                        "bonus of a new car.\n\n");
        else
            screen.write("The management want to convey their thanks "+
                        "to the hard work of all employees!\n\n");
    }

    public static void main(String[] args)
    {
        screen.showWindow();

        Employee caterer = new
        Employee("Millie Johnson","Catering",7);
        Technician lineWorker = new
        Technician("Franco Ramirez","Electronics",18);
        Manager computerManager = new
        Manager("Brian Biggins","Computing",21);

        displayDetails(caterer);
        displayDetails(lineWorker);
        displayDetails(computerManager);
    }
}
```

The following screenshot results from running the program:

In the next several sections we will introduce some advanced concepts: shadowed variables, inner classes, abstract methods and classes, and interfaces. An in-depth treatment of these concepts is beyond the scope of this book. Nevertheless, a basic understanding of them is important for anyone studying Java and object-oriented programming.

6.6 Shadowed Variables

In Section 6.3, we noticed that when the overridden method is invoked for an object of a class, the new definition of the method is called and not the old definition from the superclass. What about variables? What happens if an inherited variable has the same name as a variable of the subclass? The variable of the subclass is said to *shadow* the inherited variable with the same name. The inherited variable is visible in the subclass, yet it cannot be accessed by the same name. But what if you need to use the inherited variable in the subclass; how can it be accessed? The answer is to use the reserved word `super`. For example, if class `B` is a subclass of class `A`, and both contain a variable named `common` as follows.

```
class A
{
   protected int common;
      .
}
```

```
class B extends A
{
   // shadow the inherited variable common from class A
   protected int common;
        .
}
```

Then in class B, the variable common may be referred to by either common or this.common. However, the inherited variable common is referred to by super.common or by ((A)this).common.

Notice that the keyword this may be cast to refer to the appropriate class, in this case class A. This technique is useful if you want to refer to a variable in a class beyond the immediate superclass higher up the class hierarchy.

Although you may refer to shadowed variables by casting an object to the appropriate type, this technique cannot be used to refer to overridden methods. In Program Example_6, objectB has been cast to an object of class A and assigned to objectA. Despite the method function() being overridden in class B, objectA.function() does not invoke the original method in superclass A.

Program Example_6—Overriding is not overshadowing

```
import avi.*;

class A
{
     protected int X=2;
     public A(){}
     public int function(){return 2*X;}
}

class B extends A
{
     protected int X=3;
     public B(){}
     public int function(){return 3*X;}
}

public class Example_6
{
     static public void main(String[] args)
     {
          Window screen = new Window("Example_6.java");
          screen.showWindow();
```

```
         A objectA;
         B objectB = new B();

         screen.write("X from class B = "+objectB.X+"\n");
         screen.write("Value of function from class B = "+
                    objectB.function()+"\n");

         objectA = (A)objectB; // cast objectB to an instance of class A

         screen.write("You may refer to shadowed variables by casting\n");
         screen.write("an object of the appropriate type.\n");
         screen.write("X from class A = "+objectA.X+"\n");
         screen.write("You cannot refer to overridden methods by casting\n");
         screen.write("an object to the appropriate type.\n");
         screen.write("Value of function is still from class B = "+
                    objectA.function());
      }
}
```

Results from the program log file follow:

```
=====================================================================
                   L O G     F I L E
     audio-visual interface [avi] - Release 1.0 - by Barry Holmes
       filename: Example_6.java   date: 7/2/2000   time: 7:37:29
=====================================================================


X from class B = 3
Value of function from class B = 9
You may refer to shadowed variables by casting
an object of the appropriate type.
X from class A = 2
You cannot refer to overridden methods by casting
an object to the appropriate type.
Value of function is still from class B = 9
```

Shadowing variables results in hard-to-read code and should only be used when absolutely necessary.

6.7   Inner Classes

Java will allow an *inner class* to be nested within an outer class. This feature is useful in encapsulation, since it allows you to incorporate a class definition of data fields within the class that makes specific reference to the data fields. The inner class is known as a *member class*, and is just another class component in the same way that constants, variables, and methods are also class components. The code within a member class can implicitly refer to any of the constants, variables, and methods of its enclosing class.

Notice from the following example that in order to access the fields of the member class, it has been necessary to create an instance of the class `Center`. The instance of the member class may then be used in the enclosing class.

```
public class RoundShape
{
      // coordinates of center represented by an inner class
      protected class Center
      {
            int x,y;

            Center(){}
      }

      protected Center C = new Center();
      protected float radiusOfCircle;


      .

      .

}
```

6.8   Abstract Methods and Classes

In constructing a hierarchy of relationships among various classes, it is sometimes beneficial to include a class, normally at the top of the hierarchy, whose methods cannot be instantiated. The class acts as a blueprint for all subclasses, and as such it can be extended to suit different classes within the taxonomy.

An *abstract method* is defined by the method's signature and has no method body. An *abstract class* is a class that contains at least one abstract method. As a result, an abstract class *cannot* be instantiated since there would be no means of implementing the abstract method(s) within the class. When a class contains at least one abstract method, the class is automatically taken to be abstract. However, not all the methods of an abstract class need be abstract. There can be a mixture of constructors, implemented methods, and method signatures.

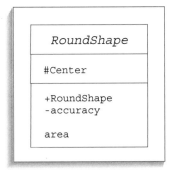

Figure 6.7 UML representation of an abstract class

The UML notation for an abstract class is depicted in Figure 6.7. Notice that the name of the class and the name of the abstract methods are written in italics to distinguish the component from a normal class.

A subclass of an abstract class may be instantiated, provided that the abstract methods of the abstract class are overridden and implemented in the subclass. If all the abstract methods are not implemented, the subclass must also be abstract.

With inheritance, you can describe *is-a* hierarchies representing many possible type variants. We have seen from Figure 6.1 that a Corvette *is-a* vehicle, a VW Beetle *is-a* vehicle, and a Porsche *is-a* vehicle. In program Example_4 we can see that a Technician *is-a*(n) Employee, and a Manager *is-a*(n) Employee.

As a rule of thumb, in the is-a hierarchy we say that inheritance is appropriate if every object of class Y may also be viewed as an object of class X. In other words "Y extends X" and "Y is-a(n) X" are consistent. In the classes that follow, the abstract class RoundShape provides the superclass for the classes Circle and Sphere. We can say that a circle is-a round shape and a sphere is-a round shape.

But the abstract class RoundShape contains an inner class Center. In considering the relationship between the class Center and the class RoundShape, it would be *incorrect* to use an is-a relationship, since RoundShape is-not-a Center. For this reason, class RoundShape did not inherit from class Center. The *has-a* relationship describes every object of a class X that *has-a* set of attributes of type Y. In program Example_7 it is correct to say that a RoundShape *has-a* Center and, therefore, the class Center may be treated as an attribute of the class RoundShape.

The class RoundShape is an abstract class; it contains an abstract method to calculate the area of a round shape. This method is implemented in the class Circle as the area of a circle, and in class Sphere as the surface area of a sphere. Figure 6.8 illustrates that both the classes Circle and Sphere inherit from the abstract class RoundShape.

Implementations of the classes follow.

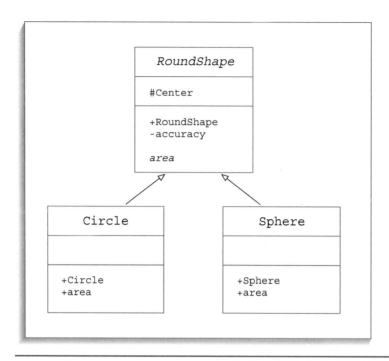

Figure 6.8 UML representation of hierarchy of classes

```
public abstract class RoundShape
{
      // coordinates of center represented by an inner class
      protected class Center
      {
            int x,y;
      }

      protected Center C = new Center();
      protected float radiusOfCircle;

      // constructor
      public RoundShape(int xCenter, int yCenter, float radius)
      {
            C.x=xCenter;
            C.y=yCenter;
            radiusOfCircle = radius;
      }

      // abstract method
      abstract public float area();
```

```
}


public class Circle extends RoundShape
{
        // constructor
        public Circle(int xCenter, int yCenter, float radius)
        {
                super(xCenter, yCenter, radius);
        }

        // return area of circle
        public float area()
        {
                float areaOfCircle =
                (float)(Math.PI*Math.pow((double)radiusOfCircle,2.0));
                return areaOfCircle;
        }
}


public class Sphere extends RoundShape
{
        // constructor
        public Sphere(int xCenter, int yCenter, float radius)
        {
                super(xCenter, yCenter, radius);
        }

        // return surface area of sphere
        public float area()
        {
                float surfaceArea =
                (float)(4.0*Math.PI*Math.pow((double)radiusOfCircle,2.0));
                return surfaceArea;
        }
}
```

In the previous chapter, you were introduced to a method of formatting numbers for output. Program `Example_7` uses a method to format decimal numbers. The package `text` contains a `DecimalFormat` class to allow decimal numbers to be output to a specified precision.

For example, if you specify an output format for numbers as "`0.##`", then `0` represents a digit, `#` is a digit (but a trailing zero appears as a space), and the period . is a placeholder for a decimal point. A number such as 18.543 would be output as 18.54, and a number such as 18.567 would be output as 18.57, and a number such as −18.543 would be output as −18.54.

NOW DO THIS ▶   Using the Java documentation you downloaded in the Introduction:

(1) Look up and read about the `DecimalFormat` class in the `text` package.

(2) Write, compile, and run a short experimental program to test the formatting of decimal numbers.

Program `Example_7` tests the methods of the `Circle` and `Sphere` classes.

```java
import avi.*;
import java.text.DecimalFormat;

public class Example_7
{
      public static void main(String[] args)
      {
            Window screen = new
            Window("Example_7.java");
            screen.showWindow();

            Circle c = new Circle(5,5,2.5f);
            Sphere s = new Sphere(5,5,2.5f);

            // display details about the circles
            DecimalFormat out = new DecimalFormat ("0.##");
            screen.write("Area of circle "+out.format(c.area())+"\n");
            screen.write("Area of sphere "+out.format(s.area()));
      }
}
```

The following results are from the log file.

```
===================================================================
                    L O G     F I L E
         audio-visual interface [avi] - Release 1.0 - by Barry Holmes
            filename: Example_7.java  date: 7/2/2000    time: 7:45:16
===================================================================

Area of circle 19.63
Area of sphere 78.54
```

CASE STUDY

Boats

Statement of the Problem   The following case study demonstrates inheritance and abstract methods. A boat may have a set of attributes such as a name, a momentary position [x,y] on a lake with respect to some origin of coordinates, a bearing (direction of travel with respect to the compass point North), and a current speed. Figure 6.9 illustrates the attributes of a boat.

Figure 6.10 illustrates how the bearing of a boat may be calculated when traveling from coordinates [x,y] to coordinates [newX, newY]. The horizontal and vertical distances between these two points in Figure 6.10 are X = newX-x, and Y = newY-y respectively. The calculation of the bearing is the angle whose tangent is X/Y, in other words the arctangent of X/Y. By simple geometry you may observe that the angle opposite side X and adjacent to side Y has the same value as the angle marked as the bearing.

Create an abstract class Boat that contains the attributes of name, position, bearing, and speed, together with instance methods to return these attributes.

A generic boat may be modeled as an object that has the instance variables of name, position, bearing, and speed. In addition to the class constructor, this class will contain methods to retrieve the data associated with a boat and calculate the bearing of the boat. The class will also contain two abstract methods to set the speed of a boat and to determine whether it is possible to travel to a particular destination on the boat (is there enough fuel or is the wind blowing in favor of the journey?). The listing of the abstract Boat class follows.

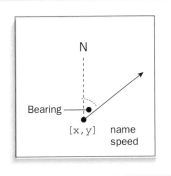

Figure 6.9 Representation of a boat   **Figure 6.10** Calculation of the bearing of a boat

```
public abstract class Boat
{
     // instance variables
     // name of boat
     protected String name;
```

```
// coordinates of current position (grid size miles)
protected float x,y;
// compass bearing from North
protected int bearing;
// speed of boat (mph)
protected int speed;

// constructor
/**
Subclasses of the abstract Boat class can create boat objects.
@param id is the name of a boat.
@param X is the x coordinate of the position of the boat
@param Y is the y coordinate of the position of the boat
*/
public Boat(String id, float X, float Y)
{
     name = id;
     x = X;
     y = Y;

     // setting default values
     bearing = 0;
     speed = 0;
}

// instance methods
/**
The method getName will return the name of the boat.
@return Returns the name of the boat.
*/
public String getName(){return name;}

/**
The method getX will return the x coordinate of the position of the
boat.
@return Returns the x coordinate.
*/
public float getX(){return x;}

/**
The method getY will return the y coordinate of the position of the
boat.
@return Returns the y coordinate.
```

```
*/
public float getY(){return y;}


/**
The method getBearing will return the bearing in degrees (with
respect to North) of the boat.
@return Returns the bearing of the boat.
*/
public int getBearing(){return bearing;}


/**
The method getSpeed will return the current speed of the boat.
@return Returns the speed of the boat.
*/
public int getSpeed(){return speed;}


/**
The method calculateBearingTo will set the instance variable bearing
to the heading a boat must make to reach the position [newX, newY]
@param newX is the x coordinate of the new position.
@param newY is the y coordinate of the new position.
*/
public void calculateBearingTo(float newX, float newY)
{
        double X = (double)(newX-x);
        double Y = (double)(newY-y);

        int angle = (int)Math.toDegrees(Math.atan(X/Y));

        // convert angle to bearing
        if (X >= 0 && Y >=0)
                bearing = angle;
        else if (Y < 0)
                bearing = 180+angle;
        else
                bearing = 360+angle;
}


// abstract methods
public abstract void setSpeed(float fractionOf);
public abstract boolean canTravelTo(float newX, float newY);
}
```

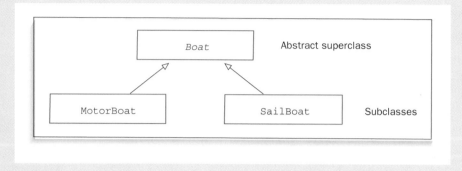

Figure 6.11 Class hierarchy

Analysis of Classes   Since the data and methods belonging to the `Boat` class are common to all boats, the abstract `Boat` class may be taken as the superclass of all lake-bound vessels. In this case study we will look at the properties of a motorboat and a sailboat, and derive classes `MotorBoat` and `SailBoat`, respectively, as subclasses of the `Boat` class, as depicted by Figure 6.11.

A characteristic that distinguishes a motorboat from the generic boat is, of course, the engine. We can now include in the `MotorBoat` class new attributes that are particular to a motorboat; these are the maximum speed of the boat, the amount of fuel it has in its tank, and the average fuel consumption. There are instance methods that enable the inspection of the fuel remaining in the tank, and the average fuel consumption.

Besides the `MotorBoat` class inheriting all the instance variables and instance methods of the superclass `Boat`, it must also implement the inherited abstract methods. Failure to perform this implementation will result in the `MotorBoat` class remaining as an abstract class.

The `setSpeed` method is implemented by setting the speed of the motorboat to a fraction of the maximum speed.

The `canTravelTo` method requires the range of the boat to be calculated and compared with the distance the boat must travel in order to reach the destination. Clearly if the range of the boat is calculated as the product of the amount of fuel remaining and the average fuel consumption, and this range is less than the distance to travel, then the journey is not possible without refueling.

Calculating the distance to travel between the current position of the boat [x,y] and the new position [newX, newY] is simply a matter of applying the Pythagorian theorem. Figure 6.12 illustrates the distances involved in this calculation. The class `MotorBoat` contains a private method to calculate this distance.

The code for `MotorBoat` follows.

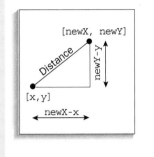

Figure 6.12 Calculation of the distance to a new position

```
public class MotorBoat extends Boat
{
      // instance variables
      protected int fastestSpeed;
      protected float fuelRemaining;
      protected float averageFuelConsumption;

      // constructor
      /**
      The MotorBoat class will create a motorboat object.
      @param id is the name of the motorboat
      @param X is the x coordinate of the position of the motorboat
      @param Y is the y coordinate of the position of the motorboat
      @param maxSpeed is the maximum speed of the motorboat (miles per
      hour)
      @param fuel is the amount of fuel in the tank of the boat (gallons)
      @param consumption is the average consumption of the fuel (miles per
      gallon)
      */
      public MotorBoat(String id, float X, float Y, int maxSpeed,
                       float fuel, float consumption)
      {
            super(id,X,Y);
            fastestSpeed = maxSpeed;
            fuelRemaining = fuel;
            averageFuelConsumption = consumption;
      }
```

```
// instance methods
/**
The method getFuelRemaining returns the amount of fuel remaining in
the motorboat's fuel tank.
@return Returns the amount of fuel (gallons) remaining.
*/
public float getFuelRemaining()
{
      return fuelRemaining;
}


/**
The method getAverageFuelConsumption returns the average fuel
consumption for the motorboat.
@return Returns the average fuel consumption (miles per gallon).
*/
public float getAverageFuelConsumption()
{
      return averageFuelConsumption;
}


/**
This is an implementation of the inherited abstract method setSpeed.
The setSpeed method sets the speed of the motorboat as a fraction
of its maximum speed.
@param fractionOfPower represents the fraction of the top speed of
the motorboat.
*/
public void setSpeed(float fractionOfPower)
{
      speed = (int)(fastestSpeed * fractionOfPower);
}


/**
This is an implementation of the inherited abstract method
canTravelTo. The canTravelTo method determines whether there is
enough fuel in the motorboat to travel to the position given by the
coordinates [newX, newY].
@param newX is the x coordinate of the destination position of the
motorboat.
@param newY is the y coordinate of the destination position of the
motorboat.
```

```
@return returns true if the motorboat has enough fuel to travel the
distance to the new position.
*/
public boolean canTravelTo(float newX, float newY)
{
        // calculate range of motorboat on remaining fuel
        float range = fuelRemaining * averageFuelConsumption;

        // check if the motorboat can travel to new destination
        return (range >= distanceToTravel(newX, newY));
}


// returns the distance between the current position of the motor-
// boat and the destination
// position of the motorboat

private float distanceToTravel(float newX, float newY)
{
        return (float)Math.sqrt((double)((newX-x)*(newX-x)+
                                         (newY-y)*(newY-y)));

}

}
```

NOW DO THIS   Write a test program to:

(1) Instantiate a `MotorBoat` object, whose name is the "Venetian Princess", at coordinates [0,0]. The boat has a maximum speed of 40 mph, a fuel tank capacity of 15 gallons, and an average fuel consumption of 15 miles per gallon.

(2) Set the speed of the boat to 70% of full power, and calculate the bearing of the boat necessary to reach a point on the lake given by the coordinates [20,15].

(3) Display all the relevant attributes of the boat and state whether it is possible to make the journey.

Now let us turn our attention to a sailboat as a lake-vessel. The sailboat has no engine and is solely reliant upon the speed and direction of the wind. The attributes of wind-speed and wind-direction belong to the wind and not the sailboat, therefore, it is fitting to examine a class for `Wind` before progressing to the `SailBoat` class.

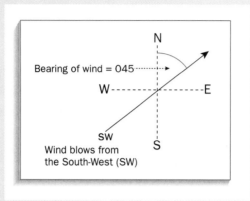

N

Bearing of wind = 045 ┈┈┈┈┈

W ┈┈┈┈┈┈ E

SW
Wind blows from
the South-West (SW)

S

Figure 6.13 Converting wind direction to a bearing

A constructor for the wind class requires two parameters, the speed of the wind and the direction the wind is blowing. When we say a wind is blowing from, say, the South-West we mean that the bearing of the wind is 45° (see Figure 6.13).

The constructor for the `Wind` class will need to convert a wind direction, specified by points on the compass, e.g. SW, into an angle in degrees that represents a bearing with respect to North.

The following code is a listing of the `Wind` class.

```
public class Wind
{
      // instance variables
      int speedOfWind;
      int directionOfWind;

      // constructor
      /**
      The Wind class will allow a wind object to be created that
      has a speed and blows from a given direction.
      @param speed is the speed of the wind in mph
      @param direction is one of eight points of the compass indicating
      the direction from which the wind is blowing.
      */
      public Wind(int speed, String direction)
      {
            speedOfWind = speed;
```

```java
        // convert direction of wind into a bearing
        direction = direction.toUpperCase();

        if (direction.equals("N"))
            directionOfWind = 180;
        else if (direction.equals("NE"))
            directionOfWind = 225;
        else if (direction.equals("E"))
            directionOfWind = 270;
        else if (direction.equals("SE"))
            directionOfWind = 315;
        else if (direction.equals("S"))
            directionOfWind = 0;
        else if (direction.equals("SW"))
            directionOfWind = 45;
        else if (direction.equals("W"))
            directionOfWind = 90;
        else if (direction.equals("NW"))
            directionOfWind = 135;
        else
            // set default of zero for incorrect direction
            directionOfWind = 0;
    }


// instance methods
/**
The method getWindSpeed returns the speed of the wind.
@return Returns the speed of the wind.
*/
public int getWindSpeed()
{
        return speedOfWind;
}


/**
The method getWindDirection returns the direction (as an angle)
the wind is blowing from.
@return Returns the direction of the wind.
*/
public int getWindDirection()
{
        return directionOfWind;
}
}
```

NOW DO THIS Examine the Java code from the `Wind` class and answer the following questions.

(1) What is the bearing of the wind when it is blowing from each of the following directions—North-East, South, West, and North-West?

(2) If the wind has a bearing of 270°, from which direction is it blowing?

Since the speed of a sailboat is dependent upon the speed of the wind, it is obvious that a `Wind` object should be included as a parameter in the `SailBoat` constructor. Remember, a class name may be treated in the same way as a primitive type, therefore, you should not be surprised at passing objects as parameters. After all you do this for `String` objects so why not for other objects? When setting the speed of the sailboat it is necessary, in the `setSpeed` method, to represent the speed as a percentage of the sail area used against the speed of the wind.

We have placed a restriction on the direction a sailboat may travel. The direction of the wind clearly has a major influence on how quickly we can reach the destination in a sailboat. If the bearing of the wind is 45° either side of the bearing of the boat, then in the `canTravelTo` method, travel is deemed to be possible, and we can reach our destination.

The Java code for the `SailBoat` class follows.

```java
public class SailBoat extends Boat
{
        // instance variables
        int windSpeed;
        int windDirection;

        // constructor
        /**
        The SailBoat class will allow a sailboat object to be created.
        @param id is the name of the sailboat.
        @param X is the x coordinate of the initial position of the sail-
        boat.
        @param Y is the y coordinate of the initial position of the sail-
        boat.
        @param power is a Wind object, where the speed and direction of the
        wind have a direct influence on the speed and direction of the sail-
        boat.
        */
        public SailBoat(String id, float X, float Y, Wind power)
        {
                super(id,X,Y);
```

```
        windSpeed = power.getWindSpeed();
        windDirection = power.getWindDirection();
}


/**
An implementation of the abstract method setSpeed, inherited from
the superclass Boat. The method set speed will adjust the speed of
the boat depending how much sail area is open to the wind.
@param fractionOfSale is the fraction of total sale area that is
open to the wind.
*/
public void setSpeed(float fractionOfSail)
{
        speed = (int)(windSpeed * fractionOfSail);
}


/**
This is an implementation of the inherited abstract method
canTravelTo. The canTravelTo method determines whether the wind
direction is favorable for the sailboat to reach position given by
the coordinates [newX, newY]. The wind direction is allowed to
vary up to 45 degrees from the bearing of the sailboat.
@param newX is the x coordinate of the destination position of the
sailboat.
@param newY is the y coordinate of the destination position of the
sailboat.
@return Returns true if the wind direction will allow the sailboat
to reach the new position.
*/
public boolean canTravelTo(float newX, float newY)
{
        // return whether wind direction is favorable to reach
        // destination
        return ((windDirection >= bearing - 45) &&
               (windDirection <= bearing + 45));
}
}
```

The full picture of the relationship between the classes is given in Figure 6.14.

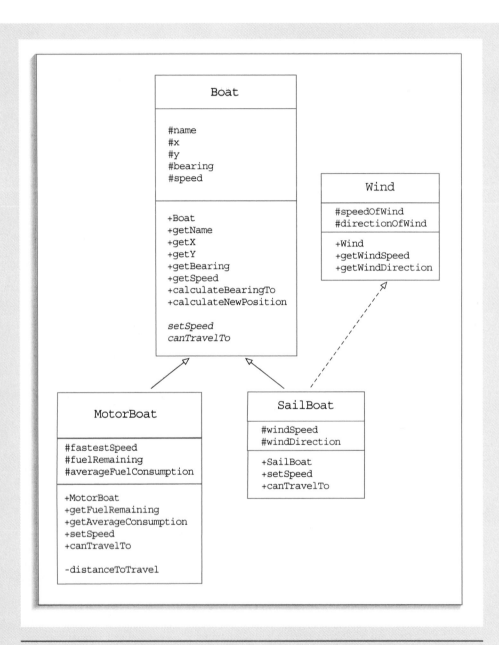

Figure 6.14 Relationships between the classes

Program Example_8 demonstrates how the methods from the various classes are tested.

```java
import avi.*;
import java.text.DecimalFormat;

class Example_8
{
    static Window screen = new Window("Example_8.java","bold","blue",24);
    static DecimalFormat out = new DecimalFormat("0.#");

    public static void displayStatistics(Boat vessel)
    {
        screen.write("Name: "+vessel.getName()+"\n");
        screen.write("Position: "+out.format(vessel.getX())+","+
                    out.format(vessel.getY())+"\n");
        screen.write("Bearing: "+vessel.getBearing()+"\n");
        screen.write("Speed: "+vessel.getSpeed()+" mph\n");

        if (vessel instanceof MotorBoat)
        {
            MotorBoat mb = (MotorBoat)vessel;
            screen.write("Fuel remaining: "+
                        out.format(mb.getFuelRemaining())+" g\n");
            screen.write("Average fuel consumption: "+
                        mb.getAverageFuelConsumption()+" mpg\n");
        }

        screen.write("\n\n");
    }

    public static void main(String[] args)
    {

        screen.showWindow();

        // create motorboat called Enigma, positioned at coordinates
        // 0,0 with a maximum speed of 25 mph, 5 gallons of fuel and an
        // average fuel consumption of 25 mpg
        MotorBoat enigma = new
        MotorBoat("Enigma",0.0f,0.0f,25,5.0f,25.0f);
```

```
        // set the Enigma on a bearing to reach the coordinates 10,10
        enigma.calculateBearingTo(10.0f,10.0f);

        //. create a light breeze at a speed of 10 mph blowing from the
        // South-East
        Wind lightBreeze = new Wind(10,"SE");

        // create a sailboat called Laser, positioned at coordinates
        // 20,0 in a light breeze
        SailBoat laser = new SailBoat("Laser",20.0f,0.0f,lightBreeze);

        // set the Laser on a bearing to reach the coordinates 10,10
        laser.calculateBearingTo(10.0f,10.0f);

        // if the Enigma has enough fuel to travel to the new position
        // then set the speed of the motorboat to 80% of its maximum
        // speed
        if (enigma.canTravelTo(10.0f,10.0f))
        {
            enigma.setSpeed(0.8f);
        }

        // if the Laser has a suitable following wind to travel to the
        // new position then set the sail area to 100% (full sail)
        if (laser.canTravelTo(10.0f,10.0f))
        {
            laser.setSpeed(1.0f);
        }

        // display the variables of the Enigma and the Laser
        displayStatistics(enigma);
        displayStatistics(laser);
    }
}
```

The following screenshot results from running program.

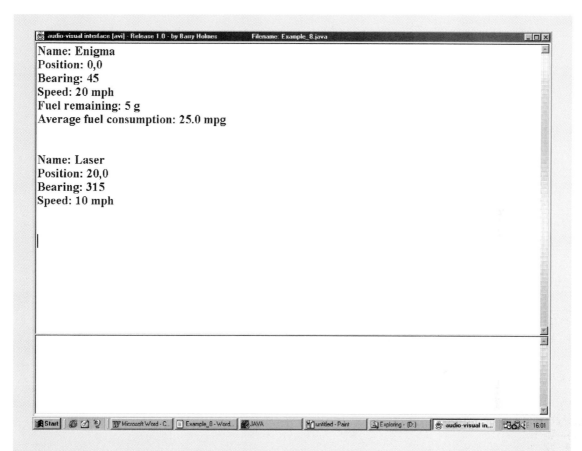

Statement of the Problem   A computer simulation is an imitation of the behavior of a system. The second half of this case study is a computer simulation of the movement of different types of boats on a lake. In this example, the course a motorboat and a sailboat travel over a predefined area will be displayed. The information output when running the simulation will be the name, position, bearing, and speed at a particular time in the simulation for each boat. In the case of the motorboat, the amount of fuel remaining will also be displayed. To ascertain the movement of boats within a predefined area, the simulation time will be a period of minutes, or even hours. However, the time it takes the simulation program to run will be several seconds.

Analysis of Classes   The simulation is used to calculate the position, bearing, and speed of a particular set of ships over a period of simulated time. Time is a suitable candidate for a class, and will contain the following constructors and methods.

The class `Time` uses two instance variables to assist in recording the passing of time—a one-dimensional array to store the hours and minutes, and a primitive variable to store the time interval.

The implementation of the class `Time` follows. Once again the coding of this class is a trivial exercise; the authors have omitted the normal stages of algorithm development for the methods in the class.

```java
public class Time
{
     // instance variables

     /**
     The array time stores the hours in time[0] and the minutes in
     time[1]
     both the hours and minutes are initialized to zero at the
     start of the simulation.
     */
     private int[] time = {0,0};

     /**
     The number of minutes the time must be updated, after the simulation
     of a set of events, such as the boats moving to a new position.
     */
     private int   timeInterval;

     // constructor
     /**
     The Time class creates an object that enables the passing of time to
     be created, for the purpose of computer simulation of events.
     @param interval is the time-lapse between observing events.
     */
     public Time(int interval)
     {
          timeInterval = interval;
     }

     // instance methods

     /**
     The method update increases the time by the time interval.
     */
     public void update()
     {
          time[1] = time[1]+timeInterval;
```

```
            if (time[1] >= 60)
            {
                    time[0] = time[0] + (int)(time[1]/60);
                    time[1] = time[1] % 60;
            }
    }


    /**
    The getHours method gets the hours component of the simulated time.
    @return Returns the hour component of elapsed time.
    */
    public int getHours()
    {
            return time[0];
    }


    /**
    The getMinutes method gets the minutes component of simulated time.
    @return Returns the minutes component of elapsed time.
    */
    public int getMinutes()
    {
            return time[1];
    }


    /**
    The method elapsedTime returns the number of minutes that have
    elapsed since the start of the simulation.
    @return Returns the elapsed time in minutes.
    */
    public int elapsedTime()
    {
            return 60*time[0] + time[1];
    }
}
```

Before we can use the `Time` class in a simulation, it is necessary to introduce a method to calculate the new position of a boat after a set period of time. The method `calculateNewPosition` can be defined in the superclass `Boat` and inherited by the subclasses `MotorBoat` and `SailBoat`.

Since both the speed of the boat and the time interval over which the boat travels are already known, the distance between the current position of the boat [x,y] and the position of the boat after a set time is calculated as a product of the speed and the time.

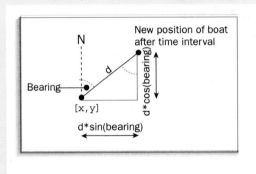

Figure 6.15 Calculation of the x and y distances traveled.

Figure 6.15 illustrates that the distance traveled and the bearing can be used to calculate the x distance traveled and the y distance traveled. Once these values are known, they are used to update the position of the boat from the current position [x,y] to the new position after the set time interval. The revised code for the `Boat` class contains the implementation of the `calculateNewPosition` method.

```
public abstract class Boat
{
        .
        .
        .

    /**
    The method calculateNewPosition will set the values of x and y to the
    new position of the boat as it moves over a period of time.
    @param timeInterval is the period of time over which the change of
    position takes place.
    */
    public void calculateNewPosition(int timeInterval)
    {
        double angle;
        double distance;

        // time interval is the number of elapsed minutes since
        // the previous distance was calculated
        distance = speed * (float)timeInterval / 60.0f;
        angle = ((double)bearing * Math.PI / 180.0);

        // calculate new position
        x = x+(float)(distance*Math.sin(angle));
        y = y+(float)(distance*Math.cos(angle));
```

```
        }



        .

        .

}
```

Now that we have a `Time` class to simulate the passing of time for the movement of a boat on the lake, it is possible to implement a method `useFuel` in the class `MotorBoat`. The distance traveled during a set time period is calculated as the product of the speed of the boat and the time interval. The quantity of fuel used is the result of the division of the distance by the average fuel consumption. This result is used to decrease the amount of fuel in the tank.

The revised code for the `MotorBoat` class contains the implementation of the `useFuel` method.

```
public class MotorBoat extends Boat
{

        .

        .

        .


        /**
        The method useFuel decreases the amount of fuel in the motorboat's
        tank over a timed interval.
        @param timeInterval is the time over which the position of the
        motorboat changes.
        */
        public void useFuel(int timeInterval)
        {
                // time interval is the number of elapsed minutes since
                // the previous distance was calculated
                float distance = speed * (float)timeInterval / 60.0f;

                // reduce fuel to cover distance
                fuelRemaining = fuelRemaining -
                                distance / averageFuelConsumption;
        }

        .

        .

        .

}
```

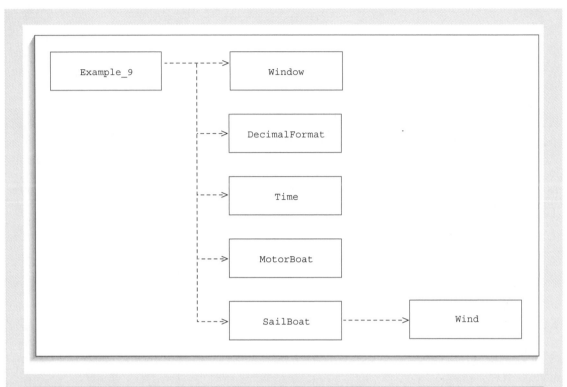

Figure 6.16 Dependency diagram

Program `Example_9` simulates the movement of a motorboat and a sailboat over 60 minutes, with the position of the boats being displayed after every minute. Figure 6.16 shows the dependencies within this program.

A listing of program `Example_9` follows.

```
import avi.*;
import java.text.DecimalFormat;

class Example_9
{
      static Window screen = new Window("Example_9.java");
      static DecimalFormat out = new DecimalFormat("00.0");

      static void boatData(Boat vessel, Time time)
      // method to display the data on any type of boat
      {
            screen.write("["+time.getHours()+":"+time.getMinutes()+"]");
            screen.write("\t"+vessel.getName());
```

```java
        screen.write("\tPosition: "+out.format(vessel.getX())+
                    ","+out.format(vessel.getY()));
        screen.write("\tBearing: "+vessel.getBearing());
        screen.write("\tSpeed: "+vessel.getSpeed());

        if (vessel instanceof MotorBoat)
        {
            MotorBoat mb = (MotorBoat)vessel;
            screen.write("\tFuel remaining: "+
                        out.format(mb.getFuelRemaining())+" g");
        }

        screen.write("\n");
    }

static public void main(String[] args)
{
    // simulation over 60 minutes
    final int MAX_SIMULATION_TIME = 60;
    // simulate movement every 1 minutes
    final int TIME_INTERVAL = 1;

    screen.showWindow();

    MotorBoat enigma = new
    MotorBoat("Enigma",0.0f,0.0f,25,5.0f,25.0f);
    enigma.calculateBearingTo(10.0f,10.0f);

    Wind moderate = new Wind(15,"SE");

    SailBoat laser = new SailBoat("Laser",20.0f,0.0f,moderate);
    laser.calculateBearingTo(10.0f,10.0f);

    if (enigma.canTravelTo(10.0f,10.0f))
    {
        enigma.setSpeed(0.8f);
    }

    if (laser.canTravelTo(10.0f,10.0f))
    {
        laser.setSpeed(1.0f);
    }

    // instantiate time
    Time simulationTime = new Time(TIME_INTERVAL);
```

```
        // display data on boats
        do
        {
                boatData(enigma,simulationTime);
                enigma.calculateNewPosition(TIME_INTERVAL);
                enigma.useFuel(TIME_INTERVAL);
                boatData(laser,simulationTime);
                laser.calculateNewPosition(TIME_INTERVAL);
                simulationTime.update();
        } while (simulationTime.elapsedTime() <= MAX_SIMULATION_TIME);
    }
}
```

Following is a screen shot from running the program. Notice that the motorboat reaches the destination whose position is given by the coordinates [10,10] at approximately 43 minutes into the simulation, and the sailboat reaches the same destination at approximately 56 minutes into the simulation.

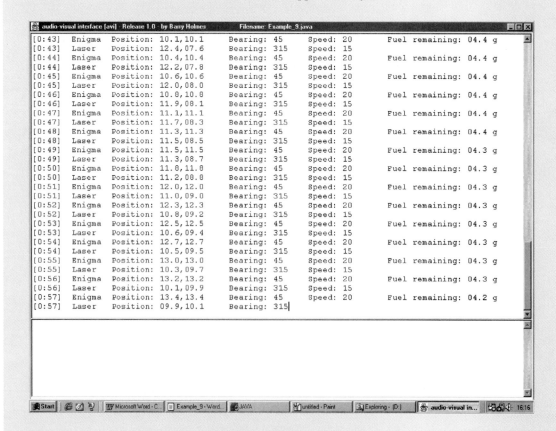

Note also that the fuel on the motorboat is gradually reduced over the timed simulation.

NOW DO THIS   Modify program `Example_9` such that:

(1) The motorboat changes its bearing at [10,10] to reach a new destination at [0,20], maintaining its current speed. At the new destination it changes its course again to a final destination at [−20,0] at full speed.

(2) The sailboat changes bearing at [10,10] also to reach a new destination at [−20,20] using full sail.

(3) Simulate the movement of the boats over 180 minutes, in 1 minute intervals, and from the output, estimate at what time and position in the simulation the boats cross paths.

6.9   Interfaces

Sometimes we want a class to inherit from more than one other class. In Java this is accomplished indirectly using an "interface." An *interface* is a class that contains only abstract methods and/or constants. The interface supplies a specification of methods and requires another class to implement the methods of the specification. The UML representations of an interface are shown in Figure 6.17.

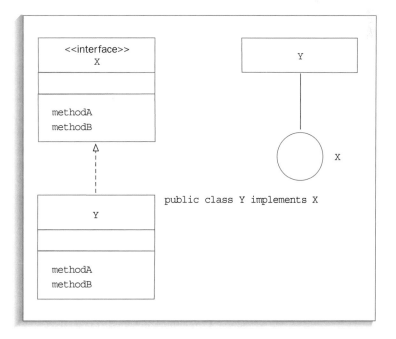

Figure 6.17 Alternative UML representations of an interface

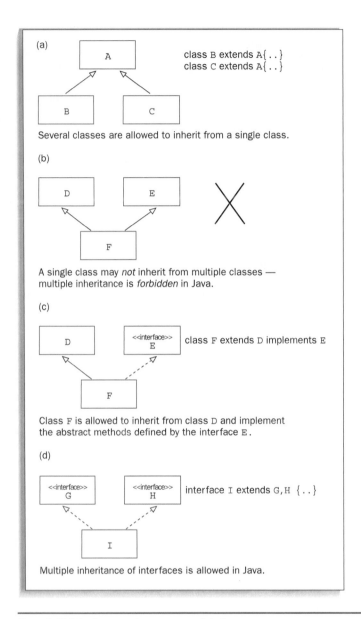

Figure 6.18 Inheritance—classes versus interfaces

The implementation of the methods of an interface may be regarded as weak inheritance, hence the use of the dashed line with the hollow arrow head pointing at the interface. Consider the following scenarios illustrated in Figure 6.18.

Part (a) illustrates that several classes may inherit from a single class. Therefore, class B can extend A, and class C can extend A. However, part (b) reveals that a single class cannot inherit from more than one class. The ability of one class to inherit from more than one superclass is known as *multiple inheritance* and is forbidden in Java. What if you have defined classes and you explicitly want them to inherit the characteristics from more than one class?

The answer is to define an *interface*. Part (c) illustrates that it is perfectly acceptable to extend class D (that is, inherit all the constants, variables, implemented constructors, and implemented methods into class F), and inherit all the constants and abstract methods from class E. That is, you can interface E with a view to implementing the undefined methods from E.

Java will permit multiple inheritance of interfaces, but not classes. In the part (d) interface, I has inherited all the abstract methods and constants from interfaces G and H. However, it is still necessary for a class to implement all the inherited abstract methods from G and H.

Note that it is possible for an interface not to contain any methods or constants.

> *i*   Interfaces are a data type, in the same way that classes are a data type. When a class implements an interface, instances of that class can be assigned to variables of the interface type.

Recall the hierarchy described in Section 6.1. If each of the subclasses Corvette, Beetle, and Porsche needed to implement a `Drawing` class, then the relationships between the classes and the interface is shown in Figure 6.19.

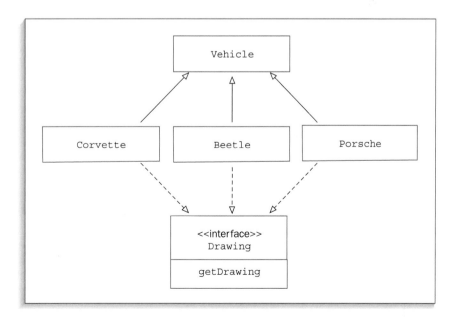

Figure 6.19 Relationship between classes and an interface

If we assume that the constructor of the `Vehicle` class allows the name of a model to be input, then the subclasses may also make reference to this constructor. The subclasses also inherit the instance method to get the name of the model. The significance of this example is not the inheritance, but how each subclass implements the interface `Drawing`.

The interface `Drawing` contains just one abstract method `getDrawing`. The implementation of `getDrawing` involves returning the name of an image file associated with a picture of the appropriate subclass.

A listing of the interface `Drawing` follows.

```
public interface Drawing
{
     public String getDrawing();
}
```

A listing of the classes in the hierarchy follows.

```
public class Vehicle
{
     String model;

     public Vehicle(String name)
     {
          model = name;
     }

     public String getName()
     {
          return model;
     }
}


public class Beetle extends Vehicle implements Drawing
{
     public Beetle(String name)
     {
          super(name);
     }

     public String getDrawing()
     {
          String image = new String("Beetle.gif");

          return image;
     }
}
```

```java
public class Corvette extends Vehicle implements Drawing
{
      public Corvette(String name)
      {
            super(name);
      }

      public String getDrawing()
      {
            String image = new String("Corvette.gif");

            return image;
      }
}

public class Porsche extends Vehicle implements Drawing
{
      public Porsche(String name)
      {
            super(name);
      }

      public String getDrawing()
      {
            String image = new String("Porsche.gif");

            return image;
      }
}
```

Program `Example_10` is used to demonstrate the use of the interface in the associated classes.

```java
import avi.*;

class Example_10
{
      public static void main(String[] args)
      {
            Window screen = new
            Window("Example_10.java","bold+italic","black",24);
            screen.showWindow();

            // instantiate car objects
            Corvette corvette = new Corvette("Corvette");
            Beetle beetle = new Beetle("Beetle");
            Porsche porsche = new Porsche("Porsche");
```

```
// create an array of image filenames for each car
String[] pictures = new String[3];
pictures[0] = corvette.getDrawing();
pictures[1] = beetle.getDrawing();
pictures[2] = porsche.getDrawing();

// instantiate a FilmStrip containing the car images
FilmStrip images = new FilmStrip(screen,pictures,140,60);

// display the names of the cars on the screen
screen.write(corvette.getName()+"\n\n");
screen.write(beetle.getName()+"\n\n");
screen.write(porsche.getName()+"\n\n");

// display the images of the cars on the screen
images.showFilmStrip();
    }
}
```

A screen shot from the program running follows.

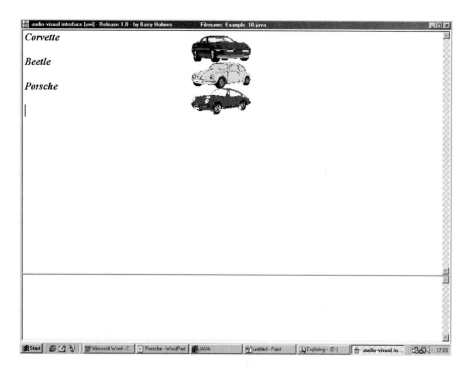

You may wonder when to use inheritance and when to use an interface:

- When we want to create a collection of closely related classes that share some behavior, we use inheritance.

- Unlike inheritance, implementing an interface does not imply any close relationship between the class and the interface(s). However, if we only want a collection of objects to be able to perform some common tasks, then using an interface is a better strategy.

If you are a beginning student, the remainder of this chapter may be omitted on the first reading.

6.10   **Constructors Revisited**

To help demonstrate the concepts described in this and the next two sections of the chapter, we will investigate the creation of a class that provides us with *rational numbers* (fractions). Such a class is often called a Rational ADT (Abstract Data Type). Java provides base types for integers and real numbers but not for rational numbers. We want to be able to create rational numbers, perform rational-number arithmetic, compare rational numbers for equality, make a copy of a rational number, and print rational numbers. In this section and the next two, we will introduce some new concepts using the rational number problem as an example; in the upcoming Case Study, we will completely develop the class `Rational`. These sections will cover many important concepts and language constructs: method overloading, method design alternatives, and copying and comparing objects.

You have already learned that a constructor is given the same name as the class, and you have probably observed that a class may contain more than one constructor. For example, if you inspect the constructors for the `String` class, you will notice there are nine constructors all with the same name, `String`. Using the same name for methods, either constructors, instance methods, or class methods, but not a mixture of all three, is known as *method overloading*.

i   Overloading a method is not the same as overriding a method, as discussed earlier. Overloading involves providing several methods with the same name, but having different formal parameter lists. In overriding, not only are the names of the methods the same, but the formal parameter lists of the overridden methods are also the same.

You may wonder how the computer can distinguish between methods of the same name. If you inspect the constructors for the `String` class, the only part of the constructor that distinguishes it from the other constructors is the formal parameter list. The number and type of parameters in the formal parameter list is the only way in which the compiler can distinguish overloaded methods.

Consider creating a class for a rational number (fraction). A natural way to do this is to create a class that contains two instance variables that together represent the fraction, a `numerator` and a `denominator`. Both instance variables are declared as `private` since access to the variables must be restricted to methods within the class.

At least two constructors may be provided for this class. The first is a default constructor that takes no parameters, yet initializes the `numerator` to zero and the `denominator` to 1. A more useful constructor has parameters that represent values for the `numerator` and `denominator` of the instantiated object. The initial steps towards the creation of the class `Rational` follow. The class contains two instance variables and two constructors:

```
public class Rational
{
    private int numerator;                  // instance variables
    private int denominator;

    public Rational()                       // default constructor
    {
        numerator = 0;
        denominator = 1;
    }

    public Rational(int num, int denom)     // specific constructor
    {
        numerator = num;

        if (denom == 0)
            denominator = 1;
        else
            denominator = denom;

        makeRational();
    }

        .
        .
```

You will note that the second constructor does not allow the creation of a rational number with a zero denominator, which is illegal in the world of mathematics. Any attempt to use a zero denominator will result in a default denominator of unity being substituted. In the next chapter you will learn the technique of exception handling to deal with erroneous data.

The class method `makeRational()` that is called in the second constructor is used to reduce the fraction to its simplest rational form (for example, the fraction 6/8 would be represented as 3/4) and for ensuring that a negative rational number is stored with a negative numerator and a positive denominator. In working with our rational number class we will always keep the representation of the rational number in this form. This approach will simplify some of the methods that we will be creating.

6.11   Instance Methods Revisited

To continue building the class `Rational`, it will be necessary to include methods that can be applied to objects of type `Rational`. The mathematics of fractions should include such operations as addition, subtraction, multiplication, and division.

> *i* Java does not allow operator overloading, so it is not possible to use the operators +, -, *, and / in the context of rational numbers. The only exception to this rule is the overloading of the + operator for string concatenation.

Suppose we have instantiated two `Rational` objects as follows:

```
Rational a = new Rational(1,2);
Rational b = new Rational(3,4);
```

and we want to add them together and put the result into the `Rational` object c. There are several ways to approach the definition of the mathematical operations, such as an `add` method. You could define an `add` instance method with only one parameter that returns the sum of the numbers, for example, c = a.add(b); or you could define an `add` class (`static`) method with two parameters that returns the sum of the numbers, for example, c = `Rational.add(a,b)`. We will use a third approach—we define an `add` instance method with two parameters that is invoked through the object that is to hold the result of the operation (for example, c.add(a,b);).

The approach you choose will depend upon the problem set being used. For example, you may want to use the `add` instance method that takes just one parameter in a problem set that contains complex expressions such as a.add(b.add(c)). In the programming problems at the end of this chapter, you are given the opportunity to rewrite the `Rational` class using the alternative definitions.

The instance method for the addition of two rational numbers follows.

```
public class Rational
{
       .

   public void add(Rational x, Rational y)
```

```
{


   numerator = x.numerator * y.denominator +
               y.numerator * x.denominator;
   denominator = x.denominator * y.denominator;
   makeRational();
}
```

.
.

If you had to add the fractions $\frac{xn}{xd} + \frac{yn}{yd}$, the result of the addition would take the form of $\frac{(xn.yd + xd.yn)}{(xd.yd)}$. Note that xn and yn refer to the numerator of the rational numbers x and y, and xd and yd refer to the denominator of the rational numbers x and y. In this method the instance variables numerator and denominator refer to the instance variables of the object c that invoked the method. These could also be expressed as this.numerator and this.denominator, respectively. Access to the corresponding numerator and denominator instance variables for the rational parameters x and y is via the dot (.) notation. Thus x.numerator refers to the numerator instance variable for object x, and y.denominator refers to the denominator instance variable for object y.

The value for the addition of the two fractions must be converted to the simplest form using the class method makeRational(). Can you write instance methods to subtract and multiply pairs of rational numbers? The answer is given in a program listing later in the chapter. The divide operation is a special case, as we will see in the next section.

6.12   Object Properties

Comparing Objects

You may recall that in Chapter 2 it was stated that class types are stored by reference, unlike primitive data types that are stored by value. Whenever an object is instantiated, all the nonstatic class variables for that object are allocated memory and initialized with data. Figure 6.20 illustrates that for the declaration of

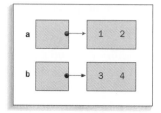

Figure 6.20 Storage of objects

the two `Rational` objects a and b, separate memory is allocated for storing the values of the two objects, and references point at the two areas of memory.

If we want to compare the two objects a and b for equality, the statement a==b will compare only the values of the references (arrowed lines in Figure 6.20) and not the contents of what is being referenced.

> The values of the references are the values of memory addresses taken from the heap. Therefore, the comparison of a==b is a comparison of whether a and b are the same memory addresses, in other words, the comparison asks if they refer to the same area of memory for storing the object's data.

To compare the two objects for equality, it is necessary to invent a new instance method that compares the values of the numerator and denominator for each object. Since all classes are subclasses of the `Object` class, a class that implements its own method to test whether two distinct objects contain the same values (a test for equality) should override the `equals` method of the `Object` class.

```
public boolean equals(Object anyObject)
{
      if (anyObject == null || ! (anyObject instanceof Rational))
            return false;
      else
      {
            Rational X = (Rational) anyObject;
            return ((this.numerator == X.numerator) &&
                  (this.denominator == X.denominator));
      }
}
```

The instance method `equals` is invoked using the statement `a.equals(b)`; it returns a `boolean` value of either `true` or `false`. In the implementation of the method, the `this` keyword refers to the object a that invoked the method. The object b is taken as the parameter x in the method. If the statement

```
((this.numerator == x.numerator) && (this.denominator == x.denominator));
```

evaluates to true, then the value `true` is returned and the contents of the two objects are the same; otherwise, if the statement evaluates to false, then the value `false` is

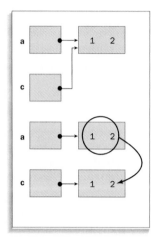

Figure 6.21 Reference versus copy (clone)

returned, indicating that the contents of the two objects differ. Note that this approach depends on the fact that both rational numbers are in simplest terms.

Copying Objects

In Chapter 2, it was stated that an assignment of one object to another does not produce a copy of the object, but only a reference to the object. For example, referring to the rational numbers, the statement c = a will only cause object c to refer to object a, as illustrated in the top diagram in Figure 6.21. Thus if the value of object a changed, then object c would no longer make reference to the original values of object a—it would refer to the new values!

If we want to make a copy of object a and assign this to object c, it is necessary to include a new instance method copy in the class Rational. A subclass that implements a method to make a copy of an object should override the clone method from the Object class. The method clone() may only be used where those subclasses have implemented the Cloneable interface. The Cloneable interface is a public interface found in the java.lang package and contains no methods.

```
public interface Cloneable{}
```

The interface simply indicates that the class that implements it may be cloned (copied) by calling the Object method clone(). Since the Rational class contains a method for copying a rational number, the class Rational may be written taking into account the inheritance of the method clone from the class Object. The inherited method is overridden, and the class must also implement the Cloneable interface.

```
class Rational extends Object implements Cloneable
{
      .
      .
      .

    public Object clone()
    {
        Object temporary = new Rational(this.numerator, this.denominator);

        return temporary;
    }
}
```

> *i* Since all classes are derived from the class `Object`, it is not strictly necessary to state that a subclass extends the `Object` class.

The instance method would be invoked using the statement `c = a.copy()`.

The object that invoked the method is `a`; therefore, any reference to the keyword `this` in the implementation of the method refers to the object `a`. Notice from the implementation that a new object `temporary` is instantiated and initialized with the data values associated with object `a`. The constructor has copied the data values of the object `a` to the object `temporary`.

The object `temporary` is then returned from the instance method and assigned to the object `c`. Object `c` now has its own copy of object `a`. Any subsequent changes made to the value of object `a` will not alter the value of object `c`.

Objects of type `Rational` can then be copied and compared for equality as follows.

```
Rational a = new Rational(1,2);
Rational b;

// copying an object
b = (Rational)a.clone();

// testing two objects for equality
if (a.equals(b))
```

Because `a.clone()` returns an object of type `Object`, it is necessary to cast the returned value before the assignment can be made.

Passing Objects as Parameters

When we pass an object as a parameter to a method, as we did in the add method in Section 6.11, the reference to the object is available to the method, not a copy of the object. Therefore, programmers must be very careful when using an object that has been passed as a parameter, particularly when changes are being made to objects of the same class.

Consider the following code to implement the divide operation for our Rational class, remembering that division of fractions is the same as multiplying by the inverse of the second fraction:

```
// NOTE - this code is incorrect
public Rational divide(Rational X, Rational Y)
{
      numerator = X.numerator * Y.denominator;
      denominator = X.denominator * Y.numerator;
      makeRational();
}
```

This code will work perfectly under most conditions but will fail under one special condition. Suppose that a, b, and c are all objects of class Rational that represent 1/2, that is, the value of each numerator is 1 and the value of each denominator is 2. If we use the statement

```
c.divide(a,b);
```

then the new value of c will be 1 as expected. But, if instead we use the statement

```
c.divide(c,c);
```

then the new value of c will be 1/2, which is incorrect! Do you see why?

The first statement of the method will change the numerator of the object c to 2 (the numerator of X, which is 1, times the denominator of Y, which is 2). In one sense, at this instant in time the c object is in an inconsistent state, since its numerator has been changed but its denominator has not been changed accordingly. Obviously, at this instant in time we should not use c. But that is exactly what we do in the next statement. Since the parameters are passed by reference, when the second statement is executed, the operand Y.numerator will be referring to *the current inconsistent contents of the object* c, not the contents of c when the method was invoked. Therefore, the second statement will set the denominator of the object c to 4 (the denominator of X, which is still 2, times the numerator of Y, which is also 2). So the object c ends up with the value 2/4 = 1/2, which is incorrect.

You will see that we avoid this problem in our implementation of the Rational class in the Case Study by using locally defined variables to hold the intermediate results.

Arithmetic of Rational Numbers

Statement of Problem   Devise a class for the addition, subtraction, multiplication, and division of rational numbers (fractions). The class should also contain methods to print a rational number and compare rational numbers for equality, as well as copy one rational number to another.

Write a test program to test all the methods of the class `Rational`.

Analysis of Classes

The arithmetic associated with rational numbers can be represented by the following expressions.

Addition	$xn/xd + yn/yd = (xn.yd+xd.yn)/(xd.yd)$
Subtraction	$xn/xd - yn/yd = (xn.yd-xd.vn)/(xd.yd)$
Multiplication	$xn/xd \cdot yn/yd = (xn.yn)/(xd.yd)$
Division	$xn/xd / yn/yd = (xn.yd)/(xd.yn)$

These expressions are used in the instance methods that provide the arithmetic operations on the rational numbers. Rational numbers must always be expressed in their simplest form. For example, the fraction $12/96$ would need to be converted to $1/8$ by finding the greatest common divisor (gcd) between the numerator and denominator and dividing both the numerator and denominator by this value. The gcd in the fraction $12/96$ is 12; thus, if both the numerator and denominator are divided by 12, the fraction is reduced to its simplest form of $1/8$.

In calculating the simplest form for a fraction, it is necessary to use two new `private` methods; the first implements Euclid's algorithm for calculating the greatest common divisor, and the second is an algorithm known as `makeRational()`, which divides both the numerator and denominator by the greatest common divisor, taking notice of the signs of the numerator and/or denominator. Figure 6.22 illustrates the UML representation of the class `Rational`.

The definition of the class `Rational` follows. Notice that it contains the two constructors, together with instance methods to perform arithmetic, comparisons for equality and object assignment discussed earlier in the chapter, and printing the value of a rational number. This is the public face of the class `Rational`. Access to the instance variables `numerator` and `denominator` and to the `private` methods `greatestCommonDivisor` and `makeRational` is denied.

```
public class Rational implements Cloneable
{
    // constructors
    public Rational();
    public Rational(int num, int denom);

    // instance methods
    public void add(Rational x, Rational y);
```

```
      public void subtract(Rational x, Rational y);
      public void multiply(Rational x, Rational y);
      public void divide(Rational x, Rational y);
      public String toString();
      public boolean equals(Object anyObject);
      public Object clone();

      // private helper methods
      private int greatestCommonDivisor(int n, int d);
      private void makeRational();
}
```

Euclid's algorithm for the method `greatestCommonDivisor` is as follows:

1. divide n by d and find the remainder
2. while remainder is not zero
3.   assign d to n
4.   assign remainder to d
5.   divide n by d and find remainder
6. assign d to gcd

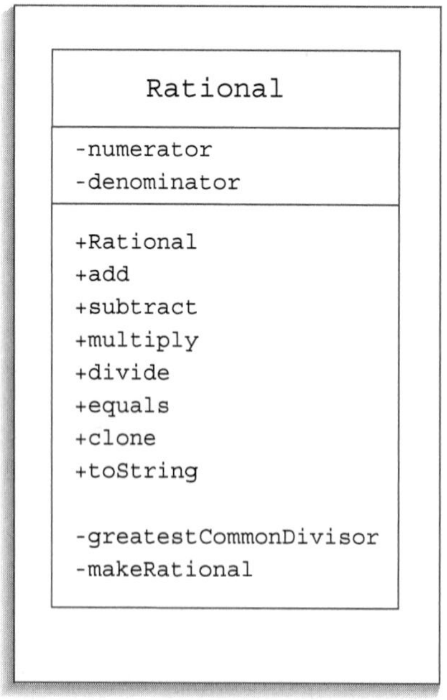

```
               Rational

     -numerator
     -denominator

     +Rational
     +add
     +subtract
     +multiply
     +divide
     +equals
     +clone
     +toString

     -greatestCommonDivisor
     -makeRational
```

Figure 6.22 UML representation of the
`Rational` class

Desk check for `greatestCommonDivisor`

n	d	remainder	(remainder==0)?	gcd
12	96	12	false	
96	12	0	true	
				12

Algorithm for the method `makeRational()`

Euclid's algorithm is used in a `private` method `makeRational()` that converts a numerator and denominator into a rational number in our standard form. The purpose of the code is to remove the negative signs if the numerator and denominator are both negative, and to move the negative sign to the numerator if the denominator is negative and the numerator isn't negative. Then the rational number is reduced by dividing by the greatest common denominator.

The algorithm for the method `makeRational()` follows.

1. if the denominator is less than zero
2.   multiply the numerator by −1
3.   multiply the denominator by −1
4. calculate the greatest common divisor for the abs value(numerator) and denominator
5. divide the numerator by the gcd
6. divide the denominator by the gcd

Desk check for `makeRational`

numerator	denominator	gcd	(denominator < 0)?
−12	−96		true
12	96	12	
1	8		

The implementation of the class `Rational` follows. Apart from the `java.lang` package, this class has no other dependencies.

```
public class Rational implements Cloneable
{
     // constant
     private static final String EMPTY_STRING = "";

     // instance variables
     private int numerator;
     private int denominator;
```

```java
// helper methods
private int greatestCommonDivisor(int n, int d)
{
      int remainder = n % d;

      while (remainder != 0)
      {
            n = d;
            d = remainder;
            remainder = n % d;
      }

      return d;
}

private void makeRational()
{
      int gcd;
      int divisor = 0;

      if (denominator < 0)
      {
            numerator = numerator * -1;
            denominator = denominator * -1;
      }

      gcd = greatestCommonDivisor(Math.abs(numerator), denominator);
      numerator = numerator / gcd;
      denominator = denominator/ gcd;
}

// constructors
/**
The rational class creates an object that represents a proper
fraction.
The default constructor sets the fraction to zero.
*/

public Rational()
{
      numerator = 0;
      denominator = 1;
      makeRational();
}
```

```
/**
The rational class creates an object that represents a proper
fraction. The denominator is not allowed to be zero.
@param num is the value of the numerator of the fraction.
@param denom is the value of the denominator of the fraction.
*/
public Rational(int num, int denom)
{
      numerator = num;
      if (denom == 0)
          denominator = 1;
      else
          denominator = denom;
      makeRational();
}


// instance methods
/**
Adds fraction X to fraction Y.
@param X is fraction X.
@param Y is fraction Y.
*/
public void add(Rational X, Rational Y)
{

      numerator = X.numerator * Y.denominator +
                  Y.numerator * X.denominator;
      denominator = X.denominator * Y.denominator;
      makeRational();
}


/**
Subtracts fraction Y from fraction X.
@param X is fraction X.
@param Y is fraction Y.
*/
public void subtract(Rational X, Rational Y)
{
      numerator = X.numerator * Y.denominator -
                  Y.numerator * X.denominator;
      denominator = X.denominator * Y.denominator;
      makeRational();
}
```

```java
/**
Multiplies fraction X by fraction Y.
@param X is fraction X.
@param Y is fraction Y.
*/
public void multiply(Rational X, Rational Y)
{
     numerator = X.numerator * Y.numerator;
     denominator = X.denominator * Y.denominator;
     makeRational();
}


/**
Divides fraction X by fraction Y.
@param X is fraction X.
@param Y is fraction Y.
*/
public void divide(Rational X, Rational Y)
{
     int holdNum;
     holdNum = X.numerator * Y.denominator;
     denominator = X.denominator * Y.numerator;
     numerator = holdNum;
     makeRational();
}


/**
@return a representation of the fraction as a string.
*/
public String toString()
{
     String result=EMPTY_STRING;

     if (denominator == 1)
          result = String.valueOf(numerator);
     else
     {
          result = result.concat(String.valueOf(numerator));
          result = result.concat("/");
          result = result.concat(String.valueOf(denominator));
     }

     return result;
}
```

```
/**
Compares two fractions for equality. The first fraction is 'this',
and the second fraction is X.
@param anyObject is one of the fractions being compared for
 equality.
@return true if the fractions are the same values, otherwise return
 false.
*/
public boolean equals(Object anyObject)
{
       if (anyObject == null || ! (anyObject instanceof Rational))
              return false;
       else
       {
              Rational X = (Rational) anyObject;
              return ((this.numerator == X.numerator) &&
                     (this.denominator == X.denominator));
       }
}


/**
Makes a copy of the 'this' fraction.
@return a copy of the 'this' fraction.
*/
public Object clone()
{
       Object temporary = new
       Rational(this.numerator, this.denominator);

       return temporary;
}
}
```

The methods of the class `Rational` require testing. Our customary practice has been to create a class, in this case `Example_11`, containing a `main` method to instantiate a number of `Rational` objects (fractions), and test the instance methods of the class. The UML diagram for `Example_11` and its dependencies are shown in Figure 6.23.

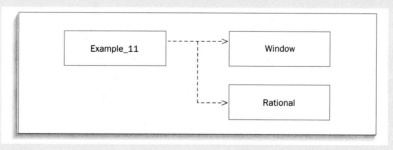

Figure 6.23 UML representations of class `Example_11` and its dependencies

```
import avi.*;

class Example_11
{
      public static void main(String[] args)
      {
            Window screen = new Window("Example_1.java");
            screen.showWindow();

            // instantiate Rational objects a, b, c and d
            Rational a = new Rational(-8,3);
            Rational b = new Rational(9,4);
            Rational c = new Rational();
            Rational d;

            // display values of fractions for a and b
            screen.write("a=" + a + "\n");
            screen.write("b=" + b + "\n");

            // display results of arithmetic on fractions
            c.add(a,b);
            screen.write("a+b=" + c + "\n");
            c.subtract(a,b);
            screen.write("a-b=" + c + "\n");
            c.multiply(a,b);
            screen.write("a*b=" + c + "\n");
            c.divide(a,b);
            screen.write("a/b=" + c + "\n");
            screen.write("c=" + c + "\n");
            c.add(c,c);
            screen.write("c+c=" + c + "\n");
            screen.write("c=" + c + "\n");
            c.divide(c,c);
            screen.write("c/c=" + c + "\n");

            // make a copy of a fraction and display the result
            d=(Rational)a.clone;
            screen.write("d=" + d + "\n");
```

```
         // compare the fractions a and d for equality
         if (d.equals(a)) screen.write("Both d and a are equal\n");
    }
}
```

Results from the log file are as follows:

```
========================================================================
                   L O G      F I L E
       audio-visual interface [avi] - Release 1.0 - by Barry Holmes
         filename: Example_11.java   date: 7/9/2000   time: 7:22:50
========================================================================


a=-8/3
b=9/4
a+b=-5/12
a-b=-59/12
a*b=-6
a/b=-32/27
c=-32/27
c+c=-64/27
c=-64/27
c/c=1
d=-8/3
Both d and a are equal
```

6.13   Garbage Collection and Object Finalization

When an object is instantiated, the system obtains space for the object from an area of memory called the heap, reserves that space for use by the object, and sets the object's pointer or reference to that space. Through combinations of cloning, uses of the = and new operations, passing objects as parameters to methods, and so forth, the number of references to a particular object space can increase and decrease. If it decreases to zero, then that space is no longer accessible to the program. We say that it is *garbage*. Space inefficiencies and program deterioration can occur if a program accumulates too much garbage.

Many programming language require the programmer to manage their own garbage. In other words, it is up to the programmer to prevent garbage from accumulating. Java, however, contains an automatic garbage collector; consequently, there are no special methods set aside for the destruction of objects and reclamation of memory to the heap when the objects are no longer required.

The Java interpreter knows which objects it has allocated and which objects it can return to the heap. When you instantiate an object, you not only get an allocation of memory from the heap, but a hidden reference counter. The counter is automatically incremented every time the object is assigned a reference. Whenever a reference to an object goes out of scope, the counter is automatically decremented. Any object with a reference count of zero is a candidate for being destroyed and its memory returned to the heap.

Java performs garbage collection at the following times.

- When the amount of memory remaining in the heap falls below a predetermined level

- When you specifically ask for garbage collection by calling `System.gc()`

- Whenever the Java system has time, generally, when the system is idle waiting for user input

Although garbage collection automatically frees up the memory resources used by objects, it cannot free up other resources that an object may hold; for example, it can't close an input stream.

Java provides a special instance method to deal with this situation. The method must be named `finalize()`, it takes no arguments and returns no value, and is automatically called before an object is returned to the heap. The following points should be kept in mind when dealing with finalizers.

- A method finalizer is automatically invoked before garbage collection of the object. There is no requirement to explicitly invoke the finalizer.

- There is no guarantee that a finalizer will be invoked (if the program terminates prematurely) or in what order finalizers will be invoked (if there are several).

i   In a Java finalizer, methods are *not* automatically chained. If you have defined a `finalize()` method in a subclass, this may override a `finalize()` method in a superclass, and as a consequence, the `finalize()` method in the superclass will never get called. To avoid this problem, always include the statement `super.finalize();` as the last statement in the finalizer of the subclass.

SUMMARY

■ Inheritance is the process by which a subclass receives the data, class methods, and instance methods from a superclass. In Java, a subclass may only inherit from one superclass; multiple class inheritance, where one subclass inherits from many superclasses, is forbidden.

■ The keyword `extends` is used to define the subclass/ superclass relationship.

■ Although `private` variables are inherited by subclass objects, such variables cannot be accessed directly by the object itself and can be accessed only through a protected or `public` access method of the superclass.

■ A `protected` variable can be accessed from any method of any class in the same package or a subclass in a different package.

■ The reserved word `super` may be used in different contexts: `super()` refers to the default, no argument constructor, of the superclass; `super` may also refer to parameterized constructors of the superclass; `super` may be used as a prefix to access inherited variables and inherited methods of a superclass in a subclass.

■ Normally, Java will automatically call a superclass default constructor from a subclass constructor. If there is no explicit call to a default superclass constructor, then Java will insert such a call. The absence of a superclass default constructor will result in a compilation error.

■ Constructor calls within a class hierarchy are automatically chained. The sequence is always subclass to superclass to superclass .. object. The execution of the bodies of the constructors starts at the object constructor, followed by the superclass constructors, and finally the subclass constructor.

■ An object of a subclass may be assigned to an object of its superclass.

■ The only superclass objects that can be assigned to a subclass-typed variable, even with an appropriate cast, are those superclass objects that are actually subclass objects.

■ A subclass may override an inherited method from a superclass. When the instance method is invoked by an object from the subclass, the overridden method is used and not the superclass method.

■ Dynamic method lookup is a technique in which each object has a table of its methods, and Java searches for the correct versions of any overridden methods at run time.

■ Java's ability to decide among methods based on the run-time class is known as polymorphism.

- Polymorphic methods must be part of the same inheritance hierarchy and support the same set of required methods.

- Classes may be nested. Every instance of a member class is internally associated with an instance of the class that defines or contains the member class.

- The methods of a member class can implicitly refer to the fields defined within the member class as well as to those defined by any enclosing class, including `private` fields of the enclosing class.

- An abstract class must contain at least one abstract method in addition to the declaration of variables, constructors, instance methods, and class methods.

- An object cannot be instantiated from an abstract class. However, an object may be declared as being of abstract type.

- Abstract classes serve as a repository of variables and methods that are common to many classes lower down the class hierarchy.

- An interface may only contain constants and/or abstract methods. The interface supplies a specification that is inherited and implemented by a subclass. A subclass is allowed to inherit and implement from many interface classes.

- A programmer may write as many constructors for a class as necessary. This implies that the name of the constructor must be overloaded (the same name used again).

- The compiler distinguishes between different overloaded constructors and methods by the number and type of parameters in the formal parameter list.

- Java does not allow operator overloading except for the use of + for both numeric addition and string concatenation.

- The `this` keyword refers to the current object for which the instance method or constructor is called.

- If two objects are to be compared for equality, then a separate method must be created. The use of the == operator will compare only the references to the objects and not the instance variables of the objects.

- Similarly, if the instance variables of one object are to be assigned to another object, then a separate method must be created. The use of the = operator will only assign the value of the reference and not allocate extra memory for the instance variables to be replicated and assigned to an object.

- When an object has gone out of scope, the automatic garbage collector will release the memory occupied by an object's data to the heap.

■ A class may contain a finalizer method for the purpose of releasing other resources used by an object that are not dealt with by automatic garbage collection.

Review Questions

True or False

1. Constructors and methods may be overloaded.

2. All operators in Java may be overloaded.

3. The operator == is used to compare the instance data of two objects.

4. All classes contain a finalizer method.

5. A finalizer method must be called from within an application program for it to be invoked.

6. A subclass inherits from a superclass.

7. A class can inherit a variable or method described as `private`.

8. Any object of a subclass can be assigned to a superclass.

9. Any object of a superclass can be assigned to a subclass.

10. Overloading and overriding a method are the same.

11. A final method may have a subclass.

12. A shadowed variable will prevent access to an inherited variable.

13. An abstract class must contain at least one abstract method.

14. It is perfectly legal to instantiate an object of type `abstract` class.

15. Several subclasses may inherit from one superclass.

16. A single subclass may inherit from several superclasses.

17. A single subclass may inherit from a single superclass, and also inherit from an interface.

18. A single subclass may inherit from any number of interfaces.

19. When a class implements an interface, instances of that class can be assigned to variables of the interface type.

Short Answers

20. How many constructors may be defined in a class?

21. Can Java automatically define its own constructor for a class if one is not present?

22. How and when is the memory allocated to an object's data released to the heap?

23. Why is it better to write a method to assign one object to another?

24. What is the purpose of the statement `System.gc()`?

25. What purpose does a default constructor serve?

26. In Figure 6.3, which class is the superclass?

27. Describe inheritance between classes.

28. Where can `protected` variables and methods be accessed?

29. Give two examples of the reserved word `super`.

30. When does Java insert a call to the default constructor of a superclass?

31. What do you call the existence of a method in a subclass with the same signature as a method in the superclass?

32. What is polymorphism?

33. Describe dynamic method lookup.

34. What methods do not use dynamic method lookup?

35. Describe how, in a subclass, you would refer to a variable that was defined far beyond the immediate superclass.

36. What is an abstract method?

37. How does an interface differ from an abstract class?

38. What is the purpose of an interface? Give one example from the Java API in which an interface is defined. State the rationale behind defining such an interface.

39. What is the `Cloneable` interface and why is it used?

Exercises

40. Devise a method to test whether a rational number is greater than another rational number.

    Desk check the skeleton programs implemented in Questions (41) through (45), stating the output in each case. Describe the principles that explain why each program functions as it does.

41.

```
class A
{
    public A(Window screen){screen.write("A");}
}
```

```
class B extends A
{
    public B(Window screen){screen.write("B");}
}

class C extends B
{
    public C(Window screen){screen.write("C");}
}

class Question_41
{
    static public void main(String[] args)
    {
        Window screen = new Window("Question 41");
        screen.showWindow();

        C object = new C(screen);
    }
}
```

42.

```
class A
{
    protected int X=25;

    public A(){}
}

class B extends A
{
    protected int X=35;

    public B(){}
}

class C extends B
{
    protected int X=45;

    public C(){}
    public void display()
    {
        Window screen = new Window("Question 42");
```

```
        screen.showWindow();

        screen.write("X in class C "+X+"\n");
        screen.write("X in class C "+this.X+"\n");
        screen.write("X in class B "+super.X+"\n");
        screen.write("X in class B "+((B)this).X+"\n");
        screen.write("X in class A "+((A)this).X+"\n");
    }
}

class Question_42
{
    static public void main(String[] args)
    {
        C object = new C();
        object.display();
    }
}
```

43.

```
class Output
{
    static Window screen = new Window("Question 43");
}

class A
{
    protected int X=25;

    public A(){}
    public int getX(){return X;}
}

class B extends A
{
    protected int X=35;

    public B(){}
    public int getX()
    {
        Output.screen.write("value of X in class A "
                            +super.getX()+"\n");
        return X;
    }
}
```

```
class Question_43
{
    static public void main(String[] args)
    {
        int X;
        B object = new B();

        Output.screen.showWindow();

        X=object.getX();
        Output.screen.write("value of X in class B "+X+"\n");
    }
}
```

44.

```
interface A
{
    static final int INTERFACE_CONSTANT = 65;
}

class B
{
    static final int CLASS_CONSTANT = 45;

    public B(){}
}


class C implements A
{
    static Window screen = new Window("Question 44");

    public C(){}
    public void displayConstants()
    {
        screen.write("value of constant from interface A "+
                    INTERFACE_CONSTANT+"\n");
        screen.write("value of constant from class B "+
                    B.CLASS_CONSTANT+"\n");
    }
}

class Question_44
{
    static public void main(String[] args)
```

```
        {
            C object = new C();

            object.displayConstants();
        }
    }
```

45.

```
    interface A
    {
        static final int CONSTANT_A = 65;
    }

    interface B
    {
        static final int CONSTANT_B = 75;
    }


    interface C extends A,B
    {
        static final int CONSTANT_C = 85;
    }

    class D implements C
    {
        static Window screen = new Window("Question 45");

        public D(){}
        public void displayConstants()
        {
            screen.showWindow();

            screen.write("value of constant from interface A "+
                        CONSTANT_A+"\n");
            screen.write("value of constant from interface B "+
                        CONSTANT_B+"\n");
            screen.write("value of constant from interface C "+
                        CONSTANT_C+"\n");


        }
    }

    class Question_45
    {
```

```
static public void main(String[] args)
{
    D object = new D();

    object.displayConstants();
}
}
```

Programming Problems

46. Devise a taxonomy of classes for two-dimensional shapes and three-dimensional shapes. Implement your classes and write a program to test each method within each class.

47. Employees in a company are divided into the classes `Employee`, `HourlyPaid`, `SalesCommissioned`, and `Executive` for the purpose of calculating their weekly wages or monthly salaries. The data to be maintained for each class may be summarized as follows:

`Employee` class	Name of employee
`HourlyPaid` class	Rate of pay
	Total weekly hours worked
`SalesCommissioned` class	Percentage commission on total sales
	Total sales for month
`Executive` class	Incremental point on annual salary scale

The methods used in each class may be summarized as follows.

`Employee` class	`getName`
	`computePay`—as an abstract method
`HourlyPaid` class	`getRate`
	`getHours`
	`computePay`
`SalesCommissioned` class	`getPercentage`
	`getSales`
	`computePay`
`Executive` class	`getIncrement`
	`computePay`

Note: To compute the monthly gross wage of an executive, it is necessary to construct a one-dimensional array containing an increasing annual salary scale. Each subscript to the array equates to an incremental point on the salary scale.

Implement the classes and write a test program to verify that the classes function correctly.

48. The characteristics of airplanes are shown in Figure 6.24.

In addition to the class `airplane`, include classes for a wide-bodied jet airliner, supersonic airliner, light jet aircraft, and a military jet.

	Boeing 747	Concorde	LearJet	Tornado
Climb rate	1400 fpm	3000 fpm	3000 fpm	2500 fpm
Cruising speed*	490 knots	563 knots	440 knots	550 knots
Vortex wake	heavy	heavy	light	small
Aircraft class	wide-bodied jet	super-sonic	jet	military jet

*Note this is only the subsonic cruising speed

Figure 6.24 Characteristics of airplanes

Write a program that simulates the movement of each type of airplane over a predefined airspace. Devise a display of the movement of each airplane in a manner similar to that used in the case study.

49. A city bank offers two different types of bank account, a savings account and a checking account. To distinguish between the two types of accounts, the savings accounts are numbered from 000001 and the checking accounts are numbered from 500000. Every time a new account is opened, the system should generate a new unique account number.

Savings accounts charge no fee, provided the account contains a balance of more than $100; otherwise, the account has an annual fee of $25.00. Savings accounts pay interest at the rate of 5% per annum.

Checking accounts pay no interest until the balance exceeds $2,500. The interest is then 2.5% per annum. Checking accounts charge a fee of $1 for every transaction.

Devise appropriate classes for the different types of account. Include methods that you think appropriate for access and manipulation of data in an account.

Write a test program to verify that the classes have been implemented correctly.

50. Rewrite the add, subtract, multiply, and divide methods of the class `Rational`, such that each method only takes one parameter. For example, the instance method `add` is invoked using the syntax `a.add(b)`, where a and b are objects of type `Rational`. The add method adds together the rational numbers a and b and returns the sum. Use more complex expressions such as `a.add(b.add(c))` when testing the newly written methods of the class `Rational`.

51. Devise a class for the addition, subtraction, multiplication, and division of complex numbers. The class should also contain a method to display complex numbers.

A complex number has two parts (A, iB), where A is the real part, B is the imaginary part, and $i = \sqrt{-1}$. The following expressions show how arithmetic can be performed on two complex numbers, so that a real part R and an imaginary I are evaluated.

Addition   R = A.real + B.real
                  I = A.imaginary + B.imaginary

Subtraction   R = A.real - B.real
                   I = A.imaginary − B.imaginary

Multiplication   R = (A.real * B.real) − (A.imaginary * B.imaginary)
                   I = (A.real * B.imaginary) + (A.imaginary * B.real)

Division   T = A * (B.real − B.imaginary)
                   N = (B.real)^2 − (B.imaginary)^2
                   R = T.real / N
                   I = T.imaginary / N

Write a program to test the instance methods in the class.

52. Devise a class `CharacterString` that has the following methods.

```
class CharacterString
{
    // constructor
    public CharacterString(char[] value);

    // instance methods
    // return the length of a CharacterString
    public int length();
    // delete N characters from this string starting at the Ith
    // character
    public CharacterString delete(int N, int I);
    // insert CharacterString A into this string, starting at
    // position I
    public CharacterString insert(CharacterString A, int I);
    // remove substring A from this string
    public CharacterString remove(CharacterString A);
    // duplicate this string
    public CharacterString duplicate();
    // test this string with string A for equality
    public boolean equals(CharacterString A);
    // display this string
    public void display();
}
```

Write a program to test all the methods of the class `CharacterString`.

CHAPTER 7

Exceptions and Streams

When designing computer programs, you need to plan for the possibility of the program failing due to the occurrence of events at run time. Examples of such events might include trying to gain access to a cell of an array through a subscript that exceeds the permitted range, dividing a number by zero in an arithmetic computation, attempting to open a file that does not exist, and so on. The full list of events that can cause a program to malfunction is quite considerable!

In this chapter we introduce Java's exception-handling feature, which when used, helps to reduce the probability of program malfunction and contributes toward the design and creation of safer computerized systems.

Additionally, we introduce the concept of data streams, which permit input from keyboard and data file sources and output to screen and data file destinations. Since the use of data streams also requires a knowledge of handling exceptions, the topics of exceptions and streams have been included in the same chapter.

By the end of the chapter you should have an understanding of the following topics:

- The hierarchy of classes that support exception handling.

- Locating in a program where an exception is handled.

- The clauses `throw`, `try`, `catch`, and `finally` used in exception handling.

- Multiple exceptions.

- Creating your own exception classes.

- Tokenizing streams.

- Input and output streams that allow reading from and writing to files.

7.1 Introduction

An *exception* is an event occurring during the execution of a program that makes continuation impossible or undesirable. Examples of exceptions include division by zero, arithmetic overflow, array reference with an index out of bounds, or a fault condition on a peripheral. Many programming languages respond to an exception by aborting execution. However, one of the design goals of Java was to provide the language with sufficient features to enable the programmer to write robust programs. An *exception handler* is a piece of program code that is automatically invoked when an exception occurs. The exception handler can take appropriate remedial action, then either allow resumption of the execution of the program (at the point where the exception occurred or elsewhere) or terminate the program in a controlled manner.

The purpose of exception handling is to allow a programmer to fix exceptions that occur under the following circumstances.

- Exceptions caused by users. A user may key in the wrong data, or supply data that is inappropriate to your system. To prevent your program from crashing you need to develop a mentality for defensive programming that relies upon exception handling.

- Exceptions that indicate program errors and are intended to serve as a mechanism for debugging a program.

- Errors outside of program control, for example a fault condition on a peripheral. A *fault-tolerant* computer system is capable of providing either full functionality or reduced functionality after a failure has occurred. Software fault tolerance may be provided using exception handling. A computer system that provides a reduced level of service in spite of the occurrence of at least one fault is said to be in a state of *graceful degradation*. Techniques to handle faults are of vital importance in the design and implementation of safety-critical computer systems where people's lives may be put at risk by the malfunction of a computer-controlled system.

- Recovery from unusual, but not unexpected events.

In this chapter we will focus primarily on exceptions caused by users, and to a lesser extent on exceptions that indicate program errors. You may have already encountered exceptions caused by program errors when writing your own programs!

An exception can be implicit, in which case it is a signal from the Java Virtual Machine to the program indicating a violation of a semantic constraint of the Java language. For example, attempting to index outside the bounds of an array would automatically throw an *index-out-of-bounds exception.*

An exception may also be explicitly thrown from within the program, to signal that an error condition exists. For example, if input data is acceptable only within a predefined range, then the programmer might create code that would throw an exception if data is found to lie outside of this range.

> *i*   In both cases it is essential to grasp the concept that an exception is thrown and must eventually be caught. If you supply an exception handler, then the exception can be dealt with in the program; otherwise, it will be thrown all the way out of the program to the Java interpreter, which will handle the exception by reporting on its cause and abandoning the program.

If a method throws an exception, then the exception has to be caught. In all the programs you have written, the Java interpreter has caught any exceptions that might have occurred. Within this chapter you will learn how to write Java code to catch exceptions.

7.2   Exception Classes

An exception is the occurrence of an event that happens when the program is running. An exception is generally an error condition that interrupts the normal execution of a program.

An exception in Java is treated as an object that is an instance of the superclass `java.lang.Throwable` or an instance of one of its subclasses. A partial listing of the class `Throwable` follows.

```
public class Throwable extends Object
{
    // constructors
    public Throwable();
    public Throwable(String  message);

    // methods
    public Throwable fillInStackTrace();
    public String getMessage();
    public void printStackTrace();
    public void printStackTrace(PrintWriter  s);
    public String toString();
        .
        .
        .
}
```

The functionality of the constructors and methods will be discussed later, in the context of the program examples found in this chapter.

The superclass `Throwable` has two immediate subclasses, `Error` and `Exception`. Generally, the first of these classes `Error` is a superclass to classes that deal with errors that are unrecoverable such as `VirtualMachineError`, which includes such subclasses as `InternalError`, `OutOfMemoryError`, `StackOverflowError`, and even `UnknownError`! The second class, `Exception`, is the superclass to a number of subclasses that support exceptions that may be detected and ultimately recovered from.

Figure 7.1 illustrates a partial class hierarchy among the top levels of exception-handling classes. However, there are many subclasses of the superclasses `Error`, `Exception`, and `RuntimeException` that are not shown in Figure 7.1. For a complete list of these classes, refer to the Java API documentation.

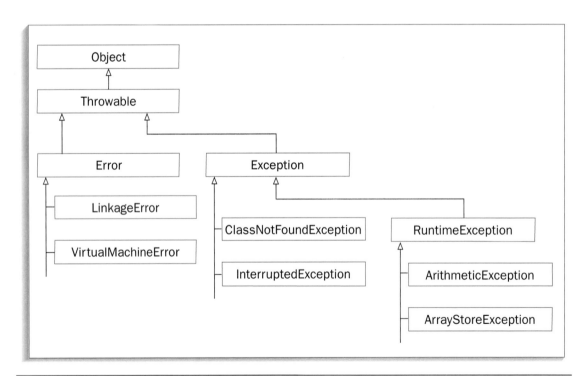

Figure 7.1 Partial class hierarchy including the `Throwable`, `Error`, and `Exception` classes

From Figure 7.1 it is clear that a number of exception classes exist that inherit from the superclass `Throwable`. The Java interpreter is capable of handling all the exceptions that may be generated. Unfortunately, the interpreter abandons the program after having warned of the exceptional condition. Unless we are using exceptions to debug parts of a program, we need to be able to catch the exception within the program and handle it ourselves.

7.3   Catching an Exception

Program `Example_1` illustrates what happens when an arithmetic exception is deliberately created. A print of the log file shows that a divisor of value zero was deliberately input to cause a run-time arithmetic exception to be thrown. This represents a typical exception generated by a user.

```
// program to demonstrate the deliberate creation of
// an arithmetic exception by dividing a number by zero

import avi.*;

class Example_1
{
      public static void main(String[] args)
      {
            Window screen = new Window("Example_1.java","bold","blue",24);
            DialogBox inputDividend = new DialogBox(screen,"Dividend?");
            DialogBox inputDivisor = new DialogBox(screen,"Divisor?");

            int dividend, divisor, quotient;

            screen.showWindow();

            inputDividend.showDialogBox();
            dividend = inputDividend.getInteger();

            inputDivisor.showDialogBox();
            divisor = inputDivisor.getInteger();

            quotient = dividend / divisor;

            screen.write(dividend+" / "+divisor+" = "+quotient+"\n");
      }
}
```

The contents of the log file from the program being executed follows.

```
================================================================================
                     L O G     F I L E
        audio-visual interface [avi] - Release 1.0 - by Barry Holmes
          filename: Example_1.java  date: 3/21/2000  time: 5:3:51
================================================================================


At the prompt: Dividend?, you input [ 25 ] at the dialog box.

At the prompt: Divisor?, you input [ 0 ] at the dialog box.
```

If you are using a PC running Microsoft Windows, inspect the contents of the MSDOS window, and you will see the following message from the Java interpreter.

```
Exception in thread "main" java.lang.ArithmeticException: / by zero
        at Example_1.main(Example_1.java:24)
```

As you can see, a divide-by-zero exception has been thrown out of the program and handled by the Java interpreter, which output the exception message. How can we incorporate into the `main` method our own code that will handle the arithmetic exception? The answer is to use a catch block. A `catch` block contains a single parameter whose type is any class from the superclass `Throwable` down through the subclass in the hierarchy.

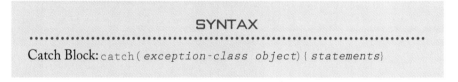

SYNTAX

••

Catch Block: `catch(`*exception-class object*`){`*statements*`}`

The `catch` block is only entered if an exception object is thrown of the same type as the class stated by the parameter, or the exception object is an instantiation   of   a   subclass   of   the   parameter.   For   example, `catch(ArithmeticException ae){..}` will allow an exception `ae` of the type `ArithmeticException` to be caught.

However, `catch(Exception e){..}` will allow an exception `e` of the type `Exception` or any type below `Exception` in the class hierarchy to be caught. Therefore, if the exception object is of type `ArithmeticException`, which is a subclass of `Exception`, the exception will still be caught.

The statements within the `catch` block may report on what caused the exception and take appropriate action to nullify the error (if appropriate). Since all the exception classes inherit from the class `Throwable`, these subclasses may use the methods defined in `Throwable` in the `catch` block to report on the error.

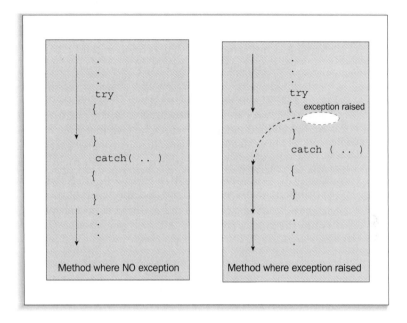

Figure 7.2 Flow of control

A `try` clause is used to delimit a block of code where the result of any method calls or other operations might cause an exception. To handle an exception, a `try` clause must have at least one `catch` block.

SYNTAX

Try Clause: `try {statements}`

Figure 7.2 illustrates the flow of control in a method that includes `try` and `catch` blocks, with and without an exception being raised. When no exception is thrown, the statements of the catch block are not executed. The computer bypasses the `catch` block and program execution resumes at the first statement that follows the end of the `catch` block (as long as it is not another `catch` block). However, when an exception is raised by a statement in the `try` block, the remaining statements in the `try` block are not executed. Control branches to the appropriate catch block that handles the exception, and the statements of the `catch` block are executed. Control then passes to the next executable statement after the `catch` block (as long as it is not another `catch` block).

Program `Example_2` is a modified version of program `Example_1`. In Program `Example_2`, a `catch` block has been coded into the `main` method to explicitly catch any arithmetic exception. Both the `try` block and the `catch` block have been embedded within a `do..while` loop controlled by a `boolean` variable. Only when valid data is input will it be possible to exit from the loop.

This technique reinforces the point made earlier, that the purpose of exception handling is to allow a programmer to fix exceptions caused by user errors.

The test run indicates that when the value of the divisor is deliberately chosen to be zero, an arithmetic exception is thrown when the interpreter attempts to divide the dividend by zero. The Java interpreter executes the code within the `catch` block associated with the arithmetic exception, then exits the `catch` block. However, the computer is still within the `do..while` loop, and the condition to exit from the loop is still false. Only when the divisor is valid is the arithmetic division performed and the result output. In these circumstances the `catch` block is never entered as there is no exception, and the computer exits from the loop.

```java
// program to demonstrate catching an exception within the program

import avi.*;

class Example_2
{
      public static void main(String[] args)
      {
            Window screen = new Window("Example_2.java","bold","blue",24);
            DialogBox inputDividend = new DialogBox(screen,"Dividend?");
            DialogBox inputDivisor = new DialogBox(screen,"Divisor?");

            int dividend, divisor, quotient;
            boolean done = false;

            screen.showWindow();

            do
            {
                  // try block
                  try
                  {
                        inputDividend.showDialogBox();
                        dividend = inputDividend.getInteger();

                        inputDivisor.showDialogBox();
                        divisor = inputDivisor.getInteger();

                        quotient = dividend / divisor;
                        screen.write(dividend+" / "+divisor+" = "
                                 +quotient+"\n");
```

```
                    done = true;
            }

            // catch block
            catch(ArithmeticException ae)
            {
                    screen.write("Exception "+ae.toString()+
                            " caught\n");
            }

        } while (! done);
    }
}
```

Since the class `Arithmetic Exception` inherits from the class `Throwable`, the method `toString()` may be used on objects of type `Arithmetic-Exception`. Remember the purpose of the method `toString()` is to convert an object to a string before it may be printed.

The contents of the log file from the running program follows.

```
=================================================================
                    L O G     F I L E
        audio-visual interface [avi] - Release 1.0 - by Barry Holmes
          filename: Example_2.java  date: 3/21/2000  time: 5:12:30
=================================================================

At the prompt: Dividend?, you input [ 25 ] at the dialog box.

At the prompt: Divisor?, you input [ 0 ] at the dialog box.

Exception java.lang.ArithmeticException: / by zero caught
At the prompt: Dividend?, you input [ 25 ] at the dialog box.

At the prompt: Divisor?, you input [ 5 ] at the dialog box.

25 / 5 = 5
```

7.4   Catching Multiple Exceptions

It is possible that other exceptions may occur when the previous program is executed. What if the character o was input instead of the digit 0 (zero)? This would generate a `NumberFormatException`, and since there is no catch block to accommodate the exception, the Java interpreter will catch the exception, display a message, and terminate the program.

You may include in a method many catch blocks to explicitly catch a number of known exceptions. The single `catch` block in Program `Example_2` may be replaced by the following code.

```
catch(ArithmeticException ae)
{
   screen.write("\nException " + ae.toString() + " caught");
}

catch(NumberFormatException nfe)
{
   screen.write("\nException " + nfe.toString() + " caught");
}
```

> *i*   When using more than one `catch` block to explicitly trap exceptions, make sure that the class type for each block is not a superclass of one of the following `catch` blocks. If you need to use a superclass in a block as a "catch all" for any exceptions that you have not explicitly coded, see that the `catch` block appears as the *last* block in the sequence.

Program `Example_3` is a modified version of program `Example_2`; the program incorporates one `try` block and two `catch` blocks. The test results show a divisor of 0 (zero) causing an arithmetic exception; a divisor of o (lower-case letter) causing a number format exception, and finally the correct result of the division.

```
// program to demonstrate catching multiple exceptions within the program

import avi.*;

class Example_3
{
      public static void main(String[] args)
      {
            Window screen = new Window("Example_3.java","bold","blue",24);
            DialogBox inputDividend = new DialogBox(screen,"Dividend?");
            DialogBox inputDivisor = new DialogBox(screen,"Divisor?");
```

```
int dividend, divisor, quotient;
boolean done = false;

screen.showWindow();

do
{
    // try block
    try
    {
        inputDividend.showDialogBox();
        dividend = new
        Integer(inputDividend.getString()).intValue();

        inputDivisor.showDialogBox();
        divisor = new
        Integer(inputDivisor.getString()).intValue();

        quotient = dividend / divisor;
        screen.write(dividend+" / "+divisor+" = "+
                     quotient+"\n");
        done = true;
    }

    // catch blocks
    catch(ArithmeticException ae)
    {
        screen.write("Arithmetic exception caught - "+
                     ae.toString()+"\n");
    }

    catch(NumberFormatException nfe)
    {
        screen.write("Number format exception caught - "+
                     nfe.toString()+"\n");
    }

} while (! done);
    }
}
```

The contents of the log file from the running program follows.

```
================================================================
               L  O  G      F  I  L  E
     audio-visual interface [avi] - Release 1.0 - by Barry Holmes
       filename: Example_3.java   date: 3/21/2000   time: 5:18:38
================================================================


At the prompt: Dividend?, you input [ 25 ] at the dialog box.

At the prompt: Divisor?, you input [ 0 ] at the dialog box.

Arithmetic exception caught - java.lang.ArithmeticException: / by zero
At the prompt: Dividend?, you input [ 25 ] at the dialog box.

At the prompt: Divisor?, you input [ o ] at the dialog box.

Number format exception caught - java.lang.NumberFormatException: o
At the prompt: Dividend?, you input [ 25 ] at the dialog box.

At the prompt: Divisor?, you input [ 5 ] at the dialog box.


25 / 5 = 5
```

NOW DO THIS   Write a program using a dialog box to input the size of an array at run-time. Also input a series of non-zero, integer values using a dialog box that are stored in the one-dimensional array. Deliberately terminate the series of integer values by a sentinel value of zero.

(1) Create an exception handler for numbers that are not in an integer format. Override the dialog box default when there is an error in the input string, so that the user is always given another opportunity for inputting a number in the correct format.

(2) Create an exception handler for the array index being out of bounds.

(3) Create an exception handler for an arithmetic exception.

(4) Calculate and output the arithmetic mean of the numbers in the array.

(5) Use data that will deliberately throw the exceptions listed in (2) and (3) to test your program, and to ensure that your exception handlers will be invoked.

7.5   Creating Your Own Exception Class

You may recall from the introduction that a predefined exception may be thrown as a result of a violation of a semantic constraint of the language. Such exceptions are covered by the predefined exception classes in the language. However, what if you want to create your own exception classes in response to various exceptions that might be thrown from a suite of your own data-validation routines? Using your own exceptions in a program will require you to create your own exception classes. Any exception class you define must be a subclass of the class `Throwable`. Naturally, the exception class will inherit all the characteristics of the class `Throwable`, unless you specifically override the methods.

The constructors of the class `Throwable` are:

```
public Throwable(); // default constructor
public Throwable(String message);
```

If the default constructor is used, then any method invoked by the object will always refer to the class of the object. For example, from the instantiation:

```
Throwable ownException = new Throwable();
```

the statement

```
screen.write(ownException.toString());
```

will display `java.lang.Throwable`.

Note that in the above example that we are explicitly calling the `toString` method, unlike the way we used `toString` in previous programs.

Suppose the constructor that takes a string argument is used this way:

```
Throwable ownException = new Throwable("THIS IS MY OWN EXCEPTION");
```

Then the statement `screen.write(ownException.toString());` will display both the name of the exception and the message that was included as the argument in the constructor:

```
java.lang.Throwable: THIS IS MY OWN EXCEPTION
```

The instance method `getMessage()` will return the message associated with the argument in the constructor. For example, the statement `screen.write(ownException.getMessage());` will display the message `THIS IS MY OWN EXCEPTION`. If the default constructor has been used, then the message is returned as `null`.

If you examine the subclasses of `Throwable`, the majority of the subclasses do not add any further functionality to this class. The classes only redefine the two constructors. Therefore, a typical class definition for your own exception class might be as follows.

```
class BadDataException extends Throwable
{
    public BadDataException()
    {
        super();
    }

    public BadDataException(String message)
    {
        super(message);
    }
}
```

Note that it is possible to extend other classes further down the hierarchy other than `Throwable`. You may care to be more specific about the type of exception you are extending. For example:

```
class BadDataException extends RuntimeException{ .. }
```

might be a better way to denote the classification of this exception. Since `RuntimeException` is a subclass of `Exception`, and `Exception` is a subclass of `Throwable`, then `BadDataException` must inherit all the functionality of `Throwable`.

User exceptions should always extend the appropriate subclass of `Throwable`. If the exception indicates a program error, it should extend a runtime exception. If it is a recoverable exception (e.g. bad data) it should extend `Exception`. However, there needs to be a decision taken that an exception is a way to handle the situation as opposed to another approach (e.g. default values on bad data as used by the `DialogBox` component of the `avi`).

Program `Example_4` invites a user to input a single integer, and the program translates the integer into the name of a day of the week. For example, 0 is translated to Sunday, 1 is translated to Monday, and so on. However, if the user inputs an integer that lies outside of the range 0 .. 6, then the method `getDayName` throws a `BadDataException`. This exception is caught within the `main` method.

Note that the `throws` clause is part of the `getDayName` method's header line. This alerts the compiler that this method throws a particular exception, in this case the `BadDataException`. Therefore, whenever the `getDayName` method is called, that exception will either have to be handled or thrown again by the method that is doing the call. More about this in the next subsection.

```java
// program to demonstrate the creation of your own exception class

import avi.*;

class Example_4
{
    static String getDayName(int dayNumber) throws BadDataException
    {
        switch (dayNumber)
        {
            case 0: return "Sunday";
            case 1: return "Monday";
            case 2: return "Tuesday";
            case 3: return "Wednesday";
            case 4: return "Thursday";
            case 5: return "Friday";
            case 6: return "Saturday";

            default: throw new BadDataException
                ("*** DAY NUMBER NOT IN RANGE 0 .. 6 ***\n");
        }
    }


    public static void main(String[] args)
    {
        Window screen = new Window("Example_4.java","bold","blue",24);
        DialogBox inputDay = new DialogBox(screen,"Day Number?");

        screen.showWindow();

        int dayNumber;
        boolean done = false;


        do
        {
            try
            {
                inputDay.showDialogBox();
                dayNumber = inputDay.getInteger();
```

```
                    screen.write("Day of week "
                            +getDayName(dayNumber)+"\n");
                    done = true;
                }

                catch(BadDataException bde)
                {
                        screen.write(bde.toString());
                }

        } while (! done);
    }
}
```

The contents of the log file from the running program follows.

```
=====================================================================
                    L O G      F I L E
         audio-visual interface [avi] - Release 1.0 - by Barry Holmes
         filename: Example_4.java    date: 3/21/2000    time: 5:46:48
=====================================================================


At the prompt: Day Number?, you input [ 7 ] at the dialog box.

BadDataException: *** DAY NUMBER NOT IN RANGE 0 .. 6 ***
At the prompt: Day Number?, you input [ 3 ] at the dialog box.

Day of week Wednesday
```

NOW DO THIS   Write a program to perform the following.

(1) Input a six-digit account number as a string.

(2) Throw a BadDataException if the string does not contain all digits.

7.6   Throwing an Exception

A simple analogy to help you understand the concept of throwing and propagating an exception follows.

A person throws a hot potato (the exception) into a small group of people. If the first person to catch the potato is wearing oven mitts (the exception handler), that person's hands do not get burned and that person can safely hold the potato (handle the exception). However, if a person in the group catches the potato and is not wearing oven mitts (no exception handler present in the method), the potato is too hot to handle and is thrown (propagated) to another person in the group. You can imagine the hot potato being thrown from person to person, until eventually it is caught by a person who can safely hold the potato (handle the exception).

A `throw` statement is executed to indicate that an exception has occurred. The `throw` statement must specify an exception object to be thrown. An exception object is any object that is instantiated from the class `Throwable` or any subclass or extension of a class in the exception classes hierarchy.

SYNTAX

....

Throw Statement: `throw exception-object`

Figure 7.3 illustrates how a thrown exception searches for a handler. The `throw` statement passes control to a `catch` block. If there is no `catch` block in the current method, the computer exits the method and returns to the calling method. Again, if there is no `catch` block to handle the exception, the computer exits the method and returns to the calling method. The process continues to pass up through the calling methods until it finds a `catch` block capable of handling the exception. Hopefully, you now see the analogy with the hot potato!

If, after returning the exception through all the calling methods, a `catch` block cannot be found, the Java interpreter will handle the exception by reporting on what caused the exception and then terminate the program.

> ⚠️ A `throws` clause *lists* the exceptions that can be thrown by a method. Do not get the `throws` clause confused with a `throw` statement, which explicitly invokes an exception.

We have seen how the `throws` clause is used to list the exceptions that are thrown by a method, that is, to list those exceptions that might be raised but not handled within the scope of the method's execution. When using the `throws` clause, you need to state only the superclass of all the exceptions that might occur within a method. Furthermore, Java does not require exceptions that refer to the subclasses of `Error` and `RuntimeException` to be declared. Practically any method can generate these exceptions, and it would become tedious to have to list all the possible subclasses of exceptions that might be thrown.

Given the restriction just mentioned, how do you know which exceptions to declare in a `throws` clause? The answer is twofold.

First, look at the documentation associated with the class methods you are using. The signatures of these methods state which methods throw exceptions.

Second, when you are developing a program, don't declare any exceptions in a `throws` clause, but wait for the compiler to tell you which exceptions you should have declared.

Program `Example_5` implements the logic behind Figure 7.3; it shows the route the computer takes to find a suitable `catch` block.

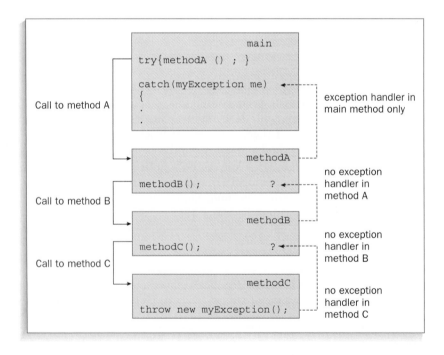

Figure 7.3 An exception searching for a handler

```
// program to demonstrate finding a catch block
import avi.*;
class MyException extends Throwable
{
      public MyException(){super();}
}
class Example_5
{
      static Window screen = new Window("Example_5.java");
      static public void main(String[] args)
      {
            try
            {
                  screen.showWindow();
                  methodA();
            }
            catch(MyException me)
            {
                  screen.write("The exception has been caught in main.\n");
            }
      }
      static void methodA() throws MyException
      {
            screen.write("method A called\n");
            methodB();
      }
      static void methodB() throws MyException
      {
            screen.write("method B called\n");
            methodC();
      }
      static void methodC() throws MyException
      {
            screen.write("method C called\n");
            // an exception must be instantiated before
            // it can exist; after which it may be thrown
            screen.write("exception thrown in method C\n");
            throw new MyException();
      }
}
```

The contents of the log file from the program being executed follows.

```
=======================================================================
                   L  O  G        F  I  L  E
          audio-visual interface [avi] - Release 1.0 - by Barry Holmes
             filename: Example_5.java    date: 3/21/2000   time: 8:0:13
=======================================================================


method A called
method B called
method C called
exception thrown in method C
The exception has been caught in main.
```

7.7 Finally Blocks

The computer will exit from a `try` block under the following circumstances.

- An exception is thrown.

- The execution of a `break`, `continue`, or `return` statement.

- Normally, after the execution of the last statement in the block in which there are no exceptions thrown.

Note a `continue` statement causes the computer to branch to the end of the last statement in a loop, but not outside the loop. A `break` statement will cause the computer to branch to outside of the loop. You should restrict your use of either the `break` or `continue` statements since they represent unconditional branching within a program and generally lead to poor programming style.

Java allows the programmer to define a block of code that is guaranteed to be executed before the computer exits from a try block, regardless of whether an exception was thrown or a `return` statement was executed within a `try` block.

The `finally` block may be used to release any permanent resources the method might have allocated, such as in closing an open file.

SYNTAX

Finally Block: `finally {statements}`

If there is a local `catch` block to handle an exception being thrown from the `try` block, the code of the `catch` block is executed before the code of the `finally` block. However, if a local `catch` block does not exist to handle the exception, then the code of the `finally` block is executed, and the computer must return to the calling method to find a `catch` clause to handle the exception.

Program `Example_6` demonstrates how a `finally` block is entered before the program is abandoned by the interpreter. Within the `try` block the method `failure()` is called. This method throws a valid Java exception, `NullPointerException`, which is usually reserved to signal an attempt to access a field or invoke a method of a null object. However, there is no handler in this program to handle a `NullPointerException`. Normally at this point the interpreter would abandon the program and display the cause of the error.

However, since a `finally` block has been included, the computer must execute the statements within this block before abandoning the program.

```java
// program to demonstrate the finally clause

import avi.*;

class Example_6
{
    static Window screen = new Window("Example_6.java");

    static void failure() throws MyException
    {
        screen.write("Entered failure() method\n");
        throw new NullPointerException();
    }

    public static void main(String[] args)
    {
        try
        {
            screen.showWindow();
            screen.write("Entered try block\n");
            failure();
        }

        catch(MyException me)
        {
            screen.write("Entered catch block with MyException\n");
        }

        finally
        {
            screen.write("Entered finally block\n");
            screen.write("Uncaught Exception - "+
                    "NullPointerException");
        }
    }
}
```

The contents of the log file from the program being executed follows.

```
============================================================================
                    L  O  G       F  I  L  E
        audio-visual interface [avi] - Release 1.0 - by Barry Holmes
          filename: Example_6.java  date: 3/22/2000   time: 1:59:28
============================================================================


Entered try block
Entered failure() method
Entered finally block
Uncaught Exception - NullPointerException
```

Here are the contents of the MSDOS window:

```
Exception in thread "main" java.lang.NullPointerException
        at Example_6.failure(Example_6.java:12)
        at Example_6.main(Example_6.java:21)
```

7.8   Using Exception Handling

Exception handling provides a unified approach for dealing with errors in a program. By adopting exception handling, you reduce the need to use *home-grown* techniques for error detection and recovery.

Never be tempted to use exception handling for purposes other than handling exceptional situations; if you do, you can reduce program clarity and program performance. For example, it is poor practice to rely upon the exception EndOfFileException to be thrown in detecting the end of file. Instead, use an appropriate method or variable that specifically detects when the end of a file has been reached.

Remember, with the prudent use of exception handling, a program may continue executing after dealing with an error situation. This helps ensure that the software you write is both robust and reliable.

When developing your own classes, state which methods are likely to throw exceptions. Do not handle the exceptions within these classes, but write the appropriate exception handlers in the program that uses the classes. Such exception handlers may be grouped together in one part of the program, thus allowing for a better organization in the layout of your code. In turn this approach will improve program clarity and enhances program modifiability.

You now have sufficient knowledge to begin to understand how parts of the `avi` package have been constructed. For example, in the `DialogBox` class, the following listing of the instance method `getInteger` illustrates how `try` and `catch` blocks are used to detect whether the input string is of the correct format to be converted into an integer. For example, if the input string represented a real number, such as 3.789, then clearly this number cannot be converted into an integer value.

The code also checks for the programmer not showing the dialog box!

```
public int getInteger()
{
    if (visible)
        visible = false;
    else
        dialogBoxNotShownError(bigBrother);

    if (inputDatum.equals(EMPTY_STRING))
        noInputError(bigBrother);

    try
    {
        return new Integer(inputDatum).intValue();
    }
    catch (NumberFormatException e)
    {
        Audio.beep(bigBrother);
        Memo error = new Memo(bigBrother,
                        "Error! "+inputDatum+" is NOT an int type",
                        "default value Integer.MIN_VALUE returned ",
                        "CLOSE to continue.",true);
        error.showMemo();
    }

    return Integer.MIN_VALUE;
}
```

Similarly, the methods `getLongInteger()`, `getFloat()`, and `getDouble()` all incorporate exception handlers for the respective number types not being in the correct numerical format. In all these methods, a default value of the minimum of the data type is returned if an error in the input string is detected.

You may wonder why these methods do not just throw an exception and allow the user to handle it; after all, this was the method advocated a little earlier in this section! Remember the `avi` package was designed for beginners to programming, and it was not expected that beginners would know how to handle exceptions until this chapter had been read and understood.

7.9   Stream Input and Output

Input and output of data, to and from a system, can be a complicated task. Java can handle both byte data, for example representing sounds or pictures, and character data, representing text. The data can be obtained from many sources, such as microphones, the keyboard, the mouse, or a file, and sent to many destinations such as the screen, the speakers, or a file. The Java I/O approach is elegant and robust. However, it can be difficult to understand, and a full treatment of it is beyond the scope of this text. In this chapter we will demonstrate one way you can do simple input and output without using our `avi` package, and we will also address text file input and output. The first topic that you need to understand is streams.

The term *stream* refers to any input source or output destination for data. The `java.io` package provides many classes that let us define and use steams. We will use two of these classes, `BufferedReader` and `PrintWriter`, for the input and output of data, respectively. The physical source and destination of the data is specified by the argument of the constructor of the appropriate class.

Input with `BufferedReader`

If we examine the class `BufferedReader`, we see that one of its constructors has the format:

```
public BufferedReader(Reader in, int bufferSize);
```

> ⚠ Do not use the alternative `BufferedReader` constructor with Microsoft Windows. Using this constructor may result in spurious errors as data is input via the keyboard. This is a well-known, and well-documented bug! A suggested work-around is to use the constructor specified here with two parameters, the second having a buffer size of unity (1).

To instantiate an object of type `BufferedReader`, you need to supply the constructor with a parameter of the correct type—`Reader`. For our purposes, we will need to associate the standard input stream, which is usually the keyboard, with this parameter. The class `java.lang.System` contains a constant in of type `InputStream` that represents the standard input stream and corresponds to the keyboard of a computer. But how can we associate something of type `InputStream` with a parameter that is of type `Reader`? The answer can be found by inspecting the hierarchy diagram in Figure 7.4. Notice that the class `Reader` is a superclass to the class `InputStreamReader`. You may recall in Chapter 6 it was stated that *an object of a subclass may be passed as an argument to a method that requires a parameter of its superclass type.* Because of this hierarchical relationship, we may fulfill the requirement for a parameter of type `Reader` with an object of type `InputStreamReader`.

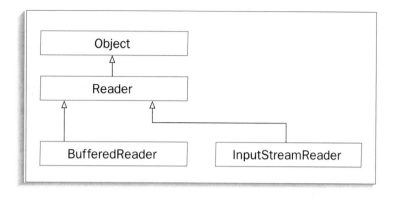

Figure 7.4 Hierarchy diagram for `java.io.BufferedReader` and
`java.io.InputStreamReader`

A constructor from the class `InputStreamReader` has the format:

```
public InputStreamReader(InputStream in);
```

Therefore, it is possible to instantiate an object of type `InputStreamReader` as follows:

```
InputStreamReader stream = new InputStreamReader(System.in);
```

The object `stream` may be used to instantiate the object `keyboard` as follows:

```
BufferedReader keyboard = new BufferedReader(stream, 1);
```

Alternatively, we can dispense with `stream` as an intermediate variable and combine the two instantiations into one as follows:

```
BufferedReader keyboard = new
BufferedReader(new InputStreamReader(System.in),1);
```

The class `BufferedReader` contains a method `readLine` that will allow you to input data of type `String` at the keyboard by using `keyboard.readLine()`. Beware! This method can throw an `IOException` that must be handled either in your program or by the Java interpreter.

So, that will take care of the input of strings. How do we input data of primitive number types such as `int`, `long`, `float`, and `double`? The answer is to input a number as a string and use the appropriate wrapper class to provide the value of the number.

If you look back at Chapter 4, you will notice that one of the constructors for the wrapper class `Integer` defines a constructor that requires a `String` type for initialization. The data we input at the keyboard is also of type `String`; therefore, this string value may be used in the constructor—for example, `new Integer(keyboard.readLine())`. We now have created an object of type `Integer`. To convert the string into a primitive data type `int`, simply use the wrapper class instance method `intValue()`. The whole operation can be performed using the following approach.

Declare a primitive type `int` `number`, then assign to the variable `number` the result of the converted string data that was input at the keyboard:

```
int number = new Integer(keyboard.readLine()).intValue();
```

This technique can also be applied to the data types `long`, `float`, and `double` since they all have the corresponding wrapper classes and methods for conversion. For example, given the declaration of the primitive type `float` `realNumber;`, the equivalent statement to input this number at the keyboard would be as follows.

```
float realNumber = new Float(keyboard.readLine()).floatValue();
```

A sample program using this input approach will be given after we cover the output side of the process.

Output with `PrintWriter`

The class `PrintStream` is a character output stream, and its position in the class hierarchy is illustrated in Figure 7.5.

The standard output stream `System.out` is a constant of type `PrintStream`. This means that the constant can be used as an object to any of

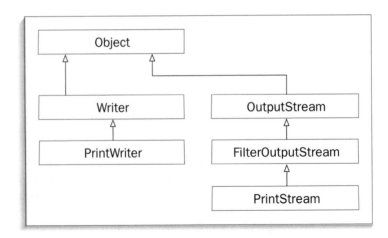

Figure 7.5 A hierarchy diagram for `java.io.PrintWriter` and `java.io.PrintStream`

the instance methods of the `PrintStream` class. Therefore, instead of instantiating our own objects of this class, we can (should) just use `System.out`. This is just as well since the two constructors of the `PrintStream` class are now *deprecated* by Sun. Deprecation means that Sun Microsystems, Inc. may not support these methods in future releases of Java, and if we used them to construct our own objects, our programs may not work correctly with future Java interpreters. It is safe to use `System.out`, however.

If you inspect the `PrintStream` class you will come across `print` and `println` instance methods that are overloaded to allow for the output of all the primitive data types and string objects. The functionality and use of the `print` method is similar to that of the `write` method of the `Window` class in the `avi` package. The output, however, is displayed at the operating system window, which is the MSDOS window in Microsoft Windows system or the terminal window in a Unix/Solaris system. The `println` method simply writes a newline after the output. This, of course, can also be achieved by the use of the escape sequence character `\n`, embedded into the end of the output string of a `print` statement.

For example,

```
System.out.print("Hello World\n");
```

will display the text HELLO WORLD *newline* in the MSDOS/terminal window. Similarly, the statement

```
float grossWage = 250.00f;
System.out.println("Gross weekly wage = " + grossWage);
```

will display the text Gross weekly wage = 250.0 *newline* in the MSDOS/terminal window.

The class `PrintWriter` is a character output stream, and its position in the class hierarchy is also illustrated in Figure 7.5. The class `PrintWriter` superseded the class `PrintStream` in Java 1.1 and therefore is the preferred approach.

A constructor for the class `PrintWriter` is:

```
public PrintWriter(OutputStream out, boolean autoFlush);
```

This constructor requires two arguments; the first argument is of type `OutputStream` and the second argument is of the type `boolean`. If you inspect the hierarchy diagram in Figure 7.5, you will notice that an object of type `OutputStream` may be replaced by an object of type `PrintStream`. (Remember that an object of a subclass may be passed as an argument to a method that requires a parameter of its superclass type.) Why should we make the substitution? Simply because we need to find a constant that will represent the standard output stream. The constant is, of course, `System.out`. You should set the autoFlush argument to true; otherwise, you may not get any information to appear in the operating system window.

Now that we have the complete picture, it is possible to instantiate an object of type PrintWriter as follows, where we refer to the generic object dosWindow to mean an operating system window.

```
PrintWriter dosWindow = new PrintWriter(System.out, true);
```

The class PrintWriter contains the same set of methods as PrintStream for displaying data as strings. Note that when using the print instance method you can follow it with the flush method. If you do not, the output may not be displayed in the operating system window until the next println statement is executed by the computer.

Program Example_7 has exactly the same functionality as program Example_4 in Chapter 2. However, Program Example_7 will allow two integers to be input via the keyboard and echoed back to the operating system window. The numbers then have the operations of addition, subtraction, multiplication, division, and remainder applied to them, and the answers are displayed in the operating system window.

This example illustrates performing input and output using the methods described in this chapter, showing that you do not have to use the components of the audio-visual interface.

```
// program to input two integer operands and perform the
// arithmetic operations of +, - *, / and % upon them

import java.io.*;

class Example_7
{
    static BufferedReader keyboard = new
    BufferedReader(new InputStreamReader(System.in),1);
    static PrintWriter dosWindow = new PrintWriter(System.out, true);

    public static void main(String[] args)
    {
        // declare two variables of type integer
        int first=0, second=0;

        // display a heading on the screen
        dosWindow.print("Simple Mathematics\n\n");
        dosWindow.flush();

        // prompt for two integers and catch any exceptions
        try
        {
```

```
            dosWindow.print("First integer? "); dosWindow.flush();
            first = new Integer(keyboard.readLine()).intValue();

            dosWindow.print("Second integer? "); dosWindow.flush();
            second = new Integer(keyboard.readLine()).intValue();
        }

    catch (Exception e)
    {
            dosWindow.println(e.toString()+" - program abandoned\n");
            System.exit(1);
    }

    // display the results of calculations
    dosWindow.println(first+" + "+second+" = "+(first+second));
    dosWindow.println(first+" - "+second+" = "+(first-second));
    dosWindow.println(first+" * "+second+" = "+(first*second));
    dosWindow.println(first+" / "+second+" = "+(first/second));
    dosWindow.println(first+" % "+second+" = "+(first%second));
        }
    }
```

The following are results from the operating system window when the program was executed.

```
Simple Mathematics

First integer? 56
Second integer? 9
56 + 9 = 65
56 - 9 = 47
56 * 9 = 504
56 / 9 = 6
56 % 9 = 2
```

NOW DO THIS   Modify program `Example_7` to perform the following.

(1) Input a long integer and input a double precision real number at either the MSDOS window or Unix terminal window, depending on the operating system you are using.

(2) Perform the computations of addition, subtraction, multiplication, division and remainder, and display the result in the same window used for data input.

7.10   The StreamTokenizer Class

An input stream can be examined and its contents broken up into tokens. For example, the stream of text:

```
To be or not to be ...
```

can be parsed and broken up into tokens of single words delimited by white-space characters.

White space is defined as the ASCII space, horizontal tab, and form-feed characters, as well as the line terminators newline LF, carriage return CR, and carriage-return line feed CRLF.

Alternatively, the stream of text can be parsed and broken up into tokens of single characters. The StreamTokenizer class parses an input stream and, depending upon the values of parameters set within the class, breaks the stream up into tokens, allowing the tokens to be inspected one at a time. This approach often makes it easier to deal with the input to a program.

For your convenience, an abridged version of the StreamTokenizer class follows. However, you are advised to take time and study the full documentation of this class.

```
public class StreamTokenizer extends Object
{
    // constants
    public static final int TT_EOF;
    public static final int TT_EOL;
    public static final int TT_NUMBER;
    public static final int TT_WORD;

    // instance variables
    public int ttype;
    public String sval;
    public double nval;

    // constructor
    public StreamTokenizer (Reader r);

    // instance methods
    .
    public void eolIsSignificant(boolean flag);
```

```
public int nextToken() throws IOException;
public void ordinaryChars(int low, int hi);
public void whitespaceChars(int low, int hi);
public void wordChars(int low, int hi);
    .
    .
    .
}
```

Basically, the constructor for this class uses the character input stream `Reader` as an argument. This can be the keyboard stream or any defined file stream. For example,

```
FileReader file = new FileReader("data.txt");
StreamTokenizer inputStream = new StreamTokenizer(file);
```

The `FileReader` class, a subclass of `Reader`, is useful when you want to read text (as opposed to binary data) from a file. The `FileReader` class is a character-based input stream used to read characters from a file. You create a `FileReader` object by specifying the file to be read. The `FileReader` constructor internally creates a `FileInputStream` to read bytes from the specified file, and use the functionality of the superclass, `InputStreamReader`, to convert those bytes from characters to the Unicode characters used by Java.

Once an object of `StreamTokenizer` has been instantiated, it can be used to provide a steady stream of tokens to the program. Methods can be used to define what you mean by a token, white space, and to move to the next token from the stream. Instance variables can be used to learn the type of the current token and to access its value.

A token's type `ttype` is either `TT_EOF`, `TT_EOL`, `TT_NUMBER`, `TT_WORD`, or a nonnegative byte value that was the first byte of the token. Whether or not the current token has an actual value associated with it, and how you access that value if it exists, depends on its type as follows:

- `TT_NUMBER`: the value of `nval` is the numerical value of the token.

- `TT_WORD` or a string quote character: the value of `sval` is the string value of the token.

- `TT_EOF`: the end of the file (stream) has been reached.

- `TT_EOL`: a line terminator has been reached.

The following methods allow you to specify how tokens are recognized.

`wordChars()` specifies a range of characters that should be treated as parts of words. For example, `inputStream.wordChars(0x20,0x7F)` specifies that all characters whose Unicodes are in the hexadecimal range 0x20 .. 0x7F (the printable characters) should be included as characters of words.

ordinaryChars() specifies characters that are never part of tokens and should be returned as is. For example, inputStream.ordinaryChars(0x00,0x7F) specifies that all the ASCII characters do not form tokens and are returned as the character. This technique is useful when you need to view the contents of a file.

eolIsSignificant() specifies whether the end-of-line is significant. If it is, then the TT_EOL constant is returned for end of lines, otherwise; the end of lines are treated as white-space characters.

The next token from the inputStream is made available by using the instance method nextToken(), which discards the current token and accesses the identified stream to obtain the next token, returning the type of that next token. For example, returning to the stream containing the text:

```
To be or not to be ...
```

this stream may be parsed and each word output separately, as follows.

```
String word;
int tokenType = inputStream.nextToken();
while (tokenType != StreamTokenizer.TT_EOF)
{
        word = inputStream.sval;
        System.out.println(word);
        tokenType = inputStream.nextToken();
}
```

When the input stream contains a mixture of numbers and words, such as:

```
395.95 television
550.00 music center
.
.
```

the stream may be parsed and each token output separately as follows:

```
inputStream.wordChars(0x20,0x7F);

float price;
String name;

int tokenType = inputStream.nextToken();
while (tokenType != StreamTokenizer.TT_EOF)
{
```

```
price = (float)inputSream.nval;
inputStream.nextToken();
name = inputStream.sval;
System.out.println(price+"\t"+name);
tokenType = inputStream.nextToken();
}
```

The next section contains a complete program example that uses the StreamTokenizer class.

7.11   Text File Processing

In this and previous chapters, input was confined to entering data through a keyboard or mouse, and output to displaying information on a screen. When there is a requirement to permanently store data, there is a need to create files. Data can be written to or read from files held on magnetic media. Common media that you are likely to use for storing your files include floppy disks that you carry around or hard disks that are part of the computer.

If the System.in and System.out values are replaced by new values that relate to computer files, then it will be possible to read input from a file in place of the keyboard and write output to a file in place of the screen.

A file must be *opened* before we can gain access to the device for reading or writing. In Java, when a file is opened, an object is created and a stream is associated with the object.

The class FileReader contains a constructor that requires the pathname (path and filename) of an input file.

```
FileReader file = new FileReader(pathname);
```

> In a Windows 95/98/NT environment, the backslash \ used in defining a pathname must be written as a double backslash \\ to avoid any confusion with an escape character in the string. If you are using a SUN Solaris system, this modification does not apply since the path names use a forward slash /.

When a file is no longer required it must be closed. The method defined in the class FileReader to do this is close().

Program Example_8 demonstrates obtaining input from a file. Suppose a text file contains data that relate to the insured values of several domestic appliances. For example, a television is insured for $395.95, a music center is insured for $550.00, a desktop computer is insured for $995.95, and so on.

```
395.95 television
550.00 music center
995.95 desktop computer
199.95 microwave oven
299.99 washing machine
149.95 freezer
```

Note that this file has been created and stored on disk using an editor, in the same way as you would create and store a program source file. The file name must be passed to the program as a parameter. For example, if the file is called goods.txt and is in the same directory as the program, you would enter:

```
java Example_8 goods.txt

// program to read a file and display a report on the screen

import avi.*;
import java.io.*;

class Example_8
{
      static public void main(String[] args) throws IOException
      {
          // instantiate input file object
          FileReader file = new FileReader(args[0]);

          // tokens in a line of the text file
          String name;
          float price;

          Window screen = new Window("Example_8.java");
          screen.showWindow();

          StreamTokenizer inputStream = new StreamTokenizer(file);
          inputStream.wordChars(0x20,0x7F);

          int tokenType;

          // headings
          screen.write("Contents of file "+args[0]+"\n\n");
          screen.write("PRICE\tAPPLIANCE\n\n");

          tokenType = inputStream.nextToken();
          while (tokenType != StreamTokenizer.TT_EOF)
          {
```

```
                 price = (float)inputStream.nval; inputStream.nextToken();
                 name = inputStream.sval;
                 screen.write(price+"\t"+name+"\n");
                 tokenType = inputStream.nextToken();
          }

          file.close();
      }
}
```

The contents of the log file from the running program are as follows.

```
======================================================================
                      L  O  G      F  I  L  E
          audio-visual interface [avi] - Release 1.0 - by Barry Holmes
              filename: Example_8.java   date: 3/22/2000   time: 3:21:18
======================================================================


Contents of file goods.txt

PRICE  APPLIANCE

395.95 television
550.00 music center
995.95 desktop computer
199.95 microwave oven
299.99 washing machine
149.95 freezer
```

NOW DO THIS   Modify program `Example_8` to include `try` and `catch` blocks, and a `finally` block.

(1) The `try` block should contain code that is likely to generate file processing exceptions; and the `finally` block should contain the code to close the file.

(2) Write exception handlers to match the exceptions that are likely to be thrown.

(3) Run the program and use test data that will deliberately throw the anticipated exceptions.

Next we will see how to write information to a file. The `FileWriter` class is a subclass of the `OutputStreamWriter` class and is useful when you want to write text (as opposed to binary data) to a file. You create a `FileWriter` object by specifying the name of the file to be written to. The `FileWriter` class creates an internal `FileOutputStream` to write bytes to the specified file, and uses the functionality of its superclass, `OutputStreamWriter` to convert the Unicode characters written to the stream characters into bytes.

The class `FileWriter` contains a constructor that requires the pathname (path and filename) of an output file. In the example that follows, the pathname could be given as `"results.txt"` as follows.

```
FileWriter output = new FileWriter("results.txt");
```

However, we have decided to allow the user of the program to pass in the output file name as a parameter, providing a more robust program. Therefore, we use

```
FileWriter output = new FileWriter("args[1]");
```

To provide the same methods that were used with screen output (`print`, `println`, `flush`) you need to use the object `output` in the constructor of the `PrintWriter`, thus creating a stream object `textFile` that is associated with writing to the disk file with the pathname specified in `args[1]` as follows:

```
PrintWriter textFile = new PrintWriter(output);
```

Program `Example_9` uses these approaches to modify the contents of the file used in the previous program so that the price of each appliance is increased by the rate of inflation; the new price and the name of the appliance are written to a different text file. For example, it could be executed by the command

```
java Example_9 goods.txt report.txt

// program to read a file and write a report

import avi.*;
import java.io.*;
import java.text.DecimalFormat;

class Example_9
{
      static public void main(String[] args) throws IOException
      {
            // instantiate input file object
            FileReader file = new FileReader(args[0]);
```

```java
        // instantiate output file object
        FileWriter output = new FileWriter(args[1]);
        PrintWriter textFile = new PrintWriter(output);

        // tokens in a line of the text file
        String name;
        float price;

        final float RATE_OF_INFLATION = 0.025f;

        Window screen = new Window("Example_9.java");
        screen.showWindow();

        StreamTokenizer inputStream = new StreamTokenizer(file);
        inputStream.wordChars(0x20,0x7F);

        int tokenType;
        DecimalFormat accuracy = new DecimalFormat("0.00");

        // print headings
        screen.write("Contents of file "+args[1]+"\n\n");
        screen.write("PRICE\tAPPLIANCE\n\n");

        tokenType = inputStream.nextToken();
        while (tokenType != StreamTokenizer.TT_EOF)
        {
            price = (float)inputStream.nval; inputStream.nextToken();
            name = inputStream.sval;
            price = price + (price * RATE_OF_INFLATION);
            screen.write(accuracy.format(price)+"\t"+name+"\n");
            textFile.println(accuracy.format(price)+"\t"+name);
            tokenType = inputStream.nextToken();
        }

        file.close();
        output.close();

        screen.write("\n\nEND OF FILES "+args[0]+" and "+args[1]);
    }
}
```

The contents of the log file from the program being executed follows.

```
================================================================================
                        L  O  G        F  I  L  E
          audio-visual interface [avi] - Release 1.0 - by Barry Holmes
             filename: Example_9.java  date: 7/15/2000   time: 4:0:9
================================================================================


Contents of file report.txt

PRICE     APPLIANCE

405.85    television
563.75    music center
1020.85   desktop computer
204.95    microwave oven
307.49    washing machine
153.70    freezer



END OF FILES goods.txt and report.txt
```

Book Example Problem

This example demonstrates the combined use of exception handling, stream tokenizing, and text file input/output.

The following listing of a text file has been created using an editor and stored under the name books.txt. Each line in the file represent the quantity in stock, the price of a book, and the title of the book. For example there is one copy, priced at $8.95, of Art in Athens.

```
1 8.95 Art in Athens
2 3.75 Birds of Prey
1 7.55 Eagles in the USA
3 5.25 Gone with the Wind
2 3.75 Hate, Lust, and Love
3 5.95 Math for Adults
3 3.75 Modern Farming
3 5.25 Raiders of Planet X
1 8.95 Splitting the Atom
1 3.75 The Invisible Man
2 3.75 The Otter
```

```
4 5.95 The Tempest
2 5.95 The Trojan Wars
2 3.75 Under the Seas
2 7.55 Vampire Bats
```

Write a program to read each line of the file and produce a text file of a report similar to that illustrated below.

```
              STOCK REPORT ON BOOKS
              =======================


*** REORDER *** 1        8.95     Art in Athens
                2        3.75     Birds of Prey
*** REORDER *** 1        7.55     Eagles in the USA
                3        5.25     Gone with the Wind
                2        3.75     Hate, Lust, and Love
                3        5.95     Math for Adults
                3        3.75     Modern Farming
                3        5.25     Raiders of Planet X
*** REORDER *** 1        8.95     Splitting the Atom
*** REORDER *** 1        3.75     The Invisible Man
                2        3.75     The Otter
                4        5.95     The Tempest
                2        5.95     The Trojan Wars
                2        3.75     Under the Seas
                2        7.55     Vampire Bats

Number of books in stock 32

Retail value of books in stock $170.60
```

Notice from the design of the document that when the stock level falls to one item, the report indicates that the stock should be replenished. Notice also that totals are calculated for the number of books and for the value of all the books in stock and printed at the end of the report.

Note: If our solution to this problem were to be used in a larger system that actually helped manage a book inventory, we would approach it in a different fashion, defining a book class, and making sure that our code interfaced well with other inventory code. However, our main concern here is to demonstrate the recently covered Java constructs, and therefore we pursue a more straightforward design.

Pseudocode of Main method

1. open files

2. tokenize input stream

3. write headings for stock report

4. get next token type

5. while token type not end of file

6.   assign token to quantity of books

7.   get next token

8.   assign token to price of book

9.   get next token

10.   assign token to title of book

11.   if quantity < re-order level

12.   write re-order to stock report

13.   else

14.   write spaces to stock report

15.   increase total quantity by quantity

16.   increase total price by price

17.   get next token type

18. write total quantity to stock report

19. write total prices to stock report

20. close files

```
// program to read a file and write a report
// any errors are reported to the operating system window

import java.io.*;
import java.text.DecimalFormat;

class Example_10
{
    static public void main(String[] args) throws IOException
    {
```

```java
final int REORDER_LEVEL = 1;

FileReader inputFile = null;
FileWriter outputFile = null;

// tokens in a line of the text file
String title;
float price;
int quantity;

int totalQuantity = 0;
float totalPrice = 0.0f;

// attempt to open the filenames specified in the command line
try
{
      inputFile = new FileReader(args[0]);
      outputFile = new FileWriter(args[1]);
}

catch(Exception e)
{
      if (e instanceof FileNotFoundException)
      {
            System.out.println("FILENAME "+args[0]+
                              " NOT FOUND");
      }

      if (e instanceof ArrayIndexOutOfBoundsException)
      {
            System.out.println("WRONG NUMBER OF FILES SPECIFIED "+
                              "IN COMMAND LINE");
      }

      System.exit(1);
}

// tokenize input stream
StreamTokenizer inputStream = new StreamTokenizer(inputFile);
inputStream.wordChars(0x20,0x7F);

// instantiate PrintWriter object
PrintWriter textFile = new PrintWriter(outputFile);

// write heading to output file
textFile.println("\t\tSTOCK REPORT ON BOOKS");
```

```
        textFile.println("\t\t====================\n");

        // WARNING! - nextToken can raise an IOException that is not
        // handled by the main method in this class.
        // get type of next token
        int tokenType = inputStream.nextToken();
        // while not end of file
        while (tokenType != StreamTokenizer.TT_EOF)
        {
                // read quantity price and title from input stream
                quantity = (int)inputStream.nval;
                inputStream.nextToken();
                price = (float)inputStream.nval;
                inputStream.nextToken();
                title = inputStream.sval;

                // test for reorder level
                if (quantity <= REORDER_LEVEL)
                        textFile.print("*** REORDER ***\t");
                else
                        textFile.print("                \t");

                // write line to output file
                textFile.println(quantity+"\t"+price+"\t"+title);

                // update cumulative quantity and price
                totalQuantity = totalQuantity+quantity;
                totalPrice = totalPrice+(price*quantity);

                // get type of next token
                tokenType = inputStream.nextToken();
        }

        // write totals to output file
        DecimalFormat accuracy = new DecimalFormat("0.00");
        textFile.println("\nNumber of books in stock "+totalQuantity);
        textFile.println("\nRetail value of books in stock $"+
                        accuracy.format(totalPrice));
        // close files
        inputFile.close();
        outputFile.close();
    }
}
```

The results from running this program four times follows.

```
D:\chap_6>java Example_10
WRONG NUMBER OF FILES SPECIFIED IN COMMAND LINE

D:\chap_6>java Example_10 books.txt
WRONG NUMBER OF FILES SPECIFIED IN COMMAND LINE

D:\chap_6>java Example_10 stock.txt
FILENAME stock.txt NOT FOUND

D:\chap_6>java Example_10 books.txt stock_report.txt

D:\chap_6>type stock_report.txt

                 STOCK REPORT ON BOOKS
                 =======================


*** REORDER *** 1      8.95     Art in Athens
                2      3.75     Birds of Prey
*** REORDER *** 1      7.55     Eagles in the USA
                3      5.25     Gone with the Wind
                2      3.75     Hate, Lust, and Love
                3      5.95     Math for Adults
                3      3.75     Modern Farming
                3      5.25     Raiders of Planet X
*** REORDER *** 1      8.95     Splitting the Atom
*** REORDER *** 1      3.75     The Invisible Man
                2      3.75     The Otter
                4      5.95     The Tempest
                2      5.95     The Trojan Wars
                2      3.75     Under the Seas
                2      7.55     Vampire Bats

Number of books in stock 32

Retail value of books in stock $170.60
```

Another Example: Using a File Viewer

Using the `StringTokenizer` class, the following handy `FileViewer` class will permit any text file to be viewed on the screen. Note that all characters are regarded as tokens and can be treated individually.

```
// Class FileViewer will display the contents of a text file on
// the screen of a window.

// FileReader throws a FileNotFoundException, and
// nextToken throws an IOException.
// Since there are no exception handlers in the class
// FileViewer the exceptions are thrown from the class.

import avi.*;
import java.io.*;

public class FileViewer
{
      private String contents=new String();

      /**
      The FileViewer class will allow an object to be created that will
      display the entire contents of a text file on the screen.
      @param filename is the pathname and filename of the text file to be
      displayed.
      */
      public FileViewer(String filename) throws FileNotFoundException,
                                                IOException
      {
            // WARNING! - FileReader throws a FileNotFoundException
            FileReader file = new FileReader(filename);
            StreamTokenizer inputStream = new StreamTokenizer(file);
            inputStream.ordinaryChars(0x00,0x7F);

            // WARNING! - nextToken throws an IOException
            int tokenType = inputStream.nextToken();
            while (tokenType != StreamTokenizer.TT_EOF)
            {
                  contents = contents+String.valueOf((char)tokenType);
                  tokenType = inputStream.nextToken();
            }
      }

      /**
      Displays the entire contents of the text file on the screen.
      @param screen is the container class for displaying the text.
      */
      public void viewFile(Window screen)
      {
            screen.write(contents);
      }
}
```

NOW DO THIS Write a program using the `FileViewer` class to display the contents of a text file of your choice.

7.12 The FileDialog Class

We have three ways to input the name of a file that we want to use in a program.

- Code the name of the file into the program during program construction. This technique is very inflexible; if you want to change the name of the file, you must amend and recompile the class.

- Pass the name of the file as an argument in the command line to the formal parameter of the `main` method. This technique will allow you to pass as many parameters as are necessary. It is an improvement over the first technique since it allows you to choose the file you will use when you execute the program.

- Input the name, as a string, to an `avi` dialog box during run time. Once again, you retain the flexibility of being able to choose the name of your file at run time. In fact, you extend the time available for entering the file name even longer than in the previous method.

Note that in the latter two approaches you need to worry about a user supplying a filename that does not exist!

An alternative way to input the name of a file is to use a pre-written Java class called the `FileDialog` class from the abstract windowing toolkit (`awt`) package. Chapter 8 is devoted to the `awt`; however, for now we will study the `FileDialog` class within this package. This class allows the user of our program to choose a file with the standard Windows approach. In other words, the user is able to browse the file system and select the file for use.

A partial listing of the `FileDialog` class follows.

```
public class FileDialog extends Dialog
{
    // constructors
    .
    public FileDialog(Frame parent, String title, int mode);
    .

    // constants
    public static final int LOAD;
    public static final int SAVE;

    // public instance methods
    .
    public String getDirectory();
```

```
public String getFile();
    .

    .
```
}

This class represents a file-selection dialog box. The constants LOAD and SAVE are values of an optional constructor argument that specifies whether the dialog box should be an *Open File* or a *Save As* dialog. Once the selection from the dialog box has been made, the name of the directory and the name of the file can be retrieved within the program by using the instance methods getDirectory() and getFile(), respectively.

In Program Example_11, a file dialog box is used to input the name of a file. The contents of this file are then displayed on the screen using the method viewFile() from the FileViewer class listed at the end of the previous section.

The constructor for the FileDialog class requires three arguments:

parent—the name of the container class for the file dialog box. Since parent is of type Frame, and the avi class Window is a subclass of Frame, we can use the screen object of the avi Window for this argument.

title—an optional string that will appear in the title bar of the file dialog box. If you use an empty string argument, the title defaults to Open.

mode—either the constant FileDialog.LOAD or the constant FileDialog.SAVE.

Note: The FileDialog class does not contain a method to show the dialog box on the screen. A show() method is inherited from a superclass in the same hierarchy. The dialog box is automatically hidden from view once the button is pressed to signify that the file should be opened.

```
// program to view the contents of a text file

import avi.*;
import java.awt.FileDialog;
import java.io.*;
class Example_11
{
    public static void main(String[] args)
    {
        Window screen = new
        Window("Example_11.java","plain","black",14);
        screen.showWindow();

        Memo error=null;

        // a FileDialog box enables a user to examine all the
        // directories, subdirectories and files on their computer
        // system
```

```
FileDialog inputFile = new
FileDialog(screen, "", FileDialog.LOAD);
inputFile.show();

// get directory and filename from the file dialog box
String directory = inputFile.getDirectory();
String filename = inputFile.getFile();

// test for user cancelling the request
if (directory == null || filename == null) System.exit(1);

try
{
     // instantiate a file viewer object
     FileViewer file = new FileViewer(directory+filename);
     // display the contents of a file on the screen
     file.viewFile(screen);
}

catch(FileNotFoundException fnfe)
{
     error = new Memo(screen,directory+filename,
                       "not found","CLOSE TO QUIT",true);
     error.showMemo();
}

catch(IOException ioe)
{
     error = new Memo(screen,"IO exception","",
                       "CLOSE TO QUIT",true);
     error.showMemo();
}
   }
 }
```

Note: If the user chooses to press the CANCEL button on the `FileDialog` box, this will generate a null directory and a null filename entry. Program `Example_11` explicitly checks for this condition, and exits from the program back to the operating system. The statement `System.exit(1)` will allow the execution of a program to be terminated.

Screenshots from the running program follow:

CASE STUDY

Reporting on the Statistics of a Text File

Statement of the Problem

Create a class `TextFileAnalyzer` that will read a text file and return the number of characters and vowels, and also return the frequency of occurrence of vowels, consonants, and words in the text file.

Create a second class to test the functionality of all the methods of the `TextFileAnalyzer` class, and also display the contents of the file.

Identification of classes and methods

The problem has stated the two classes to be created—(1) `TextFileAnalyzer` and (2) a class containing a `main` method to test the functionality of the methods of the `TextFileAnalyzer` class; this second class we will call `Example_12`. Note that one of the functions of `Example_12` is to display the contents of the file. However, we have already created a class `FileViewer` to display the contents of any text file; therefore, it would be prudent to reuse this class in `Example_12`.

If we examine the verbs in the description of the problem, then it is clear that *read* and *return* may offer suitable candidate methods. The class constructor will enable text to be read from a file. The methods of the class must return the number of characters (this includes all the nonprinting characters such as `CR` and `LF`), return the number of vowels, return the classification of the frequency of vowels, return the number of consonants, and return the number of words.

The constructor and methods for class `TextFileAnalyzer` follow. For the UML diagram, see Figure 7.6.

```
public class TextFileAnalyzer
{
      public TextFileAnalyzer(String filename) throws FileNotFoundException,
                                            IOException;

      public int getCharacters();
      public int getVowels();
      public int[] getVowelFrequency();
      public int getWords();
      public int getConsonants();
}
```

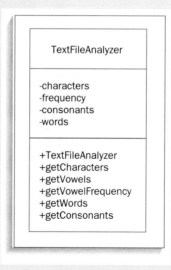

Figure 7.6 The UML diagram for the class `TextFileAnalyzer`

The parameter of the constructor is the name of the text file. Since this file needs to be opened and read by the constructor, the `FileReader` constructor might throw an exception if the file cannot be found, and the `nextToken` method from the `StreamTokenizer` class might throw an exception when reading tokens from a stream. These exceptions are not handled by the constructor; therefore, should either exception occur, the constructor throws a `FileNotFoundException` and an `IOException`.

The instance methods to `getCharacters`, `getVowels`, `getVowelFrequency`, `getWords`, and `getConsonants` all return the values of their respective instance variables. The coding of these methods is so trivial that their respective designs will not be considered here. The majority of the text analysis is performed by the constructor. Therefore, its design and testing is included here in detail. Note that the instance variable frequency is a one-dimensional array for storing the frequency of occurrence of each vowel.

Algorithm Development for the Constructor

1. open input stream
2. read stream and split line into tokens
3. read next token
4. while token type not end of file
5.   get character from stream
6.   convert character to lowercase
7.   increase character count by 1
8.   test character for vowel
9.   test character for consonant
10.   test character for end of word delimiter
11.   read next token
12. close input stream

Parts of this algorithm can be refined further.

8. test character for a vowel
8.1   for each vowel
8.2   if character is vowel
8.3   increase frequency of vowel by 1

9. test character for consonant
9.1   if character in range 'b' .. 'd' or
9.2   character in range 'f' .. 'h' or
9.3   character in range 'j' .. 'n' or
9.4   character in range 'p' .. 't' or
9.5   character in range 'v' .. 'z' then
9.6   increase consonant counter by 1

10. test character for end of word delimiter
10.1   if character is a SPACE or

10.2   character is end of line then
10.3   increase word counter by 1

Testing the Constructor

The test data is the phrase `To be or not to be`*CRLFeof*.

identifiers	value(s)										
characters	0	1	2	3	4	5	6	7	8	9	10
frequency[0]	0										
frequency[1]	0					1					
frequency[2]	0										
frequency[3]	0		1					2			
frequency[4]	0										
consonants	0	1			2				3		4
words	0			1			2			3	

inputStream	To be or not to be *CRLFeof*									
character	T	o	(space)	b	e	(space)	o	r	(space)	n
end of file?	false	false	false	false	false	false	false	false	false	false
character (to lowercase)	t	o	(space)	b	e	(space)	o	r	(space)	n
vowel?	false	true	false	false	true	false	true	false	false	false
consonant?	true	false	false	true	false	false	false	true	false	true
word delimiter?	false	false	true	false	false	true	false	false	true	false

identifiers	value(s)										
characters	10	11	12	13	14	15	16	17	18	19	20
frequency[0]	0										0
frequency[1]	1								2		2
frequency[2]	0										0
frequency[3]	2	3				4					4
frequency[4]	0										0
consonants	4		5		6			7			7
words	3			4			5			6	6

inputStream	To be or not to be*CRLFeof*									
character		o	t	(space)	t	o	(space)	b	e	*CR*	*LF*
end of file?		false	false	false	false	false	false	false	false	false	false

character (to lowercase)		o	t	(space)	t	o	(space)	b	e	-	-
vowel?		true	false	false	false	true	false	false	true	false	false
consonant?		false	true	false	true	false	false	true	false	false	false
word delimiter?		false	false	true	false	false	true	false	false	true	false

Note that the next character to be analyzed after the LF (line feed) is the end-of-file character. At this point, the condition to test for the end of file will be true and the while loop will terminate. The dependencies for the TextFileAnalyzer class are depicted in Figure 7.7.

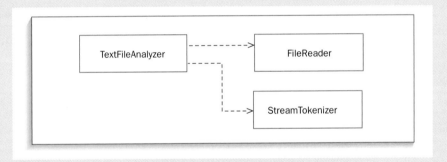

Figure 7.7 UML dependency diagram for the TextFileAnalyzer class

```java
import java.io.*;

public class TextFileAnalyzer
{
    // class constant
    private static int SPACE = 0x0020;
    private static char[] vowels = {'a','e','i','o','u'};

    // instance variables
    private int characters;                    // character counter
    private int[] frequency = new int[5];      // occurrence of each
                                               //    vowel
    private int consonants;                    // consonant counter
    private int words;                         // word counter
```

```
/**
The TextFileAnalyzer class will allow an object to be created from a
text file and return the following data about the text file:
        - the number of characters;
        - the number of vowels;
        - the frequency of each vowel;
        - the number of consonants;
        - the number of words.

@param filename is the pathname and filename of the text file to be
analyzed.
*/
public TextFileAnalyzer(String filename) throws
                                        FileNotFoundException,
                                        IOException
{
        char character;

        // WARNING! - FileReader throws a FileNotFoundException
        FileReader file = new FileReader(filename);
        StreamTokenizer inputStream = new StreamTokenizer(file);
        inputStream.ordinaryChars(0x00,0x7F);
        inputStream.eolIsSignificant(true);

        // WARNING! - nextToken throws an IOException
        int tokenType = inputStream.nextToken();
        while (tokenType != StreamTokenizer.TT_EOF)
        {
                // convert token type to primitive char type
                character = (char)tokenType;

                // convert character to lowercase for purposes of
                // comparison
                character = Character.toLowerCase(character);

                // increase character counter
                characters++;

                // process vowels
                for (int index=0; index != vowels.length; index++)
                {
                        if (character == vowels[index])
```

```
                    {
                            frequency[index]++;
                            break;
                    }
            }

            // process consonants
            if ((character >= 'b' && character <= 'd') ||
                (character >= 'f' && character <= 'h') ||
                (character >= 'j' && character <= 'n') ||
                (character >= 'p' && character <= 't') ||
                (character >= 'v' && character <= 'z'))
            {
                    consonants++;
            }

            // process words
            if ((character == (char)SPACE) ||
                (tokenType == StreamTokenizer.TT_EOL)) words++;

            tokenType = inputStream.nextToken();
        }

    file.close();
}

/**
Return the total number of characters in the text.
@return The number of characters in the text file.
*/
public int getCharacters()
{
    return characters;
}

/**
Return the total number of vowels in the text.
@return The number of vowels in the text file.
*/
public int getVowels()
{
    int sum=0;
```

```
        for (int index=0; index != frequency.length; index++)
            sum = sum + frequency[index];

        return sum;
    }


    /**
    Return the frequency of occurrence of vowels in the text.
    @return The frequency of occurrence of vowels in the text file.
    */
    public int[] getVowelFrequency()
    {
        return frequency;
    }


    /**
    Return the total number of words in text file.
    @return The total number of words in text file.
    */
    public int getWords()
    {
        return words;
    }


    /**
    Return the total number of consonants in text file.
    @return The total number of consonants in text file.
    */
    public int getConsonants()
    {
        return consonants;
    }


    /**
    Return the literal values of the vowels.
    @return The literal values of each vowel.
    */
    public static char[] getVowelLiterals()
    {
        return vowels;
    }
}
```

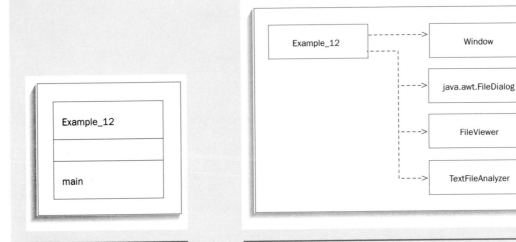

Figure 7.8 UML class diagram for `Example_12`

Figure 7.9 UML dependency diagram for the class `Example_12`

Figures 7.8 and 7.9 depict the class and dependency diagrams for the class `Example_12`.

```java
import avi.*;
import java.awt.FileDialog;
import java.io.*;

class Example_12
{
      public static void main(String[] args)
      {
            int[] frequency;
            char[] vowels = TextFileAnalyzer.getVowelLiterals();
            // open window
            Window screen = new
            Window("Example_12.java","plain","black",14);
            screen.showWindow();

            // open file dialog box
            FileDialog file = new FileDialog(screen,"",FileDialog.LOAD);
            file.show();

            String pathname = file.getDirectory();
            String filename = file.getFile();
```

```
try
{
        // create FileViewer and TextFileAnalyzer objects
        FileViewer passageFromShakespeare = new
        FileViewer(pathname+filename);
        TextFileAnalyzer aLittleShakespeare = new
        TextFileAnalyzer(pathname+filename);

        // output information about file
        screen.write("Name of file being analyzed: "+
                        filename+"\n\n");
        screen.write("Contents of file ..\n\n");
        passageFromShakespeare.viewFile(screen);

        screen.write("\n\nStatistics from the file - "+
                        "numbers of\n\n");
        screen.write("\tcharacters "+
                        aLittleShakespeare.getCharacters()+"\n");
        screen.write("\twords "+aLittleShakespeare.getWords()+
                        "\n");
        screen.write("\tconsonants"+
                        aLittleShakespeare.getConsonants()+"\n");
        screen.write("\tvowels "+aLittleShakespeare.getVowels()+
                        "\n\n");

        frequency = aLittleShakespeare.getVowelFrequency();
        screen.write("vowel\tnumber\n");
        for (int index=0; index != frequency.length; index++)
            screen.write(vowels[index]+"\t"+
                        frequency[index]+"\n");

        screen.write("\n\n\n\nCLOSE WINDOW TO QUIT");
}

catch(Exception e)
{
        Memo error=null;

        if (e instanceof FileNotFoundException)
        {
                error = new Memo(screen,pathname+filename,
                                "NOT FOUND","CLOSE TO QUIT",
                                true);
        }
```

```
                    if (e instanceof IOException)
                    {
                            error = new Memo(screen,"","IO Exception raised",
                                            "CLOSE TO QUIT",true);
                    }

                    error.showMemo();
                    screen.closeWindowAndExit();
            }
        }
}
```

A screen shot from the running program follows.

NOW DO THIS Create your own text file and re-run program `Example_12` using the new text file.

SUMMARY

- An exception is the occurrence of an event that happens when the program is running.

- In Java, an exception is treated as an object that is an instance of the superclass `Throwable`, or an instance of one of its subclasses.

- The superclass `Throwable` has two subclasses, `Error` and `Exception`.

- There exists a list of subclasses to `RuntimeException`, which itself is a subclass of `Exception`.

- As a general rule, programmers should handle explicit exceptions from the subclass of `Exception` and not the subclass of `Error` or `RuntimeException`.

- All exceptions that are thrown must be eventually caught.

- A method might not always handle an exception but instead propagates it for another method to eventually handle.

- Exceptions are handled using a `catch` block.

- Only an exception that is the same class, or a subclass, of the `catch` block parameter may be handled by the `catch` block.

- A `try` clause is used to delimit a block of code in which the result of a method call or other operation might cause an exception.

- If an exception is raised within a `try` block, then the computer branches to the corresponding `catch` block. After the execution of the appropriate `catch` block, the computer does *not* return to the next executable statement in the `try` block, but continues to execute statements that follow the `catch` block.

- When there is no exception raised within a `try` block, the corresponding `catch` block is ignored and the computer continues to execute statements after the `catch` block.

- Whenever there are multiple `catch` blocks, the `catch` block with the lowest subclass parameter must be placed first in the order of the `catch` blocks. The `catch` block with a superclass parameter must be placed last in the order of the `catch` blocks. Failure to observe this rule will result in a superclass `catch` block overshadowing a subclass `catch` block and the compiler reporting this occurrence as an error.

- Multiple exceptions may be caught by either the use of multiple `catch` blocks or by a single superclass `catch` block, with sufficient logic to determine which exception was thrown.

- You may create your own exception classes; however, these classes should extend one of the superclasses such as `Throwable` or `Exception`.

- An exception is explicitly thrown using a `throw` statement. A `throw` statement must specify an exception object to be thrown.

- A `throws` clause lists the exceptions that can be thrown by a method.

- The instance method `toString()` in the class `Throwable` returns as a string the name of the exception class.

- The instance method `getMessage()` in the class `Throwable` returns the message used in the instantiation of the exception object.

- Whenever a block of statements needs to be executed before the computer exits from a try block, declare these statements in a `finally` block.

- Good practice dictates that you should state which methods in a class throw exceptions. Write the exception handlers for these exceptions in the program that uses the methods.

- A keyboard may be replaced by a file for the input of data to a program.

- A screen may be replaced by a file for the output of the results from a program.

- Files must be opened before they can be used and closed when no longer needed in a program.

- A line of text may be divided into individual tokens, where each token represents an item of data.

Review Questions

True or False

1. A `RuntimeException` is a superclass of an `ArithmeticException`.

2. The order of `try` and `catch` blocks is of no significance.

3. A single `try` block may have corresponding multiple `catch` blocks.

4. The `throws` clause invokes an exception.

5. A `catch` clause may have more than one parameter.

6. Catch blocks must immediately follow a `try` block.

7. A `catch` block is never executed if the corresponding exception is not raised.

Short Answer

8. What is an exception?

9. How is an exception invoked?

10. If a method cannot handle an exception, what happens to the exception?

11. Inspect the class `java.lang.Math`. State which of the class methods throw exceptions, and why you think the methods need to do this.

12. Repeat the previous question, but this time look at the methods in the class `java.lang.String`.

13. Define `try`, `catch`, and `finally` blocks.

14. What is the function of the instance method `toString()` and when is it used?

15. What does the `instanceof` operator return?

16. Why do the methods found in Java classes throw exceptions rather than handling them within the class?

17. How should multiple `catch` blocks be arranged?

18. What restrictions are imposed on creating your own exception class?

19. What is the difference between a `throw` clause and a `throws` clause?

20. If a `catch` block does not exist in a method, how is the corresponding `throws` clause handled?

21. What is a text file?

22. What is a token?

23. What is wrong with the following declaration?

    ```
    static BufferedReader keyboard = new BufferedReader(System.out);
    ```

24. If you inspect the class `PrintStream`, why is it possible to use the methods `print` and `println` to output numbers of type `int`, `long`, `real`, and `double`?

Exercises

25. Detect the error in the following code.

    ```
    try
    {
        methodA();
    }
    ```

```
   methodB();

   catch(Throwable t){}
```

26. Detect the error in the following code.

```
try
{
   FileReader file = new FileReader("data.bin");
   BufferedReader input = new BufferedReader(file);
}
catch(FileNotFoundException f){System.exit(1);}
Record data = new Record();
data.readRecord(input);
```

27. Is the following structure of `try` and `catch` blocks legal?

```
try
{
   .
   .
   try
   {
      .
      .
   }
   catch(..){}
   .
   .
}
catch (..){}
```

28. Detect the error in the following `catch` block.

```
catch (Error e)
{
   if (e instanceof ArithmeticException) ..
   if (e instanceof ArrayStoreException) ..
}
```

29. Comment upon the legality of the following `catch` blocks.

```
try
{
   .
   .
}
catch (Throwable t){..}
catch (Exception e){..}
```

```
catch (ClassNotFoundException c){..}
catch (InterruptedException i){..}
```

30. Detect the errors in the following code.

```
static public void main(String[] args)
{
    methodA();
}


static void methodA() throw newTypeOfException
{

    .

    .

    throws newTypeOfException;
}
```

31. Desk check the following code. What type of exception will cause the `catch` block to be executed?

```
int[] array = {1,2,3,4,5};
int   index = 0;

for (;;)
{
    try
    {
        screen.println(array[index]);
        index++;
    }
    catch(Exception e)
    {
        System.out.println(e.toString());
        return;
    }
}
```

32. How would you expect the following output statements to display information?

    a. `System.out.println("Hello World");`

    b. `System.out.println("\tname: ");`

    c. `System.out.println("\tname:   "  +  name);` where `name` is declared as `String name = "Mickey Mouse";`

33. Using the declaration for `dosWindow` given in the text, state the output from the following statements.

   a.   `dosWindow.println("a=" + a + " b=" + b + " c=" + c);` where a = 3, b = 4, and c = 5.

   b.   `dosWindow.print("area covered " + area); screen.flush();` where area = 635.8658.

   c.   `dosWindow.println("\u0041\u0042\u0043");`

34. Detect the errors in the following statements.

   a.   `println("value of beta is ", beta);`

   b.   `String alpha = 'X';`

   c.   `int beta = new Float(keyboard.readLine()).intValue();`

35. Draw hierarchy diagrams for the following classes.

   a.   `Float`   b.   `BufferedOutputStream`

Programming Problems

36. Write a program to prove that the order in which `catch` blocks are written is of importance.

37. Write and test separate segments of program code to input a string and throw the appropriate exception if the string cannot be:

   a.   converted to a number.

   b.   converted to an integer.

   c.   converted to a real number.

Allow the number to be reinput until it is accepted as a number in a valid format.

38. Write an exception class for a time of day not represented in the correct 24-hour format. Write a program to input various times in the 24-hour format and throw an exception for those times that are in error.

39. Rewrite the case study from this chapter; however, do not use command-line arguments for the input of the file name. Instead, allow a user to type the name of the text file to be processed when the program is running. If the file does not exist, allow the user to either enter a new file name or to choose to quit the program.

40. A text file contains records with the following fields:

     stock number—four digits followed by a modulus-11 check digit

     quantity of stock—three digit positive integer

     distribution code—two digit positive integer

Create a test data file having records with the stated format. However, you should include in your file a number of records that do not conform to the format. For example, a stock number may have the wrong modulus-11 check digit, implying that the number was incorrectly transcribed; a quantity of stock may not lie within the prescribed limits; and a distribution code may not be a two-digit number.

Write a program to read the records from the stock file. Filter only those records that contain no errors into another file. Before writing each record to the new file, translate the two-digit distribution code into a textual description of the area for distribution. The names of the distribution points are stored in a one-dimensional array. Beware— this is another source of error since the distribution code may generate an index-out-of-bounds exception.

Records that are in error should be displayed on the screen stating the nature of the error.

Note: A modulus-11 check digit provides a means for the computer to check that a number has not had any digits transposed when it has been input to the computer. The check-digit method ensures a detection of all transcription and transposition errors and 91% of random errors.

The modulus-11 check digit for a stock number is calculated as follows. Using the code number 9118 as an example, multiply each digit by its associated weight, and calculate the sum of the partial products. The weights are 5, 4, 3, and 2, with the most significant digit in the number having the weight of 5 and the least significant digit in the number having the weight of 2.

$$(5 \times 9) + (4 \times 1) + (3 \times 1) + (2 \times 8) = 68$$

The sum 68 is then divided by 11 and the remainder 2 is then subtracted from 11; the result, 9, is the check digit. The stock number, including the check digit as the last digit, is 91189. If the value of the check digit is computed to be 10, this is replaced by the letter X.

To check whether a stock number has been entered into the computer correctly, a similar calculation is carried out. Each digit is multiplied by a weight, the check digit has a weight of 1, and the sum of the partial products is calculated.

$$(5 \times 9) + (4 \times 1) + (3 \times 1) + (2 \times 8) + (1 \times 9) = 77$$

The sum 77 is divided by 11 and the remainder is zero. If the remainder was nonzero, then a transcription error would have been made when entering the number into the computer.

41. Use an editor to create a file `booze.txt` that contains the details of items of stock in a bar. Each line in the file contains the following data: stock quantity, unit price, and description. For example, a line of text might contain: 3 30.00 Brandy, which represents 3 bottles of Brandy at $30.00 per bottle.

Write a program to read each line from the text file `booze.txt` and create a report `stock.txt` similar in layout and content to that illustrated in Figure 7.10, where the value of the stock is the product of the respective quantity and price.

```
                    Report Layout Document

12345678901234567890123456789012345678901234567890

            BAR  STOCK  REPORT

QUANTITY    PRICE    VALUE    DESCRIPTION
3           30.00    90.00    Brandy
5           18.50    92.50    Gin
5           17.00    85.00    Rum
10          15.50    155.00   Vodka
8           25.00    200.00   Whiskey

TOTAL                $622.50
```

Figure 7.10 Stock report

42. A text file `viewers.txt` contains the following three items per line:

    category code of program

    estimated size of viewing audience (millions)

    name of television program

    The category of program is coded with a single character as follows.

    D—drama

    L—light entertainment

    M—music

    S—science fiction

    A typical record from the file might contain the following data:

    `D 5.25 NYPD Blue`

    The data indicate that 5.25 million viewers watched the television program NYPD Blue and that the show is a drama.

    Use an editor to create the text file with programs of your own choice so that the contents of your file are ordered on the category code as the key. Group all the drama programs together, all the light-entertainment programs together, and so on.

    Write a computer program to input a category code and generate output similar to that shown in Figure 7.11. This output lists the names of all the programs in the chosen category, the audience viewing figures, and the total number of viewers who watched programs in that category.

```
┌─────────────────────────────────────────────────────────────┐
│                 Screen Layout Document                       │
├─────────────────────────────────────────────────────────────┤
│ 12345678901234567890123456789012345678901234567890           │
│                                                              │
│ CATEGORY - DRAMA                                             │
│                                                              │
│ audience          program                                    │
│ 5.25              NYPD Blue                                  │
│ 7.45              Murder She Wrote                           │
│ 7.50              L.A.Law                                    │
│                                                              │
│ 20.20 millions total audience                                │
│                                                              │
│                                                              │
│                                                              │
└─────────────────────────────────────────────────────────────┘
```

Figure 7.11 Audience viewing figures

CHAPTER 8

An Introduction to the `java.awt` Package

Within this chapter you will be introduced to many of the Java components for constructing *graphical user interfaces* (*GUIs*). You are already familiar with the use of some of these components through the audio-visual interface. With the information in this chapter you will be able to develop your own GUIs.

A GUI is an interface between a user and a computer that makes use of input devices other than the keyboard, and presentation techniques other than alphanumeric characters. Typical GUIs involve the use of windows, menus, and pointing devices. The windows can contain control objects such as slider bars, radio buttons, check boxes, and pick lists, as well as textual or graphical information. The objects forming the interface have the ability to be resized, moved around the display, shrunk down to an icon, or given different colors.

Throughout the chapter you are required to modify the classes and example programs to gain a better understanding of how the `awt` components are used.

By the end of this chapter you should have an understanding of the following topics.

- The hierarchy of components found in the `java.awt` package known as the Abstract Windowing Toolkit (AWT).

- The creation of a container class.

- Adding awt components such as buttons, labels, text fields, check boxes, radio buttons, and lists to a container.

- Handling events described in the java.awt.event package.

- The use of two layout-manager classes for positioning components in a container.

- The creation of reusable GUI components from awt components, including dialog boxes, text areas, and scrollbars.

8.1   Creating a Container

In this section you will see how to create a container in the form of a window that will appear on the screen; it is into this window that we will add the various awt objects. Figure 8.1 illustrates some of the classes from the AWT found in the package java.awt used to build GUIs.

In Figure 8.1 the Component class has been shaded and expanded to indicate that it is of special significance in the construction of a graphical user interface. Subclasses of the Component class include a Container class, which itself has subclasses that include Window (not to be confused with the avi Window), Frame, and Dialog classes. Both the Component and Container classes contain a large number of methods that are inherited by their subclasses.

In creating a graphical user interface, we need to create a container object into which we will place other objects. The Container class is defined as an abstract class, and therefore it cannot be instantiated directly. However, any of the subclasses of Container can be instantiated. To begin, we will concentrate on creating our own container class, called MyWindow, which is a subclass of Frame. This may be coded as:

```
public class MyWindow extends Frame
```

The Frame class represents an optionally resizable top-level application window with a title bar and contains two constructors.

```
public Frame();
public Frame(String title);
```

The first constructor is the default constructor that takes no arguments. The second constructor takes a string argument that represents the text stored in the title bar. In creating the constructor for our MyWindow container class we will code:

```
public MyWindow(int width, int height, int x, int y)
{
    super("My Window");
    .
    .
```

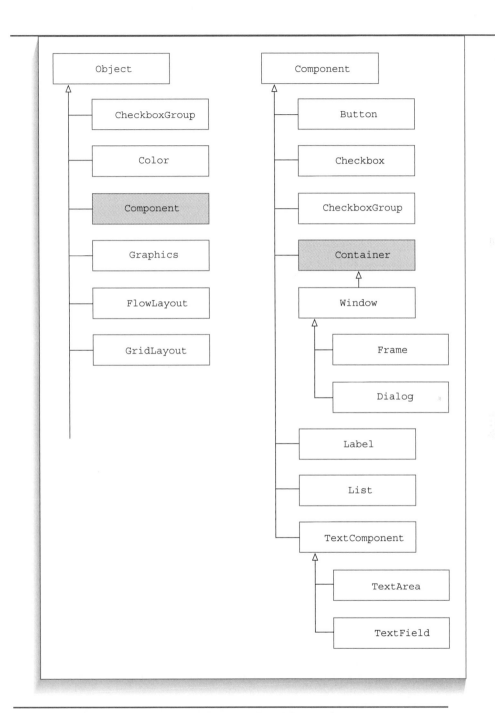

Figure 8.1 A selection of classes in the AWT package for building interfaces

Remember the reserved word `super` invokes the constructor of the superclass. In this case this constructor will be `Frame(String title)`. The text that will appear in the title bar of our container window will be `My Window`.

The dimensions of the container are passed as the parameters `width` and `height`. We need to use a method inherited by `Frame` from the `Component` class—`setSize`—to set the dimensions of the `MyWindow` container. If you inspect the Java documentation, you will notice that `setSize` can take either a single argument of type `Dimension` or two arguments specifying the `width` and `height` of type integer. We will choose to use the second option. Hence, the coding to set the size of the window container is:

```
setSize(width,height);
```

The window container also has other attributes besides size; it has the color of the foreground and the color of the background. Once again, the `Frame` class has inherited the methods `setForeground` and `setBackground` from the `Component` class; these methods will be used to set the color attributes of the window container `MyWindow`. Both methods take an argument that represents the color of the foreground and the color of the background. Color is specified as a public constant from the `Color` class that also forms part of the `awt` package. The coding to set the foreground and background colors of the `MyWindow` class is:

```
setForeground(Color.black);
setBackground(Color.yellow);
```

If you inspect the Java documentation for the `Color` class, you have a choice of 13 different color constants. The colors used for the window container `MyWindow` are the authors' choice.

Java will allow the programmer to specify where to place the window container on the screen. The constructor for the class `MyWindow` has two parameters `x` and `y` that represent the coordinates of the top left-hand corner of the window. The method `setLocation`, inherited from the `Component` class, fixes the position of the top left-hand corner of the window container with respect to the screen of the monitor. The statement is coded as:

```
setLocation(x,y);
```

i The origin of coordinates is taken to be the upper left-hand corner of the screen. You may think of the x-axis as the top edge of the screen and the y-axis as the left-hand edge of the screen, where the positive x-axis is to the right of the origin and the positive y-axis is below the origin.

Although this position is fixed initially, the user can drag the window container anywhere on the screen by pressing the left mouse button over the window bar and moving the mouse until you release the button.

Although the constructor builds a window container, it does not display the container on the screen of the monitor. The display must be done using the `show` method inherited by `Frame` from the `Window` class. The statement is coded as:

```
this.show();
```

where the keyword `this` refers to the `MyWindow` object. It is good practice to create an instance method `showWindow` to display the container on the screen rather than code the `show` method in the constructor. The reasons for this may not be obvious for a container; however, as you will see towards the end of the chapter, it is important for reusable components that appear in a container.

If we put all these pieces of code together, the first attempt at coding the `MyWindow` class is written as follows. Note that class `Example_1` is included to test the methods of the new container class.

```java
// program to create a window container

import java.awt.*;

class MyNewWindow extends Frame
{
    // constructor
    public MyNewWindow(int width, int height, int x, int y)
    {
        // call Frame's constructor
        super("My Window");

        // set colors of window
        setBackground(Color.yellow);
        setForeground(Color.black);

        // set dimensions and position of window on screen
        setSize(width, height);
        setLocation(x,y);       }

    // instance method to display window on screen
    public void showWindow()
    {
        this.show();
    }
}
```

```
public class Example_1
{
      public static void main(String[] args)
      {
            MyNewWindow window = new MyNewWindow(300,100,200,200);
            window.showWindow();
      }
}
```

When you attempt to execute Program `Example_1`, you soon find that you run into trouble! The window container appears correctly on the screen of the monitor, but any attempt to close the window is in vain. You can keep pressing the close window icon marked X, or click-on X Close in the drop-down menu, or press the Alt+F4 keys together, as depicted by Figure 8.2; however, the window container will not close. In the end you have to resort to clicking on the MSDOS/terminal window so that you can type the Ctrl+C keys together to abandon the running program.

8.2 Handling an Event

Let us tackle the problem of trying to close the window container. All the time you were trying to close the window, by either moving the mouse pointer over the close icon X and pressing the window close button, or by moving the mouse pointer over the X Close window menu option and selecting this option by clicking on the mouse button, or by pressing Alt+F4 keys, you were generating events that the computer program failed to recognize. The events you were generating were a result of actions taking place such as pressing a mouse button or pressing a key. What was missing from the program was the ability to detect the events and act upon them.

The event-handling model in versions of Java later than 1.0 is based upon the concept of an *event listener*.

An *event* occurs when an `awt` component receives some message from the mouse or keyboard. A listener can be used to respond to these events. Graphical

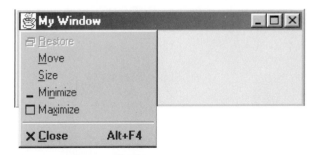

Figure 8.2 Various options for closing a window

user interfaces are event-driven because they respond to events on their components such as a button being pressed.

A *listener* is an object that responds to an event taking place in an awt graphical user interface. Listeners respond to events such as window-close buttons being pressed and mouse button clicks.

If you want to listen for a particular type of event within a class you have written, the class must implement the correct listener interface for the type of event you want to handle. For example, when a window-close button is pressed, it generates a WindowEvent object. A component such as MyWindow must listen for such events by implementing the WindowListener interface.

The WindowListener is an interface that contains a set of abstract methods that must be implemented by any class that uses a window listener. The abstract methods for the class WindowListener are as follows:

```
public abstract void windowClosed(WindowEvent event);
public abstract void windowDeiconified(WindowEvent event);
public abstract void windowIconified(WindowEvent event);
public abstract void windowActivated(WindowEvent event);
public abstract void windowDeactivated(WindowEvent event);
public abstract void windowOpened(WindowEvent event);
public abstract void windowClosing(WindowEvent event);
```

You may wonder about the inclusion of so many WindowListener methods when we only require to implement the method windowClosing in this example. There is a way to implement the MyWindow class without having to explicitly handle all of the methods. The java.awt.event package contains adapter classes for all event-listener interfaces that have at least two methods. The WindowAdapter class implements all the WindowListener methods by including a set of do-nothing methods. By creating your own class, say, CloseMyWindow that extends the WindowAdapter class, you can override only those methods that are of use to you in your program.

Furthermore, if this class is implemented as an inner class, then it has access to all the variables of the outer class. An object of an inner class CloseMyWindow can refer to an object of an outer class MyWindow to which it is associated by the syntax MyWindow.this. The coding of the CloseMyWindow class follows.

```
private class CloseMyWindow extends WindowAdapter
{
      // overridden method of superclass
      public void windowClosing(WindowEvent event)
      {
            MyWindow.this.dispose();
            System.exit(0);
      }
}
```

The implementation of the `windowClosing` method determines how the event will be processed. In this method we need to return any system resources being used by the window. This is accomplished by invoking the object's `dispose` method—in this case, `dispose` is inherited from `Window`. It is always a good idea to call `dispose` when a window is no longer needed in order to free its windowing system resources. Finally, we must also call the `System.exit` method; it will terminate the currently executing program. We pass it the exit value 0, which indicates normal termination.

We now need to create a `CloseMyWindow` object and add this as a window listener to the `MyWindow` class by calling the `addWindowListener` method. Remember to import the `java.awt.event` package to allow us to use events.

The original code for the `MyWindow` class has been modified to include an event listener. Class `Example_2` is included to test the creation of the container `MyWindow`.

```java
// program to create a window container

import java.awt.*;
import java.awt.event.*;

class MyWindow extends Frame
{
      // constructor
      public MyWindow(int width, int height, int x, int y)
      {
            // call Frame's constructor
            super("My Window");

            // set colors of window
            setBackground(Color.yellow);
            setForeground(Color.black);

            // set dimensions and position of window on screen
            setSize(width, height);
            setLocation(x,y);

            // add listener to detect window being closed
            addWindowListener(new CloseMyWindow());
      }
      // instance method to display window on screen
      public void showWindow()
      {
            this.show();
      }

      // subclass of WindowAdapter
```

```
    private class CloseMyWindow extends WindowAdapter
    {
        // overridden method of superclass
        public void windowClosing(WindowEvent event)
        {
            MyWindow.this.dispose();
            System.exit(0);
        }
    }
}


public class Example_2
{
    public static void main(String[] args)
    {
        MyWindow window = new MyWindow(300,100,200,200);
        window.showWindow();
    }
}
```

NOW DO THIS   Modify the classes `MyWindow` and `Example_2` as follows.

(1) Change the background color of the window to red.

(2) Change the dimensions of the window to 100 × 400, and change the position of the window on the screen to (300,50).

(3) When your program is running, press the Maximize button on the title bar of `MyWindow`—this should fill the screen with a red window.

(4) Continue by pressing the Restore button on the title bar of `MyWindow`—this should restore the window to its original size.

(5) Finally, press the Minimize button on the title bar of `MyWindow`—this should shrink the window to an icon. Mouse-click on the icon to restore `MyWindow` to its original size; then close `MyWindow`.

8.3 Adding a Button to the Container

Having successfully created a container class `MyWindow`, it is now possible to add a push button to the container. Figure 8.3 indicates the appearance of this component.

This new component is created from the awt `Button` class. The default constructor `Button()` creates a button with no label, whereas the constructor `Button(String label)` creates a button with the string argument as the label.

Figure 8.3 Adding a button to a window container

Notice a recurring theme in the use of components. All awt components inherit methods from the abstract Component class—therefore, setBackground and setForeground are also used by the Button object in the following code.

```
// create a button object
Button pushButton = new Button("press me");

// set colors of button
pushButton.setBackground(Color.cyan);
pushButton.setForeground(Color.black);
```

Before the button is added to the container we need to establish the size of the button and its placement in the container. There is no reason why the methods setSize and setLocation, used for the window container, should not also be used for the button. However, for the moment we will take a simpler approach by using a layout manager, and then we will return to using the methods setSize and setLocation later in the chapter.

A *layout manager* is an interface (java.awt.LayoutManager) that defines the methods necessary for a class to be able to arrange component objects within a container object. There are five predefined layout classes that implement the interface LayoutManager.

Each of these describes a different way that components are physically laid out within a container. Of the five layout classes illustrated in Figure 8.4, we will examine the FlowLayout class now and the GridLayout class in the next section. Once you understand what a layout manager does, you should be able to study the Java documentation relating to the remaining three layout classes.

When using the FlowLayout class, components are added to the container one after another in rows, and when a row is full, the next component is added to the next row.

The FlowLayout class has three constructors.

```
public FlowLayout();
public FlowLayout(int align);
public FlowLayout(int align, int hGap, int vGap);
```

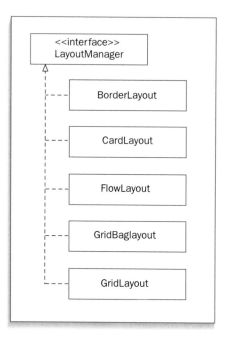

Figure 8.4 Five implementations of the layout manager

The argument `align` may be any one of the three class constants `LEFT`, `RIGHT`, or `CENTER` (default). It specifies whether the alignment of the components will be left justified, right justified, or centralized with respect to the edge of the container.

The arguments `hGap` and `vGap` specify the number of horizontal and vertical pixels between components.

The code used to set the flow layout manager for the button in the `MyWindowWithButton` class is:

```
setLayout(new FlowLayout());
```

The button is added to the `MyWindowWithButton` container, using the `add` method inherited from the `Container` class.

```
// add push button to the container
add(pushButton);
```

A button has a different event listener than a window. Figure 8.5 illustrates the event and listener methods associated with each component. For example, a button when pressed generates an `ActionEvent` object. `ActionListener` is an interface that contains a single method `actionPerformed`, which is automatically invoked when a button is pressed. Because `ActionListener` is an interface, the method `actionPerformed` must be implemented by the programmer. However, the `ActionListener` interface contains only one method, so the method can be implemented directly in the `MyWindowWithButton` class. The action listener is added to the `MyWindowWithButton` class with the following code.

```
pushButton.addActionListener(this);
```

The source of the event may be established by invoking the method `getActionCommand()` from the `ActionEvent` class. This way it is possible to determine which of several buttons have been pressed. Note, both classes `ActionEvent` and `ActionListener` can be found in the package `java.awt.event`.

To detect the event of a button being pushed we must do the following:

- Import the `java.awt.event` package.
- Add an action listener to the class `MyWindowWithButton`.
- Since `ActionListener` is an interface, we must implement its method by the appropriate class (in this example, the `MyWindowWithButton` class).
- Process the event. The implementation of the `actionPerformed` method determines how the event will be processed.

We will design the `MyWindowWithButton` class so that when you press the button, the computer generates the sound associated with Unicode \u0007 (the BELL character) and displays the message `button pressed` in the MSDOS/terminal window.

The complete code for the `MyWindowWithButton` class follows together with class `Example_3`, which is needed to test the GUI.

```java
// program to create a window container and add a push button to the
// container

import java.awt.*;
import java.awt.event.*;

class MyWindowWithButton extends Frame implements ActionListener
{
      // constructor
      public MyWindowWithButton(int width, int height, int x, int y)
      {
```

```
        // call Frame's constructor
        super("My Window with button");

        // set colors of window
        setBackground(Color.yellow);
        setForeground(Color.black);

        // set dimensions and position of window on screen
        setSize(width, height);
        setLocation(x,y);

        // add listener to detect window being closed
        addWindowListener(new CloseMyWindow());

        // use flow layout manager
        setLayout(new FlowLayout());

        // create a button object
        Button pushButton = new Button("press me");

        // set colors of button
        pushButton.setBackground(Color.cyan);
        pushButton.setForeground(Color.black);

        // add push button to the container
        add(pushButton);

        // add listener to detect button being pushed
        pushButton.addActionListener(this);
    }

// instance method to display window on screen
public void showWindow()
{
        this.show();
}


// subclass of WindowAdapter
private class CloseMyWindow extends WindowAdapter
{
        // overridden method of superclass
        public void windowClosing(WindowEvent event)
        {
            MyWindowWithButton.this.dispose();
            System.exit(0);
        }
}
}
```

```
// implementation of Action Listener method
public void actionPerformed(ActionEvent event)
{
        final char BELL = '\u0007';

        if (event.getActionCommand().equals("press me"))
        {
                System.out.println(BELL+"button pressed");
        }

    }
}


public class Example_3
{
    public static void main(String[] args)
    {
        MyWindowWithButton window = new
        MyWindowWithButton(300,100,200,200);
        window.showWindow();

    }
}
```

NOW DO THIS   Modify the class `MyWindowWithButton` as follows.

(1) Create two buttons called STOP and GO. The background color of the STOP button is red, and the background color of the GO button is green. You don't need to code an entry for the foreground colors of the buttons; they will be taken as black by default.

(2) Add these buttons to the container and remember to add action listeners for each button. When the STOP button is pressed, print the message `Red is for Danger`, and when the GO button is pressed print the message `Green is for Eco-friendly`. Both messages are displayed in the MSDOS/terminal window.

Figure 8.5 lists a number of components from the Abstract Windowing Toolkit. Note that although both a key (from the keyboard) and a mouse are external to the GUI and are not components within the AWT, they are still capable of generating events that must be handled within your program.

Component	Events Generated	Listener Interface	Listener Methods
Button	ActionEvent	ActionListener	actionPerformed
Checkbox	ItemEvent	ItemListener	itemStateChanged
CheckboxMenuItem	ItemEvent	ItemListener	itemStateChanged
Choice	ItemEvent	ItemListener	itemStateChanged
Component	ComponentEvent	ComponentListener	componentHidden
.	.	.	componentMoved
.	.	.	componentResized
.	.	.	componentShown
.	FocusEvent	FocusListener	focusGained
.	.	.	focusLost
Container	ContainerEvent	ContainerListener	componentAdded
.	.	.	componentRemoved
[key]	KeyEvent	KeyListener	keyPressed
.	.	.	keyReleased
.	.	.	keyTyped
List	ActionEvent	ActionListener	actionPerformed
.	ItemEvent	ItemListener	itemStateChanged
MenuItem	ActionEvent	ActionListener	actionPerformed
[mouse]	MouseEvent	MouseListener	mouseClicked
.	.	.	mouseEntered
.	.	.	mouseExited
.	.	.	mousePressed
.	.	.	mouseReleased
.	.	MouseMotionListener	mouseDragged
.	.		mouseMoved
Scrollbar	AdjustmentEvent	AdjustmentListener	adjustmentValueChanged
TextComponent	TextEvent	TextListener	textValueChanged
TextField	ActionEvent	ActionListener	actionPerformed
Window	WindowEvent	WindowListener	windowActivated
			windowClosed
			windowClosing
			windowDeactivated
			windowDeiconified
			windowIconified
			windowOpened

Figure 8.5 Components, events, and listener methods

8.4   Adding Labels, Fonts, and Text Fields to a Container

Labels

Labels are text strings that may be used to label other components. Figure 8.6 illustrates two labels appearing in a window container.

An object from the `Label` class is instantiated using one of the following constructors.

```
public Label();
public Label(String label);
public Label(String label, int alignment);
```

Figure 8.6 Labels written to a window container

where alignment is one of the class constants CENTER, LEFT, and RIGHT. The code used to create the labels shown in Figure 8.6 follows.

```
Label name = new Label("Name");
Label address = new Label("Address");
```

Fonts

Before the label is displayed in the window container, it is often desirable, but not necessary, to set the font for writing the label. The constructor for the Font class is:

```
public Font(String name, int style, int size);
```

where name is either "Serif", "SansSerif", "Monospaced", "Dialog", or "DialogInput"; style is one of the class constants BOLD, ITALIC, or PLAIN, and size is the point size of the font. Note that a one-inch-high character has a point size of 72.

In this example we will set the font name to SansSerif, style to ITALIC, and the font size to 14 points.

```
Font label = new Font("SansSerif",Font.ITALIC,14);
```

Before we add the labels to window container, it is necessary to decide where on the container the labels will be written. At this point we will consider the second of the layout managers—GridLayout.

With the GridLayout manager, the components are placed into the respective cells of a grid. When the cells of the first row are filled, the components continue to be placed in the next row, and so on, until eventually there are no further components to place on the grid.

The constructor for the GridLayout class is:

```
public GridLayout(int rows, int columns);
public GridLayout(int rows, int columns, int hGap, int vGap)
```

where the parameters `rows` and `columns` specify the size of the grid and `hGap` and `vGap` specify the distance in pixels between the components.

If we want each label to be placed in a separate row, then we can code the layout manager using two rows and one column as:

```
setLayout(new GridLayout(2,1));
```

The labels are added to the window container using the following code:

```
add(name);
add(address);
```

The following classes, `MyWindowWithLabels` and `Example_4`, are used to generate the graphical interface shown in Figure 8.6.

```java
// program to create a window container and add labels to the container

import java.awt.*;
import java.awt.event.*;

class MyWindowWithLabels extends Frame
{
    // constructor
    public MyWindowWithLabels(int width, int height, int x, int y)
    {
        // call Frame's constructor
        super("My Window with labels");

        // set colors of window
        setBackground(Color.yellow);
        setForeground(Color.black);

        // set dimensions and position of window on screen
        setSize(width, height);
        setLocation(x,y);

        // add listener to detect window being closed
        addWindowListener(new CloseMyWindow());

        // use grid layout manager
        setLayout(new GridLayout(2,1));

        // create font for labels
        Font label = new Font("SansSerif",Font.ITALIC,14);
```

```java
        // create labels
        Label name = new Label("Name");
        Label address = new Label("Address");

        // set font of labels
        name.setFont(label);
        address.setFont(label);

        // add labels to container
        add(name);
        add(address);
    }

    // instance method to display window on screen
    public void showWindow()
    {
        this.show();
    }

    // subclass of WindowAdapter
    private class CloseMyWindow extends WindowAdapter
    {
        // overridden method of superclass
        public void windowClosing(WindowEvent event)
        {
            MyWindowWithLabels.this.dispose();
            System.exit(0);
        }
    }
}

public class Example_4
{
    public static void main(String[] args)
    {
        MyWindowWithLabels window = new
        MyWindowWithLabels(300,100,200,200);
        window.showWindow();
    }
}
```

NOW DO THIS   Modify classes `MyWindowWithLabels` and `Example_4` as follows.

(1) Add extra labels to the window container for a telephone number and date of birth.

(2) Modify the grid layout to cater for 4 rows and 1 column.

(3) Experiment with the use of different fonts for the labels.

Text Fields

A `TextField` allows you to either input or output textual information. Figure 8.7 illustrates how labels may be used in conjunction with text fields to describe what the text field contains. Regardless of the length of a text field, Java will allow you to enter text that is physically longer than the text field. Although part of the text becomes obscured, the complete line of text can still be retrieved.

An object from the `TextField` class can be instantiated using the following constructor.

```
public TextField();
```

The following constructors were used to create the text fields illustrated in Figure 8.7.

```
TextField nameField = new TextField();
TextField addressField = new TextField();
```

Assume that text has been input into the appropriate text field. Pressing the return key is an action that generates an event. Provided an action listener is associated with the text field, the event can be handled by implementing the `actionPerformed` method of the `ActionListener` interface. You, of course, need to add an action listener for each text field object as:

```
nameField.addActionListener(this);
addressField.addActionListener(this);
```

The `ActionListener` interface contains only one method to be implemented—`actionPerformed`. Notice in this implementation that when the event of pressing the Return key is detected, the information that had been typed into the text field is retrieved by the `getText` method inherited by the class `TextField` from the `TextComponent` class.

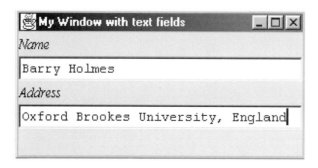

Figure 8.7 Labels and text fields in a window container

```
// implementation of action listener class
public void actionPerformed(ActionEvent event)
{
     System.out.println("Name: "+nameField.getText());
     System.out.println("Address: "+addressField.getText());
}
```

The classes `MyWindowWithTextFields` and `Example_5` together form the components illustrated in Figure 8.7. When Program `Example_5` is executed, whatever is typed in the text field is displayed in the MSDOS/terminal window.

```
// program to create a window container and add labels and text fields to
// the container

import java.awt.*;
import java.awt.event.*;

class MyWindowWithTextFields extends Frame implements ActionListener
{
     private TextField nameField;
     private TextField addressField;
     // constructor
     public MyWindowWithTextFields(int width, int height, int x, int y)
     {
          // call Frame's constructor
          super("My Window with text fields");

          // set colors of window
          setBackground(Color.yellow);
          setForeground(Color.black);

          // set dimensions and position of window on screen
          setSize(width, height);
          setLocation(x,y);

          // add listener to detect window being closed
          addWindowListener(new CloseMyWindow());

          // create fonts for labels and text fields
          Font label = new Font("SansSerif",Font.ITALIC,14);
          Font text = new Font("Monospaced",Font.PLAIN,14);

          // use grid layout manager
          setLayout(new GridLayout(5,2));

          // create labels
```

```java
        Label name = new Label("Name");
        Label address = new Label("Address");

        // set font of labels
        name.setFont(label); address.setFont(label);

        // create text fields
        nameField = new TextField();
        addressField = new TextField();

        // set font of text fields
        nameField.setFont(text); addressField.setFont(text);

        // add labels and text fields to container
        add(name); add(nameField);
        add(address); add(addressField);

        // add listeners to detect input in both fields
        nameField.addActionListener(this);
        addressField.addActionListener(this);
    }
    // instance method to display window on screen
    public void showWindow()
    {
        this.show();
    }
    // subclass of WindowAdapter
    private class CloseMyWindow extends WindowAdapter
    {
        // overridden method of superclass
        public void windowClosing(WindowEvent event)
        {
            MyWindowWithTextFields.this.dispose();
            System.exit(0);
        }
    }
    // implementation of action listener class
    public void actionPerformed(ActionEvent event)
    {
        System.out.println("Name: "+nameField.getText());
        System.out.println("Address: "+addressField.getText());
    }
}


public class Example_5
{
```

```
public static void main(String[] args)
{
        MyWindowWithTextFields window = new
        MyWindowWithTextFields(300,150,200,200);
        window.showWindow();
    }
}
```

> **NOW DO THIS**   Modify classes `MyWindowWithTextFields` and `Example_5` as follows.

(1) Add labels and text fields for a telephone number and date of birth; then display the contents of what is input into each field.

(2) Modify the grid layout to cater for 9 rows and 1 column.

(3) Experiment with typing text that is longer than the length of the text field.

(4) Experiment with changing the foreground and background colors of the fields.

To write text into a text field from within a program, use the method `setText` inherited by `TextField` from the `TextComponent` class. The signature of the method is:

```
public synchronized void setText(String text);
```

The method `setEditable`, also inherited by `TextField` from the `TextComponent` class, specifies whether the text in a text field can be edited. The signature of this method is:

```
public synchronized void setEditable(boolean value);
```

> **NOW DO THIS**

(1) Devise a new class `MyWindowWithNewTextFields` to display within five different text fields data about the name of a country, the size of its population, the name of the capital of the country, and the size of the population living within the capital. Calculate the percentage of the population living in the capital and display this figure in the fifth text field.

(2) The data for this problem should be input at the command line of the MSDOS/terminal window, and the user should not be allowed to edit any of the text fields.

8.5 Adding Check Boxes, Radio Buttons, and Lists to a Container

Check Boxes

Check boxes are components that have two states; on or off (true or false). The check boxes illustrated in Figure 8.8 may be selected nonexclusively, implying that any check box may be selected.

An object from the `awt Checkbox` class is instantiated using one of the following constructors.

```
public Checkbox();
public Checkbox(String label);
public Checkbox(String label, boolean state);
```

The `label` parameter specifies a text literal for a check box. The `state` parameter indicates whether the checkbox should be preselected (true) or not (false).

There are five constructors in total. The remaining two constructors will be considered later under the discussion of radio buttons.

The following skeletal code shows how two of the check boxes illustrated in Figure 8.8 were created.

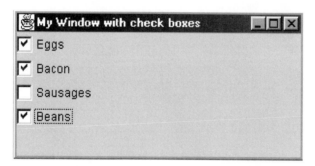

Figure 8.8 Adding check boxes to a window container

```
// select grid layout manager
setLayout(new GridLayout(5,1));

// create check boxes
Checkbox eggs = new Checkbox("Eggs");
Checkbox bacon = new Checkbox("Bacon");
.
.

// add check boxes to window container
```

```
add(eggs);
add(bacon);
    .
    .
    .
// add listeners for each check box
eggs.addItemListener(this);
bacon.addItemListener(this);
    .
    .
    .
```

A mouse is used to point at and click-select the appropriate boxes. Figure 8.8 illustrates that three breakfast foods—Eggs, Bacon, and Beans—have been chosen from the selection. The events of a check box are detected by the method `itemStateChanged` defined in the interface `ItemListener`. The class `ItemEvent` contains class constants that specify whether an item is DESEL-ECTED or SELECTED. There are two methods, `getStateChange` and `getItem`, to determine which items have been selected. The `itemStateChanged` method would be implemented as follows, to detect and print only those items that have been selected.

```
// implementation of Item Listener method
public void itemStateChanged(ItemEvent event)
{
        if (event.getStateChange() == ItemEvent.SELECTED)
        {
                String item = (String)event.getItem();
                System.out.println(item);
        }
}
```

The following classes, `MyWindowWithCheckBoxes` and `Example_6`, are used to generate the GUI shown in Figure 8.8.

```
// program to create a window and add check boxes to it

import java.awt.*;
import java.awt.event.*;

class MyWindowWithCheckBoxes extends Frame implements ItemListener
{
        // constructor
        public MyWindowWithCheckBoxes(int width, int height, int x, int y)
        {
                // call Frame's constructor
                super("My Window with check boxes");
```

```
// set colors of window
setBackground(Color.yellow);
setForeground(Color.black);

// set dimensions and position of window on screen
setSize(width, height);
setLocation(x,y);

// add listener to detect window being closed
addWindowListener(new CloseMyWindow());

// select grid layout manager
setLayout(new GridLayout(5,1));

// create check boxes
Checkbox eggs = new Checkbox("Eggs");
Checkbox bacon = new Checkbox("Bacon");
Checkbox sausages = new Checkbox("Sausages");
Checkbox beans = new Checkbox("Beans");

// add check boxes to window container
add(eggs);
add(bacon);
add(sausages);
add(beans);

// add listeners for each check box
eggs.addItemListener(this);
bacon.addItemListener(this);
sausages.addItemListener(this);
beans.addItemListener(this);          }
// instance method to display window on screen
public void showWindow()
{
     this.show();
}
// subclass of WindowAdapter
private class CloseMyWindow extends WindowAdapter
{
     // overridden method of superclass
     public void windowClosing(WindowEvent event)
     {
          MyWindowWithCheckBoxes.this.dispose();
          System.exit(0);
     }
```

```
        }
        // implementation of Item Listener method
        public void itemStateChanged(ItemEvent event)
        {
                if (event.getStateChange() == ItemEvent.SELECTED)
                {
                        String item = (String)event.getItem();
                        System.out.println(item);
                }
        }

}


public class Example_6
{
        public static void main(String[] args)
        {
                MyWindowWithCheckBoxes window = new
                MyWindowWithCheckBoxes(300,150,200,200);
                window.showWindow();
        }
}
```

NOW DO THIS   Modify classes `MyWindowWithCheckBoxes` and `Example_6` as follows.

(1) Create check boxes for the names of your favorite music stars.

(2) In your code, preselect one of the boxes and change the font of the labels for the boxes.

(3) Experiment with a different number of rows and columns in the `GridLayout` object and note the changes to the layout of the check boxes.

Radio Buttons

Radio buttons, unlike check boxes, allow only one button to be chosen from a series of buttons. Switching any one button on will switch off the remaining buttons. Hence, only one button can be set on; it will exclude all the remaining buttons from being set on. Figure 8.9 illustrates a group of radio buttons added to a window container.

To create a set of radio buttons, first instantiate an object from the `CheckboxGroup` class. A `CheckboxGroup` object enforces mutual exclusion (also known as radio-button behavior) among any number of `Checkbox` but-

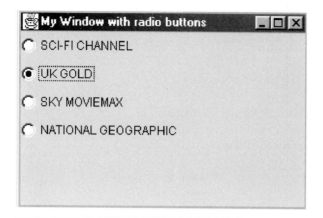

Figure 8.9 Adding radio buttons to a window container

tons. There is only one constructor for the `CheckboxGroup` class, and its signature is `public CheckboxGroup();`.

The `Checkbox` class has two more constructors in addition to the three constructors previously described.

```
public Checkbox(String label, boolean state, CheckboxGroup group);
public Checkbox(String label, CheckboxGroup group, boolean state);
```

Clearly these two constructors contain an extra parameter to ensure that a check box is part of a `CheckboxGroup` and hence will enforce mutual exclusion (radio-button behavior) within the components of the group. The parameters `label` and `state` serve the same purpose as previously described for a check box. The following skeletal code shows how two of the radio buttons illustrated in Figure 8.9 were created.

```
// create check box group
CheckboxGroup cbg = new CheckboxGroup();

// create individual check boxes as part of check box group
Checkbox sciFi = new Checkbox("SCI-FI CHANNEL",false,cbg);
Checkbox ukGold = new Checkbox("UK GOLD",false,cbg);
.
.
.

// add check boxes to window container
add(sciFi);
add(ukGold);
.
.
.
```

```
// add listeners for each check box
sciFi.addItemListener(this);
ukGold.addItemListener(this);
.
.
```

Since we are dealing with `Checkbox` components, the method of detecting and dealing with events is similar to the previous example. The following code detects and prints only those items that are selected.

```
// implementation of Item Listener method
public void itemStateChanged(ItemEvent event)
{
        if (event.getStateChange() == ItemEvent.SELECTED)
        {
                String item = (String)event.getItem();
                System.out.println(item);
        }
}
```

The following program demonstrates how all of the radio buttons illustrated in Figure 8.9 were created and handled.

```
// program to create a window and add radio buttons to the container

import java.awt.*;
import java.awt.event.*;

class MyWindowWithRadioButtons extends Frame implements ItemListener
{
        // constructor
        public MyWindowWithRadioButtons(int width, int height, int x, int y)
        {
                // call Frame's constructor
                super("My Window with radio buttons");

                // set colors of window
                setBackground(Color.yellow);
                setForeground(Color.black);

                // set dimensions and position of window on screen
                setSize(width, height);
                setLocation(x,y);
```

```
        // add listener to detect window being closed
        addWindowListener(new CloseMyWindow());

        // select grid layout manager
        setLayout(new GridLayout(6,1));

        // create check box group
        CheckboxGroup cbg = new CheckboxGroup();

        // create individual check boxes as part of check box group
        Checkbox sciFi = new Checkbox("SCI-FI CHANNEL",false,cbg);
        Checkbox ukGold = new Checkbox("UK GOLD",false,cbg);
        Checkbox skyMovie = new Checkbox("SKY MOVIEMAX",false,cbg);
        Checkbox natGeo = new Checkbox("NATIONAL GEOGRAPHIC",
                                      false,cbg);

        // add check boxes to window container
        add(sciFi);
        add(ukGold);
        add(skyMovie);
        add(natGeo);

        // add listeners for each check box
        sciFi.addItemListener(this);
        ukGold.addItemListener(this);
        skyMovie.addItemListener(this);
        natGeo.addItemListener(this);
}
// instance method to display window on screen
public void showWindow()
{
        this.show();
}
// subclass of WindowAdapter
private class CloseMyWindow extends WindowAdapter
{
        // overridden method of superclass
        public void windowClosing(WindowEvent event)
        {
                MyWindowWithRadioButtons.this.dispose();
                System.exit(0);
        }
}
// implementation of Item Listener method
```

```
public void itemStateChanged(ItemEvent event)
{
    if (event.getStateChange() == ItemEvent.SELECTED)
    {
        String item = (String)event.getItem();
        System.out.println(item);
    }
}

}

public class Example_7
{
    public static void main(String[] args)
    {
        MyWindowWithRadioButtons window = new
        MyWindowWithRadioButtons(300,200,200,200);
        window.showWindow();
    }
}
```

NOW DO THIS   Modify classes MyWindowWithRadioButtons and Example_7
as follows.

(1) Create radio buttons for all the colors defined by the Color class in the awt
    package.
(2) Change the number of rows in the GridLayout manager and the height of
    the window container to accommodate all the colors.

List

A *list* is illustrated in Figure 8.10. If the number of items in the list is larger than
the size of the list box, a scrollbar is automatically inserted to allow inspection of
the other items in the list. A list can be defined for the selection of either single
or multiple items from the list.

An awt List component has the following constructors.

```
public List();
public List(int rows, boolean multipleSelections);
```

where rows represents the minimum number of visible entries before a vertical
scroll bar is automatically inserted. multipleSelections is set to true if you
want to choose more than one item from the list; otherwise it is set to false.

The following code shows how six items are added to the list to produce the
scrolling list illustrated in Figure 8.10.

Figure 8.10 Adding a list to a window container

```
// create a list with multiple selection and with 4 items visible
List shopping = new List(4,true);

// add items to the list
shopping.add("lettuce");
shopping.add("cucumber");
shopping.add("tomatoes");
shopping.add("peppers");
shopping.add("coleslaw");
shopping.add("onions");

// add the list to the window container
add(shopping);
```

You may have noticed from Figure 8.5 that a list may generate two different types of events. Hence you need to implement an `ActionListener` and an `ItemListener`. You must add a listener for an item being selected and add another listener for an action being performed.

```
// listen for item being selected
shopping.addItemListener(this);

// listen for double-click on item
shopping.addActionListener(this);
```

When you single-click select an item from the menu with a mouse-pointer, a change of state for that item takes place. This event is handled by the item listener and by the implemented `itemStateChanged` method. To identify which item has been selected, use the instance method `getItem()` from the class `java.awt.event.ItemEvent`. The method `getItem()` will return the position of the item in the list. The first item is located at position 0 (zero), the second item is located at position 1, and so on.

```
// implementation of Item Listener method
public void itemStateChanged(ItemEvent event)
```

```
{
        int position = ((Integer)event.getItem()).intValue();

        System.out.println("you selected the item at position "+
                              position+" in the list");
}
```

However, when you double-click select an item, the first click is handled by the item listener and the second click by the action listener. The following code can be used to determine the name of the item selected from the menu.

```
// implementation of Action Listener method
public void actionPerformed(ActionEvent event)
{
        System.out.println("you double-clicked on "+
                              event.getActionCommand());
}
```

The following program demonstrates how the radio buttons illustrated in Figure 8.10 were created.

```
// program to create a window and add a list to the container

import java.awt.*;
import java.awt.event.*;

class MyWindowWithList extends Frame implements ActionListener,
                                                ItemListener
{
        // constructor
        public MyWindowWithList(int width, int height, int x, int y)
        {
                // call Frame's constructor
                super("My Window with list");

                // set colors of window
                setBackground(Color.yellow);
                setForeground(Color.black);

                // set dimensions and position of window on screen
                setSize(width, height);
                setLocation(x,y);

                // add listener to detect window being closed
                addWindowListener(new CloseMyWindow());
```

```java
    // select grid layout manager
    setLayout(new FlowLayout());

    // create a list with multiple selection and with 4 items
    // visible
    List shopping = new List(4,true);

    // add items to the list
    shopping.add("lettuce");
    shopping.add("cucumber");
    shopping.add("tomatoes");
    shopping.add("peppers");
    shopping.add("coleslaw");
    shopping.add("onions");

    // add the list to the window container
    add(shopping);

    // listen for item being selected
    shopping.addItemListener(this);

    // listen for double-click on item
    shopping.addActionListener(this);
}
// instance method to display window on screen
public void showWindow()
{
    this.show();
}
// subclass of WindowAdapter
private class CloseMyWindow extends WindowAdapter
{
    // overridden method of superclass
    public void windowClosing(WindowEvent event)
    {
        MyWindowWithList.this.dispose();
        System.exit(0);
    }
}
// implementation of Item Listener method
public void itemStateChanged(ItemEvent event)
{
    int position = ((Integer)event.getItem()).intValue();
```

```
                System.out.println("you selected the item at position "+
                                   position+" in the list");
        }
    // implementation of Action Listener method
     public void actionPerformed(ActionEvent event)
     {
                System.out.println("you double-clicked on "+
                                   event.getActionCommand());

        }
}


public class Example_8
{
    public static void main(String[] args)
    {
        MyWindowWithList window = new
        MyWindowWithList(200,130,200,200);
        window.showWindow();

    }
}
```

NOW DO THIS   Modify classes `MyWindowWithList` and `Example_8` as follows.

(1) Create a list containing all your favorite foods.

(2) Experiment with changing the background and foreground colors of the list and the font of the items in the list.

8.6   Creating a Reusable Container

The `MyWindow...` classes were created to allow you to experiment with adding components to the `MyWindow` container. In all these examples, the data for the classes was "hard-coded" into classes. For example, the text fields were predefined with Name and Address, the check boxes with Eggs, Bacon, Sausages, and Beans, and so on. Because of the hard-coding of the data, the classes cannot be reused in other examples. This approach somewhat defeats one of the objectives of object-oriented programming—to create classes that can be reused wherever possible.

Now that you have had time to use and understand some of the `awt` components, you are able to build new general-purpose components that can be reused in many applications.

To begin, we will concentrate on creating our own container class, called WindowPane, which is a subclass of Frame. This may be coded as:

```
public class WindowPane extends Frame
```

In creating the constructor for our WindowPane container class we will code:

```
public WindowPane()
{
        super("    This is a WindowPane ..");
        .
```

Remember the reserved word super invokes the constructor of the superclass. In this case the constructor is Frame(String title). The text that will appear in the title bar of our container window will be This is a WindowPane ...

The next stage in building our constructor is to determine the size of the WindowPane.

> *i*   Good practice dictates that you should acquire the size of the screen of the monitor and base all your component measurements as percentages of the screen size. If you use this technique and then run your application on different sized screens, you will always have the components of your graphical user interface correctly proportioned.

To acquire the size of the screen, we need the help of the Toolkit class that is part of the awt package. A Toolkit is an abstract class that defines method signatures for creating standard GUI components and obtaining information about them. The Component class defines a getToolkit method that is overridden by the Window class, and the overridden method is thus inherited by the Frame class. The getToolkit method will return the Toolkit of the frame. To create a Toolkit object we code:

```
Toolkit tools = this.getToolkit();
```

The keyword this refers to the current WindowPane object. You may wonder why we did not use the constructor of the Toolkit class, that is, why we didn't just code:

```
Toolkit tools = new Toolkit();
```

If you inspect the Java documentation for this class, you will see that only a default constructor is supplied that is useless for our requirements.

The Java documentation for the `Toolkit` class reveals a host of many useful methods of which the `getScreenSize` method is just one. The data type returned by this method is the class `Dimension`, which is yet another class within the `awt` package. The `Dimension` class has two public instance variables that describe the `width` and `height` of an object. Therefore, to get the width and height of the screen of a monitor we need the following code:

```
Dimension size = tools.getScreenSize();
width = size.width;
height = size.height;
```

Now that we know the size of the screen, we want to set the size of the `WindowPane`. Hence, the coding to set the size of the window pane is:

```
this.setSize(width,height);
```

The effect of all of this work is that our `WindowPane` will be set to the size of the monitor.

The coding to set the foreground and background colors of the `WindowPane` class is:

```
setForeground(Color.blue);
setBackground(Color.black);
```

We have already seen that Java allows the programmer to specify different approaches for placing components into a container by using the method `setLayout`, inherited by `Frame` from the `Container` class. If we want to ignore any predefined layout, then we code:

```
setLayout(null);
```

The window pane is displayed using the instance method `showWindowPane` that contains the `show` method inherited by `Frame` from the `Window` class. The statement is coded as:

```
this.show();
```

Two other instance methods, `getWidth` and `getHeight`, get the width and the height of the window pane, respectively, and these methods can also be included in the `WindowPane` class.

However, you will need to create a `CloseWindowPane` object and add this as a window listener to the window pane by calling the `addWindowListener` method. The code is very similar to that discussed at the beginning of the chapter for the class `MyWindow`. The code for the `WindowPane` class also incorporates an inner class to handle the window event.

```java
import java.awt.*;
import java.awt.event.*;

public class WindowPane extends Frame
{
    // size of window
    private static int width;
    private static int height;
    /**
    The WindowPane class enables an object that represents a
    container for holding graphical components. The object takes
    the dimensions of the screen of the monitor.
    */
    public WindowPane()
    {
        super("   This is a WindowPane ..");

        // add window listener
        addWindowListener(new CloseWindowPane());

        // get size of screen
        Toolkit tools = this.getToolkit();
        Dimension size = tools.getScreenSize();
        width = size.width;
        height = size.height;
        this.setSize(width,height);

        // set foreground color and size of window
        setForeground(Color.blue);
        setBackground(Color.black);
        setLayout(null);
    }
    /**
    Show the window pane on the screen of the monitor
    */
    public void showWindowPane()
    {
        this.setVisible(true);
    }
    /**
    Get the width of the container.
    @return The width of the container.
    */
```

```
public int getWidth()
{
      return width;
}
/**
Get the height of the container.
@return The height of the container
*/
public int getHeight()
{
      return height;
}
// inner class used to handle event
private class CloseWindowPane extends WindowAdapter
{
      public void windowClosing(WindowEvent event)
      {
            WindowPane.this.dispose();
            System.exit(0);
      }
}
}
```

8.7   Creating a Reusable WritingPad Component

In creating the `WindowPane` class we have provided no methods for outputting text to the screen. This ploy is quite deliberate. Remember `WindowPane` is a container—it is not meant for writing on, but is meant for containing other objects. In order to display text on the screen we need to create a new component out of `awt` components, one that can be placed in the container `WindowPane`. This new component is composed from three standard `awt` components—the `Dialog` class, the `Font` class, and the `TextArea` class.

As you can see from Figure 8.1, the `Dialog` class is a subclass of the `Window` class. The class represents a window with a title bar. However, a `Dialog` window may be *modal* so that it blocks user input to all other windows until dismissed. A `Dialog` object is an `awt` container, and `awt` component objects can be added to it.

The `Dialog` class has four constructors. The only one that is of interest in this example has the following signature:

```
public Dialog(Frame parent, String title, boolean modal);
```

where `parent` is the container class for this new window. In other words, you can create a window appearing on a window. In this context `parent` will be a `WindowPane` object, but equally it could be any container object that has a `Frame` as its superclass. The string `title` is suitable text for the title bar of the `Dialog` window, and `modal`, when set `true`, will cause all input to other windows to be blocked until the `Dialog` window is closed. When `modal` is set to `false`, it is possible to interact with other windows.

The initial coding of the constructor for the `WritingPad` class contains the following code.

```
public WritingPad(Frame parent)
{
      super(parent, " This is a WritingPad ..", false);
      int screenWidth = parent.getWidth();
      int screenHeight = parent.getHeight();
      // set location and size of dialog box
      int xLocationOfBox = (int)(0.075f * screenWidth);
      int yLocationOfBox = (int)(0.1f * screenHeight);
      int widthOfBox     = (int)(0.4f * screenWidth);
      int heightOfBox    = (int)(0.7f * screenHeight);
      // construct a dialog box
      this.setLayout(null);
      this.setBackground(Color.lightGray);
      this.setForeground(Color.blue);
      this.setLocation(xLocationOfBox,yLocationOfBox);
      this.setSize(widthOfBox,heightOfBox);
      .
      .
      .
```

Notice that, within the constructor, the location of the top left-hand corner of the `Dialog` window and the size of the `Dialog` window have been initialized. Don't be put off by the numbers used in the initialization of the coordinates of the top left-hand corner and by the width and height of the `Dialog` window. These numbers are not *magic numbers* (numeric literals that appear in a program without any explanation or declaration as constants); they simply represent the percentage of the screen width and height of the `WindowPane` object on which the `Dialog` window will appear. For example, the width of the `Dialog` window is 40% of the width of the `WindowPane`, and the height of the `Dialog` window is 70% of the height of the `WindowPane`.

A dialog window is more commonly referred to as a dialog box; hence, the coding in the constructor refers to `widthOfBox` and `heightOfBox`.

As the name suggests, `setLocation` fixes the position of the top left-hand corner of the `Dialog` window, with respect to the `WindowPane`. Although this position is fixed initially, it is possible to drag the `Dialog` window anywhere within the `WindowPane` by pressing the left mouse button over the dialog window bar and moving the mouse until you release the button.

In the coding for drawing the dialog window, the keyword `this` refers to the object that invoked the constructor—this is a `WritingPad` object. Hence, a `WritingPad` object has a light gray background, blue foreground, set size and location, and does not use any of the regimes for placing components into the `Dialog` window.

The next phase in the construction of the `WritingPad` constructor is to specify a font for printing text. In this example we will set the font name to `Serif`, style to `BOLD`, and the font `size` to 16 points.

```
Font type = new Font("Serif",Font.BOLD,16);
```

The final phase in the construction of the `WritingPad` constructor is to specify a component that can be placed in the `Dialog` window and used for writing text. The name of the component is `TextArea`, and many of its useful methods are defined in its superclass `TextComponent`.

The `TextArea` class has five constructors; we are interested only in the one constructor whose signature is:

```
public TextArea(String text, int rows, int columns, int scrollbars);
```

where `text` is the text to be displayed, `rows` and `columns` represent the number of rows and columns of text, and `scrollbars` is a constant determining the scrollbars regime. In this example, the text string is set to null, the number of rows and columns is set at unity, and only a vertical scroll bar is required. The code to define the text area in the constructor is written as:

```
TextArea writingArea = new
TextArea("",1,1,TextArea.SCROLLBARS_VERTICAL_ONLY);

writingArea.setLocation(X_TOP_LH_CORNER,Y_TOP_LH_CORNER);
writingArea.setSize((int)(widthOfBox-SCREEN_TRIM_SIZE/2),
                    heightOfBox-HEIGHT_OF_BAR);

writingArea.setBackground(Color.white);
writingArea.setForeground(Color.blue);
writingArea.setEditable(false);

this.add(writingArea);
```

Notice that since `TextArea` is a subclass of `Component`, it may also use the inherited methods `setLocation`, `setSize`, `setBackground`, and `setForeground`. The method `setEditable` is inherited from its immediate superclass `TextComponent` and will allow the text to be edited when the parameter is set to `true`. In this example, the text displayed in the `TextArea` is not to be edited; hence the parameter is set to `false`.

Finally, any component can be added to a container class through the inherited method `add` from the `Container` class. Thus, the statement `this.add(writingArea)` adds the object `writingArea` to the `Dialog` window of the `WritingPad` object.

The `WritingPad` class will require instance methods to show the writing pad in the parent container, write strings to the text area, and erase the text area. The method `setVisible` will be used to show the writing pad. The method `append` from the class `TextArea` will be used to append text to the writing area. The method `setText` from the class `TextComponent` will be used to set the text in the writing area to the `null` string, thus effectively erasing the text from the window.

The completed coding for the `WritingPad` class follows.

```java
import java.awt.*;
import java.awt.event.*;

public class WritingPad extends Dialog
{
        private static int X_TOP_LH_CORNER = 5;
        private static int Y_TOP_LH_CORNER = 25;
        private static int SCREEN_TRIM_SIZE = 20;
        private static int HEIGHT_OF_BAR = 30;
        private static String EMPTY_STRING = "";
        private static TextArea writingArea;
        /**
        The WritingPad class enables an object that represents an
        area of text for writing string data.
        @param parent is the container on which the writing pad object
        is added.
        */
        public WritingPad(Frame parent)
        {
                super(parent, " This is a WritingPad ..", false);

                // get the size of the parent screen
                int screenWidth = parent.getWidth();
                int screenHeight = parent.getHeight();

                // set location and size of dialog box
                int xLocationOfBox = (int)(0.075f * screenWidth);
                int yLocationOfBox = (int)(0.1f * screenHeight);
                int widthOfBox     = (int)(0.4f * screenWidth);
                int heightOfBox    = (int)(0.7f * screenHeight);

                // draw dialog box
                this.setLayout(null);
                this.setBackground(Color.lightGray);
                this.setForeground(Color.blue);
                this.setLocation(xLocationOfBox,yLocationOfBox);
                this.setSize(widthOfBox,heightOfBox);

                // set font for writing pad
                Font type = new Font("SansSerif",Font.PLAIN,14);
```

```java
        // set location and size of writing area
        writingArea = new
        TextArea("",1,1,TextArea.SCROLLBARS_VERTICAL_ONLY);
        writingArea.setLocation(X_TOP_LH_CORNER,Y_TOP_LH_CORNER);
        writingArea.setSize((int)(widthOfBox-SCREEN_TRIM_SIZE/2),
                            heightOfBox-HEIGHT_OF_BAR);

        // create writing area
        writingArea.setFont(type);
        writingArea.setBackground(Color.white);
        writingArea.setForeground(Color.blue);
        writingArea.setEditable(false);
        this.add(writingArea);

        // add window listener
        addWindowListener(new CloseWritingPad());
    }
    /**
    Makes the writing pad visible on the container.
    */
    public void showWritingPad()
    {
        this.setVisible(true);
    }
    /**
    Writes a string to the writing pad.
    @param datum is the string to be written.
    */
    public void write(String datum)
    {
        writingArea.append(datum);
    }
    /**
    Clears the entire area of the writing pad.
    */
    public void erase()
    {
        writingArea.setText(EMPTY_STRING);
    }
    // inner class to handle event listener
    public class CloseWritingPad extends WindowAdapter
    {
        public void windowClosing(WindowEvent event)
        {
            WritingPad.this.setVisible(false);
        }
    }
}
```

The event listener to close the writing pad has been stored in the inner class `CloseWritingPad`. Notice that, in closing the writing pad, it is not disposed of, as with the `WindowPane`, but merely hidden from view using `setVisible(false)`. The rationale behind this approach is that if the writing pad is ever needed again in the same application, you need only invoke `showWritingPad` without having to create a new writing-pad object.

The Program `Example_9` is used to test the methods of the `WritingPad` class.

```
class Example_9
{
    public static void main(String[] args)
    {
        WindowPane screen = new WindowPane();
        screen.showWindowPane();

        int width = screen.getWidth();
        int height = screen.getHeight();

        WritingPad notes = new WritingPad(screen);
        notes.showWritingPad();

        notes.write("\n\nWidth of window pane: "+
                    String.valueOf(width)+" pixels");
        notes.write("\n\nHeight of window pane: "+
                    String.valueOf(height)+" pixels");
    }
}
```

Part of the screen shot from the running program is shown below.

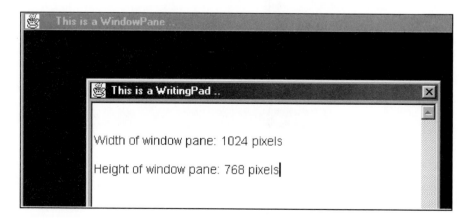

8.8   Creating a Reusable DialogBox Component

Figure 8.11 illustrates how a Dialog window, Label object, and TextField object can be used together to provide a reusable TextInput component.

If a Dialog window container has already been created with dimensions widthOfBox and heightOfBox, then the location and size of the label can be coded as follows.

```
// set location and size of label
int xLocationOfLabel    = (int)(0.05f * widthOfBox);
int yLocationOfLabel    = (int)(0.3f * heightOfBox);
int widthOfLabel        = (int)(0.9f * widthOfBox);
int heightOfLabel       = (int)(0.25f * heightOfBox);
```

The numbers in these statements refer to the percentage width and the percentage height of the Dialog window.

Before the label can be displayed in the Dialog window, you must set the font for writing the label. The following code uses the standard Dialog font described in the Font class:

```
Font dialog = new Font("Dialog", Font.BOLD, FONT_SIZE);
```

The label can now be put into the Dialog window container. Notice the reuse of the inherited methods setLocation, setSize, setForeground, and setFont from the Component class and the inherited method add from the Container class.

The actual text for the label is the variable prompt that was passed to the TextInput constructor as an argument.

```
// insert prompt into dialog box
textLabel = new Label(prompt, Label.LEFT);
textLabel.setLocation(xLocationOfLabel, yLocationOfLabel);
textLabel.setSize(widthOfLabel,heightOfLabel);
textLabel.setForeground(Color.black);
textLabel.setFont(dialog);
this.add(textLabel);
```

Figure 8.11 An example of a TextInput component

The following code illustrates how the text field in Figure 8.11 was created. First, it is necessary to specify the location and size of the text field with respect to the size of the `Dialog` window. Remember the numbers represent the percentages of the width and height of the `Dialog` window.

```
// set location and size of text field
int xLocationOfField = (int)(0.05f * widthOfBox);
int yLocationOfField = (int)(0.6 * heightOfBox);
int widthOfField     = (int)(0.9f * widthOfBox);
int heightOfField    = (int)(0.25f * heightOfBox);
```

Before we draw the text field in the `Dialog` window, we need to specify the font of the text to be displayed. We use the standard `DialogInput` font described in the `Font` class.

```
Font dialogInput = new Font("DialogInput", Font.PLAIN, FONT_SIZE);
```

The methods used to include the `TextField` component in the `Dialog` window should be very familiar to you now.

```
// draw text field in dialog box
datum = new TextField(EMPTY_STRING);
datum.setLocation(xLocationOfField, yLocationOfField);
datum.setSize(widthOfField, heightOfField);
datum.setBackground(Color.white);
datum.setForeground(Color.blue);
datum.setFont(dialogInput);
this.add(datum);
```

After text has been input into the appropriate text field, pressing the Return key generates an event. Provided an action listener is associated with the text field, the event can be handled by implementing the `actionPerformed` method of the `ActionListener` interface. You, of course, need to add the action listener for the text field object as:

```
datum.addActionListener(this);
```

If you want to find the particular source of an event, the class `EventObject` in the package `java.util` contains an instance method `getSource()` that returns a type `Object`. The class `ActionEvent` is a subclass of `AWTEvent`, and `AWTEvent` is a subclass of `EventObject`. Therefore, the instance method `getSource()` is applicable to `ActionEvent` objects. All the events described in the package `java.awt.event` are either subclasses of the class `AWTEvent` or exist further down this hierarchy, in which case the instance method getSource() is also applicable to the event classes in the `java.awt.event` package.

The `ActionListener` interface contains only one method to be implemented—actionPerformed. Notice in this implementation that when the event of pressing the Return key is detected, the information that had been typed into the text field is retrieved by the `getText` method inherited by the class `TextField` from the `TextComponent` class and stored in the instance variable inputDatum. After the text has been retrieved, the text field is re-initialized with the empty string (ready for further use in an application), and the `TextInput` component (this object) is hidden from view.

```
public void actionPerformed(ActionEvent event)
{
      if (event.getSource().equals(datum))
      {
            inputDatum = new String(datum.getText());
            datum.setText(EMPTY_STRING);
            this.setVisible(false);
      }
}
```

By using the `getSource` method we can discriminate between text fields when a multifield text-input component is created. The complete code for the `TextInput` class follows. Notice that the class implements the `ActionListener` interface.

```
import java.awt.*;
import java.awt.event.*;

public class TextInput extends Dialog implements ActionListener
{
      // constants
      private static final int FONT_SIZE = 11;
      private static final String EMPTY_STRING = "";

      // instance variables
      private String inputDatum = EMPTY_STRING;
      private TextField datum;
      private Label textLabel;

      /**
      The TextInput class enables an object that represents a combination
      of a label and text field stored in a dialog box window. Text can be
      input into this component.
      @param parent is the container that a TextInput object may be added.
      @param prompt is a label indicating the nature of the data to be
```

```java
input.
*/
public TextInput(Frame parent, String prompt)
{
        super(parent, " Input the following datum ..", true);

        // set width and height of screen
        int screenWidth  = parent.getWidth();
        int screenHeight = parent.getHeight();

        // set location and size of dialog box
        int xLocationOfBox = (int)(0.7f * screenWidth);
        int yLocationOfBox = (int)(0.1f * screenHeight);
        int widthOfBox     = (int)(0.25f * screenWidth);
        int heightOfBox    = (int)(0.125f * screenHeight);

        // set location and size of label
        int xLocationOfLabel = (int)(0.05f * widthOfBox);
        int yLocationOfLabel = (int)(0.3f * heightOfBox);
        int widthOfLabel     = (int)(0.9f * widthOfBox);
        int heightOfLabel    = (int)(0.25f * heightOfBox);

        // set location and size of text field
        int xLocationOfField = (int)(0.05f * widthOfBox);
        int yLocationOfField = (int)(0.6 * heightOfBox);
        int widthOfField     = (int)(0.9f * widthOfBox);
        int heightOfField    = (int)(0.25f * heightOfBox);

        // set fonts
        Font dialog = new Font("Dialog", Font.BOLD, FONT_SIZE);
        Font dialogInput = new Font("DialogInput", Font.PLAIN,
                                    FONT_SIZE);

        // draw dialog box
        this.setLayout(null);
        this.setBackground(Color.lightGray);
        this.setForeground(Color.blue);
        this.setLocation(xLocationOfBox,yLocationOfBox);
        this.setSize(widthOfBox,heightOfBox);

        // insert prompt into dialog box
        textLabel = new Label(prompt, Label.LEFT);
        textLabel.setLocation(xLocationOfLabel, yLocationOfLabel);
        textLabel.setSize(widthOfLabel,heightOfLabel);
        textLabel.setForeground(Color.black);
        textLabel.setFont(dialog);
```

```
     this.add(textLabel);

     // draw text field in dialog box
     datum = new TextField(EMPTY_STRING);
     datum.setLocation(xLocationOfField, yLocationOfField);
     datum.setSize(widthOfField, heightOfField);
     datum.setBackground(Color.white);
     datum.setForeground(Color.blue);
     datum.setFont(dialogInput);
     this.add(datum);

     // add action listener for text field
     datum.addActionListener(this);
     // add the window listener for the Dialog window
     addWindowListener(new CloseTextInput());
}
/**
Display the text input box on the container.
*/
public void showTextInput()
{
     this.setVisible(true);
}
/**
Get the contents of the text input box.
@return Returns the contents of the text field.
*/
public String getString()
{
     return inputDatum;
}
public void actionPerformed(ActionEvent event)
{
     if (event.getSource().equals(datum))
     {
          inputDatum = new String(datum.getText());
          datum.setText(EMPTY_STRING);
          this.setVisible(false);
     }
}
private class CloseTextInput extends WindowAdapter
{
     public void windowClosing(WindowEvent event)
     {
          inputDatum = new String(datum.getText());
          datum.setText(EMPTY_STRING);
```

```
                TextInput.this.setVisible(false);
            }
        }
    }
```

NOW DO THIS   Write a class containing a `main` method to perform the following.

(1) Create `WindowPane`, `WritingPad`, and `TextInput` objects.

(2) Input a line of text at the `TextInput` object, and write this text to the `WritingPad` object. You may repeat your code for many different lines of text.

8.9   Creating a Reusable CheckBoxes Component

The `CheckBoxes` component illustrated in Figure 8.12 was composed from the `awt` components `Dialog`, `Label`, and `Checkbox`.

Since you already know how to create a `Dialog` window and a `Label`, we will concentrate on the creation of the check boxes for the component `CheckBoxes`. The signature of the `CheckBoxes` constructor is:

```
public CheckBoxes(Frame parent, String prompt, String[] itemsInList);
```

Figure 8.12 An example of the `CheckBoxes` component

where `parent` is a container for the `CheckBoxes` component, `prompt` describes the context of the check boxes, for example Jazz musicians in Figure 8.12, and `itemsInList` is a one-dimensional array of strings to store in the respective awt check-box components.

The check boxes illustrated in Figure 8.12 were created using the following code.

```
// instantiate a one-dimensional array item of type Checkbox to store
// individual check box components
item = new Checkbox[numberOfItems];

// for every item in the list
for (int index=0; index != numberOfItems; index++)
{
     // instantiate an awt Checkbox object
     item[index] = new Checkbox(itemsInList[index],false);

     // set the location and size of the awt Checkbox object
     item[index].setLocation(xLocationOfItem,
                             yLocationOfItem+(index*heightOfItem));
     item[index].setSize(widthOfItem, heightOfItem);

     // add the Checkbox to the Dialog window
     this.add(item[index]);

     // create an item listener for the Checkbox
     item[index].addItemListener(this);
}
```

A mouse is used to point at and click-select the appropriate boxes. Figure 8.12 illustrates that four jazz musicians have been chosen from the selection. The events of a check box are detected by the method `itemStateChanged` defined in the interface `ItemListener`. The class `ItemEvent` contains class constants that specify whether an item is `DESELECTED` or `SELECTED`. There are two methods, `getStateChange` and `getItem`, to determine which items have been selected. The `itemStateChanged` method would be implemented as follows.

```
public void itemStateChanged(ItemEvent event)
{
     int indexOfSelection = 0;

     // get the name of the item selected
     String item = (String)event.getItem();
     // search the array of items for the position in the array
     // of the selected item
     for (int index=0; index != numberOfItems; index++)
```

```
    {
        if (item.equals(namesOfItems[index]))
            indexOfSelection = index;
    }
    // indicate in a boolean array of selected items which items were
    // chosen from the check boxes
    if (event.getStateChange() == ItemEvent.SELECTED)
        selectedItems[indexOfSelection] = true;
    else if (event.getStateChange() == ItemEvent.DESELECTED)
        selectedItems[indexOfSelection] = false;
}
```

The `boolean` array `selectedItems` contains as many cells as there are check-box components. From Figure 8.12 this would be eight cells. A cell is set to `true` if an item is selected from the corresponding check box; otherwise, the cell is set to `false`. The array `selectedItems` can be returned by an instance method of the nonstandard component `CheckBoxes`.

The complete listing of the `CheckBoxes` component follows.

```
import java.awt.*;
import java.awt.event.*;

public class CheckBoxes extends Dialog implements ItemListener
{
    private static final int POINT_SIZE = 12;
    private static final int HEIGHT_OF_BAR = 20;

    private boolean[] selectedItems;
    private String[] namesOfItems;
    private Label textLabel;
    private Checkbox[] item;
    private int numberOfItems;
    /**
    The CheckBoxes class enables an object that represents a label and
    any number of check boxes defined by the programmer to be
    represented in a dialog box.
    @param parent is the container to which the CheckBoxes object is
    added.
    @param prompt is a text prompt indicating the generic content of the
    check box labels.
    @param itemsInList is an array of labels for the check boxes.
    */
    public CheckBoxes(Frame parent, String prompt, String[] itemsInList)
    {
        super(parent, " Select item(s) then CLOSE ..", true);
        numberOfItems = itemsInList.length;
```

```
addWindowListener(new CloseDialogWindow());
namesOfItems = itemsInList;
selectedItems = new boolean[numberOfItems];

// set width and height of dialog box
int screenWidth = parent.getWidth();
int screenHeight = parent.getHeight();

// set location and size of dialog box
int xLocationOfBox = (int)(0.7f * screenWidth);
int yLocationOfBox = (int)(0.1f * screenHeight);
int widthOfBox     = (int)(0.25f * screenWidth);
int heightOfBox    = (int)((screenHeight/24)*(numberOfItems))+
                         3*HEIGHT_OF_BAR;

// set location and size of label
int xLocationOfLabel = (int)(0.125f * widthOfBox);
int yLocationOfLabel = (int)(1.5*HEIGHT_OF_BAR);
int widthOfLabel     = (int)(0.9f * widthOfBox);
int heightOfLabel    = (int)(HEIGHT_OF_BAR);

// set size and location of first item
int heightOfItem     = (int)(screenHeight/24);
int widthOfItem      = (int)(0.9f * widthOfBox);
int xLocationOfItem  = (int)(0.05f * widthOfBox);
int yLocationOfItem  = (int)(2*HEIGHT_OF_BAR+
                         (int)(heightOfItem/4));

// set fonts
Font dialog = new Font("Dialog", Font.PLAIN, POINT_SIZE);
Font dialogInput = new Font("DialogInput", Font.BOLD,
                              POINT_SIZE);

// set parameters of dialog box
this.setBackground(Color.lightGray);
this.setForeground(Color.black);
this.setLocation(xLocationOfBox,yLocationOfBox);
this.setSize(widthOfBox,heightOfBox);
this.setFont(dialog);
setLayout(null);

// insert prompt into dialog box
textLabel = new Label(prompt, Label.LEFT);
textLabel.setLocation(xLocationOfLabel, yLocationOfLabel);
textLabel.setSize(widthOfLabel,heightOfLabel);
textLabel.setFont(dialogInput);
textLabel.setForeground(Color.black);
this.add(textLabel);
```

```
        // insert a check box for each item
        item = new Checkbox[numberOfItems];
        for (int index=0; index != numberOfItems; index++)
        {
                item[index] = new Checkbox(itemsInList[index],false);

                item[index].setLocation(xLocationOfItem, yLocationOfItem+
                                        (index*heightOfItem));
                item[index].setSize(widthOfItem, heightOfItem);

                this.add(item[index]);
                item[index].addItemListener(this);
        }
}
/**
Display the check boxes on the container.
*/
public void showCheckBoxes()
{
        for (int index=0; index != numberOfItems; index++)
            selectedItems[index] = false;

        this.setVisible(true);
}
/**
Get a boolean array containing true for all those boxes checked,
and false if the boxes are not checked.
@return Returns a boolean array of items set to true that have been
checked.
*/
public boolean[] getCheckedBoxes()
{
        return selectedItems;
}

public void itemStateChanged(ItemEvent event)
{
        int indexOfSelection = 0;
        String item = (String)event.getItem();

        for (int index=0; index != numberOfItems; index++)
        {
                if (item.equals(namesOfItems[index]))
                        indexOfSelection = index;
        }
```

```
        if (event.getStateChange() == ItemEvent.SELECTED)
            selectedItems[indexOfSelection] = true;
        else if (event.getStateChange() == ItemEvent.DESELECTED)
            selectedItems[indexOfSelection] = false;
    }
    // inner class to handle closing dialog box event
    private class CloseDialogWindow extends WindowAdapter
    {
        public void windowClosing(WindowEvent event)
        {
            boolean boxesChecked = false;

            // check to see if any boxes are checked
            for (int index=0; index != numberOfItems; index++)
            {
                if (item[index].getState())
                {
                    boxesChecked = true;
                    break;
                }
            }

            if (boxesChecked)
            {
                CheckBoxes.this.setVisible(false);

                for (int index=0; index != numberOfItems; index++)
                {
                    item[index].setState(false);
                }
            }
        }
    }
}
```

NOW DO THIS   Using the code from the class `CheckBoxes` as a template perform the following.

(1) Create files for a `RadioButtons` class and a `ScrollableList` class.

(2) Write programs to test the validity of your classes.

Note that if you need assistance with your answers, the code for both the `RadioButtons` and `ScrollableList` classes are available on the CD that accompanies this book.

8.10   Java Swing

A successful computer language will evolve over time. The Java language was introduced in 1995, and is already in its third major version. When a new version of a language is released it usually means that new features are added, and new standard libraries are available. Sometimes the controlling organization will also announce that some features are "deprecated," i.e., that those features may no longer be supported by future compilers and they should no longer be used.

When Java was first released by Sun Microsystems it provided only one way to create graphical user interfaces—the AWT (Abstract Windowing Toolkit) that we have been using in this text. Since then however, Sun has added another component library, commonly known as Java Swing, which can also be used for GUI development.

It is important to note that Java Swing is not a replacement for the AWT, since it is actually built on top of the core 1.1 and 1.2 AWT libraries, and depends extensively on the current event handling mechanism of AWT 1.1.

Java Swing is merely an alternative. In one sense it is an extension. Sun continues to support the AWT and software developers continue to use it. We do not believe the AWT will be deprecated by Sun in the foreseeable future. In fact, the Java Swing classes rely on concepts established for the AWT, and are based on the same general programming model. For this reason, we have decided in this textbook to use the original AWT approach. We believe that a solid foundation in this approach will prepare those students interested in continuing their studies of Java to be able to master the nuances of the Swing libraries with a reasonable effort.

In general, Swing components are more versatile than their AWT counterparts. Using them, a developer can create a more polished user interface than can be created with the AWT. You can usually spot a Swing component within the code of a system, because most of them begin with the letter 'J'. For example, the button class provided by Swing is called `JButton`, as opposed to the regular `Button` class of the AWT.

SUMMARY

- A graphical user interface (GUI) replaces the traditional input of data via a keyboard and the display of information in textual form on a screen.

- A GUI typically consists of a container, such as a window or frame into which components, such as buttons, check boxes, radio buttons, lists, text fields, and text areas are added.

- The information gathered from the components in a GUI represent data input. Output from a GUI may take the form of text written into new windows, text fields, and text areas.

- The Abstract Windowing Toolkit (AWT) contains classes that enable a programmer to build GUIs.

- A container class is created by inheriting all the characteristics of a superclass, such as the `Frame` class, and by specifying in the constructor such features as the size, location, foreground and background colors of the container, and type of layout manager used for the components.

- Always build GUI components as standalone classes. Using an `awt` component directly with the "base" container will reduce the reusability of the component with another application.

- Always capture the size of the monitor and base all dimensions of components relative to it. This will enable you to port your applications between different-sized monitors without having to rescale all the components in your application.

- A GUI component is created by instantiating a variable of the appropriate class to create an object. The object is added to the container by using the `add` method from the `Container` class.

- When a user interacts with a GUI component, for example by pressing a button, the action of the user creates an event.

- Associated with every event is an event class. The source and characteristics of the event may be obtained through constants and methods found in the appropriate event class. For example, the action of pressing a button generates an `ActionEvent`. The source of the event may be determined from the `getActionCommand()` instance method in the `ActionEvent` class.

- An event is detected through an event listener. Every event has a corresponding event listener whose methods must be implemented in a manner applicable to handling the event for the action on that component. For example, the action of pressing a button generates an `ActionEvent` that is detected by the `ActionListener`. The `ActionListener` method `actionPerformed` must be implemented in a way that deals with the button being pressed.

- The event and event listener classes are contained in the package `java.awt.event`.

- The selection of components examined in detail in this chapter have been labels, check boxes, radio buttons, text fields, text areas, and lists. If you examine the `java.awt package`, you may notice these are not the only components available in Java.

■ Components are added to a container in a sequence predetermined by the appropriate layout manager in use. If you wish to specify the position and size of each component in the container, then set the layout manager to `null`.

Review Questions

True or false

1. `Component` is an abstract class.

2. A button component is added to a container using the `add` method from the `Component` class.

3. `Button`, `Checkbox`, and `Label` classes all inherit from the `Component` class.

4. A `Frame` inherits from a `Window` class.

5. A `Checkbox` generates an `ActionEvent`.

6. It is not necessary to implement all the listener methods of the `MouseListener` interface.

Short Answer

7. Using your Java documentation, how many different event listeners are there?

8. What instance method would you use to set the size of a `Frame`?

9. How do you make a `Frame` visible?

10. How would you set the background color of a `Frame` to red?

11. How would you set the size and location of a component in a container?

12. What listener methods must be implemented for the `KeyListener` interface?

13. What is a `Label`?

14. What is nonexclusive check-box selection?

15. How does a radio button differ from a check box?

16. In a program, how can you retrieve the chosen items from a `List`?

17. How do you prevent the displayed text in either a `TextField` or `TextArea` from being overwritten?

18. How can you find the source of an event?

19. What is the difference between `FlowLayout` and `GridLayout`?

20. What is the purpose of a `WindowAdapter` class?

21. Why should you want to extend a `WindowAdapter` class?

Exercises

22. Modify the `TextInput` class to contain instance methods that will return the input string as either an integer or a floating-point real number. Allow the class to throw an exception if either an integer or a real number is in the wrong format.

23. Create and test a reusable component containing a label, text field, and a push button. The purpose of the push button is to clear the text field.

24. Create and test your own reusable `Slider` class, similar in appearance to that used in the `avi` package.

25. Set up a list containing the names of countries. In the same GUI, transfer any three countries from the list to a separate text area.

26. Use the Java documentation to investigate the `BorderLayout` manager. Write code to demonstrate the functionality of the `BorderLayout` manager.

Programming Problems

27. Create a GUI that will allow a user to type his or her name and password. Read the documentation of `java.awt.TextField` class to see how to obscure the password from being seen on the screen. After the input is completed, display both the name and password in the MSDOS/terminal window.

28. Create a reusable component containing a text field and two check boxes. The first check box represents the bold style of font and the second check box the italic style of font. You can select the style of font as plain (no boxes are checked); bold, italic, or bold and italic (both boxes are checked). The text field contains a message that changes in style according to the boxes that are checked.

29. Extend your answer to Question 28 to include a list that contains different fonts.

30. Extend your answer to Question 24 to create three text fields, as well as the slider bar. The first text field contains a temperature in degrees Fahrenheit, controlled by the position of the slider. The second text field the value of the equivalent temperature in degrees Celsius, and the third text field the value in degrees Kelvin.

31. Create a currency conversion gui as a reusable component that will allow you to select from a list of world currencies. The GUI should contain a text field to input the current conversion rate against the US dollar, a text field that allows you to input the number of dollars, and a text field containing the equivalent amount of money in the currency of your choice.

32. Create and test a reusable component containing three text areas. The first area allows you to input a passage of text. The second area displays a frequency analysis of the letters used in the text. The third text area contains a frequency analysis of the word sizes.
    Add push buttons to analyze the text and to clear the three text areas.

CHAPTER 9

Vectors, Serialization, and the `java.awt` Graphics Class

The chapter is split logically into three parts. The first part explains how objects may be saved in a data structure similar to a one-dimensional array but with the property of growing or shrinking in size according to the amount of data there is to store at run-time. This data structure is known as a vector. A case study is used to extend the work of the previous chapter on graphical user interfaces, and show how a vector may be used in practice. The case study helps to emphasize a natural progression from storing objects in a data structure to storing objects permanently in a serializable data file.

The `Graphics` class is yet another class of the `awt` package. The class contains methods to draw lines and shapes in two-dimensions on the screen, where the position and size of these shapes can be controlled by a mouse. The second part of the chapter contains a number of programs to show you how to draw shapes on the screen, use a mouse to define the envelope of a shape, and an alternative method of selecting items from a graphical user interface by using a pop-up menu.

The third and final part of the chapter explains how Java paints the screen, and examines a technique for preventing the contents of a screen from being erased by other objects. Another application for the serialization of objects in a file explains how drawings may be permanently stored and retrieved. Finally, having created a drawing, you are shown how to output the graphics to a printer.

By the end of this chapter you should have an understanding of the following topics.

- The `Vector` class and the serialization of objects.

- Drawing two-dimensional graphical shapes.

- Using a mouse to set the location and size of a graphical shape.

- The creation of pop-up menus.

- The techniques of painting and refreshing the screen.

- Printing graphics.

9.1   Vectors

Although the declaration of the size of an array may be performed at run-time, the size of the array is then fixed for the duration of the executing program. An object instantiated as a `Vector`, however, will allow for the storage of objects in a similar data structure to a one-dimensional array, when the number of objects is not known. A partial listing for the class `Vector` follows.

```
public class Vector extends Object implements Cloneable
{
    // constructor(s)
    public Vector(int initialCapacity);

    // methods
    public final synchronized void addElement(Object obj);
    public final int capacity();
    public final synchronized void copyInto(Object[] anArray);
    public final synchronized Object elementAt(int index);
    public final synchronized Object firstElement();
    public final int indexOf(Object elem);
    public final synchronized Object lastElement();
    public final int size();
    public final synchronized void trimToSize();

        .

        .

}
```

Notice that the constructor will allow you to specify the initial capacity of the vector. However, when the vector cannot store any more data, the vector automatically doubles in size to accommodate further data storage, assuming there is enough computer memory available. A partial listing of the class's methods includes the following.

addElement(Object obj)—insert an object into the next free location in the vector.

capacity()—return the capacity of the Vector.

copyInto(Object[] anArray)—copy the contents of the vector into an array.

elementAt(int index)—return the object stored in the vector at the position index.

firstElement()—return the object stored at index position 0 (zero).

indexOf(Object elem)—return the index of the object element stored in the Vector.

lastElement()—return the object element stored at the position size-1.

size()—return the number of object elements stored in the Vector.

trimToSize()—reduce the capacity of the Vector to the number of elements stored in the Vector.

Program Example_1 allows a user to input as many single words into a vector as they wish and display a list of the words. The program demonstrates some of the methods defined in the Vector class and shows that individual cells of a vector may be accessed in a similar manner to accessing a one-dimensional array. Finally the program shows how to copy the contents of a vector into a one-dimensional array, and re-display the contents on the screen.

```
// program to demonstrate storing and retrieving data from a Vector

import avi.*;
import java.util.*;

class Example_1
{
    static public void main(String[] args)
    {
        // initial size of vector
        final int INITIAL_SIZE = 4;

        Window screen = new Window("Example_1.java");
        DialogBox inputWord = new DialogBox(screen,"Name of fruit?");

        String[] reply = {"continue?","quit?"};
```

```
RadioButtons buttons = new
RadioButtons(screen,"What next?",reply);

Vector dataStore = new Vector(INITIAL_SIZE);
int    sizeOfVector;
String word;

screen.showWindow();

do
{
    inputWord.showDialogBox();
    word = inputWord.getString();

    dataStore.addElement(word);
    screen.write("index "+dataStore.indexOf(word)+
                "\tcontents "+word+
                "\tcapacity of vector "+
                    dataStore.capacity()+"\n");

    buttons.showRadioButtons();
}while (buttons.getNameOfButton().equals("continue?"));

// display size, capacity, first element and last element of
// vector
screen.write("\nsize of vector " + dataStore.size()+"\n");
screen.write("capacity of vector " +
            dataStore.capacity()+"\n");
screen.write("first element " + dataStore.firstElement()+"\n");
screen.write("last element " + dataStore.lastElement()+"\n");

// input any position within bounds of vector
DialogBox inputPosition = new
DialogBox(screen,"Any position in vector");
int position;
do
{
    inputPosition.showDialogBox();
    position = inputPosition.getInteger();
} while (position < 0 || position >= dataStore.size());

// display item at given position in vector
screen.write("element at position "+position+" "+
            dataStore.elementAt(position)+"\n");
```

```
// reduce the capacity of the vector to the size of the vector
dataStore.trimToSize();
sizeOfVector = dataStore.capacity();

// display the new capacity of the trimmed vector
screen.write("\ntrimmed size capacity "+sizeOfVector+"\n");

// list the contents of the vector
screen.write("Contents of Vector\n");
for (int index=0; index != sizeOfVector; index++)
    screen.write(dataStore.elementAt(index) + " ");

// copy contents of vector into an array
String[] array = new String[sizeOfVector];
dataStore.copyInto((String[])array);

// list the contents of the array
screen.write("\n\nContents of array initialized from the "+
            "vector\n");
for (int index=0; index != array.length; index++)
    screen.write(array[index]+" ");
    }

}
```

Notice the capacity of the vector was initially set to 4 by the constructor. After four items of data had been input, the capacity of the vector was automatically increased to eight. After eight items of data had been input, the capacity of the vector was doubled again to sixteen.

By specifying the name of an object in the method `indexOf`, it is possible to obtain the index of the cell containing the object.

The `size` of the vector indicates the number of items of data stored, whereas the `capacity` of the vector indicates the total number of cells, whether occupied by data or not.

It is possible to access any cell within the vector by using the appropriate class methods. In this example, the methods `firstElement`, `lastElement`, and `elementAt` have been used to find the elements at index 0, 8 and the range 0..8 respectively.

Once a vector has been filled with data and there are wasted cells not being used, it is possible to trim the vector to the size of the array by using the method `trimToSize`.

The contents of the vector can be copied into an array using the method `copyInto`; the array may then be processed in the normal manner.

Screen shots from the program being run follow.

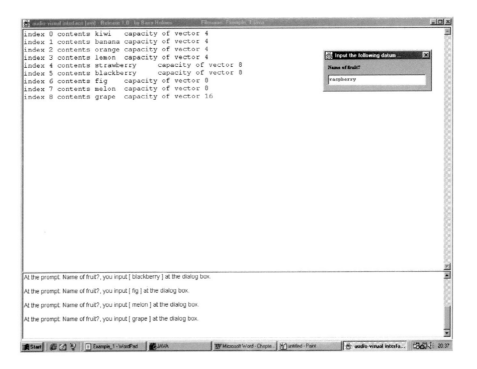

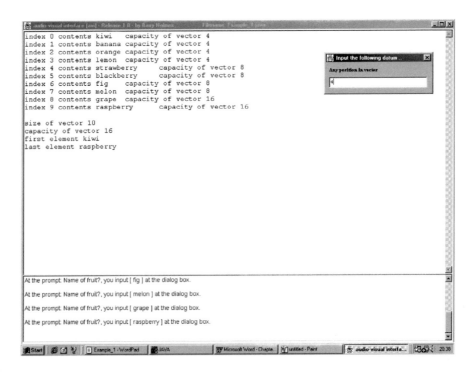

```
index 0 contents kiwi    capacity of vector 4
index 1 contents banana capacity of vector 4
index 2 contents orange capacity of vector 4
index 3 contents lemon  capacity of vector 4
index 4 contents strawberry    capacity of vector 8
index 5 contents blackberry    capacity of vector 8
index 6 contents fig    capacity of vector 8
index 7 contents melon  capacity of vector 8
index 8 contents grape  capacity of vector 16
index 9 contents raspberry     capacity of vector 16

size of vector 10
capacity of vector 16
first element kiwi
last element raspberry
element at position 4 strawberry

trimmed size capacity 10
Contents of Vector
kiwi banana orange lemon strawberry blackberry fig melon grape raspberry

Contents of array initialized from the vector
kiwi banana orange lemon strawberry blackberry fig melon grape raspberry |
```

At the prompt: Name of fruit?, you input [melon] at the dialog box.

At the prompt: Name of fruit?, you input [grape] at the dialog box.

At the prompt: Name of fruit?, you input [raspberry] at the dialog box.

At the prompt: Any position in vector, you input [4] at the dialog box.

NOW DO THIS

(1) Create a class `Subscriber` containing instance variables name, address, and telephone number, and a constructor and instance methods to retrieve the variables.

Using program `Example_1` for reference, write a program to perform the following.

(2) Create a vector containing telephone Subscriber objects.

(3) Display the entire contents of the vector.

(4) Input the name of a subscriber and display the corresponding address and telephone number.

The completion of the above exercise will help you to understand the use of vectors in following case study.

CASE STUDY

Chemical Elements

Statement of the Problem   Write a program to store attributes of chemical elements in a vector. The program should be capable of adding different chemical elements to the vector, selecting and displaying individual elements from the vector, listing the entire contents of the vector, and returning back to the operating system.

The program must use a graphical user interface to communicate with the user of the program.

Before we delve into the graphical components required to create the interface, we need to examine the attributes of a chemical element. We classify a chemical element by its name, chemical symbol, and atomic weight; now we can create a class ChemicalElement that encapsulates this data.

```java
public class ChemicalElement
{

    private String nameOfElement;
    private String chemicalSymbol;
    private String atomicNumber;


    /**
    The ChemicalElement class enables an object that represents a
    chemical element from the periodic table of elements.
    @param name is the name of the element.
    @param symbol is the chemical symbol of the element.
    @param number is the atomic number of the element.
    */
    public ChemicalElement(String name, String symbol, String number)
    {

        nameOfElement = name;
        chemicalSymbol = symbol;
        atomicNumber = number;

    }


    /**
    @return The name of the element.
    */
    public String getName()
    {

        return nameOfElement;

    }
```

```
/**
@return The chemical symbol of the element.
*/
public String getSymbol()
{
      return chemicalSymbol;
}

/**
@return the atomic number of the element.
*/
public String getNumber()
{
      return atomicNumber;
}
}
```

The data for each chemical element needs to be input via a reusable graphical component. The only component we have created that can be used to input specific data for an element is the `TextInput` component. The limitation of this component is that we have to create three different components for the three different attributes of a chemical element.

How much better it would be to create a reusable component similar to the one depicted in Figure 9.1. By combining labels, text fields, and buttons we can create a very useful graphical component for the input of any number of text fields. Figure 9.1 illustrates a `DataInputBox` component; the number of labels and text fields are not fixed, but are input as arguments to the constructor.

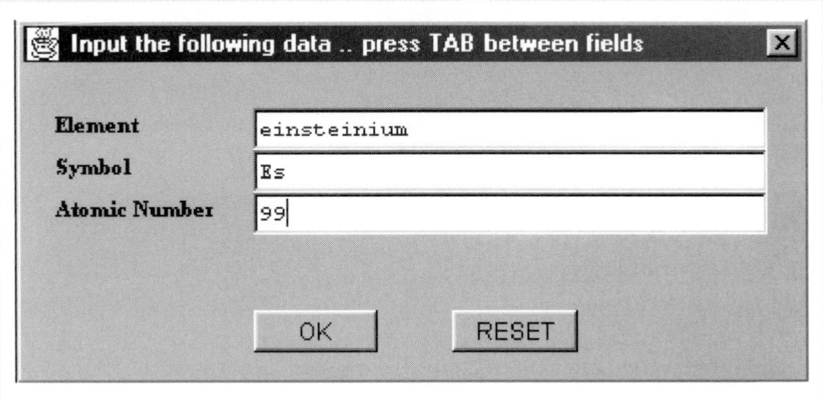

Figure 9.1 A `DataInputBox` component

If you have prepared a GUI where data is to be input to a number of fields, move the cursor to the next field using the TAB key rather than using the mouse pointer. This technique is quicker for data entry.

The complete listing of the `DataInputBox` component follows. The component is composed from the `awt` `Dialog`, `Label`, `TextField`, and `Button` components. You have been given enough information in the previous chapter to be able to read about and understand the construction of the `DataInputBox` component.

```java
import java.awt.*;
import java.awt.event.*;

public class DataInputBox extends Dialog implements ActionListener
{
        // constants
        private static final int FONT_SIZE = 11;
        private static final int HEIGHT_OF_BAR = 20;
        private static final String EMPTY_STRING = "";

        // instance variables
        private String[] inputData;
        private TextField[] data;
        private Label[] textLabels;
        private int numberOfItems;

        /**
        The DataInputBox class enables an object that represents as many
        labelled text fields as required, to be used to input textual data.
        An indication that the text fields are complete with data is made by
        pressing an "OK" button. The contents of the text fields may be
        cleared at any time by pressing the "RESET" button.
        @param parent is the container on which to add the data input box.
        @param prompts is an array of labels for the text fields.
        */
        public DataInputBox(Frame parent, String[] prompts)
        {
                super(parent,
                " Input the following data .. press TAB between fields",
                  true);
                numberOfItems = prompts.length;
```

```
inputData = new String[numberOfItems];
addWindowListener(new CloseDataInput());

// set width and height of screen
int screenWidth  = parent.getWidth();
int screenHeight = parent.getHeight();

// set location and size of dialog box
int xLocationOfBox = (int)(0.4f * screenWidth);
int yLocationOfBox = (int)(0.1f * screenHeight);
int widthOfBox     = (int)(0.4f * screenWidth);
int heightOfBox    = (int)(screenHeight/36)*
                          (numberOfItems)+6*HEIGHT_OF_BAR;

// set location and size of first label
int xLocationOfLabel = (int)(0.05f * widthOfBox);
int yLocationOfLabel = (int)(2.0f * screenHeight/36);
int widthOfLabel     = (int)(0.2f * widthOfBox);
int heightOfLabel    = (int)(screenHeight/36);

// set location and size of first text field
int widthOfField     = (int)(0.65f * widthOfBox);
int heightOfField    = (int)(screenHeight/36);
int xLocationOfField = (int)(0.3f * widthOfBox);
int yLocationOfField = (int)(2*HEIGHT_OF_BAR+
                          (int)(heightOfField/4));

// set fonts
Font dialog = new Font("Dialog", Font.BOLD, FONT_SIZE);
Font dialogInput = new Font("DialogInput", Font.PLAIN,
                          FONT_SIZE);

// draw dialog box
this.setLayout(null);
this.setBackground(Color.lightGray);
this.setForeground(Color.blue);
this.setLocation(xLocationOfBox,yLocationOfBox);
this.setSize(widthOfBox,heightOfBox);

// set location and size of "OK" button
int xLocationOfOKButton = (int)(0.30f*widthOfBox);
int yLocationOfOKButton = (int)(0.8f*heightOfBox);
int widthOfButton = (int)(0.8f*widthOfLabel);
int heightOfButton = (int)(heightOfLabel);
```

```
// create button
Button okButton = new Button("OK");
okButton.setLocation(xLocationOfOKButton,
                     yLocationOfOKButton);
okButton.setSize(widthOfButton, heightOfButton);
okButton.setBackground(Color.lightGray);
okButton.setForeground(Color.black);

// add push button to dialog box and action listener for
// button
this.add(okButton);
okButton.addActionListener(this);


// set location and size of "RESET" button
int xLocationOfResetButton = (int)(0.55f*widthOfBox);
int yLocationOfResetButton = (int)(0.8f*heightOfBox);

// create button
Button resetButton = new Button("RESET");
resetButton.setLocation(xLocationOfResetButton,
                        yLocationOfResetButton);
resetButton.setSize(widthOfButton, heightOfButton);
resetButton.setBackground(Color.lightGray);
resetButton.setForeground(Color.black);

// add push button to dialog box and action listener for
// button
this.add(resetButton);
resetButton.addActionListener(this);

// insert a label and a text field for each item
// draw text field in dialog box
textLabels = new Label[numberOfItems];
data = new TextField[numberOfItems];

for (int index=0; index != numberOfItems; index++)
{
    // insert prompt(s)
    textLabels[index] = new Label(prompts[index],
                                  Label.LEFT);
    textLabels[index].setLocation(xLocationOfLabel,
                yLocationOfLabel+(index*heightOfLabel));
    textLabels[index].setSize(widthOfLabel, heightOfLabel);
```

```
        textLabels[index].setForeground(Color.black);
        textLabels[index].setFont(dialog);
        this.add(textLabels[index]);

        // insert text field(s)
        data[index] = new TextField(EMPTY_STRING,widthOfField);
        data[index].setLocation(xLocationOfField,
                    yLocationOfField+(index*heightOfField));
        data[index].setSize(widthOfField, heightOfField);
        data[index].setBackground(Color.white);
        data[index].setForeground(Color.blue);
        data[index].setFont(dialogInput);
        this.add(data[index]);
    }
}

/**
Display the DataInputBox on the container.
*/
public void showDataInputBox()
{
    this.setVisible(true);
}


/**
Get the contents of the text fields.
@return Returns an array of strings representing the contents of the
text fields taken in consecutive order. The contents of the first
text field are stored in cell 0, the contents of the second text
field are stored in cell 1, and so on.
*/
public String[] getFields()
{
    return inputData;
}


public void actionPerformed(ActionEvent event)
{
    if (event.getActionCommand().equals("OK"))
    {
        for (int index=0; index != numberOfItems; index++)
        {
            inputData[index] = new
            String(data[index].getText());
```

```
                            data[index].setText(EMPTY_STRING);
                    }

                    this.setVisible(false);
            }
            else if (event.getActionCommand().equals("RESET"))
            {
                    for (int index=0; index != numberOfItems; index++)
                    {
                            data[index].setText(EMPTY_STRING);
                            inputData[index] = EMPTY_STRING;
                    }
            }
    }


    // inner class to handle window event
    public class CloseDataInput extends WindowAdapter
    {
            public void windowClosing(WindowEvent event)
            {
                    DataInputBox.this.setVisible(false);
            }
    }
}
```

A text field is capable of displaying information as well as having data typed into the field. The Case Study problem states that the program selects an individual chemical element and display the attributes of the element. If the selection of an individual element is to be based upon the name of the element, then a `TextInput` component can be used to input a single name. Although it is possible to write the attributes of a chemical element to a `WritingPad` object, it would be far better to output the attributes to a set of labeled text fields, occupying a separate graphical component. Figure 9.2 illustrates a `DataOutputBox` component. You will

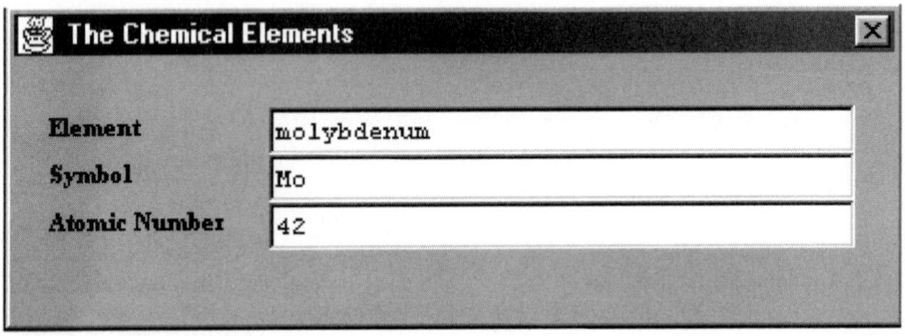

Figure 9.2 A `DataOutputBox` component

notice that it resembles the `DataInputBox`, but it is without the press buttons and displays a different message in the title bar.

NOW DO THIS▶ Use the code from the class `DataInputBox` as a template to perform the following.

(1) Create a class `DataOutputBox`. You need to edit out the creation of the two buttons, allow for any title to be input in the title bar of the dialog box, and transfer the contents of a string array to a method in the class to permit each respective text field to be set to the text stored in the array.

Once again, if you need assistance with your answer, the code for the `DataOutputBox` is available on the CD that accompanies this book.

In Chapter 8 you were asked to write a class `RadioButtons`. This class can be used in the program to allow a user to select one of the options to insert a chemical element into the vector, select an element from the vector, list the entire contents of the vector, or quit the program and return back to the operating system.

Figure 9.3 illustrates how a `RadioButtons` object can be used to offer this choice in the program.

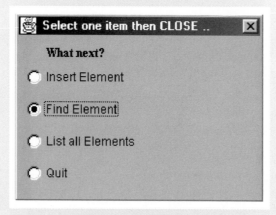

Figure 9.3 A `RadioButtons` component

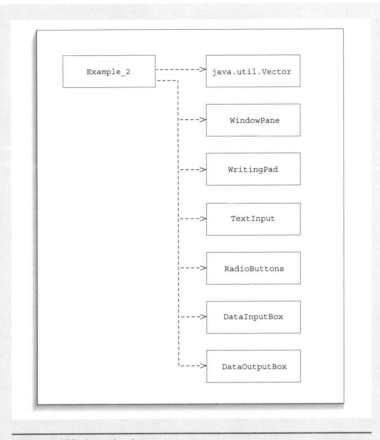

Figure 9.4 UML dependencies

There are no further graphical components to consider in this program. To summarize, Figure 9.4 illustrates the dependencies class `Example_2` has on the `Vector` class and the graphical components created in this and the previous chapter.

The pseudocode for the test program `Example_2` follows.

1. show the window pane
2. show the radio buttons
3. get choice from radio buttons
4. while choice is not to quit
5.   if choice is to insert chemical element into vector
6.   show data input box
7.   get contents of fields from box
8.   create chemical element object and add this to the vector

9.   else if choice is to find a chemical element
10.   show text input box
11.   get name of chemical element
12.   for every element in the vector
13.   get a chemical element object from the vector
14.   if name of element is the same as the name from the object
15.   show the data output box
16.   build an array from the attributes of the object in the vector
17.   set the text fields of the data output box from the array
18.   else if choice is to list all the elements
19.   show the writing pad
20.   for every element in the vector
21.   get a chemical element object from the vector
22.   write the attributes of the chemical element object
23.   show the radio buttons
24.   get choice from radio buttons

A listing of the test program `Example_2` follows.

```java
import java.util.Vector;

class Example_2
{
    public static void main(String[] args)
    {
        // arrays used in graphical components
        String[] prompts = {"Element","Symbol","Atomic Number"};
        String[] whatNext = {"Insert Element","Find Element",
                            "List all Elements","Quit"};

        // array to store data for an element
        String[] fields = new String[3];

        // create a vector to store ChemicalElement objects
        Vector dataStore = new Vector();

        // instantiate a number of graphical components for use in the
        // GUI
        WindowPane screen = new WindowPane();
        RadioButtons buttons = new
        RadioButtons(screen, "What next?", whatNext);
        TextInput element = new TextInput(screen, "Element?");
        DataInputBox input = new DataInputBox(screen, prompts);
        DataOutputBox output = new
```

```
DataOutputBox(screen, prompts, "The Chemical Elements");
WritingPad notes = new WritingPad(screen);

// show the screen and get the initial choice
screen.showWindowPane();
buttons.showRadioButtons();
String choice = buttons.getNameOfButton();

while (! choice.equals("Quit"))
{
      // insert a ChemicalElement object into the vector
      if (choice.equals("Insert Element"))
      {
            // input data of chemical element
            input.showDataInputBox();
            fields = input.getFields();

            // store chemical element object in vector
            dataStore.addElement(new
            ChemicalElement(fields[0],fields[1],fields[2]));
      }

      // search the vector for a chemical element
      else if (choice.equals("Find Element"))
      {
            element.showTextInput();
            String nameOfElement = element.getString();

            // search through vector
            for (int index=0; index != dataStore.size();
                  index++)
            {
                  ChemicalElement datum = (ChemicalElement)
                  dataStore.elementAt(index);

                  // check on the name of the element
                  if (nameOfElement.equals(datum.getName()))
                  {
                        output.showDataOutputBox();
                        fields[0] = datum.getName();
                        fields[1] = datum.getSymbol();
                        fields[2] = datum.getNumber();
```

```
                              // display chosen chemical element
                              output.setFields(fields);
                    }
               }
          }


          // list the contents of the vector
          else if (choice.equals("List all Elements"))
          {
               ChemicalElement datum;

               notes.showWritingPad();
               for (int index=0; index != dataStore.size();
                         index++)
               {
                    datum = (ChemicalElement)
                              dataStore.elementAt(index);
                    notes.write(datum.getName()+
                              " "+datum.getSymbol()+
                              " "+datum.getNumber()+"\n");
               }
               notes.write("\n");
          }


          // get next choice of what to do
          buttons.showRadioButtons();
          choice = buttons.getNameOfButton();
     }
   }
}
```

A screen shot from the running program follows.

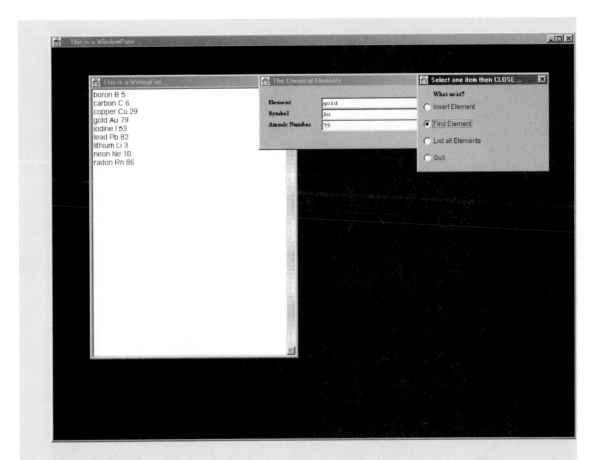

After running this program several times, you may feel the need to be able to store the contents of the vector in a file so that it can be retrieved at a later time and re-loaded into the vector. This feature will be dealt with in the next section under serializable files.

9.2 Saving and Loading Serializable Objects

The only saving of data in files that we have done so far in the book is saving text in a text file. Saving objects in a file is a new experience!

The process of saving objects to a stream is called *serialization* because each object is assigned a serial number on the stream

Object streams are far easier to use than the text streams that we looked at in Chapter 7. One big advantage is that you don't need to separate numbers and strings when writing to or reading from a file. The serialization mechanism takes care of this automatically. You simply write and read objects. For this to work, each of the classes whose objects are to be stored must implement the `Serializable` interface. In our example the `ChemicalElements` class must implement the `Serializable` interface. The `Serializable` interface defines no methods or constants. Any class that implements `Serializable` may have its object written to and read from a stream using classes found in the `java.io` package.

To save objects to a disk file you should store all the objects in a single structure such as a vector and write the vector to the file. The process of saving an objects to a file may be divided into the following stages.

■ Create a name under which to save the file, where `screen` is the name of the container class on which to draw the `FileDialog` object.

```
FileDialog file = new FileDialog(screen,"",FileDialog.SAVE);
file.show();

String filename = file.getFile();
```

■ Create an output stream.

```
FileOutputStream fos = new FileOutputStream(filename);
```

■ Write the entire data structure (vector `store`) to the output file, flush the buffer, and the close stream.

```
ObjectOutputStream out = new ObjectOutputStream(fos);

out.writeObject(store);
out.flush();
out.close();
```

The `ObjectOutputStream` is used to serialize objects to a stream. The `writeObject` method serializes an object, the `flush` method writes any remaining data on the stream to the file, and the `close` method closes the stream.

Loading objects may be thought of as the reverse of saving objects, and can be broken down into the following stages.

■ Obtaining the name of the file to be loaded.

```
FileDialog file = new FileDialog(screen,"",FileDialog.LOAD);
file.show();

String filename = file.getFile();
```

■ Create a file input stream.

```
FileInputStream fis = new FileInputStream(filename);
```

■ Create an object input stream, read the objects into a vector `newStore`, and close the stream.

```
ObjectInputStream in = new ObjectInputStream(fis);

Vector newStore = (Vector)in.readObject();
in.close();
```

The `ObjectInputStream` is used to deserialize objects to a stream. The `readObject` method deserializes an object; the `close` method closes the stream.

NOW DO THIS   Modify program `Example_2` as follows.

(1) Add two more buttons to the radio buttons class—"Load Elements" and "Save Elements".

(2) Insert the following code to load elements.

```
// load the contents of the file into the vector
else if (choice.equals("Load Elements"))
{
        FileDialog file = new
        FileDialog(screen,"",FileDialog.LOAD);
        file.show();

        String filename = file.getFile();
        if (filename != null)
        {
                try
                {
                        FileInputStream fis = new
                        FileInputStream(filename);
                        ObjectInputStream in = new
                        ObjectInputStream(fis);

                        Vector newStore = (Vector)in.readObject();
                        in.close();
                        dataStore = newStore;
                }
```

(continued)

NOW DO THIS   *(continued)*

```
            catch (Exception e){}
        }
    }
```

(3) Insert the following code to save elements.

```
// save the contents of the vector in a serializable file
else if (choice.equals("Save Elements"))
{
        FileDialog file = new
        FileDialog(screen,"",FileDialog.SAVE);
        file.show();

        String filename = file.getFile();
        if (filename != null)
        {
            try
            {
                    FileOutputStream fos = new
                    FileOutputStream(filename);
                    ObjectOutputStream out = new
                    ObjectOutputStream(fos);
                    out.writeObject(dataStore);
                    out.flush();
                    out.close();
            }
            catch (IOException e){}
        }
    }
```

(4) Modify the `ChemicalElement` class to implement the `Serializable` interface.

(5) Save the modifications to `Example_2` using a different filename, remember to change the class name from `Example_2` to the new name; compile and run the program.

9.3 The Graphics Class

Within the `java.awt` package is an abstract `Graphics` class that specifies methods for doing line drawing, area filling, image painting, area copying, graphics-output clipping, and displaying strings. A partial listing of the `Graphics` class follows, showing some of the methods we will be using to output strings and draw straight lines, squares, rectangles, circles, and ellipses. For a full description of the `Graphics` class, turn to your downloaded Java documentation.

```
public abstract class Graphics extends Object
{
      // instance methods
      .

      .

      public abstract void drawLine(int x1,int y1,int x2,int y2);
      public abstract void drawOval(int x,int y,int width,int height);
      public void drawRect(int x,int y,int width,int height);
      public abstract void drawString(String str,int x,int y);

      .

      .


}
```

The next program in this chapter creates a window on which to draw shapes from the `Graphics` class. Notice that a new method, `paint`, has been coded in the class `MyGraphicsWindow` without any visible means of invoking the method from within either the class or from the `main` method of class `Example_3`.

The `Graphics` class contains the method `paint` that is automatically invoked by the window manager; it should not normally be invoked directly from within a program. You may override the `paint` method in your own program and let the window manager invoke the method automatically.

```
// program to create a window container and draw two-dimensional shapes
// from the Graphics class

import java.awt.*;
import java.awt.event.*;

class MyGraphicsWindow extends Frame
}
      private MyGraphicsWindow bigBrother;

      // constructor
      public MyGraphicsWindow(int width, int height, int x, int y)
      {
```

```
        // call Frame's constructor
        super("My graphics window");

        // set colors of window
        setBackground(Color.yellow);
        setForeground(Color.black);

        // set dimensions and position of window on screen
        setSize(width, height);
        setLocation(x,y);

        // store object that invoked constructor
        bigBrother = this;

        // add listener to detect window being closed
        addWindowListener(new CloseMyWindow());
}

// instance method to display window on screen
public void showWindow()
{
        this.show();
}

public void paint(Graphics g)
{
        // draw a pair of lines
        g.drawLine(50,50,350,50);
        g.drawLine(300,25,300,250);

        // draw a rectangle
        g.drawRect(50,75,200,150);

        // draw an ellipse
        g.drawOval(75,90,150,80);

        // draw a circle
        g.drawOval(150,125,40,40);

        // print text in the graphics window
        g.drawString("A masterpiece in contemporary art !",50,250);
}

// subclass of WindowAdapter
private class CloseMyWindow extends WindowAdapter
```

```
        {
                // overridden method of superclass
                public void windowClosing(WindowEvent event)
                {
                        bigBrother.dispose();
                        System.exit(0);
                }
        }
}

public class Example_3
{
        public static void main(String[] args)
        {
                MyGraphicsWindow window = new MyGraphicsWindow(400,300,50,50);
                window.showWindow();
        }
}
```

Results from the running program follow.

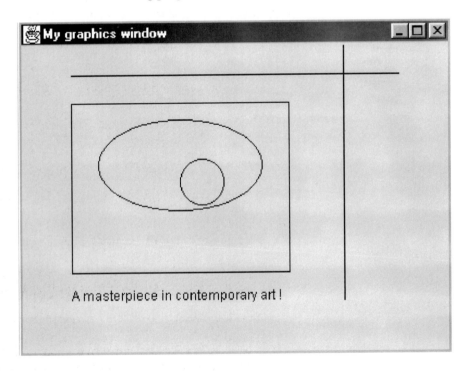

NOW DO THIS   Read the Java documentation of the `Graphics` class to modify program `Example_3` to perform the following.

(1) Remove the code to draw the shapes and text shown in the screen output.

(2) Experiment by drawing shapes for a polygon and a polyline. You must choose the number of sides for each component.

(3) Experiment by drawing shapes for a raised filled 3D rectangle, and a filled arc.

9.4 Mouse Events

For interactive drawing of shapes on the screen, the position of the mouse can provide the coordinates for drawing a shape.

Actions such as clicking, releasing, and pressing the mouse button all generate mouse events that can be detected by the mouse listener. The appropriate method from the following `MouseListener` interface is then implemented as a reaction to the event taking place.

```
public abstract interface MouseListener extends EventListener
{
    // public instance methods
    public abstract void mouseClicked(MouseEvent e);
    public abstract void mouseEntered(MouseEvent e);
    public abstract void mouseExited(MouseEvent e);
    public abstract void mousePressed(MouseEvent e);
    public abstract void mouseReleased(MouseEvent e);
}
```

These methods are implemented in the `java.awt.event` package as do-nothing methods in the `MouseAdapter` class. As with the `WindowAdapter` class, the `MouseAdapter` class will also be extended to create appropriate mouse-listener methods.

The `MouseEvent` class, in the package `java.awt.event`, describes two instance methods that allow us to examine the position of the mouse in relationship to the coordinates of the screen. These methods are:

```
public int getX();
public int getY();
```

The class `WhereIsTheMouse` implements the `mousePressed` method to draw a string on the screen indicating the position of the mouse when the left-button is pressed. The methods `getX()` and `getY()` are from the class `MouseEvent`, and the method `drawString` is from the `Graphics` class. Notice that the `WhereIsTheMouse` class extends the `WindowPane` class in order to be able to draw on a screen.

> *i*   A Graphics object cannot be created directly though a constructor—it can be obtained with the `getGraphics()` method of `Component`. In the programs that follow, a `Graphics` object g is created using the statement `Graphics g = getGraphics()`.

```
// program to plot mouse coordinates on the screen

import java.awt.*;
import java.awt.event.*;

class WhereIsTheMouse extends WindowPane
{
    // constructor
    public WhereIsTheMouse()
    {
        super();
        this.setForeground(Color.white);
        addMouseListener(new HandleMouseEvents());
    }

    public void begin()
    {
        this.showWindowPane();
    }

    private class HandleMouseEvents extends MouseAdapter
    {
        public void mousePressed(MouseEvent event)
        {
            // get coordinates of mouse
            int x = event.getX();
            int y = event.getY();

            Graphics g = getGraphics();

            // display message on screen
            g.drawString("+ ["+String.valueOf(x)+","+
                            String.valueOf(y)+"]",x,y);
        }
    }
}
```

Program `Example_4` is used to test the methods of the `WhereIsTheMouse` class.

```
class Example_4
{
     public static void main(String[] args)
     {
          WhereIsTheMouse mouseFinder = new WhereIsTheMouse();
          mouseFinder.begin();
     }
}
```

Here is a screen shot from a running program.

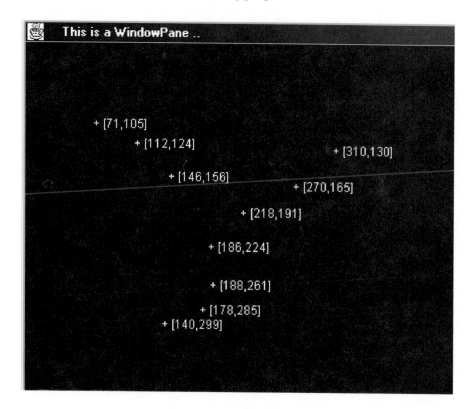

The origin of coordinates is taken to be the upper left-hand corner of the screen. From the screen shot you will notice that the positive x-axis is to the right of the origin and the positive y-axis is below the origin. You may think of the x-axis as the top edge of the screen and the y-axis as the left-hand edge of the screen.

The following technique uses a mouse to determine the coordinates of two points on the screen. Pressing the mouse button determines the position of the first point. Dragging the mouse (moving the mouse with the button kept

pressed) to another location on the screen and releasing the mouse button determines the position of the second point. It is necessary to listen for two types of
events—pressing the mouse button and releasing the mouse button.

> The events of dragging a mouse and moving a mouse are also `MouseEvents`. The appropri-
> ate listener for these two mouse events is the `MouseMotionListener` interface. Any class
> implementing this interface must implement the listener methods `mouseDragged` and
> `mouseMoved`. A `MouseMotionAdapter` class exists that contains do-nothing implementations of
> these two listener methods. Therefore, it is possible to subclass the `MouseMotionAdapter`
> class and override either of the two listener methods.

Upon detecting the mouse button being pressed or released, the methods
`getX()` and `getY()` from the class `MouseEvent` can capture the position of the
mouse. The two points formed by pressing the mouse button, dragging the
mouse, and then releasing the mouse button form opposite corners of an imaginary rectangle. The calculations of the coordinates for the upper left-hand corner and the width and height of the imaginary rectangle will vary when you are
dragging the mouse either up or down the screen and to the right or left as
depicted in Figure 9.5.

Note the coordinates [x1,y1] of a point refer to the horizontal position x_1 and
the vertical position y_1 of the point from the origin of coordinates. The difference $y_1 - y_2$ represents the vertical distance between two points provided $y_1 > y_2$.

The coordinates of the upper left-hand corner and the width and height of
the imaginary rectangle can be calculated using the following expressions, irre-
spective of the direction of the movement of the mouse.

```
upperLeftX = Math.min(x1,x2); upperLeftY = Math.min(y1,y2);
width = Math.abs(x1-x2);       height = Math.abs(y1-y2);
```

Note that the mathematical class method `min` will return the smaller of two
numbers, and the method `abs` will return the positive value of the difference
between two numbers.

We can capture the coordinates of the mouse at the point where it is pressed
using the following `mousePressed` implementation.

```
public void mousePressed(MouseEvent event)
{
        upperLeftX=0; upperLeftY=0; width=0; height=0;

    x1=event.getX();
    y1=event.getY();
}
```

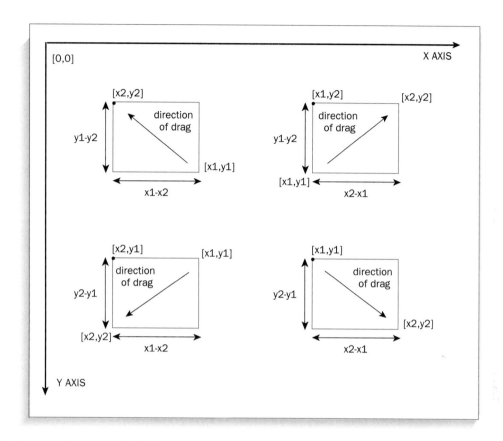

Figure 9.5 Constructing rectangles

We can also capture the coordinates of the mouse at the point where the mouse button is released (having first dragged the mouse to a new position) using the following mouseReleased implementation.

```
public void mouseReleased(MouseEvent event)
{
      x2=event.getX();
      y2=event.getY();

      upperLeftX = Math.min(x1,x2);
      upperLeftY = Math.min(y1,y2);
      width = Math.abs(x1-x2);
      height = Math.abs(y1-y2);


      .
      .
```

Now that we have defined an imaginary rectangle into which we can draw a figure, we can (in the same `mouseReleased` implementation) draw the appropriate shape using the methods from the `Graphics` class. The following code from the `mouseReleased` class is used to draw a rectangle.

.

.

```
Graphics g = getGraphics();

g.drawRect(upperLeftX,upperLeftY,width,height);
}
```

The `ElasticRectangle` class brings together the skeletal code developed in this section and a class that will permit drawing a rectangle of any size anywhere on the screen.

```
// program to draw any-sized rectangle on the screen

import java.awt.*;
import java.awt.event.*;

public class ElasticRectangle extends WindowPane
{
      // coordinate of upper-left hand corner of a rectangle
      private int upperLeftX, upperLeftY;
      // size of surrounding rectangle
      private int width, height;
      // coordinates of two selected points
      private int x1,y1,x2,y2;

      // constructor
      public ElasticRectangle()
      {
            super();
            setForeground(Color.white);
            addMouseListener(new HandleMouseEvents());
      }

      // instance method
      public void draw()
      {
            this.show();
      }
```

```
// inner classes to handle mouse and window events
private class HandleMouseEvents extends MouseAdapter
{
      // capture initial coordinates of mouse
      public void mousePressed(MouseEvent event)
      {
            upperLeftX=0; upperLeftY=0; width=0; height=0;

            x1=event.getX();
            y1=event.getY();
      }

      // draw the appropriate shape when mouse button released;
      // shape will be drawn between the coordinates (x1,y1) and
      // (x2,y2)
      public void mouseReleased(MouseEvent event)
      {
            Graphics g = getGraphics();
            x2=event.getX();
            y2=event.getY();
            upperLeftX = Math.min(x1,x2);
            upperLeftY = Math.min(y1,y2);
            width = Math.abs(x1-x2);
            height = Math.abs(y1-y2);
            g.drawRect(upperLeftX,upperLeftY,width,height);
      }
   }
}
```

Program `Example_5` is used to test the validity of the methods of our `ElasticRectangle` class.

```
class Example_5
{
      public static void main(String[] args)
      {
            ElasticRectangle shape = new ElasticRectangle();
            shape.draw();
      }
}
```

A partial screen shot from running program follows.

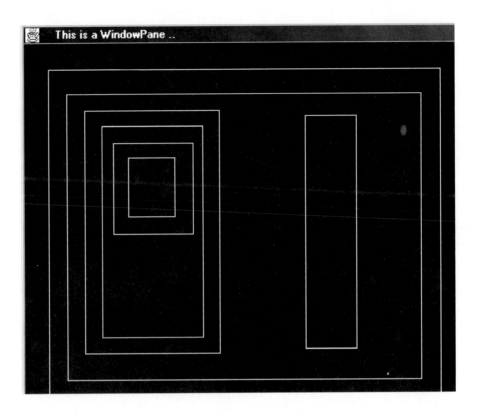

9.5 Pop-Up Menus

We previously defined an imaginary rectangle into which we can draw a figure. However, there is no need to be limited to drawing a rectangular shape; it is also possible in the same `mouseReleased` implementation to draw an appropriate straight line, square, rectangle, circle, or ellipse using the appropriate methods from the `Graphics` class. The following partial implementation of the `mouseReleased` method assumes the existence of a string variable `drawShape` that has prerecorded the type of shape to be drawn.

```
public void mouseReleased(MouseEvent event)
{
        .
        .

        Graphics g = getGraphics();

        if (drawShape.equals("line"))
                g.drawLine(x1,y1,x2,y2);
```

```
else if (drawShape.equals("square"))
      g.drawRect(upperLeftX,upperLeftY,width,width);
else if (drawShape.equals("rectangle"))
      g.drawRect(upperLeftX,upperLeftY,width,height);
else if (drawShape.equals("circle"))
      g.drawOval(upperLeftX,upperLeftY,width,width);
else if (drawShape.equals("ellipse"))
      g.drawOval(upperLeftX,upperLeftY,width,height);
}
```

In developing a program to draw various shapes on the screen, we must give the user a choice of what to draw and also a choice of what color to use in drawing the shape. A pop-up menu will appear in response to some trigger event, such as pressing the right button on the mouse. Figure 9.6 shows the set of pop-up menus used in this section.

The pop-up menus illustrated in Figure 9.6 were created using the following code. The contents of the pop-up menus are stored as strings in one-dimensional arrays.

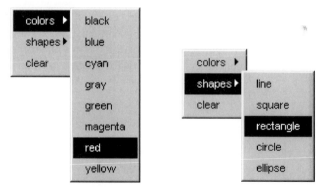

Figure 9.6 Examples of pop-up menus

```
String[] colorNames = {"black","blue","cyan","gray","green",
                       "magenta","red","yellow"};
String[] shapeNames = {"line","square","rectangle","circle","ellipse"};
```

An abridged version of the class `PopupMenu` from the `java.awt` package follows:

```
public class PopupMenu ..
{
     // constructors
     public PopupMenu();
         public Popupmenu(String label);
```

```
            // instance method(s)
            public void show(Component origin, int x, int y);
                .

                .
}
```

To create a pop-up menu, create a `PopupMenu` object:

```
PopupMenu menu = new PopupMenu();
```

Create two further submenu objects and add these to the main menu:

```
PopupMenu colors = new PopupMenu("colors");
menu.add(colors);
PopupMenu shapes = new PopupMenu("shapes");
menu.add(shapes);
```

Using the methods from the `MenuItem` class, create `MenuItem` objects. This class encapsulates a menu item with a specified textual label. Use the `setActionCommand` to specify an identifying string that is included in `ActionEvent` events generated by the menu item.

Build the menu for the color of the shapes:

```
for (int index=0; index != colorNames.length; index++)
{
      MenuItem mi = new MenuItem(colorNames[index]);
      mi.setActionCommand(colorNames[index]);
      mi.addActionListener(this);
      colors.add(mi);
}
```

Then build the menu for the names of the shapes:

```
for (int index=0; index != shapeNames.length; index++)
{
      MenuItem mi = new MenuItem(shapeNames[index]);
      mi.setActionCommand(shapeNames[index]);
      mi.addActionListener(this);
      shapes.add(mi);
}
```

Add the last menu item to the main menu that does not require a submenu:

```
MenuItem mi = new MenuItem("clear");
mi.setActionCommand("clear");
mi.addActionListener(this);
menu.add(mi);
```

Finally, add the pop-up menu with the component that it appears over:

```
this.add(menu);
```

When an `AWTEvent` is delivered to a component, there is some default processing that goes on before the event is dispatched to the appropriate event listeners. The Java run-time system will dispatch a mouse event to either the `processMouseEvent()` method or `processMouseMotionEvent()`, depending upon the type of the mouse event that occurred. Each of these methods will send the event object to the appropriate listener. By overriding either of the methods you can intercept the event object before it is passed on to a listener.

The `MouseEvent` class contains a method `isPopupTrigger` that will detect whether a specific mouse event was, in fact, a trigger event. By overriding the `processMouseEvent` method it is possible to detect whether a mouse button has acted as a trigger.

```
public void processMouseEvent(MouseEvent event)
{
     if (event.isPopupTrigger())

          // popup the menu over the container item
          menu.show(this,event.getX(), event.getY());
     else
          // invoke the superclass version of the processMouseEvent
          // to deal with mouse events other than a popup trigger
          super.processMouseEvent(event);
}
```

The `SketchPad` class that follows contains pop-up menus that allow a user to select the color and name of a shape to draw on the screen. Once a shape has been chosen, the mouse is used to define two points on the screen that define the size of the shape to be drawn. Several different geometrical shapes can be drawn on the sketch pad. To erase the shapes, the user can select Clear from the main pop-up menu. You now have enough information to be able to read through the following code and understand its functionality.

```java
import java.awt.*;
import java.awt.event.*;

public class SketchPad extends Dialog implements ActionListener
{
      private static int X_TOP_LH_CORNER = 5;
      private static int Y_TOP_LH_CORNER = 25;
      private static int SCREEN_TRIM_SIZE = 20;
      private static int HEIGHT_OF_BAR = 30;

      private int widthOfBox;
      private int heightOfBox;

      // coordinate of upper-left hand corner of a rectangle
      private int upperLeftX, upperLeftY;
      // size of surrounding rectangle
      private int width, height;
      // coordinates of two selected points
      private int x1,y1,x2,y2;

      // chosen color and shape - initialized to default values
      String drawColor = new String("black");
      String drawShape = new String("line");

      // contents of the popup menus stored in arrays
      String[] colorNames =
      {"black","blue","cyan","gray","green","magenta","red","yellow"};
      String[] shapeNames =
      {"line","square","rectangle","circle","ellipse"};

      PopupMenu menu;

      /**
      The SketchPad class enables an object that allows drawings of two-
      dimensional shapes.
      The shapes are contained within their own window.
      @param parent is the container for the SketchPad window.
      @param mode indicates whether the SketchPad is modal.
      */
      public SketchPad(Frame parent, boolean mode)
      {
            super(parent," This is a SketchPad .. right-click mouse button "+
                  "for menu", mode);

            int screenWidth = parent.getWidth();
            int screenHeight = parent.getHeight();
```

```
        // set location and size of dialog box
        int xLocationOfBox = (int)(0.075f * screenWidth);
        int yLocationOfBox = (int)(0.1f * screenHeight);
        widthOfBox     = (int)(0.4f * screenWidth);
        heightOfBox    = (int)(0.7f * screenHeight);

        // draw dialog box
        this.setLayout(null);
        this.setBackground(Color.white);
        this.setForeground(Color.blue);
        this.setLocation(xLocationOfBox,yLocationOfBox);
        this.setSize(widthOfBox,heightOfBox);

        // initialize components
        initializeMenuComponents();

        // set up remaining listeners
        addMouseListener(new HandleMouseEvents());
        addWindowListener(new CloseSketchPad());
}


/**
Display the SketchPad object on the screen.
*/
public void showSketchPad()
{
        this.setVisible(true);
}


// helper methods
private void initializeMenuComponents()
{
        // instantiate main popup menu
        menu = new PopupMenu();

        // add colors and shapes to the main menu
        PopupMenu colors = new PopupMenu("colors");
        menu.add(colors);
        PopupMenu shapes = new PopupMenu("shapes");
        menu.add(shapes);

        for (int index=0; index != colorNames.length; index++)
        {
                MenuItem mi = new MenuItem(colorNames[index]);
                mi.setActionCommand(colorNames[index]);
                mi.addActionListener(this);
```

```
                colors.add(mi);
        }


        for (int index=0; index != shapeNames.length; index++)
        {
                MenuItem mi = new MenuItem(shapeNames[index]);
                mi.setActionCommand(shapeNames[index]);
                mi.addActionListener(this);
                shapes.add(mi);
        }


        MenuItem mi = new MenuItem("clear");
        mi.setActionCommand("clear");
        mi.addActionListener(this);
        menu.add(mi);

        this.add(menu);
}


/**
Changes the color of a graphic to correspond with chosen color from
the menu.
@param g is a graphics object.
*/
protected void selectColor(Graphics g)
{
        for (int index=0; index != colorNames.length; index++)
        {
                if (drawColor.equals(colorNames[index]))
                {
                        switch (index)
                        {
                                case 0: g.setColor(Color.black);break;
                                case 1: g.setColor(Color.blue);break;
                                case 2: g.setColor(Color.cyan);break;
                                case 3: g.setColor(Color.gray);break;
                                case 4: g.setColor(Color.green);break;
                                case 5: g.setColor(Color.magenta);break;
                                case 6: g.setColor(Color.red);break;
                                case 7: g.setColor(Color.yellow);
                        }
                }
        }
}
```

```
public void actionPerformed(ActionEvent event)
// method to detect which item is chosen from a menu
{
      Graphics g = getGraphics();
      Object source = event.getActionCommand();

      // check for color chosen
      for (int index=0; index != colorNames.length; index++)
          if (source.equals(colorNames[index]))
          {
                drawColor =colorNames[index];
                return;
          }

      // check for shape chosen
      for (int index=0; index != shapeNames.length; index++)
          if (source.equals(shapeNames[index]))
          {
                drawShape = shapeNames[index];
                return;
          }

      // check for clear
      if (source.equals("clear"))
      {
            g.clearRect(0,0,widthOfBox,heightOfBox);
            return;
      }
}


public void processMouseEvent(MouseEvent event)
{
      if (event.isPopupTrigger())
            menu.show(this,event.getX(), event.getY());
      else
            super.processMouseEvent(event);
}

// inner classes to handle mouse and window events
private class HandleMouseEvents extends MouseAdapter
{
      // capture initial coordinates of mouse
      public void mousePressed(MouseEvent event)
```

```
        {
                upperLeftX=0; upperLeftY=0; width=0; height=0;

                x1=event.getX();
                y1=event.getY();
        }

        // draw the appropriate shape when mouse button released;
        // shape will be drawn between the coordinates (x1,y1) and
        // (x2,y2)
        public void mouseReleased(MouseEvent event)
        {
                Graphics g = getGraphics();

                selectColor(g);
                x2=event.getX();
                y2=event.getY();

                upperLeftX = Math.min(x1,x2);
                upperLeftY = Math.min(y1,y2);
                width = Math.abs(x1-x2);
                height = Math.abs(y1-y2);

                // draw appropriate shape
                if (drawShape.equals("line"))
                        g.drawLine(x1,y1,x2,y2);
                else if (drawShape.equals("square"))
                        g.drawRect(upperLeftX,upperLeftY,width,width);
                else if (drawShape.equals("rectangle"))
                        g.drawRect(upperLeftX,upperLeftY,width,height);
                else if (drawShape.equals("circle"))
                        g.drawOval(upperLeftX,upperLeftY,width,width);
                else if (drawShape.equals("ellipse"))
                        g.drawOval(upperLeftX,upperLeftY,width,height);
        }
}

private class CloseSketchPad extends WindowAdapter
{
        public void windowClosing(WindowEvent event)
        {
                SketchPad.this.dispose();
        }
}
}
```

Program `Example_6` tests the methods of the class `SketchPad`.

```
class Example_6
{
      public static void main(String[] args)
      {
            WindowPane screen = new WindowPane();
            screen.showWindowPane();

            SketchPad geoShapes = new SketchPad(screen, false);
            geoShapes.showSketchPad();
      }
}
```

Here is a screen shot of the running program.

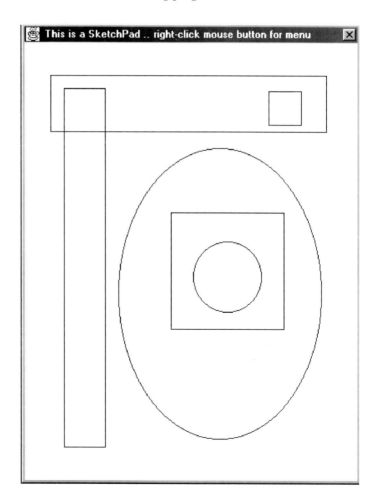

NOW DO THIS   Modify `SketchPad` to allow for drawing regular polygons.

9.6   Painting the Screen

There is one major drawback with the `SketchPad` class. To see what the drawback is, modify Program `Example_6` to create two `SketchPad` objects. Run the program; both sketch pads will appear, one on top of the other. Move the top sketch pad and place it alongside the lower sketchpad. Draw shapes on the lower sketch pad. Move the upper sketch pad back over the lower pad, and then away from the lower pad. You will notice that the original drawings of the shapes have been erased. What can be the reason for this behavior?

As you have just witnessed, when you make a change to a drawing, your drawing is not automatically updated. A window is automatically painted by the window manager whenever the window appears for the first time or when it is minimized, then maximized again. In the case of the sketch pad, we needed to deliberately repaint the screen after the upper sketch-pad object has been moved away from the lower sketch-pad object, thereby restoring the previously drawn shapes.

The `Graphics` class contains two methods, `paint` and `repaint`, that will allow the programmer to paint the window when necessary. However, the `paint` method is automatically invoked by the window manager and should not normally be invoked directly from within a program. If you want a window to be repainted, then call `repaint`, which will in turn invoke the `paint` method for you.

Alternatively, you can override the `paint` method in your own program and let the window manager invoke the method automatically. However, remember not to invoke the `paint` method directly in your program.

The `SketchPad` class did not contain any data structure for storing the drawings of the shapes, so there was no means of referring back to the history of what had already been drawn. If we had overridden the `paint` method in the `SketchPad` class, then there would be no means of retrieving previously drawn shapes in order to repaint them on the screen.

Before we can save graphical objects in a data structure we first need to create them. In fact, it is necessary to create new classes of `Line`, `Square`, `Rectangle`, `Circle`, and `Ellipse`. These classes all inherit from the superclass `Shape`, which also needs to created. Figure 9.7 illustrates the hierarchy of these shape classes.

The implementation of the superclass `Shape` follows.

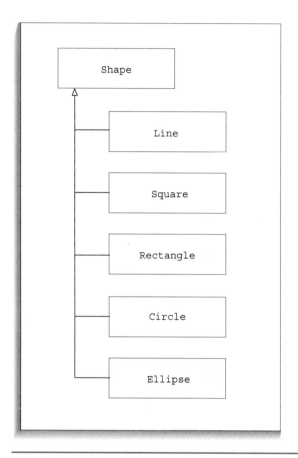

Figure 9.7 A hierarchy of shapes

```
import java.io.*;
import java.awt.*;

abstract class Shape implements Serializable
{
      protected int x1,y1,x2,y2;
      protected Color color;

      public Shape(){};
      public abstract void drawShape(Graphics g);

}
```

As you can see, the abstract class declares the basic attributes of a shape, such as the coordinates of two points needed to form the shape and the color of the shape. The class also declares an abstract method for drawing a shape. As an example of the coding of the subclasses, consider the contents of the class Rectangle that inherits from the class Shape.

```java
import java.io.*;
import java.awt.*;

public class Rectangle extends Shape implements Serializable
{
      public Rectangle(int x1,int y1,int x2,int y2,Color c)
      {
            this.x1=x1; this.y1=y1; this.x2=x2; this.y2=y2;
            this.color = c;
      }

      public void drawShape(Graphics g)
      {
            g.drawRect(x1,y1,x2,y2);
      }
}
```

Once the coordinates of the two points for drawing a rectangle and the color of the shape have been established, a Rectangle object is created by invoking the constructor and storing the data as instance variables.

NOW DO THIS   Complete the classes for a Line, Square, Circle, and Ellipse.

On every occasion of drawing a shape on the screen, an object of the same shape is instantiated and stored in a vector. Having a vector store every shape object that is drawn can be used to your advantage. First, the repository of shapes can be used to update the paint method, so that a full history of all the shapes drawn is always maintained on the screen. And second, we now have a repository of shapes that can be saved to a file.

Assuming that we have instantiated the following vector

```java
private Vector store = new Vector();
```

the mouseReleased method used to draw a shape on the screen is amended to instantiate a shape and store this shape in the vector in the code that follows. Apart from the changes shown, this code is identical to that for the SketchPad class.

```
public void mouseReleased(MouseEvent event)
{
        .
        .
        .

      // draw appropriate shape and save shape
      if (drawShape.equals("line"))
      {
            Line l = new Line(x1,y1,x2,y2,color);
            l.drawShape(g);
            store.addElement(l);
      }
      else if (drawShape.equals("square"))
      {
            Square s = new
            Square(upperLeftX,upperLeftY,width,height,color);
            s.drawShape(g);
            store.addElement(s);
      }
      else if (drawShape.equals("rectangle"))
      {
            Rectangle r =
                      new Rectangle(upperLeftX,upperLeftY,width,height,color);
            r.drawShape(g);
            store.addElement(r);
      }

        .
        .
        .

}
```

Now that we have created a vector of shapes that grows in size every time a new shape is drawn on the screen, we can use this vector to update the `paint` method as follows. Notice that the code makes particular use of polymorphism for the method `drawShape`.

```
public void paint(Graphics g)
{
      for (int index=0; index != store.size(); index++)
      {
            Shape shape = (Shape)store.elementAt(index);
            g.setColor(shape.color);

            shape.drawShape(g);
      }
}
```

Remember the window manager automatically invokes the `paint` method, so you do not need to invoke it directly from within the program. Simply overriding the `paint` method and including it in the `SketchPad` class is all that needs to be done.

9.7   Printing Objects

Before you start printing an object you must first set up a "print job." First invoke the system dialog box that requests information about a print job. This is performed by invoking the `getPrintJob` from the `Toolkit` class.

```
Toolkit toolkit = this.getToolkit();
PrintJob job = toolkit.getPrintJob(bigBrother,"",new Properties());
```

The `Properties` class is used to implement the system properties list, which supports user customization by allowing programs to look up the value of named resources. In this example we simply create a `Properties` object using the default constructor of the `Properties` class.

A `PrintJob` object represents a single printing session or "job." The `PrintJob` class is abstract; therefore, it cannot be instantiated directly and hence we need to invoke the `getPrintJob` method of the `Toolkit` class.

The `PrintJob` class contains a `getGraphics` method to allow for the creation of a graphics page.

```
Graphics page = job.getGraphics();
```

We next obtain the size of the page and center the output on the page.

```
Dimension size = this.getSize();
Dimension pageSize = job.getPageDimension();
page.translate((pageSize.width-size.width)/2,
               (pageSize.height-size.height)/2);
```

Finally, we print the page, dispose of the page object, and end the print job.

```
this.print(page);
page.dispose();
job.end();
```

Using the changes developed in this and the previous two sections, we have rewritten the `SketchPad` class as the `DrawingPad` class. The coding of the `DrawingPad` class follows.

```
import java.awt.*;
import java.awt.event.*;
```

```java
import java.io.*;
import java.util.*;

public class DrawingPad extends Dialog implements ActionListener
{
        private static int X_TOP_LH_CORNER = 5;
        private static int Y_TOP_LH_CORNER = 25;
        private static int SCREEN_TRIM_SIZE = 20;
        private static int HEIGHT_OF_BAR = 30;

        private int widthOfBox;
        private int heightOfBox;
        private Frame container;

        // coordinate of upper-left hand corner of a rectangle
        private int upperLeftX, upperLeftY;
        // size of surrounding rectangle
        private int width, height;
        // coordinates of two selected points
        private int x1,y1,x2,y2;
        // vector for storing geometrical shapes
        private Vector store = new Vector();

        // chosen color and shape - initialized to default values
        String drawColor = new String("black");
        Color  color     = Color.black;
        String drawShape = new String("line");

        // contents of the popup menus stored in arrays
        String[] colorNames  = {"black","blue","cyan","gray","green",
                                "magenta","red","yellow"};
        String[] shapeNames  = {"line","square","rectangle",
                                "circle","ellipse"};
        String[] optionNames = {"clear","save","load","print"};

        PopupMenu menu;

        // constructor
        public DrawingPad(Frame parent, boolean mode)
        {
                super(parent,
                " This is a DrawingPad .. right-click mouse for menu", mode);
                container = parent;

                int screenWidth = parent.getWidth();
                int screenHeight = parent.getHeight();
```

```
      // set location and size of dialog box
      int xLocationOfBox = (int)(0.075f * screenWidth);
      int yLocationOfBox = (int)(0.1f * screenHeight);
      widthOfBox     = (int)(0.4f * screenWidth);
      heightOfBox    = (int)(0.7f * screenHeight);

      // draw dialog box
      this.setLayout(null);
      this.setBackground(Color.white);
      this.setForeground(Color.blue);
      this.setLocation(xLocationOfBox,yLocationOfBox);
      this.setSize(widthOfBox,heightOfBox);

      // initialize components
      initializeMenuComponents();

      // set up remaining listeners
      addMouseListener(new HandleMouseEvents());
      addWindowListener(new CloseDrawingPad());
}

// instance method
public void showDrawingPad()
{
      this.setVisible(true);
}

// helper methods
private void initializeMenuComponents()
{
      // instantiate main popup menu
      menu = new PopupMenu();

      // to the main menu
      PopupMenu colors = new PopupMenu("colors");
      menu.add(colors);
      PopupMenu shapes = new PopupMenu("shapes");
      menu.add(shapes);
      PopupMenu options = new PopupMenu("options");
      menu.add(options);

      for (int index=0; index != colorNames.length; index++)
      {
            MenuItem mi = new MenuItem(colorNames[index]);
            mi.setActionCommand(colorNames[index]);
            mi.addActionListener(this);
```

```
                colors.add(mi);
        }


        for (int index=0; index != shapeNames.length; index++)
        {
                MenuItem mi = new MenuItem(shapeNames[index]);
                mi.setActionCommand(shapeNames[index]);
                mi.addActionListener(this);
                shapes.add(mi);
        }


        for (int index=0; index != optionNames.length; index++)
        {
                MenuItem mi = new MenuItem(optionNames[index]);
                mi.setActionCommand(optionNames[index]);
                mi.addActionListener(this);
                options.add(mi);
        }


        this.add(menu);
}


// method to change color of graphic to correspond
// with chosen menu item
protected void selectColor(Graphics g)
{
        for (int index=0; index != colorNames.length; index++)
        {
                if (drawColor.equals(colorNames[index]))
                {
                        switch (index)
                        {
                                case 0: color=Color.black;
                                        g.setColor(color);break;
                                case 1: color=Color.blue;
                                        g.setColor(color);break;
                                case 2: color=Color.cyan;
                                        g.setColor(color);break;
                                case 3: color=Color.gray;
                                        g.setColor(color);break;
                                case 4: color=Color.green;
                                        g.setColor(color);break;
                                case 5: color=Color.magenta;
                                        g.setColor(color);break;
                                case 6: color=Color.red;
```

```
                                    g.setColor(color);break;
                    case 7: color=Color.yellow;
                                    g.setColor(color);

                }
            }
        }
    }

public void actionPerformed(ActionEvent event)
// method to detect which item is chosen from a menu
{
        Object source = event.getActionCommand();

        // check for color chosen
        for (int index=0; index != colorNames.length; index++)
            if (source.equals(colorNames[index]))
            {
                    drawColor =colorNames[index];
                    return;
            }

        // check for shape chosen
        for (int index=0; index != shapeNames.length; index++)
            if (source.equals(shapeNames[index]))
            {
                    drawShape = shapeNames[index];
                    return;
            }

        // check for clear
        if (source.equals("clear"))
        {
            // clear contents of vector for storing shapes
            store.removeAllElements();
            repaint();
            return;
        }

        // check for save
        if (source.equals("save"))
        {
            FileDialog file = new
            FileDialog(container,"",FileDialog.SAVE);
            file.show();
```

```
String filename = file.getFile();
if (filename != null)
{
      try
      {
            FileOutputStream fos = new
            FileOutputStream(filename);
            ObjectOutputStream out = new
            ObjectOutputStream(fos);
            out.writeObject(store);
            out.flush();
            out.close();
      }
      catch (IOException e){}
}

return;
}

// check for load
if (source.equals("load"))
{
   FileDialog file = new
   FileDialog(container,"",FileDialog.LOAD);
   file.show();

   String filename = file.getFile();

   if (filename != null)
   {
      try
      {
            FileInputStream fis = new
            FileInputStream(filename);
            ObjectInputStream in = new
            ObjectInputStream(fis);

            Vector newStore = (Vector)in.readObject();
            in.close();
            store = newStore;
            repaint();
      }
      catch (Exception e){}
   }
```

```java
            return;
    }


    // check for print
    if (source.equals("print"))
    {
            // get a print job object
            Toolkit toolkit = this.getToolkit();
            PrintJob job = toolkit.getPrintJob(container,"",
                                            new Properties());

            // check if the user clicked Cancel in the print dialog
            if (job == null) return;

            // get a Graphics object for the first page of output
            Graphics page = job.getGraphics();

            // check the size of the drawing and the page
            Dimension size = this.getSize();
            Dimension pageSize = job.getPageDimension();

            // center the output on the page
            page.translate((pageSize.width-size.width)/2,
                        (pageSize.height-size.height)/2);

            // print the drawing
            this.print(page);

            // clean up
            page.dispose();
            job.end();

            return;
    }

}


public void paint(Graphics g)
{
    for (int index=0; index != store.size(); index++)
    {
            Shape shape = (Shape)store.elementAt(index);
            g.setColor(shape.color);

            shape.drawShape(g);
    }
}
```

```
public void processMouseEvent(MouseEvent event)
{
    if (event.isPopupTrigger())
        menu.show(this,event.getX(), event.getY());
    else
        super.processMouseEvent(event);
}

private class HandleMouseEvents extends MouseAdapter
{
    // capture initial coordinates of mouse
    public void mousePressed(MouseEvent event)
    {
        upperLeftX=0; upperLeftY=0; width=0; height=0;

        x1=event.getX();
        y1=event.getY();
    }

    // draw the appropriate shape when mouse button released;
    // shape will be drawn between the coordinates (x1,y1) and
    // (x2,y2)
    public void mouseReleased(MouseEvent event)
    {
        Graphics g = getGraphics();

        selectColor(g);
        x2=event.getX();
        y2=event.getY();

        upperLeftX = Math.min(x1,x2);
        upperLeftY = Math.min(y1,y2);
        width = Math.abs(x1-x2);
        height = Math.abs(y1-y2);

        // draw appropriate shape and save shape
        if (drawShape.equals("line"))
        {
            Line l = new Line(x1,y1,x2,y2,color);
            l.drawShape(g);
            store.addElement(l);
        }
        else if (drawShape.equals("square"))
        {
            Square s = new
            Square(upperLeftX,upperLeftY,width,height,color);
```

```
                        s.drawShape(g);
                        store.addElement(s);
                }
                else if (drawShape.equals("rectangle"))
                {
                        Rectangle r = new Rectangle(upperLeftX,upperLeftY,
                                              width,height,color);
                        r.drawShape(g);
                        store.addElement(r);
                }
                else if (drawShape.equals("circle"))
                {
                        Circle c = new Circle(upperLeftX,upperLeftY,
                                          width,height,color);
                        c.drawShape(g);
                        store.addElement(c);
                }
                else if (drawShape.equals("ellipse"))
                {
                        Ellipse e = new Ellipse(upperLeftX,upperLeftY,
                                           width,height,color);
                        e.drawShape(g);
                        store.addElement(e);
                }
            }
        }

        private class CloseDrawingPad extends WindowAdapter
        {
                public void windowClosing(WindowEvent event)
                {
                        DrawingPad.this.dispose();
                }
        }
}
```

Program `Example_7` is used to test the methods of the `DrawingPad` class.

```
class Example_7
{
        public static void main(String[] args)
        {
                WindowPane screen = new WindowPane();
                screen.showWindowPane();
```

```
        DrawingPad geoShapes = new DrawingPad(screen, false);
        geoShapes.showDrawingPad();
    }
}
```

A screen shot of the running program follows.

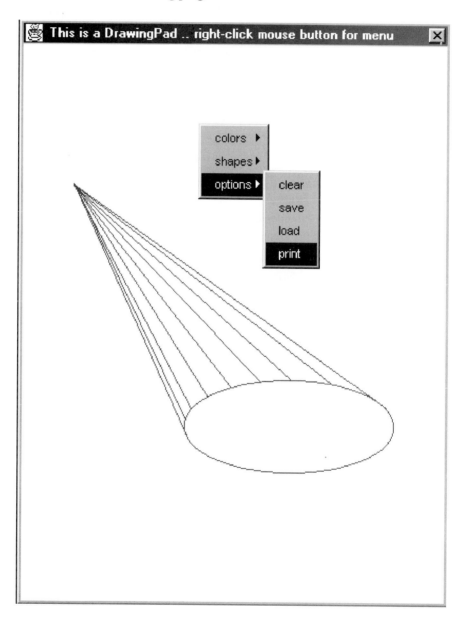

SUMMARY

- A Vector structure is similar to a one-dimensional array, with the exception that it is truly dynamic since it will grow with the amount of data that is being added to it.

- The contents of a vector may be copied into a one-dimensional array.

- The vector class contains many instance methods that permit information to be obtained about the vector and the data stored in the vector.

- A `Graphics` class is available for drawing shapes. To create an object of type `Graphics` it is necessary to call the method `getGraphics()`.

- The `Graphics` class contains methods to draw a variety of shapes that include a straight line, rectangle, ellipse, and polygon.

- Mouse events have two listener interfaces—(1) `MouseListener` to listen for mouse button activity such as pressed, clicked, and released and (2) `MouseMotionListener` to listen for the mouse being dragged or moved.

- The position of the mouse can be obtained from the methods `getX` and `getY` in the `MouseEvent` class.

- A window manager automatically paints a window when an event such as resizing the window takes place. Never call the `paint` method directly in a program. Either use the `repaint` method or just override the `paint` method in the program and let the window manager call it automatically.

- Objects that implement the `Serializable` interface may be stored in serial files.

- Objects are written to a serial file using the `writeObject` method from the `ObjectOutput` class. They are read from a serial file using the `readObject` method from the `ObjectInput` class. Both classes are found in the `java.io` package.

- The `PrintJob` class from the `awt` contains methods that will permit details of objects to be printed on a page.

Review Questions

1. How does a vector differ from an array?

2. Distinguish between the instance methods `size` and `capacity` in the class `Vector`.

3. What is the fundamental error in the following statement?

   ```
   Graphics g = new Graphics();
   ```

4. Code a `Graphics` method to draw a straight line between the points [50,50] and [250,250].

5. Repeat Question 4 to draw a rectangle between the stated points.

6. Code a `Graphics` method to draw the string `"HELLO WORLD"` from the coordinates [100,50].

7. Code a `Graphics` method to draw a rectangle, given the coordinates of the bottom right-hand corner as (x1,y1) and the coordinates of the top left-hand corner as (x2,y2).

8. What is the purpose of the `paint` method?

9. How do you invoke the `paint` method?

10. What is the difference between a mouse being dragged and a mouse being moved?

11. How can you obtain the values of mouse coordinates?

12. What is the `MouseMotionAdapter` class?

13. What two methods must be implemented in the `MouseMotionListener` interface?

14. Use skeletal code to explain how a `MouseMotionAdapter` class can be used to implement the event of a mouse being moved.

15. What is a pop-up menu and what triggers it?

16. In the `MouseEvent` class, what method will detect whether a mouse event was a trigger event?

17. What must a class implement for its objects to be written to a serial file?

18. List, in order, the operations for storing objects in a serializable file.

19. List, in order, the operations for retrieving objects from a serializable file.

20. What is a `PrintJob` object?

Exercises

21. Using the Java documentation for the class `Vector`, describe the functions of the following methods.

    (a) `public final boolean contains(Object elem);`

    (b) `public final synchronized void copyInto(Object[] anArray);`

    (c) `public final boolean isEmpty();`

    (d) `public final int lastIndexOf(Object elem);`

22. Desk check the following program segment; explain the meaning of the statements, and draw the contents of the vector `dataStore` after the execution of each statement.

```
Vector dataStore = new Vector(1);
dataStore.addElement("Sybil");
dataStore.addElement("Basil");
dataStore.addElement("Polly");
```

In Questions 23 and 24, you should write Java code to do the following.

23. Set up three text fields labeled `Red`, `Green`, and `Blue`. Input numbers in the range 0—-255 in each box. Display a square area of the screen that represents the RGB color. Read your Java documentation to find a suitable method in the class `Color` that computes RGB color.

24. Rotate a compass needle on the screen about a fixed point in response to the mouse being moved around the screen.

Programming Problems

25. Devise a system for maintaining a file of subscribers to a telephone directory. Pay particular attention to always entering your data into a vector so that it remains in ascending order of the surname of the subscriber. Use a full graphical interface in your system.

In Questions 26 to 30, remember with nonevent-driven graphical output to override the `paint` method for displaying the graphical information.

26. Write a program to plot the path of a small circle moving around the circumference of a larger circle.

27. Use the polar equation

$$r = a(1 + e.\cos\theta)$$

where

$$0 \le \theta \le 2\pi$$

and

$$x = r \cdot \sin\theta \text{ and } y = r \cdot \cos\theta.$$

Write a program to plot graphs of the equation for $e = 0.5$, 1, and 2. Select a value for a so that the graphs are large enough to fill the screen. *Hint:* Try values of a between 20 and 100.

28. An analysis of examination results at a school gave the following distribution of grades for all subjects taken in one year.

Grade	%
A	10
B	25
C	45
D	20

Write a program to represent the distribution of each grade in a pie chart, where each slice of pie is drawn in a different color.

29. The monthly sales figures (units sold) for a computer manufacturing company are as follows.

Jan	Feb	Mar	Apr	May	Jun	Jul	Aug	Sep	Oct	Nov	Dec
20	25	37	27	19	25	34	40	50	60	55	42

Write a program to plot a histogram of the sales.

30. Return to your answer to Question 48 in Chapter 6. Replace the textual output with a graphical output that plots the movement of the airplanes on their various courses.

CHAPTER 10

Objects Working Together

Classes on their own have very limited use. Generally, systems are built from many cooperating classes, where objects work together to form the functionality of a complete system.

This chapter brings your knowledge of object-oriented programming to a level where you can start to build software systems that comprise many related classes. By the end of the chapter you will have gained knowledge in the following areas.

- The creation of programmer-defined packages containing classes that are related through a common theme.

- A technique using CRC cards for discovering classes, methods, and relationships with other classes.

- The concept of a class being formed by the sum of its associated component classes.

- An understanding of "whole—part" relationships between classes.

- Further UML notation for the development and documentation of software.

- Panel and pull-down menu classes from the `java.awt` package.

- The development of a small management system.

10.1 Packages

Now that we have created several useful graphical user interface classes in Chapters 8 and 9 (such as `CheckBoxes`, `DataInputBox`, `ScrollableList`, `RadioButtons`, `WritingPad`, and `WindowPane`), it would be helpful to be able to use these classes in other chapters of the book without needing to copy the class files to the subdirectories in which they are to be used. In other words, we need a mechanism for creating class files that can be stored in only one subdirectory and yet used by Java programs stored in any subdirectory on your computer, as was done with the `avi` package used throughout this book.

You are already familiar with importing some of Java's standard API packages into a program, for example:

```
import java.io.*;
import java.util.*;
import java.awt.*;
import java.awt.event.*;
```

and using the classes defined in the respective packages. Java also permits the inclusion of programmer-defined packages, so you can define a package containing the implementation of your own classes.

Just as the authors created the `avi` package, you can create a package for holding the components developed in the previous two chapters. The classes created in Chapters 8 and 9 were in the context of a graphical user interface (GUI); therefore, it would be appropriate to create a package called `gui` to contain the classes from those chapters that are itemized above.

To include the implementation of these classes as part of the package `gui`, we need to use a `package` statement at the beginning of each class file. The `package` statement must appear as the first noncomment, nonblank line in a Java source code file. For example, the class `WindowPane` would contain the `package` statement at the beginning of the source file, as follows.

```
package gui;

import java.awt.*;
import java.awt.event.*;

public class WindowPane extends Frame
{
    // size of window
    private static int width;
    private static int height;

    .
    .
```

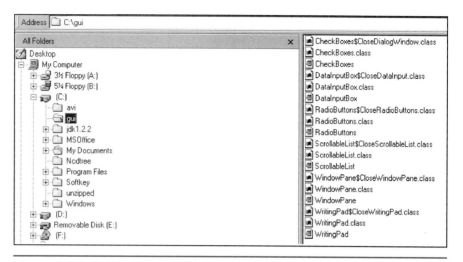

Figure 10.1 The contents of the `gui` subdirectory

Java places each package in its own subdirectory, where the name of the subdirectory is the same as the package name. The modified source file `WindowPane.java` must be moved to the subdirectory `gui` that has already been created.

The modified source file is then compiled using the `javac` command in the normal way. Figure 10.1 illustrates the contents of the `gui` subdirectory. Six of the class files developed in Chapters 8 and 9 have been modified to include the `package gui;` statement at the beginning of each file. The files were then moved into the `gui` subdirectory and separately compiled. Notice that any defined inner classes, such as the `CloseDialogueWindow` class, are translated into separate `.class` files by the compiler. The names of these `.class` files include the name of the outer class, followed by a `$`, followed by the name of the inner class.

Since Java is designed to be independent from any one environment, a `CLASSPATH` environmental variable is used to determine where the Java compiler is to start looking for programmer-defined classes. The `CLASSPATH` entry associated with the `avi` package used throughout this book was set to `CLASSPATH=.;c:\` in the `autoexec.bat` file.

The interpretation of this `CLASSPATH` entry follows. The pathways are separated by the semicolon, and hence there are two pathways the computer should use when searching for the named packages. The first pathway is signified by the use of a period (`.`) that implies the current directory. The computer first searches all subdirectories of the current subdirectory to find the subdirectory of the named package.

The second pathway is signified by `c:\` which is the root directory of the C drive. The computer will search all the subdirectories of the root directory to find the subdirectory of the named package.

A subdirectory `gui` is created at the same level as the subdirectory `avi`; in other words, both subdirectories are at the first level down the tree from the root directory on drive `C`; it is not necessary to change the settings of the `CLASSPATH` variable in the `autoexec.bat` file from the original setting you created in the Introduction at the beginning of the book.

> ⚠ The setting of the `CLASSPATH` environmental variable will differ in a Windows environment and a UNIX environment; consult the appropriate manual for the UNIX system you are using.

The first program in this chapter uses the classes `ScrollableList`, `WindowPane`, and `WritingPad` that now form part of the `gui` package. The program invites a user to select from a scrollable list any number of classical musicians; when the selection is complete, the names of those musicians chosen are displayed on the `WritingPad` object. Remember: The subdirectory containing class `Example_1` does not contain any of the classes used in the `main` method. All these classes are available in the `gui` package, and hence you need to use `import gui.*` at the beginning of the program.

```java
import gui.*;

public class Example_1
{
    public static void main(String[] args)
    {
        String[] names =
        {"Chopin", "Mozart","Bach","Debussy","Bruch","Tchaikovsky",
         "Schubert","Elgar","Britten","Beethoven","Holst","Smetana",
         "Handel","Prokofiev","Rossini","Brahms","Gershwin","Dvorak"};

        WindowPane screen = new WindowPane();
        screen.showWindowPane();
        WritingPad notes = new WritingPad(screen);
        notes.showWritingPad();
        ScrollableList inputNames = new
        ScrollableList(screen, "Classical musicians ..", names);
        inputNames.showList();

        boolean[] chosenFew = new boolean[names.length];
        chosenFew = inputNames.getSelectedItems();

        notes.write("\n\nList of chosen classical musicians\n\n");
```

```
for (int index=0; index != chosenFew.length; index++)
{
        if (chosenFew[index])
              notes.write(names[index]+"\n");
}
    }
}
```

Two screen shots from the running program follow:

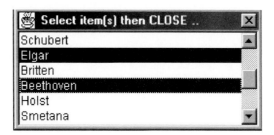

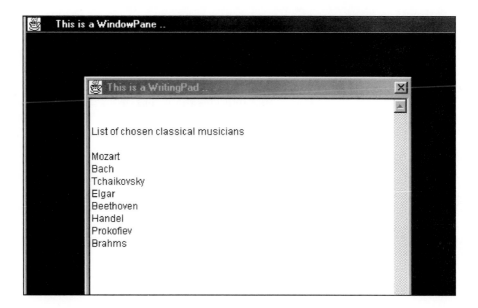

Instead of using the * wildcard in the statement import gui.*; you can list each of the specific classes that are being imported. Program Example_1 could be modified to:

```
import gui.WindowPane;
import gui.WritingPad;
import gui.ScrollableList;
```

This style of coding has the advantage that you see exactly what classes you are importing from the package and, therefore, you have documented the dependencies the current class has on other classes. For example, class `Example_1` is dependent upon the classes `WindowPane`, `WritingPad`, and `ScrollableList`.

You may wonder about the outcome of importing several packages that contain classes that have the same name. One solution to the problem is to invent unique names for the classes in programmer-defined classes.

Alternatively, if you find there is a clash between two class names from different packages, then simply qualify the names with the name of the package. For example, the `Window` class occurs in both the `java.awt` package and the `avi` package. In coding the `FilmStrip` class of the `avi` package we used the `Window` class of the `java.awt` package. The clash of names was resolved as follows:

```
package avi;        // the avi package already contains a Window class
import java.awt.*;  // the java.awt package also contains a Window class
.

public class FilmStrip extends java.awt.Window
{
    .

    .
```

The `FilmStrip` class needed to use the methods of the `java.awt.Window` class and not the methods of the `avi.Window` class, and so we included the qualification of which `Window` class to use.

Figure 10.2 indicates the names of the classes within the `gui` package that are available for public use. This figure uses the UML notation for describing a package. The package name is contained within a tab drawn on the top left-hand side of a larger rectangle, thus representing a folder icon. Each class is

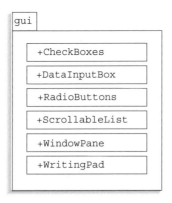

Figure 10.2 UML representation of the package `gui`

labeled within an inner rectangle. The + sign in front of the name of a class indicates that the class has been written for `public` use.

A *dependency* between two packages exists if any dependency exists between any two classes in the packages. If you inspect the source listings of the classes of the `gui` package, you will notice that they all import from the `java.awt` package and the `java.awt.event` package. Additionally, all classes import from the `java.lang` package by default. These dependencies can be shown by the UML diagram in Figure 10.3.

Notice that, because the `java.awt.event` package is stored as a subdirectory of the `java.awt` package, the `event` package is nested within the `awt` package.

If there are any future changes to any of the classes in the `awt` and `event` packages, both of which are used by classes in the `gui` package, then the changes would have an effect on the classes in the `gui` package. Such changes to future versions of Java cannot be ruled out; however, such changes to `awt` and `event` at this stage in the development of the language are thought to be unlikely.

The use of packages is vital in the development of large projects. The grouping together of related classes in a single package improves the development and management of a project and helps create a reusable library of components.

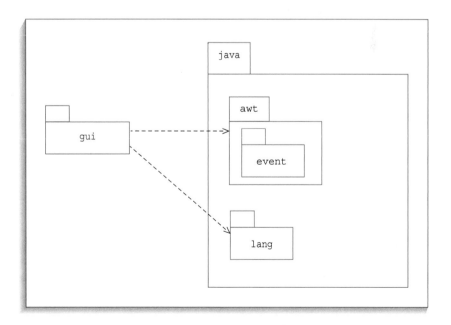

Figure 10.3 UML diagram showing dependencies between packages

In summary, the use of packages provides you with the following benefits.

- The ability to use any of the classes in a package, in any classes in other directories on your computer.

- A means of resolving name clashes between classes. For example, both the `java.awt` and `avi` packages contain a `Window` class.

- Improved management of software.

NOW DO THIS

(1) Invent your own class called `SimpleMath` that contains methods to perform simple arithmetic on double-precision numbers.

(2) Create a package named `arithmetic`, and include the `SimpleMath` class in this package.

(3) Adjust your `CLASSPATH` variable accordingly.

(4) Compile the `SimpleMath` class.

(5) Write a separate program, stored in a different subdirectory from your package, that imports `arithmetic.*`, and test the invocation of the methods of your `SimpleMath` class.

10.2 Associations

Imagine that we are required to write a program to create a numeric calculator as a graphical object. Figure 10.4 illustrates such a calculator.

The calculator is built from several components. From Figure 10.4 it is evident that the calculator contains a numeric key pad for input of the digits of a number, a negative sign, a decimal point, and the option to cancel a number; a function pad to select an operator and hence perform a calculation on a pair of numbers; and a display to show the number as it is entered into the calculator, or to show the result of a calculation.

In writing a program to create a calculator as a graphical object, we will need to design classes that represent a `Calculator` as the container class to allow objects of type `NumericKeyPad`, `FunctionPad`, and `Display` to be held by the container.

Let's consider the methods required for each class. The `Calculator` class needs only to show itself on the screen; hence a method `showCalculator` is required. Since we need to be able to read data from and write data to the display, we need to include methods to `read` and `write` in the `Display` class. The `FunctionPad` class contains a method to calculate the value for whatever two

Figure 10.4 A numeric calculator

numbers have been entered into the calculator and to display the result. Finally, the `NumericKeyPad` class is required to show the digits of a number on the display when the appropriate numeric keys are pressed.

Until now we have tended to develop classes that have been independent of each other. As we develop more complex programs it is necessary for objects from one class to work together with objects of another class. An *association* is a structural relationship that specifies objects from one class that are connected to objects of another class. Associations form the "glue" that holds objects from different classes together to build a computer program.

The associations of the calculator, the numeric key pad, the function pad, and the display are depicted by the UML class diagram illustrated in Figure 10.5.

An association can be given a name to describe the relationship between two objects. The name contains a direction triangle that points in the direction you want to read. For example, from Figure 10.5, a `Display` object is *part of* a `Calculator` object, a `FunctionPad` object is *part of* a `Calculator` object, and a `NumericKeyPad` is *part of* a `Calculator` object.

In an association it is important to state how many objects may be connected across the instance of an association. The number of objects in an association is known as the *multiplicity* of an association and is written as an expression that evaluates to a range of values. In Figure 10.5, the use of the expression containing just 1 represents a single `Display` object, a single `FunctionPad` object, and a single `Display` object. Further examples using multiplicity will be given later in this chapter.

The `Calculator` class will extend the `Dialog` class in order to create a graphical component that can be moved about any parent container object. This

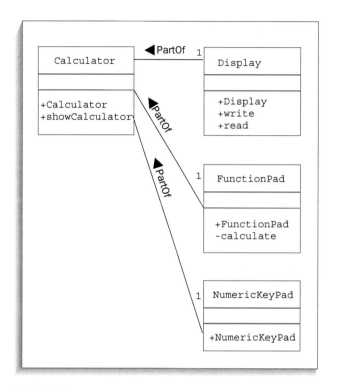

Figure 10.5 UML class diagram showing the associations between the classes

technique is the same as that practiced for all of the graphical objects implemented in Chapter 9. The location, size, and color of the `Calculator` container is also established.

Having created the `Calculator` container, we can easily instantiate objects for the `Display`, `NumericKeyPad`, and `FunctionPad` and set the location and size of these objects in the `Calculator` container. The skeletal code that describes this operation follows.

```
public class Calculator extends Dialog
{
        .

    public Calculator(Frame parent)
    {
            .
            .

        // set location and size of calculator

        // add display to calculator
        Display display = new Display();
```

```
        display.setLocation(1,25);
        display.setSize(150,30);
        add(display);

        // add numeric keypad to calculator
        NumericKeyPad keys = new NumericKeyPad(display);
        keys.setLocation(15,65);
        keys.setSize(90,150);
        add(keys);

        // add function pad to calculator
        FunctionPad functions = new FunctionPad(display);
        functions.setLocation(110,65);
        functions.setSize(30,150);
        add(functions);
    }

        .
        .
        .
```

Before we continue with the coding of the three component classes, we need to introduce a new container class `Panel` from the `java.awt` package.

A `Panel` class is a container that does not create a separate window of its own but is itself contained within a container. `Panel` is suitable for holding portions of a larger graphical user interface within a parent container. The actual panel is invisible unless you set the background color of the panel. The panel serves as a convenient container, allowing subsets of components to be arranged and placed within a larger container.

The `Display`, `FunctionPad`, and `NumericKeyPad` classes should all extend the `Panel` class in order to place their respective components into a container that is a `Panel`. The coding for the `Display` class follows; this is the shortest and simplest class to understand.

```
import java.awt.*;

public class Display extends Panel
{
    TextField data;

    /**
    The Display class enables a text field to be added to a panel.
    */
    public Display()
    {
        super();
        setLayout(new FlowLayout(FlowLayout.CENTER));
```

```
        data = new TextField("",16);
        this.add(data);
}


/**
Writes a string to the display.
@param value of the string to be written.
*/
public void write(String datum)
{
        data.setText(datum);
}


/**
Reads the datum stored in the display.
@return The string stored in the display.
*/
public String read()
{
        return data.getText();
}
}
```

In the `Display` class, a text field is set up within the panel; a string can be written to the text field, and the contents of the text field can be read as a string of information. If you examine the skeletal coding of the `Calculator` class, you will notice how simple it is to add a `Display` component to the class:

```
// add display to calculator
Display display = new Display();
display.setLocation(1,25);
display.setSize(150,30);
add(display);
```

This is a matter of instantiating a `Display` object, which of course comes with its own panel, setting the location and size of the `Display` object, then adding the object to the calculator container.

The `NumericKeyPad` class is dependent upon the `Display` class. The complete listing of the `NumericKeyPad` source code follows.

Note that the constructor uses a grid layout to arrange the buttons, with the buttons inserted into the grid from left to right, top to bottom.

An `actionPerformed` method handles the event of a button being pressed. Whenever either a numeric key, negative sign of the number key, or decimal point key on the pad is pressed, the value associated with the key is written as either a digit, minus sign, or period on the display, respectively. The display must first be read, its string contents are then concatenated with the character associated with the key being pressed, and the new string is then written back to the display. If the key to cancel the number being displayed is pressed, the display is cleared by writing an empty string to it.

```java
import java.awt.*;
import java.awt.event.*;

public class NumericKeyPad extends Panel implements ActionListener
{
        Button[] button = new Button[15];
        Display datum;

        /**
        The NumericKeyPad class enables a panel containing numeric keys, a
        minus sign, decimal point and clear keys to be created.
        @param display is the name of the object that shows the number
        chosen.
        */
        public NumericKeyPad(Display display)
        {
                super();
                datum = display;

                setLayout(new GridLayout(5,3));
                Font font = new Font("SansSerif",Font.BOLD,16);
                setFont(font);

                // create buttons 7 .. 9
                for (int index = 7; index < 10; index++)
                {
                        button[index] = new Button(String.valueOf(index));
                        button[index].addActionListener(this);
                        button[index].setForeground(Color.black);
                        button[index].setBackground(Color.cyan);
                        this.add(button[index]);
                }

                // create buttons 4 .. 6
                for (int index = 4; index < 7; index++)
                {
                        button[index] = new Button(String.valueOf(index));
                        button[index].addActionListener(this);
                        button[index].setForeground(Color.black);
                        button[index].setBackground(Color.cyan);
                        this.add(button[index]);
                }
```

```
                // create buttons 1 .. 3
                for (int index = 1; index < 4; index++)
                {
                        button[index] = new Button(String.valueOf(index));
                        button[index].addActionListener(this);
                        button[index].setForeground(Color.black);
                        button[index].setBackground(Color.cyan);
                        this.add(button[index]);
                }

                // create numeric buttons 0
                button[0] = new Button("0");
                button[0].addActionListener(this);
                button[0].setForeground(Color.black);
                button[0].setBackground(Color.cyan);
                this.add(button[0]);

                // create two blank buttons
                for (int index = 10; index < 12; index++)
                {
                        button[index] = new Button("");
                        button[index].setBackground(Color.lightGray);
                        this.add(button[index]);
                }

                // create bottom row of special buttons
                button[12] = new Button("-");
                button[13] = new Button("C");
                button[14] = new Button(".");

                for (int index = 12; index < 15; index++)
                {
                        button[index].setForeground(Color.black);
                        button[index].setBackground(Color.lightGray);
                        button[index].addActionListener(this);
                        this.add(button[index]);
                }
        }

public void actionPerformed(ActionEvent event)
{
        String buttonPressed;

        // process numeric buttons
        for (int index=0; index < 10; index++)
```

```
        {
                buttonPressed = String.valueOf(index);

                if (event.getActionCommand().equals(buttonPressed))
                {
                        datum.write(datum.read()+buttonPressed);
                        return;
                }
        }

        // process buttons on bottom row
        if (event.getActionCommand().equals("-"))
        {
                datum.write(datum.read()+"-");
        }
        else if (event.getActionCommand().equals("C"))
        {
                datum.write("");
        }
        else if (event.getActionCommand().equals("."))
        {
                datum.write(datum.read()+".");
        }
    }
}
```

Finally, the FunctionPad class is also dependent upon the Display class. When one of the arithmetic function keys is pressed, the value of the operator is stored and the contents of the display is read, converted from a string to a real number, and stored as the first operand for later use.

When the equals key is pressed, the contents of the display are read and converted from a string to a real number and stored as the second operand. The operator that was previously stored is then used to determine the operation to perform on the two operands. The calculation is computed, and the result is written to the display.

The complete listing of the FunctionPad source code follows. Note that the actionPerformed method uses the private method calculator to perform the arithmetic operations.

```
import java.awt.*;
import java.awt.event.*;

public class FunctionPad extends Panel implements ActionListener
{
        private char[] functions = {'+','-','x','/','='};
        private Button[] button;
        private Display datum;
```

```
private double operand1, operand2;
private char arithmeticOperator;

/**
The FunctionPad class enables a panel containing function keys to be
created.
@param display is the name of the object that shows the result of the
function chosen.
*/

public FunctionPad(Display display)
{
     super();
     datum = display;
     button = new Button[functions.length];

     setLayout(new GridLayout(functions.length,1));
     Font font = new Font("Monospaced",Font.BOLD,24);
     setFont(font);

     for (int index = 0; index != functions.length; index++)
     {
          button[index] = new
          Button(String.valueOf(functions[index]));
          button[index].addActionListener(this);
          button[index].setForeground(Color.red);
          button[index].setBackground(Color.lightGray);
          this.add(button[index]);
     }
}

public void actionPerformed(ActionEvent event)
{
     // get operator of key pressed
     char operator = event.getActionCommand().charAt(0);

     switch (operator)
     {
          case '+':
          case '-':
          case 'x':
          case '/': try
                    {
                              operand1 = Double.valueOf
                              (datum.read()).doubleValue();
                    }
```

```
                catch (NumberFormatException nfe)
                {
                        datum.write("  not a number");
                        return;
                }

                arithmeticOperator = operator;
                datum.write("");
                return;
        case '=': try
                {
                        operand2 = Double.valueOf
                        (datum.read()).doubleValue();
                }
                catch (NumberFormatException nfe)
                {
                        datum.write("  not a number");
                        return;
                }

                double result = calculate(operand1, operand2);
                datum.write(String.valueOf(result));
    }
}

/**
Calculate and return the result of the function being applied to the
two operands.
@param operand1 is the first number to be keyed into the calculator;
@param operand2 is the second number to be keyed into the calculator;
@return Result of the calculation on operand1 and operand2.
*/
private double calculate(double operand1, double operand2)
{
    double answer = 0.0;

    switch (arithmeticOperator)
    {
            case '+': answer = operand1+operand2; break;
            case '-': answer = operand1-operand2; break;
            case 'x': answer = operand1*operand2; break;
            case '/': answer = operand1/operand2;
    }

    return answer;
}
}
```

Finally, a full source listing of the `Calculator` class follows. It consists primarily of setting up the calculator container and adding the interrelated graphical objects to it. Of course, it also includes methods to show the calculator and to dispose of it.

```java
import java.awt.*;
import java.awt.event.*;

public class Calculator extends Dialog
{
    /**
    The Calculator class enables a small pocket numeric calculator to be
    created and displayed on the screen.
    @param parent is the name of the container on which to display the
    calculator.
    */
    public Calculator(Frame parent)
    {
        super(parent,"Calculator ..",true);
        addWindowListener(new CloseCalculator());

        Toolkit tools = parent.getToolkit();
        Dimension size = tools.getScreenSize();
        int screenWidth = size.width;
        int screenHeight = size.height;

        // set location and size of calculator
        int xLocationOfCalc = (int)(0.7f * screenWidth);
        int yLocationOfCalc = (int)(0.2f * screenHeight);
        int widthOfCalc = (int)(0.15f * screenWidth);
        int depthOfCalc = (int)(0.3f * screenHeight);

        // draw calculator
        setLayout(null);
        setLocation(xLocationOfCalc,yLocationOfCalc);
        setSize(widthOfCalc,depthOfCalc);
        setForeground(Color.blue);
        setBackground(Color.lightGray);

        // add display
        Display display = new Display();
        display.setLocation(1,25);
        display.setSize(150,30);
        add(display);
```

```
            // add numeric keypad
            NumericKeyPad keys = new NumericKeyPad(display);
            keys.setLocation(15,65);
            keys.setSize(90,150);
            add(keys);

            // add function pad
            FunctionPad functions = new FunctionPad(display);
            functions.setLocation(110,65);
            functions.setSize(30,150);
            add(functions);
    }


    /**
    Show the calculator on the screen
    */
    public void showCalculator()
    {
            this.setVisible(true);
    }

    private class CloseCalculator extends WindowAdapter
    {
            public void windowClosing(WindowEvent event)
            {
                Calculator.this.dispose();
                System.exit(0);
            }
    }
}
```

The program to test the `Calculator` class is trivial:

```
import gui.*;

public class Example_2
{
    public static void main(String[] args)
    {
            WindowPane screen = new WindowPane();
            screen.showWindowPane();
            Calculator machine = new Calculator(screen);
            machine.showCalculator();
    }
}
```

NOW DO THIS Run program `Example_2`. A calculator similar to that shown in Figure 10.4 should appear on a `WindowPane`.

10.3 CRC Cards

So far the method used throughout the book to discover classes was to analyze the text of the stated problem and use the nouns in the text to represent a number of candidate classes. The candidate classes were then examined further to determine their suitability for the solution to the problem. The next stage was to re-examine the text of the stated problem and use the verbs in the text to represent the possible methods. This approach works fine for small problems, but the ability to find associations between the appropriate classes becomes more difficult as the complexity of the problems increases. An alternate method that works well with more complex problems is to use Classes, Responsibilities, and Collaborators (CRC) cards.

The *CRC card technique* is a means of discovering classes, responsibilities (the methods of the class), and collaborators (those classes that are also needed to fulfill the responsibilities, revealing the associations between classes when designing an object-oriented system). Figure 10.6 illustrates the layout of a CRC card.

i

CRC cards are not part of the UML notation. They were first described by Beck and Cunningham in 1989—see `http://c2.com/doc/oopsla89/paper.html`. Beck and Cunningham used a small 6" × 4" index card to document the name of the class and list the responsibilities of that class. Alongside each responsibility they wrote down whether any other classes were also needed to permit the responsibility to be implemented.

For each class there was an index card, so it was possible to build up a pack of cards representing all the classes of the project. Cards could be grouped into classes that exhibited some form of commonality and thus be implemented as a package. By inspecting the responsibilities on each card and looking for repeated responsibilities or responsibilities that could be used in other cards, the programmer could make decisions on which class would form a subclass of another. CRC cards provide a good medium for project teams where decisions about the design of an object-oriented system are forced to be made up-front in a nonrestrictive and informal group.

Consider the following scenario. A college offers a number of degrees. Each degree is composed of a number of topic modules (or courses depending upon which part of the world you live in). Not all degrees are made up from the same number of modules. Each degree has a unique name, and each module has a unique name.

The grade for a module will be based on a weighted combination of an exam mark and a coursework mark. The weight given to each of these grade compo-

Class	
Responsibilities	Collaborators

Figure 10.6 The layout of an index card to represent a CRC card

nents can differ from one module to the next and is part of the defining characteristics of a module. Marks are based on the standard scale of 100 points. Module grade cutoffs are: A 85, B+ 70, B 55, C 40, F below 40.

For example, if a module uses a 60% weight for exams (and therefore a 40% weight for coursework) and a student has received a mark of 80 for exams and a mark of 90 for coursework, then the student's total score is $(0.6 * 80) + (0.4 * 90)$ = 84 and receives a grade of B+.

We want to create a program system that will let us define, update, and report on various students' degrees of study. Obvious candidate classes are `Degree` and `Module`. The `Degree` class would contain information about the name of the degree and the modules that comprise the degree. In addition to the constructor for the `Degree` class, we will want to create instance methods to add individual modules to the degree, get the name of the degree, and get the modules that the degree comprises. This information is documented on a CRC card as shown in Figure 10.7. Notice that if we want to add a module to the degree, then it is necessary to collaborate with the candidate class `Module`.

Degree	
Responsibilities	Collaborators
Course	-
add module	Module
get name of course	-
get course of modules	-

Figure 10.7 CRC card for the `Degree` class

Module	
Responsibilities	Collaborators
Module	-
get module name	-
get exam ratio	-
get coursework ratio	-

Figure 10.8 CRC card for the `Module` class

A `Module` class should contain the name of the module and information about the assessment ratio between the weight of the examination mark and the weight of the coursework mark. The ratio of the examination marks and the coursework mark is used in computing the total mark for a module. In addition to using the constructor for the `Module` class, we need to supply methods to get the name of the module, the exam weight, and coursework weight assessment ratios. This information is documented on the CRC card shown in Figure 10.8.

From the collaborators column of the `Degree` card in Figure 10.7 you can see that there is an *association* between the `Degree` class and the `Module` class shown in Figure 10.8.

Continuing the scenario: When a student registers for a college degree you must store such information as the name of the student and the name of the degree for which the student is registering. You must also be able to add the results for the student for each of the modules in the registered degree. If `StudentProgram`, representing a student's program of study, can be regarded as another candidate class, then in addition to its constructor, we might want methods for four other actions—to get the name of the student, get the degree on which the student is registered, add the results of an assessment for a module to the class, and get the results of those modules that have been examined. This information is documented on the CRC card shown in Figure 10.9.

Once again, if you look down the collaborators column of the card, you can see that there are relationships between the class `StudentProgram` and the classes `Degree`, `Module`, and `ModuleResult`. You may notice that the class `ModuleResult` has not been mentioned before, and you should question what it represents!

We do not have a class that represents the results for a particular module studied. Such a class should store the module, the percentage exam mark, and the percentage coursework mark. Ultimately, a module result will be stored as an object in a vector in the class `StudentProgram`. The vector will eventually con-

StudentProgram	
Responsibilities	Collaborators
StudentProgram	Degree
get student name	-
get course	Degree
add module result	Module,ModuleResult
get student results	-

Figure 10.9 CRC card for the StudentProgram class

tain all the assessments of all the modules the student has studied on a degree. You can argue that since the StudentProgram class contains a method to add the module results to the student's program, then this new class should be an inner class of the StudentProgram class. If this were the case, there would be no means of making this new class public so that it could be used by other classes.

The ModuleResult class not only allows objects to be created and stored in a vector, but also enables the retrieval of information from a student program. In addition to the constructor for the class, the ModuleResults class contains methods to get the name of the module, get the exam mark, get the coursework mark, get the total mark, and get the grade based upon the total mark. This information is documented on the CRC card shown in Figure 10.10.

ModuleResult	
Responsibilities	Collaborators
ModuleResult	Module
get module name	-
get exam mark	-
get coursework mark	-
get total mark	-
get grade	-

Figure 10.10 CRC card to represent the class ModuleResults

By inspecting the collaborators column of the `ModuleResults` class it is clear that there is a relationship between the `ModuleResults` class and the `Module` class.

The calculation of the total mark is not simply a matter of summing the exam mark and the coursework mark since a weight is applied to both of these components of assessment. For example, if the exam weight is 60% and the coursework weight is 40%, then the total is calculated as 60% of the exam mark, plus 40% of the coursework mark. If the `ModuleResults` class is to calculate the total mark, then it requires the exam and coursework weightings for the assessment. Methods to supply these values are found in the `Module` class.

Since both the `Module` and `ModuleResults` classes need to share methods, it is reasonable for the `ModuleResults` class to have an instance variable of type `Module`. That way, the `ModuleResults` class has access to the instance variables of a module. It would be wrong to treat `ModuleResults` as a subclass of `Module`, since the "is-a" relationship does not apply.

Once the relationships between the classes have been discovered, we can move towards the next stage in the design by drawing the class diagrams and showing the associations and dependencies. For each CRC card there will be the representation of a class. The relationships between classes are taken from the collaborators columns of the cards and drawn as either an association or a dependency on the class diagram. The methods for each class are taken directly from the responsibilities column of each card.

We will continue with this example in the next section.

NOW DO THIS   A variation on CRC cards subdivides responsibilities into two subsections: "responsibilities for knowing" and "responsibilities for doing." The " .. for knowing" leads to the discovery of instance variables and the " .. for doing" leads to the methods.

(1) Repeat the work of Section 10.3 using the "responsibilities for knowing" and establish the instance variables for each class.

10.4 Aggregation

Sometimes you will want to model a whole-part relationship in which one class represents a larger thing (the whole) that consists of smaller things (the parts). This kind of relationship is called an *aggregation*, which represents a has-a relationship (see Section 6.8), meaning that an object of the whole has objects of the parts. In other words, aggregation is a method of recording that an object of one class is part of an object of another class. Aggregation is a special kind of

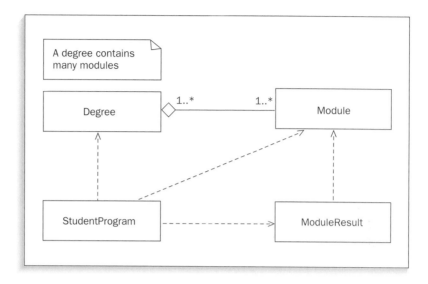

Figure 10.11 A UML class-relationship diagram

association; it is specified by drawing an open diamond at the "whole" end on the relationship diagram (see Figure 10.11).

In the scenario described in the previous section, there is an association between two classes that form an aggregation. The aggregation is between the `Degree` and `Module` classes. A degree (the whole) has-a number of modules (the parts). The notation 1..* means that a degree is composed from at least 1 module. The * implies any number. In practice, a degree is normally composed from at least, say, six modules, in which case the notation would change to 6..*. A class-relationship diagram for the scenario is shown in Figure 10.11.

Note the symbol shown in Figure 10.11 as

This symbol may be used to add notes to a diagram and is used to append notes to a UML diagram.

A detailed UML diagram showing the methods of each class of our example and the relationships between each class is given in Figure 10.12.

The implementation of each class follows. Each class implements the `serializable` interface because, later in the development of the scenario, objects can be written to or read from `serializable` files.

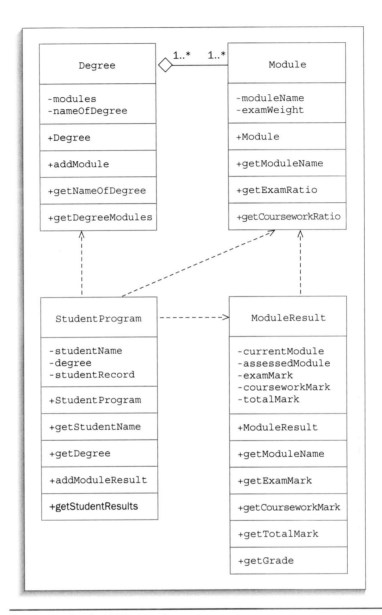

Figure 10.12 Detailed UML class diagram

```java
import java.io.*;
import java.util.*;

public class Degree implements Serializable
{
        private Vector modules;
        private String nameOfDegree;
```

```java
/**
The Degree class enables an object that represents
a college degree containing a number of pre-defined
modules.
@param name is the name of the degree
*/
public Degree(String name)
{
      nameOfDegree = name;
      modules = new Vector();
}

// instance methods
/**
Add a module to the degree.
@param module is the module to be added
*/
public void addModule(Module module)
{
      modules.add(module);
}

/**
Returns the name of the degree.
@return name of the degree.
*/
public String getNameOfDegree()
{
      return nameOfDegree;
}

/**
Returns a vector containing the names of the modules
that form the degree.
@return A vector containing the names of the degree modules.
*/
public Vector getDegreeModules()
{
      return modules;
}
}
```

```java
import java.io.*;

public class Module implements Serializable
```

```
{
      protected String moduleName;
      protected int examWeight;

      // default constructor
      public Module(){}
      /**
      The Module class enables an object that represents a study
      unit within a degree. A single degree consists of at least
      one module.
      @param name is the name of the module.
      @param weight is the proportion of the assessment that is
      examination based e.g. a weight of 60 implies that the assessment
      is 60% examination 40% coursework.
      */
      public Module(String name, int weight)
      {
            moduleName = name;
            examWeight = weight;
      }


      // instance methods
      /**
      Returns the name of the module.
      @return The name of the module.
      */
      public String getModuleName()
      {
            return moduleName;
      }


      /**
      Returns the proportion of the assessment that is examination.
      @return An integer representing the percentage of the assessment
      based upon the examination.
      */
      public int getExamRatio()
      {
            return examWeight;
      }

      /**
      Returns the proportion of the assessment that is coursework.
      @return An integer representing the percentage of the assessment
```

```
        based upon the coursework.
        */
        public int getCourseworkRatio()
        {
                return 100-examWeight;
        }
}
```

```
import java.io.*;

public class ModuleResult implements Serializable
{
        private Module currentModule;
        private String assessedModule;
        private int examMark;
        private int courseworkMark;
        private int totalMark;

        /**
        The ModuleResult class enables an object that represents the
        statistics of an assessment for a single module.
        @param module is the Module being assessed.
        @param exam is the percentage examination mark.
        @param coursework is the percentage coursework mark.
        */
        public ModuleResult(Module module, int exam, int coursework)
        {
                currentModule = module;
                assessedModule = currentModule.getModuleName();
                examMark = exam;
                courseworkMark = coursework;
                totalMark = (currentModule.getExamRatio() * examMark /100) +
                        (currentModule.getCourseworkRatio() *
                         courseworkMark / 100);
        }

        /**
        Get name of module that was assessed.
        @return The name of the module.
        */
        public String getModuleName()
        {
                return assessedModule;
        }
```

```
/**
Get the percentage examination mark.
@return The percentage examination mark.
*/
public int getExamMark()
{
        return examMark;
}


/**
Get the percentage coursework mark.
@return The percentage coursework mark.
*/
public int getCourseworkMark()
{
        return courseworkMark;
}


/**
Get the total mark after the examination and coursework weightings
have been applied.
@return Total mark as a percentage.
*/
public int getTotalMark()
{
        return totalMark;
}


/**
Compute the grade based upon the total mark.
@return The grade.
*/
public String getGrade()
{
        if      (totalMark >= 85) return "A";
        else if (totalMark >= 70) return "B+";
        else if (totalMark >= 55) return "B";
        else if (totalMark >= 40) return "C";
        else                      return "F";
}
}
```

```
import java.io.*;
import java.util.*;
```

```
public class StudentProgram implements Serializable
{
      private String studentName;
      private Degree degree;
      private Vector studentRecord;

      /**
      The StudentProgram class enables an object that represents
      the registration of a student on a degree. This object also
      maintains a record of the student's progress by recording
      details of the modules assessed.
      @param name is the name of the student.
      @param registeredOn is the degree the student has joined.
      */
      public StudentProgram(String name, Degree registeredOn)
      {
           studentName = name;
           degree = registeredOn;
           studentRecord = new Vector();
      }


      // instance methods
      /**
      Gets the name of the student.
      @return The name of the student.
      */
      public String getStudentName()
      {
           return studentName;
      }


      /**
      Gets the degree the student has registered on.
      @return The degree the students has registered on.
      */
      public Degree getDegree()
      {
           return degree;
      }


      /**
      Add the result from a module to the student program.
      @param module is the Module being assessed.
      @param exam is the percentage mark for the examination.
      @param coursework is the percentage mark for the coursework.
```

```
    */
    public void addModuleResult(Module module, int exam, int coursework)
    {
        ModuleResult result = new
        ModuleResult(module, exam, coursework);
        studentRecord.add(result);
    }


    /**
    Get the results from every module on the degree.
    @return A vector containing the result for each module taken.
    */
    public Vector getStudentResults()
    {
        return studentRecord;
    }

}
```

Program `Example_3` is a program to test the methods of the four classes. Note that it uses the `gui` package developed in the first two sections of this chapter. The program is split into two class methods. In the first method, `createData()`, the program creates two degrees—mathematics and computing. The mathematics degree contains the modules calculus, algebra, and trigonometry, and the computing degree contains the modules programming, architecture, data structures, expert systems, and networks.

A one-dimensional array is used to store two student programs. The first student takes the mathematics degree and the second student takes the computing degree. The results of the assessments for both students are added to each student's program.

In the second method, `displayResults()`, the details of each student program are output to the screen. A vector is created that contains all the modules the student has studied. The details of the results are output for each module studied.

```
import gui.*;
import java.util.*;

public class Example_3
{
    static Degree mathematics, computing;
    static Module calculus, algebra, trigonometry, programming,
            architecture, dataStructures, expertSystems, networks;
    static StudentProgram[] students = new StudentProgram[2];

    static void createData()
    {
        // create degrees called Mathematics and Computing
```

```
      mathematics = new Degree("Mathematics");
      computing = new Degree("Computing");

      // create modules
      calculus = new Module("Calculus",70);
      algebra = new Module("Algebra",50);
      trigonometry = new Module("Trigonometry",100);
      programming = new Module("Programming",50);
      dataStructures = new Module("Data Structures",70);
      architecture = new Module("Computer Architecture",100);
      expertSystems = new Module("Expert Systems",70);
      networks = new Module("Networks",100);

      // add modules to the mathematics degree
      mathematics.addModule(calculus);
      mathematics.addModule(algebra);
      mathematics.addModule(trigonometry);

      // add modules to the computing degree
      computing.addModule(programming);
      computing.addModule(architecture);
      computing.addModule(dataStructures);
      computing.addModule(expertSystems);
      computing.addModule(networks);

      // create student records and store in an array
      students[0] = new StudentProgram("Jane Morgan", mathematics);
      students[1] = new StudentProgram("Barry Freeman", computing);

      // add results to Jane's student record
      students[0].addModuleResult(calculus,45,60);
      students[0].addModuleResult(algebra,65,90);
      students[0].addModuleResult(trigonometry,85,0);

      // add results to Barry's student record
      students[1].addModuleResult(programming,90,95);
      students[1].addModuleResult(dataStructures,70,90);
      students[1].addModuleResult(networks,65,0);
   }

static void displayResults()
{
      // print out details of program for each student
      WindowPane screen = new WindowPane();
      screen.showWindowPane();
      WritingPad pad = new WritingPad(screen);
```

```
pad.showWritingPad();

// for each student
for (int number=0; number != students.length; number++)
{
    // write name of student and name of degree
    pad.write("Name: "+students[number].getStudentName()+
            "        Degree: "+
        students[number].getDegree().getNameOfDegree()+"\n");

    // create a vector of the modules required by the degree
    Vector namesOfModules =
    students[number].getDegree().getDegreeModules();
    int sizeOfVector = namesOfModules.size();

    // display those modules that are required by the degree
    pad.write("Modules to be studied on the degree\n");
    for (int index=0; index != sizeOfVector; index++)
    {
        Module name =
        (Module)namesOfModules.elementAt(index);
        pad.write("            "+name.getModuleName()+" ["+
            String.valueOf(name.getExamRatio())+":"+
            String.valueOf(name.getCourseworkRatio())+"]\n");
    }


    // create a vector of the results of those modules
    // already assessed
    Vector resultsOfModules =
    students[number].getStudentResults();
    sizeOfVector = resultsOfModules.size();

    // write the assessment details of the modules studied
    pad.write("Assessment details to date\n");
    for (int index=0; index != sizeOfVector; index++)
    {
        ModuleResult result =
        (ModuleResult)resultsOfModules.elementAt(index);
        pad.write("            "+
            result.getModuleName()+" ex: "+
            String.valueOf(result.getExamMark())+" cw: "+
            String.valueOf(result.getCourseworkMark())+
            " total: "+String.valueOf(result.getTotalMark())+
            " grade: "+result.getGrade()+"\n");
```

```
            }

        pad.write("\n\n");
    }
}

public static void main(String[] args)
{
    createData();
    displayResults();
}
}
```

A screen shot for the running program follows.

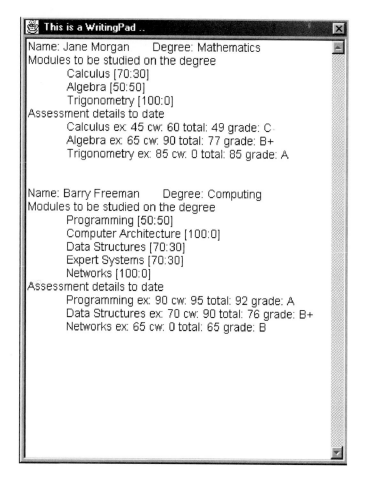

`NOW DO THIS▶`   Modify program `Example_3` as follows.

(1) Include degrees and modules of your own choice.

(2) Create a different layout for the data on the writing pad.

10.5 Composition

In aggregation, groups of objects are used as components to make some larger object; for example, a group of modules forms a degree. However, different permutations of modules may be used to form different degrees; in other words, in aggregation one object may own other objects but they may also have an independent lifetime and other associations.

For example, a Mathematics degree may contain the modules Algebra, Calculus and Logic; yet a Computing degree might also contain the module on Logic, in addition to other modules on say, Programming, Data Structures, and Computer Architecture. In our aggregations, not only does the module Logic have an independent lifetime, that is if the Mathematics degree is scrapped, the Logic module lives on in the Computing degree; but the number of modules also differs between the degrees.

If we want a tighter alliance between objects such that the "whole" owns its "parts", their lifetimes are identical, and it is unlikely that the parts have any relationships with other objects outside of the alliance, then the association is known as a composition. One example of a composition is the buttons on the function pad of the calculator (see Figure 10.4). The `FunctionPad` object owns 5 function `Button` objects. The lifetime of both objects is identical. When the function pad is disposed of, then the function buttons also cease to exist. The function buttons do not form part of the numeric buttons (even the functionality of the minus signs between the numeric key pad and the function pad are different). Hence the function buttons cannot be used as part of the numeric key pad.

Composition is a special kind of association, and is specified by drawing a closed diamond at the "whole" end (see Figure 10.13).

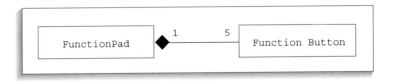

Figure 10.13 Composition relationship between the function pad and its buttons

10.6 Building a Student Management System

Since most of the data in the class `Example_3` was hard-coded into the program, the program could not be used to handle any changes to the number of modules, degrees, or students at run time. It could only test the methods of the defined classes. But the classes `Degree`, `Module`, `StudentProgram`, and `ModuleResult` form the fundamental building blocks of a larger student management system. However, if such a system is to be truly usable, it will be necessary for it to store and retrieve the data it manipulates between one use of the system and the next. Therefore, it must use permanent files to hold the data. The data in the files will need to be read and stored in appropriate data structures so that it can be accessed and manipulated before eventually being written back to the files to enable the preservation of an up-to-date student management system.

The classes `Degree`, `Module`, and `StudentProgram` do not contain the functionality to manage more than one object; nor should they! What is needed are new modules, known as *managers*, to organize the storage and manipulation of many objects for each of the respective classes. As an example, we will look at the functionality of just one manager, the module manager.

The `ModuleManager` is a class that is responsible for initializing a vector with any previously defined module objects that have been stored in a `serializable` file. This new manager class will allow module objects to be inserted into the vector in alphabetical sequence, allow module objects to be deleted from the vector, allow any modules to be selected and returned from the vector, return all the modules stored in the vector, return the number of modules stored in the vector, and finally save the contents of the vector in a `serializable` file. You may have noticed that the class `Module` implemented the `Serializable` interface; this is necessary if module objects are to be stored in a `serializable` file.

A complete source listing of the `ModuleManager` class follows.

```
import gui.*;
import java.io.*;
import java.util.*;

public class ModuleManager
{
        static String nameOfFile = "MODULES.STREAM";
        static WindowPane bigBrother;

        // vector used to store all the modules
        Vector moduleStore = new Vector();

        /**
        The ModuleManager class enables an object that manages the vector
        used to store the modules. Management involves initializing the
```

```
vector from a serializable file; inserting new modules in
alphabetical order into the vector; deleting modules from the vector;
selecting any number of modules from the vector; returning the number
of modules stored in the vector; returning all the modules stored in
the vector; and finally copying the contents of the vector to the
original serializable file.
@param parent is the name of the container class.
*/
public ModuleManager(WindowPane parent) throws Exception
{
       bigBrother = parent;

       // open a predefined file
       File f = new File(nameOfFile);

       // only if the file exists should its contents be copied to the
       // vector
       if (f.exists())
       {
              FileInputStream fis = new FileInputStream(nameOfFile);
              ObjectInputStream in = new ObjectInputStream(fis);

              moduleStore = (Vector)in.readObject();
              in.close();
              fis.close();
       }
}


/**
Add any number of modules to the vector
*/
public void addModules()
{
       String[] choice = {"yes","no"};
       RadioButtons reply = new RadioButtons(bigBrother,
                              "Add another module?", choice);
       String[] items = {"Module name","Exam weight"};
       DataInputBox modules = new DataInputBox(bigBrother, items);

       do
       {
              // input data for a module according to the names of the
              // fields displayed by the data input box
              modules.showDataInputBox();
```

```
        String[] values = new String[items.length];
        values = modules.getFields();

        // get name of module
        String name = values[0];

        // get exam weighting for module, if error use
        // Integer.MAX_VALUE
        int weight;
        try
        {
            weight = new Integer(values[1]).intValue();
        }
        catch (Exception e)
        {
            weight = Integer.MAX_VALUE;
        }

        // instantiate new module
        Module mod = new Module(name, weight);

        // insert the module into the vector in alphabetical
        // sequence
        // ordered on the name of the module
        insertInOrder(mod);

        // request for more modules
        reply.showRadioButtons();
    } while (reply.getNameOfButton().equals("yes"));
}

/**
Inserts a module into the vector in alphabetical sequence
@param mod is the module to be inserted
*/
private void insertInOrder(Module mod)
{
    String nameOfModule;
    int sizeOfVector = moduleStore.size();

    // if the vector is empty then just add the module to the
    // vector
    if (sizeOfVector == 0)
```

```
        {
             moduleStore.addElement(mod);
             return;
        }

        // compare the name of the module to be inserted with the name
        // of each module stored in the vector; if the name of new
        // module is less than or equal to the name of the module being
        // compared, then insert the module into vector
        for (int index=0; index != sizeOfVector; index++)
        {
             nameOfModule =
             ((Module)moduleStore.elementAt(index)).getModuleName();
             if ((mod.getModuleName().toUpperCase()).
                  compareTo(nameOfModule.toUpperCase()) <= 0)
             {
                  moduleStore.insertElementAt((Module)mod,index);
                  return;
             }
        }

        // new module is inserted at the end of the vector
        moduleStore.addElement(mod);
    }

    /**
    Delete a number of modules from the vector.
    */
    public void deleteModules()
    {
        String nameOfModule;
        int length = moduleStore.size();

        // if the vector is not empty
        if (length != 0)
        {
             // request which modules are to be deleted
             boolean[] selection = this.selectModules();

             // since the vector will shrink in size after each
             // deletion, it is necessary to delete the selected
             // modules in reverse order
             for (int index=length-1; index >= 0; index--)
             {
                  if (selection[index])
                  {
```

```
                                    moduleStore.removeElementAt(index);
                            }
                    }
            }
}


/**
Write the modules as objects in a serializable file
*/
public void saveModules() throws Exception
{
        FileOutputStream fos = new FileOutputStream(nameOfFile);
        ObjectOutputStream out = new ObjectOutputStream(fos);
        out.writeObject(moduleStore);
        out.flush();
        out.close();
        fos.close();
}


/**
Select any number of modules from the vector.
@return a boolean array indicating which modules have been selected
*/
public boolean[] selectModules()
{
        String[] moduleNames;

        int sizeOfVector = moduleStore.size();

        // if vector contains at least one module
        if (sizeOfVector != 0)
        {
                // instantiate an array to store the names of the modules
                moduleNames = new String[sizeOfVector];

                // store the names of all the modules found in the vector
                // in the array
                for (int index=0; index != sizeOfVector; index++)
                {
                        Module name = (Module)moduleStore.elementAt(index);
                        moduleNames[index] = name.getModuleName();
                }

                // instantiate a list to enable module names to be
                // selected
                ScrollableList modules = new
```

```
            ScrollableList(bigBrother, "Modules", moduleNames);
            modules.showList();

            // return a boolean array indicating which module names
            // have been chosen
            return modules.getSelectedItems();
        }
        // if vector is empty then return a single-celled boolean array
        // set to false
        else
        {
            boolean[] noItems = {false};
            return noItems;
        }
    }


/**
Return the number of modules stored in the vector.
@return number of modules
*/
public int getNumberOfModules()
{
    return moduleStore.size();
}


/**
Return all the modules stored in the vector.
@return vector containing all the modules
*/
public Vector getModulesStored()
{
    return moduleStore;
}
}
```

NOW DO THIS   Using the `ModuleManager` class as reference, create and desk-check the Java code for the class of `DegreeManager`.

10.7   Menus Revisited

A modern-day student management system must have its own graphical user interface that will allow a user to choose between activities that involve either degrees, modules, or students programs. In the previous chapter you were introduced to pop-up menus; in this chapter we will look at menus that *drop-down* from a menu bar situated along the top of a container.

The `MenuBar` class, from the `awt` package, will allow a `MenuBar` object to be displayed within a `Frame` by passing it to `Frame.setMenuBar()`.

The `Menu` class, also from the `awt` package, represents a drop-down menu pane that appears within a `MenuBar`.

The following code will create a `MenuBar` object containing just one menu-bar item.

```
MenuBar bar = new MenuBar();
```

To the menu bar is added a drop-down menu containing the string literals contained within the array `moduleItems`.

```
String[] moduleItems = {"add new modules", "delete modules",
                   "list all modules", "list selected modules",
                   "exit"};

Menu modules = new Menu("Modules");
for (int index=0; index != moduleItems.length; index++)
     modules.add(moduleItems[index]);

bar.add(modules);
```

The menu bar is then added to the container, which must be a subclass of `Frame`.

```
setMenuBar(bar);
```

When a mouse-button is clicked over the name of the menu, the menu drops down to allow a further selection of items. The container class with a menu must implement the `ActionListener` interface by adding an action listener; otherwise, pressing the mouse button of a selected item on the drop-down menu will result in the creation of an event that cannot be handled.

```
modules.addActionListener(this);
```

Figure 10.14 illustrates the drop-down menu for the modules.

Rather than writing a new container class that contains a menu bar and drop-down menus from scratch, we can easily create a new class `WindowWithMenuBar` that is a subclass of the class `WindowPane`. The listing of the source code for the `WindowWithMenuBar` class follows. Notice that although three drop-down menus have been created for degrees, modules, and students, only the modules menu has given the user any choice.

```
import gui.*;
import java.awt.*;
import java.awt.event.*;
```

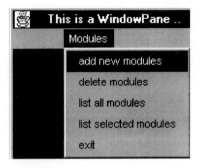

Figure 10.14 An Example of a drop-down menu

```
public class WindowWithMenuBar extends WindowPane implements ActionListener
{
      static String NO_ITEM_SELECTED = "";

      // contents of drop-down menus
      String[] menuBarItems = {"Degrees","Modules","Students"};
      String[] degreeItems = {"not yet implemented"};
      String[] moduleItems = {"add new modules", "delete modules",
                              "list all modules", "list selected modules",
                              "exit"};
      String[] studentItems = {"not yet implemented"};

      // selected item from menu
      String menuItem = NO_ITEM_SELECTED;

      /**
      The WindowWithMenuBar class enables an object that represents
      a WindowPane that contains a number of drop-down menus.
      */
      public WindowWithMenuBar()
      {
            super();

            // instantiate menu bar object
            MenuBar bar = new MenuBar();

            // add degree items to menu bar
            Menu degrees = new Menu(menuBarItems[0]);
            degrees.add(degreeItems[0]);
            bar.add(degrees);
```

```java
        // add module items to menu bar
        Menu modules = new Menu(menuBarItems[1]);
        for (int index=0; index != moduleItems.length; index++)
                modules.add(moduleItems[index]);
        bar.add(modules);

        // add student items to menu bar
        Menu students = new Menu(menuBarItems[2]);
        students.add(studentItems[0]);
        bar.add(students);

        // set menu bar into frame
        setMenuBar(bar);

        // add action listeners for each menu
        degrees.addActionListener(this);
        modules.addActionListener(this);
        students.addActionListener(this);

    }


/**
Returns the selection from one of the drop-down menus.
@return A string containing the name of the selected item from a
menu.
*/
public String getMenuItem()
{
        return menuItem;
}

// overridden method to detect which item is chosen from the menu bar
public void actionPerformed(ActionEvent event)
{
        Object source = event.getActionCommand();

        // check for degree items
        if (source.equals(degreeItems[0]))
        {
                menuItem = (String)source;
                return;
        }
```

```
// check for module items
for (int index=0; index != moduleItems.length; index++)
{
        if (source.equals(moduleItems[index]))
        {
                menuItem = (String)source;
                return;
        }
}

// check for student items
if (source.equals(studentItems[0]))
{
        menuItem = (String)source;
        return;
}
        }
}
```

NOW DO THIS   Modify the `WindowWithMenuBar` class to complete the drop-down menus for the degrees and students.

10.8   Testing the Student Management System

The methods from the classes `ModuleManager` and `WindowWithMenuBar` can now be tested. Each of the menu items for the `Modules` drop-down menu is implemented in the test program, with the results of each test being written to a `WritingPad` object.

Figure 10.15 illustrates the relationships and dependencies between the various classes developed in this section.

The source code for the test program `Example_4` follows. Having created objects for a window with a menu bar and a module manager, the user is given a choice of adding new modules, deleting modules, listing all modules, listing only selected modules, or saving the current state of the modules and exiting from the system.

```
import gui.*;
import java.util.*;

public class Example_4
{
      public static void main(String[] args) throws Exception
```

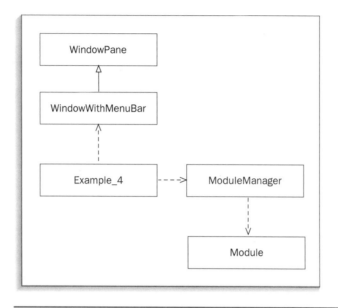

Figure 10.15 Relationships between classes

```
{
    // Open a window pane containing drop down menus
    WindowWithMenuBar screen = new WindowWithMenuBar();
    screen.showWindowPane();

    // initialize menu item
    String menuItem = WindowWithMenuBar.NO_ITEM_SELECTED;

    // initialize previously chosen menu item, and initialize
    // that no change in menu items selected has yet taken place
    String previousMenuItem = menuItem;
    boolean change = false;

    // create a writing pad to display information
    WritingPad pad = new WritingPad(screen);
    pad.showWritingPad();

    // create an object to manage the various transactions on
    // modules
    ModuleManager mm = new ModuleManager(screen);
```

```
// get a selection from a drop-down menu
menuItem = screen.getMenuItem();
while (true)
{
        // test to see if this is a new selection
        if (menuItem.equals(previousMenuItem))
                change = false;
        else
        {
                change = true;
                previousMenuItem = menuItem;
        }

        // add new modules
        if (change && menuItem.equals("add new modules"))
        {
                mm.addModules();
        }

        // delete modules
        else if (change && menuItem.equals("delete modules"))
        {
                mm.deleteModules();
        }

        // list all modules
        else if (change && menuItem.equals("list all modules"))
        {
                // create a vector of all the modules
                Vector modules = mm.getModulesStored();
                int length = mm.getNumberOfModules();

                // if vector empty then no modules stored
                if (length == 0)
                {
                        pad.write("[no modules listed]\n");
                }

                // display each module stored in the vector
                for (int index=0; index != length; index++)
                {
                        Module module =
                        (Module)modules.elementAt(index);
```

```
                    pad.write(module.getModuleName()+" "+
                            module.getExamRatio()+":"+
                            module.getCourseworkRatio()+"\n");
        }
        pad.write("\n");
}


// list only selected modules
else if (change &&
        menuItem.equals("list selected modules"))
{
        // test for the existence of any modules to select
        if (mm.getNumberOfModules() == 0)
        {
                pad.write("[no modules to select]\n");
        }
        else
        {
                // modules selected are stored as true,
                // otherwise stored as false; the boolean
                // array is the same length as the total
                // number of modules
                boolean[] selection = mm.selectModules();

                int length = selection.length;

                // store all the modules in a vector
                Vector modules = mm.getModulesStored();

                // for each module selected, display
                // information about the module
                for (int index=0; index != length; index++)
                {
                        if (selection[index])
                        {
                                // create a new module from the
                                // module selected
                                Module module =
                                (Module)modules.elementAt(index);

                                // display the information on the
                                // selected module
```

```
                            pad.write(module.getModuleName()+
                            " "+module.getExamRatio()+":"+
                            module.getCourseworkRatio()+"\n");
                 }
             }
         }
         pad.write("\n");
     }

     // save the current state of the module manager object
     // and exit
     else if (change && menuItem.equals("exit"))
     {
         mm.saveModules();
         System.exit(0);
     }

     // get selection from a drop-down menu
     menuItem = screen.getMenuItem();
         }
     }
 }
```

Screen shots follow that were taken when the program was running. You should run this program to get a feel for the functionality of the system before attempting the programming questions at the end of the chapter.

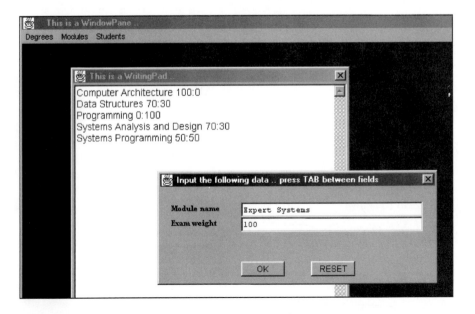

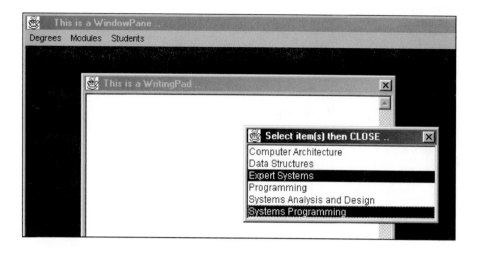

NOW DO THIS Run program `Example_4` using your own test data.

SUMMARY

- A number of classes that have a common theme may be grouped together into a package. The package can be imported into any program that requires the use of any of the classes that it contains.

- For a class to be contained within a package it must have the keyword `package` inserted at the beginning of the class's source file.

- The package is stored in the same subdirectory as the package name.

- Access to any class within the package is made possible by modifying the `CLASSPATH` directive to indicate the correct search paths the compiler must use when reconciling the packages specified in the import statements.

- The entire Java development environment is based upon the concept of packages.

- To resolve any clash between two classes with the same names in two different packages, simply qualify one of the classes with the name of the package from which it is contained.

- If there exists a dependency between two classes from different packages, then a dependency between the packages is said to exist.

- A single class on its own is not of much use. Classes work together to build programs. An association is a structural relationship that specifies objects from one class that are connected to objects of another class. Associations are the "glue" that holds objects from different classes together to build a computer program.

- An association in which one class represents the whole and is composed from many parts is known as an aggregation. The number of parts is known as the multiplicity of the association.

- If the lifetime of the whole and the parts is the same, and the parts do not form part of another association with another class, then the association is known as a composition, and not an aggregation.

- A useful "group" technique for determining classes, methods, and their relationships with other classes is the use of CRC cards.

- CRC cards help to identify (1) a commonality between classes and hence group them into packages, (2) a commonality between methods of different classes, and hence a hierarchy of classes, and (3) other classes that are required to implement any dependencies, hence the associations with other classes.

- The `Panel` class from the `awt` package does not create a separate window, yet is a container that must form a component within another container. The use of the `Panel` as a superclass to a component is sufficient for items that make up that component to be placed on to the `Panel`.

- Drop-down menus may be used on any window that supports a menu bar.

Review Questions

True or False

1. CRC cards are used after classes and methods have been discovered.

2. CRC cards are used by project teams in designing object-oriented systems.

3. The UML notation for a composition is an empty diamond shape.

Short Answer

4. What is a package?

5. How do you declare a class to be part of a package?

6. How is a package stored in relation to its name?

7. How do you nest a package within a package?

8. What are the advantages of storing classes within a package?

9. How does the Java system make use of packages?

10. What is the condition for dependency between two packages?

11. Discuss the term association in relation to classes.

12. What is aggregation?

13. How does composition differ from aggregation?

14. What is a `Panel` class?

15. How do you use a `Panel` class?

16. What does a CRC card represent?

17. What is a drop-down menu?

18. What are the restrictions on the use of a drop-down menu compared with a pop-up menu?

Exercises

19. Look up the `Applet` package from your Java documentation. Draw a UML diagram showing the dependencies between the `Applet` package and associated packages within Java. The answer to this question serves as a primer to the next chapter.

20. Use UML notation to show the relationship between:

    (a) a `Polygon` class and a `Side` class;

    (b) a Company and an Employee;

    (c) a Company and its Departments;

    (d) a half adder and two AND gates, an OR gate, and a NOT gate (see Figure 10.16).

21. Use CRC cards in the design of an information system for a school. You may want to structure your answer using the classes `School`, `Department`, `Student`, `Course`, and `Instructor`.

22. Based upon your answer to Question 21, draw a UML class diagram showing the relationships between the classes `School`, `Department`, `Student`, `Course`, and `Instructor`.

23. Use CRC cards in the design of an Automatic Teller Machine (ATM) in a bank. You may want to structure your answer using the classes `ATM`, `Bank`, `Bank Account`, and `Customer`.

24. Based upon your answer to Question 23, draw a UML class diagram showing the relationships between the classes mentioned in that question.

Programming Problems

25. Return to Section 10.2 and redevelop some of the classes of the `Calculator` for its use with rational numbers only. Reuse the `Rational` class developed in Chapter 5. You should display the fractions being computed as rational numbers, together with the arithmetic operation selected and the result of the computation. For example, the display part of the `Calculator` might contain the following output:

$$-8/3 + 9/4 = -5/12$$

26. Return to Section 10.6 and write a class for the `StudentProgramManager`.

27. Return to Section 10.8 and complete the `WindowWithMenuBar` class so that it includes all the functionality in the menus for both the `DegreeManager` and `StudentProgram-Manager` classes.

28. Write a new class `StudentManagementSystem` that uses the manager classes for `Degree`, `Module`, and `StudentProgram` and the revised `WindowWithMenuBar` class to produce a complete student management system.

29. Return to your designs from Questions 23 and 24 and create a simulation of a banking system that uses an ATM.

30. (a) Figure 10.16 illustrates the logic circuitry of a half adder. Implement a `HalfAdder` class that comprises objects from `ANDgate`, `ORgate`, and `NOTgate` classes. Test the `HalfAdder` class.

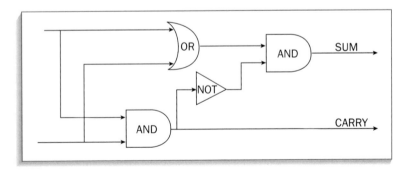

Figure 10.16 A half adder

(b) Figure 10.17 illustrates the logic circuitry of a full adder composed of two half
adders and an OR gate. Using the classes you implemented in part (a), write a
`FullAdder` class.

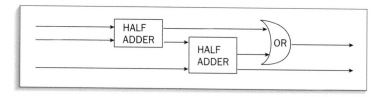

Figure 10.17 A four-bit full adder

(c) Devise a graphical interface to input two four-bit numbers and, using the
`FullAdder` class developed in part (b), show the result of adding the numbers.

CHAPTER 11

Applets and Threads

All the programs you have written up to this chapter have been application programs—each program was compiled into Java byte codes and run using a Java interpreter.

This chapter introduces you to writing *applet programs* that are designed to be run either by a Web browser or by an applet viewer. Your knowledge of creating and implementing classes, handling exceptions, and devising graphical user interfaces may also be used in conjunction with writing applets. In addition to having these features, an applet will also allow you to play sounds and display images.

Before we write applets that can successfully run on a computer we need to introduce a feature of programming that will permit quasi-concurrency through the use of threads.

By the end of this chapter you should have an understanding of the following topics.

- An introduction to the terminology of the World Wide Web.

- The construction of applets.

- Multimedia applets with sound and images.

- Arrays revisited.

- Image maps.

- An introduction to the meaning and use of threads.

- Animation of images.

- The limitations of applets.

- Sounds and images, with applications.

11.1   Introduction

The *Internet* is an international network of computers, or, more accurately, a network of networks. For example, the network at Oxford Brookes University is joined, via the Internet, to other networks all over the world, giving users global access to people and information. The Internet is the hardware of network cables, hubs, repeaters, and so on that enable computers from all around the world to communicate with one another.

There are various resources available on the Internet, including e-mail, FTP, Gopher, and Telnet.

E-mail is an electronic mailing system that allows you to send a message to anyone that is connected to the Internet.

A *File Transfer Protocol* (FTP) server is a computer on the Internet that stores a collection of files. Using FTP software, you can connect to any FTP server, browse through the directories, and download files to your local machine. Provided you have the access rights, you can also transfer files from your local machine to the FTP server.

Gopher allows you to search for files and documents about a particular topic.

Telnet provides you with a method to log on to a computer on a remote site. When you telnet to another computer, the resulting link is just like using a terminal at the remote site.

The four Internet resources described (and there are others), all require dedicated software tools, with each resource having its own user interface. As a result, the different Internet resources with their different interfaces can at times present a confusing system. The World Wide Web combines many of the Internet resources into a consistent, user-friendly front end that is much easier to use.

The *World Wide Web* (WWW, the Web, or W3) is a distributed information service on the Internet that allows access to documents containing links. Information on the Web is displayed in the form of hypertext and hypermedia documents.

Using the Web, you can access information located anywhere in the world. The level of user interaction on the Web ranges from the simple selection and retrieval of Web documents to the submission of completed forms, the inquiry of databases, and the ability to access multimedia computer-based learning packages.

A *hypertext* document may be entered at many points and may be browsed in any order by interactively choosing highlighted words or phrases to jump to the next text or image to be viewed. The highlighted word or phrase in a hypertext document is a *hot link*, and when selected by using a mouse, usually causes information relevant to the word or phrase to be displayed.

Hypermedia is a more accurate term than hypertext since the links in the WWW are not constrained to being text only. Links can also be made with still images, sound, and video clips.

The *Hyper-Text Mark-up Language* (HTML) is the language that is used to write WWW documents. In the context of this book, you are not expected to understand the syntax of HTML. However, if you would like to know more about HTML you can find an abundance of documentation and tutorials on the

Web. You can also download editors from the Web that write the HTML syntax for you, allowing you to concentrate on the contents of the document.

The user-friendly front end of the Web is a *browser*. This is the software package that reads and formats the HTML pages to be viewed. There are several popular browsers, such as Sun's HotJava, Netscape's Navigator, and Microsoft's Internet Explorer.

A Web browser provides the means to perform at least the following tasks.

- Search the Web for information—known as *surfing the net*.

- Use links in a hypertext document to move to different networked sites on the Web.

- Access any site on the Web.

- Send and receive electronic mail (this is a secondary feature and is not available on all browsers).

- Download files from other sites on the Web.

- Interpret a text file written in HTML.

A fifth resource of the Internet, not previously mentioned, is the *Hyper-Text Transfer Protocol* (HTTP). This is the set of rules that defines and controls the flow of information via the Web. Both the Web server and Web browser understand the HTTP language, and they use it to communicate with one another. Part of the server's job is to store Web documents; the other part is to deliver the documents over the network to the Web browser making a request for the documents.

To gain access to other sites on the Web, you must provide a *Uniform Resource Locator* (URL). Think of a URL as a networked extension of the hierarchical filename concept; not only can you specify a file in a directory, but that file and that directory can exist on any machine on the network. A URL comprises the following four parts that specify the unique address of a document on the Web.

Resource descriptor	`http:`
Separator	`//`
Resource address	`www.users.globalnet.co.uk`
Pathname	`/~bjholmes`

If you want to know more about the authors of this textbook, then enter the full URL at a browser as:

```
http://www.users.globalnet.co.uk/~bjholmes
```

to visit Barry's home page on his Web site. If you visit his home page you can mouse-click on hot links to the Jones and Bartlett Web site (the publishers of this book), Oxford Brookes University (where he works), and Letts Educational (another publisher for whom he writes textbooks).

If you enter the URL

```
http://www.csc.villanova.edu/~joyce
```

you can visit Dan's home page at Villanova University.

11.2   Applets

An *applet* is a Java program designed to be run by a Java-enabled Web browser or an applet viewer. A call to an applet is embedded in an HTML script file. When a Web page is loaded that contains a reference to an applet, the browser downloads the applet from the Web server and executes the applet on the client's machine. Having a piece of software invade your computer like this, from anywhere on the Web, is a frightening prospect! To avoid the possibility of the applet causing havoc on your computer, there are certain restrictions imposed on what an applet is allowed to do. Towards the end of this chapter we will briefly discuss what these restrictions are.

Before we start writing applets, it is necessary to consider how an applet is called from an HTML script file. The only HTML you need to know to follow this chapter is the ⟨APPLET⟩ tag, illustrated below. The following HTML script file calls the file Example_1.class containing the Java byte codes of the compiled applet. The applet source code would be stored in a file named Example_1.java, and it would be compiled in the same manner as a Java application program.

```
<HTML>
<BODY>

<APPLET code=Example_1.class width=300 height=75>
</APPLET>

</BODY>
</HTML>
```

A Java applet is included in a Web page using the ⟨APPLET⟩ tag, which has the following minimal syntax.

SYNTAX

Applet tag:
```
<APPLET code = applet-filename
        width = pixel-width
        height = pixel-height>
</APPLET>
```

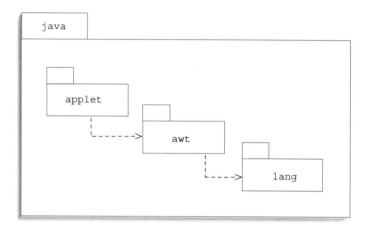

Figure 11.1 The dependency of an `applet` class

where the `width` and `height` refer to the initial width and height that the applet requires in the browser's window. The `java.applet` package contains the following classes—`Applet`, `AppletContext`, `AppletStub`, and `AudioClip`. Figure 11.1 shows the dependency of the `Applet` package to the Java system.

Figure 11.2 shows the inheritance hierarchy of the `Applet` class.

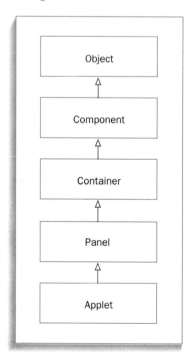

Figure 11.2 `Applet` class hierarchy

Applet inherits from the Panel class (found in the awt package). Panel is a container class, but unlike the Frame and Dialog classes, Panel does not create a separate window of its own. A Panel is suitable for containing information within a larger interface. For example, applets are displayed in a Panel that is contained within a Web browser or applet viewer.

Because Panel is a container, it is possible to add all the awt graphical components, discussed in Chapter 8, directly to the applet.

An abridged listing of the Applet class follows. For a complete listing, refer to your Java documentation.

```
public class Applet extends Panel
{
    // Default Constructor
    public Applet();

    // Instance Methods
    public void destroy();
    public AppletContext getAppletContext();
    public String getAppletInfo();
    public AudioClip getAudioClip(URL  url, String  name);
    public URL getCodeBase();
    public URL getDocumentBase();
    public Image getImage(URL  url, String  name);
    public String getParameter(String  name);
    public void init();
    public void play(URL  url);
    public void play(URL  url, String  name);
    public void start();
    public void stop();

        .
        .
        .

}
```

To create an applet you must create a subclass of Applet and override some or all of the following methods:

- init()—called after the constructor is invoked, when the applet first starts.

- start()—called when the browser opens the applet's window.

- `stop()`—called when the browser changes to a new HTML page, making the applet temporarily hidden.

- `destroy()`—called when the applet exits; reverses any actions taken by `init()`, freeing all resources the applet is holding.

The applet also overrides the `paint()` method from the `java.awt.Component` class to draw an applet on the screen.

> ⚠ You do not need to explicitly call the methods `init( )`, `start( )`, `stop( )`, `destroy( )`, or `paint( )` since they are automatically called for you.
>
> There is no `main` method in a Java applet, as there is in a Java application. Hence, it has become common practice to override methods from the appropriate classes and allow the system to call the methods automatically.

Since the `Applet` class inherits from the `Panel` class, which in turn inherits from the `Container`, `Component`, and `Object` classes, respectively, you are at liberty to override any of the methods found in these classes in an applet.

Program `Example_1` illustrates how to write a simple applet for displaying the familiar phrase "Hello World" in an applet viewer window.

```
// applet to display Hello World in a window

import java.awt.*;
import java.applet.*;

public class Example_1 extends Applet
{
    Font font;

    // override init() method
    public void init()
    {
        setBackground(Color.black);
        font = new Font("SansSerif", Font.BOLD+Font.ITALIC, 36);
    }

    // override paint() method to automatically display information
    // in the applet's window
    public void paint(Graphics g)
```

```
{
      // set font, and color and display message on
      // the panel of the applet at position 50,50
      g.setFont(font);
      g.setColor(Color.yellow);
      g.drawString("Hello World",50,50);
   }
}
```

The applet was stored in a source file called `Example_1.java` and compiled using the same `javac` command as for a Java application—for example `javac Example_1.java`. The compiler produced a Java byte-code file called `Example_1.class`. It is the file `Example_1.class` that is called from within the HTML script file, saved as `Example_1.html`, that was shown earlier. Note that, for each of the `.java` examples of this chapter, there is a corresponding `.html` file that can be used to test the example provided.

After a successful compilation, the applet may be run on an applet viewer by using the command `appletviewer Example_1.html`. Alternatively, the applet may be run on a Java-enabled Web browser by opening the file `Example_1.html` in the browser.

An applet viewer is software that will enable you to load and run applets on your computer. An applet viewer was also downloaded as part of the Java 2 SDK from Sun Microsystems Inc.

Not all the applets developed in this chapter will run on all Web browsers; therefore, you are advised to run the applets using Sun's applet viewer.

A screen shot from the running applet is shown below:

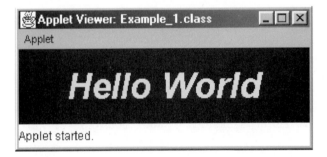

What lessons can we learn from this simple applet?

As you can see, we have used the methods `getFont`, `setColor`, and `drawString` from the `Graphics` class, yet no attempt was made to set up a window on which to draw the graphics! After the program has run, we can close down the window by pointing at the X button in the top right-hand corner of the window or by invoking the drop-down menu from the applet viewer to close the window; yet no window or event listeners have been declared in the program!

Since Java applets run inside a Web browser or applet viewer, the applets take full advantage of the following facilities offered by the host software.

- Applets may run in the browser's window.

- Event-handling (such as closing down a window) already exists for the browser and may be shared by the applet.

- The `Graphics` class may be used in the context of the browser's window.

- The interface of the Web browser or applet viewer may also be used to control the applet—for example, to stop the applet from running.

As an illustration of this last point, Figure 11.3 illustrates a drop-down menu that may be used to control an applet running on the Sun applet viewer.

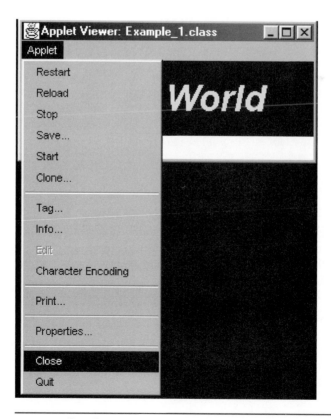

Figure 11.3 Drop-down menu from the applet viewer

The applet is a subclass of the class `java.applet.Applet` and as such inherits all the methods from its superclass.

The method `init()`, inherited from the superclass, has been overridden to set the background color of the applet viewer's window to black, the font to SansSerif with a bold, italic style and a point size of 36.

The Web browser or applet viewer invokes the `paint()` method automatically to allow the applet to draw itself in the browser's window. By overriding the `paint()` method, we can get the browser to draw what we want.

NOW DO THIS   `Example_1` used the `awt` Graphics class to draw a string in the applet's window. Modify `Example_1` to draw shapes, such as rectangles, circles, and polygons.

11.3   Input to Applets

An HTML script file may pass values to an applet, just as arguments may appear in the command line to run a Java application program. The syntax to define arguments in an HTML script file, to be passed to an applet, follows.

SYNTAX

Passing parameters to applets:

```
<APPLET code = .. >
<PARAM NAME=parameter-name VALUE=parameter-value>
.

.
</APPLET>
```

For example, if we wanted to modify Program `Example_1` to accept parameters for defining the size of a character, the font, the color of the letters, the color of the background, and the message, then we would modify the HTML script file as follows.

```
<HTML>
<BODY>

<APPLET code=Example_2.class width=350 height=80>

<PARAM NAME=size VALUE="24">
<PARAM NAME=font VALUE="Serif">
```

```
<PARAM NAME=color VALUE="yellow">
<PARAM NAME=background VALUE="black">
<PARAM NAME=message VALUE="The truth is out there!">

</APPLET>

</BODY>
</HTML>
```

Notice that each parameter is given a name, and the value of the parameter is always treated as a string in the HTML script file.

Within the applet, the value of the parameter is obtained by using the getParameter applet class method. For example, to obtain the point size of a character you would use:

```
int sizeParameter = new Integer(getParameter("size")).intValue();
```

The getParameter method returns the value of the parameter as a string. Therefore, when dealing with numbers, the string will need to be converted into a number of the appropriate type.

Clearly, in the case of the remaining four parameters in the HTML script file, when a parameter is a string type there is no need for any further type conversion. For example,

```
String messageParameter = getParameter("message");
```

The names given to the parameters in the HTML script file need not be the same as the names given to the variables within the applet.

Notice from Program Example_2 that it is perfectly legal to include your own methods in an applet. You are not confined to the predefined methods already mentioned in this chapter. The method convertColorString does just what the name implies—it takes a string parameter that represents the name of a color and returns the appropriate Color constant.

```
// applet to display a message in a window; the font style, font size,
// background and foreground colors and the message are input as parameters
// to the applet

import java.awt.*;
import java.applet.*;

public class Example_2 extends Applet
{
```

```
int    sizeParameter;
String colorParameter;
String backgroundParameter;
String messageParameter;
Font font;

private Color convertColorString(String color)
// method to convert the string name of a color to a Color object
// if the string name does not exist return the Color black
{
    if      (color.equals("red"))     return Color.red;
    else if (color.equals("yellow"))  return Color.yellow;
    else if (color.equals("blue"))    return Color.blue;
    else if (color.equals("magenta")) return Color.magenta;
    else                              return Color.black;

}

// override init method to assign the values of the parameters
// from the HTML file to variables within the applet
public void init()
{
    sizeParameter = new Integer(getParameter("size")).intValue();
    colorParameter = getParameter("color");
    backgroundParameter = getParameter("background");
    messageParameter = getParameter("message");
    font = new Font(getParameter("font"), Font.BOLD,
                    sizeParameter);

}

public void paint(Graphics g)
{
    // set font, color, background color and display
    // a message on the screen at position 50,50
    g.setFont(font);
    g.setColor(convertColorString(colorParameter));
    setBackground(convertColorString(backgroundParameter));

    g.drawString(messageParameter,50,50);

}

}
```

The best way to view the output from this program is to run the program. You will then observe that the background is colored black and the message is written using the color yellow.

Here is a screen shot of the running applet:

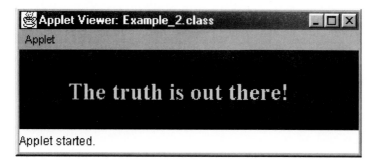

NOW DO THIS▶   Edit the parameters in the HTML script file, choose a different point size, foreground and background colors, and a new message. Save the file and open the HTML script file in either a Web browser or applet viewer. Notice that without changing the Java applet, the appearance of the screen has changed.

Input to applets can also be through any graphical input components displayed in the applet's window, such as dialog boxes, radio buttons, and check boxes. In the next example we choose to use scrollbars for user input. You are already familiar with using a scrollbar for input when you used the `Slider` class from the `avi` package. Using your Java documentation, look up the `java.awt.Scrollbar` class and study the descriptions of the methods in conjunction with the next program.

Program `Example_3` takes the use of graphics with applets a little further. In this program scroll bars are used to input the intensities for three colors—red, green, and blue. The colors are electronically mixed and the resultant color is displayed.

i   Projected light, the type you find on a television screen or computer monitor, uses the primary colors of Red, Green, and Blue (RGB). Reflected light, the type you find on a painting or photograph, uses the primary colors of Red, Yellow, and Blue (RYB).

The `Color` class in the `awt` package contains a constructor to allow you to create a `Color` object from the intensities of the three colors of the RGB system. This `Color` object may then be used as a parameter to set the fill color of a shape from the `Graphics` class using the method `setColor`.

Although the Web browser or applet viewer can handle the events created by closing a window in an applet, an event listener must be used when inputting data via a scroll bar.

```java
// applet to display a color swatch

import java.awt.*;
import java.awt.event.*;
import java.applet.*;

public class Example_3 extends Applet implements AdjustmentListener
{
    Label redLabel = new Label("red");
    Label greenLabel = new Label("green");
    Label blueLabel = new Label("blue");

    TextField redValue = new TextField(4);
    TextField greenValue = new TextField(4);
    TextField blueValue = new TextField(4);

    Scrollbar redBar = new Scrollbar(Scrollbar.HORIZONTAL, 0,1,0,256);
    Scrollbar greenBar = new Scrollbar(Scrollbar.HORIZONTAL,0,1,0,256);
    Scrollbar blueBar = new Scrollbar(Scrollbar.HORIZONTAL,0,1,0,256);

    int red, green, blue;

    public void init()

    {
        setLayout(new FlowLayout(FlowLayout.LEFT));
        setBackground(Color.white);

        // add a text field, label and scrollbar for each of the RGB
        // colors to the panel
        add(redValue); add(redBar);   add(redLabel);
        redBar.setVisible(true);
        add(greenValue); add(greenBar); add(greenLabel);
        greenBar.setVisible(true);
        add(blueValue); add(blueBar);   add(blueLabel);
        blueBar.setVisible(true);
```

```
        // add listeners for each of the RGB scrollbars
        redBar.addAdjustmentListener(this);
        greenBar.addAdjustmentListener(this);
        blueBar.addAdjustmentListener(this);
    }

    public void paint(Graphics g)
    {
        // create a Color object from the intensities of the RGB colors
        Color rgb = new Color(red,green,blue);

        // set the fill color
        g.setColor(rgb);

        // draw a filled 3D rectangle in the panel
        g.fill3DRect(10,100,155,100,true);
    }

    public void adjustmentValueChanged(AdjustmentEvent event)
    {
        // depending upon which scrollbar was moved get the
        // intensity of the color, and set the text field
        // of the RGB color to this value
        if (event.getAdjustable() == redBar)
        {
            red = event.getValue();
            redValue.setText(String.valueOf(red));
        }
        else if (event.getAdjustable() == greenBar)
        {
            green = event.getValue();
            greenValue.setText(String.valueOf(green));
        }
        else
        {
            blue = event.getValue();
            blueValue.setText(String.valueOf(blue));
        }

        // call repaint that will automatically call the overridden
        // paint method
        repaint();
    }
}
```

A screen shot of the running applet follows:

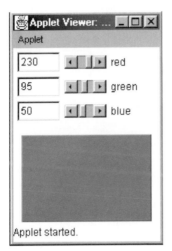

The RGB mix of 230 red, 95 green, and 50 blue gives a burnt-orange/light-brown color.

NOW DO THIS Return to your modified version of program `Example_1`, where you drew different shapes in the applet's window. Introduce a set of radio buttons to input a fill color for the shapes you used. Re-draw all the shapes as filled shapes using the color input from the radio button. If you cannot remember how to construct radio buttons, turn back to Chapter 8 and re-read Section 8.5.

11.4 Playing Sounds

If you examine the methods of the `Applet` class you cannot fail to notice such methods as `getAudioClip` and `play`. Java applets have the ability to play sounds on your computer.

File formats for audio files have already been described in Chapter 3. *AU sound files* use an audio format developed for Sun workstations and are often used to distribute sound clips via the Web.

Ten sounds, ranging from a dog barking to a train whistling, have been downloaded from the Oxford University Sound Archive. This archive allows you public access to many useful sounds. If you want to visit this site, the URL is:

`http://www.comlab.ox.ac.uk/archive/sound.html`

The sounds used in Program `Example_4` may be found under the hot key *Sun demonstration sounds* on this site.

There are three statements necessary to play an audio clip:

1. `AudioClip sound;`

2. `sound = getAudioClip(getCodeBase(), source+".au");`

3. `sound.play();`

The first statement declares a variable `sound` of type `AudioClip`. The class `AudioClip` is part of the `applet` package and contains the following methods.

```
public interface AudioClip
{
    // methods
    public abstract void loop();
    public abstract void play();
    public abstract void stop();
}
```

The second statement initializes the variable `sound` with an `AudioClip` file. The format of the `getAudioClip` method that is invoked in the second statement is:

```
public AudioClip getAudioClip(URL url, String name);
```

As you can see, this method requires two parameters, one of type `URL` and one of type `string`. In our example statement we use the method `getCodeBase()` to provide the required `URL`—it returns the URL from which the applet's code was loaded. The string parameter refers to the directory and filename of a particular `AU` sound file. The string is composed from a concatenation of the name on the button (source of the event) and the type of file (`.au`). In our example:

```
source+".au"
```

The third statement, `play`, executes the `sound` variable by playing the contents of the `AudioClip` file.

```
// program to demonstrate the use of sound in an applet

import java.awt.*;
import java.awt.event.*;
import java.applet.*;

public class Example_4 extends Applet implements ActionListener
{
    // initialize an array with the names of the sounds
    String[] soundNames = {"bark","computer","crash","cuckoo","doorbell",
                           "drip","gong", "ring","spacemusic","train"};
```

```java
// instantiate an array of buttons
Button[] button = new Button[soundNames.length];

AudioClip sound;

// override init method to display an array of buttons
// with the names of the sounds written on the buttons
public void init()
{
    setLayout(null);
    setBackground(Color.white);

    for (int index=0; index != soundNames.length; index++)
    {
        button[index] = new Button(soundNames[index]);
        button[index].setLocation(20,25*index);
        button[index].setSize(100,20);
        button[index].setForeground(Color.white);
        button[index].setBackground(Color.black);
        button[index].addActionListener(this);
        add(button[index]);
    }
}

// use an implementation of the actionPerformed method taken
// from the ActionListener abstract class
public void actionPerformed(ActionEvent event)
{
    // find the name of the button that was pressed
    String source = event.getActionCommand();

    for (int index=0; index != soundNames.length; index++)
    {
        // inspect each sound name with the sound names in the
        // array
        if (source.equals(soundNames[index]))
        {
            // play the appropriate audio clip
            sound = getAudioClip(getCodeBase(),source+".au");
            sound.play();
            return;
        }
    }
}
}
```

Obviously, the results from this applet can be heard only by running the program on a multimedia computer (one that includes a sound card and speakers). The layout of the buttons on the applet follows.

Note that the class `AudioClip` also contains methods `loop()` (to repeatedly play a sound) and `stop()` (to terminate a sound).

NOW DO THIS   Surf the internet for new sources of `.au` sound files. Pay attention to any copyright notices and infringements before you download a new set of sound files. Modify program `Example_4`, re-label the buttons, and play the new sounds of your choice.

11.5   Displaying Images

Let us turn our attention to using applets to display images on the screen. Image files are limited to GIF files (Graphic Interchange Format)—a commonly used file-compression format developed by CompuServe for transferring graphics files to and from online services, and JPEG files (Joint Photographic Experts Group), an image-compression format used to transfer color and monochrome photographs and images over computer networks. Along with GIF, the JPEG format is one of the most common ways photographs are moved over the Web.

The `Applet` class provides a method to read an image over a network and return the corresponding Java object. The signature of the `getImage` method is:

```
public Image getImage(URL url, String name);
```

The `url` is returned by the `Applet` class method `getDocumentBase`. This method returns the base URL from which the HTML document containing the applet was loaded, in other words the `url` of the document in which the applet is embedded.

The `name` refers to the filename of the image.

Within the `java.awt` package is an `Image` class. An `Image` object may not be instantiated directly through a constructor; it must be obtained through a method call, such as `Applet.getImage()`. The `Graphics` class defines several methods for drawing an image; the method used in the following examples has the format:

```
public abstract boolean drawImage(Image img,
                        int x, int y,
                        int width, int height,
                        ImageObserver observer);
```

Program `Example_5` uses these ideas in a program to display three JPEG images on the screen.

```java
// applet to display photographic images on the screen

import java.awt.*;
import java.applet.*;

public class Example_5 extends Applet
{
    // declare names of three Image variables
    Image dancers, mask, figure;

    // override init method to assign the image files to the three
    // variables
    public void init()
    {
        dancers = getImage(getDocumentBase(),"fig1.jpg");
        mask    = getImage(getDocumentBase(),"fig2.jpg");
        figure  = getImage(getDocumentBase(),"fig3.jpg");
    }

    // display the three images on the screen
```

```
public void paint(Graphics g)
{
        g.drawImage(dancers,50,50,150,120,this);
        g.drawImage(mask, 250,50,150,120,this);
        g.drawImage(figure, 450,50,150,120, this);
}
}
```

The following screen shot shows the results of running the program.

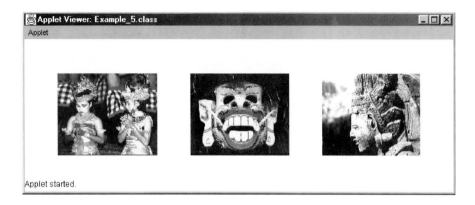

You may have noticed that during the running of this applet the three images did not appear on the screen simultaneously.

11.6 Loading Images

When a program is loading images, due to timing and communication problems, the images may often appear as partial images. To eliminate partial images being displayed, use MediaTracker to load one or more images and wait until those images have been completely loaded and are ready to use. The methods from the `MediaTracker` class keep track of the status of any number of `Image` objects. A partial listing of the `MediaTracker` class follows. For the full documentation, refer to the Sun SDK API documentation.

```
public class MediaTracker extends Object
{
      // fields
      public final static int ABORTED;
      public final static int COMPLETE;
      public final static int ERRORED;
      public final static int LOADING;

      // constructor
```

```
public MediaTracker(Component  comp);

// methods
public void addImage(Image  image, int  id);
public boolean isErrorAny();
public int statusAll(boolean  load);
public void waitForAll() throws InterruptedException;

        .
        .
        .
}
```

Here are descriptions of some of the more important methods:

- addImage() method registers an image to be loaded and tracked and assigns it a specified identifier value.

- isErrorAny() method checks whether any errors have occurred when loading images.

- statusAll() method returns the status of all images, and returns one of the field constants.

- waitForAll() method loads all images and returns when all images have been loaded or received an error. Since you are putting the application program into a waiting state, this method is capable of throwing an interrupted exception that may occur during the running of the application program.

Code to retrieve images from files and to store the images in an array can be written making full use of the methods in the MediaTracker class.

In this segment of code, the filenames of the images are stored in a one-dimensional array called filenames, and the images themselves are stored in a one-dimensional array called photos.

```
// instantiate an object of the MediaTracker class
MediaTracker tracker = new MediaTracker(this);

// declare a one-dimensional array to contain the images of the photos
Image[] photos = new Image[filenames.length];

// for each image file
for (int index=0; index != filenames.length; index++)
{
     // get the image object from the file and store it in the array
     photos[index] = getImage(getDocumentBase(),filenames[index]);
     // register an image to be loaded and tracked
     tracker.addImage(photos[index],index);
```

```
}

// wait for all images to be loaded
try
{
        tracker.waitForAll();
}

catch (InterruptedException e){}
```

NOW DO THIS   Modify program `Example_5` by incorporating the media tracker code. Re-compile and run the program. Do you notice how smoothly the images are displayed on the screen?

11.7   Arrays Revisited

Up to now we have managed to use one-dimensional arrays for storing either primitive data types or objects. Now is the time to increase your knowledge of arrays by investigating two-dimensional arrays. The topic of two-dimensional arrays has nothing to do with applets and threads, however, it is necessary to introduce the ideas of a two-dimensional array before solving the next problem on image maps.

An array is not confined to one dimension (one index). In fact, an array can be extended to two dimensions and beyond in order to provide a flexible data structure for the solution to a problem. A *two-dimensional array* is a repetition of one-dimensional arrays. The structure can be thought of as a matrix or grid. In Figure 11.4 the two-dimensional array represents the average monthly rainfall over four regions of an island and is composed from four one-dimensional arrays, where each one-dimensional array is represented by a row. Each row represents a region of the island—row 0 is North, row 1 is South, row 2 is East, and row 3 is West. Each column represents the average rainfall for one month—column 0 is January, column 1 is February, column 2 is March, and so on up to and including column 11 which represents December.

The array may be initialized at its point of declaration as follows.

```
int[][] rainfall = {{14,13,11,9,5,3,1,1,4,8,9,12},
                    {17,18,15,13,11,9,7,8,9,10,13,15},
                    {9,8,6,4,2,1,0,1,3,7,9,10},
                    {12,11,9,6,4,2,1,3,5,8,10,13}};
```

	0	1	2	3	4	5	6	7	8	9	10	11
0	14	13	11	9	5	3	1	1	4	8	9	12
1	17	18	15	13	11	9	7	8	9	10	13	15
2	9	8	6	4	2	1	0	1	3	7	9	10
3	12	11	9	6	4	2	1	3	5	8	10	13

rows (left label); columns (bottom label)

Figure 11.4   A two-dimensional array storing average rainfall values

Alternatively the array may be declared

```
static final int REGIONS = 4;
static final int MONTHS = 12;

int[][]rainfall = new float[REGIONS][MONTHS];
```

where there are 4 regions and 12 months and the data for the average rainfall can be stored in the array having first been read from a data stream.

Access to any cell in the two-dimensional array is by row and then by column. For example, the rainfall for the North region (row 0) in the month of May (column 4) is 5. This array element is written as `rainfall[0][4]`.

What is the average rainfall for the following:

(i) South region, during March?   Answer - rainfall[1][2] = 15

(ii) East region during September?   Answer - rainfall[2][8] = 3

Access to each cell, in turn, within the two-dimensional array is possible using two `for` loops. An outer `for` loop is used to process each row, and an inner `for` loop processes each cell within the one-dimensional array depicted by the row. For example, the contents of the two-dimensional array illustrated in Figure 11.4 can be output using the following code.

```
for (int row=0; row != REGIONS; row++)
{
   for (int column=0; column != MONTHS; column++)
   {
      screen.write(rainfall[row][column] + " ");
   }

   screen.write("\n");
}
```

If you perform a desk check on this code, you will end up with the following values.

row	0												
(row != 4)?	true												
column	0	1	2	3	4	5	6	7	8	9	10	11	12
(column != 12)?	true	true	true	true	true	true	true	true	true	true	true	true	false
rainfall[row][column]	14	13	11	9	5	3	1	1	4	8	9	12	

row	1												
(row != 4)?	true												
column	0	1	2	3	4	5	6	7	8	9	10	11	12
(column != 12)?	true	true	true	true	true	true	true	true	true	true	true	true	false
rainfall[row][column]	17	18	15	13	11	9	7	8	9	10	13	15	

row	2												
(row != 4)?	true												
column	0	1	2	3	4	5	6	7	8	9	10	11	12
(column != 12)?	true	true	true	true	true	true	true	true	true	true	true	true	false
rainfall[row][column]	9	8	6	4	2	1	0	1	3	7	9	10	

row	3												
(row != 4)?	true												
column	0	1	2	3	4	5	6	7	8	9	10	11	12
(column != 12)?	true	true	true	true	true	true	true	true	true	true	true	true	false
rainfall[row][column]	12	11	9	6	4	2	1	3	5	8	10	13	

row	4
(row != 4)?	false

It is also possible to use two `for` loops to access each cell in order to add together every number to compute the total of all the rainfall averages for the island.

```
int total = 0;

for (int row=0; row != REGIONS; row++)
{
    for (int column=0; column != MONTHS; column++)
    {
        total = total + rainfall[row][column];
    }
}
```

You should desk check the code so that you understand how all the numbers in a single row are added together before progressing to the next row.

Using just a single `for` loop to control access to each column, it is possible to calculate the total of all the rainfall averages for any region, provided the region is first translated into a `row` value.

```
for (int column = 0; column != MONTHS; column++)
    regionalTotal = regionalTotal + rainfall[row][column];
```

Similarly, using a single `for` loop to control access to each row, it is possible to calculate the total of all the rainfall averages for any month over the island, provided the month is first translated into a `column` value.

```
for (int row = 0; row != REGIONS; row++)
    monthlyTotal = monthlyTotal + rainfall[row][column];
```

NOW DO THIS   Write an applet to store the average rainfall data, and calculate and display the following information.

(1) The total average rainfall for the island.

(2) The total average rainfall for each region.

(3) The total average rainfall for each month.

(4) The driest month on the island.

Hint—store the names of the months in a one-dimensional array so you can use the names of the months for output when required.

11.8   Image Maps

The topics covered in the previous two sections on loading images and two-dimensional arrays can be put into practice in the solution to the next problem.

To create an image map, first an image is displayed on the screen. The coordinates of the parts of the image where you want events to occur, such as displaying further information, are stored in a two-dimensional array for future use.

When a mouse-pointer passes over the image on the screen, the coordinates of the mouse in relation to the parts of the image where events occur are known and can be compared. If the mouse-pointer is within a set region, then it is possible to, say, display new information on the screen relating to that part of the image.

In the following example, an image of the World is displayed on the screen, and when a mouse passes over the image, the coordinates of the mouse in relation to the image are known, and the event of a mouse button being pressed can be used to display information on the screen relating to that part of the World image selected by the mouse pointer. In this example, when the mouse button is pressed over a country of the World, the national flag and the name of the country are displayed in the top right-hand corner of the screen.

The position of the approximate center of each country is stored as percentages of the width and height of the World image in a two-dimensional array. Upon receiving a mouse-button pressed event, the coordinates of the position of the mouse are compared to the position of the center of each country. If the position of the mouse pointer is within pre-defined limits, then the image of the country's national flag and the name of the country are displayed on the screen.

In this example, images of eight national flags are stored in the `gifImage` array; a ninth image, that of the World map, is stored in the last cell `gifImage[8]` of the array.

```
// program to demonstrate image maps

import java.awt.*;
import java.awt.event.*;
import java.applet.*;

public class Example_6 extends Applet
{
      static final int NUMBER_OF_IMAGES = 9;

      String[] countries = {"Australia","Canada","India","Japan",
                      "New Zealand","Spain","UK","USA"};
      double[][] mapRef  = {{0.77,0.54},{0.27,0.26},{0.65,0.4},{0.74,0.33},
                      {0.84,0.6},{0.5,0.32},{0.5,0.28},{0.28,0.32}};
```

```
Image[] gifImages  = new Image[NUMBER_OF_IMAGES];

Applet applet;
MediaTracker tracker;

int width, height;
int x,y,screenX, screenY;

public void init()
{
      applet = this;
      Toolkit tools = this.getToolkit();
      Dimension size = tools.getScreenSize();
      width = size.width;
      height = size.height;

      tracker = new MediaTracker(this);

      // get images from the files and assign to the gifImages array

      for (int index=0; index != gifImages.length; index++)
      {
            gifImages[index] = getImage(getDocumentBase(),
                                     "image"+index+".gif");
            tracker.addImage(gifImages[index],index);
      }

      try
      {
            tracker.waitForAll();
      }
      catch (InterruptedException e){}

      addMouseListener(new HandleMouseEvents());
}

// paint single image of World map
public void paint(Graphics g)
{
      g.drawImage(gifImages[8],100,150,800,400,this);
}

private class HandleMouseEvents extends MouseAdapter
```

```
{
    public void mousePressed(MouseEvent event)
    {
        Image flag = null;
        String country = null;

        x=event.getX();
        y=event.getY();
        Graphics g = getGraphics();

        // erase previous flag from window
        g.setColor(Color.white);
        g.fillRect(750,25,120,130);
        g.setColor(Color.black);

        for (int index=0; index != countries.length; index++)
        {
            screenX = (int)(width*mapRef[index][0]);
            screenY = (int)(height*mapRef[index][1]);

            if ((x >= screenX-15 && x < screenX+15) &&
                (y >= screenY-15 && y < screenY+15))
            {
                flag = gifImages[index];
                country = countries[index];
            }
        }

        if (flag != null)
        {
            g.drawImage(flag,750,25,120,90,applet);
            g.drawString(country,750,125);
        }
    }
}
}
```

Here is a screen shot from running the applet and selecting a map position within Canada.

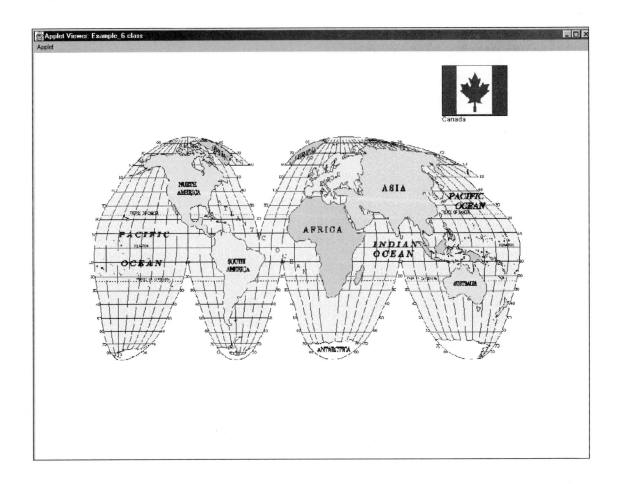

NOW DO THIS   Modify program `Example_6` by increasing the number of map references in the two-dimensional array where the flags of new countries will be displayed. Supply a set of new images for the new flags.

i   Multimedia programs often require a large number of media files to be downloaded with an applet. Normally, each file is transferred in a uncompressed form. To improve the efficiency of data transfer and data storage, all dependent files may be combined into one single compressed Java Archive (JAR) file. The single compressed file can be transferred from the Web server to the Web browser more efficiently. See your JDK documentation for further information.

11.9 Threads

Program `Example_7` is written to simulate a digital clock that contains a display for hours, minutes, and seconds. The class `Calendar` found in the `java.util` package contains many methods and constants to represent the date and time.

The constructors are protected in the `Calendar` class, and it is necessary to use the `getInstance()` method that returns an instance of a `Calendar` subclass. For example,

```
Calendar time=Calendar.getInstance();
```

If you inspect the contents of the `Calendar` class, you may notice a list of field constants, among which you will find the integer class constants `HOUR`, `MINUTE`, and `SECOND`. You need to use the instance method `get` to obtain a value for the three field constants. For example,

```
int hours = time.get(Calendar.HOUR);
int mins = time.get(Calendar.MINUTE);
int secs = time.get(Calendar.SECOND);
```

With this newfound knowledge, you may think it is very straightforward to write an applet to regularly sample the time of day and display the values for hours, minutes, and seconds. Indeed, the program is straightforward, and chances are you may create a program similar to Program `Example_7`. You may recall that the `paint` method is called by `Java` whenever an applet needs to be painted. However, telling the applet to continuously paint the new time requires a call to the method `repaint()` found in the `Container` class. The `repaint()` method in turn automatically calls the `update()` method that clears the screen and then calls `paint`.

In the program, the `paint` method is overridden and contains the code to display the time on the screen. After the time (hours, minutes, and seconds) has been updated, there always follows a call to `repaint`.

```
// applet to demonstrate the need for threads when
// continuously repainting a window

import java.applet.*;
import java.awt.*;
import java.util.*;

public class Example_7 extends Applet
{
      Font font = new Font("Monospaced",Font.BOLD,16);

      int hours, mins, secs;
```

```java
// override the start method to calculate the time of day
// and call the repaint() method to display the time
public void start()
{
    while (true)
    {
        Calendar time=Calendar.getInstance();

        hours = time.get(Calendar.HOUR);
        mins = time.get(Calendar.MINUTE);
        secs = time.get(Calendar.SECOND);

        repaint();
    }
}

// display the time of day on the screen
public void paint(Graphics g)
{
    g.setFont(font);
    g.drawString(String.valueOf(hours)+":"+
                 String.valueOf(mins)+":"+
                 String.valueOf(secs),50,50);
}
}
```

A screen shot from running the applet follows:

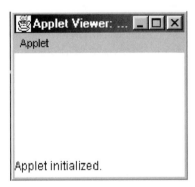

Oh, the results did not work out quite as expected! The applet window has been displayed; however, there is no sight of the time! When you attempt to stop the applet running, you continue to press the mouse button over the window-close symbol, and if you are lucky, after a short while the window closes and the program stops running. This is not a very satisfactory outcome to what appeared to be a simple solution to the problem.

What has gone wrong?

An applet does not have a `main` method. Instead, we override the methods `init()`, `start()`, `stop()`, and so on and let the Web browser or applet viewer invoke these overridden methods. In other words, the running of the applet is dependent upon when the browser or viewer decides to execute methods like `init()`, `start()`, `stop()`. An applet, unlike an application, is not in control of itself; it simply responds when told to do so by the Web browser or applet viewer.

Because the Web browser or applet viewer is in control, it is necessary that the methods you override should take very little time to execute. These methods should not enter into time-consuming work.

The method `repaint()` is a request for the applet viewer or Web browser to repaint your applet as soon as it can. The important words are "as soon as it can." In Program `Example_7`, the Web browser or applet viewer cannot regain control and find time to execute `repaint()` since it is stuck in an infinite loop. To prove the point, insert the statement `System.out.println("start method");` anywhere inside the `while` loop; recompile the applet, then execute the corresponding HTML source file. We know that the applet window remains blank, but just look at the terminal or MSDOS window—the statement `start method` is displayed over and over again, indicating that the applet is still running, but the Web browser or applet viewer has no spare time to execute the `repaint()` method. Convinced?

To resolve this problem we turn to Java threads. Most desktop PCs contain a single processor; however, the illusion of several programs running at once can be produced by rapidly swapping between the programs that have been loaded, allocating a few milliseconds to each program in rotation. The technique is known as *multitasking* and is operating-system dependent. Each process runs in its *own* memory space under a single *thread* of control.

As a thread executes code, it carries out a sequence of actions; it does the following:

- Uses the value of a variable.

- Assigns a value to a variable.

- Performs arithmetic operations.

- Performs conditional tests.

- Performs method invocations.

Within a program there are often separate actions that are more or less independent of each other and that could be run as separate *subprocesses* within the overall program. (Often it is useful to think of a subprocess as a thread.) This approach is called *multithreading*.

The technique of multithreading depends more on the language in which the program was written than on the operating system being used. Java is an implicitly threaded language—several threads are started automatically every time you run a Java applet or application. For example, there will be separate threads for each of the following:

- Events generated by users (pressing buttons in a graphical user interface).

- Automatic garbage collection (watching for previously allocated memory that is no longer needed and freeing it up).

- Creation of a programmer's own threads for running sections of a program independently.

You may wonder how the computer can cope with more than one thread of execution at any one time. Thread objects allow multithreaded Java programming, where a single Java Virtual Machine can execute many threads in an interleaved or concurrent manner. Threads independently execute Java code that operates on Java values and objects residing in shared memory.

The computer must share its time between executing the code running in different threads. Unfortunately, different operating systems have different approaches for coping with multithreading. As an example, both Windows 95 and Windows NT give each thread a portion (or slice) of time to use the processor; at the end of the time slice, the code running in that thread is suspended (swapped from the processor) and the code for the next thread that is ready to run is given a slice of time on the processor. The business of running program code on the processor for different threads of execution continues in a round-robin manner until program execution is completed or the program is abandoned.

A thread has a life cycle:

- A thread must be created (born) using an appropriate constructor.

- A thread must be started; however, depending on the availability of the processor, the thread may only go into a ready (to be run) state.

- A thread can be running (the program code associated with the thread is being executed on the processor).

- After a thread has been running, it can go into one of several states.

  - Ready (to be run when it is the thread's turn and a processor becomes free).

  - Sleeping (not requiring the processor until it wakes up after a stated time period).

  - Suspended (not requiring the processor until it is resumed at some later time).

  - Waiting (not requiring the processor until notified that it may be transferred to a ready state).

- Blocked (not requiring the processor until the completion of an I/O operation).

- A thread can die when it is no longer required. The garbage collector will return the unwanted memory space back to the heap.

To solve the problem of the digital clock not appearing, we need to allow the applet to run in parallel with the Web browser. In other words, we need to give the applet its own thread of execution to run alongside the Web browser.

The `java.lang.Thread` class encapsulates all the information about a single thread running on the Java interpreter. To create a thread you must pass a `Runnable` object (an object that implements the `Runnable` interface by defining a `run()` method) to the `Thread` constructor, or you must subclass `Thread` so that it defines its own `run()` method.

The `run()` method of the `Thread` or of the specified runnable object is the body of the thread—it begins executing when the `start()` method of the `Thread` object is called, and it executes until either the `run()` method returns or the `stop()` method of the `Thread` object is called. An abridged listing of the `Thread` class follows. For a complete listing, consult your Java documentation.

```
public class Thread extends Object implements Runnable
{
    // constructor(s)
    public Thread();
    public Thread(String name);
    public Thread(Runnable target);
    .
    // class methods
    public static native Thread currentThread();
    public static native void sleep(long millis) throws
    InterruptedException;
    .
    // public instance methods
    public void destroy();
    public final String getName();
    public final native boolean isAlive();
    public final void resume();
    public void run();
    public synchronized native void start();
    public final void stop();
    public final void suspend();
    .
}
```

A thread is declared as a variable of type `Thread`, for example, as `Thread appletThread`. Until the variable has been instantiated, it will have a `null` reference.

A thread can be started—for example, `appletThread.start()`. Don't become confused over the `start()` methods; this one is from the class `Thread` and not from the class `Applet`. *After a thread has been started, it automatically invokes the* `run()` *method*.

The code of a thread may be executed by ensuring that it is included within the `run()` method. The method `run()` is the only method in the interface `java.lang.Runnable` and must be implemented in the applet containing the thread.

A thread may sleep for a stated number of milliseconds. For example, the thread currently executing the code contained in the `run` method would sleep for one second by including the statement `Thread.sleep(1000)`. The danger in putting a thread to sleep stems from the fact that a program may be interrupted (for example, by using the Ctrl C keys to abandon program execution), in which case the thread needs to be cleared from the system. Whenever you use the class method `sleep`, you must always provide an exception handler should an interrupt exception occur.

> *i* When a thread is in sleep mode, the processor is free to work on other tasks. As a result, sleeping is a very useful (non) activity for threads to do when not needed.

A thread may be stopped by invoking `appletThread.stop()`. Don't become confused over the `stop()` methods; this one is from the class `Thread` and not from the class `Applet`.

Program `Example_8` is a modification of Program `Example_7` and includes a thread for the running of the applet to allow the Web browser or applet viewer to run in parallel, and hence process the request to repaint the screen.

Notice that the standard applet method `init()` has been used to create a thread and start it running, and `destroy()` has been used to stop a thread. The method `run()` from the `Runnable` interface has also been overridden.

```
// program to display a digital clock allowing the calculation of
// the time and displaying the value to run in its own thread of
// execution

import java.applet.*;
import java.awt.*;
import java.util.*;

public class Example_8 extends Applet implements Runnable
{
        Thread appletThread;
```

```
Font font = new Font("Monospaced",Font.BOLD,16);

int hours, mins, secs;

// override the init() method to initialize and start
// a thread of execution
public void init()
{
      if (appletThread == null)
      {
            appletThread = new Thread(this);
            appletThread.start(); // start from class Thread
      }
}


// calculate the time of day, and call the repaint method to
// display the time
public void run() // implemented from the interface Runnable
{
      while (true)
      {
            Calendar time=Calendar.getInstance();

            hours = time.get(Calendar.HOUR);
            mins = time.get(Calendar.MINUTE);
            secs = time.get(Calendar.SECOND);

            repaint();

            // generate a short pause by letting the thread sleep
            try{Thread.sleep(1000);}
            catch(InterruptedException i){System.exit(1);}
      }
}

// override the destroy() method to stop the execution of the thread
// and nullify the thread
public void destroy()
{
      if (appletThread != null)
      {
            appletThread.stop();
            appletThread = null;
      }
```

```
}

// display the time in the applet's window
public void paint(Graphics g)
{
        g.setFont(font);
        g.drawString(String.valueOf(hours)+":"+
                    String.valueOf(mins)+":"+
                        String.valueOf(secs),50,50);

}
}
```

You are advised to run the program to verify that it does accurately display the time of day. Because the applet is running in its own thread, the Web browser or applet viewer can react to the mouse button being pressed over the X to close the applet window. Closing the applet window will result in the `destroy` method being called and the thread of execution being terminated.

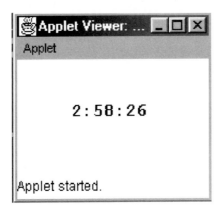

Always get into the habit of running an applet in its own thread. You may want to run more than one applet on a Web page, so concurrent processing becomes almost mandatory!

> ⚠️ The methods `stop()` and `stop(Throwable)` from the class `java.lang.Thread` have been *deprecated* in Java 1.2. Deprecation means that Sun Microsystems, Inc., may not support these methods in future releases of Java. When the programs containing the `stop` method were compiled, the deprecation was flagged as a warning after compilation. All the programs containing the `stop` method still ran correctly using the Java 1.2 interpreter.

CASE STUDY

An Example of Multithreading

Statement of the Problem   Write a program to display three frames in an applet's window. Each frame has a solid black rectangle (that appears as a bar and increases in length with time. Associated with each frame is a separate thread of execution. The threads are given different attributes of sleepiness. Some threads may sleep for a long time before doing any active work in increasing the length of the rectangle; other threads require less sleep and are always adding to the length of the rectangle.

The time each thread is given to sleep can be calculated as a random number. If the maximum sleeping period of a thread is 5,000 ms, then a random number generated between 0.0 and 5.0 will scale the time to sleep between 0 and 5,000 ms. You will rarely get three random numbers generated with the same value; therefore, you will nearly always create threads that sleep for longer periods than other threads.

Identification of Classes and Methods

The solution to this problem uses three classes:

- A class to create a `RectangularWindow` object from a frame with a method to increment and draw a solid rectangle.

- A class to create a `GraphicThread` that has instance variables of `timeAsleep` and a `threadFrame`, with a method `run` that implements the Runnable interface. All objects of this class will execute the `run` method automatically. Hence, all objects will go through a period of sleeping, followed by drawing of their extended rectangle in the frame.

- A class that extends the `Applet` class. Its function is to instantiate and start the three threads, and when the applet window is closed, to destroy the three threads. Since the third class is trivial, it will not be discussed further, but implemented directly in the coding section.

Algorithm Development

The constructor and methods for the class `RectangularWindow` follow.

```
public class RectangularWindow extends Frame
{
    public RectangularWindow(String s);
    public void drawInWindow();
}
```

The UML representation of the constructor is shown in Figure 11.5.

The instance variables of the `RectangularWindow` class contains the dimensions of the frame and the dimensions of the rectangle. The width and height of the frame are initialized

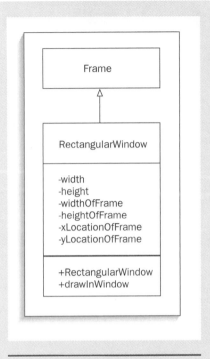

Figure 11.5 UML representation of the
class `RectangularWindow`

from the Toolkit methods, and the width and height of the rectangle are based upon percentages of the width and height of the frame.

The horizontal (x-axis) position of a rectangle is fixed as a percentage of the width of the frame; however, the vertical (y-axis) position of the rectangle with respect to the applet's window must be declared as a `static` integer variable to prevent different frames from being drawn one on top of another.

The parameter of the constructor is any message that you want to display in the window.

Algorithm for the Constructor

1. set the size of the frame
2. set the location of the frame
3. update the position of the next frame so there is no frame overlap
4. set the background color of the frame

Since this method is responsible for drawing the solid rectangle, there is a need to create a variable of type `Graphic` and hence the local declaration of

```
Graphics g = getGraphics();
```

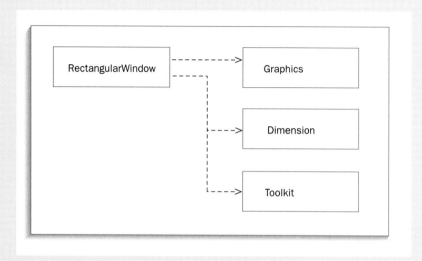

Figure 11.6 UML dependencies

Algorithm for the Method `drawInWindow`

1. get an instance of a graphic
2. set the graphic to the color black
3. increase the length of the rectangle by the incremental length
4. draw the rectangle at a set position within the frame

```java
import java.awt.*;

public class RectangularWindow extends Frame
{

        static final int INCREMENTAL_LENGTH = 5;    // size bar increases
        static final int WIDTH_OF_BAR = 10;         // width of bar

        private int width;
        private int height;
        private int widthOfFrame;
        private int heightOfFrame;
        private int xLocationOfFrame;

        static int yLocationOfFrame = 250; // unique y coordinate of top-LH
                                           // corner for each frame
        int lengthOfBar = 0;               // initial length of bar
```

```
      public RectangularWindow(String s)
      {
            super(s);

            Toolkit tools = this.getToolkit();
            Dimension size = tools.getScreenSize();
            width = size.width;
            height = size.height;

            widthOfFrame = (int)(0.9f*width);        // 90% width of screen
            heightOfFrame = (int)(0.10f*height);     // 10% height of
                                                     //   screen
            xLocationOfFrame = (int)(0.05f*width);   // 5% width of screen

            // set up attributes of a single frame
            setSize(widthOfFrame,heightOfFrame);
            setLocation(xLocationOfFrame, yLocationOfFrame);
            yLocationOfFrame = yLocationOfFrame+heightOfFrame;
            setBackground(Color.yellow);
      }


      public void drawInWindow()
      // method to draw a black rectangle in the frame
      {
            // coordinates of top-LH corner of bar
            final int X = (int)(0.01f*widthOfFrame);
            final int Y = (int)(0.55f*heightOfFrame);

            Graphics g = getGraphics();

            g.setColor(Color.black);
            lengthOfBar=lengthOfBar+INCREMENTAL_LENGTH;
            g.fillRect(X,Y,lengthOfBar,WIDTH_OF_BAR);
      }
}
```

The constructor and method of the `GraphicThread` class follow.

```
public class GraphicThread extends Thread implements Runnable
{
      public GraphicThread();
      public void run();
}
```

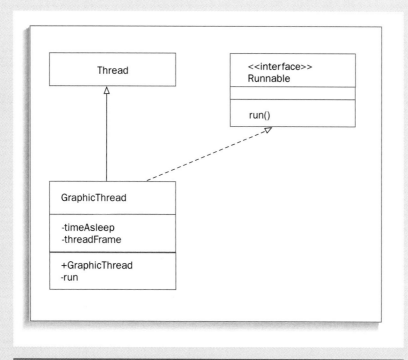

Figure 11.7 UML representation of the class `GraphicThread`

Notice that the method `run` is not available for public use from the class `GraphicThread`. The `run` method cannot be described as `private` since it must implement a predefined signature from the `Runnable` interface. This class contains an integer constant representing the maximum time a thread will spend asleep (5,000 ms) and an instance variable representing the time asleep. Since every thread has its own frame, an instance variable must be declared of type `RectangularWindow`.

Algorithm for the Constructor `GraphicThread`
1. calculate the time a thread spends asleep by using a random number generator
2. instantiate a new frame for the thread

Algorithm for the Method `run`
1. while true
2.   thread sleeps predefined time
3.   set threads frame visible
4.   draw solid rectangle for threads frame

```
public class GraphicThread extends Thread implements Runnable
{
      static final int DELAY = 5000;    // maximum delay of 5 seconds
      int timeAsleep;                   // time a thread spends asleep
      RectangularWindow threadFrame;    // the frame used by a thread

      public GraphicThread()
      {
            super();

            // calculate sleep time for thread
            timeAsleep = (int)(DELAY*Math.random());
            // instantiate and set the attributes of a frame
            threadFrame = new
            RectangularWindow("Thread sleeps for "+
                           String.valueOf(timeAsleep)+" milliseconds");
      }

      // each thread will be scheduled an amount of time to run by the
      // operating system, however some threads will remain asleep during
      // their allocated amount of time
      public void run()
      {
            while (true)
            {
                  try{sleep(timeAsleep);}
                  catch(InterruptedException i){System.exit(1);}
                  // set frame visible and extend length of rectangle
```

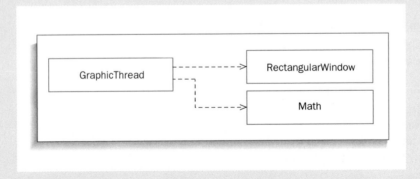

Figure 11.8 UML dependencies

```
                        threadFrame.setVisible(true);
                        threadFrame.drawInWindow();
                }
        }
}
```

Testing

Up to now all our desk checking activities have been confined to programs that run in a single thread. In this example we have three threads to consider. In constructing a table of results we will show elapsed time over a short period.

During this time period different events of drawing and sleeping will take place for each thread. We may assume that the time spent asleep for each thread is 1s, 2s, and 3s, respectively, and the amount of drawing a thread can perform in 1s is just one rectangle.

The test data represents the time spent asleep for each thread. Let thread1 = 1s, thread2 = 2s, and thread3 = 3s.

time interval	0	1	2	3	4	5	6	7	8	9
thread1 (position)	0									
asleep	1									
lengthOfRectangle	0	5	10	15	20	25	30	35	40	45
thread2 (position)	100									
asleep	2									
lengthOfRectangle	0	0	5	5	10	10	15	15	20	20
thread3 (position)	200									
asleep	3									
lengthOfRectangle	0	0	0	5	5	5	10	10	10	15

The coding of the applet used to test the methods in the classes RectangularWindow and GraphicThread follows:

```
// applet to demonstrate three threads of execution;
// each thread makes different rates of progress in drawing a
// solid rectangle in its own window;
// the thread given less time to sleep will draw the longest
// rectangle compared with the thread that sleeps for longer periods
// of time
```

```
import java.applet.*;

public class Example_9 extends Applet
{
        GraphicThread firstThread, secondThread, thirdThread;

        // override init() method to instantiate and start three threads
        public void init()
        {
                firstThread = new GraphicThread();
                secondThread = new GraphicThread();
                thirdThread = new GraphicThread();

                firstThread.start();
                secondThread.start();
                thirdThread.start();
        }

        // override destroy() method to stop the three threads running
        public void destroy()
        {
                firstThread.stop();
                secondThread.stop();
                thirdThread.stop();
        }
}
```

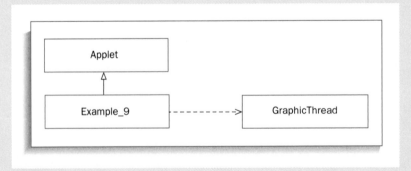

Figure 11.9 UML Dependencies

A screen shot from the running applet follows. Once again, we recommend that you run this program to gain a better insight into the functionality of threads. If you edit the program so that none of the threads sleep, you will get an idea of how your operating system schedules the running of many threads.

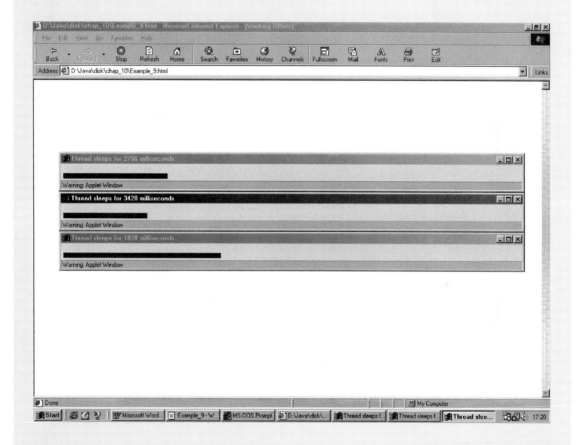

Threads are not unique to applets. The following application program uses the classes `RectangularWindow` and `GraphicThread` to demonstrate the same functionality as the previous applet. Notice that despite a radio-button component being used in a modal form, it cannot block the running of the three graphic threads since they are scheduled to run independently of the application program. Only when the radio button is pressed will the remainder of the code that follows the statement `endProgram.showradioButtons()` be executed. The remainder of the code in the application then kills off the three graphic threads.

```
// application to demonstrate three threads of execution;

public class Example_10
{
    static public void main(String[] args)
    {
        String[] quit = {"EXIT PROGRAM"};

        WindowPane screen = new WindowPane();
        screen.showWindowPane();
        RadioButtons endProgram = new
        RadioButtons(screen,"What next?",quit);

        GraphicThread firstThread = new GraphicThread();
        GraphicThread secondThread = new GraphicThread();
        GraphicThread thirdThread = new GraphicThread();

        firstThread.start();
        secondThread.start();
        thirdThread.start();

        endProgram.showRadioButtons();

        firstThread.stop();
        secondThread.stop();
        thirdThread.stop();
    }
}
```

A screen shot of the program running follows.

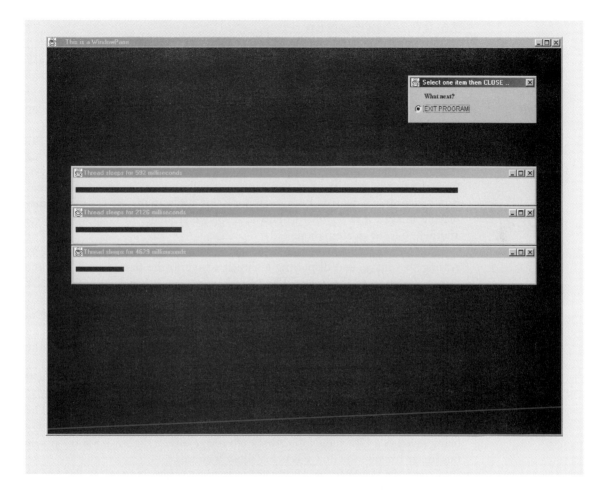

NOW DO THIS   Using the `RectangularWindow` class and the `GraphicThread` class for reference:

(1) Create a `Circle` class that contains a constructor to set the coordinates of the center of the circle, set the fill color of the circle, and initialize the radius of the circle. The class also contains a method to draw the circle. Every time the method to draw the circle is called, the radius of the circle is increased by a small incremental amount, up to an upper limit. When the upper limit for the radius of the circle has been reached, the radius of the circle is decreased by a small incremental amount down to a lower limit. The effect is to re-draw a circle many times so that it appears to pulsate between the lower and upper limits of its radius.

(2) Create a `GraphicThread` class that instantiates a `Circle` class, and will allow the circle to pulsate.

(3) Write a test program to display pulsating circles of different colors in different parts of the screen.

11.10   Animation

One of the simplest techniques for animation is to display an animated GIF image from an applet. The disadvantage of embedding an animated GIF into an applet lies in the amount of flicker you get from the picture as the screen is redrawn. It is better to use animated GIFs directly in HTML files rather than trying to use them in applets.

You may recall seeing children's books in which a series of single pictures are drawn on, say, the odd-numbered pages of the book, with each picture differing very slightly from the previous picture. By rapidly thumbing through the pages, from the first page to the last, you can get the illusion of movement or animation of the drawn figures. Because applets and applications are capable of displaying images, it is possible in Java to display a sequence of images, one after another, to form an animation.

The technique involves the sequence of displaying an image, followed by erasing the image, and displaying a similar image to the first apart from some minor alteration to the image. The technique is repeated until all images have been shown.

This technique is fine in theory, but very disappointing to implement in practice since it suffers from a considerable amount of flicker caused by an image being cleared from the screen and a new image being drawn on the screen.

Let us tackle the problem of flicker by looking at a worked example. We will store a series of GIF images, 16 images to be precise, in an array, and display each image from the array. The first four images are shown in Figure 11.10. The image is the 3-D word Java, produced using a drawing package, with each image being saved as a GIF file. Notice that each image differs slightly from the previous image because the image is being tilted forwards.

The code you may intuitively write to display the images on the screen might follow the same technique as for displaying the digital clock. You override the `paint` method with the code required to display each image, and you call the `repaint()` method from within an overridden `run()` method. Your code might look something like this.

```
public void paint(Graphics g)
{
    // draw image on the applet's screen
    g.drawImage(gifImages[index],0,0,width,height,this);
}
```

Note that `index` is a class variable that is incremented from within the `run()` method. The `run()` method may be overridden with the following code.

image java0.gif

image java1.gif

image java2.gif

image java3.gif

Figure 11.10 A selection of GIF images used in the animation in Program Example_11

```
public void run()
{
    Graphics g = getGraphics();

    while (true)
    {
        repaint();
        index++;
        index = index % 16;

        try{appletThread.sleep(100);} catch (InterruptedException e){}
    }
}
```

The code will produce an animation; however, there is a discernible flicker between the drawing and clearing of the images. The call to `repaint()` automatically calls the method `update()`. The `update()` method clears the area of the screen in use and then automatically calls the `paint()` method. The `update()` method is the method responsible for the flicker; you perceive an image, followed by a blank screen, followed by another image.

A trick to reduce flicker is not to use `repaint()` but to override the `paint()` method with a technique called graphical double-buffering. The `paint()` method is then called directly.

Graphical double-buffering uses two drawing areas—one off screen and the other on the applet's screen. All erasure of images and drawing of images is performed off screen; the created off-screen image is then drawn on the applet's screen. With this technique there is no erasure of images on the applet's screen; hence, flicker is reduced. The technique requires two instance variables being declared, one to hold the image off screen and one to hold the graphics off screen. For example:

```
Image offScreenImage;
Graphics offScreenGraphics;
```

During the applet's initialization phase, both these objects can be initialized with values. For example:

```
offScreenImage = createImage(width,height);
offScreenGraphics = offScreenImage.getGraphics();
```

where `createImage(width, height)` from the `Component` class will create an image that may be used off screen. The `getGraphics()` method returns a `Graphics` object that can be used for drawing into off-screen images.

The `paint()` method is overridden as follows.

```
public void paint(Graphics g)
{
        int topLeftX=75;  // abscissa of top left-hand corner of image
        int topLeftY=40;  // ordinate top left-hand corner of image

        int imageWidth = gifImages[index].getWidth(this);
        int imageHeight = gifImages[index].getHeight(this);

        // erase previous image from off screen graphics area
        offScreenGraphics.setColor(Color.white);
        offScreenGraphics.fillRect(0,0,width,height);

        // draw next image in off screen graphics area
        offScreenGraphics.drawImage(gifImages[index],
              topLeftX,topLeftY,imageWidth,imageHeight,this);

        // draw image on the applet's screen
        g.drawImage(offScreenImage,0,0,width,height,this);
}
```

Program Example_11 brings together the points discussed above and demonstrates animation using the 16 GIF files. Notice that the example combines the
techniques of (1) allowing an applet to run in its own thread, (2) using a multimedia tracker to prevent partial images being displayed when the images are
being loaded, and (3) using graphical double-buffering to reduce the flicker of
animated images.

```java
// program to demonstrate animation techniques

import java.awt.*;
import java.applet.*;

public class Example_11 extends Applet implements Runnable
{
      static final int NUMBER_OF_FRAMES = 16;
      static final int TIME_ASLEEP = 100; // 100 milliseconds sleep time

      Image[] gifImages = new Image[NUMBER_OF_FRAMES];

      int index = 0;     // index to gifImages array

      int width = 250;  // width of offscreen graphics area
      int height = 100; // height of offscreen graphics area

      Image        offScreenImage;
      Graphics     offScreenGraphics;
      MediaTracker tracker;

      Thread appletThread;

      public void init()
      {
          // load images into array
          tracker = new MediaTracker(this);
          for (int index=0; index != gifImages.length; index++)
          {
                  gifImages[index] = getImage(getDocumentBase(),
                                              "java"+index+".gif");
                  tracker.addImage(gifImages[index],index);
          }

          try
          {
                  tracker.waitForAll();
          }
```

```
            catch (InterruptedException e){}

            offScreenImage = createImage(width,height);
            offScreenGraphics = offScreenImage.getGraphics();
}


public void paint(Graphics g)
{
        int topLeftX=75;  // abscissa of top left-hand corner of image
        int topLeftY=40;  // ordinate top left-hand corner of image

        int imageWidth = gifImages[index].getWidth(this);
        int imageHeight = gifImages[index].getHeight(this);

        // erase previous image from off screen graphics area
        offScreenGraphics.setColor(Color.white);
        offScreenGraphics.fillRect(0,0,width,height);

        // draw next image in off screen graphics area
        offScreenGraphics.drawImage(gifImages[index],
        topLeftX,topLeftY,imageWidth,imageHeight,this);

        // draw image on the applet's screen
        g.drawImage(offScreenImage,0,0,width,height,this);
}

// create new thread
public void start()
{
        if (appletThread == null)
        {
                appletThread=new Thread(this);
                appletThread.start();
        }
}

// override run() method to display the images on the screen
public void run()
{
        Graphics g = getGraphics();
        while (true)
        {
                paint(g);
                index++;
                index = index % NUMBER_OF_FRAMES;
```

```
        try{appletThread.sleep(TIME_ASLEEP);}
        catch (InterruptedException e){}
    }
}

public void destroy()
{
    if (appletThread != null)
    {
        appletThread.stop();
        appletThread=null;
    }
}
}
```

The results of this applet are best viewed with the applet running. When the applet runs, the 3-D word Java appears to take a bow. The screen shot shows just one image being displayed by an applet viewer.

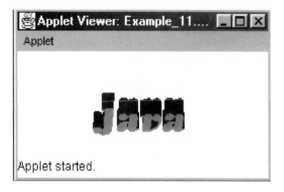

NOW DO THIS▶ Return to the `SketchPad` class developed in Chapter 9. You may recall that with this class no re-drawing of the shapes occurred. Modify the `SketchPad` class to use a double buffer, draw the shapes on an off-screen image and redraw from that image.

11.11 Restrictions

When you surf the Web and download documents, you have probably noticed that your browser literally comes into life with superb text and graphics, displayed in brilliant colors, possibly with sound, photographs, videos, and animated pictures. You now know that the text is based on an HTML script file, and the photographs and some animation are likely to come from GIF files. However, there may be a number of applets that have been downloaded and are running on your computer.

As mentioned earlier in this chapter, to avoid the possibility of a downloaded applet causing havoc on your computer, there are certain restrictions imposed on what an applet is allowed to do.

Different Web browsers and applet viewers may impose different security restrictions on applets. Applets downloaded over the network must be considered as *untrusted code*, and you should assume that any applet will be restricted by the following security measures. Applets that are considered to be untrusted code are subject to stringent restrictions. They *cannot* do the following:

- Access the local file system on your computer.

- Perform networking operations.

- Use system facilities.

- Use certain AWT facilities.

- Access certain system properties.

- Create threads or access threads or thread groups outside of the thread group in which the applet is running.

- Access certain classes and packages.

When an applet is loaded from the file system on your computer, it is assumed that the code is likely to be more trustworthy than an anonymous downloaded applet over the network. In this case, Web browsers and applet viewers may relax some of the restrictions listed above.

> *i*   It is possible to attach a digital signature to a Java Archive (JAR) file, as a means of specifying that the applet(s) contained within the JAR file have trusted code. The Web browser may then grant special privileges to such applet(s). See your SDK documentation for further information.

11.12   Sound and Images with Applications

Within this chapter the use of audio files and image files has been confined to applets. However, the audio visual interface contains the class `Audio` to allow the playing of AU and WAV files, and also contains the class `FilmStrip` to allow the viewing of JPEG and GIF images on the screen. As you have experienced, these two classes have been used extensively with Java applications.

Sound

A new method in the class `java.applet.Applet` enables applications as well as applets to create `AudioClips`. The signature of the class method is:

```
public static final AudioClip newAudioClip(URL url);
```

You may wonder how you transform the filename of an audio file into a URL. The class `File` in the package `java.io` contains a method that converts a file-name into a URL; the signature of the method is:

```
public URL toURL();
```

The method throws a `MalformedURLException`. For example, to convert the filename—represented as a string—of an audio file into a URL we would code:

```
File f = new File(filename);
try{myUrl = f.toURL();}
catch (MalformedURLException e}
```

The creation of an `AudioClip` from a sound file is achieved by writing:

```
AudioClip sound = Applet.newAudioClip(myUrl);
```

The audio clip can use any of the methods described in this chapter for playing a sound—`loop()`, `play()`, and `stop()`.

When you are creating a class, such as `Audio`, for playing sounds, it is good practice to have the sound play in its own thread. For example, the `Audio` class extends the `Thread` class and overrides the `run` method from the `Thread` class to play the audio clip.

Images

The techniques of displaying images in applications are the same as we have encountered in this chapter for displaying images within applets.

In the `Toolkit` class of the `awt` package you will find two `getImage` meth-ods that use either a string filename or a URL as an argument. Both methods return an `Image` object.

The `FilmStrip` class uses the methods of the `MediaTracker` class to load all the image objects before displaying any of them.

```
// load all images into the array visual before displaying them
Toolkit tools = parent.getToolkit();
MediaTracker tracker = new MediaTracker(this);
for (int index=0; index != numberOfFrames; index++)
{
      // convert filename to URL
```

```
        File file = new File(filenames[index]);
        if (! file.exists())
        {
                .

                .

                parent.closeWindowAndExit();
        }

        try{url = file.toURL();}
        catch (MalformedURLException e)
        {
                .

                .

                parent.closeWindowAndExit();
        }

        visual[index] = tools.getImage(url);
        tracker.addImage(visual[index],index);
}
try{tracker.waitForAll();}
catch (InterruptedException e){}
```

To reduce flicker when showing a sequence of images, the `FilmStrip` class also utilizes the technique of double buffering. It is necessary to first create an off-screen image using the `createImage` method from the `Container` class. An off-screen graphics object is then created from this off-screen image. Individual images can then be drawn on the off-screen graphics object using the `drawImage` method from the `Graphics` class in the `awt` package. Finally, the completed off-screen images are painted.

11.13   Conclusion

In Chapter 2 it was stated that by the time that you have read through this book you would be able to understand how the `avi` package was written, and you would have enough knowledge of the Java language to write your own package for input and output.

The `avi` package contains nine classes. In this chapter you have learned how to play audio sounds and display images. These techniques are at the heart of the `Audio` and `Filmstrip` classes. In Chapters 8 and 9 you learned how to create a `WindowPane` class and add to the window components to represent `CheckBoxes`, a `WritingPad`, a `DialogBox`, and `RadioButtons`. These are some of the basic ingredients of the audio-visual interface.

The `avi` also contains other classes such as the `Memo`, `Slider`, and `Timer`. However, these use similar techniques to those already learned.

Your knowledge of the Java language, and the construction of object-oriented programs has come a long way since you first opened the book and started to understand this modern-day approach to programming. However, this is only the beginning of your programming experience with Java. Every year the number of packages that is added to the language continues to grow. The diversity of applications for Java will also continue to grow as man's ingenuity with computers continues to increase.

In your quest to learn more about Java, we hope this book has given you a foundation that will allow you to continue to expand your knowledge of programming over the next few years.

SUMMARY

- The Internet is an international network of computers in which the structure permits networks within networks. The Internet refers to the hardware needed to support the linking together of many computers to form networks and the linking of the networks together.

- There are various resources available on the Internet—E-mail, File Transfer Protocol (FTP), Gopher, Telnet, and Hyper-Text Transfer Protocol (HTTP).

- The World Wide Web (WWW) is a distributed information service on the Internet that uses browsers to interpret documents written in Hyper-Text Mark-up Language (HTML).

- An HTML script file may contain references to text, images, video clips, and applets.

- A Uniform Resource Locator (URL) is a means of addressing any site on the Web.

- An applet is a program designed to be run by a Java-enabled Web browser or applet viewer.

- There are two parts to creating an applet. The first is the applet code itself, which is compiled using a Java compiler. The second is an HTML file that contains a call to the applet, together with any parameters that the applet requires. The HTML file is executed by the Web browser of applet viewer.

- The `Applet` class contains a set of methods that may be overridden by a subclass of the `Applet` class. The most important standard methods to override are `init()`, `start()`, `stop()`, and `destroy()`.

- There is no concept of a `main` method in an applet as there is with an application. Control of the computer must be made through automatic calls to the standard methods of the applet.

- Applets run in either a Web browser or an applet viewer; they make use of such facilities as (1) the browser's window, to implement GUIs and draw graphics, (2) the browser's event handling of its window, and (3) the browser's interface for controlling the applet.

- Both HTML files and applets may be used to incorporate multimedia into Web-based documents.

- An array can have more than one dimension.

- A two-dimensional array may be thought of as a repetition of one-dimensional arrays.

- Arrays of any dimension may be initialized at the point of declaration.

- An applet may set up listeners to control input and output in a graphical user interface.

- The position of a mouse may be used in conjunction with an image map to trigger other media being shown or played.

- A thread is a single sequential flow of control. Since the Web browser or applet viewer controls the applet, it is important for an applet to have at least one thread to run in to allow the browser time to perform useful work, such as implementing `repaint`.

- A thread has a life cycle—it is created, starts, runs, and enters any of several states. In these states the thread might be ready to be run, be asleep, suspended, waiting, or blocked, and eventually it must die.

- An applet that uses threads must ensure that the functionality of the applet is controlled from within the `run` method.

- Images may be animated within applets. To ensure flicker-free animation, do not clear the image on the browser's drawing surface. Instead, clear the image behind the scenes by using double buffering.

- To prevent images from being partially shown during the loading process, use the `MediaTracker` class to monitor the loading of the images.

- Applets that are downloaded to a local machine have severe restrictions of access imposed upon them as a means of protecting the host machine from untrusted code.

- Applets that have been loaded from a local machine are regarded as being trustworthy and are subject to less stringent restrictions.

Review Questions

True or False

1. A Web browser interprets an HTML script file.

2. An applet does not require an HTML script file in order to run.

3. A Web browser and an applet viewer have the same functionality.

4. You must override the standard methods `init()`, `start()`, `stop()`, and `destroy()` in an applet before it can be executed.

5. There is no `main` method in an applet.

6. Data stored in a vector may be accessed the same as data stored in a two-dimensional array.

Short Answers

7. What is the Internet, and how does it differ from the Word Wide Web?

8. Describe any three resources on the Internet.

9. What is hypertext, and how does it differ from hypermedia?

10. What is a HTML script file, and why is it used?

11. Describe three tasks that a Web browser enables you to perform.

12. What is Hyper-Text Transfer Protocol (HTTP)?

13. Discuss the format and purpose of a Uniform Resource Locator (URL).

14. What is the purpose of the parameters width and height in a HTML applet tag?

15. State two advantages of running an applet in a Web browser or applet viewer compared with running an application.

16. What is the purpose of NAME and VALUE in an HTML parameter tag?

17. How do you play an audio clip in an applet?

18. Define a two-dimensional array.

19. What is an image map?

20. Why is it important for an applet to run in its own thread?

21. Discuss briefly the life cycle of a thread.

22. What is the major cause of flicker in image animation when applets are used?

23. Discuss graphical double buffering.

24. What is the purpose of a `MediaTracker` object?

25. State any three limitations imposed upon an applet that is downloaded from the Web to a local computer.

Exercises

26. Comment on the error in the following URL—java.sun.com.

27. The following HTML script contains errors. What are the errors?

```
<BODY>
<APPLET> code=Ex_27.java>
</HTML>
```

28. Desk check the following HTML script file and applet. Use your Java SDK documentation to look up the classes and methods that are not explained in the chapter.

```
<HTML>
<BODY>
<APPLET code=Ex_28.class width=500 height=300>
<PARAM NAME=url VALUE="http://www.windows95.com">
</APPLET>
</BODY>
</HTML>
```

```
public class Ex_28 extends Applet
{
    public void init()
    {
        try
        {
            URL site = new URL(getParameter("url"));
            getAppletContext().showDocument(site);
        }
        catch (MalformedURLException m){System.exit(1);}
    }
}
```

What do the HTML script file and applet do? How could you change the value of the URL without having to edit and recompile the applet?

29. Desk check the following code. Explain any errors that you find.

```
public class Ex_29 extends Applet
{
    String name;

    public void paint()
    {
        Font font = new Font("Monospaced, Font.ITALIC, 36);
```

```
        setFont(font);
        setBackground(yellow);
        setColor(red);
        drawString(name);
    }
}
```

30. Rewrite the applet in Question 29, so that it is error free; supply a value for the variable `name` from the parameter list in the corresponding HTML script file.

31. Modify your program in Question 30 so that a value for the variable `name` can be input at the time of running the applet.

32. Suppose the value of the `String` variable `source` is "`dialtone`" and the AU sound file `dialtone.au` is stored in the same directory as the applet containing the following statements:

```
AudioClip sound = getAudioClip(getCodebase(), souce+"au");
sound.play();
```

Why doesn't the applet make a sound when it is executed? (This is a very simple error, but one that is very easy to make!)

33. Use the data from Figure 11.4 to determine the values of the following expressions.

```
rainfall[3][8]; rainfall[0][11]; rainfall[1][5].
```

Use Figure 11.4 to determine the value of `sum` after the following code is executed.

```
int sum = 0;
for (int column=0; column != 3; column++)
{
    for (int row=0; row != 4; row ++)
        sum = sum + rainfall[row][column];
}
```

34. Figure 11.11 indicates the strength of the sun protection factor that you should use in your sun-block cream to protect against harmful UV radiation.

uv Index range	category of skin			
	1	2	3	4
0..2	3	2	2	1
2..4	6	4	3	2
4..7	11	8	5	4
7..9	14	10	7	5
9+	18	12	8	7

Figure 11.11 Table showing Recommended Sun Protection Factor

Write an applet to store the contents of this table in a two-dimensional array, input the type of skin and a value for the current UV index, and display the sun protection factor that you should use to protect against UV radiation under those conditions.

35. Comment on the errors in the following applet. Rewrite the code using a thread to control the repainting of the screen.

```
public class Ex_35 extends Applet
{
    Thread appletThread;
    int length = 1;

    public start()
    {
        while (true)
        {
            repaint();
            length++;

            Thread.sleep(5000);
        }
    }

    public void paint(Graphics g)
    {
        g.fillRect(10,50,length,5);
    }
}
```

Programming Problems

36. Improve the digital clock applet. The clock should be given a set of buttons that control an alarm.

37. Design and write a program to display an analog clock on the screen. Give the clock a sweeping seconds hand and program the clock to chime every quarter hour as well as hourly.

38. Design and write a program to display the buttons from a digital telephone. As you dial a number, play the correct tone. After a six-digit number is input, the program plays either a ringing or busy tone. Download the tone-dialing sounds from a sound archive of your choice.

39. Design and write a class for a graphical component that shows the progression of a computer operation such as loading a set of images. Write an applet to show this graphical component running in parallel with the operation of loading images.

40. (a) Design and write a class that simulates an image of an airplane flying across the screen. Create an applet containing several airplane objects flying in different directions across the screen.

   (b) Design and write a class to display the attributes of a plane in a separate window and to be able to modify certain attributes such as the speed and direction of the plane. When the user points and clicks the mouse-button over a plane, the new window is activated.

41. A computerized minefield, divided into a 10 × 10 matrix as illustrated in Figure 11.12, may be considered as an object. Devise a class `Minefield` containing methods that will allow you to plot a path through the mines and display your route.

   The position of the mines is generated at random. The number of mines is also generated at random, and will be a value in the range 1 to 10. A person plotting a path through the minefield is allowed to input pairs of coordinates of a path. The computer generates the starting position at any column in row 9 of the matrix, and the only legal move is to any adjacent cell in the matrix. The idea behind the simulation is to trace a path through a minefield without stepping on a mine, and to finish at the northern perimeter of the matrix. Only at the end of the simulation should the computer reveal the position of the mines.

   Write an applet to test the instance methods of the class by simulating tracing a path though the minefield.

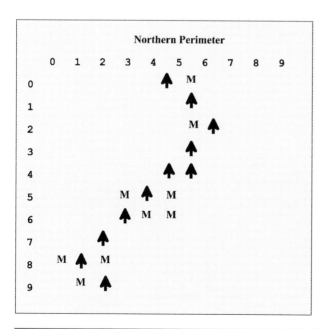

Figure 11.12 Matrix of a minefield

42. Design and write your own space-invaders game. Control a gun sight by moving the mouse over the enemy space-craft to zap the invaders. Invader space craft should be generated at random intervals and at random positions on the screen. Display on the screen the number of seconds remaining before the game finishes and the number of invader space-craft zapped. You might also allow different levels of difficulty.

     This problem gives you plenty of opportunity to experiment with sounds and graphics. Remember to use threads in this problem.

43. Write a computer program to play the game of Tic-Tac-Toe (also known as Noughts and Crosses) against the computer. Develop your answer around such classes as a `Board`, a `Square`, a `Token`, a `Move`, and a `Game`. Use a mouse pointer to choose a square on the board. In this problem, look at the possibility of displaying a square on a canvas. Study the `Canvas` class in your Java documentation.

CHAPTER 12

Sorting, Searching, and Dynamic Data Structures

This final chapter is optional.

The chapter provides an introduction to a number of sorting and searching algorithms and dynamic data structures you may find useful when you write computer programs. The approach we take is to cover how to implement some important algorithms and data structures "from scratch" and how to use Java's built-in predefined implementations of algorithms and data structures. As computer students you need to understand both.

Sorting and searching are two of the most common activities performed on data with computers. In this chapter we not only see how to design and code a sorting algorithm—the selection sort, we also see how to use some of Java's built-in sorting routines. A similar approach is taken with the topic of searching, where we code our own sequential search and learn how to use the library's binary search. We also analyze all of these algorithms with respect to their execution efficiency.

One of the most versatile ways to structure data for computer processing is to link related data together. In this chapter we learn how to implement linked lists in Java, building our own generic linked list ADT. We also see how to use one of the Java `util` package's built-in data structures, the `Stack`. By the end of the chapter you should have an understanding of the following topics.

- Writing a sorting algorithm.

- The `Sort` class, and a comparison of the efficiencies of its algorithms.

- Writing a searching algorithm.

- The `BinarySearch` class, and a comparison of the efficiencies of its algorithms.

- A linked list dynamic data structure.

- The `Stack` class.

12.1   Sorting

There is a basic requirement when storing data to keep the values organized by some form of relationship. You can imagine the problems encountered if the entries in a telephone directory were not sorted into alphabetical sequence by the names of the telephone subscribers. Attempting to find the name and number of a subscriber could prove to be very time-consuming since the entries in the telephone directory would appear at random.

If the data have been sorted on the surname of the subscriber into an alphabetical sequence in the telephone directory, you can simply turn the pages in the directory to match the first few letters of the surname, then perform a one-by-one name search through several entries to find the name you are looking for. Listed against the name will be the telephone number and address of the person you want to call.

Sorting is one of the techniques used to organize data. Despite there being numerous sorting techniques available for the programmer to use, we will consider just one of the simplest sorting techniques to implement on the computer. The first sorting technique we will examine is the *selection sort*.

Figure 12.1 illustrates the movement of integers in a one-dimensional array, when a selection sort is used to place the integers into ascending order (lowest to highest values). The contents of the cells from 0 to 4 are inspected for the largest number (18), which is swapped with the number in cell 4. The contents of the cells from 0 to 3 are inspected for the largest number (15), which is swapped with the number in cell 3. The contents of the cells from 0 to 2 are inspected for the largest number (13), which is swapped with the number in cell 2. The contents of the cells from 0 to 1 are inspected for the largest number (8), which is swapped with the number in cell 1. When only the contents of cell 0 remain to be inspected, the numbers are assumed to have been sorted into ascending order.

To generalize, if N represents the number of integers to be sorted in the cells of an array from subscripts 0 to $N - 1$, the largest number in the cells subscripted 0 to $N - 1$ is found and swapped with the number in cell $N - 1$. The process is repeated with N being decreased by 1 each time until $N = 0$. The name of this approach is based on the idea that we select the largest remaining number and swap it into its correct location.

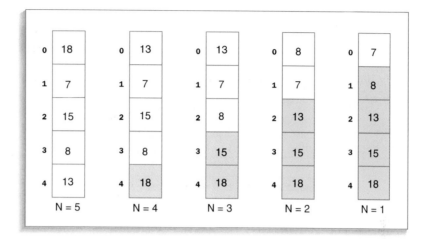

Figure 12.1 A selection sort

Although the selection sort can be implemented as a single method, it is clearer if the implementation is based on two methods. The first method positionOfLargest will return the subscript of the largest number in an array numbers of size limit.

The selection sort algorithm has been coded as class methods within the class named SortingAlgorithms. The method selectionSort calls the method positionOfLargest to find the largest number in the N-element array, where N is equal to size. This number is then swapped with the number at the end of the array. The process is repeated for $N - 1$ elements, then $N - 2$ elements, and so on, until N is reduced to zero.

Notice that the array to be sorted is a parameter of both methods in the class. You would expect the sorted array to be returned by the class method selectionSort, yet inspection of the class method shows that the return type has been defined as void. You may wonder: How do the sorted values in the array get returned?

A technique of passing arguments to a called method relates to all those items of data that are stored by *reference*. These are strings, arrays, and in fact, any objects. (Refer back to Figure 2.3, Objects stored by reference, and Figure 5.5, Declaration of an array of integers.) In such circumstances it is the reference to the object or array that is passed and not the specific values of the object or array. This technique implies that any changes made to the values of the parameters in the called method will result in changes being made to the values of the corresponding arguments in the calling method. These facts are illustrated in Figure 12.2, where a reference to an array (the arrowed line) is passed as an argument to the class method selectionSort. The class method selectionSort changes the values in respective cells of this array, and conse-

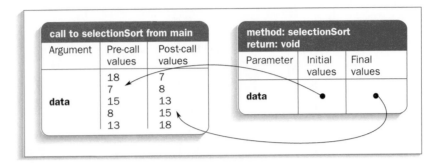

Figure 12.2 Passing an array by reference

quently the original values in the array associated with the main method have changed.

The following code shows the class SortingAlgorithms, which includes the selection sort:

```
public class SortingAlgorithms
{
    static int positionOfLargest(int[] data, int limit)
    // method to return the position of the largest item
    // in the data with bounds 0..limit
    {
        int largest = data[0];
        int indexOfLargest = 0;

        for (int index=1; index <= limit; index++)
        {
            if (data[index]> largest)
            {
                largest = data[index];
                indexOfLargest = index;
            }
        }

        return indexOfLargest;
    }

    public static void selectionSort(int[] data)
    // method to sort the contents of a data into ascending order
    {
        int temporary;
        int position;
        int size=data.length;
```

```
        for (int index=size-1; index > 0; index--)
        {
                position=positionOfLargest(data, index);

                // swap numbers
                if (index != position)
                {
                        temporary = data[index];
                        data[index] = data[position];
                        data[position] = temporary;
                }
        }
    }
}
```

Program `Example_1` illustrates how an array of numbers is passed by reference to the class method `selectionSort`. Notice in this program that the values of the array have been displayed before and after the call to the method `convert`. Notice also that another class method has been used to display the contents of the array. A method for displaying the data was used to reduce the amount of repeated coding that would otherwise be necessary.

```
// program to demonstrate the selection sort

import avi.*;

class Example_1
{
        static Window screen = new Window("Example_1.java");

        // method to display the contents of an array
        static void displayData(int[] data)
        {
                for (int index=0; index != data.length; index++)
                        screen.write(data[index]+"\t");

                screen.write("\n");
        }

        public static void main(String[] args)
        {
                int[] data = {18,7,15,8,13};

                screen.showWindow();
                screen.write("numbers before being sorted\n");
                displayData(data);
```

```
// call bubble sort
SortingAlgorithms.selectionSort(data);

screen.write("numbers after being sorted\n");
displayData(data);
    }
}
```

You are advised to desk check program `Example_1` using the test data illustrated in Figure 12.1.

Contents of the log file from the program being executed are shown below.

```
==================================================================================
                      L  O  G        F  I  L  E
         audio-visual interface [avi] - Release 1.0 - by Barry Holmes
            filename: Example_1.java    date: 7/22/2000    time: 2:24:3
==================================================================================


numbers before being sorted
18      7       15      8       13
numbers after being sorted
7       8       13      15      18
```

In attempting to compare the efficiency of two algorithms for solving the same problem—in this case, sorting—we want to see which algorithm is more time efficient. Intuitively, you might want to code both algorithms and perform a comparison on the time it takes to run both programs. However, there are problems with this approach:

- How should the algorithms be coded? In comparing the running times, we are comparing the implementations of the algorithms and not the algorithms.

- What computer should you use? The operations used by one algorithm might run faster on one machine than on another.

- What data should be used to compare the two algorithms? The values of the data will influence the timings of the algorithms. Ideally our analysis should be independent of specific data.

To analyze algorithms independently of specific implementations, computers or data, the time requirement of an algorithm is taken to be a function of the size of the problem. Size, in this case, is measured as the number of items in an array. We need to establish how quickly an algorithm's time requirement grows as a function of the size of the problem. For example, making the statement that *algorithm A requires time proportional to N^2* is exactly the kind of statement that characterizes the inherent efficiency of an algorithm; it is independent of such factors as implementations, computers, and specific data.

In analyzing the efficiency of the selection sort, we will look at the number of comparisons on the data being sorted.

If there are N items of data, then:

The number of comparisons on the first pass through the array is $N - 1$.

The number of comparisons on the second pass through the array is $N - 2$.

The number of comparisons on the third pass through the array is $N - 3$.

.

.

.

The number of comparisons on the $N - 1$th pass through the array is 1.

The selection sort algorithm is blind to the original order of the numbers. The number of comparisons, regardless of the order of the numbers, will be

$$(N-1)+(N-2)+\cdots+1 \sum_{1}^{N-1} i = N(N-1)/2 = \left(N^2/2\right)-\left(N/2\right)$$

You can verify this equation in any discrete mathematics textbook. If we omit the fractional part of this expression, we may conclude that the selection sort has an order of magnitude of N^2 comparisons. This is referred to as a *quadratic algorithm*. The time it takes to sort an array will be proportional to the amount of work the computer must do to compare and swap data. For example, doubling the size of the input causes a quadrupling of the time it takes to sort the data.

The algorithm is suitable for sorting only a small amount of data; otherwise, the time taken to complete the sorting algorithm, proportional to N^2, will become lengthy.

12.2   Class Java.util.Arrays—Sort

The Java library contains two efficient sorting algorithms for sorting large volumes of data. These are a *tuned* version of the *Quicksort* for sorting data of a primitive type, such as integers; and a *modified* version of the *Mergesort* for sorting objects, such as strings. A description of both of these algorithms is beyond the scope of this chapter; they are not normally covered in introductory courses to programming. You will certainly learn more about them if you continue your study of computing. Meanwhile, since both algorithms are built into the `Arrays` class in the predefined Java `util` package, you can use these algorithms without completely understanding all of their details. Such is the beauty of abstraction. Note that the `Arrays` class is not used for creating arrays—you already learned how to do that in Chapter 5. The `Arrays` class simply provides methods for manipulating arrays.

The efficiency of the *tuned* Quicksort is of the order of $n * \log_2(n)$; and for the *modified* Mergesort the efficiency is also $n * \log_2(n)$, where n represents the numbers of items of data to be sorted. These expressions of the efficiencies of the algorithms represent the average case and not the worst case scenarios. In the case of the Mergesort, if the original data is almost sorted, then the efficiency of the Mergesort approaches *n*.

If you inspect the documentation for the class `Arrays`, found in the package `util`, you will notice that all the class methods are overloaded to account for all the primitive data types, and they are overloaded to account for objects. The method used to perform sorting is simply called `sort`. If it is passed an array of primitive data types, it will use Quicksort; if it is passed an array of objects, it will use Mergesort.

Program `Example_2` is a repeated version of program `Example_1`, however, the selection sort is replaced by the Java library version of the Quicksort.

```java
// program to demonstrate the use of Quicksort from the class
// java.util.Arrays

import avi.*;
import java.util.Arrays;

class Example_2
{
    static Window screen = new Window("Example_2.java");

    // method to display the contents of an array
    static void displayData(int[] data)
    {
        for (int index=0; index != data.length; index++)
            screen.write(data[index]+"\t");

        screen.write("\n");
    }
    public static void main(String[] args)
    {
        int[] data = {18,7,15,8,13};

        screen.showWindow();
        screen.write("numbers before being sorted\n");
        displayData(data);

        // call Quicksort
        Arrays.sort(data);

        screen.write("numbers after being sorted\n");
        displayData(data);
    }
}
```

N	N² Selection sort	Nlog₂ N Quicksort
32	1024	160
64	4,096	384
128	16,384	896
256	65,536	2,048
512	262,144	4,608

Figure 12.3 Average-case efficiency of sorting algorithms

If you run this program, you will find the results are identical to those from `Example_1`.

The Quicksort algorithm works more efficiently for some arrays than it does for others. The best time for a Quicksort is proportional to the order of $n * \log_2 n$ where n is the number of elements to be sorted.

The worst results occur when the array is already sorted or is in reverse order—the efficiency drops to the order of N^2. In such cases, the time to perform the Quicksort is no faster than the time to perform the selection sort since the efficiency has deteriorated to the order N^2. Figure 12.3 illustrates the comparative average-case efficiency of the selection sort and the Quicksort for increasing values of N. Notice that the time to sort identical arrays is proportional to N^2 and $N \log_2 N$, respectively, and increases dramatically for the selection sort as the number of elements N increases.

So far we have concentrated on sorting numbers; however, it is also possible to sort objects including strings. In fact, the solution to this problem is a great example of the power of using the Java interface construct, which was introduced in Chapter 6. Upon inspecting the overloaded sort methods in `java.util.Arrays`, you will notice that a set of sort methods explicitly handles sorting objects.

```java
// program to demonstrate the Mergesort from the class
// java.util.Arrays

import avi.*;
import java.util.Arrays;

class Example_3
{
    static Window screen = new Window("Example_3.java");

    // method to display the contents of an array
    static void displayData(String[] data)
```

```
    {
            for (int index=0; index != data.length; index++)
                    screen.write(data[index]+"\t");

            screen.write("\n\n");
    }

    public static void main(String[] args)
    {
            String[] data = {"Mowbray","Adams","Quayle","Peters",
                            "Fogg","Jones","Rankin","Fellows",
                            "Evans","Hewitt","Davies"};

            screen.showWindow();
            screen.write("Strings BEFORE being sorted\n\n");
            displayData(data);

            // call merge sort
            Arrays.sort(data);

            screen.write("Strings AFTER being sorted\n\n");
            displayData(data);
    }
}
```

Contents of the log file from the program being executed are as follows.

```
================================================================================
                        L O G     F I L E
        audio-visual interface [avi] - Release 1.0 - by Barry Holmes
        filename: Example_3.java    date: 7/22/2000    time: 2:33:5
================================================================================


Strings BEFORE being sorted

Mowbray Adams Quayle Peters Fogg Jones Rankin Fellows Evans Hewitt Davies


Strings AFTER being sorted

Adams Davies Evans Fellows Fogg Hewitt Jones Mowbray Peters Quayle Rankin
```

Regardless of the algorithm being used, there will be a need to compare two items of data and determine which is the largest. The Java coding of this comparison will depend upon the type of data being sorted. For example, if two items of data A and B are numerical, then the comparisons A<B, A==B, and A>B will hold for all numerical types. However, if the two items of data are strings, then a comparison using the > symbol is illegal and the instance method compareTo from the String class must be used. The need to use two different statements for comparing numerical data and string data implies that two different versions of the same sorting algorithm must be coded. That might not seem too bad, but what of objects other than numbers and strings? Suppose you want to compare two student records or two bank accounts? For every class of objects you define that you want to sort, you will have to create yet another version of the sorting algorithm.

The way around this unacceptable situation is provided by the Java interface construct. The Comparable interface defined in the java.lang package contains a method, compareTo. Remember what this means—the Comparable interface does not itself define the method, but it does define the interface of the method. Any class that implements the Comparable interface must provide its own code for implementing the method and must follow the method signature defined in the interface.

The required method signature for compareTo is:

```
public int compareTo(Object obj)
```

The associated method description is "Compares this object with the obj object for order. Returns a negative integer, zero, or a positive integer as this object is less than, equal to, or greater than the obj object respectively."

So if you define a class of objects that you wish to pass to a generic sorting method, define the class so that it implements the Comparable interface. Then, within the sorting method, you can safely use a method call to compareTo as needed to perform the sort. If you study the sort methods defined in the Arrays class, you will see that many of them use this approach.

Consider the following class Telephone, which through its constructor creates an object containing the name, telephone number, and address of a subscriber to a telephone company.

```
import java.lang.*;

public class Telephone implements Comparable
{
      // instance variables
      String name;
      String teleNumber;
      String address;

      // constructor
```

```
public Telephone(String person, String number, String home)
{
        name = person;
        teleNumber = number;
        address = home;
}

// implemented method of class Comparable
public int compareTo(Object object)
{
        return
        (((Telephone)this).name).compareTo(((Telephone)object).name);

}
}
```

To be able to compare `Telephone` objects we need to state that the class implements `Comparable` and we need to implement the method `compareTo` from the interface within the class `Telephone`. Notice that in the `compareTo` method, it is the `this` object that passed a message to the method that is being compared with the `name`. Since the signature of the method indicates that an object from the superclass `Object` is passed as an argument, we must cast the object to the `Telephone` class, hence the use of `((Telephone)this)` and `((Telephone)object)`. To avoid any confusion, remember the instance variable `name` is defined as a string; therefore, it is appropriate that the instance method `compareTo`, from the class `String`, is used within the implementation of the interface's `compareTo` method.

Note that if the key had been numeric, it would still have been necessary to implement the `Comparable` interface.

A text data file named `subscribers.txt`, contains the following lines of text.

```
Mowbray    "Ashford 134581"  "45 Brookside Avenue"
Adams      "Watford 129099"  "18 Milestone Road"
Quayle     "Perth 12124"     "212 Wiltshire Boulevard"
Peters     "Glasgow 776543"  "113 Flemming Road"
Fogg       "Poole 9001"      "10 Almond Avenue"
Jones      "Ripon 83765"     "336 Cornwallis Road"
Rankin     "Plymouth 42212"  "732 High  Street"
Fellows    "Hull 496112"     "21 Turnpike Boulevard"
Evans      "Truro 334466"    "433 Lake Street"
Hewitt     "Hamble 7854312"  "30 Chester Street"
Davies     "Bath 8009211"    "72 Sherwood Avenue"
```

where each line of text represents the name, telephone number, and address of a subscriber to the telephone company. Since spaces are embedded within the strings for telephone numbers and addresses, it has been necessary to delimit

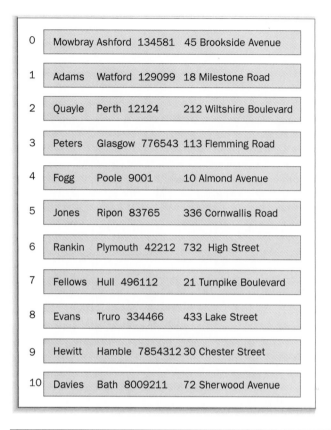

0	Mowbray Ashford 134581 45 Brookside Avenue
1	Adams Watford 129099 18 Milestone Road
2	Quayle Perth 12124 212 Wiltshire Boulevard
3	Peters Glasgow 776543 113 Flemming Road
4	Fogg Poole 9001 10 Almond Avenue
5	Jones Ripon 83765 336 Cornwallis Road
6	Rankin Plymouth 42212 732 High Street
7	Fellows Hull 496112 21 Turnpike Boulevard
8	Evans Truro 334466 433 Lake Street
9	Hewitt Hamble 7854312 30 Chester Street
10	Davies Bath 8009211 72 Sherwood Avenue

Figure 12.4 A one-dimensional arrays containing `Telephone` objects

these strings with quotes. Failure to delimit these strings would mean that the embedded spaces would be used as token delimiters in the `StreamTokenizer` class that is used to process the text file.

The `subscribers.txt` file is to be read, and its contents transferred as objects of type `Telephone` to the one-dimensional array depicted in Figure 12.4.

The following program reads the file line by line and creates objects of type `Telephone`. Each object, after it has been instantiated, is stored in a respective cell of the one-dimensional array. After the array has been filled with 11 `Telephone` objects, the contents of the array are sorted on the subscribers' names as keys; then the contents of the sorted array are displayed.

The overloaded sorting method has the following signature:

```
public static void sort(Object[] array);
```

where array is a one-dimensional array containing the data to be sorted.

```java
// program to demonstrate the Mergesort from the class
// java.util.Arrays, on keys of name from the Telephone class

import avi.*;
import java.io.*;
import java.awt.FileDialog;
import java.util.*;

class Example_4
{
      static Window screen = new Window("Example_4.java");
      static final int SIZE_OF_ARRAY = 11;

      // method to display the contents of an array
      static void displayData(Telephone[] data)
      {
            for (int index=0; index != data.length; index++)
                  screen.write(data[index].name+"\t\t"+
                                  data[index].teleNumber+"\t"+
                                  data[index].address+"\n");

            screen.write("\n");
      }

      public static void main(String[] args)throws Exception
      {
            Telephone[] data = new Telephone[SIZE_OF_ARRAY];
            String person;
            String number;
            String home;

            screen.showWindow();

            FileDialog inputFile = new
            FileDialog(screen,"",FileDialog.LOAD);
            inputFile.show();

            String directory = inputFile.getDirectory();
            String filename = inputFile.getFile();

            FileReader file = new FileReader(directory+filename);
            StreamTokenizer inputStream = new StreamTokenizer(file);

            int index = 0;
            int tokenType = inputStream.nextToken();
            while (tokenType != StreamTokenizer.TT_EOF)
```

```
{
        person = inputStream.sval;
        inputStream.nextToken();
        number = inputStream.sval;
        inputStream.nextToken();
        home = inputStream.sval;

        data[index] = new Telephone(person, number, home);
        tokenType = inputStream.nextToken();
        index++;
    }

    file.close();

    screen.write("Records BEFORE being sorted\n\n");
    displayData(data);

    // call merge sort
    Arrays.sort(data);

    screen.write("Records AFTER being sorted on name as key\n\n");
    displayData(data);
    }
}
```

Here is a screen shot from the running program:

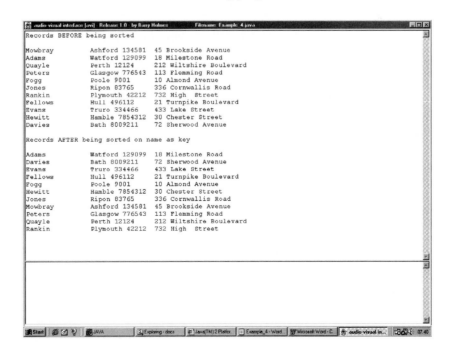

12.3   Sequential Search

Imagine that information is stored in an array without any regard to the order of the keys to the data. For example, the names of telephone subscribers do not appear in alphabetical sequence. In attempting to search for a key that does not exist in an array, it is necessary to compare every key in the array before you discover that the key cannot be found in the array!

When the information held in an array is sorted into search key order, it is not always necessary to search through the entire array before discovering that a particular piece of the information is not present. Consider for a moment the information held in the array depicted in Figure 12.5. Alphabetically, Adams is before Davies, Davies is before Evans, Evans is before Fellows, and so on.

If we search the contents of the sequential array for the key Ellis, then we must perform the following comparisons, illustrated in the rightmost column of

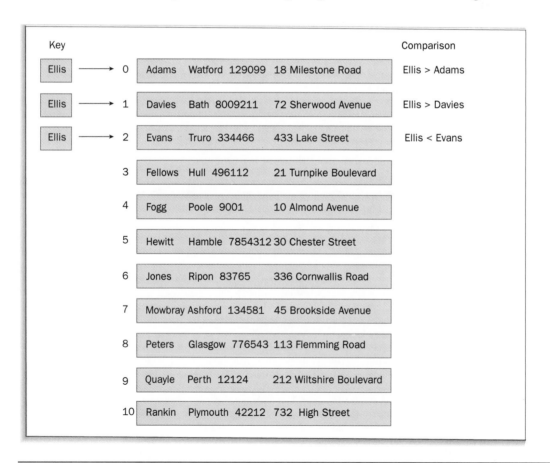

Figure 12.5 A sequential search on an array of records

Figure 12.5, before we discover that Ellis is not in the array. Ellis is alphabetically greater than both Adams and Davies, and so may be found further on in the array. Ellis is alphabetically less than Evans; therefore, an entry for Ellis cannot exist in the array beyond Evans because the names are ordered into alphabetical sequence. By sorting the contents of the array into alphabetical order on the name of each person as the key, only three key comparisons are necessary to discover that Ellis does not exist in the array. If the array was not sorted by name, then we would have to check every name in the array before we discovered that Ellis does not exist in the array.

Assume that the records are stored into consecutive array locations from 0 to 10; the following algorithm can be used in searching for a surname in the array. Note that, in this example, the size of the array is 11 and that the string compareTo method will return 0, a negative number, or a positive number if the string parameter is equal to, less than, or greater than the string being used to invoke the method.

```
public class SearchingAlgorithms
{
    // method to search the records of an ordered array
    // for a key; if not found return the size of the array
    // otherwise return the position in the array of the match

    static public int sequential(Telephone[] array,
                                 int size,String nameKey)
    {
        int index = 0;
        int resultOfComparison;

        while (index < size)
        {
            // compare key with key in array
            resultOfComparison=nameKey.compareTo(array[index].name);

            // keys match
            if (resultOfComparison == 0)
                return index;

            // search key less than key in array, therefore,
            // key cannot exist in array
            else if (resultOfComparison < 0)
                return size;

            // search key greater than key in array, therefore,
            // key may exist further down the array
```

```
            else
                index++;
      }

      // return the size of the array to show that no key
      // match was possible
      return size;
   }
}
```

The index used to access each cell of the array is initialized to 0, the first cell position of the array.

Although the value of the index is within the limits of the array [0..10], the search for the key continues. In the cell being examined, if the key is equal to the surname, the position in the array of the located record, that is the value of the index, is returned.

In the cell being examined, if the key is less than the name field, then the surname cannot exist in the array; the search must stop, and the size of the array is returned. The size of the array is not a legal subscript to the array; it is used to signify that no match for the key was found.

In the cell being examined, if the key is greater than the name of the field, then the surname may exist further down the array, and the value of the index is increased to retrieve the contents of the next cell.

The algorithm is implemented as the method `sequential` in the class `SearchingAlgorithms`. The following program stores 11 objects containing names, telephone numbers, and addresses in alphabetical order by surname in a one-dimensional array. A user is invited to input a name, and the array is searched for a key match. If the key is found, the corresponding telephone number and address is output. If the key is not found, an appropriate message is output.

```
// program to demonstrate the sequential search

import avi.*;
import java.io.*;
import java.awt.FileDialog;
import java.util.*;


class Example_5
{
      static final int SIZE_OF_ARRAY = 11;

      public static void main(String[] args)throws Exception
      {
            Telephone[] data = new Telephone[SIZE_OF_ARRAY];
            String person;
            String number;
```

```java
String home;

Window screen = new Window("Example_5.java");
DialogBox inputKey = new DialogBox(screen,"Key?");

String[] reply = {"continue?","quit?"};
RadioButtons buttons = new
RadioButtons(screen,"What next?",reply);

screen.showWindow();

FileDialog inputFile = new
FileDialog(screen,"",FileDialog.LOAD);
inputFile.show();

String directory = inputFile.getDirectory();
String filename = inputFile.getFile();

FileReader file = new FileReader(directory+filename);
StreamTokenizer inputStream = new StreamTokenizer(file);

int index = 0;
int tokenType = inputStream.nextToken();
while (tokenType != StreamTokenizer.TT_EOF)
{
      person = inputStream.sval;
      inputStream.nextToken();
      number = inputStream.sval;
      inputStream.nextToken();
      home = inputStream.sval;

      data[index] = new Telephone(person, number, home);
      tokenType = inputStream.nextToken();

      index++;
}

file.close();

// call merge sort
Arrays.sort(data);

do
{
      // show dialog box
      inputKey.showDialogBox();
```

```
String key = inputKey.getString();

// call sequential search
int position =
SearchingAlgorithms.sequential(data,data.length,key);

// write value
if (position != data.length)
    screen.write("name:                "+data[position].name+
            "\n"+"telephone number: "+
            data[position].teleNumber+"\n"+
            "address:            "+data[position].address+
            "\n\n");
else
    screen.write(key+" not found\n\n");

// show radio buttons
buttons.showRadioButtons();
}while (buttons.getNameOfButton().equals("continue?"));
}
}
```

A screen shot from the running program follows.

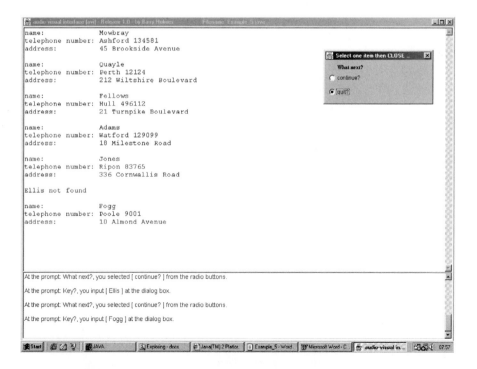

12.4   Class Java.util.Arrays—Binary Search

The sequential search algorithm is nice, but it is not the best approach to use when there is a large amount of sorted data. For example, suppose you wanted to look up the phone number of a friend in a telephone book. You would not start at the beginning of the book and look at each name until you either found your friend or determined that the name and number were not in the book, would you? Instead, you would jump into the pages at about the place you thought your friend would be listed, and then you would jump around using educated guesses as to where you were heading, until you zeroed in on your friend's name. The idea of jumping over and eliminating many names in a single step is the basis behind the binary search algorithm.

The *binary search algorithm* requires the keys to be sorted prior to the search and the information to be stored in an array. Suppose we wanted to search the array shown in Figure 12.6 for the entry `Quayle`. First the array is divided into two parts by the midpoint. The midpoint is calculated as (first + last)/2, and in this example it is assigned to the variable `location`. The key `Quayle` is compared with the key at `location`. Since `Quayle` > `Hewitt`, `Quayle` might be found in the lower subarray within the bounds (location+1..last) but will definitely not be found in the upper subarray. We have eliminated half the array with a single comparison! This process is repeated using only the lower subarray, with a new midpoint being calculated as (location+1 + last)/2 and assigned to the variable `location`. The key `Quayle` is compared with the key at the new location. Since `Quayle` > `Peters`, `Quayle` may be found in the lower subarray within the bounds (location+1..last). We have now eliminated half of the remaining array. The process is repeated again with a new midpoint being calculated. Note when a sublist contains an even number of keys, the midpoint may be taken to be the next lowest key from the center. A match for the key `Quayle` exists at `location` = 9. If the value for `first` had exceeded the value for `last`, then no match would be found for the key. Notice that only three comparisons are necessary with this approach, compared with 10 comparisons if a serial or sequential search had been performed.

The binary search algorithm is very important, and it is widely used. It is provided in the Java `utils` package in the `Arrays` class. Upon inspection of the documentation for the `Arrays` class, you will find overloaded methods for the `binarySearch` algorithm.

The signature of one of the overloaded methods to search for an instance variable of an object is:

```
public static int binarySearch(Object[] array, Object key);
```

Program `Example_5` has been rewritten as `Example_6` to incorporate the changes necessary to use the binary search method from the class `Arrays`. Program `Example_6` is shown as skeletal code, showing the changes that have been made to Program `Example_5`.

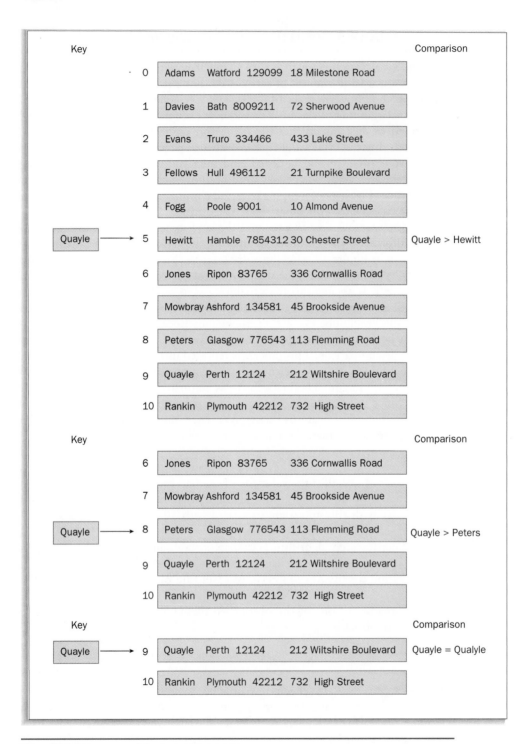

Figure 12.6 A binary search for a name in an array

```
// program to demonstrate the binary search from the class java.util.Arrays

.
.

class Example_6
{
      static final int SIZE_OF_ARRAY = 11;

      public static void main(String[] args) throws Exception
      {
            Telephone[] data = new Telephone[SIZE_OF_ARRAY];

            .
            .
            .


            // call merge sort
            Arrays.sort(data);

            do
            {
                  // show dialog box
                  inputKey.showDialogBox();
                  String key = inputKey.getString();
                  Telephone searchKey = new Telephone(key,"","");

                  // call binary search
                  int position =
                  Arrays.binarySearch(data, searchKey);

                  // write value
                  if (position >= 0)
                        screen.write("name:            "+
                                    data[position].name+"\n"+
                                    "telephone number: "+
                                    data[position].teleNumber+"\n"+
                                    "address:         "+
                                    data[position].address+"\n\n");
                  else
                        screen.write(key+" not found\n\n");

                  // show radio buttons
                  buttons.showRadioButtons();
            }while (buttons.getNameOfButton().equals("continue?"));
      }
}
```

N	N sequential search	$\log_2 N$ binary search
32	32	5
64	64	6
128	128	7
256	256	8
512	512	9

Figure 12.7 Worst-case efficiency of searching algorithms

When this program is run, the results are similar to those illustrated for program `Example_5`.

Finally, Figure 12.7 illustrates the performance of a sequential search and a binary search for different amounts of data.

If there are N records in an array, then applying a sequential search will result in the worst-case search time proportional to N comparisons of keys, since we may need to search through the entire array. However, using the binary search, if there are N records in an array, then the average number of key comparisons will be $\log_2 N$.

To justify this last statistic, remember that with the binary search, each time we do a comparison we eliminate half the remaining array. How many times can you cut an array of size N in half? The answer is $\log_2 N$. For example, consider an array containing eight records. Provided the key can be matched with a record in the array, the worst-case scenario is obtained as follows. We find the midpoint and make a key comparison; divide the array by 2, giving four records; find the midpoint and make a key comparison; divide the array by 2, giving two records; find the midpoint and make a key comparison. You are left with just one record—the one you are searching for! The number of key comparisons we made was 3—($\log_2(8) = 3$). If the array contained N records, then it would be necessary to make $\log_2 N$ comparisons.

An examination of this table makes the importance of algorithm efficiency very clear.

12.5 Linked Lists

Figure 12.8 illustrates an object containing two variables; the first `datum` may store an item of any type, and the second `link` is a reference to another object of the same type. The figure illustrates that the object structure known as a `Node` is referred to by a variable named `head`. The class `Node` may be defined as follows.

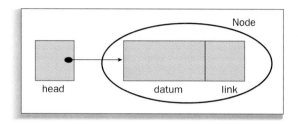

Figure 12.8 A single node

```
class Node
{
    private Object datum;
    private Node    link;

    public Node(Object item, Node pointer)
    {
        datum = item;
        link = pointer;
    }
}
```

The declaration `Node head = new Node();` would create the structure shown in Figure 12.8.

Since the structure contains the field `link`, which is a reference to another structure of the same data type `Node`, the record is known as a *self-referential structure*.

A *linked list* is a sequence of nodes in which each node is linked or connected to the node following it, as illustrated in Figure 12.9. This list has a head referencing the first node in the list. The first node contains the word *apple* and a reference to the second node in the list. The second node contains the word *banana* and a reference to the third node in the list. The third node contains the word *date* and a null reference. The `null` reference indicates that the link does not reference another node, and the list is terminated. To summarize, the linked list illustrated in Figure 12.9 has the following constructional features.

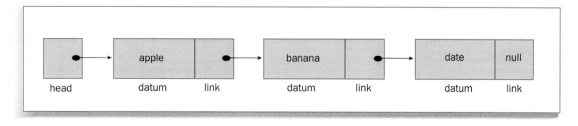

Figure 12.9 An example of a linked list

- A *named reference variable head* that points to the first node in the linked list

- A *list* in which the order of the nodes is determined by an explicit reference field within each record, rather than by the physical order of the components in memory (as in the case of an array)

- A `null` *reference* indicating the end of the linked list

A linked list may be used instead of an array for storing data in main memory when the following circumstances apply.

- The number of data records to be stored is not known in advance of the program being executed. The linked list is truly a dynamic data structure, since main memory is allocated for storing the records at run time without having to specify the number of nodes in the list.

- Nodes need to be inserted into a list or deleted from a list. During the insertion or deletion of nodes in a linked list, there is no movement of the data records in memory, only changes in reference (link) values. By contrast, the insertion or deletion of records in an array would involve the movement of many records in main memory.

Since a linked list in Java may be thought of as a collection of objects, the implementation of the data structure is very straightforward. If `Node` has been declared as above, building the linked list shown in Figure 12.9 is simply a matter of specifying three objects as follows.

```
Node head = null;

head = new Node("date", head);
head = new Node("banana", head);
head = new Node("apple", head);
```

Figure 12.10 illustrates how this code is used to build the linked list—the constructor `Node(Object item, Node pointer);` uses the link pointer to "join together" the nodes. Initially, `head` is set to a `null` reference. This value is passed to the first constructor, and the resultant node object is then assigned to `head`. This new value of `head` is then passed as an argument to the second constructor to preserve the link with the previous object, and the second new object is then assigned to `head`. Notice that the first object has been pushed down the list. Finally, the new value of `head` is passed as an argument to the third constructor to preserve the link with the previous object, and the third new object is assigned to `head`.

Now that the linked list has been built, it is possible to traverse the list, starting at the head, and finishing when the `null` reference in the last object is detected. Each time we visit a node, the contents of the datum field may be displayed. The following code traverses a linked list and displays the data stored at each node.

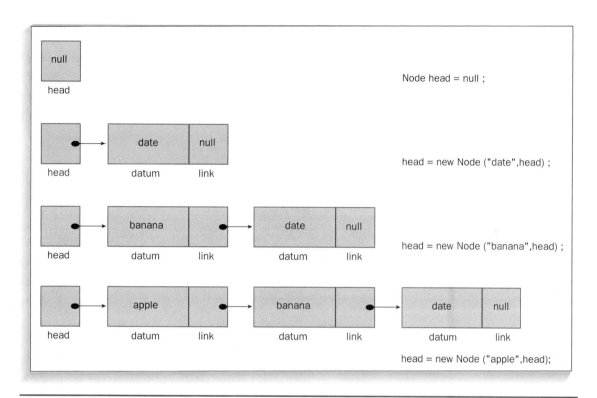

Figure 12.10 Building a linked list

```
Node temporary = head;

while (temporary != null)
{
    screen.write(temporary.datum);
    temporary = temporary.link;
}
```

You are advised to desk check this code, using the data from Figure 12.9, before progressing with the remainder of this section.

The following code shows how all of this comes together to define the class Node.

```
import avi.*;

public class Node
{
    private Object datum;
```

```
private Node    link;

public Node(){}

public Node(Object item, Node pointer)
{
      datum = item;
      link = pointer;
}

public void displayList(Window screen)
{
      Node temporary = this;

      while (temporary != null)
      {
            screen.write(temporary.datum+"\n");
            temporary = temporary.link;
      }
}
}
```

When you inspect the code we used to build the linked list, you can see that it is very repetitive. If we were to build a list of different items, only the arguments used in the constructors would change. If these arguments are represented in a program as variables, then it is possible to build a linked list of any number of nodes (subject to the size of the memory allocated to building objects!). Program Example_7 builds and displays a linked list.

```
import avi.*;

class Example_7
{
      static public void main(String[] args)
      {
            String[] answer = {"yes","no"};

            Window screen = new Window("Example_7.java");
            DialogBox inputFruit = new DialogBox(screen,"Name of fruit?");
            RadioButtons more = new
            RadioButtons(screen,"More data?",answer);

            Node list=null;
            String datum;
```

```
        screen.showWindow();

        do
        {
              inputFruit.showDialogBox();
              datum = inputFruit.getString();
              list = new Node(datum,list);
              more.showRadioButtons();
        } while (more.getNameOfButton().equals("yes"));

        // display contents of list
        list.displayList(screen);
    }
}
```

Results from the log file follow:

```
=======================================================================
                    L  O  G      F  I  L  E
      audio-visual interface [avi] - Release 1.0 - by Barry Holmes
        filename: Example_7.java   date: 7/22/2000    time: 3:10:57


=======================================================================

At the prompt: Name of fruit?, you input [ date ] at the dialog box.

At the prompt: More data?, you selected [ yes ] from the radio buttons.

At the prompt: Name of fruit?, you input [ banana ] at the dialog box.

At the prompt: More data?, you selected [ yes ] from the radio buttons.

At the prompt: Name of fruit?, you input [ apple ] at the dialog box.

At the prompt: More data?, you selected [ no ] from the radio buttons.

apple
banana
date
```

Program Example_7 uses the Node class to create and traverse a linked list. Following the object-oriented philosophy, we want to create a separate linked list class, essentially a linked list abstract data type (ADT). The first consideration to address is the relationship between the linked list class and the Node class that has already been defined.

Java will allow an inner class to be nested within an outer class. The inner class is sometimes referred to as a "member" class of the outer class. A *member class* is just another class component, in the same way that constants, variables, and methods are class components. The code within a member class can implicitly refer to any of the constants, variables, and methods of its enclosing class.

Since we have defined the class Node in the previous program, a LinkedList class should nest the class Node as an inner class. In addition, it should be able to offer methods to append a node to the list, delete a node from the list, return the number of nodes, and return whether the list is empty. In the definition of the LinkedList class that follows, the method to display the linked list has been removed from the class Node and implemented in the class LinkedList.

```
public class LinkedList
{
    public LinkedList()
    public void append(Object datum)
    public boolean delete(Object scrap)
    public void displayList()
    public boolean isEmpty()
    public int numberOfNodes()
}
```

Figure 12.11 illustrates the variables used to build and maintain a linked list LL. Within the implementation of the class LinkedList, these variables are defined as follows.

```
private Node head;      // references the first node of the list
private Node tail;      // references the last node of the list
private Node temporary; // used for node manipulation
```

The code used to append a node into the linked list follows. This should be read in conjunction with Figure 12.12. Each drawing in this figure depicts the effects of a separate line of the following code.

```
public void append(Object datum)
{
    if (head==null) // list empty
    {
        head=new Node(datum,head);
        tail=head;
    }
}
```

```
else
{
        temporary = new Node(datum,temporary);
        tail.link = temporary;
        tail = temporary;
        temporary = null;
}

nodeCount++;
}
```

Notice that the nodes are appended into the linked list, unlike the previous algorithm in which the nodes were inserted into the head of the linked. After appending a node, the class variable `nodeCount` is increased.

The removal of any node from any position in the linked list is slightly more tricky than the removal of a node from the head of the list.

There are three cases to consider.

■ The removal of a node at the head of the list: The head must point to the next node in the list if one exists. The value of the head of the list must always be preserved; otherwise, there is no means of accessing the linked list.

■ The removal of a node from the middle of the list, that is, excluding the head or tail nodes. The previous node to the one being removed must point to the successor node (the node after the one to be removed).

■ The removal of the last node in the list. The penultimate node becomes the last node in the list.

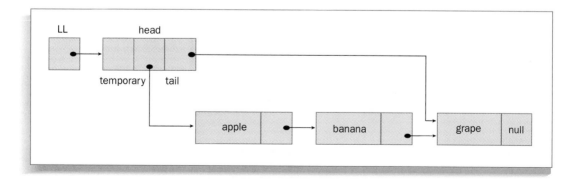

Figure 12.11 Class variables associated with the linked list

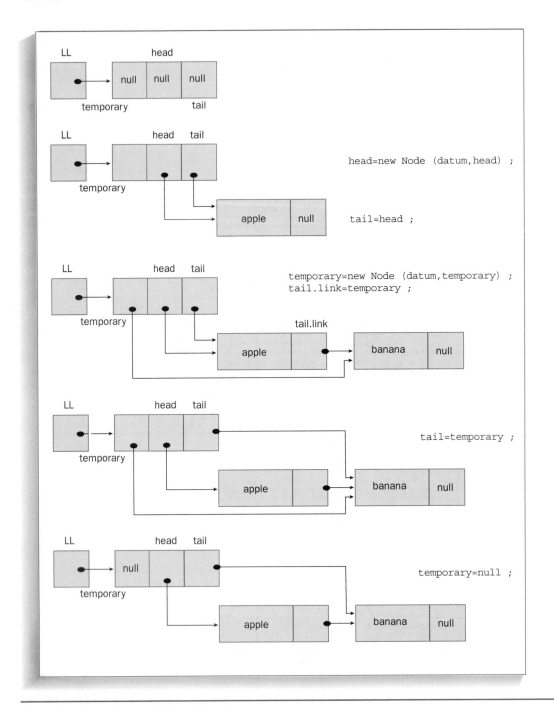

Figure 12.12 Appending a node into a linked list

The code used to delete any node from the linked list follows. Notice that it is necessary to include two local references in this code, one to point at the current node (the node being inspected), and one to point at the previous node (the node previously inspected if not at the head of the list).

```java
public boolean delete(Object scrap)
{
      Node previous = head;

      for (Node current=head; current != null; current=current.link)
      {
            // node to be deleted is at the head of the list
            if (current.datum.equals(scrap) && previous==current)
            {
                  head = current.link;
                  if (head == null) tail = null;
                  nodeCount--;
                  return true;
            }

            // node to be deleted is after the first node and before the last
            else if (current.datum.equals(scrap) && (current.link != null))
            {
                  previous.link = current.link;
                  nodeCount--;
                  return true;
            }

            // node to be deleted is at the end of the list
            else if (current.datum.equals(scrap) && (current.link == null))
            {
                  tail = previous;
                  previous.link = null;
                  nodeCount--;
                  return true;
            }

            previous = current;
      }

      return false;
}
```

You should desk check the code while following Figures 12.13, 12.14, and 12.15.

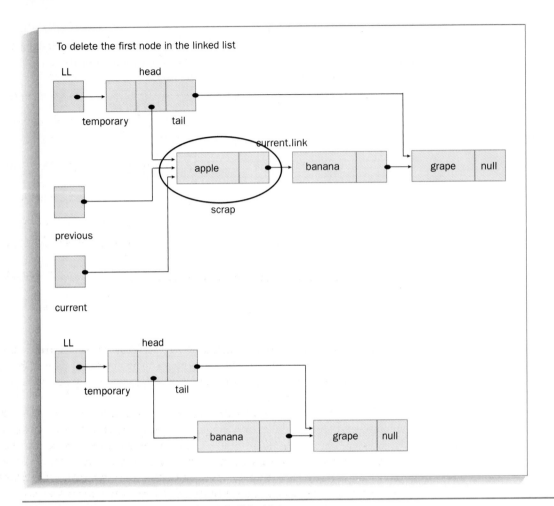

Figure 12.13 Deleting a node from the front of a linked list

LinkedList class

Here is the complete version of the `LinkedList` class:

```
import avi.*;

public class LinkedList
{
      class Node
      {
            protected Object datum;
            protected Node    link;
```

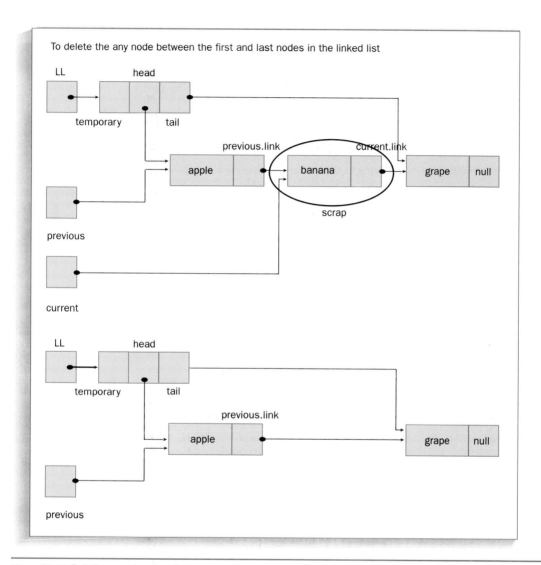

Figure 12.14 Deleting a node other than at the head or tail

```
public Node(){}

public Node(Object item, Node pointer)
{
      datum = item;
      link = pointer;
}
}
```

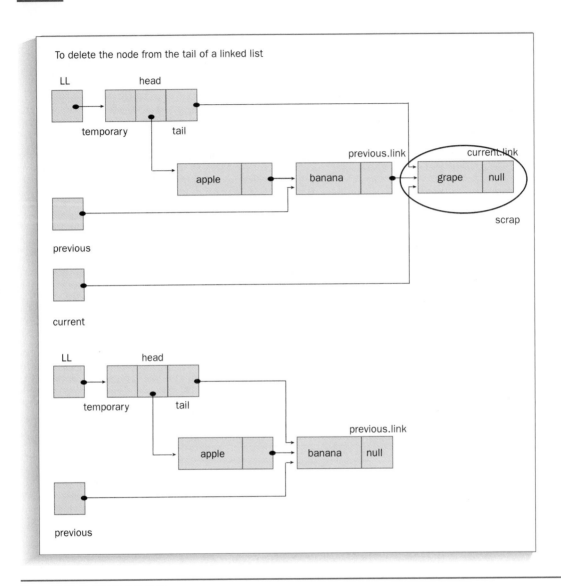

Figure 12.15 Deleting a tail node

```
private Node head;
private Node tail;
private Node temporary;
private int nodeCount;


// constructor
/**
The LinkedList class will create a linked list object,
```

```
that contains no nodes.
*/
public LinkedList()
{
      head = null;
      tail = null;
      temporary = null;
      nodeCount = 0;
}


/**
The method append will add an object into the end of the linked list;
the method will allow for multiple entries of the same object.
@param datum is the object to be added into the end of the list.
*/
public void append(Object datum)
{
      if (head==null) // list empty
      {
            head=new Node(datum,head);
            tail=head;
      }
      else
      {
            temporary = new Node(datum,temporary);
            tail.link = temporary;
            tail = temporary;
            temporary = null;
      }
      nodeCount++;
}

/**
The method delete removes an object from the linked list.
@param scrap is the object to be removed.
@return Returns true if the object could be found and successfully
deleted.
*/
public boolean delete(Object scrap)
{
      Node previous = head;

      // for every node in the linked list
      for (Node current=head; current != null; current=current.link)
      {
```

```
            // node to be deleted is at the head of the list
            if (current.datum.equals(scrap) && previous==current)
            {
                    head = current.link;
                    if (head == null) tail = null;
                    nodeCount--;
                    return true;
            }
            // node to be deleted is after the first node and before
            // the last
            else if (current.datum.equals(scrap) &&
                    (current.link != null))
            {
                    previous.link = current.link;
                    nodeCount--;
                    return true;
            }
            // node to be deleted is at the end of the list
            else if (current.datum.equals(scrap) &&
                    (current.link == null))
            {
                    tail = previous;
                    previous.link = null;
                    nodeCount--;
                    return true;
            }

            previous = current;
    }

    return false;
}


/**
The method displayList displays the contents of a linked list
from the first node through to the last node.
@param screen is the container of the text area on which to write
the information.
*/
public void displayList(Window screen)
{
        Node temporary = head;

        if (head == null)
```

```
            {
                    screen.write("linked list is empty\n");
                    return;
            }

            screen.write("\nContents of linked list\n");
            screen.write("=======================\n");
            while (temporary != null)
            {
                    screen.write((String)temporary.datum+"\n");
                    temporary = temporary.link;
            }
            screen.write("=======================\n\n");
    }

    /**
    The method isEmpty will return whether the linked list is empty.
    @return Returns true if the list is empty, otherwise return false.
    */
    public boolean isEmpty()
    {
            return (nodeCount == 0);
    }

    /**
    The method numberOfNodes returns the number of nodes in the linked
    list.
    @return Returns the number of nodes in the linked list.
    */
    public int numberOfNodes()
    {
            return nodeCount;
    }
}
```

Program `Example_8` tests the methods of the class `LinkedList`.

```
// case study - linked lists
import avi.*;

class Example_8
{
      static public void main(String[] args)
      {
```

```
String[] reply = {"Append item to list",
                  "Delete item from list",
                  "Display the list",
                  "Display number of nodes",
                  "Quit to inspect I/O"};
String[] answer = {"yes","no"};

Window screen = new Window("Example_8.java");
DialogBox inputFruit = new
DialogBox(screen,"Name of fruit?");
RadioButtons menu = new
RadioButtons(screen,"What next?",reply);
RadioButtons more = new
RadioButtons(screen,"More data?",answer);

LinkedList list = new LinkedList();
String datum;
String choice;

screen.showWindow();

do
{
    menu.showRadioButtons();
    choice = menu.getNameOfButton();

    if (choice.equals("Append item to list"))
    {
        do
        {
            inputFruit.showDialogBox();
            datum = inputFruit.getString();
            list.append(datum);
            screen.write(datum+
                    " was appended to list\n");
            more.showRadioButtons();
        } while (more.getNameOfButton().equals("yes"));
    }
    else if (choice.equals("Delete item from list") &&
            !list.isEmpty())
    {
        do
        {
            inputFruit.showDialogBox();
            datum = inputFruit.getString();
```

```
                    if (list.delete(datum))
                    {
                            screen.write(datum+
                                    " was scrapped from list\n");
                    }
                    more.showRadioButtons();
              } while (more.getNameOfButton().equals("yes"));
        }
        else if (choice.equals("Display the list"))
        {
                list.displayList(screen);
        }
        else if (choice.equals("Display number of nodes"))
        {
                screen.write("number of nodes "+
                        list.numberOfNodes()+"\n");
        }
    } while (!choice.equals("Quit to inspect I/O"));
  }
}
```

A screen shot follows from the running program.

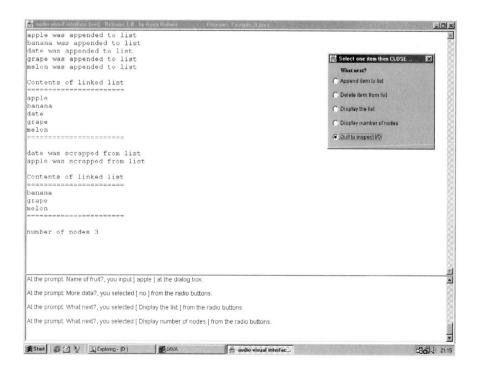

We have designed, coded, and tested our own linked list class. It is important for you, as a student of computing, to learn the basic approaches we have illustrated and to see how they all work together to provide a useful class. You should know, however, that a good linked list class also comes with the `java.util` package. You may want to investigate this class in case you have opportunities to use it in your future programs.

12.6 Stacks

The linked list is a general list structure. Several specialized list structures are important in computer program design, namely the queue and the stack. The *queue* is a list in which we append items at one end of the list and remove them from the other end. It is a First In First Out or FIFO list. It is useful for holding a list of jobs that must be executed, for example. The *stack* is a list in which we insert items at one end of the list and remove them from the same end. It is a Last In First Out or LIFO list. It is useful for holding the list of return addresses to be used when following a sequence of nested methods calls, for example.

Figure 12.16 illustrates a stack. As you can see, the stack operates on the LIFO principle. The entry/exit point of the stack is known as the stack top. An item that joins the stack is said to be *pushed* on to the stack. An item that leaves the stack is said to be *popped* from the stack. It is also possible to *peek* (look at) at the item on the top of the stack without removing the item.

Figure 12.17 illustrates the movement of the stack top as data is pushed and popped to and from the stack.

You may create a stack from a linked list; in fact, we have already gone part way in doing so. If you examine the code in the class `LinkedList`, you may

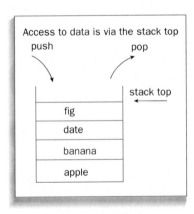

Figure 12.16 Access to a stack is from one end only

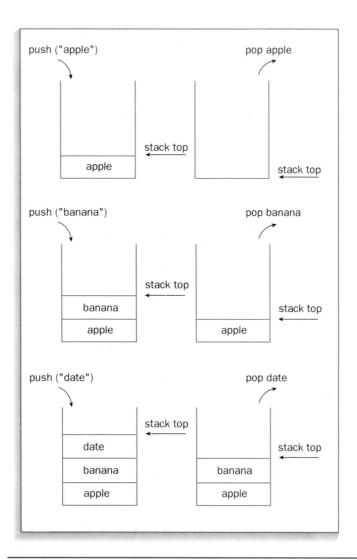

Figure 12.17 Pushing and popping items to and from a stack

observe that we can already insert and delete a node from the front of a linked list. If we treat the front of the linked list as the stack top, then we already have the code we need for manipulating data on a stack.

Alternatively, the Java `util` package contains the following `Stack` class.

```
public class Stack extends Vector
{
    // Constructors
    public Stack();

    // Methods
    public boolean empty();
    public Object peek();
    public Object pop();
    public Object push(Object  item);
    public int search(Object  o);
}
```

Stacks are used by the Java language in tracing the route the computer takes through the methods in attempting to find a *catch* block to handle the exception. The output from the stack trace is always displayed in the order of visiting the methods, with the last method visited being displayed first. This is a typical characteristic of a stack—the last item stored in the stack is the first item to be retrieved from the stack.

CASE STUDY

Using a Stack for Converting Algebraic Expressions

Background Information

Normal algebraic notation is often termed *infix* notation, since the binary arithmetic operator appears between (inside) the two operands to which it is being applied. Infix notation may require parentheses to specify the desired order of operations. For example, in the expression a/b+c, the division will occur first, followed by the addition. If we want the addition to occur first, we must parenthesize the expression as a/(b+c).

Using postfix notation (also called reverse Polish notation after the nationality of its originator Jan Lukasiewicz), the need for parentheses is eliminated because the operator is placed directly after the two operands to which it applies.

The infix expression a/b+c would be written as the postfix expression ab/c+, which is interpreted as divide a by b and add c to the result.

The infix expression a/(b+c) would be written as abc+/ in postfix notation, which is interpreted as add b to c and then divide that result into a.

The Railway Shunting-Yard Algorithm

In compiler writing it is more convenient to evaluate arithmetic expressions written in reverse Polish notation than it is to evaluate arithmetic expressions written in infix notation. The

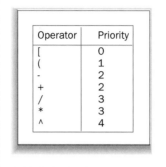

Operator	Priority
[	0
(	1
-	2
+	2
/	3
*	3
^	4

Figure 12.18 Operator priorities

following algorithm, known as the Railway Shunting-Yard algorithm (since data are shunted to and from a stack), can be used to convert infix notations to reverse Polish notations.

The operators [and] are used to delimit the infix expression. For example, the expression a*(b+c/d) will be coded as [a*(b+c/d)]. The algorithm uses operator priorities as defined in Figure 12.18.

Use Figure 12.19 to trace the following explanation of the algorithm. The figure shows the steps followed by the algorithm to convert the infix expression a*(b+c/d) into the equivalent postfix expression abcd/+*.

Diagram (i): If brackets [or (are encountered, each is pushed on to the stack.

Diagram (ii): All operands that are encountered (for example a, b, and c) are stored in a string buffer.

Diagrams (iii), (iv), and (v): When an operator is encountered, its priority is compared with that of the operator's priority at the top of the stack.

Diagram (vi): If, when comparing priorities, the operator encountered is not greater than the operator on the top of the stack, the operator on the top of the stack is popped and added to the string buffer. This process is repeated until the encountered operator has a higher priority than the stack top operator. The encountered operator is then pushed on to the stack.

Diagrams (v) and (vi): When a) is encountered, all the operators up to but not including (are popped from the stack one at a time and stored in the string buffer. The operator (is then deleted from the stack.

Diagrams (vi) and (vii): When the operator] is encountered, all the remaining operators, up to but not including [, are popped from the stack one at a time and stored in the string buffer. The string of characters that is displayed will be the reverse Polish string.

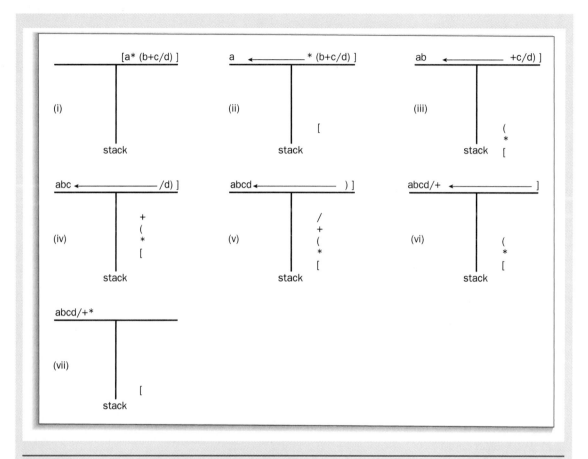

Figure 12.19 The use of a stack in the reverse Polish algorithm

Statement of the Problem   Create a class `ReversePolish` that contains methods to permit an arithmetic expression written in infix notation to be converted to a postfix notation expression. Create an additional class to test the methods of the `ReversePolish` class.

Analysis of Classes

Naturally, the Java class `Stack` will be used in the solution to this problem. However, the algorithm to convert an infix string to a postfix string will be an instance method in a class `ReversePolish`. The UML representation of the class `ReversePolish` and its dependencies are shown in Figure 12.20.

The signatures of the constructor and method for this class follow.

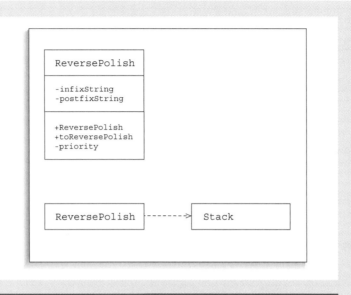

Figure 12.20 UML representation of the class `ReversePolish` and its dependencies

```
class ReversePolish
{
    // constructor
    public ReversePolish(String infixExpression);

    // method to return a reverse Polish string
    public String toReversePolish();

    // method to return the numerical priority of an operator
    private int priority(char operator)

}
```

Algorithm for the Constructor `ReversePolish`

The purpose of the constructor is to input the infix string as a parameter, and store the string as a `StringBuffer` object. The `StringBuffer` class represents a string of characters. It differs from the `String` class in that its contents may be modified. A `StringBuffer` object grows in length as necessary. The string stored in a `StringBuffer` object may be inspected character-by-character with the `charAt()` method and modified in place with the `append()` method.

1. copy formal parameter string to local variable of type string buffer.

Algorithm for the Method `toReversePolish`

This algorithm is a representation of the logic expressed when describing the functionality of Figure 12.19. It describes how the stack is used as the siding to temporarily store operators.

```
 1. for every character in the infix expression
 2.     if next character is closing parenthesis ')'
 3.         pop operator from stack
 4.         while operator not opening parenthesis '('
 5.             store operator in string buffer
 6.             pop operator from stack
 7.     else if next character is closing bracket ']'
 8.         pop operator from stack
 9.         while operator not opening bracket '['
10.             store operator in string buffer
11.             pop operator from stack
12.     else if next character is opening parenthesis '(' or opening bracket '['
13.         push next character on to stack
14.     else if next character arithmetic operator
15.         while priority of next character is < = to priority of stack top operator
16.             pop operator from stack
17.             store operator in string buffer
18.         push next character on to stack
19.     else
20.         store next character in string buffer
```

Algorithm for the Method `private priority`

To effectively push and pop operators onto the stack it is necessary to compare the priority of the incoming operator with the stack top operator. The purpose of the `private` helper method `priority` is to return the priority of an operator.

```
1. switch operator
2.  [ :        return 0
3.  ( :        return 1
4.  -, + :     return 2
5.  /, * :     return 3
6.  ^ :        return 4
7. default :   return -1
```

Desk Check of the Method `toReversePolish`

The test data is `[a*(b+c/d)]`.

Diagram (Figure 12.19)	(i)	(ii)			(iii)		(iv)	
nextCharacter	[	a	*	(	b	+	c	/
nextCharacter == ')'?	false	false	false	false	false	false	false	false
nextCharacter == ']'?	false	false	false	false	false	false	false	false
nextCharacter == '(' | '['?	true	false	false	true	false	false	false	false
arithmetic operator?		false	true		false	true	false	true
popped operator								
operator != '('								
operator != '['								
priority <= priority stack top			false			false		false
contents of stack	[		[*	[*(		[*(+		[*(+/
contents of string buffer	a			ab		abc		

Diagram (Figure 12.19) (cont)	(v)	(vi)			(vii)	
nextCharacter	d	)			]	
nextCharacter == ')'?	false	true			false	
nextCharacter == ']'?	false				true	
nextCharacter == '(' | '['?	false					
arithmetic operator?	false					
popped operator		/	+	(	*	[
operator != '('		false	false	false	true	
operator != '['						false
priority <= priority stack top						
contents of stack		[*(+	[*(	[*	[	
character stored in buffer	abcd	abcd/	abcd/+		abcd/+*	

```java
import java.util.*;

public class ReversePolish
{
    private StringBuffer infixString   = new StringBuffer();
    private StringBuffer postfixString = new StringBuffer();

    // constructor
    /**
    The ReversePolish class will create a reverse Polish object.
    @param A string representing the infix expression to be converted.
    */
    public ReversePolish(String infixExpression)
    {
        infixString.append(infixExpression);
    }
```

```
/**
The method toReversePolish converts the infix expression into a
reverse Polish string.
@return Return the reverse Polish string.
*/
public String toReversePolish()
{
    char      nextCharacter;
    char      operator='\u0000';

    int lengthOfExpression = infixString.length();

    // instantiate stack object siding
    Stack siding = new Stack();

    for (int index=0; index != lengthOfExpression; index++)
    {
        // get next nextCharacter from
        nextCharacter = infixString.charAt(index);

        if (nextCharacter == ')')
        {
            // pop character from stack
            operator = ((Character)siding.pop()).charValue();
            while (operator != '(')
            {
                // store operator in string buffer
                postfixString.append(operator);
                // pop character from stack
                operator =
                ((Character)siding.pop()).charValue();
            }
        }
        else if (nextCharacter == ']')
        {
            // pop character from stack
            operator = ((Character)siding.pop()).charValue();
            while (operator != '[')
            {
                // store operator in string buffer
                postfixString.append(operator);
                // pop character from stack
                operator =
                ((Character)siding.pop()).charValue();
            }
        }
```

```
            else if (nextCharacter == '(' || nextCharacter == '[')
            {
                    // push character on to stack
                    siding.push(new Character(nextCharacter));
            }
            else if (nextCharacter == '^' || nextCharacter == '*' ||
                    nextCharacter == '/' || nextCharacter == '+' ||
                    nextCharacter == '-')
            {
                    while (priority(nextCharacter) <=
                            priority(((Character)siding.peek()).
                                            charValue()))
                    {
                            // pop character from stack
                            operator = ((Character)siding.pop()).
                                            charValue();
                            // store operator in string buffer
                            postfixString.append(operator);
                    }

                    // push character on to stack
                    siding.push(new Character(nextCharacter));
            }
            else
                    // store operand in string buffer
                    postfixString.append(nextCharacter);
        }

        return postfixString.toString();
}

// method to return the priority of an operator
private int priority(char operator)
{
        switch (operator)
        {
        case '[':               return 0;
        case '(':               return 1;
        case '-': case '+':     return 2;
        case '/': case '*':     return 3;
        case '^':               return 4;
        default :               return -1;
        }
    }
}
}
```

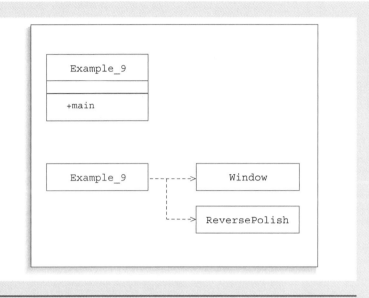

Figure 12.21 UML representation of the class `Example_9` and its dependencies

The UML diagram for the class used to test the methods of the `ReversePolish` class is seen in Figure 12.21.

```
import avi.*;

class Example_9
{
      public static void main(String[] args)
      {
          // store infix expressions into an array
          String[] infixExpression = {"[a*b+c]","[a*(b+c/d)]",
                                "[a*b+c/d]","[u+f*t]",
                                "[b^2-4*a*c]","[h*(a+4*b+c)/3]",
                                "[w*1-1/(w*c)]"};

          Window screen = new Window("Example_9.java");
          screen.showWindow();

          for (int index=0; index != infixExpression.length; index++)
          {
```

```
                // display an infix expression
                screen.write("infix: "+infixExpression[index]+"\n");

                // instantiate a ReversePolish object
                ReversePolish expression = new
                ReversePolish(infixExpression[index]);

                // convert the infix expression to reverse Polish and
                // display on the screen
                screen.write("reverse Polish: "+
                            expression.toReversePolish()+"\n\n");
            }
        }
}
```

Results from the log file follow:

```
===============================================================================
                    L O G   F I L E
        audio-visual interface [avi] - Release 1.0 - by Barry Holmes
         filename: Example_9.java   date: 7/22/2000   time: 3:57:44
===============================================================================

infix: [a*b+c]
reverse Polish: ab*c+

infix: [a*(b+c/d)]
reverse Polish: abcd/+*

infix: [a*b+c/d]
reverse Polish: ab*cd/+

infix: [u+f*t]
reverse Polish: uft*+

infix: [b^2-4*a*c]
reverse Polish: b2^4a*c*-

infix: [h*(a+4*b+c)/3]
reverse Polish: ha4b*+c+*3/

infix: [w*1-1/(w*c)]
reverse Polish: w1*1wc*/-
```

SUMMARY

- In the selection sort, the largest item of data found in the cells $0..N - 1$ of an array is transferred to cell $N - 1$. The algorithm is repeated for the items of data in cells $0 .. N - 2$, and the largest item of data is transferred to cell $N - 2$. The algorithm is repeated until there is only one number to consider in cell 0.

- The selection sort has an efficiency of the order on N^2, and are known as quadratic algorithms.

- Searching for data held in an array is made more efficient when the data is ordered on key value. If the value of the key is greater than the item being inspected, then the key may be found further on in the array. However, if the value of the key is less than the item being inspected, then the key cannot exist in the array and the search must be abandoned.

- The binary-search algorithm relies upon the fact that the contents of the array must be ordered. The technique repeatedly divides an array into smaller arrays that are likely to contain the key until either a key match is possible or the array cannot be subdivided further.

- For large amounts of data, a Quicksort ($N \log_2 N$) is an efficient algorithm for sorting data, and a binary search ($\log_2 N$) is an efficient algorithm for searching for a piece of data.

- A node may be regarded as a self-referential record since it contains a field with a reference to the same record.

- A linked list is a sequence of nodes in which each node is linked or connected to the node following it. A named reference variable points to the first node in the linked list. A null reference is used to indicate the end of the linked list.

- A linked list offers the following advantages over an array:
  - A list is created at run time through dynamic memory allocation.
  - The insertion and deletion of nodes in a list requires changing reference variables and not moving data about main memory.
  - A linked list may be used to represent queues and stacks.

- A stack is a data structure in which access to objects is from one end only. A stack works on the LIFO principle that the last object inserted into the stack is the first object removed from the stack. Objects are said to be pushed onto the stack (for storage) and popped from the stack (for access and removal). See `java.util.Stack`.

Review Questions

Short Answer

1. If an array contained 1,024 integers, how much longer proportionally would it take to sort the numbers using a selection sort than with a Quicksort?

2. What changes would you make to the selection sort to reverse the order of the sorted numbers, that is, highest to lowest?

3. What is a sequential search?

4. What is the proportional saving in time when using a sequential search versus a binary search to search for an item that does not exist?

5. How many key comparisons are necessary in a binary search when there are 1,024 items in an array and the key does not exist in the array?

6. Explain the term self-referential structure.

7. How do you make a reference to a linked list?

8. Why is it easier to insert or delete nodes in a linked list rather than to insert or delete items in an array?

9. Give three methods for implementing a stack using the Java language.

Exercises

10. Implement a class `Queue`, based upon a linked list, which allows objects to join at the rear of the list and leave from the front of the list. In addition to the constructor, you should devise methods to test whether the queue is empty, to insert and delete objects from the queue, and to display the values of the objects in the list.

Programming Problems

11. Create a class `Friend` that contains data fields (instance variables) for the name (surname followed by first name), address, telephone number, birthday, and name of the image file (JPEG or TIF) of the friend's photograph. Remember to create a constructor for this class that will initialize the data fields and create methods to retrieve the data from the data fields.

    Create your own text file containing the data fields of the `Friend` class for any number of your own friends. You will also need to digitize the photographs of your friends and store these images in the same directory as the text file.

    Create a class to read the text file, create `Friend` objects, and store each object in consecutive cells of a one-dimensional array; sort the array on the surname of the friend. The class should contain a method for you to get the contents of the sorted array.

Write a main method to input the name of a friend, and use the prewritten binary search method to search the array for the name of the friend. If the name is found, then display all the personal details about the friend, including the photograph.

12. Using the class `Friend` and the text file created in Question 11, modify both the `LinkedList` class and program `Example_8` to store the `Friend` objects in a linked list and maintain the linked list.

13. Write a program to create a linked list of nonzero integer random numbers stored in key disorder. Build a second linked list that contains the integers from the first linked list sorted into key order. Find the largest number in the first linked list and copy this to the second linked list. As each integer is used from the first linked list, delete it from the first linked list. Repeat the process until the first linked list is empty. Display the contents of the second linked list.

Scenario for Questions 14 to 16

A supermarket has a fixed number of checkout lanes. Customers wanting to pay for their goods normally choose the lane that has the shortest queue.

The queues of customers waiting to pay for their goods at a supermarket lane can be simulated on a computer.

The data structures that represent the customers queuing at the lanes are shown in Figure 12.22. All queues are organized on a first in first out (FIFO) basis. New customers must join the queue at the rear, and only a customer at the head of the queue can be removed from the queue.

14. Implement a class `BadDataException`.

A `BadDataException` may be thrown from any method in which:

- the checkout number is not in the range `0 .. lane-1`

- the number of checkouts is less than the minimum stated

- the time of day is not in the range `0 .. 2359`

- an attempt is made to insert a customer into a checkout that does not exist

- an attempt is made to remove a customer from an empty queue

Note that you are *not* expected to validate the time order in which a customer enters or leaves a queue.

15. Implement a class `SupermarketQueue` that contains the following constructor and methods.

```
public class SupermarketQueue
{
    // constructor
    public SupermarketQueue(int numberOfCheckouts) throws

BadDataException;
```

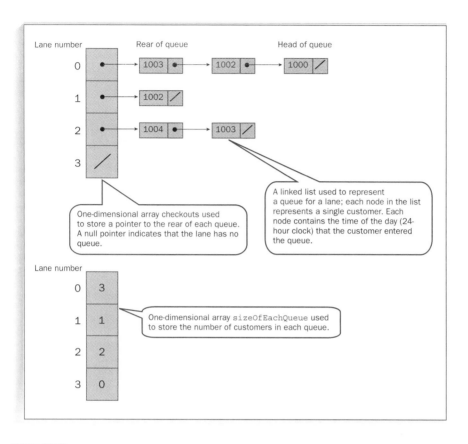

Lane number　　　　Rear of queue　　　　　　　Head of queue

A linked list used to represent a queue for a lane; each node in the list represents a single customer. Each node contains the time of the day (24-hour clock) that the customer entered the queue.

One-dimensional array checkouts used to store a pointer to the rear of each queue. A null pointer indicates that the lane has no queue.

Lane number

One-dimensional array `sizeOfEachQueue` used to store the number of customers in each queue.

Figure 12.22

```
// instance methods
// input a customer into a queue for a given checkout at a
   // given time
   public void queue(int checkoutNumber,
                     int timeOfDay) throws BadDataException;

// remove a customer from the head of a given checkout at a given
   // time and return (in minutes) the time spent queuing
public int leave(int checkoutNumber,
                 int timeOfDay) throws BadDataException;

// method that returns true if customers are queuing at a
  // checkout
```

```
    public boolean queueFormed(int checkoutNumber) throws

BadDataException;

    // return the number of the checkout with the smallest queue
    public int checkoutWithSmallestQueue();

    // display the time each customer entered a queue for all the
        // lanes
    public void displayQueues();
}
```

16. Write a `main` method that uses the public methods of the classes to test *all* the construc-
    tors and *all* the methods defined in the classes `BadDataException` and
    `SupermarketQueue`.

17. Figure 12.23 illustrates a circular doubly linked list structure containing a dummy node
    at the head of the list.

    Rewrite Program `Example_8` to maintain data in this structure. Examine the con-
    tents of the list both in order, ascending and descending.

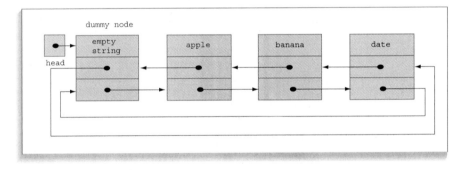

Figure 12.23 A circular double linked list

Tables

Unicode	Octal	character	Unicode	Octal	character	Unicode	Octal	character
0000	000	NUL	0030	060	0	0060	140	'
0001	001	SOH	0031	061	1	0061	141	a
0002	002	STX	0032	062	2	0062	142	b
0003	003	ETX	0033	063	3	0063	143	c
0004	004	EOT	0034	064	4	0064	144	d
0005	005	ENQ	0035	065	5	0065	145	e
0006	006	ACK	0036	066	6	0066	146	f
0007	007	BEL	0037	067	7	0067	147	g
0008	010	BS	0038	070	8	0068	150	h
0009	011	HT	0039	071	9	0069	151	i
000A	012	LF	003A	072	:	006A	152	j
000B	013	VT	003B	073	;	006B	153	k
000C	014	FF	003C	074	<	006C	154	l
000D	015	CR	003D	075	=	006D	155	m
000E	016	SO	003E	076	>	006E	156	n
000F	017	SI	003F	077	?	006F	157	o
0010	020	DLE	0040	100	@	0070	160	p
0011	021	DC1	0041	101	A	0071	161	q
0012	022	DC2	0042	102	B	0072	162	r
0013	023	DC3	0043	103	C	0073	163	s
0014	024	DC4	0044	104	D	0074	164	t
0015	025	NAK	0045	105	E	0075	165	u
0016	026	STN	0046	106	F	0076	166	v
0017	027	ETB	0047	107	G	0077	167	w
0018	030	AN	0048	110	H	0078	170	x
0019	031	EM	0049	111	I	0079	171	y
001A	032	SUB	004A	112	J	007A	172	z
001B	033	ESC	004B	113	K	007B	173	{
001C	034	FS	004C	114	L	007C	174		
001D	035	GS	004D	115	M	007D	175	}
001E	036	RS	004E	116	N	007E	176	~
001F	037	US	004F	117	O	007F	177	del
0020	040	space	0050	120	P			
0021	041	!	0051	121	Q			
0022	042	"	0052	122	R			
0023	043	#	0053	123	S			
0024	044	$	0054	124	T			
0025	045	%	0055	125	U			
0026	046	&	0056	126	V			
0027	047	'	0057	127	W			
0028	050	(	0058	130	X			
0029	051	)	0059	131	Y			
002A	052	*	005A	132	Z			
002B	053	+	005B	133	[			
002C	054	,	005C	134	\			
002D	055	-	005D	135	]			
002E	056	.	005E	136	^			
002F	057	/	005F	137	_			

Table A.1 ASCII characters and their respective hexadecimal and octal codes

type	contains	default	size	range
boolean	true or false	false	1 bit	not applicable
char	Unicode character	\u0000	16 bits	\u0000 .. \uFFFF
byte	signed integer	0	8 bits	-128 .. +127
short	signed integer	0	16 bits	-32768 .. +32767
int	signed integer	0	32 bits	-2147483648 .. +2147483647
long	signed integer	0	64 bits	-9223372036854775808 .. +9223372036854775807
float	IEEE 754 floating-point	0.0	32 bits	± 1.40239846E-45 .. ± 3.40282347E+38
double	IEEE 754 floating-point	0.0	64 bits	± 4.94065645841246544E-324 ± 1.79769313486231570e+308

Table A.2 Java primitive data types

priority level	operator	operand type(s)	associativity	operation performed
1	++	*arithmetic*	**R**	unary pre or post increment
	--	*arithmetic*	**R**	unary pre or post decrement
	+ -	*arithmetic*	**R**	unary plus, unary minus
	~	*integral*	**R**	unary bitwise complement
	!	*boolean*	**R**	unary logical complement
	(type)	*any*	**R**	cast
2	* / %	*arithmetic*	**L**	multiplication, division, remainder
3	+ -	*arithmetic*	**L**	addition, subtraction
	+	*string*	**L**	string concatenation
4	<<	*integral*	**L**	left shift
	>>	*integral*	**L**	right shift with sign extension
	>>>	*integral*	**L**	right shift with zero extension
5	< <=	*arithmetic*	**L**	less than, less than or equal
	> >=	*arithmetic*	**L**	greater than, greater than or equal
6	**instanceof**	*object, type*	**L**	type comparison
	==	*primitive*	**L**	equal (have identical values)
	!=	*primitive*	**L**	not equal (have different values)
	==	*object*	**L**	equal (refer to same object)
7	!=	*object*	**L**	not equal (refer to different objects)
	&	*integral*	**L**	bitwise AND
8	&	*boolean*	**L**	boolean AND
	^	*integral*	**L**	bitwise XOR
9	^	*boolean*	**L**	boolean XOR
	|	*integral*	**L**	bitwise OR
10	|	*boolean*	**L**	boolean OR
11	&&	*boolean*	**L**	conditional AND
12	||	*boolean*	**L**	condirional OR
13	?:	*boolean any any*	**L**	conditional tenary operator
	=	*variable any*	**R**	assignment
	*= /= %=	*variable any*	**R**	assignment with operation
	+= -=			
	<<= >>=			
	>>>= &=			
	^= |=			

Table A.3 Operator priorities

escape sequence	character value
\b	backspace
\t	horizontal tab
\n	newline
\f	form feed
\r	carriage return
\"	double quote
\'	single quote
\\	backslash
\xxx	the character corresponding to the octal value xxx, where xxx is in the range 000 .. 0377
\uxxxx	the Unicode character with encoding xxxx, where xxxx is one to four hexadecimal digits. Unicode escapes are distinct from other escape types listed here.

Table A.4 Escape-sequence characters

Syntax of Java

Within the syntax description we use both terminal symbols and nonterminal symbols. The terminal symbols are shown in color, and nonterminal symbols in an *italic typeface*. Terminal symbols cannot be defined further, unlike nonterminal symbols that can be defined in other syntax definitions.

B.1 Productions from Lexical Structures

Literal:
> *IntegerLiteral*
> *FloatingPointLiteral*
> *BooleanLiteral*
> *CharacterLiteral*
> *StringLiteral*
> *NullLiteral*

B.2 Productions from Types, Values, and Variables

Type:
> *PrimitiveType*
> *ReferenceType*

PrimitiveType:
> *NumericType*
> `boolean`

NumericType:
> *IntegralType*
> *FloatingPointType*

IntegralType: one of
> `byte short int long char`

FloatingPointType: one of
> `float double`

ReferenceType:
> *ClassOrInterfaceType*
> *ArrayType*

ClassOrInterfaceType:
> *Name*

ClassType:
> *ClassOrInterfaceType*

ArrayType:
> *PrimitiveType* [ ]
> *Name* [ ]
> *ArrayType* [ ]

B.3   Productions from Names

Name:
> *SimpleName*
> *QualifiedName*

SimpleName:
> *Identifier*

QualifiedName:
> *Name . Identifier*

B.4   Productions from Packages

CompilationUnit:
> *PackageDeclaration* $_{opt}$ *ImportDeclaration* $_{opt}$ *TypeDeclaration* $_{opt}$

ImportDeclarations:
> *ImportDeclaration*
> *TypeDeclarations TypeDeclaration*

TypeDeclarations:
  TypeDeclaration
  TypeDeclarations TypeDeclaration

PackageDeclarations:
  `package` *Name* `;`

ImportDeclaration:
  SingleTypeImportDeclaration
  TypeImportOnDemandDeclaration

SingleTypeImportDeclaration:
  `import` *Name* `;`

TypeImportOnDEmandDEclaration:
  `import` *Name* `.` `*` `;`

TypeDeclaration:
  ClassDeclaration
  InterfaceDeclaration
  `;`

B.5 Productions Used Only in the LALR(1) Grammar

Modifiers:
  Modifier
  Modifiers, Modifier

Modifier: one of
  `public protected private`
  `static`
  `abstract final native synchronized transient volatile`

B.6 Productions from Classes

Productions from Class Declarations

ClassDeclarations:
  Modifiers$_{opt}$ `class` *Identifier Super$_{opt}$ Interfaces$_{opt}$ ClassBody*

Super:
  `extends` *ClassType*

Interfaces:
        `implements` *InterfaceTypeList*

InterfaceTypeList:
        InterfaceType
        InterfaceTypeList , InterfaceType

ClassBody:
        { *ClassBodyDeclaration$_{opt}$* }

ClassBodyDeclarations:
        ClassBodyDeclaration
        ClassBodyDeclarations ClassBodyDeclaration

ClassBodyDeclaration:
        ClassMemberDeclaration
        StaticInitializer
        ConstructorDeclaration

ClassMemberDeclaration:
        FieldDeclaration
        MethodDeclaration

Productions from Field Declarations

FieldDeclaration:
        Modifiers$_{opt}$ Type variableDeclarators ;

VariableDeclarators:
        VariableDeclarator
        VariableDeclarators , VariableDeclarator

VariableDeclarator:
        VariableDeclaratorId
        VariableDeclaratorId = VariableInitializer

VariableDeclaratorId:
        Identifier
        VariableDeclaratorId [ ]

VariableInitializer:
        Expression
        ArrayInitializer

Productions from Method Declarations

MethodDeclaration:
> *MethodHeader MethodBody*

MethodHeader:
> *Modifiers$_{opt}$ Type MethodDeclarator Throws$_{opt}$*
> *Modifiers$_{opt}$* `void` *MethodDeclarator Throws$_{opt}$*

MethodDeclarator:
> *Identifier* (*FormalParameterList$_{opt}$*)
> *MethodDeclarator* []

FormalParameterList:
> *FormalParameter*
> *FormalParameterList* , *FormalParameter*

FormalParameter:
> *Type VariableDeclaratorId*

Throws:
> `throws` *ClassTypeList*

ClassTypeList:
> *ClassType*
> *ClassTypeList* , *ClassType*

MethodBody:
> *Block*
> ;

Productions from Static Initializers

StaticInitializer:
> `static` *Block*

Productions from Constructor Declarations

ConstructorDeclaration:
> *Modifiers$_{opt}$ ConstructorDeclarator Throws$_{opt}$ ConstructorBody*

ConstructorDeclarator:
> *SimpleName* (*FormalParameterList$_{opt}$*)

ConstructorBody:
> { *ExplicitConstructorInvocation$_{opt}$ BlockStatements$_{opt}$* }

ExplicitConstructorInvocation:
    this (*ArgumentList*$_{opt}$);
    super (*ArgumentList*$_{opt}$);

B.7   Productions from Interfaces

Productions from Interface Declarations

InterfaceDeclaration:
    Modifiers$_{opt}$ interface *Identifier ExtendsInterfaces*$_{opt}$ *InterfaceBody*

ExtendsInterfaces:
    extends *InterfaceType*
    ExtendsInterfaces , *InterfaceType*

InterfaceBody:
    { *InterfaceMemberDeclaration*$_{opt}$ }

InterfaceMemberDeclarations:
    InterfaceMemberDeclaration
    InterfacememberDeclarations InterfaceMemberDeclaration

InterfaceMemberDeclaration:
    ConstantDeclaration
    AbstractMethodDeclaration

ConstantDeclaration:
    FieldDeclaration

AbstractMethodDeclaration:
    MethodHeader ;

B.8   Productions from Arrays

ArrayInitializer:
    { *VariableInitializers*$_{opt}$,$_{opt}$ }

VariableInitializers:
    VariableInitializer
    VariableInitializers , *VariableInitializer*

B.9   Productions from Blocks and Statements

Block:
> { *BlockStatements*_{opt} }

BlockStatements:
> *BlockStatement*
> *BlockStatements BlockStatement*

BlockStatement:
> *LocalVariableDeclarationsStatement*
> *Statement*

LocalVariableDeclarationsStatement:
> *LocalvariableDeclaration* ;

LocalVariableDeclaration:
> *Type VariableDeclarators*

Statement:
> *StatementWithoutTrailingSubstatement*
> *LabeledStatement*
> *IfThenStatement*
> *IfThenElseStatement*
> *WhileStatement*
> *ForStatement*

StatementNoShortIf:
> *StatementWithoutTrailingSubstatement*
> *LabeledStatementNoShortIf*
> *IfThenElseStatementNoShortIf*
> *WhileStatementNoShortIf*
> *ForStatementNoShortIf*

StatementWithoutTrailingSubstatement:
> *Block*
> *EmptyStatements*
> *ExpressionStatements*
> *SwitchStatement*
> *DoStatement*
> *BreakStatement*
> *ContinueStatement*
> *ReturnStatement*
> *SynchronizedStatement*
> *ThrowStatement*
> *TryStatement*

EmptyStatement:
　　;

LabeledStatement:
　　Identifier : *Statement*

LabeledStatementNoShortIf:
　　Identifier : *StatementNoShortIf*

ExpressionStatement:
　　Statementexpression ;

StatementExpression:
　　Assignment
　　PreIncrementExpression
　　PreDecrementExpression
　　PostIncrementExpression
　　PostDecrementExpression
　　MethodInvocation
　　ClassInstanceCreationExpression

IfThenStatement:
　　if (*Expression*) *Statement*

IfThenElseStatement:
　　if (*Expression*) *StatementNoShortIf* else *Statement*

IfThenElseStatementNoShortIf:
　　if (*Expression*) *StatementNoShortIf* else *StatementNoShortIf*

Switch statement:
　　switch (*Expression*) *SwitchBlock*

SwitchBlock:
　　{ *SwitchBlockStatementGroups*_{opt} *SwitchLabels*_{opt} }

SwitchBlockstatementGroups:
　　SwitchBlockStatementGroup
　　SwitchBlockStatementGroups SwitchBlockStatementGroup

SwitchBlockStatementGroup:
　　Switchlabels BlockStatements

SwitchLabels:
　　SwitchLabel
　　SwitchLabels SwitchLabel

SwitchLabel:
        `case` *ConstantExpression* `:`
        `default :`

WhileStatement:
        `while (` *Expression* `)` *statement*

WhileStatementNoShortIf:
        `while (` *Expression* `)` *statementNoShortIf*

DoStatement:
        `do` *statement* `while (` *expression* `)` `;`

ForStatement:
        `for (` *ForInit$_{opt}$* `;` *Expression$_{opt}$* `;` *ForUpdate$_{opt}$* `)` *Statement*

ForStatementNoShortIf:
        `for (` *ForInit$_{opt}$* `;` *Expression$_{opt}$* `;` *ForUpdate$_{opt}$* `)` *StatementNoShortIf*

ForInit:
        StatementExpressionList
        LocalVariableDeclarations

ForUpdate:
        StatementExpressionList

StatementExpressionList:
        StatementExpression
        StatementExpressionList `,` *StatementExpression*

BreakStatement:
        `break` *Identifier$_{opt}$* `;`

ContinueStatement:
        `continue` *Identifier$_{opt}$* `;`

ReturnStatement:
        `return` *Expression$_{opt}$* `;`

ThrowStatement:
        `throw` *Expression* `;`

SynchronizedStatement:
        `synchronized (` *Expression* `)` *Block*

TryStatement:
      `try` *Block Catches*
      `try` *Block Catches*$_{opt}$ *Finally*

Catches:
      CatchClause
      Catches CatchClause

CatchClause:
      `catch` (*FormalParameter*) *Block*

Finally:
      `finally` *Block*

B.10   Productions from Expressions

Primary:
      PrimaryNoNewArray
      ArrayCreationExpression

PrimaryNoNewArray:
      Literal
      `this`
      (*Expression*)
      ClassInstanceCreationExpression
      FieldAccess
      MethodInvocation
      ArrayAccess

ClassInstanceCreationExpression:
      `new` *ClassType* (*ArgumentList*$_{opt}$)

ArgumentList:
      Expression
      ArgumentList , *Expression*

ArrayCreationExpression:
      `new` *PrimitiveType DimensionExpression DimensionExpression*$_{opt}$
      `new` *ClassOrInterfaceType DimensionExpression DimensionExpression*$_{opt}$

DimensionExpressions:
      DimensionExpression
      DimensionExpressions DimensionExpression

DimensionExpression:
    [*Expression*]

Dimensions:
    []
    Dimensions []

FieldAccess:
    Primary . Identifier
    super *. Identifier*

MethodInvocation:
    Name (*ArgumentList$_{opt}$*)
    Primary . Identifier (*ArgumentList$_{opt}$*)
    super *. Identifier* (*ArgumentList$_{opt}$*)

ArrayAccess:
    Name [*Expression*]
    PrimaryNoNewArray [*Expression*]

Postfix Expressions:
    Primary
    Name
    PostIncrementExpression
    PostDecrementExpression

PostIncrementExpression:
    PostfixExpression ++

PostDecrementExpression:
    PostFixExpression --

UnaryExpression:
    PreIncrementExpression
    PreDecrementExpression
    + *Unary Expression*
    - *Unary Expression*
    UnaryExpressionNotPlusMinus

PreIncrementExpression:
    ++ *UnaryExpression*

PreDecrementExpression:
    -- *UnaryExpression*

UnaryExpressionNotPlusMinus:
 PostfixExpression
 ~ UnaryExpression
 ! UnaryExpression
 CastExpression

CastExpression:
 (*PrimitiveType Dimensions$_{opt}$*) *UnaryExpression*
 (*Expression*) *UnaryExpressionNotPlusMinus*
 (*Name Dimensions*) *UnaryExpressionNotPlusMinus*

MultiplicationExpression:
 UnaryExpression
 *MultiplicativeExpression * UnaryExpression*
 MultiplicativeExpression / UnaryExpression
 MultiplicativeExpression % UnaryExpression

AdditiveExpression:
 MultiplicativeExpression
 AdditiveExpression + MultiplicativeExpression
 AdditiveExpression - MultiplicativeExpression

ShiftExpression:
 AdditiveExpression
 ShiftExpression << AdditiveExpression
 ShiftExpression >> AdditiveExpression
 ShiftExpression >>> AdditiveExpression

RelationalExpression:
 ShiftExpression
 RelationalExpression < ShiftExpression
 RelationalExpression > ShiftExpression
 RelationalExpression <= ShiftExpression
 RelationalExpression >= ShiftExpression
 RelationalExpression `instanceof` *ReferenceType*

EqualityExpression:
 RelationalExpression
 EqualityExpression == RelationalExpression
 EqualityExpression != RelationalExpression

AndExpression:
 EqualityExpression
 AndExpression & EqualityExpression

ExclusiveOrExpression:
    AndExpression
    ExclusiveOrExpression ^ *AndExpression*

InclusiveOrExpression:
    ExclusiveOrExpression
    InclusiveOrExpression | *ExclusiveOrExpression*

ConditionalAndExpression:
    InclusiveOrExpression
    ConditionalAndExpression && *InclusiveOrExpression*

ConditionalOrExpression:
    ConditionalAndExpression
    ConditionalOrExpression || *ConditionalAndExpression*

ConditionalExpression:
    ConditionalOrExpression
    ConditionalOrExpression ? *Expression* : *ConditionalExpression*

AssignmentExpression:
    ConditionalExpression
    Assignment

Assignment:
    LeftHandSide AssignmentOperator AssignmentExpression

LeftHandSide:
    Name
    FieldAccess
    ArrayAccess

AssignmentOperator: one of
    = *= /= %= += -= <<= >>= >>>= &= ^= |=

Expression:
    AssignmentExpression

ConstantExpression:
    Expression

Source: The Java Language Specification, James Gosling, Bill Joy and Guy Steele, Addison-Wesley 1996.

Answers to Exercises

Chapter 1

27. Figure 1.14—Zone is an integer; One-way, Half-fare, Monthly-pass, and Family-fare are all real numbers.

```
int zone;
float oneWay, halfFare, monthlyPass, familyFare;
```

28. (b) `net-pay` (Embedded hyphen is illegal.)

    (d) `cost of paper` (Embedded spaces are illegal.)

    (f) `?X?Y` (Characters other than alphabetic, numeric digits, underscore, or $ are illegal.)

    (g) `1856AD` (Identifier must begin with a nondigit legal character.)

    (h) `float` is a keyword, and therefore an illegal identifier.

29. (a) `int`   (b) `char`   (c) `int`   (d) `long`   (e) `double`   (f) `float`
    (g) `int`   (h) `float`

30. (a) 0041   (b) 004D   (c) 002A   (d) 0061   (e) 006D   (f) 0039

31. (a) −8.74458E+02   (b) +1.23456E-03   (c) 1.23456789E+08

32. (a) 2   (b) 2.5f   (c) 26   (d) 38

33. (a) `final int INT_NUMBER = -45678;`

    (b) `final int HEX_NUMBER = 0xFABC;`

    (c) `final double PI = 3.14159;`

    (d) `final char UNI_CHAR = '\u0041';`

34. (a) 255 (b) 6700 (c) 0×73 (d) $0 \times 730F$

35. (a) | A | B | C | D |
    |---|---|---|---|
    | 36 | 36 | 36 | 36 |

    (b) | A | B | C | D |
    |---|---|---|---|
    | 10 | 14 | 29 | 89 |

    (c) | A | B |
    |---|---|
    | 48 | 50 |

    (d) | X | Y |
    |---|---|
    | 19 | −13 |

    (e) | X | Y | Z |
    |---|---|---|
    | 18 | 3 | 54 |

    (f) | A | B |
    |---|---|
    | 12.5 | 2.0 |

    (g) | A | B | X (assuming A, B, and X are integers) |
    |---|---|---|
    | 16 | 3 | 5 |

    (h) | C | D | Y |
    |---|---|---|
    | 19 | 5 | 4 |

    (i) | D |
    |---|
    | 35 |

36. (a) (A+B)/C

    (b) (W−X)/(Y+Z)

    (c) (D−B)/(2*A)

    (d) (A*A+B*B)/2

    (e) (A−B)*(C−D)

    (f) B*B−(4*A*C)

    (g) (A*X*X)+(B*X)+C

37. (a) X+(2/Y)+4

    (b) (A*B)/(C+2)

    (c) (U/V)*(W/X)

    (d) (B*B)−(4*A*C)

    (e) (A/B)+(C/D)+(E/F)

Chapter 2

14. Figure 2.13—`city` is a string; high and low temperatures are both integers; abbreviations are strings.

```
String city;
int     high, low;
String weatherCondition;
```

15. (a) Object screen missing.

    (b) Wrong number of arguments in constructor—normally one argument expected.

    (c) Wrong number of arguments in constructor—normally four arguments expected.

    (d) Wrong data type in argument list—screen is an Window object and not a string literal.

    (e) Wrong number of arguments in the constructor—object for container class is missing.

    (f) Wrong number of arguments in the constructor—prompt is missing.

16. Note in the answers that the underscore _ represents the position of the cursor.

    (a) `Hello World_`

    (b) `   name: _`

    (c) `   name: Mickey Mouse_`

    (d) `a=3 b=4 c=5`

         `_`

    (e) `area covered 635.8658_`

    (f) `ABC_`

17. (a) Missing parentheses `()` in method `getString`.

    (b) Wrong method—should be `getInteger()`. Alternatively, wrong type—should be `float`.

    (c) Wrong method—should be `getString()`. Alternatively, wrong type—should be `char`.

    (d) Type `double` begins with a lowercase d, not spelled as `Double`.

    (e) Wrong method—should be `getFloat()`. Alternatively, wrong type—should be `double`.

Chapter 3

35. 25   Note that the method returns the sum of A and B.

36. `Hello World`   Note: The argument `Hello World` is passed to the parameter message. The cursor moves to the next line.

37. 38   Note: The arguments 25 and 13 are passed to the parameters A and B.

    29   Note: The arguments 12 and 17 are passed to the parameters A and B.

38. `[valueOnly]`   A=40 B=30

    `[main]`   A=41 B=29

39. (a) Missing parentheses in call to `alpha`—should be `alpha();`

    (b) No formal parameter list in the method `beta`.

    (c) The order of the arguments is wrong—an integer argument must *follow* a character argument in the method call to `delta`.

    (d) The data type of the arguments in the call to `gamma` do not match the formal parameters in the method `gamma`. The formal parameter is an array of integers, yet the actual parameters are two variables.

`40. The method `alpha` does not return a value (void); therefore, `return 2*number` cannot be possible. The method signature should be changed to: `static int alpha(int number);`

41. 56   Note: The class scope version of global is hidden by the declaration within the block.

42. value of x is 0

    value of x is 1

    value of x is 2

43. value of x is 0

    value of x is 1

    value of x is 1

Chapter 4

15. (a) false   (b) true   (c) true   (d) true   (e) true   (f) true   (g) true

16. (a) `X==Y`   (b) `X!=Y`   (c) `A<=B`   (d) `Q<=T`   (e) `X>=Y`   (f) `(X<=Y && A!=B)`

    (g) `(A>18 && H>68 && W>75)`   (h) `(G<100 && G>50)`   (i) `(H<50 || H>100)`

17.

	A	B	C	output
(a)	16	16	32	y
(b)	16	−18	32	x
(c)	−2	−4	16	z

18. (a) capital letters   (b) error in data   (c) small letters

19.

```
if (y > 25)
{
    x = 16;
    screen.write("x = " + x);
}
else
    y = 20;
```

20.

1. input length of side 1

2. input length of side 2

3. input length of side 3

4. input length of side 4

5. input internal angle

6. if internal angle is a right angle

7.   if side 1 equals side 2 and side 2 equals side 3 and side 3 equals side 4

8.   output square

9.   else if side 1 equals side 3 and side 2 equals side 4

10.   output rectangle

11.   else

12.   output irregular

13. else

14.   if side 1 equals side 2 and side 2 equals side 3 and side 3 equals side 4

15.   output rhombus

16.   else if side 1 equals side 3 and side 2 equals side 4

17.   output parallelogram

18.   else

19.   output irregular

Test Data

side 1	side 2	side 3	side 4	internal angle
1	1	1	1	90
1	2	1	2	90
1	1	1	1	120
1	2	1	2	120
1	1.5	2	1.75	90
1	1.5	2	1.75	120

Desk Check

side 1	1	1	1	1
side 2	1	2	1	2
side 3	1	1	1	1
side 4	1	2	1	2
internal angle	90	90	120	120
right angle?	true	true	false	false
all sides equal?	true	false	true	false
opposite sides equal?		true		true
shape	square	rectangle	rhombus	parallelogram

side 1	1	1
side 2	1.5	1.5
side 3	2	2
side 4	1.75	1.75
internal angle	90	120
right angle?	true	false
all sides equal?	false	false
opposite sides equal?	false	false
shape	irregular	irregular

Chapter 5

18. Output from the `while` loop is

    1   3   5   7   9

19. The loop is a validation loop; termination from the loop is only possible when a digit in the range 0 to 9 is input.

20. Output from the `for` loop is the alphabet in lowercase.

    abcdefghijklmnopqrstuvwxyz

21. (a) This is a classical error of placing a semicolon after the condition in the `while` loop. The result of this error is to create an infinite loop.

    (b) This is a similar error to that found in (a); the semicolon at the end of the statement

    ```
    for (i=10; i>0; i--);
    ```

marks the end of the scope of the `for` statement. The behavior of the segment of code differs from that of (a). The value of `i` will be counted down to zero, and the line `T minus 0 and counting` will be output.

22.

```
for (int x=30; x>=3; x--)
    screen.write(x);
```

23.

1. input decimal number D

2. do

3.   divide D by 16 giving quotient Q and remainder R

4.   if remainder R > 9

5.   R is assigned the character whose decimal code is R+55

6.   else

7.   R is assigned the character whose decimal code is R+48

8.   output R as the next least significant digit of the hexadecimal value

9.   assign Q to D

10. while Q is not zero

Desk Check

D	3947		246		15	
Q	246		15		0	
R	11	66	6	54	15	70
R>9?	true		false		true	
output		B		6		F
Q != 0		true		true		false

Note: By adding 48 to R, you are creating the decimal code for the character that represents the digit R; by adding 55 to R, you are creating the decimal code for the character that represents the hexadecimal digit from A..F.

The value of the remainder is displayed with the least significant digit of the hexadecimal number first and finally the most significant digit last. Therefore, when it comes to writing a program for this algorithm, it is necessary to reverse the output, by printing from right to left and not left to right in the conventional sense.

24.

alpha[0]	−10
alpha[1]	16
alpha[2]	19
alpha[3]	−15
alpha[4]	20

index	0	1	2	3	4	5
value	0	−10	6	25	10	30

The final value of the identifier value is 30.

25. −31

26. The type declaration is wrong. The correct answer is:

```
String string = "abracadabra";
```

27. The method `toCharArray()` will store a string as a sequence of characters in a one-dimensional array. Therefore, the string "Ten green bottles standing on the wall." will be stored as consecutive characters in the character array `string` as follows.

string[0]	T
string[1]	e
string[2]	n
string[3]	(space)
string[4]	g

.

.

28. Length of the array `string` is 39.

29.

numbers[0]	5					5
numbers[1]	2					2
numbers[2]	8					8
numbers[3]	7				8	8
numbers[4]	0		2			2
numbers[5]	3	5				5
left	0	1	2	3		
right	5	4	3	2		
left <= right?	true	true	true	false		

Chapter 6

40. In this answer it is necessary to create a private helper method to return whether a rational number is positive, in addition to the public method that tests whether one rational number is greater than another rational number.

```
private boolean positive(Rational number)
{
    return (number.numerator > 0 && number.denominator > 0);
}

public boolean greaterThan(Rational x)
{
    if (positive(this) && !positive(x)) return true;
    if (!positive(this) && positive(x)) return false;

    // subtract rational numbers
    numerator = this.numerator * x.denominator -
                x.numerator * this.denominator;
    denominator = this.denominator * x.denominator;

    // create temporary rational number
    Rational difference = new Rational(numerator, denominator);

    if (positive(this) && positive(x) && positive(difference))
        return true;
    if (positive(this) && positive(x) && !positive(difference))
        return false;
    if (!positive(this) && !positive(x) && positive(difference))
        return true;
    if (!positive(this) && !positive(x) && !positive(difference))
        return false;

    return true;
}
```

41. The output from the program is:

```
A
B
C
```

A hierarchical relationship exists between the classes A, B, and C. When the constructor for class C is invoked, the system will automatically chain the constructor calls to classes B and A. The constructor in class A is executed first, followed by the constructor for class B and finally the constructor for class C.

42. The output from the program is:

```
X in class C 45
X in class C 45
X in class B 35
X in class B 35
X in class A 25
```

This problem is all about how to access shadowed variables in a hierarchy of classes. Variable X in class C may be accessed directly using the name X, or by using the implicit this object, `this.X`. Access to the variable X in class B (the superclass of class C) is made possible by using the reserved word `super`, `super.X`. Access is also possible by casting class B, `((B)this).X`. A similar technique is used to access the variable X in class A, `((A)this).X`.

43. The output from the program is:

```
value of X in class A 25
value of X in class B 35
```

This is a problem of accessing shadowed variables and overriding superclass methods. The variable object of type B is instantiated. The call to `getX` invokes the instance method in class B, which calls the `getX` method from class A. The `getX` method in class A returns the value of X (25) in A. This value is displayed from class B. The computer then returns the value of the variable X (35) in B to the `main` method. The value of X from class B is then displayed.

44. The output from the program is:

```
value of constant from interface A 65
value of constant from class B 45
```

This is a problem of accessing constants from an interface and a class. Since class C implements the interface A, the constants defined in the interface may be used without qualification in class C. However, since there is no hierarchical relationship between class B and class C, it is necessary to qualify the constant from class B.

45. The output from the program is:

```
value of constant from interface A 65
value of constant from interface B 75
value of constant from interface C 85
```

This is a problem of inheritance of constants from interfaces. Interface C inherits from interface A and from interface B. This implies that the constants from both interfaces are now accessible in interface C. Class D implements interface C and therefore has access to all the constants defined in interfaces A, B, and C.

Chapter 7

25. A catch block must immediately follow the corresponding try block.

26. The declaration of the object `input` has taken place in a try block, and consequently is not visible outside of this block. Any attempt to access the variable `input` outside of the try block will generate a syntax error.

27. Yes. The outer try block is followed by a catch block, and the inner try block is followed by a catch block; therefore, the structure is legal.

28. The class `Error` is not a superclass of either the classes `ArithmeticException` or `ArrayStoreException`; therefore, the `instanceof` operator is not valid.

29. The statements are legal; however, the class `Throwable`, in the first catch block, is the superclass of all the classes in the subsequent catch blocks. As a consequence, only the first block will ever be executed when an exception is raised. The superclass should appear as the last class in this program segment. The arrangement of the classes in the blocks should be `ClassNotFoundException`, `InterruptedException`, `Exception`, and `Throwable`.

30. The throw and throws clauses should be interchanged. A throws clause lists the exceptions that can be thrown by a method. The throw statement explicitly invokes an exception. The throw statement must instantiate an exception object to be thrown.

31. Desk-checking the code shows that the value of the index goes out of bounds as soon as it becomes 5. The exception to cause the catch block to be executed is `ArrayIndexOutOfBoundsException`.

32. Note in the following answers that the underscore _ represents the position of the cursor.

    (a) `Hello World`

        _

    (b) `    name:`

        _

    (c) `    name: Mickey Mouse`

        _

33.

    (a) `a=3 b=4 c=5`

        _

    (b) `area covered 635.8658_`

    (c) `ABC`

        _

34.

    (a) The object `dosWindow` is missing; the comma should be replaced by a +:

        `dosWindow.println("value of beta is " + beta);`

    (b) The delimiters should be double quotes: `"X"`.

    (c) The wrapper class should be `Integer`.

35.

(a) Hierarchy diagram for the wrapper class `java.lang.Float`:

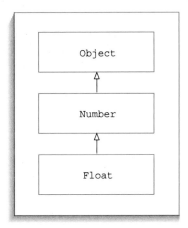

(b) Hierarchy diagram for the class `java.io.BufferedOutputStream`:

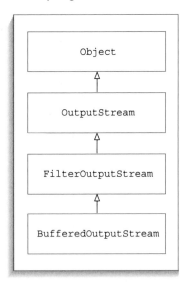

Chapter 8

22. The `TextInput` class should include the following methods.

```
public int getInteger() throws NumberFormatException
{
        return new Integer(inputDatum).intValue();
}
```

```
public float getFloat() throws NumberFormatException
{
       return new Float(inputDatum).floatValue();
}
```

23.

```
import java.awt.*;
import java.awt.event.*;

public class InputBox extends Dialog implements ActionListener
{
       // constants
       private static final int FONT_SIZE = 11;
       private static final int HEIGHT_OF_BAR = 20;
       private static final String EMPTY_STRING = "";
       private static final int NUMBER_OF_ITEMS = 1;

       // instance variables
       private String inputDatum;
       private TextField datum;
       private Label textLabel;

       public InputBox(Frame parent, String prompts)
       {
              super(parent, " Input the following datum .. then CLOSE",
                     true);
              addWindowListener(new CloseInputBox());

              // set width and height of screen
              int screenWidth  = parent.getWidth();
              int screenHeight = parent.getHeight();

              // set location and size of dialog box
              int xLocationOfBox = (int)(0.4f * screenWidth);
              int yLocationOfBox = (int)(0.1f * screenHeight);
              int widthOfBox     = (int)(0.4f * screenWidth);
              int heightOfBox    =
              (int)(screenHeight/36)*(NUMBER_OF_ITEMS)+6*HEIGHT_OF_BAR;

              // set location and size of label
              int xLocationOfLabel = (int)(0.05f * widthOfBox);
              int yLocationOfLabel = (int)(2.0f * screenHeight/36);
              int widthOfLabel     = (int)(0.2f * widthOfBox);
              int heightOfLabel    = (int)(screenHeight/36);
```

```
            // set location and size of text field
            int widthOfField     = (int)(0.65f * widthOfBox);
            int heightOfField    = (int)(screenHeight/36);
            int xLocationOfField = (int)(0.3f * widthOfBox);
            int yLocationOfField =
            (int)(2*HEIGHT_OF_BAR+(int)(heightOfField/4));

            // draw dialog box
            this.setLayout(null);
            this.setBackground(Color.lightGray);
            this.setForeground(Color.blue);
            this.setLocation(xLocationOfBox,yLocationOfBox);
            this.setSize(widthOfBox,heightOfBox);

            // insert label and text field
            textLabel = new Label(prompts, Label.LEFT);
            textLabel.setLocation(xLocationOfLabel, yLocationOfLabel);
            textLabel.setSize(widthOfLabel, heightOfLabel);
            this.add(textLabel);

            datum = new TextField(EMPTY_STRING, widthOfField);
            datum.setLocation(xLocationOfField, yLocationOfField);
            datum.setSize(widthOfField, heightOfField);
            this.add(datum);

            // set location and size of "CLEAR" button
            int xLocationOfResetButton = (int)(0.4f*widthOfBox);
            int yLocationOfResetButton = (int)(0.8f*heightOfBox);
            int widthOfButton = (int)(0.8f*widthOfLabel);
            int heightOfButton = (int)(heightOfLabel);

            // create button
            Button resetButton = new Button("CLEAR");
            resetButton.setLocation(xLocationOfResetButton,
                                    yLocationOfResetButton);
            resetButton.setSize(widthOfButton, heightOfButton);
            resetButton.setBackground(Color.lightGray);
            resetButton.setForeground(Color.black);

            // add push button to dialog box and action listener for button
            this.add(resetButton);
            resetButton.addActionListener(this);
        }
```

```
        public void showInputBox()
        {
               this.setVisible(true);
        }


        public String getInput()
        {
               return inputDatum;
        }


        public void actionPerformed(ActionEvent event)
        {
               if (event.getActionCommand().equals("CLEAR"))
               {
                      datum.setText(EMPTY_STRING);
                      inputDatum = EMPTY_STRING;
               }
        }


        public class CloseInputBox extends WindowAdapter
        {
               public void windowClosing(WindowEvent event)
               {
                      inputDatum = new String(datum.getText());
                      datum.setText(EMPTY_STRING);
                      InputBox.this.setVisible(false);
               }
        }
}



class Chap8Ans23
{
        public static void main(String[] args)
        {
               WindowPane screen = new WindowPane();
               screen.showWindowPane();

               InputBox data = new InputBox(screen,"Name");
               data.showInputBox();

               System.out.println(data.getInput());
        }
}
```

24.

```java
import java.awt.*;
import java.awt.event.*;

public class Slider extends Dialog implements AdjustmentListener
{
        private static final String SPACE = " ";
        private static final int FONT_SIZE = 12;

        private TextField position;
        private int value;
        private String cue;

        public Slider(Frame parent, String prompt, int minValue,
        int maxValue, int increment) throws Exception
        {
                super(parent, " Move slider, then CLOSE ..", true);

                if (increment <= 0 || minValue >= maxValue)
                throw new Exception("Incremental value out of range");

                addWindowListener(new CloseSlider());
                cue = prompt;

                // set and assign fonts
                Font dialog = new Font("Dialog", Font.BOLD, FONT_SIZE);
                Font dialogInput = new
                Font("DialogInput", Font.PLAIN, FONT_SIZE);

                // set width and height of screen
                int screenWidth  = parent.getWidth();
                int screenHeight = parent.getHeight();

                // set location and size of dialog box
                int xLocationOfBox = (int)(0.7f * screenWidth);
                int yLocationOfBox = (int)(0.1f * screenHeight);
                int widthOfBox     = (int)(0.25f * screenWidth);
                int heightOfBox    = (int)(0.125f * screenHeight);

                // set location and size of label
                int xLocationOfLabel = (int)(0.1f * widthOfBox);
                int yLocationOfLabel = (int)(0.3f * heightOfBox);
                int widthOfLabel     = (int)(0.6f * widthOfBox);
                int heightOfLabel    = (int)(0.25f * heightOfBox);
```

```
// set location and size of text field
int xLocationOfField = (int)(0.7f * widthOfBox);
int yLocationOfField = (int)(0.3f * heightOfBox);
int widthOfField    = (int)(0.19f * widthOfBox);
int heightOfField   = (int)(0.25f * heightOfBox);

// set location and size of slider
int xLocationOfSlider = (int)(0.1f * widthOfBox);
int yLocationOfSlider = (int)(0.6f * heightOfBox);
int widthOfSlider     = (int)(0.8f * widthOfBox);
int heightOfSlider    = (int)(0.2f * heightOfBox);

// initial position of slider
int initialValue = (int)(minValue+maxValue)/2;

// set parameters of dialog box
this.setBackground(Color.lightGray);
this.setForeground(Color.black);
this.setLocation(xLocationOfBox,yLocationOfBox);
this.setSize(widthOfBox, heightOfBox);

// draw slider
Scrollbar slide = new
Scrollbar(Scrollbar.HORIZONTAL, initialValue,
         increment, minValue, maxValue+increment);
setLayout(null);
slide.setLocation(xLocationOfSlider, yLocationOfSlider);
slide.setSize(widthOfSlider, heightOfSlider);
slide.setBackground(Color.white);
slide.setUnitIncrement(increment);
add(slide);

// display title
Label title = new Label(prompt);
title.setLocation(xLocationOfLabel,yLocationOfLabel);
title.setSize(widthOfLabel,heightOfLabel);
title.setFont(dialog);
add(title);

// display position of slider
value = initialValue;
position = new TextField();
position.setLocation(xLocationOfField, yLocationOfField);
position.setSize(widthOfField, heightOfField);
position.setBackground(Color.white);
```

```java
            position.setForeground(Color.blue);
            position.setText(SPACE+String.valueOf(value));
            position.setEditable(false);
            position.setFont(dialogInput);
            add(position);

            slide.addAdjustmentListener(this);

        }

        public void showSlider()
        {
            this.setVisible(true);
        }

        public int getValue()
        {
            return value;
        }

        public void adjustmentValueChanged(AdjustmentEvent event)
        {
            value = event.getValue();
            position.setText(SPACE+String.valueOf(value));
        }

        public class CloseSlider extends WindowAdapter
        {
            public void windowClosing(WindowEvent event)
            {
                Slider.this.setVisible(false);
            }
        }
    }
```

25.

```java
// chap_8\Ans_25.java
// lists and text areas

import java.awt.*;
import java.awt.event.*;

class Gui extends Frame implements ItemListener
{
```

```
static final int NUMBER_OF_MENU_ITEMS = 10;
static final int MAX_SELECTION = 3;

List      countries = new List(NUMBER_OF_MENU_ITEMS, true);
TextArea  selection = new TextArea();
int       counter = 0;

static String[] countryNames = {"Australia","Brazil",
                                "Chile","France","Greece",
                                "Japan","Norway","Spain",
                                "Switzerland","Zimbabwe"};

public Gui(String s)
{
super(s);
setBackground(Color.yellow);
setLayout(null);

// display list
setUpList();

// display selection
add(selection);
addWindowListener(new CloseWindow());
}

// method to display the countries on screen
private void setUpList()
{

    for (int index=0; index != NUMBER_OF_MENU_ITEMS; index++)
    {
       countries.add(countryNames[index]);
    }

    countries.setLocation(10,50);
    countries.setSize(100,50);
    add(countries);
    countries.addItemListener(this);
}
```

```
    // method to display the selected countries
    private void displaySelection()
    {

        int[] listArray = countries.getSelectedIndexes();

        selection.setLocation(200,50);
        selection.setSize(100,75);
        selection.setEditable(false);

        // display selected countries
        for (int index=0; index != listArray.length; index++)
        {
            selection.append(countries.getItem(listArray[index])+"\n");
        }
    }


    private class CloseWindow extends WindowAdapter
    {
        public void windowClosing(WindowEvent event)
        {
            System.exit(0);
        }
    }


    // method to detect when a selection has been made and increase
    // the counter by 1; when three countries have been selected
    // display the selection in a text area
    public void itemStateChanged(ItemEvent event)
    {
        if (event.getStateChange() == ItemEvent.SELECTED) counter++;

        if (counter==MAX_SELECTION)
        {
            displaySelection();
        }
    }
}



class Chap8Ans25
{

    public static void main(String[] args)
```

```
    {
        Gui screen = new Gui("Example 25");

        screen.setSize(400,200);
        screen.setVisible(true);
    }
}
```

26. `BorderLayout` is the default layout manager for Windows and the `Window` subclass `Frame`. There are up to five areas in a `BorderLayout`. When all five are used, the arrangement will look like that pictured below. If the East or West areas are missing, the Center expands to fill up the space. If the North or South are missing, the Center and East/West fill the remaining space.

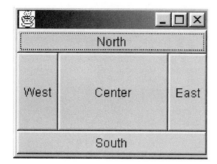

The signatures of the constructors are:

```
public BorderLayout();
public BorderLayout(int hgap, int vgap);
```

There are a set of static constants NORTH, SOUTH, EAST, WEST, and CENTER used to position elements in the container.

Components can be added to the container using the `add` method inherited from the `Container` class whose signature is given as:

```
public void add(Component comp, Object constraints);
```

where constraints can be one of the `static` constants to define the position of the component.

An example program follows.

```
import java.awt.*;
import java.awt.event.*;

class DirectionalButtons extends Frame implements ActionListener
{
    public DirectionalButtons(int width, int height, int x, int y)
    {
        super();
        setSize(width, height);
```

```
        setLocation(x,y);
        addWindowListener(new CloseWindow());

        setLayout(new BorderLayout());

        String[] direction = {"North","South","East","West","Center"};
        Button[] button = new Button[direction.length];

        for (int index=0; index != direction.length; index++)
        {
            button[index] = new Button(direction[index]);
            button[index].addActionListener(this);
        }

        add(button[0], BorderLayout.NORTH);
        add(button[1], BorderLayout.SOUTH);
        add(button[2], BorderLayout.EAST);
        add(button[3], BorderLayout.WEST);
        add(button[4], BorderLayout.CENTER);
    }

    public void showButtons()
    {
        this.show();
    }

    public void actionPerformed(ActionEvent event)
    {
        System.out.println(event.getActionCommand());
    }

    private class CloseWindow extends WindowAdapter
    {
        public void windowClosing(WindowEvent event)
        {
            DirectionalButtons.this.dispose();
            System.exit(0);
        }
    }
}


public class Chap8Ans26
{
    public static void main(String[] args)
```

```
    {
            DirectionalButtons buttons = new
            DirectionalButtons(200,150,50,50);
            buttons.show();
    }
}
```

Chapter 9

21.

    (a) `contains`—tests if the specified object is a component in this vector.

    (b) `copyInto`—copies the components of this vector into the specified array.

    (c) `isEmpty`—tests if this vector has no components.

    (d) `lastIndexOf`—returns the index of the last occurrence of the specified object in this vector.

22. `Vector dataStore = new Vector(1);`   instantiate the object dataStore containing 1 cell.

    `dataStore.addElement("Sybil");`   insert the string `"Sybil"` into cell 0

    `dataStore.addElement("Basil");`   the vector will double in size, to just 2 cells, and the string `"Basil"` will be inserted into cell 1

    `dataStore.addElement("Polly");`   the vector will double in size, to just 4 cells, and the string `"Polly"` will be inserted into cell 2.

23.

```
// chap_9\Ans_23.java
// program to input RGB color data via three text fields
// and display the color in a rectangle

import java.awt.*;
import java.awt.event.*;
import java.io.*;

class Gui extends Frame implements ActionListener
{
    static PrintWriter screen = new PrintWriter(System.out,true);

    // define name and size of each text field
    TextField red = new TextField(5);
    TextField green = new TextField(5);
    TextField blue = new TextField(5);

    // initialize the contents of each text field
    String redField ="0";
    String greenField ="0";
```

```
String blueField ="0";

Color value;

// constructor
public Gui(String s)
{
    super(s);
    setLayout(new FlowLayout());

    // display text fields
    add(new Label("Red      "));
    add(red);
    red.addActionListener(this);

    add(new Label("Green    "));
    add(green);
    green.addActionListener(this);

    add(new Label("Blue     "));
    add(blue);
    blue.addActionListener(this);

    addWindowListener(new CloseWindow());
}

// if numeric value for color is not in range return
// zero, otherwise return value of color
static int validateColor(int colorValue)
{
    if (colorValue < 0 || colorValue > 255)
        return 0;
    else
        return colorValue;
}

public void actionPerformed(ActionEvent event)
{
    Graphics g = getGraphics();

    int redValue, greenValue, blueValue;

    // capture data
    if (event.getSource() == red)
        redField = new String(red.getText());
```

```
        if (event.getSource() == green)
            greenField = new String(green.getText());
        if (event.getSource() == blue)
            blueField = new String(blue.getText());

        // convert captured data to numbers and validate value
        redValue = validateColor(new Integer(redField).intValue());
        greenValue = validateColor(new Integer(greenField).intValue());
        blueValue = validateColor(new Integer(blueField).intValue());

        // create an RGB color
        value = new Color(redValue, greenValue, blueValue);

        // display color
        g.setColor(value);
        g.fillRect(100,100,300,50);
    }

    private class CloseWindow extends WindowAdapter
    {
        public void windowClosing(WindowEvent event)
        {
            System.exit(0);
        }
    }
}

class Chap9Ans23
{
    public static void main(String[] args)
    {
        Gui screen = new Gui("Answer 23");

        screen.setSize(500,200);
        screen.setVisible(true);
    }
}
```

24.

```
// chap_9\Ans_24.java
// program to simulate a directional compass

import java.awt.*;
import java.awt.event.*;
```

```
class Gui extends Frame implements MouseMotionListener
{
    // center of compass
    int x=500;
    int y=400;

    // half-length of compass needle
    int halfLength=50;

    // old coordinates of mouse prior to new position
    int xOld = 0;
    int yOld = 0;

    // constructor
    public Gui(String s)
    {
        super(s);
        addMouseListener(new HandleMouseEvents());
        addMouseMotionListener(this);
    }


    public void mouseDragged(MouseEvent event){}

    public void mouseMoved(MouseEvent event)
    {
        // get current coordinates of mouse
        int xValue=event.getX();
        int yValue=event.getY();

        // erase old position of compass needle
        drawNeedle(xOld,yOld,Color.white);
        // draw new position of compass needle
        drawNeedle(xValue, yValue, Color.red);
        drawCompassPoints();
    }


    // draw a needle on the screen using the color hue, at the
    // position corresponding to the coordinates of the mouse
    public void drawNeedle(int xValue, int yValue, Color hue)
    {
        Graphics g = getGraphics();

        double angle;
```

```
    int vertDist, horizDist;
    int x1,y1,x2,y2;

    // calculate the angle of compass needle to the horizontal
    angle = Math.atan((double)Math.abs(yValue-y)/Math.abs(xValue-x));

    // calculate the horizontal and vertical distances of the tip of the
    // needle from the centre of the needle
    vertDist = (int)(halfLength * Math.sin(angle));
    horizDist = (int)(halfLength * Math.cos(angle));

    // calculate the coordinates of the ends of the compass needle with
    // respect to the position of the mouse
    if ((xValue>x && yValue<y) || (xValue<x && yValue > y))
    {
        x1=x-horizDist; y1=y+vertDist;
        x2=x+horizDist; y2=y-vertDist;

    }
    else
    {
        x1=x-horizDist; y1=y-vertDist;
        x2=x+horizDist; y2=y+vertDist;
    }


    // draw the compass needle
    g.setColor(hue);
    g.drawLine(x1,y1,x2,y2);

    // store the current coordinates of the mouse
    xOld=xValue;
    yOld=yValue;
}


// display the points of the compass
private void drawCompassPoints()
{
    Graphics g = getGraphics();

    g.setColor(Color.black);
    g.drawLine(x-30,y,x+30,y);
    g.drawLine(x,y-50,x,y+50);
    g.drawString("N",x-4,y-52);
    g.fillOval(x-2,y-2,4,4);
}
```

```
    private class HandleMouseEvents extends MouseAdapter
    {
        public void mousePressed(MouseEvent event)
        {
            System.exit(0);
        }
    }
}

class Chap9Ans24
{
    public static void main(String[] args)
    {
        Gui screen = new
        Gui("Example 24  .. PRESS MOUSE BUTTON TO CLOSE WINDOW");

        screen.setSize(1000,800);
        screen.setVisible(true);
    }
}
```

Chapter 10

19.

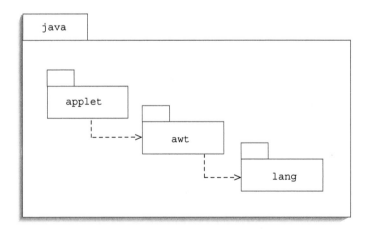

20.

(a)

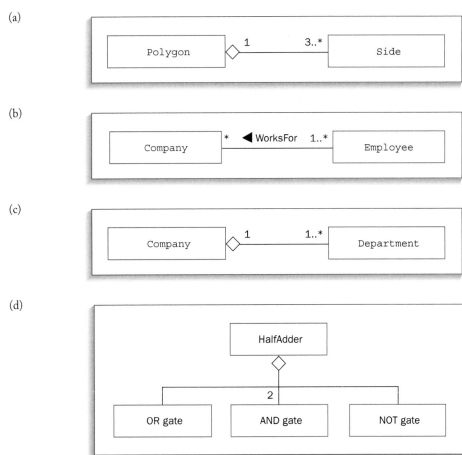

(b)

(c)

(d)

21. The contents of the CRC cards are by no means final. The answer is intended to promote further discussion about the relationships and methods of the classes.

School	
Responsibilities	Collaborators
add student	Student
remove student	Student
get student	
get all students	
add department	Department
remove department	Department
get department	
get all departments	

Department	
Responsibilities	Collaborators
add instructor	Instructor
remove instructor	Instructor
get instructor	
get all instructors	

Student	
Responsibilities	Collaborators
create student	
get student	
assign to course	Course
get courses	
get results	

Instructor	
Responsibilities	**Collaborators**
create instructor	
get instructor	
assign to course	Course
get courses taught	

Course	
Responsibilities	**Collaborators**
create course	
get course	
get assessment criteria	
get instructor	Instructor
get students on course	Student

22. The instances of the following classes are intended to live in a database or a serializable file that is used to create arrays or vectors.

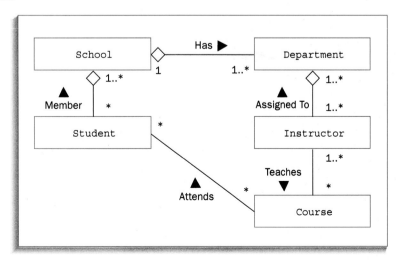

23. The contents of the CRC cards are by no means final. The answer is intended to promote further discussion about the relationships and methods of the classes.

ATM	
Responsibilities	**Collaborators**
find customer	Bank, Customer, Keypad
find account	Customer, BankAccount,
	Keypad
withdraw	BankAccount, Keypad
deposit	BankAccount, Keypad

Bank	
Responsibilities	**Collaborators**
search for customer	Customer
get customer details	Customer

BankAccount	
Responsibilities	**Collaborators**
get balance	
deposit	
withdraw	

Customer	
Responsibilities	Collaborators
get customer account	BankAccount
match a/c number	
match PIN	

Keypad	
Responsibilities	Collaborators
get value input	

24. The aggregation relationships follow from:

- a bank has-(a) customer

- a customer has-(a) accounts

- an ATM has-(a) keypad

The dependencies are obtained from the collaborator columns of the CRC cards:

- ATM uses `Keypad`, `Bank`, `Customer`, and `BankAccount`

- `Bank` uses `Customer`

Note: The aggregations are regarded as stronger relationships than the dependencies when drawing the class diagram; hence `Bank` and `Customer` are drawn as an aggregation and not a dependency.

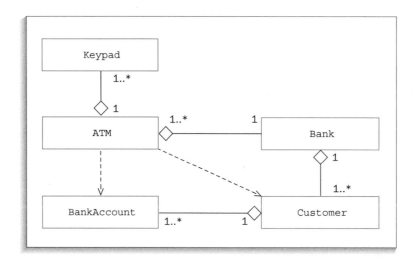

Chapter 11

26. The resource descriptor and separator are missing. The correct URL is:

```
http://java.sun.com
```

27. The `HTML`, `APPLET`, and `BODY` tags are not nested correctly; there is no `width` and `height` specified for the applet window. The filename for the applet is incorrect; it should refer to the bytecode file and not the java source code file. The correct code is:

```
<HTML>
<BODY>
<APPLET code=Ex_27.class width=900 height=300>
</APPLET>
</BODY>
</HTML>
```

28. The `HTML` file provides a parameter for the applet. The value of the parameter is a `URL`. The applet attempts to link to the Web site specified by the `URL` and display the home page of the site. If the `URL` is incorrect, the computer will exit from the applet.

   To change the `URL`, and hence change the Web site to visit, simply edit the value specified in the `HTML` file.

29. If the code in the question represents the contents of the source file, then the need to import classes from the packages `java.awt` and `java.applet` is absent.

   The name given to the applet class must match the name given to the applet file. It might be better to rename the class `Ans_29`, and hence the filename as `Ans_29.java`.

   The variable name is not initialized in the declaration. Without any parameter passing from the corresponding HTML file, the name cannot take a value and will result in a run-time error.

The `paint` method must take a formal parameter of type `Graphics`. This parameter is absent from the methods `setFont`, `setColor`, and `drawString`.

A string terminator " is missing after the font name `Monospaced`.

The `drawString` method does not contain coordinates describing where to draw the string on the screen.

30.

```
// chap_11\Ans_30.java

import java.awt.*;
import java.applet.*;

public class Ans_30 extends Applet
{
    String name;

    public void init()
    {
        name = getParameter("name");
    }

    public void paint(Graphics g)
    {
        Font font = new Font("Monospaced", Font.ITALIC, 36);

        g.setFont(font);
        setBackground(Color.yellow);
        g.setColor(Color.red);
        g.drawString(name, 75,100);
    }
}
```

```
<HTML>
<BODY>
<APPLET code=Ans_30.class width=700 height=250>
<PARAM NAME=name VALUE="Programming with Java">
</APPLET>
</BODY>
</HTML>
```

31.

```
// chap_11\Ans_31.java

import java.awt.*;
import java.awt.event.*;
import java.applet.*;

public class Ans_31 extends Applet implements ActionListener
{
        TextField nameField = new TextField(30);

        public void init()
        {
                add(new Label("NAME "));
                add(nameField);
                nameField.addActionListener(this);
                setBackground(Color.yellow);
        }

        public void actionPerformed(ActionEvent event)
        {
                Font font    = new Font("Monospaced", Font.ITALIC, 36);
                String name = nameField.getText();

                Graphics g = getGraphics();

                g.setFont(font);
                g.setColor(Color.red);
                g.drawString(name,75,100);
        }
}

<HTML>
<BODY>
<APPLET code=Ans_31.class width=700 height=250>
</APPLET>
</BODY>
</HTML>
```

32. The error is forgetting to include the dot (`.`) separator between the name of the file and the postfix abbreviation. For example, the file is normally referred to by `dialtone.au`; the coding `source+"au"` will result in the filename being constructed as `dialtoneau`, which of course does not exist. The code requires an amendment of `source+".au"`.

33. Values from the two-dimensional array are 5, 12, and 9, respectively.

Value of the variable sum is 143 .

34.

```
// chap_11/Ans_34.java

import java.applet.*;
import java.awt.*;
import java.awt.event.*;

public class Chap11Ans34 extends Applet implements ItemListener
{
      // array for uv index
      String[] uvIndex = {"0..2","3..4","5..7","8..9","9+"};

      // array for skin category
      String[] skinCat = {"1","2","3","4"};

      CheckboxGroup cb1 = new CheckboxGroup();
      CheckboxGroup cb2 = new CheckboxGroup();

      Checkbox[] uvIndexRanges = new Checkbox[uvIndex.length];
      Checkbox[] skinCatData = new Checkbox[skinCat.length];

      // 2-D array for storing sun protection factor
      int[][] sunProtFact =
      {{3,2,2,1},{6,4,3,2},{11,8,5,4},{14,10,7,5},{18,12,8,7}};

      int uv=0, category=0;
      TextField spf = new TextField();

      public void init()
      {
            setLayout(new GridLayout(10,5));
            setBackground(Color.red);

            Label uvRange = new Label("uv range");
            add(uvRange);

            for (int index=0; index != uvIndex.length; index++)
            {
                  uvIndexRanges[index] = new
                  Checkbox(uvIndex[index],false,cb1);
                  add(uvIndexRanges[index]);
                  uvIndexRanges[index].addItemListener(this);
            }
```

```
        uvIndexRanges[0].setState(true);

        Label skin = new Label("skin category");
        add(skin);

        for (int index=0; index != skinCat.length; index++)
        {
             skinCatData[index] = new
             Checkbox(skinCat[index],false,cb2);
             add(skinCatData[index]);
             skinCatData[index].addItemListener(this);
        }

        skinCatData[0].setState(true);

        spf.setBackground(Color.yellow);
        add(spf);
        spf.setText("SKIN PF = "+
        String.valueOf(sunProtFact[uv][category]));
    }



public void itemStateChanged(ItemEvent event)
{
        if (event.getStateChange() == ItemEvent.SELECTED)
        {
             String item = (String)event.getItem();

             for (int index=0; index != uvIndex.length; index++)
             {
                  if (item.equals(uvIndex[index])) uv=index;
             }

             for (int index=0; index != skinCat.length; index++)
             {
                  if (item.equals(skinCat[index])) category=index;
             }

             spf.setText("SKIN PF = "+
             String.valueOf(sunProtFact[uv][category]));
        }
    }
}
```

35. The errors are as follows:

The applet needs to implement the `Runnable` interface, and the `run()` method must be overridden in the applet. Without this implementation the code of a thread cannot be executed.

There is no code to correctly start a thread or stop a thread.

The reference to a thread sleeping, without any means of trapping an interrupted exception, will generate a syntax error.

The correct solution to this program follows.

```
// chap_11\Ans_35.java

import java.awt.*;
import java.applet.*;

public class Ans_35 extends Applet implements Runnable
{
    Thread appletThread;

    int length=1;

    public void start()
    {
        if (appletThread == null)
        {
            appletThread = new Thread(this);
            appletThread.start();
        }
    }

    public void run()
    {
        while (true)
        {
            repaint();
            length++;

            try{Thread.sleep(50);}
            catch(InterruptedException i){System.exit(1);}
        }
    }

    public void stop()
    {
        if (appletThread != null)
```

```
      {
         appletThread.stop();
         appletThread=null;
      }
   }

   public void paint(Graphics g)
   {
      //g.setColor(Color.black);
      g.fillRect(10,50,length,5);
   }
}
```

Chapter 12

10.

```
// chap_12\Ans_10.java
// program to demonstrate the creation and maintenance of a FIFO queue using a linked
// list

import avi.*;

class Queue
{
   class Node
   {
      protected Object datum;
      protected Node    link;

      public Node(){}

      public Node(Object item, Node pointer)
      {
         datum = item;
         link = pointer;
      }
   }

   private Node head;
   private Node tail;
   private Node temporary;
   private int nodeCount = 0;

   // constructor
   public Queue()
```

```
{
    head = null;
    tail = null;
    temporary = null;
}

// method to insert an object into the tail of FIFO queue
public void join(Object datum)
{
    if (head==null) // queue empty
    {
        head=new Node(datum,head);
        tail=head;
    }
    else
    {
        temporary = new Node(datum,temporary);
        tail.link = temporary;
        tail = temporary;
        temporary = null;
    }
    nodeCount++;
}


// method to delete an object from the head of a FIFO queue
public Object leave()
{
    temporary = head;

    // test for empty queue
    if (head == null) return null;

    // point head at next node in queue
    head = temporary.link;

    // test for end of queue
    if (head == null) tail = null;

    nodeCount--;
    return temporary.datum;
}

// method to display the contents of a queue from the head to the tail
public void displayQueue(Window screen)
```

```
    {
        temporary = head;

        if (head == null)
        {
            screen.write("queue is empty\n");
            return;
        }

        while (temporary != null)
        {
            screen.write(temporary.datum+"\n");
            temporary = temporary.link;
        }
    }

    // method to return true if the queue is empty otherwise return false
    public boolean isEmpty()
    {
        return (nodeCount == 0);
    }

    // method to return the size of the queue
    public int size()
    {
        return nodeCount;
    }
}


class Ans_10
{
    static public void main(String[] args)
    {
        String[] choice =
        {"Join the queue","Leave the queue","Display the queue",
         "Exit from program"};
        String nameOfButton;
        int positionOfButton;

        Window screen = new Window("Answer_10.java");
        screen.showWindow();

        RadioButtons menu = new RadioButtons(screen,"",choice);
        DialogBox input = new DialogBox(screen,"");
```

```
Queue fifo = new Queue();
String datum;

menu.showRadioButtons();
positionOfButton = menu.getPositionOfButton();

while (! choice[positionOfButton].equals("Exit from program"))
{
    switch (positionOfButton)
    {
      case 0 : {
                  input.showDialogBox();
                  datum = input.getString();
                  fifo.join(datum);

                  break;
               }
      case 1 : {
                  // if queue is empty deletion is not possible
                  if (fifo.isEmpty())
                  {
                        screen.write("queue is empty\n");
                        break;
                  }
                  else
                  {
                        datum = (String)fifo.leave();
                        screen.write(datum+" left the queue\n");
                  }

                  break;
               }
      case 2 : {
                  fifo.displayQueue(screen);
                  screen.write("size of queue "+fifo.size()+"\n");
               }
    }

    menu.showRadioButtons();
    positionOfButton = menu.getPositionOfButton();
}
}
}
```

Index

A

Abstract class(es), 289, 312, 364
 UML representation of, *313*
Abstract data types, 87, 88-90, 713
Abstraction, 88
Abstract method, 312, 313, 364
Abstract Windowing Toolkit, 443, 497, 498
 components from, *457*
 FileDialog class from, 419
`ActionEvent` class, 454, 487, 498
`ActionEvent` object, 453
`ActionListener` class, 454, 473
`ActionListener` interface, 453, 454, 461, 487, 488, 605
`ActionListener` method, 474, 498
Action listeners, 605
 adding for text field objects, 461, 487
`actionPerformed` method, 454, 574
Addition (+), 35, 45
Additive operators, 35, 40
`addWindowListener` method, 450, 478
ADTs. *See* Abstract data types
Aggregation, 586-598, 614
Algebraic expressions
 stack for conversion of, 728-737
Algorithm development, 111-112
 for body-mass index case study, 186-188
 for date validation case study, 197-200
 for die rolling simulation, 136-142
 and log cutting case study, 118-119

Algorithms
efficiency of, 708
time efficiency analysis for, 690
American Standard Code for Information
Interchange. *See* ASCII character code
Analysis phase
in software development, 106, 145
AND (&&) logical operator, 173, 209
Animated GIF images, 130
Animation, 668-673, 678
API. *See* Application Programming Interface
append() method, 483, 731
Applet class, 677
dependency of, *623*
hierarchy, *624*
Applet programs, 619
Applets, 2, 62, 622-628, 677
creating, 624-625, 677
defined, 622
to display color swatch, 632
input to, 628-634
multimedia, 619
restrictions on, 673-674, 678
Applet viewer, 626, 678
drop-down menu from, *627*
Application programming, 62
Application Programming Interface, 52
Archival mode
original file saved in, 15, 16
Area copying and filling, 524
args array, 77
args parameter
illustration of main method, *76*
Arithmetic Exception class, 383
Arithmetic mean of numbers in array program,
250-251
screen shot from, *252*
Arithmetic operations, 35-39
Arithmetic statements program, 38
Array of integers
declaration of, *243*
Arrays, 241-242
advantages of linked lists over, 738
binary search for name in, *706*
conceptual representation of numbers in, *243*
defined, 77
initializing, 124
of integers, *132*

methods for declaring/initializing, 242-244
passing by reference, *688*
productions from, 752
sounds, *128*
using, 245-261. *See also* One-dimensional arrays;
Two-dimensional arrays
Arrays class, 691, 692
binary search algorithm in, 705
Array size/declaration program, 246-247
screen shot from, *247*
Array size program, 249
screen shot from, *250*
ASCII character code, 24
ASCII characters
respective hexadecimal/octal codes for, 743
Assignment statement, 29
Association, 570-582, 584, 586, 614
UML class diagram showing, *572. See also*
Composition
Audio class, 674, 675, 676
AudioClip class, 637
Audio clips, 675
playing, 635
Audio files
using Audio class, 127
Audio-Visual Interface (AVI) package, 1, 17, 443,
674, 676
copying and installing, 7-9. *See also* avi package
AU files, 674
au format audio files, 127
AU sound files, 634
autoexec.bat file, 8, 9, 12
autoFlush argument, 402
AVI. *See* Audio-visual interface package
avi classes
CheckBox, 217, 261-264
Memo, 194-195
RadioButtons, 156-160
Slider, 154-156
avi directory, 7
contents of, *8*
avi package, 51, 63-64, 87, 88, 111, 124-135, 153,
397
Audio class in, 87, 124, 125-127
Checkbox object from, *262*
classes within, 676
FilmStrip class in, 87, 124, 130-135
RadioButtons object from, *157*

`Slider` object from, *154*
`Timer` class in, 87, 124, 127-130, 224
Awt. *See* Abstract windowing toolkit
`awt` package
`Panel` class from, 614

B
Backslash, 407
Base class, 291
and derived classes, *290*
Beaufort Wind Speed Scale, 214
Ben's Breakfast Bar
case study, 267-281
screen shot from program, *279*
Binary additive operators, 35
Binary digit (bit), 22
Binary multiplicative operators, 35
Binary number system, 23, 24
Binary search, *708*
for name in array, *706*
Binary search algorithm, 705, 738
`BinarySearch` class, 686
Bird songs program, 159-160
Bits, 22, 23
Blocks
productions from, 753-756
statements treated as, 168
Block scope, 106, 145
Boats case study, 317-339
relationships between classes, *328*
Body mass index case study, 185-194
BOLD+ITALIC style, 66
BOLD style, 66
Book example problem, 412-417
`Boolean` array, 263, 264
`Boolean` class, 185
`boolean` data type, 153, 177-178
Braces, 168, 170, 172
Bracket notation, 75
Branching, unconditional, 394
`break` statement, 180, 236, 282, 394
`BufferedReader`
input with, 398-400
Bugs
and `BufferedReader` constructor, 398
`Button` class, 451, 497
`Button` object, 452

Buttons, 444
adding to containers, 451-456, 497
`Byte` class, 185
`Byte` data, 398
Bytes, 23

C
C, 2
`Calculator` class, 570, 571, 574
source listing of, 580-581
`Calendar` class, 649
CANCEL button
on `FileDialog` box, 421
Case labels, 183, 209
Case-sensitivity, 27, 81
Case statements, 180
Case studies
arithmetic of rational numbers, 353-361
Ben's Breakfast Bar, 267-281
boats, 317-339
body mass index, 185-194
chemical elements, 508-520
cutting logs, 116-124
date validation (including leap years), 196-209
die rolling simulation, 135-143
multithreading example, 657-667
palindrome, 253-261
stack for converting algebraic expressions, 728-737
text file statistics, 422-432
Casting, 42-45
Cast operation syntax, 42
`catch` block, 381, 382, 397, 409, 433
and exception handling, 391
finding, 393
and stacks, 728
syntax for, 380
for trapping exceptions, 384
`catch` clause, 375
CDs
copying/editing programs from, 15-16
`Character` class, 185
`Character` data, 398
Character literal, 25
Character(s), 20, 24-25
`charAt()` method, 731
`char` data type, 25, 27
`CheckBox` class, 217, 261-264

Check boxes, 443, 444
    adding to containers, 465-468, 497
    adding to window container, *465*
CheckBoxes component
    example of, *491*
    listing of, 493-496
    reusable, 491-496
CheckBoxes constructor, 263
CheckBoxes object
    in Ben's Breakfast Bar case study, 268-269
CheckboxGroup class, 468, 469
CheckBox objects
    from avi package, *262*
    creating, 262-263
ChemicalElement class, 508
Chemical elements case study, 508-520
Chip, 22, 25
Circle class, 315, 316, 544
Circles
    drawing, 524, 534, 628
Class declaration
    productions from, 749-750
Class(es), 51, 82
    hiding implementation details of, 88
    identifying, 109
    identifying in log cutting case study, 117
    instance methods of, 83
    items defined by, *104*
    naming, 63
    nesting, 364
    in packages, 613
    productions from, 749
    relationship between interface and, *342*
    relationships between, in Student Management
        Class, *609*
    UML class diagram showing associations
        between, *572*
    UML representation of, *109, 110*
    UML representation of dependencies between,
        111
    "whole-part" relationships between, 563
    wrapper, 184-185. *See also* Data types
Classes, Responsibilities, and Collaborators cards. *See*
        CRC cards
Class methods, 87, 101-104, 144
CLASSPATH directive, 613
CLASSPATH entry, 12
    interpretation of, 8-9, 565-566
Class scope, 106, 145
Class variables, 118

clearImages() method, 132
clearTextArea() method, 68
Cloneable interface, 350
clone method, 350
Cloning, 361
CloseDialogWindow class, 565
close method, 521, 522
CloseMyWindow class, 449
closeWindowAndExit() method, 68
CloseWritingPad, 485
Coding, 107
Collaborators
    and CRC card technique, 582, 584
Color
    for applets, 631
    foreground/background, 446
    images, 131
    parameter, 66
    for shapes, 535, 536
Color class, 446, 632
Color constant, 629
Color object, 632
Command line arguments, 75-78, 83
Command message, 59
Comments, 62
Comparable interface, 695
compareTo method, 163, 695, 696
Compilation and execution, 112
Compiler, 10, 12
Compiling
    Java program, 10-12
    tools for, 14
Component class, 444, 452, 477
Composition, 598, 614
    relationship between function pad and its but-
        tons, *598*
CompuServe, 131, 637
Computer memory, *22*
Computer programs, 20, 88
Concatenation, 302
Conditional expressions, 153, 163, 172-175, 209
    for controlling number of repetitions, 282
    and indentation, 168
Conditional statements program, 173-174
Condition X, 178
Condition Y, 178
Constant declaration, 246
    syntax for, 32
Constants, 32-33, 37, 145
    initializing, 46

Constructor calls, 297
Constructor declarations
    productions from, 751-752
Constructors, 55, 56-58, 82, 87, 89, 90-93, 125, 144,
    345-347
Container class, 444
    add method from, 498
    `createImage` method from, 676
    creating, 443, 498
Containers
    `awt` components added to, 444
    buttons added to, 451-456
    check boxes added to, 465-468, 497
    components added to, 499
    creating, 444-448
    fonts added to, 458-460
    labels added to, 457-458
    lists added to, 472-476, 497
    menu bars added to, 605
    radio buttons added to, 468-472, 497
    reusable, 476-480
    text fields added to, 461-464
`continue` statement, 394
Control variable identifiers, 245, 248
Coordinates, mouse, 528-530, *531*
Copying
    objects, 350-351
    programs from CD, 15-16
Copyright-free
    images, 135
    sound clips, 126, 130
Correlation coefficient, 402
Counters
    while loop controlled by, 220
Counting demonstration program, 237-238
CRC cards, 563, 582-586, 614
    for `Degree` class, *583*
    index card layout for representing, *583*
    for `Module` class, *584*
    for `ModuleResults` class, *585*
    for `StudentProgram` class, *585*
CRC card technique, 582
`createData()` method, 594, 595
`createImage` method, 676
Currency formatting, 265

D

Data, 20-21, 45
    encapsulation of, 88
    input and output, 398

    names, 45
Data controlled loop, 220-223, *229*
Data controlled while loop program, 222
    screen shot from, *224*
Data declarations, 31
`DataInputBox`, 515
`DataInputBox` component, *509*
    listing of, 510-514
`DataOutputBox` component, *514*
Data storage, 21-27
    number systems, 23-27
Data streams, 375
Data types, 23, 51, 52, 53, 82, 88-90, 144, 563. *See*
    also Classes
Data validation case study, 196-209
`DecimalFormat` class, 315, 316
Decimal integer literals, 25
Decimal number system, 23, 24
Decision symbol, 227
Declarations, 95
    arrays, 241, 253
    one-dimensional arrays, 242, 243, 244
    objects, 54
`DecorateRoom` class, 124
    creating, 98
Decreasing function, 354
Decrement postfix operators, 217, 233, 282
Decrement prefix operators, 233
Default statement, 180
Default superclass constructor, 363
Degree class, 599
    CRC card for, *583*
`delay` class method, 127
Dependencies, 586
    between classes, 145
    between packages, 569, 613
    UML representation of, between classes,
        111
    UML representation of `DateString` class,
        201
Dependency diagram
    in Boats case study, *336*
Deprecation, 401, 497, 656
Derived classes, 290
Design and programming parts
    of software development life cycle, 108
Design phase
    in software development, 107, 145
Desk checking, 112, 145
    of `cut()` instance method, 120

Destination, of assignment, 36
Dialog box, 68, 444, 481
   example of, *69*
   input of number into, *72*
   input to, 69-72
   visibility of, 70
`DialogBox` class, 64, 69, 73, 397
`DialogBox` component
   reusable, 486-491
`DialogBox` object creation, 70
`Dialog` class, 444, 480, 481
Dialog font, 486
Dialog window
   drawing, 481
   label for, 486
   width and height of, 486, 487
Die rolling simulation case study, 135-143
Die rolling simulation program extension, 230-231
   screen shot from, *232*
Digital, 21
Dimension class, 478
Directories
   class storage in, 97
`Display` class, 570, 573-574
`displayDetails` method, 307
`displayList` method, 722
`displayResults()` method, 594, 595
`displayStatistics` class method, 103, 104
`dispose` method, 450
Divide-by-zero exception, 380
Divide operation, 348, 352
Division (/), 35, 45
Documentation, 113-116
Double backslash, 407
Double-branch selection, *164*
Double buffering, 676
Double class, 185
double data type, 27
Double equals sign (==), 170
double number type, 399, 400
Double-precision form, 32
Double-precision literal, 27
`double` type, 26
Doubling time, 390
`do..while` loop, 227-231, 240, 282
`do..while` statement, 217
`drawImage` method, 676
Drawing
   circles, 628

   and mouse events, 527-533
   polygons, 628
   rectangles, 532-533, 628
   and storage/retrieval, 502
   shapes from Graphics class, 524
   two-dimensional shapes, 502
`DrawingPad` class, 548-557
`drawInWindow` method
   algorithm for, 659
`drawShape` method, 547
`drawShape` variable, 534
`drawString` method, 528
driver class, 97, 101
Drop-down menus, 605, *606*, 614
   from applet viewer, *627*
   example of, *606*
Dynamic array, 250
Dynamic data structure, 710
Dynamic memory allocation, 738
Dynamic method lookup, 305, 363

E

Editing programs from CD, 15-16
Editor program, 9
`ElasticRectangle` class, 532, 533
`Ellipse` class, 544
Ellipses
   drawing, 524, 534, 558
`else` clause, 171, 172
`else if` statements, 176
`else` keyword, 176, 209
`else` statements, 175
E-mail, 620, 621, 677
Embedded selection statements, 153
Encapsulation, 88, 144
   of data, 52
   data and methods, *89*
   and inner classes, 312
`EndOfFileException`, 396
Environmental Protection Agency Web site, 86, 214
`eolIsSignificant()` method, 406
`equalsIgnoreCase` method, 163
`equals` method, 163, 349
Equals sign (=)
   for assignment, 170
`Error` class, 378
Error message
   for data in incorrect format, *72*
Errors, 51, 78-82, 376

detection of, 153
logical, 82, 83, 112
run-time, 82, 83
syntax, 78-81, 83, 112. *See also* Exceptions
Error subclass, 433
Escape-sequence characters, 66, 746
Euclid's algorithm, 353
    for greatestCommonDivisor method, 354
    for makeRational() method, 355
Event class, 498
Event handling, 444
    and applets, 627
    in java.awt package, 448-451
Event listener, 448, 498
Events
    and program malfunctions, 375
Example_2.java, 15-16
    screen shot from running program, *16*
Exception classes, 377-379
    creating own, 387-390
Exception handlers, 376, 409
Exception handling, 375, 412
    purpose of, 376
    and throwing exception, 391
    using, 396-397
Exception-handling classes
    partial class hierarchy for, *378*
Exception object, 391
Exception(s)
    catching, 377, 379-383, 433
    catching multiple, 383-386, 433
    creating own, 376
    defined, 376, 433
    and flow of control, *381*
    search for handler by, *392*
    throwing, 390-394, 433
Exception subclass, 433
Exception superclass, 434
Expressions
    evaluating, 40
    productions from, 756-759
extends keyword, 363

F

failure() method, 395
Fault handling techniques, 376
Fault-tolerant computer system, 376
Field declarations
    productions from, 750

FIFO list, 726
FileDialog class, 419-422
FileInputStream, 405
filename parameter, 65, 66
filenames, 131
FileNotFoundException, 424
FileOutputStream, 410
FileReader class, 405, 407
FileReader object creation, 405
Files
    creation of, 407
    inputting name of, 419
    objects saved to, 521
File Transfer Protocol, 620, 677
FileWriter class, 410
FileWriter object creation, 410
FilmStrip class, 568, 674, 675, 676
FilmStrip object, 130
finalize() method, 362
Finalizers, 362
finally block, 394-396, 409, 434
finally clause, 375
First In First Out list. *See* FIFO list
Flicker
    reducing, 668-670, 676
Float class, 185
float number type, 399, 400
float type, 26, 42, 67
Floppy disks, 407
FlowLayout class, 452
flush method, 402, 521
Font class, 480, 486
Fonts
    adding to containers, 458-460
    size of, 78
fontSize parameter, 66
for loop, 235-239, 240-241, 245, 282
    and index control, 248
    and two-dimensional arrays, 642, 644
    and while loop, 236, 239
formal-parameter-list, 55, 94
Formal parameters, 144
for statement, 217
    to control index to array, 248
    loop control variable in, 282
    syntax for, 235
Forward slash, 407
Four-bit full adder, *617*
Frame class, 444

FTP. *See* File Transfer Protocol
FunctionPad class, 570, 573
FunctionPad object, 598
FunctionPad source code, 577-579

G

Garbage, 361, 362
    collection of, 106, 145, 361-362, 364, 365, 652
Generalization, 290
getActionCommand() method, 454
getAudioClip method, 634, 635
getDate() method, 128
getDirectory() method, 420
getDouble() method, 397
getFile() method, 420
getFloat() method, 397
getGraphics method, 528, 548, 558
getHeight() method, 68, 478
getHour() method, 127
getImage method, 638
getInteger method, 397
getItem method, 466, 473, 492
getLongInteger() method, 397
getMinute() method, 127
getNameOfButton method, 158
getParameter method, 629
GetPrintJob
    from Toolkit class, 548
getScreenSize method, 478
getSecond() method, 127
getSource() method, 487, 488
getStateChange method, 466, 492
getText method, 461
getTime() method, 128
getToolkit method, 477
getValue() method, 155
getWidth() method, 68, 478
GIF files, 637, 668, 674
GIF images, 130, *669*, 674
Gopher, 620, 677
Gosling, James, 2
Graceful degradation, 376
Grammatical errors, 10-11, 78. *See also* Syntax
Graphical double-buffering, 670, 671
Graphical objects, 65
    creating/saving, 544
Graphical user interfaces, 51, 443, 497, 564, 678
    in chemical elements case study, 508-510
    proportioning components of, 477

for student management systems, 604
Graphic Interchange Format files. *See* GIF files
Graphics
    printing, 502
Graphics class, 501, 524-527, 558
    drawImage method from, 676
    drawing two-dimensional shapes in, 534
    image drawing methods defined by, 638
    methods in, 626
Graphics-output clipping, 524
GraphicThread class, 665, 667
    constructor and method of, 660
    UML dependencies, *662*
    UML representation of, *661*
GridLayout manager, 458-459
GUI components
    creating, 498
    reusable, 444
    as standalone classes, 498
GUI development
    Java Swing for, 497
gui package, 594
    UML representation of, *568*
GUIs. *See* Graphical user interfaces
gui subdirectory, 566
    contents of, *565*

H

Half-adder, *616*
Half-life, 398
Hard-coding data, 73
Hard disks, 407
has-a relationship, 313, 586
Heap, 91, 145, 361, 362
heightOfFrame, 131
height parameter, 446
HELLO WORLD, 68-69
    applet for displaying in window, 625-626
    executing, 12
    screen shot from running program, *13*
    string display, *67*
helper method, 101, 103, 111
    and pseudocode, 112
Hexadecimal number system, 24
Hierarchy
    object assignment over, 298
Hierarchy class diagrams, *294, 295*
Hierarchy diagram
    superclass/subclass relationship, *291*

Home-grown techniques, 396
HotJava (Sun), 2, 621
Hot link, 620
HTML. *See* Hyper-Text Mark-up Language
HTTP. *See* Hyper-Text Transfer Protocol
Hypermedia, 620
Hypertext document, 620
Hyper-Text Mark-up Language, 620, 673, 677
Hyper-Text Transfer Protocol, 621, 677

I

Identifiers, 27-28, 45
    numbers stored by, 36
    to represent data, *28*
    scope and lifetime of, 87, 104-106
if..else statement, 153, 161-166
    program, 164-165
    syntax of, 165
If Java statement program, 162
if keyword, 176, 209
If statements
    nesting of, 171, 209
    syntax for, 163
Illegal identifiers, 31
Image maps, 645-648, 678
    screen shot, *648*
Image painting, 524
Images
    animation of, 678
    with applications, 675-676
    displaying, 637-639, 675-676
    files of, 15
    loading, 639-641
    three, on screen, *134*
Import list, 62-63
import statement, 62, 83
Increasing function, 354
Increment postfix operators, 217, 233, 282
Increment prefix operators, 233
Indentation
    with else if statements, 176
    with if statements, 168, 171
    and while loop, 221
Index, 253
index loop control variable, 246
indexOf method, 505
Index-out-of-bounds exception, 377
Index page
    iconizing, 14

Infinite loop, 236, 237, 282
Infix notation, 728, 729
Inheritance, 289, 290-299, 363
    classes *versus* interfaces, *340*
    between Employee and Technician classes, 296
    example of, 292-299
    Java syntax for, 291
    multiple, 341
    when to use, 344
Initialization
    of alphabet, 56
    of arrays, 124
    of instance variables of class, 144
    of loop control variables, 219
    of one-dimensional arrays, 242, 243, 244
    of variables, 32
Inner classes, 312
Input and output, 64
InputStream, 398
InputStreamReader, 398, 405
    format of constructor from, 399
Instance methods, 55, 58-61, 82, 83, 87, 89, 93-101, 103, 144, 347-348
    in Audio class, 125
    differentiation of, from class method, 101
Instance of class, 56
instanceof operator, 307-309
Instances, of class, 52
Instance variables, 90, 586
Instantiation, 52, 90, 91, 144
Instructions, 31
int data type, 27
Integer class, 184, 185
Integer data types, 25, 45
Integer numbers, 25
Integer object, 184
Integers, 20, 45
    array of, *132*
    program for inputting/performing operations on, 73-74
Integer type
    object creation for, 399-400
Integer wrapper class
    use of, *185*
Integrated circuits, 22, 25
Interfaces, 289, 339-345, 364
    alternative UML representations of, *339*
    classes in AWT package for building, *445*
    productions from, 752

Interfaces *(continued)*
    relationship between classes and, *342*
    when to use, 345
Internet, 2, 677
    defined, 620
    using, 3
Internet browser, 3
Internet provider accounts, 3
Interpreter, 12
int number type, 399, 400
int primitive, 57
int type, 42
intValue() method, 184
int values, 25
IOException, 424
    and readLine method, 399
is-a hierarchies, 313
isEmpty method, 723
isPopupTrigger method, 537
ITALIC typeface style, 29, 66
ItemListener method, 466, 470, 473-474
itemStateChanged method, 466, 473, 492

J

Java, 1, 52
    applets, 2
    as case-sensitive language, 81
    description of, 2-3
    diversity of applications for, 677
    finalizer methods in, 362
    input/output, 398
    string literal in, 54. *See also* Syntax of Java
Java API, 52, 53
    documentation generator (javadoc), 113
    reusing methods defined by, 145
java.applet package, 623
Java application program
    format for simple, 33-35
Java Archive (JAR) file, 648
    digital signature attached to, 674
java.awt.event package, 454, 498
    event classes in, 487, 488
    event-listener interfaces in, 449
java.awt package, 443
    buttons added to containers, 451-457
    check boxes, radio buttons, and lists added to
        containers, 465-476
    container creation, 444-448
    event handling, 448-451

Graphics class within, 524
Java Swing, 497
labels, fonts, and text fields added to containers,
    457-464
reusable CheckBoxes component creation,
    491-496
reusable container creation, 476-480
reusable DialogBox component creation,
    486-491
reusable WritingPad component creation,
    480-485
Java byte codes, 10, 12
javac command, 11, 95, 97, 565
Java code, 111
    documenting, 14
java command, 12
Java components, 19-49
    arithmetic, 35-39
    casting, 42-45
    data, 20-21
    data storage, 21-27
    format of simple program, 33-35
    identifiers, 27-28
    operator precedence, 40-41
    syntax, 29-31
    variables and constants, 31-33
javac tool, 14
Java Dialog font, 66
javadoc, 14, 113
    sample online documentation generated by, *116*
Java interface construct, 693, 695
Java interpreter, 384
    and exception handling, 379, 380, 382, 391
Java Interpreter (java), 14
java.io.BufferedReader
    hierarchy diagram for, *399*
java.io.InputStreamReader
    hierarchy diagram for, *399*
java.io package, 398
    and Serializable interface, 521
java.io.PrintStream
    hierarchy diagram for, *400*
java.io.PrintWriter
    hierarchy diagram for, *400*
java.lang, 6
java.lang package, 53, 63
    Comparable interface defined in, 695
java.lang.Runnable, 654
java.lang.Thread class, 653

Java Language Compiler (javac), 14
Java library
    NumberFormat class, 217
Java primitive data types, 744
Java program
    compiling, 10-12
    executing (running), 12-14
    general structure of, 61-63
    inputting/saving, 9-10
Java software development environment
    creating, 5-6
java.string, 6
.java suffix
    saving program as text file with, 10
Java.sun.com Web site, 17
Java Swing, 407
java tool, 14
Java 2 Software Development Kit, 1
Java 2 Software Development Kit documentation
    downloading, 4, 6
    introductory page, 7
    opening page of, 6
java.util, 6
java.util.Arrays, 693
java.util.Arrays—Binary search class, 705-708
java.util.Arrays—Sort class, 691-699
Java Virtual Machine, 10, 652
    and exceptions, 376
JButton class, 497
Joint Photographic Experts Group files (JPEG files),
    637, 674
JPEG images, 130
jpg image files, 131

K

Keyboard input, 375
Keyboard object
    instantiating of, by object stream, 399
Keywords, 27-28, *28*

L

Labels, 444
    added to containers, 457-458
    for Dialog window, 486
    parameters, 465, 469
    in window container, *461*
    written to window container, *458*
LALR(1) grammar
    productions from, 749

Last In First Out list. *See* LIFO list
Layout manager, 452
    five implementations of, *453*
LayoutManager interface, 452
Length, of array, 241
length variable, 282
Lexical structures
    productions from, 747
Lifetime of identifier, 106
LIFO list, 726
Linear models, 403
Line class, 544
Line drawing, 524, 534, 558
Linked list, 685, 686, 708-726
    building, *711*, 712-713
    class variables associated with, *715*
    node appended into, 714, *716*
    node deleted between first/last in, *719*
    node deleted from front of, 718
    node deleted from tail of, *720*
    stack created from, 726
    use of, 710
LinkedList class, 714, 718-725, 726
Linux platform, 5
    downloading Java 2 SDK on, 4
Linux users
    inputting/saving Java program, 9
List component constructors, 472
Listeners, 449
Lists, 444, 710
    adding to containers, 472-476, 497
    adding to window containers, *473*
Literal, 25
LOAD constant, 420
Log class
    listing of, 120
    program demonstrating use of, 122-123
Log cutting case study, 116-124
Log files
    arithmetic exception, 380
    arithmetic of rational numbers, 361
    array size/declaration program, 248
    from Ben's Breakfast Bar program, 280-281
    bird songs program, 160
    for body-mass index case study, 193
    conditional statements program, 174
    counting demonstration program, 239
    data controlled while loop program, 223
    date validation case study, 208-209

Log files   *(continued)*
    die rolling simulation, 143
    for `Employee` and `Technician` classes, 297
    example of, *75*
    exception catching, 383
    exception class creation, 390
    `finally` clause, 396
    finding catch block, 394
    `if...else` statement, 165
    `if` statement, 162
    image files, 134
    input obtained from file, 409
    linked lists, 713
    Mergesort demonstration, 694
    multiple exceptions catching, 386
    object assignment over hierarchy, 299
    one-dimensional array and initialization program, 245
    overriding is not overshadowing program, 311
    overriding superclass methods program, 301
    polymorphism program, 306
    read file/write report, 410-411
    `ReversePolish` class, 737
    selections sort, 690
    `switch` statement program, 182
    temperature conversion program, 156
    what to wear program, 168
    `while` loop for alarm clock program, 226-227
LOG_FILE.TXT, 74
Logical AND (&&)
    and `else if` statements, 176
    truth table for, *175*, 178
Logical errors, 51, 82, 83, 112
Logical operators, 153
    AND (&&), 173, 178, 209
    OR, 177, 178, 209
Logical OR
    truth table for, 177, *178*
Logistic growth models, 399-401
Long class, 185
long data type, 27
Long evaluation, 209
Long integer literal, 25
long number type, 399, 400
long type, 25
Loop control variable, *218*, 218-219, 282
Loop structure, 218-220
    best choice for, 239-241

Loop variable
    controlled by data, *219*
Lukasiewicz, Jan, 728

M

`main` method, 63, 75, 77, 78, 83, 91, 96, 103, 112, 241, 242
    within driver class, 97
    helper method called from, 101
    and inputting name of file, 419
    pseudocode of, in book example problem, 414
Maintenance phase
    in software development, 107, 145
`makeRational()` algorithm, 353
`makeRational()` class method, 346, 348
`MalformedURLException`, 675
`Manager` class
    coding of, 303-305
    as subclass of `Employee` class, *304*
Managers, 599
Mantissa, 26
Maximum constants, 184
Maximum numbers
    in array, 252
MediaTracker, 639
`MediaTracker` class, 639, 675, 678
    instantiating object of, 640-641
    methods in, 640
`Member` class, 312, 714
`Memo` class, 194-195, 676
`Memo` object
    creating, 195
    example of, *194*
Memory, *22*, 45
    addresses, 349
    real number stored in, 26
`MenuBar` class, 605
`MenuBar` object, 605
Menu bars, 605, 614
`MenuItem` objects, 536
Menus, 443, 604-608
    drop-down, 605, *606*, 614
Mergesort
    modified version of, 691, 692
Message passing, 60
Messages, 59
Method call, 87, 145

Method declarations
     productions from, 751
Method definition
     syntax, 94
Method finalizer, 362
method-name, 55
Method overloading, 289, 345
Methods, 52
     calling and declaring, 144
     classifying, 103
     within DialogBox class, 69
     identifying, 109
     identifying in log cutting case study, 117
     and parameters, 54-55
     value returned from, 87
     in Window class, 65
Method signature, 54
Microsoft Internet Explorer, 3, 621
Microsoft 95/98, 5
Minimum constants, 184
Minimum numbers
     in array, 252
Modal windows, 480, 481
Modem, 3
Modifiers, 54, 144
Module class, 583, 584, 599
     CRC card for, 584
ModuleManager class, 608
     source listing of, 599-604
ModuleResults class, 586, 599
     CRC card representing, 585
Modules menu, 605
Monitors
     and dimensions of components, 498
     screen size, component measurements and, 477
     and size of window pane, 478
Mouse
     and location/size of graphical shape, 502
MouseAdapter class, 527
mouseDragged method, 530
MouseEvent class, 527, 528, 537, 558
MouseEvents, 530
Mouse events, 527-533
     listener interfaces for, 558
MouseListener, 558
MouseListener interface, 527
MouseMotionAdapter class, 530
MouseMotionListener, 558

MouseMotionListener interface, 530
mouseMoved method, 530
Mouse position
     and image maps, 678
mousePressed method, 527
mouseReleased method, 534, 546
MSDOS window
     errors listed in, 11-12
     execute command java to run program from, 13
Multimedia applets, 619
Multimedia interfaces, 51
Multi-media tracker, 671
Multiple exceptions, 376
     catching, 383-386
Multiple inheritance, 341
Multiple selection, 181
Multiplication (*), 35, 45
Multiplicative operators, 35, 40
Multiplicity of an association, 571, 614
Multitasking, 651
Multithreading, 651-652
     case study, 657-667
Music, 126, 127
MyWindow class
     foreground/background colors set for, 446
     modifying, 451
MyWindow container, 446
MyWindowWithButton class, 454
     modifying, 454-456
MyWindowWithCheckBoxes class, 466
     modifying, 468
MyWindowWithLabels class
     modifying, 460
MyWindowWithList class
     modifying, 476
MyWindowWithNewTextFields class, 464
MyWindowWithRadioButtons class
     modifying, 472
MyWindowWithTextFields class, 462
     modifying, 464

N

Named reference variable head, 709, 738
Name input
     dialog box used for, 16
Names
     for class, 63
     constructor, 91

Names *(continued)*
    of identifiers, 144
    productions from, 748
    resolving clash of, 568
    for shapes, 536
National Oceanic and Atmospheric Administration,
    214
National Weather Service, 86
Nested classes, 364
Nested `if..else` statements program, 167-168
Nested if statements, 166-172, 209
Nested selections, *166*
Nested selection statements, 153
Netscape Navigator, 3, 621
`new` keyword, 282
New operator
    array instantiated with, 253
`newString` variable, 59
`nextToken()` method, 406
NOAA. *See* National Oceanic and Atmospheric
    Administration
Node class, 708, 711-712, 713
    relationship between linked list class and, 714
`NodeCount` variable, 715
Nodes, 709, 710, 738
    appending into linked lists, 714, *716*
    code for deleting from linked list, 717
    data stored at, 711
    deleting between first and last nodes in linked
        list, *719*
    deleting from front of, *718*
    deleting from tail of linked list, *720*
    removal of, from any position in linked list, 715
Non-terminal symbols, 29
NotePad, 8, 9
NOT operator (!), 177
Noun identification, 110
NT Windows, 5
`NullPointerException`, 395
Null reference, 709, 710
`NumberFormat` class, 217, 264, 265, 283
    in Ben's Breakfast Bar case study, 267-279
`NumberFormatException`, 383
Numbers
    formatting for output, 264-266
    strings converted to, 72-75
Number systems, 23-27
    characters, 24-25
    integer numbers, 25
    real numbers, 26-27

Numeric calculator, 570, *571*
`NumericKeyPad` class, 571, 573, 574
`NumericKeyPad` source code, 575-577

O

Oak, 2
Object
    creating, 56
    stored by reference, *57*
Object assignment, 297
    over hierarchy, 298
Object class, 292, 349
Object finalization, 362, 365
`ObjectInput` class, 558
`ObjectInputStream`, 522
Object-oriented language, 52
Object-oriented program design, 108-124, 145
    algorithm development, 111-112
    classes/methods identified, 109-111
    compilation and execution, 112
    documentation, 113-116
    testing, 112
Object-oriented programming, 1, 2, 4, 87-151, 289
    abstract data type, 88-90
    avi package revisited, 124-143
    class methods, 101-104
    constructors, 90-93
    instance methods, 93-101
    learning, with Java, 15
    object-oriented program design, 108-124
    and reusable classes, 476
    scope and lifetime of identifiers, 104-106
    software development, 106-108
`ObjectOutput` class, 558
`ObjectOutputStream`, 521
Object properties, 289, 348-352
    comparing objects, 348-350
    copying objects, 350-351
    passing objects as parameters, 352
Objects, 51-86
    association and connecting of, 571
    AVI package, 63-64
    command line arguments, 75-78
    converting strings to numbers, 72-75
    copying, 350-351
    declaring, 53-61, 54
    and errors, 78-82
    identification of, 109
    input to a dialog box, 69-72
    instantiating, 52

introduction to, 52-53
passing as parameters, 289, 352
printing, 548-557
saving and loading serializable, 520-523
serialization of, 502
simple program revisited, 61-63
storage of, *348*, 687
string class, 53-61
`Window` class, 65-69
Object streams
versus text streams, 520
"Off by one" errors, 241
One-dimensional array declaration
syntax of, 243
One-dimensional arrays, 75, 217, 241, 252-253, 282,
558, 641
for Ben's Breakfast Bar, 274
declaring and initializing, 242-245
and initialization program, 244
Telephone objects within, *697*
Online documentation
illustration of, *116*
Operator overloading, 347, 364
Operator precedence, 40-41, 45
Operator priorities, 40, 745
Ordinal type, 179, 183, 209
Ordinal value, 179
`ordinaryChars()` method, 406
OR logical operator, 209
OR operator, 177
Output
formatting numbers for, 264-266
Window class for, 65
Output format options program, 265-266
`OutputStreamWriter` class, 410
Overloaded constructors, 364
Overloading methods, 345
Overridden methods, 299
Overriding is not overshadowing program, 310-311
Overriding superclass methods
program demonstrating, 301
Oxford University Sound Archive, 634
Ozone levels
and UV index, 214

P

`package` keyword, 613
Packages, 52, 53, 82, 293, 564-570, 613
benefits of, 569-570
productions from, 748-749

UML diagram of dependencies between, *569*
`package` statement, 564
Painting screen, 502, 544-548
`paint` method, 524, 544, 546, 548, 558, 628, 649
overriding, 668, 670
Palindrome case study, 253-261
screen shot for, *261*
`Panel` class, 573, 614, 623, 625
Parameters
and methods, 54-55
objects passed as, 289, 352
Parentheses
and order of precedence, 40
parent type, 70
parent-Window type, 130
Partial images, 639
Pascal, 2
Password, 3
PCM coded data, 127
Peeking, at item in stack, 726
Per-group inspection, 112
Photographs
moving over Web, 637
Pick lists, 443
PLAIN style, 66
Plus sign (+), 25, 67
and classes for public use, 569
Pointing devices, 443
Polygons, 628
drawing, 558
Polymorphic methods, 364
Polymorphism, 289, 303-306, 363, 547
program example, 306
Popping from stack, 726, *727*
`PopupMenu` object
creating, 536
Pop-up menus, 501, 502, 534-544
examples of, *535*
Portable between two computers, 10
`positionOfLargest` method, 687
Positive integer literals, 25
Postfix notation, 728
Primitive data types, 27
wrapper classes for, 185, 209
and write method, 67
Primitive data values, 53
Primitive types
stored by value, *57*
and wrapper classes, 184
Principal, 357

Printing
    graphics, 502
    objects, 548-557
print instance method, 401, 402
PrintJob class, 558
PrintJob object, 548
Print jobs, 548
println instance method, 401
println statement, 402
PrintStream
    and deprecation, 401
PrintWriter
    output with, 400-403
private fields
    of enclosing class, 364
Private method, 90, 103, 144
private priority method
    algorithm for, 732
private variables, 293, 363
Problem analysis, 109
processMouseEvent() method, 537
processMouseMotionEvent() method, 537
Program, computer, 20
Program failure
    and events, 375
Program implementation
    phases of, 13, *14*
Programmer-defined classes
    names for classes in, 568
Programmer-defined packages, 564
Programming phase
    of software project development, 107, *108*,
    145
Programming stages, 145
Programs
    animation techniques, 671-673
    arithmetic exception creation, 379
    arithmetic statements, 38
    arrays, 246-247, 249, 250-252
    binary search, 707
    class creation, 113
    class scope for window object, 105
    command line parameters, 77
    conditional statements, 173
    counting, 237
    die rolling simulation, 230
    digital clock, 654-656
    exception catching within program, 382
    exception class creation, 389

finally clause, 395
finding catch block, 393
if..else statement, 164
if statement, 162
image display, 133
image maps, 645-647
inheritance, 296
input obtained from file, 408-409
instanceof operator, 308
integer operands and arithmetic operations, 73,
    402-403
Mergesort demonstration, 693-694
mouse coordinates plotted on screen, 528-529
multiple exception catching within program,
    384-385
nested if..else statements, 167
newspaper names/prices, 79
numbers calculations, 43-44
object assignment over hierarchy, 298
output format options, 265-266
overriding is not overshadowing, 310
overriding superclass methods, 301
polymorphism, 306
Quicksort demonstration, 692
radio buttons, 159
read file/write report, 410-411
selections sort, 689-690
sequential search demonstration, 702-704
slider to input temperature, 155
storing/retrieving data from Vector, 503-505
String class and instance methods, 60
SwimmingPool class, 97, 102
switch statement, 180
Telephone class, 698-699
testing, 112
text file contents viewing, 420-421
Timer class and playing sounds, 128
two-dimensional shapes drawn from Graphics
    class, 524-526
wav sound file playing, 126
while, do..while loops and
    increment/decrement operators, 233
while loop controlled by input data, 222
while loop for alarm clock, 225
window container creation, 447, 450
window container creation and labels added,
    459-460
window container creation and push button,
    454-456

window container creation with added labels/text fields, 462-464

window creation and list added to container, 474-476

window creation with radio buttons added to container, 470-472

Projected light, 631

prompt, 70

Properties class, 548

protected variable, 293, 363

Pseudocode, 111

public access method, 363

Public class, 90, 144

Public method, 90, 94, 103, 144

Pushing from stack, 726, *727*

Q

Quadratic algorithms, 691, 738

Query message, 59

Queue, 726

Quicksort
    algorithm, 738
    tuned version of, 691, 693

R

Radio buttons, 443, 444
    added to containers, 468-472, 497
    adding to window container, *469*
    behavior of, 468

RadioButtons class, 156-160, 496

RadioButtons component, *515*

Radio-buttons object
    creating, 158

Railway Shunting-Yard algorithm, 728-729

Rational ADT (Abstract Data Type), 345

Rational class, 345, 346, 347, 352, 353
    definition of, 353
    implementation of, 355-359
    methods of, 359
    UML representation of, *354*

Rational numbers, 345
    arithmetic of (case study), 353-361
    case study, 353-361
    instance method for addition of, 347

Reader class, 398

readLine method, 399

readObject method, 522, 558

Real-number literal, 27

Real numbers, 20, 26-27

Rectangle class, 544, 546

Rectangles
    constructing, *531*, 532-533
    drawing, 524, 534, 558, 628

RectangularWindow class, 657, 659-660, 665, 667
    UML dependencies, *659*
    UML representation of, *658*

Red, Green, and Blue (RGB), 631, 632

Red, Yellow, and Blue (RYB), 631

Reference
    copy *versus*, *350*
    passing array by, *688*
    storage by, 687
    to value, 58

Reference counter, hidden, 362

Reflected light, 631

Reflecting, 354, 366, 367

Relational operators, *170*

Remainder operator (%), 35, 41, 45

repaint() method LC, 544, 558, 649, 651

Resource Information File Format, 127

Restrictions, 673-674, 678

Return statement, 145
    syntax of, 95

return-type, 55
    and value, 94, 95

Reusable containers
    creating, 476-480

Reverse Polish algorithm
    stack used in, *730*

ReversePolish class, 730-731, 733
    UML representation of, and dependencies, *731*, *736*

ReversePolish constructor
    algorithm for, 731

Reverse Polish notation, 728, 729

RIFF. *See* Resource Information File Format

RoundShape class, 313, 314

Run() method, 653, 654, 678

Run-time errors, 51, 82, 83

RuntimeException
    list of subclasses to, 433

S

Sailboat class
    Java code for, 326-327

SAVE constant, 420

Scope
    of identifier, 106

Screens
    output to, 375
    painting, 502
    `Window` object, 66
Screen size
    and component measurements, 477
`ScrollableList` class, 496, 566, 568
Scrollbars, 68, 444
SDK. *See* Java 2 Software Development Kit
SDK Tool Documentation
    index page for, 14
SDK tools, 14
Searching, 685
Searching algorithms
    worst-case efficiency, *708*
`SearchingAlgorithms` class, 701-702
Selection, 153-215
    boolean data type, 177-178
    conditional expressions, 172-175
    `else if` statements, 176
    `if-else` statements, 161-166
    `Memo` class, 194-195
    nested `if` statements, 166-172
    `Slider` class, 154-160
    `switch` statements, 179-183
    `this` object, 195-196
    wrapper classes, 184-194
Selection sort, 686, *687*, 738
`selectionSort` method, 687, 689
Self-extracting programs, 5
Self-referential structure, 709
Semiconductor device, 22
Sentinel value, 220
`sequential` method, 702
Sequential search, 700-704, *708*
    on array of records, *700*
Serializable interface, 521, 558, 587, 588-593
Serializable objects
    saving and loading, 520-523
Serialization, 502, 520
`setActionCommand`, 536
`setBackground` component, 452
`setBackground` method, 446, 482
`setEditable` method, 464, 482
`setForeground` component, 452
`setForeground` method, 446, 482
`setLayout` method, 478
`setLocation` method, 446, 482
`setSize` method, 446, 482

`setText` method, 464
Shadowed variables, 309-311
`Shape` class, 546
Shapes
    drawing on sketch pad, 537-543
    hierarchy of, *545*
    repository of, 546
`Shape` superclass
    implementation of, 545
Short-circuit evaluation, 178, 209
`Short` class, 185
`showCheckBoxes()` method, 263
`showDialogBox()` method, 70, 71
`showSlider` method, 155
Signature syntax, 54
Single-branch selection, *161*
Single-precision literal, 27
Single-precision value, 32
Siple, Paul A., 86
SIZE constant, 246
`SketchPad` class, 537, 546, 548, 673
    drawbacks with, 544
    screen shot, *543*
sleep method, 654
Slider bars, 443
`Slider` class, 154-156, 676
`Slider` object
    creating, 154
Sliders, 233, 245
Software development, 106-108
    life cycle, *107*
    stages within, 145
`Sort` class, 686
Sorting, 685, 686-691
Sorting algorithm, 685, 686
    average-case efficiency of, *693*
`sortingAlgorithms` class, 687, 688
`sort` method, 692
Sound
    with applications, 674-675, 675
    clips, 127
    links with, 620
    playing, 634-637
    program for playing succession of, 128-130
Sound files, 15
    AudioClip created from, 675
Sphere class, 315, 316
Squares
    drawing, 524, 534

Stack class, 686
Stack list, 727-728
Stacks, 726-728, 738
    access to, *726*
    for converting algebraic expressions, 728-737
    operator priorities, *729*
    in reverse Polish algorithm, *730*
start() method
    of Thread object, 653
Statements
    productions from, 753-756
State parameter, 465, 469
Static arrays, 282
Static initializers
    productions from, 751
Static method, 101, 103
Static modifier, 63
stop method
    and deprecation, 656
Storage, 97
    of real numbers, 171
Storage space
    and new keyword, 282
Stored by reference object, *57*
Stream input and output, 398-403
    input with BufferedReader, 398-400
    output with PrintWriter, 400-403
stream object
    keyboard object instantiated by, 399
Streams, 375, 398
StreamTokenizer class, 404-407, 424, 697
Stream tokenizing, 376, 412
String, 20
    alphabet, 56
    array, 83
    assignment, *58*
    concatenating, 67-68
    converting to numbers, 72-75
    defined, 53
    displaying, 524
    instantiation, 70
StringBuffer object, 731
String class, 51, 53-61, 89, 163
    compareTo method from, 695, 696
    constructors for, 56-58, 345
    declaring objects, 54
    instance method, 58-61
    methods and parameters, 54-55
    program demonstrating, 60

string assignment, 58
String concatenation operator, 67
String data
    and command line, 75
String data type, 58, 83
String literals, 54
String methods, 59
String objects, 52
StringTokenizer class
    and FileViewer class, 417
Student Management Class
    screen shots, *612*, *613*
Student management system
    building, 599-604
    testing, 608-613
StudentProgram class, 599
    CRC card for, *585*
style parameter, 66
Subclasses, 289, 291, 363
    of abstract class, 313
    constructor for, 297
    finalizer of, 362
Subdirectories
    class storage in, 97
    packages placed in, 565
Subprocesses, 651
Subscriber class, 507
Subtraction (-), 35, 45
Sun Microsystems, Inc., 1, 2, 401, 497, 626, 656
    Web site, 5, 113
Superclasses, 289, 291, 363
    constructor for, 297
    overriding methods, 299-303
super keyword, 295, 303
super reserved word, 309, 363, 446, 477
Surfing the net, 621
SwimmingPool class, 92, 95, 113
    creation of, 96-97
switch statement, 153, 179-183, 209
    program to demonstrate, 180, 182
    syntax for, 179
Syntax, 29-31
    for applet tag, 622
    of cast operation, 42
    catch block, 380
    constructor, 91
    for declaration of one-dimensional array, 243
    do..while loop, 228

Syntax   *(continued)*
    errors, 51, 78-81, 83, 112
    `finally` block, 394
    `if..else` statement, 165
    for inheritance, 291
    `instanceof` operator, 307
    method definition, 94
    passing message to object by instance method, 59
    for passing parameters to applets, 628
    to produce Java documentation, 115
    return statement, 95
    of signature, 54
    of for statement, 235
    for `switch` statement, 179
    for `throw` statement, 391
    for variable declaration, 31
    of `while` loop, 220
Syntax of Java, 747-759
    productions from arrays, 752
    productions from blocks and statements,
        753-756
    productions from classes, 749-750
    productions from constructor declarations,
        751-752
    productions from expressions, 756-759
    productions from field declarations, 750
    productions from interfaces, 752
    productions from lexical structures, 747
    productions from method declarations, 751
    productions from names, 748
    productions from packages, 748-749
    productions from static initializers, 751
    productions from types, values, and variables,
        747-748
    productions used only in LALR(1) grammar, 749
`System.out`, 401

T

Tab
    for Ben's Breakfast Bar, *273, 274, 275*
`Technician` class
    modifications to, *300*
`Telephone` class, 695-696
`Telephone` objects
    within one-dimensional array, *697*
Telnet, 620, 677
Temperature
    conversion program, 155-156
    wind chill, 86

Terminal symbols, 29, 30
Testing, 112
    for body-mass index case study, 188
    for date validation case study, 201
    for log cutting case study, 120
    multithreading example case study, 663-664
    software project, 107
    student management system, 608-612
Text
    outputting, 67
    writing into text field, 464
`TextArea` class, 480, 482
Text areas, 444
`TextComponent` class, 461, 464
Text document
    saving program as, 10
`TextField` class, 461
`TextField` component
    in dialog window, 487
Text fields, 444
    added to containers, 461-464
    in window container, *461*
`TextFileAnalyzer` class, 422
    UML dependency diagram for, *426*
    UML diagram for, *423*
Text file input/output, 412
Text file processing, 407-419
    book example problem, 412-417
    `FileViewer` usage, 417-419
Text file statistics reporting case study, 422-432
`TextInput` class, 488-491
`TextInput` component
    example of, *486*
Text streams
    versus object streams, 520
`this` keyword, 196, 209, 310, 349, 364, 481
`this` object, 153, 195-196
`Thread` class, 675
    listing of, 653
Thread life cycle, 652-653
Threads, 649-667, 678
    code executed by, 651
    creating, 653
    in sleep mode, 654, 657
    starting, 654
`Throwable` class, 377, 378, 379, 383
    constructors of, 387
    extending subclasses of, 388
    `toString()` method in, 434

`Throwable` superclass, 433, 434
`throws` clause, 375, 388, 391-392, 434
  exceptions to declare in, 392
`throw` statement, 434
  syntax for, 391
`Time` class, 332, 333
`Timer` class, 224, 676
Tokenizing streams, 376
Tokens, 404, 434
`Toolkit` class, 477, 478
  `getPrintJob` from, 548
`toReversePolish` method
  algorithm for, 732
`toString()` method, 302-303, 305
  purpose of, 383
  in `Throwable` class, 434
Truth table
  for logical AND, *175*, 178
  for logical OR, 177, *178*
`try` block, 382, 384, 397, 409
  exiting from, 394
`try` clause, 375, 381, 433
TT_EOF, 405
TT_EOL, 405
TT_NUMBER, 405
TT_WORD, 405
Two-dimensional arrays, 641, *642*, 643, 678
  and image maps, 645
Two-dimensional shapes
  drawing, 502, 534-535
Type conversion, 42, 46
Type declarations, 23, 25
Types
  productions from, 747

U

UML, 64
  class diagrams, *136*
  dependency diagrams, *141*
  palindrome study representation of classes, *254*
  representation of classes, *109, 110*
  representation of classes, in log cutting case study, *118*
  representation of dependencies between classes, *111*
  representation of dependencies in log cutting case study, *122*
UML class diagram, detailed, *588*
UML class-relationship diagram, *587*

UML dependencies
  for class Tab, *276*
Unary minus (-), 35
Unary operators, 35, 40
Unary plus (+), 35
Unicode character set, 24, 25, 233
Unicode Worldwide Character Standard, 25
Uniform Resource Locator, 621, 677
Universal Modeling Language. *See* UML
Unix platform, 5
  downloading Java 2 SDK on, 4
Unix users
  inputting/saving Java program by, 9
Untrusted code, 674
URL. *See* Uniform Resource Locator
User errors
  and exception handling, 382
User id, 3
Users
  exceptions caused by, 376
UV index, 214-215

V

Value added tax (VAT), 37
Value of integer variable counter
  increasing/decreasing, 232
Values
  primitive data stored by, 57
  productions from, 747
  return-type and, 94, 95
  of strings, 163
Variable declarations, 46, 95
Variables, 23, 25, 31-32, 145
  initializing, 32
  productions from, 747
`Vector` class, 502
  methods of, 503, 505
  UML dependencies on, *516*
Vectors, 501, 502-507
  loading elements into, 522
  saving elements to, 523
  screen shots for storing/retrieving data from, *506, 507*
  shape objects stored in, 546
  structure of, 558
Verb identification, 109, 110
Video clips
  links with, 620

W

wav audio files, 127
WAV files, 674
Web browser, 621
    applets run in, 678
Web server, 621
What to wear program, 167-168
WhereIsTheMouse class, 528
while loop, 220-227, 240, 282
    for alarm clock program, 225-226
    data controlled, 220-223, 220-224
    and for loop, 236, 239
while statement, 217
White space, 404
"Whole-part" relationships
    between classes, 563
widthOfFrame, 131
width parameter, 446
Wildcard
    defined, 63
Wind chill temperature, 86
WindowAdapter class, 449
Window class, 64, 65-69, 111, 444
windowClosing method, 449, 450
Window container object
    creating, 65
WindowEvent object, 449
WindowListener interface, 449
Window objects, 65
    format of, *67*
    program demonstrating class scope for, 105
WindowPane class, 477, 479, 480, 528, 564, 566,
    568, 605, 676

WindowPane.java, 565
Window pane size, 478
Windows, 443
    closing options, *448*
Windows platform
    downloading Java 2 SDK on, 4
WindowWithMenuBar class, 608
    source code listing for, 605, 606-608
WinZip, 4, 6
wordChars() method, 405
WordPad, 9
World Wide Web, 2, 619, 620, 677
    connecting to, 3
    photographs moved over, 637
    terminology of, 620-621
Wrapper classes, 153, 184-185, 209, 399-400
write method, 67
writeObject method, 521, 558
WritingPad class, 481, 482, 483-485, 566,
    568
    screen shot for, *597*
WritingPad component
    reusable, 480-485
WritingPad constructor
    construction of, 481-482
WritingPad object, 481, 608
WWW. *See* World Wide Web

Z

Zero
    and behavior of while loop, 221
Zip utilities, 4